The
Managerial Economics
Reader

Edited by

Douglas J. Lamdin
Economics Department
University of Maryland Baltimore County

BLACKWELL
Publishers

First published 1994
First published by Blackwell Publishers Ltd 1996

Blackwell Publishers Ltd
108 Cowley Road
Oxford OX4 1JF, UK

Blackwell Publishers Inc.
238 Main Street
Cambridge, Massachusetts 02142, USA

British Library Cataloguing in Publication Data
A CIP catalogue record for this book is available from the British Library

Library of Congress Cataloging in Publication Data
Library of Congress Catalog Card Number 93–80416

ISBN 1–878975–37–4

Printed and bound in Great Britain by Athenæum Press Ltd, Gateshead, Tyne & Wear

This book is printed on acid-free paper

A list of sources appears on pages 393–6 at the end of this text.

Preface

Managerial economics is a standard course in graduate schools of business and undergraduate programs in economics. The purpose of the course is to provide the student with an understanding of the tools of economics that can aid the manager of a firm in making decisions. Perusal of textbooks in the field confirms this purpose. The emphasis placed on various topics in textbooks differs as does the emphasis of the instructors who use these texts. Textbooks cover in varying degrees: relevant aspects of microeconomic theory such as consumer theory, production theory, cost, market structure, pricing, and regulation; quantitative tools including econometrics, forecasting, optimization, and linear programming; investment project evaluation; and increasingly, international issues that bear upon managerial decisions.

The goal of this reader is to provide a selection of articles that cover most of the topics that fall under the purview of managerial economics. As a supplement to a textbook, this reader extends and illustrates the concepts and techniques of managerial economics that textbooks simply do not have the space to cover adequately. A balance between two general approaches to managerial economics was desired in article selection. Numerous articles that are descriptive in nature are included for courses that focus on the economic environment in which managers of firms operate. For courses that are more concerned with the application of empirical techniques, many articles that apply these techniques are included.

All of the articles either discuss or illustrate a concept or technique that may be useful to a current or potential manager. Special effort was made to select articles that show applications in a variety of industries and markets. For example, the housing, cable television, professional baseball, and nursing home industries are subjects of articles. The increasing importance of international issues to the manager and to managerial economics is reflected in the many articles with an international focus. Finally, some articles are concerned with public sector issues. This reflects the reality of both the pervasive nature of the government in a mixed economy, and the use of the tools of the managerial economist by managers in the public sector.

The reader contains 37 articles that are organized into eight sections shown as follows. A brief discussion of each section is included.

Section I
The Firm, Managers, and Managerial Economists

This section includes articles that discuss the theory of the firm, the changing role of the corporation, and corporate managers. An article that illustrates the role of an economist within a firm is included to further define the scope of managerial economics.

Section II
Demand Estimation and other Applications of Econometrics

A basic tool of the managerial economist, namely econometrics, is the focus of this section. Articles that illustrate the way econometrics is used to estimate demand functions and demand elasticities are included, as are articles that show other applications of econometrics.

Section III
Forecasting

The role of forecasting is the focus of this section. Articles that describe and illustrate forecasting techniques are included.

Section IV
Production, Cost, and Related Topics

Empirical applications of production and cost analysis are illustrated in this section. Articles on linear programming and the learning curve are also in this section.

Section V
Market Structure, Pricing, and Related Topics

Prices, and the effect of the extent of competition on market prices, is the concern of articles in this section. An article that discusses the takeover wave of the 1980s is also included.

Section VI
Regulation

Environmental regulation, utility regulation, and the effect of other forms of government regulation are the focus of the articles in this section.

Section VII
Investment Decisions and Benefit–Cost Analysis

The investment decisions of firms are discussed in the articles in this section. In addition, articles that are concerned with the public sector analog of private sector investment analysis, benefit–cost analysis, are included.

Section VIII
International Issues

Issues of both international finance and international trade relevant to managerial decisions are the focus of the articles in this section.

Many people helped me put together this reader. I wish to thank Kateri Davis, Bob Kolb, and the staff at Kolb Publishing. My colleagues at UMBC provided valuable assistance with and suggestions for the project as have students in my ECON 408 classes. Thanks also to Todd Weller for his research assistance. Financial support for this project, provided by my Department Chairman, Alan Sorkin; Dean, Jo Ann Argersinger; and Dean of the Graduate School, Joann Boughman, is gratefully acknowledged. The ultimate acknowledgement must go to both the authors of the articles in the reader and the publications where the articles appeared originally. A book of readings such as this one would not be possible without them.

Douglas J. Lamdin
University of Maryland Baltimore County

Contents

Section I
The Firm, Managers, and Managerial Economists

An introduction to the field of managerial economics is provided in this section. The firm, the managers of firms, and the activities of economists who are employed by firms are the topics. The section begins with "An Economist's Perspective on the Theory of the Firm," by Oliver Hart. His article is a primer on the current views of economists on the theory of the firm. He begins with a discussion of the neoclassical theory. This is the standard view of the firm presented in microeconomics textbooks. Summaries of recent and more realistic approaches to the theory of the firm follow. These alternatives are principal–agent theory, transactions cost economics, the firm as a nexus of contracts, and the property rights approach.

   The theme of the nature of the firm continues in the next article, "Eclipse of the Public Corporation," by Michael C. Jensen. He argues that the primary weakness of the public corporation is that owners and managers struggle over corporate resource allocation and control. According to Jensen, recent corporate restructuring brought about by takeovers, spinoffs, and publicly traded corporations going private, reduce the owner–manager conflict and enhance the performance of the firm.

   The compensation of corporate chief executive officers is the topic of "CEO Incentives—It's Not How Much You Pay, But How," by Michael C. Jensen and Kevin J. Murphy. Jensen and Murphy believe that organizational success depends in part on compensation policy. The results of their survey reveal that chief executive officer (CEO) compensation is not as excessive as popular press reports imply. They find that changes in the performance of the corporation are not generally reflected in changes in CEO compensation.

   The last article in this section provides a view of managerial economics from the trenches. Anthony Finizza describes his duties and responsibilities as an economist in "The Business Economist at Work: Atlantic Richfield Company."

Article 1

AN ECONOMIST'S PERSPECTIVE ON THE THEORY OF THE FIRM

*Oliver Hart**

An outsider to the field of economics would probably take it for granted that economists have a highly developed theory of the firm. After all, firms are the engines of growth of modern capitalistic economies, and so economists must surely have fairly sophisticated views of how they behave. In fact, little could be further from the truth. Most formal models of the firm are extremely rudimentary, capable only of portraying hypothetical firms that bear little relation to the complex organizations we see in the world. Furthermore, theories that attempt to incorporate real world features of corporations, partnerships and the like often lack precision and rigor, and have therefore failed, by and large, to be accepted by the theoretical mainstream.

This Article attempts to give lawyers a sense of how economists think about firms. It does not pretend to offer a systematic survey of the area; rather, it highlights several ideas of particular importance, and then explores an alternative theoretical perspective from which to view the firm.[1] Part I introduces various established economic theories of the firm. Part II turns to a newer theory of the firm, based not upon human capital structures, but rather upon property rights. Part III synthesizes this property rights-based theory of the firm with more established theories.

I. ESTABLISHED THEORIES

A. *Neoclassical Theory*

Any discussion of theories of the firm must start with the neoclassical approach, the staple diet of modern economists. Developed over the last one hundred years or so, this approach can be found in any

* Professor of Economics, Massachusetts Institute of Technology. B.A. 1969, Cambridge University; M.A. 1972, Warwick University; Ph.D. 1974, Princeton University. Helpful comments from Jeffrey Gordon, Bengt Holmstrom and Jean Tirole are gratefully acknowledged. This Article is based in part on the author's Fisher-Schultze lecture delivered to the Econometric Society in Bologna, Italy in August 1988. Some of the work was done while the author was visiting the Harvard Business School as a Marvin Bower Fellow. He would like to thank that institution for its hospitality and financial support. The author would also like to acknowledge financial assistance from the Guggenheim and Olin Foundations, the Center for Energy and Policy Research at MIT and the National Science Foundation.

1. Several recent surveys provide other perspectives on this material. See, e.g., Holmstrom & Tirole, The Theory of the Firm, *in* 1 Handbook of Industrial Organization (R. Schmalensee & R. Willig eds., forthcoming 1989); Milgrom & Roberts, Economic Theories of the Firm: Past, Present and Future, 21 Can. J. Econ. 444 (1988); Williamson, The Logic of Economic Organization, 4 J.L. Econ. & Organization 65 (1988).

modern-day textbook; in fact, in most textbooks, it is the *only* theory of the firm presented.[2]

Neoclassical theory views the firm as a set of feasible production plans.[3] A manager presides over this production set, buying and selling inputs and outputs in a spot market and choosing the plan that maximizes owners' welfare. Welfare is usually represented by profit, or, if profit is uncertain so that profit-maximization is not well defined, by expected net present value of future profit (possibly discounted for risk) or by market value.

To many lawyers and economists, this is a caricature of the modern firm; it is rigorous but rudimentary. At least three reasons help explain its prolonged survival. First, the theory lends itself to an elegant and general mathematical formalization. Second, it is very useful for analyzing how a firm's production choices respond to exogenous change in the environment, such as an increase in wages or a sales tax.[4] Finally, the theory is also very useful for analyzing the consequences of strategic interaction between firms under conditions of imperfect competition;[5] for example, it can help us understand the relationship between the degree of concentration in an industry and that industry's output and price level.

Granted these strengths, neoclassical theory has some very clear weaknesses. It does not explain how production is organized within a firm, how conflicts of interest between the firm's various constituencies—its owners, managers, workers, and consumers—are resolved, or, more generally, how the goal of profit-maximization is achieved. More subtly, neoclassical theory begs the question of what defines a given firm or what determines its boundaries. Since the theory does not address the issue of each firm's size or extent, it does not explain the consequences of two firms choosing to merge, or of one firm splitting itself into two or more smaller firms. Neoclassical theory describes in rudimentary terms how firms function, but contributes little to any meaningful picture of their structure.

B. *Principal-Agent Theory*

Principal-agent theory, an important development of the last fifteen years, addresses some of the weaknesses of the neoclassical approach.[6] Principal-agent theory recognizes conflicts of interest

---

2. See, e.g., J. Henderson & R. Quandt, Microeconomic Theory: A Mathematical Approach 64–134 (1980); H. Varian, Microeconomic Analysis 6–78 (1984).

3. For example, one feasible plan might be to use 10 person-hours and one acre of land to produce one hundred pounds of wheat, while another feasible plan might be to use 12 person-hours and one and one-half acres to produce fifty pounds of corn.

4. See H. Varian, supra note 2, at 47; Bishop, The Effects of Specific and Ad Valorem Taxes, 82 Q.J. Econ. 198 (1968).

5. See J. Tirole, The Theory of Industrial Organization 205–301 (1988).

6. See, e.g., Holmstrom, Moral Hazard and Observability, 10 Bell J. Econ. 74

between different economic actors, formalizing these conflicts through the inclusion of observability problems and asymmetries of information. The theory still views the firm as a production set, but now a professional manager makes production choices, such as investment or effort allocations, that the firm's owners do not observe. Because the manager deals with the day-to-day operations of the firm, she also is presumed to have information about the firm's profitability that the owners lack. In addition, the manager has other goals in mind beyond the owners' welfare, such as on-the-job perks, an easy life, empire building, and so on. Under these conditions, principal-agent theory argues that it will be impossible for the owners to implement their own profit-maximizing plan directly, through a contract with the manager—in general, the owners will not even be able to tell ex post whether the manager has chosen the right plan. Instead, the owners will try to align the manager's objectives with their own by putting the manager on an incentive scheme. Even under an optimal incentive scheme, however, the manager will put some weight on her own objectives at the expense of those of the owners, and conflicting interests remain. Hence, we have the beginnings of a managerial theory of the firm.[7]

Principal-agent theory enriches neoclassical theory significantly, but still fails to answer the vital questions of what defines a firm and where the boundaries of its structure are located. To see why, consider the example of Fisher Body, which for many years has supplied car bodies to General Motors.[8] Principal-agent theory can explain why it might make sense for GM and Fisher to write a profit-sharing agreement, whereby part of Fisher Body's reward is based on GM's profit from car sales: this encourages Fisher to supply high-quality inputs. The theory does not tell us, however, whether it matters if this profit-sharing agreement is accomplished through the merger of Fisher and GM into a single firm, with GM having authority over Fisher management; or whether GM and Fisher should remain as separate firms; or whether GM and Fisher should merge, with Fisher management having authority over GM management.[9] In other words, principal-agent theory tells

---

(1979); Shavell, Risk Sharing and Incentives in the Principal and Agent Relationship, 10 Bell J. Econ. 55 (1979). For a recent survey, see Hart & Holmstrom, The Theory of Contracts, in Advances in Economic Theory: Fifth World Congress 71, 75–106 (T. Bewley ed. 1987).

7. It is also possible to extend the principal-agent view of the firm to analyze conflicts of interests between managers and workers, and those between managers and consumers. See Calvo & Wellisz, Supervision, Loss of Control and the Optimum Size of the Firm, 86 J. Pol. Econ. 943 (1978).

8. I will discuss the GM-Fisher Body relationship at several points in the text. In doing so, I draw on material from Klein, Crawford & Alchian, Vertical Integration, Appropriable Rents, and the Competitive Contracting Process, 21 J.L. & Econ. 297, 308–10 (1978); Klein, Vertical Integration as Organizational Ownership: The Fisher Body-General Motors Relationship Revisited, 4 J.L. Econ. & Organization 199 (1988).

9. As a matter of history, GM and Fisher started off as separate firms linked by a

us about optimal incentive schemes, but not (at least directly) about organizational form. Hence, in the absence of a parallel between the two, which turns out to be difficult to draw, principal-agent theory provides no predictions about the nature and extent of the firm.[10]

C. *Transaction Cost Economics*

While the neoclassical paradigm, modified by principal-agent theory, progressed along the above lines, a very different approach to the theory of the firm developed under the heading of transaction cost economics. Introduced in Coase's famous 1937 article,[11] transaction cost economics traces the existence of firms to the thinking, planning and contracting costs that accompany any transaction, costs usually ignored by the neoclassical paradigm. The idea is that in some situations these costs will be lower if a transaction is carried out within a firm rather than in the market. According to Coase, the main cost of transacting in the market is the cost of learning about and haggling over the terms of trade; this cost can be particularly large if the transaction is a long-term one in which learning and haggling must be performed repeatedly.[12] Transaction costs can be reduced by giving one party authority over the terms of trade, at least within limits. But, according to Coase, this authority is precisely what defines a firm: within a firm, transactions occur as a result of instructions or orders issued by a boss, and the price mechanism is suppressed.[13]

Such an arrangement, however, brings costs of its own. Concentrating authority in one person's hands is likely to increase the cost of errors and lead to greater administrative rigidity. In Coase's view, the boundaries of the firm occur at the point where the marginal cost savings from transacting within the firm equal these additional error and

---

long-term contract, but after a dispute GM bought Fisher in 1926. Klein, Crawford & Alchian, supra note 8, at 310.

10. Drawing a parallel might be possible if, say, profit- or cost-sharing arrangements were only found within a single firm. This is not the case, however. For example, consider cost-plus contracts between the United States Government and private defense contractors. See generally F. Scherer, The Weapons Acquisition Process: Economic Incentives 131–309 (1964) for a discussion of defense contracts.

11. Coase, The Nature of the Firm, 4 Economica 386 (1937).

12. One can distinguish between learning and haggling costs incurred at the beginning of the relationship when the parties reach an initial agreement and those incurred as the relationship proceeds and the parties revise their agreement. For present purposes, the latter costs are more important.

13. A related idea can be found in Simon, A Formal Theory of the Employment Relationship, 19 Econometrica 293 (1951) (arguing that it is efficient for employee to accept employer's authority if employee is approximately indifferent about tasks he performs, but employer has a strict preference) It is also worth noting that the superior adaptive properties of the employment relation were emphasized by Chester Barnard at around the same time that Coase was writing. See C. Barnard, The Functions of the Executive 139–60 (1938) (discussing incentives necessary to induce individuals to contribute to organizations).

rigidity costs.[14]

Coase's ideas, although recognized as highly original, took a long time to catch on.[15] There are probably two reasons for this. First, they remain to this day very hard to formalize. Second, there is a conceptual weakness, pointed out by Alchian and Demsetz,[16] in the theory's dichotomy between the role of authority within the firm and the role of consensual trade within the market. Consider, for example, Coase's notion that an employer has authority over an employee—an employer can tell an employee what to do.[17] Alchian and Demsetz questioned this, asking what ensures that the employee obeys the employer's instructions. To put it another way, what happens to the employee if he disobeys these instructions? Will he be sued for breach of contract? Unlikely. Probably the worst that can happen is the employee will be fired. But firing is typically the sanction that one independent contractor will impose on another whose performance he does not like. To paraphrase Alchian and Demsetz's criticism, it is not clear that an employer can tell an employee what to do, any more than a consumer can tell her grocer what to do (what vegetables to sell at what prices); in either case, a refusal will likely lead to a termination of the relationship, a firing. In the case of the grocer, this means that the consumer shops at another grocer.[18] Thus, according to Alchian and Demsetz's argument, Coase's view that firms are characterized by authority relations does not really stand up.[19]

Finding Coase's characterization of the firm wanting, Alchian and Demsetz developed their own theory, based on joint production and monitoring. Transactions involving joint or team production require careful monitoring so that each actor's contribution can be assessed. According to Alchian and Demsetz, the best way to provide the monitor with appropriate incentives is to give him the following bundle of rights, which effectively define ownership of the capitalist firm: 1) to be a residual claimant; 2) to observe input behavior; 3) to be the central

---

14. Coase, supra note 11, at 395.

15. In Coase's words, they were "much cited and little used" (until the 1970s). Coase, The Nature of the Firm: Influence, 4 J.L. Econ. & Organization 33, 33 (1988).

16. Alchian & Demsetz, Production, Information Costs, and Economic Organization, 62 Am. Econ. Rev. 777 (1972).

17. Coase, supra note 11, at 404.

18. Alchian & Demsetz, supra note 16, at 777–78, 783–84. But cf. Masten, A Legal Basis for the Firm, 4 J.L. Econ. & Organization 181, 186–87 (1988) (law makes a distinction between an employer-employee relationship and one between independent contractors, in that an employee owes her employer duties of loyalty and obedience that do not exist between independent contractors).

19. It bears noting that the second part of Coase's thesis, maintaining that firms suppress the price mechanism, is also flawed. The use of prices to allocate resources within a multidivisional firm—the phenomenon of transfer pricing, probably more common now than it was when Coase wrote—seems a fairly immediate counterexample. For a recent discussion of the use of transfer pricing, see Eccles & White, Price and Authority in Inter-Profit Center Transactions, 94 Am. J. Soc. S17 (Supp. 1988).

party common to all contracts with inputs; 4) to alter membership of the team; and, 5) to sell rights 1–4.[20] We will return to some of these ideas below, but at this stage it suffices to note that the theory suffers from the same criticism levelled at Coase: it is unclear why the problems of joint production and monitoring must be solved through the firm and cannot be solved through the market. In fact, one does not need to look far to see examples of market solutions to these problems, such as auditing between independent contractors.

At the same time that doubts were being expressed about the specifics of Coase's theory, Coase's major idea—that firms arise to economize on transaction costs—was increasingly accepted. The exact nature of these transaction costs, however, remained unclear. What lay beyond the learning and haggling costs that, according to Coase, are a major component of market transactions? Professor Oliver Williamson has offered the deepest and most far-reaching analysis of these costs.[21] Williamson recognized that transaction costs may assume particular importance in situations where economic actors make relationship-specific investments—investments to some extent specific to a particular set of individuals or assets.[22] Examples of such investments include locating an electricity generating plant adjacent to a coal mine that is going to supply it; a firm's expanding capacity to satisfy a particular customer's demands; training a worker to operate a particular set of machines or to work with a particular group of individuals; or a worker's relocating to a town where he has a new job.[23]

In situations like these, there may be plenty of competition before the investments are made—there may be many coal mines next to which an electricity generating plant could locate or many towns to which a worker could move. But once the parties sink their investments, they are to some extent locked into each other. As a result, external markets will not provide a guide to the parties' opportunity costs once the relationship is underway. This lack of information takes on great significance, since, in view of the size and degree of the specific investment, one would expect relationships like these to be long lasting.[24]

In an ideal world, the lack of ex post market signals would pose no problem, since the parties could always write a long-term contract in advance of the investment, spelling out each agent's obligations and

---

20. See Alchian & Demsetz, supra note 16, at 783.

21. See generally O. Williamson, The Economic Institutions of Capitalism (1985) [hereinafter Economic Institutions]; O. Williamson, Markets and Hierarchies: Analysis and Antitrust Implications (1975). For another significant analysis of these costs, see generally Klein, Crawford & Alchian, supra note 8.

22. See Economic Institutions, supra note 21, at 30.

23. Id. at 95–96.

24. Id. at 61. For empirical evidence on the importance of relationship-specific investments and lock-in effects, see Joskow, Asset Specificity and the Structure of Vertical Relationships: Empirical Evidence, 4 J.L. Econ. & Organization 95 (1988).

the terms of the trade in every conceivable situation. In practice, however, thinking, negotiation and enforcement costs will usually make such a contract prohibitively expensive. As a result, parties must negotiate many of the terms of the relationship as they go along. Williamson argues that this leads to two sorts of costs. First, there will be costs associated with the ex post negotiation itself—the parties may engage in collectively wasteful activities to try to increase their own share of the ex post surplus; also, asymmetries of information may make some gains from trade difficult to realize.[25] Second, and perhaps more fundamental, since a party's bargaining power and resulting share of the ex post surplus may bear little relation to his ex ante investment, parties will have the wrong investment incentives at the ex ante stage.[26] In particular, a far-sighted agent will choose her investment inefficiently from the point of view of her contracting partners, given that she realizes that these partners could expropriate part of her investment at the ex post stage.[27]

In Williamson's view, bringing a transaction from the market into the firm—the phenomenon of integration—mitigates this opportunistic behavior and improves investment incentives. Agent A is less likely to hold up agent B if A is an employee of B than if A is an independent contractor. However, Williamson does not spell out in precise terms the mechanism by which this reduction in opportunism occurs. Moreover, certain costs presumably accompany integration. Otherwise, all transactions would be carried out in firms, and the market would not be used at all. Williamson, however, leaves the precise nature of these costs unclear.[28]

D. *The Firm as a Nexus of Contracts*

All the theories discussed so far suffer from the same weakness:

---

25. Economic Institutions, supra note 21, at 21.
26. Id. at 88–89.
27. Id. at 30–32.
28. Williamson argues that a major benefit of integration comes from the fact that the party with authority can resolve disputes by fiat (as opposed to litigation), while a major cost comes from the fact that the party with authority cannot commit himself to intervene selectively in the affairs of other parties. See id. at 76, 133–35. Williamson, however, is not very clear about what mechanisms are at work here. For example, a boss may try to resolve a dispute, but what guarantee is there that the parties will follow his edicts? To paraphrase Alchian and Demsetz, what disciplinary power does a boss have that an independent contractor does not? A similar issue arises with regard to selective intervention. In what activities will the boss intervene, and how will this intervention be enforced? What power to intervene does a boss have that an independent contractor does not have? See supra notes 16–18 and accompanying text.

The greater powers of a boss relative to an independent contractor can be understood if one takes a property rights-based view of the firm—in particular, if one recognizes that a firm consists of nonhuman assets as well as human assets and that a boss typically has control over these nonhuman assets. See infra notes 33–46 and accompanying text.

while they throw light on the nature of contractual failure, none explains in a convincing or rigorous manner how bringing a transaction into the firm mitigates this failure.

One reaction to this weakness is to argue that it is not really a weakness at all. According to this point of view, the firm is simply a nexus of contracts,[29] and there is therefore little point in trying to distinguish between transactions within a firm and those between firms. Rather, both categories of transactions are part of a continuum of types of contractual relations, with different firms or organizations representing different points on this continuum.[30] In other words, each type of business organization represents nothing more than a particular "standard form" contract. One such "standard form" contract is a public corporation, characterized by limited liability, indefinite life, and freely transferable shares and votes. In principle it would be possible to create a contract with these characteristics each time it is needed, but, given that these characteristics are likely to be useful in many different contexts, it is much more convenient to be able to appeal to a "standard form." Closely held corporations or partnerships are other examples of useful "standard forms."

Viewing the firm as a nexus of contracts is helpful in drawing attention to the fact that contractual relations with employees, suppliers, customers, creditors and others are an essential aspect of the firm. Also, it

> serves to make it clear that the personalization of the firm implied by asking questions such as "what should be the objective function of the firm" . . . is seriously misleading. *The firm is not an individual* . . . . The "behavior" of the firm is like the behavior of a market, i.e., the outcome of a complex equilibrium process.[31]

At the same time, the nexus of contracts approach does less to resolve the questions of what a firm is than to shift the terms of the debate. In particular, it leaves open the question of why particular "standard forms" are chosen. Perhaps more fundamentally, it begs the question of what limits the set of activities covered by a "standard form." For example, corporations are characterized by limited liability, free transferability of shares, and indefinite life. But what limits the size of a corporation—what are the economic consequences of two corpora-

---

29. The nexus of contract theory is often associated with Jensen and Meckling. See Jensen & Meckling, Theory of the Firm: Managerial Behavior, Agency Costs and Ownership Structure, 3 J. Fin. Econ. 305, 310 (1976).

30. Note that lawyers' and economists' ideas of what constitutes a contract may differ. Economists tend to view contracts as relationships characterized by reciprocal expectations and behavior; lawyers consider the enforceable legal duties implicit in such relationships and look for formalization through the standard indicia of contract formation, such as offer and acceptance. See Gordon, The Mandatory Structure of Corporate Law, 89 Colum. L. Rev. 1549, 1549-50 (1989).

31. Jensen & Meckling, supra note 29, at 311.

tions merging or of one corporation splitting itself into two? Given that mergers and breakups occur all the time, and at considerable transaction cost, it seems unlikely that such changes are cosmetic. Presumably they have some real effects on incentives and opportunistic behavior, but these effects remain unexplained.

II. A PROPERTY RIGHTS APPROACH TO THE FIRM

One way to resolve the question of how integration changes incentives is spelled out in recent literature that views the firm as a set of property rights.[32] This approach is very much in the spirit of the transaction cost literature of Coase and Williamson, but differs by focusing attention on the role of physical, that is, nonhuman, assets in a contractual relationship.

Consider an economic relationship of the type analyzed by Williamson, where relationship-specific investments are important and transaction costs make it impossible to write a comprehensive longterm contract to govern the terms of the relationship. Consider also the nonhuman assets that, in the postinvestment stage, make up this relationship. Given that the initial contract has gaps, missing provisions, or ambiguities, situations will typically occur in which some aspects of the use of these assets are not specified. For example, a contract between GM and Fisher might leave open certain aspects of maintenance policy for Fisher machines, or might not specify the speed of the production line or the number of shifts per day.

Take the position that the right to choose these missing aspects of usage resides with the *owner* of the asset. That is, ownership of an asset goes together with the possession of residual rights of control over that asset; the owner has the right to use the asset in any way not inconsistent with a prior contract, custom, or any law. Thus, the owner of Fisher assets would have the right to choose maintenance policy and production line speed to the extent that the initial contract was silent about these.[33]

---

32. See generally Grossman & Hart, The Costs and Benefits of Ownership: A Theory of Vertical and Lateral Integration, 94 J. Pol. Econ. 691 (1986); Holmstrom & Tirole, supra note 1; O. Hart & J. Moore, Property Rights and the Nature of the Firm (Massachusetts Institute of Technology, Dep't of Economics Working Paper No. 495, 1988). This literature owes much to the earlier property rights literature on the efficiency of private property in an externality-free world. See, e.g., Demsetz, Toward a Theory of Property Rights, Am. Econ. Rev., May 1967, at 347.

33. This view of ownership seems consistent with the standard one adopted by lawyers:

> But what are the rights of ownership? They are substantially the same as those incident to possession. Within the limits prescribed by policy, the owner is allowed to exercise his natural powers over the subject-matter uninterfered with, and is more or less protected in excluding other people from such interference.
> The owner is allowed to exclude all, and is accountable to no one.

O. Holmes, The Common Law 193 (1963 ed.).

Finally, identify a firm with all the nonhuman assets that belong to it, assets that the firm's owners possess by virtue of being owners of the firm. Included in this category are machines, inventories, buildings or locations, cash, client lists, patents, copyrights, and the rights and obligations embodied in outstanding contracts to the extent that these are also transferred with ownership. Human assets, however, are not included. Since human assets cannot be bought or sold, management and workers presumably own their human capital both before and after any merger.

We now have the basic ingredients of a theory of the firm. In a world of transaction costs and incomplete contracts, ex post residual rights of control will be important because, through their influence on asset usage, they will affect ex post bargaining power and the division of ex post surplus in a relationship. This division in turn will affect the incentives of actors to invest in that relationship. Hence, when contracts are incomplete, the boundaries of firms matter in that these boundaries determine who owns and controls which assets.[34] In particular, a merger of two firms does not yield unambiguous benefits: to the extent that the (owner-)manager of the acquired firm loses control rights, his incentive to invest in the relationship will decrease. In addition, the shift in control may lower the investment incentives of workers in the acquired firm. In some cases these reductions in investment will be sufficiently great that nonintegration is preferable to integration.[35]

Note that, according to this theory, when assessing the effects of integration, one must know not only the characteristics of the merging firms, but also who will own the merged company. If firms A and B integrate and A becomes the owner of the merged company, then A will presumably control the residual rights in the new firm. A can then use those rights to hold up the managers and workers of firm B. Should the

---

34. This consolidation of ownership and control points to an important lacuna in the property rights approach. The approach makes no distinction between ownership and control, assuming that both rest with the same entity. In most of the formal models that have been developed, such an arrangement turns out to be optimal since agents are assumed to be risk-neutral and to have sufficient wealth to buy any asset. If managers were risk-averse and had limited wealth, however, this conclusion would no longer be valid. Moreover, from a descriptive point of view, the assumption that owners manage is seriously inadequate; while it may apply to small firms such as partnerships or closed corporations, it certainly does not apply to large, publicly held corporations. For how the ownership/control dichotomy might affect the property rights approach, see infra notes 58–59 and accompanying text.

35. It is important to emphasize that the property rights approach distinguishes between ownership in the sense of possession of residual control rights over assets and ownership in the sense of entitlement to a firm's (verifiable) profit stream. In practice, these rights will often go together, but they do not have to. The property rights approach takes the point of view that the possession of control rights is crucial for the integration decision. That is, if firm A wants to acquire part of firm B's (verifiable) profit stream, it can always do this by contract. It is only if firm A wants to acquire control over firm B's assets that it needs to integrate.

situation be reversed, a different set of control relations would result in *B* exercising control over *A*, and *A*'s workers and managers would be liable to holdups by *B*.

It will be helpful to illustrate these ideas in the context of the Fisher Body-General Motors relationship.[36] Suppose these companies have an initial contract that requires Fisher to supply GM with a certain number of car bodies each week. Imagine that demand for GM cars now rises and GM wants Fisher to increase the quantity it supplies. Suppose also that the initial contract is silent about this possibility, perhaps because of a difficulty in predicting Fisher's costs of increasing supply. If Fisher is a separate company, GM presumably must secure Fisher's permission to increase supply. That is, the status quo point in any contract renegotiation is where Fisher does *not* provide the extra bodies. In particular, GM does not have the right to go into Fisher's factory and set the production line to supply the extra bodies; Fisher, as owner, has this residual right of control. The situation is very different if Fisher is a subdivision or subsidiary of GM, so that GM owns Fisher's factory. In this case, if Fisher management refuses to supply the extra bodies, GM always has the option to fire management and hire someone else to supervise the factory and supply extra bodies (they could even run Fisher themselves on a temporary basis). The status quo point in the contract renegotiation is therefore quite different.

To put it very simply, if Fisher is a separate firm, Fisher management can threaten to make both Fisher assets and their own labor unavailable for the uncontracted-for supply increase. In contrast, if Fisher belongs to GM, Fisher management can only threaten to make their own labor unavailable. The latter threat will generally be much weaker than the former.[37]

Although the status quo point in the contract renegotiation may depend on whether GM and Fisher are one firm rather than two, it does not follow that the outcomes after renegotiation will differ. In fact, if the benefits to GM of the extra car bodies exceed the costs to Fisher of supplying them, we might expect the parties to agree that the bodies should be supplied, regardless of the status quo point. However, the divisions of surplus in the two cases will be very different. If GM and Fisher are separate, GM may have to pay Fisher a large sum to persuade it to supply the extra bodies. In contrast, if GM owns Fisher's plant, it may be able to enforce the extra supply at much lower cost since, as we have seen in this case, Fisher management has much reduced bargaining and threat power.

Anticipating the way surplus is divided, GM will typically be much more prepared to invest in machinery that is specifically geared to

---

36. See supra note 8.

37. If current Fisher management is indispensable for the operation of Fisher assets, there is, of course, no difference between the two threats. It is rare, however, that current management is completely irreplaceable.

Fisher bodies if it owns Fisher than if Fisher is independent, since the threat of expropriation is reduced.[38] The incentives for Fisher, however, may be quite the opposite. Fisher management will generally be much more willing to come up with cost-saving or quality-enhancing innovations if Fisher is an independent firm than if it is part of GM, because Fisher management is more likely to see a return on its activities. If Fisher is independent, it can extract some of GM's surplus by threatening to deny GM access to the assets embodying these innovations. In contrast, if GM owns the assets, Fisher management faces total expropriation of the value of the innovation to the extent that the innovation is asset-specific rather than management-specific, and GM can threaten to hire a new management team to incorporate the innovation.[39]

So far, we have discussed the effects of control changes on the incentives of top management. But workers' incentives will also be affected. Consider, for example, the incentive of someone who works with Fisher assets to improve the quality of Fisher's output by better learning some aspect of the production process. Suppose further that GM has a specific interest in this improvement in car body quality, and that none of Fisher's other customers cares about it. There are many ways in which the worker might be rewarded for this, but one important reward is likely to come from the fact that the worker's value to the Fisher-GM venture will rise in the future and, due to his additional skills, the worker will be able to extract some of these benefits through a higher wage or promotion. Note, however, that the worker's ability to do this is greater if GM controls the assets than if Fisher does. In the former case, the worker will bargain directly with GM, the party that

---

38. It should be emphasized that there is no inconsistency in assuming that an initial contract is incomplete and at the same time that the parties anticipate how the ex post surplus will be divided up as a result of this incompleteness. For example, suppose there are many individually unlikely states with similar characteristics to an uncontracted-for increase in demand. It may be prohibitively expensive for the parties to contract for each of these states, and yet they may be well aware of the average degree to which their investments will be expropriated as a result of not contracting for these states.

39. Under some conditions expropriation problems can be avoided regardless of organizational form. One possibility is for the parties to write an ex ante profit-sharing agreement. However, a profit-sharing agreement may be insufficient to encourage ex ante investments to the extent that some returns from an asset's use are unverifiable. Examples of unverifiable returns are effort costs, nonmonetary rewards such as perks, and monetary returns that can be diverted so that they do not show up in the firm's accounts.

Another way the parties might overcome expropriation problems is to share investment expenditures. For example, if Fisher and GM are independent, Fisher could compensate GM for its later hold-up power by contributing towards GM's initial Fisher-specific investment. Note, however, that this strategy will work only to the extent that either GM contractually agrees to make the investment or Fisher can make part of the investment on GM's behalf. Otherwise, GM could use an up-front payment from Fisher to make a *non*-relationship-specific investment.

benefits from the worker's increased skill.[40] In the latter case, the worker will bargain with Fisher, who only receives a fraction of these benefits, since it must in turn bargain with GM to parlay these benefits into dollars. In consequence, the worker will typically capture a lower share of the surplus, and his incentive to make the improvement in the first place will fall.

In other words, given that the worker may be held up no matter who owns the Fisher assets—assuming that he, himself, does not—his incentives are greater if the number of possible hold-ups is smaller rather than larger. With Fisher management in control of the assets, there are two potential hold-ups: Fisher can deny the worker access to the assets, and GM can decline to pay more for the improved product.[41] As a result, we might expect the worker to get, say, a third of his increased marginal product (supposing equal division with Fisher and GM). With GM management in control of the Fisher assets, there is only one potential hold-up, since the power to deny the worker his increased marginal product is concentrated in one agent's hands. As a result, the worker in this case might be able to capture half of his increased marginal product (supposing equal division with GM).[42]

The above reasoning applies to the case in which the improvement is specific to GM. Exactly the opposite conclusion would be reached, however, if the improvement were specific to Fisher, such as the worker learning how to reduce Fisher management's costs of making car bodies, regardless of Fisher's final customer (a cost reduction, furthermore, which could not be enjoyed by any substitute for Fisher management). In that event, the number of hold-ups is reduced by giving control of Fisher assets to Fisher management rather than GM. The reason is that with Fisher management in control, the worker bargains with the party who benefits directly from his increased productivity, whereas with GM management in control, he must bargain with an indirect recipient; GM must in turn bargain with Fisher management to benefit from the reduction in costs.

---

40. This is not quite correct since the worker will actually bargain with GM management rather than with GM shareholders, who are arguably the ultimate beneficiaries. However, it is approximately correct to the extent that, perhaps because GM management is on an incentive scheme, GM management benefits from an increase in GM's profit or market value. For the remainder of the discussion, we will, at a cost both in precision and realism, ignore the distinction between management and shareholders, and also treat management as a monolithic group. But see supra note 34; infra note 46 (explaining how this analysis can be generalized to include more complicated forms of group ownership); infra notes 58–59 and accompanying text.

41. We assume that no payment was specified for the improved product in the initial contract.

42. For a formal treatment of the division of surplus, see O. Hart & J. Moore, supra note 32, at 11. The numbers one-half and one-third should not be taken too seriously. The important point is that, in the context described, the worker is likely to get a larger share of his increased marginal product when GM controls the assets than when Fisher does.

Up to this point we have assumed that GM management will control GM assets. This, however, need not be the case; in some situations it might make more sense for Fisher management to control these assets—for Fisher to buy up GM. One thing we can be sure of is that if GM and Fisher assets are sufficiently complementary, and initial contracts sufficiently incomplete, then the two sets of assets should be under common control. With extreme complementarity, no agent—whether manager or worker—can benefit from any increase in his marginal productivity unless he has access to both sets of assets (by the definition of extreme complementarity, each asset, by itself, is useless). Giving control of these assets to two different management teams is therefore bound to be detrimental to actors' incentives, since it increases the number of parties with hold-up power.[43] This result confirms the notion that when lock-in effects[44] are extreme, integration will dominate nonintegration.[45]

These ideas can be used to construct a theory of the firm's boundaries. First, as we have seen, highly complementary assets should be owned in common, which may provide a minimum size for the firm. Second, as the firm grows beyond a certain point, the manager at the center will become less and less important with regard to operations at the periphery in the sense that increases in marginal product at the periphery are unlikely to be specific either to this manager or to the assets at the center. At this stage, a new firm should be created since giving the central manager control of the periphery will increase hold-up problems without any compensating gains. It should also be clear from this line of argument that, in the absence of significant lock-in effects, nonintegration is always better than integration—it is optimal to do things through the market, for integration only increases the number of potential hold-ups without any compensating gains.[46]

Finally, it is worth noting that the property rights approach can explain how the purchase of physical assets leads to control over human assets. To see this, consider again the GM-Fisher hypothetical. We showed that someone working with Fisher assets is more likely to

---

43. See id. at 11, 19.

44. For examples of lock-in effects, see supra notes 22–24 and accompanying text.

45. Klein, Crawford & Alchian, supra note 8, at 300. However, Klein, Crawford and Alchian fail to provide a formal justification for this notion.

46. In the above we have concentrated on ownership by an individual or by a homogeneous and monolithic group ("management"). However, the analysis can be generalized to include more complicated forms of group ownership, such as partnerships, or worker-, manager-, or consumer-cooperatives. It turns out that these will be efficient when increases in agents' marginal products are specific to a group of individuals of variable composition, rather than to a fixed group. For example, if the increase in an agent's marginal product can be realized only if the agent has access to a majority of the members of a management team, as well as to a particular asset, then it will be optimal to give each of the managers an equal ownership share in the asset and equal voting rights, and adopt majority rule. See O. Hart & J. Moore, supra note 32, at 19.

improve Fisher's output in a way that is specifically of value to GM if GM owns these assets than if Fisher does. This result can be expressed more informally as follows: a worker will put more weight on an actor's objectives if that actor is the worker's boss, that is, if that actor controls the assets the worker works with, than otherwise. The conclusion is quite Coasian in spirit, but the logic underlying it is very different. Coase reaches this conclusion by assuming that a boss can tell a worker what to do; in contrast, the property rights approach reaches it by showing that it is in a worker's self-interest to behave in this way, since it puts him in a stronger bargaining position with his boss later on.

To put it slightly differently, the reason an employee is likely to be more responsive to what his employer wants than a grocer is to what his customer wants is that the employer has much more leverage over his employee than the customer has over his grocer. In particular, the employer can deprive the employee of the assets he works with and hire another employee to work with these assets, while the customer can only deprive the grocer of his custom and as long as the customer is small, it is presumably not very difficult for the grocer to find another customer.

III. Property Rights and the Established Theories of the Firm

The property rights approach has features in common with each of the approaches described previously.[47] It is based on maximizing behavior (like the neoclassical approach); it emphasizes incentive issues (like the principal-agent approach); it emphasizes contracting costs (like the transaction cost approach); it treats the firm as a "standard form" contract (like the nexus of contracts approach);[48] and, it relies on the idea that a firm's owner has the right to alter membership of the firm: the owner has the right to decide who uses the firm's assets and who doesn't.[49] Its advantage over these other approaches, however, is its ability to explain both the costs and the benefits of integration; in particular, it shows how incentives change when one firm buys up another one.

Some react skeptically to the notion that a firm can be characterized completely by the nonhuman assets under its control.[50] That is, there is a feeling that one should be able to make sense of a firm as a mode of organization, even if there are no definable assets on the scene. In his analysis of GM's decision to acquire Fisher Body in 1926, Professor Klein argues that getting control over Fisher's organizational

---

47. See supra notes 2–31 and accompanying text.

48. In the language of the property rights approach, "firm" is shorthand for a collection of assets; "ownership" is shorthand for the possession of residual rights of control over these assets.

49. See Alchian & Demsetz, supra note 16, at 783 (manager should have right to alter membership of production team).

50. See, e.g., Klein, supra note 8, at 205–08.

assets rather than their physical capital was the crucial motivating factor:

> By integrating with Fisher, General Motors acquired the Fisher Body organizational capital. This organization is embedded in the human capital of the employees at Fisher but is in some sense greater than the sum of its parts. The employees come and go but the organization maintains the memory of past trials and the knowledge of how to best do something (that is, how to make automobile bodies).[51]

Klein's conclusion is in no way inconsistent with the property rights approach. The control of physical capital can lead to control of human assets in the form of organizational capital.[52] However, Klein appears to argue that his conclusion would hold true even if physical assets were irrelevant.[53] The problem with this point of view is that, in the absence of physical assets, it is unclear how GM can get control over an intangible asset like organizational capital by purchasing Fisher. For example, what is to stop Fisher management from trying to reassert control of the organizational capital after the merger? Klein writes:

> A threat that all the individuals will simultaneously shirk or leave if their wages were not increased to reflect the quasi-rents on the organizational capital generally will not be credible. After vertical integration the Fisher brothers will not be able to hold up General Motors by telling all the employees to leave General Motors and show up on Monday morning at a new address.[54]

This conclusion is reasonable when physical capital is important since it would be difficult at best for Fisher employees to find a substitute for this capital, particularly by Monday morning. However, it is not reasonable in the absence of physical assets. In this case, to paraphrase Alchian and Demsetz, the Fisher brothers have no more ability to hold up GM by telling all the employees to leave GM or, more generally, by countermanding GM's instructions, when Fisher is separate than when Fisher belongs to GM. Their ability to do so will be determined by factors such as the motivation, talent, knowledge and charisma of the Fisher brothers; the quality of worker information;[55] and the degree of worker inertia—factors that do not seem to have anything

---

51. Id. at 208.

52. See supra notes 32–46 and accompanying text. Note that the observation that the whole of organizational capital is typically greater than the sum of its parts is equivalent to the observation that the total output of a group of workers typically exceeds the sum of the workers' individual outputs, to the extent that there are complementarities.

53. Klein, supra note 8, at 208 n.11.

54. Id. at 208.

55. See G. Mailath & A. Postlewaite, Workers Versus Firms: Bargaining Over a Firm's Value 14 (University of Pennsylvania, Center for Analytic Research in Economics and the Social Sciences Working Paper No. 88–11, 1988).

to do with ownership structure. To put it another way, GM's response to a hold-up attempt by the Fisher brothers will be the same whether GM owns Fisher or Fisher is independent: to try to persuade Fisher workers to desert the Fisher brothers and join GM.[56]

As noted previously, one of the weaknesses of the property rights approach as described here is that it does not take account of the separation of ownership and control present in large, publicly held corporations.[57] In principle, it should be possible to extend the existing analysis to such situations. A public corporation can still be usefully considered a collection of assets, with ownership providing control rights over these assets. Now, however, the picture is more complicated. Although owners (shareholders) typically retain some control rights, such as the right to replace the board of directors, in practice they delegate many others to management, at least on a day-to-day basis.[58] In addition, some of the shareholders' rights shift to creditors during periods of financial distress. Developing a formal model of the firm that contains all these features, and that includes also an explanation of the firm's financial structure, is an important and challenging task for future research. Fortunately, recent work suggests that the task is not an impossible one.[59]

CONCLUSION

This Article began with the observation that the portrayal of the firm in neoclassical economics is a caricature of the modern firm. It then went on to discuss some other approaches that attempt to develop a more realistic picture. The end product to date is still, in many ways,

---

56. This is not without qualification. It can be argued that if GM acquires Fisher, Fisher workers become liable for damages if they try to organize a new firm since, as employees, they owe GM a duty of loyalty. See Masten, supra note 18, at 189. But, in practice, employees *do* leave to form new firms. Moreover, the courts facilitate this process by sometimes hesitating to enforce covenants not to compete even when such covenants are explicit. See, e.g., E. Farnsworth, Contracts § 5.3, at 337–38 (1982) (courts enforce non-compete covenants "only if . . . employee acquired confidential information" in course of employment). Thus, it is unclear how important this factor could have been in the GM-Fisher acquisition.

57. See supra note 34.

58. See, e.g., Clark, Agency Costs Versus Fiduciary Duties, in Principals and Agents: The Structure of Business 55 (J. Pratt & R. Zeckhauser eds. 1985); Easterbrook & Fischel, Voting in Corporate Law, 26 J.L. & Econ. 395 (1983); Fama & Jensen, Separation of Ownership and Control, 26 J.L. & Econ. 301 (1983).

59. See, e.g., Grossman & Hart, One Share-One Vote and the Market for Corporate Control, 20 J. Fin. Econ. 175 (1988); Harris & Raviv, Corporate Governance: Voting Rights and Majority Rules, 20 J. Fin. Econ. 203 (1988); P. Aghion & P. Bolton, An 'Incomplete Contract' Approach to Bankruptcy and the Financial Structure of the Firm (Stanford University, Institute for Mathematical Studies in the Social Sciences Technical Report No. 536, 1988); C. Kahn & G. Huberman, Default, Foreclosure, and Strategic Renegotiation (paper presented at Conference on Economics of Contract Law, Duke University, March 1988).

a caricature, but perhaps not such an unreasonable one. One promising sign is that the different approaches economists have used to address this issue—neoclassical, principal-agent, transaction cost, nexus of contracts, property rights—appear to be converging. It is to be hoped that in the next few years the best aspects of each of these approaches can be drawn on to develop a more comprehensive and realistic theory of the firm. Such a theory would capture the salient features both of modern corporations and of owner-managed firms, and would illuminate the issues for economists and lawyers alike.

Article 2

Eclipse of the Public Corporation

by Michael C. Jensen

The publicly held corporation, the main engine of economic progress in the United States for a century, has outlived its usefulness in many sectors of the economy and is being eclipsed.

New organizations are emerging in its place—organizations that are corporate in form but have no public shareholders and are not listed or traded on organized exchanges. These organizations use public and private debt, rather than public equity, as their major source of capital. Their primary owners are not households but large institutions and entrepreneurs that designate agents to manage and monitor on their behalf and bind those agents with large equity interests and contracts governing the use and distribution of cash.

Takeovers, corporate breakups, divisional spin-offs, leveraged buyouts, and going-private transactions are the most visible manifestations of a massive organizational change in the economy. These

Michael C. Jensen is the Edsel Bryant Ford Professor of Business Administration at the Harvard Business School and founding editor of the Journal of Financial Economics. His research and writing have figured prominently in the national debate over corporate governance and mergers and acquisitions. This article draws from Mr. Jensen's book, Organizational Change and the Market for Corporate Control, to be published by Basil Blackwell in 1990.

transactions have inspired criticism, even outrage, among many business leaders and government officials, who have called for regulatory and legislative restrictions. The backlash is understandable. Change is threatening; in this case, the threat is aimed at the senior executives of many of our largest companies.

Despite the protests, this organizational innovation should be encouraged. By resolving the central weakness of the public corporation—the con-

> New organizations resolve the central weakness of the public corporation:
> the struggle between owners and managers.

flict between owners and managers over the control and use of corporate resources—these new organizations are making remarkable gains in operating efficiency, employee productivity, and shareholder

The Privatization of Equity

The last share of publicly traded common stock owned by an individual will be sold in the year 2003, if current trends persist. This forecast may be fanciful (short-term trends never persist), but the basic direction is clear. By the turn of the century, the primacy of public stock ownership in the United States may have all but disappeared.

Households have been liquidating their direct holdings and indirect positions (through channels like mutual funds) at an unprecedented rate. Over the last five years, they have been net sellers of more than $500 billion of common stock, 38% of their holdings at the beginning of 1984.

Why have stock prices risen sharply despite this massive sell-off? Because there has been one huge buyer – corporations themselves. LBOs, MBOs, share repurchases, leveraged mergers and acquisitions, and takeovers have been contracting the supply of publicly held equity. In 1988, 5% of the market value of public equity (more than $130 billion) disappeared through these kinds of transactions, even after adding back all of the new issues brought to market during the year.

Of course, the risks and returns from the underlying corporate assets have not disappeared. To some extent they now reside in quasi-equity debt instruments like high-yield bonds, whose total market value exceeds $200 billion. But many of the risks and returns still exist as equity; they just take the form of large positions of privately held equity. The "privatization of equity" is now a central feature of corporate ownership in the United States.

Historically, public stock markets dominated by individual investors developed to a greater extent in the United States than in any other country. Broad public ownership offered managers a reasonably priced source of more or less permanent equity capital that could buffer the company against adversity in a way debt could not. Share ownership allowed individual investors to participate in equity returns and get the benefits of liquidity (because they could sell their shares) and diversification (because they could hold a small number of shares from many corporations).

The virtues of broad public ownership are not what they used to be, for managers or investors. One important factor is the emergence of an active market for corporate control. A capital structure consisting mostly of equity still offers managers protection against the risks of economic downturn. But it also carries substantial risks of inviting a hostile takeover or other threats to management control.

The role of the public market has also changed because investors themselves have changed. For decades, stock ownership has been migrating from direct holdings by millions of individuals to indirect beneficial ownership through large pools of capital – in particular, the huge corporate and governmental pension funds whose total value exceeded $1.5 trillion in 1988. These institutional funds, which now comprise more than 40% of total stock ownership, used to behave like large public investors. They kept diversified by retaining many different investment managers, each of whom traded an array of highly liquid public securities. But their investment philosophy has been evolving in recent years to include participation in a select number of

---

value. Over the long term, they will enhance U.S. economic performance relative to our most formidable international competitor, Japan, whose companies are moving in the opposite direction. The governance and financial structures of Japan's public companies increasingly resemble U.S. companies of the mid-1960s and early 1970s – an era of gross corporate waste and mismanagement that triggered the organizational transformation now under way in the United States.

Consider these developments in the 1980s:
□ The capital markets are in transition. The total market value of equity in publicly held companies has tripled over the past decade – from $1 trillion in 1979 to more than $3 trillion in 1989. But newly acquired capital comes increasingly from private placements, which have expanded more than ten times since 1980, to a rate of $200 billion in 1988. Private placements of debt and equity now account for more than 40% of annual corporate financings. Meanwhile, in every year since 1983, at least 5% of the outstanding value of corporate equity has disappeared through stock repurchases, takeovers, and going-private transactions. Finally, households are sharply reducing their stock holdings.[1] (See the insert, "The Privatization of Equity.")

□ The most widespread going-private transaction, the leveraged buyout, is becoming larger and more frequent. In 1988, the total value of the 214 public-company and divisional buyouts exceeded $77 billion – nearly one-third of the value of all mergers and acquisitions. The total value of the 75 buyouts in 1979 was only $1.3 billion (in constant 1988 dollars), while the 175 buyouts completed in 1983

private illiquid investments and private pools of equity capital. This new investment philosophy makes broad public markets less essential for institutions.

Large pools of capital such as pension funds and endowments don't really need the liquidity the public market offers. Liquidity serves two basic purposes. It allows investors to meet unexpected cash needs and to trade their stocks. Unlike individuals, the large funds can project their cash needs well into the future based on predictable factors such as employee demographics, life expectancies, and health trends. So they can take a long-term view of investment returns and keep their holdings in illiquid assets.

Fund managers are also realizing that trading is a tough discipline in which they hold little comparative advantage. Trading is a zero-sum game played in a fairly efficient market against equally talented rivals. Worse still, large funds face diseconomies of scale when executing trades. The larger a fund, the more difficult it is to trade quickly, based on transient information advantages. The very act of trading moves markets.

Still, these managers remain charged with generating returns in excess of passive benchmarks. Enter the market for private assets such as real estate, venture capital, and, more recently, the market for corporate control and restructurings. Instead of trading a large number of small, liquid positions, the funds can buy and own smaller numbers of large, illiquid positions in a form where they (or, more likely, their agents) participate more actively with management in the control of the assets.

This alternative can be a positive-sum game; real changes in corporate policies can be a route to enhanced value. The very large funds also have a competitive advantage here. The larger their positions, the more actively they can participate in the ownership and management of the underlying assets. In the extreme, as with LBO funds, these changes can be dramatic. The LBO fund itself becomes the managing owner in partnership with company managers. In short, large institutional funds can behave more like owners and less like traders.

The same basic changes are at work in a wide variety of corporate recapitalizations where outside (or related) parties acquire large, relatively nontraded equity positions. Large pools of capital can participate in these private equity positions yet remain diversified by virtue of their own enormous size. Smaller funds and households cannot.

In the short run, this new investment philosophy has been, in the aggregate, a great success. Without the sobering influence of an economic contraction, the returns from these private investments have been very attractive. In the long run, the institutions' new philosophy is ushering in a system of equity ownership dominated by "private positions" that resembles ownership systems in Germany and Japan. Individual investors in this system will increasingly be free riders on the coattails of a small number of very large private investors rather than the central feature of the financial markets.

–JAY O. LIGHT

Jay O. Light is the George Fisher Baker, Jr. Professor of Business Administration at the Harvard Business School.

had a total value of $16.6 billion. This process is just getting started; the $77 billion of LBOs in 1988 represented only 2.5% of outstanding public-company equity. (See the table, "Rise of the LBO.")

☐ Entire industries are being reshaped. Just five years ago, the leading U.S. truck and automobile tire manufacturers were independent and diversified public companies. Today each is a vastly different enterprise. Uniroyal went private in 1985 and later merged its tire-making operations with those of B.F. Goodrich to form a new private company called Uniroyal Goodrich. In late 1986, Goodyear borrowed $2.6 billion and repurchased nearly half its outstanding shares to fend off a hostile tender offer by Sir James Goldsmith. It retained its core tire and rubber business while moving to divest an array of unrelated operations, including its Celeron oil and gas subsidiary,

California-to-Texas oil pipeline, aerospace operation, and Arizona resort hotel. In 1987, GenCorp issued $1.75 billion of debt to repurchase more than half its outstanding shares. It divested several operations, including its General Tire subsidiary, to pay down the debt and focus on aerospace and defense. Last year, Firestone was sold to Bridgestone, Japan's largest tiremaker, for $2.6 billion, a transaction that created shareholder gains of $1.6 billion.

Developments as striking as the restructuring of our financial markets and major industries reflect underlying economic forces more fundamental and powerful than financial manipulation, management greed, reckless speculation, and the other colorful epithets used by defenders of the corporate status quo. The forces behind the decline of the public corporation differ from industry to industry. But its decline is real, enduring, and highly productive. It is not merely a function of the tax deductibility of interest. Nor does it reflect a transitory LBO phase through which companies pass before investment bankers and managers cash out by taking them public again. Nor, finally, is it premised on a systematic fleecing of shareholders and bondholders by managers and other insiders with superior information about the true value of corporate assets.

The current trends do not imply that the public corporation has no future. The conventional twentieth-century model of corporate governance – dispersed public ownership, professional managers without substantial equity holdings, a board of directors dominated by management-appointed outsiders – remains a viable option in some areas of the economy, particularly for growth companies whose profitable investment opportunities exceed the cash they generate internally. Such companies can be found in industries like computers and electronics, biotechnology, pharmaceuticals, and financial services. Companies choosing among a surplus of profitable projects are unlikely to invest systemat-

> **The public corporation will decline in industries such as aerospace, banking, and food processing.**

ically in unprofitable ones, especially when they must regularly turn to the capital markets to raise investment funds.

The public corporation is not suitable in industries where long-term growth is slow, where internally generated funds outstrip the opportunities to invest them profitably, or where downsizing is the most productive long-term strategy. In the tire industry, the shift to radials, which last three times longer than bias-ply tires, meant that manufacturers needed less capacity to meet world demand. Overcapacity inevitably forced a restructuring. The tenfold increase in oil prices from 1973 to 1981, which triggered worldwide conservation measures, forced oil producers into a similar retrenchment.[2]

Industries under similar pressure today include steel, chemicals, brewing, tobacco, television and radio broadcasting, wood and paper products. In these and other cash-rich, low-growth or declining sectors, the pressures on management to waste cash flow through organizational slack or investments in unsound projects is often irresistible. It is in precisely these sectors that the publicly held corporation has

declined most rapidly. Barring regulatory interference, the public corporation is also likely to decline in industries such as aerospace, automobiles and auto parts, banking, electric power generation, food processing, industrial and farm implements, and transportation equipment.

The public corporation is a social invention of vast historical importance. Its genius is rooted in its capacity to spread financial risk over the diversified portfolios of millions of individuals and institutions and to allow investors to customize risk to their unique circumstances and predilections. By diversifying risks that would otherwise be borne by owner-entrepreneurs and by facilitating the creation of a liquid market for exchanging risk, the public corporation lowered the cost of capital. These tradable claims on corporate ownership (common stock) also allowed risk to be borne by investors best able to bear it, without requiring them to manage the corporations they owned.

From the beginning, though, these risk-bearing benefits came at a cost. Tradable ownership claims create fundamental conflicts of interest between those who bear risk (the shareholders) and those who manage risk (the executives). The genius of the new organizations is that they eliminate much of the loss created by conflicts between owners and managers, without eliminating the vital functions of risk diversification and liquidity once performed exclusively by the public equity markets.

In theory, these new organizations should not be necessary. Three major forces are said to control management in the public corporation: the product markets, internal control systems led by the board of directors, and the capital markets. But product markets often have not played a disciplining role. For most of the last 60 years, a large and vibrant domestic market created for U.S. companies economies of scale and significant cost advantages over foreign rivals. Recent reversals at the hands of the Japanese and others have not been severe enough to sap most companies of their financial independence. The idea that outside directors with little or no equity stake in the company could effectively monitor and discipline the managers who selected them has proven hollow at best. In practice, only the capital markets have played much of a control function – and for a long time they were hampered by legal constraints.

Indeed, the fact that takeover and LBO premiums average 50% above market price illustrates how much value public-company managers can destroy before they face a serious threat of disturbance. Takeovers and buyouts both create new value and unlock value destroyed by management through misguided policies. I estimate that transactions associated with the market for corporate control unlocked shareholder gains (in target companies alone) of more than $500 billion between 1977 and 1988 – more than 50% of the cash dividends paid by the entire corporate sector over this same period.

The widespread waste and inefficiency of the public corporation and its inability to adapt to changing economic circumstances have generated a wave of organizational innovation over the last 15 years – innovation driven by the rebirth of "active investors." By active investors I mean investors who hold large equity or debt positions, sit on boards of directors, monitor and sometimes dismiss management, are involved with the long-term strategic direction of the companies they invest in, and sometimes manage the companies themselves.

Active investors are creating a new model of general management. These investors include LBO partnerships such as Kohlberg Kravis Roberts and Clayton & Dubilier; entrepreneurs such as Carl Icahn, Ronald Perelman, Laurence Tisch, Robert Bass, William Simon, Irwin Jacobs, and Warren Buffett; the merchant banking arms of Wall Street houses such as Morgan Stanley, Lazard Frères, and Merrill Lynch; and family funds such as those controlled by the Pritzkers and the Bronfmans. Their model is built around highly leveraged financial structures, pay-for-performance compensation systems, substantial equity ownership by managers and directors, and contracts with owners and creditors that limit both cross-subsidization among business units and the waste of free cash flow. Consistent with modern finance theory, these organizations are not managed to maximize earnings per share but rather to maximize *value*, with a strong emphasis on cash flow.

More than any other factor, these organizations' resolution of the owner-manager conflict explains how they can motivate the same people, managing the same resources, to perform so much more effectively under private ownership than in the publicly held corporate form.

In effect, LBO partnerships and the merchant banks are rediscovering the role played by active investors prior to 1940, when Wall Street banks such as J.P. Morgan & Company were directly involved in the strategy and governance of the public companies they helped create. At the height of his prominence, Morgan and his small group of partners served on the boards of U.S. Steel, International Harvester, First National Bank of New York, and a host of railroads, and were a powerful management force in these and other companies.

Morgan's model of investor activism disappeared largely as a result of populist laws and regulations approved in the wake of the Great Depression. These laws and regulations – including the Glass-Steagall Banking Act of 1933, the Securities Act of 1933, the Securities Exchange Act of 1934, the Chandler Bankruptcy Revision Act of 1938, and the Investment Company Act of 1940 – may have once had their place. But they also created an intricate web of restrictions on company "insiders" (corporate officers, directors, or investors with more than a 10% ownership interest), restrictions on bank involvement in

Rise of the LBO

| Year | Public–Company Buyouts | | Divisional Buyouts | | Total Value of Buyouts (In billions of 1988 dollars) |
	Number	Average Value (In millions of 1988 dollars)	Number	Average Value (In millions of 1988 dollars)	
1979	16	$ 64.9	59	$ 5.4	$ 1.4
1980	13	106.0	47	34.5	3.0
1981	17	179.1	83	21.0	4.8
1982	31	112.2	115	40.7	8.2
1983	36	235.8	139	58.2	16.6
1984	57	473.6	122	104.0	39.7
1985	76	349.4	132	110.1	41.0
1986	76	303.3	144	180.7	49.0
1987	47	488.7	90	144.2	36.0
1988	125	487.4	89	181.3	77.0

Source: George P. Baker, "Management Compensation and Divisional Leveraged Buyouts," unpublished dissertation, Harvard Business School, 1986. Updates from W. T. Grimm, *Mergerstat Review 1988*. Transactions with no public data are valued at the average price of public transactions.

corporate reorganizations, court precedents, and business practices that raised the cost of being an active investor. Their long-term effect has been to insulate management from effective monitoring and to set the stage for the eclipse of the public corporation.

Indeed, the high cost of being an active investor has left financial institutions and money management firms, which control more than 40% of all corporate equity in the United States, almost completely uninvolved in the major decisions and long-term strategies of the companies their clients own. They are almost never represented on corporate boards. They use the proxy mechanism rarely and usually ineffectively, notwithstanding recent efforts by the Council of Institutional Investors and other shareholder activists to gain a larger voice in corporate affairs.

All told, institutional investors are remarkably powerless; they have few options to express dissatisfaction with management other than to sell their shares and vote with their feet. Corporate managers criticize institutional sell-offs as examples of portfolio churning and short-term investor horizons. One guesses these same managers much prefer churning to a system in which large investors on the boards of their companies have direct power to monitor and correct mistakes. Managers really want passive investors who can't sell their shares.

The absence of effective monitoring led to such large inefficiencies that the new generation of active investors arose to recapture the lost value. These investors overcome the costs of the outmoded legal constraints by purchasing entire companies – and using debt and high equity ownership to force effective self-monitoring.

A central weakness and source of waste in the public corporation is the conflict between shareholders and managers over the payout of free cash flow – that is, cash flow in excess of that required to fund all investment projects with positive net present values when discounted at the relevant cost of capital. For a company to operate efficiently and maximize value, free cash flow must be distributed to shareholders rather than retained. But this happens infrequently; senior management has few incentives to distribute the funds, and there exist few mechanisms to compel distribution.

A vivid example is the senior management of Ford Motor Company, which sits on nearly $15 billion in cash and marketable securities in an industry with excess capacity. Ford's management has been deliberating about acquiring financial service companies, aerospace companies, or making some other multibillion-dollar diversification move – rather than deliberating about effectively distributing Ford's excess cash to its owners so they can decide how to reinvest it.

Ford is not alone. Corporate managers generally don't disgorge cash unless they are forced to do so. In 1988, the 1,000 largest public companies (by sales) generated total funds of $1.6 trillion. Yet they distributed only $108 billion as dividends and another $51 billion through share repurchases.[3]

Managers have incentives to retain cash in part because cash reserves increase their autonomy vis-à-vis the capital markets. Large cash balances (and independence from the capital markets) can serve a competitive purpose, but they often lead to waste and inefficiency. Consider a hypothetical world in which companies distribute excess cash to shareholders and then must convince the capital markets to supply

---

Institutional investors are powerless. Their only option is to vote with their feet.

---

funds as sound economic projects arise. Shareholders are at a great advantage in this world, where management's plans are subject to enhanced monitoring by the capital markets. Wall Street's analytical, due diligence, and pricing disciplines give shareholders more power to quash wasteful projects.

Managers also resist distributing cash to shareholders because retaining cash increases the size of the companies they run – and managers have many incentives to expand company size beyond that which maximizes shareholder wealth. Compensation is one of the most important incentives. Many studies document that increases in executive pay are strongly related to increases in corporate size rather than value.[4]

The tendency of companies to reward middle managers through promotions rather than annual performance bonuses also creates a cultural bias toward growth. Organizations must grow in order to generate new positions to feed their promotion-based reward systems.

Finally, corporate growth enhances the social prominence, public prestige, and political power of senior executives. Rare is the CEO who wants to be remembered as presiding over an enterprise that makes fewer products in fewer plants in fewer countries than when he or she took office – even when such a course increases productivity and adds hundreds of millions of dollars of shareholder value. The perquisites of the executive suite can be substantial, and they usually increase with company size.

The struggle over free cash flow is at the heart of the role of debt in the decline of the public corporation. Bank loans, mezzanine securities, and high-yield bonds have fueled the wave of takeovers, restructurings, and going-private transactions. The combined borrowings of all nonfinancial corporations in the United States approached $2 trillion in 1988, up from $835 billion in 1979. The interest charges on these borrowings represent more than 20% of corporate cash flows, high by historical standards.[5]

This perceived "leveraging of corporate America" is perhaps the central source of anxiety among defenders of the public corporation and critics of the new organizational forms. But most critics miss three important points. First, the trebling of the market value of public-company equity over the last decade means that corporate borrowing had to increase to avoid a major *de*leveraging.

Second, debt creation *without retention of the proceeds of the issue* helps limit the waste of free cash flow by compelling managers to pay out funds they would otherwise retain. Debt is in effect a substitute for dividends—a mechanism to force managers to disgorge cash rather than spend it on empire-building projects with low or negative returns, bloated staffs, indulgent perquisites, and organizational inefficiencies.

By issuing debt in exchange for stock, companies bond their managers' promise to pay out future cash flows in a way that simple dividend increases do not. "Permanent" dividend increases or multiyear share repurchase programs (two ways public companies can distribute excess cash to shareholders) involve no contractual commitments by managers to owners. It's easy for managers to cut dividends or scale back share repurchases.

Take the case of General Motors. On March 3, 1987, several months after the departure of GM's only active investor, H. Ross Perot, the company announced a program to repurchase up to 20% of its common stock by the end of 1990. As of mid-1989, GM had purchased only 5% of its outstanding common shares, even though its $6.8 billion cash balance was more than enough to complete the program. Given management's poor performance over the past decade, shareholders would be better off making their own investment decisions with the cash GM is retaining. From 1977 to 1987, the company made capital expenditures of $77.5 billion while its U.S. market share declined by 10 points.

Borrowing allows for no such managerial discretion. Companies whose managers fail to make promised interest and principal payments can be declared insolvent and possibly hauled into bankruptcy court.

In the imagery of G. Bennett Stewart and David M. Glassman, "Equity is soft, debt hard. Equity is forgiving, debt insistent. Equity is a pillow, debt a sword."[6] Some may find it curious that a company's creditors wield far more power over managers than its public shareholders, but it is also undeniable.

Third, debt is a powerful agent for change. For all the deeply felt anxiety about excessive borrowing, "overleveraging" can be desirable and effective when it makes economic sense to break up a company, sell off parts of the business, and refocus its energies on a few core operations. Companies that assume so much debt they cannot meet the debt service payments out of operating cash flow force themselves to rethink their entire strategy and structure. Overleveraging creates the crisis atmosphere managers require to slash unsound investment programs, shrink overhead, and dispose of assets that are more valuable outside the company. The proceeds generated by these overdue restructurings can then be used to reduce debt to more sustainable levels, creating a leaner, more efficient and competitive organization.

In other circumstances, the violation of debt covenants creates a board-level crisis that brings new actors onto the scene, motivates a fresh review of top management and strategy, and accelerates response. The case of Revco D.S., Inc., one of the handful of leveraged buyouts to reach formal bankruptcy, makes the point well.

> **Efficient companies distribute free cash flow to shareholders. So why is Ford sitting on $15 billion?**

Critics cite Revco's bankruptcy petition, filed in July 1988, as an example of the financial perils associated with LBO debt. I take a different view. The $1.25 billion buyout, announced in December 1986, did dramatically increase Revco's annual interest charges. But several other factors contributed to its troubles, including management's decision to overhaul pricing, stocking, and merchandise layout in the company's drugstore chain. This mistaken strategic redirection left customers confused and dissatisfied, and Revco's performance suffered. Before the buyout, and without the burden of interest payments, management could have pursued these policies for a long period of time, destroying much of the company's value in the process. Within six months, however, debt served as a brake on management's mistakes, motivating the board and creditors to reorganize the company before even more value was lost.[7]

Developments at Goodyear also illustrate how debt can force managers to adopt value-creating policies they would otherwise resist. Soon after his company warded off Sir James Goldsmith's tender offer, Goodyear chairman Robert Mercer offered his version of the raiders' creed: "Give me your undervalued assets, your plants, your expenditures for technology, research and development, the hopes and aspirations of your people, your stake with your customers, your pension funds, and I will enhance myself and the dealmakers."[8]

What Mr. Mercer failed to note is that Goodyear's forced restructuring dramatically increased the company's value to shareholders by compelling him to disgorge cash and shed unproductive assets. Two years after this bitter complaint, Tom Barrett, who succeeded Mercer as Goodyear's CEO, was asked whether the company's restructuring had hurt the quality of its tires or the efficiency of its plants. "No," he replied. "We've been able to invest and continue to invest and do the things we've needed to do to be competitive."[9]

Robert Mercer's harsh words are characteristic of the business establishment's response to the eclipse of the public corporation. What explains such vehement opposition to a trend that clearly benefits shareholders and the economy? One important factor, as my Harvard Business School colleague Amar Bhide suggests, is that Wall Street now competes directly with senior management as a steward of shareholder wealth. With its vast increases in data, talent, and technology, Wall Street can allocate capital among competing businesses and monitor and discipline management more effectively than the CEO and headquarters staff of the typical diversified company. KKR's New York offices and Irwin Jacobs' Minneapolis base are direct substitutes for corporate headquarters in Akron or Peoria. CEOs worry that they and their staffs will lose lucrative jobs in favor of competing organizations. Many are right to worry; the performance of active investors versus the public corporation leaves little doubt as to which is superior.

Active investors are creating new models of general management, the most widespread of which I call the LBO Association. A typical LBO Association consists of three main constituencies: an LBO partnership that sponsors going-private transactions and counsels and monitors management in an ongoing cooperative relationship; company managers who hold substantial equity stakes in an LBO division and stay on after the buyout; and institutional investors (insurance companies, pension funds, and money management firms) that fund the limited partner-

ships that purchase equity and lend money (along with banks) to finance the transactions.

Much like a traditional conglomerate, LBO Associations have many divisions or business units, companies they have taken private at different points in time. KKR, for example, controls a diverse collection of 19 businesses including all or part of Beatrice, Duracell, Motel 6, Owens-Illinois, RJR Nabisco, and Safeway. But LBO Associations differ from publicly held conglomerates in at least four important respects. (See the illustration, "Public Company vs. LBO Association.")

> ## Debt is a substitute for dividends. It forces managers to disgorge cash rather than waste it.

Management incentives are built around a strong relationship between pay and performance. Compensation systems in LBO Associations usually have higher upper bounds than do public companies (or no upper bounds at all), tie bonuses much more closely to cash flow and debt retirement than to accounting earnings, and otherwise closely link management pay to divisional performance. Unfortunately, because these companies are private, little data are available on salaries and bonuses.

Public data are available on stock ownership, however, and equity holdings are a vital part of the reward system in LBO Associations. The University of Chicago's Steven Kaplan studied all public-company buyouts from 1979 through 1985 with a purchase price of at least $50 million.[10] Business-unit chiefs hold a median equity position of 6.4% in their unit. Even without considering bonus and incentive plans, a $1,000 increase in shareholder value triggers a $64 increase in the personal wealth of business-unit chiefs. The median public-company CEO holds only .25% of the company's equity. Counting *all* sources of compensation—including salary, bonus, deferred compensation, stock options, and dismissal penalties—the personal wealth of the median public-company CEO increases by only $3.25 for a $1,000 increase in shareholder value.[11]

Thus the salary of the typical LBO business-unit manager is almost 20 times more sensitive to performance than that of the typical public-company manager. This comparison understates the true differences in compensation. The personal wealth of managing partners in an LBO partnership (in effect, the CEOs of the LBO Associations) is tied almost exclusively to the performance of the companies they control. The general partners in an LBO Association typically receive (through overrides and direct equity holdings) 20% or more of the gains in the value of the divisions they help manage. This implies a pay-for-performance sensitivity of $200 for every $1,000 in added shareholder value. It's not hard to understand why an executive who receives $200 for every $1,000 increase in shareholder value will unlock more value than an executive who receives $3.25.

LBO Associations are more decentralized than publicly held conglomerates. The LBO Association substitutes compensation incentives and ownership for direct monitoring by headquarters. The headquarters of KKR, the world's largest LBO partnership, has only 16 professionals and 44 additional employees. In contrast, the Atlanta headquarters of RJR Nabisco employed 470 people when KKR took it private last year in a $25 billion transaction. At the time of the Goldsmith tender offer for Goodyear, the company's Akron headquarters had more than 5,000 people on its salaried payroll.

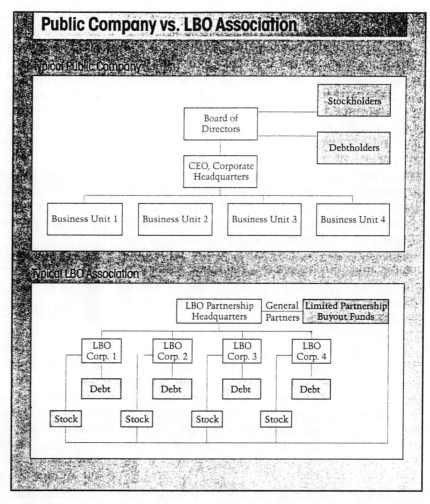

Public Company vs. LBO Association

Typical Public Company

Stockholders

Board of Directors

Debtholders

CEO, Corporate Headquarters

Business Unit 1 — Business Unit 2 — Business Unit 3 — Business Unit 4

Typical LBO Association

LBO Partnership Headquarters — General Partners — Limited Partnership Buyout Funds

LBO Corp. 1 — LBO Corp. 2 — LBO Corp. 3 — LBO Corp. 4

Debt — Debt — Debt — Debt

Stock — Stock — Stock — Stock

It is physically impossible for KKR and other LBO partnerships to become intimately involved in the day-to-day decisions of their operating units. They rely instead on stock ownership, incentive pay that rewards cash flow, and other compensation techniques to motivate managers to maximize value without bureaucratic oversight. My survey of 7 LBO partnerships found an average headquarters staff of 13 professionals and 19 nonprofessionals that oversees almost 24 business units with total annual sales of more than $11 billion. (See the table, "LBO Partnerships Keep Staff Lean.")

LBO Associations rely heavily on leverage. The average debt ratio (long-term debt as a percentage of debt plus equity) for public companies prior to a buyout is about 20%. The Kaplan study shows the average debt ratio for an LBO is 85% on completion of the buyout.

Intensive use of debt dramatically shrinks the amount of equity in a company. This allows the LBO general partners and divisional managers to control a large fraction of the total ownership without requiring huge investments they would be unable to make or large grants of free equity. For example, in a company with $1 billion in assets and a debt ratio of 20%, management would have to raise $80 million to buy 10% of the equity. If that same company had a debt ratio of 90%, management would have to raise only $10 million to control a 10% stake. By concentrating equity holdings among managers and LBO partners, debt intensifies the ownership incentives that are so important to efficiency.

High debt also allows LBO Associations and other private organizations to tap the benefits of risk diversification once provided only by the public equity market. Intensive use of debt means much of it must be in the form of public, high-yield, noninvestment-grade securities, better known as junk bonds. This debt, which was pioneered by Drexel Burnham Lambert, reflects more of the risk borne by shareholders in the typical public company. Placing this public debt in the well-diversified portfolios of large financial institutions spreads equitylike risk among millions of investors, who are the ultimate beneficiaries of mutual funds and pension funds – without requiring those risks to be held as equity. Indeed, high-yield debt is probably the most important and productive capital market innovation in the last 40 years.

LBO Associations have well-defined obligations to their creditors and residual claimants. Most buyout funds are organized as limited partnerships in which the partners of the sponsoring LBO firm serve as general partners. The buyout fund purchases most of the equity and sometimes provides debt financing. The limited partnership agreement denies the general partner the right to transfer cash or other resources from one LBO division to another. That is, all returns from a business must be distributed to the limited partners and other equity holders of that business. Such binding agreements reduce the risk of unproductive reinvestment by prohibiting cross-subsidization among LBO units. In effect, the LBO sponsor must ask its institutional investors for permission to reinvest funds, a striking difference from the power of public-company managers to freely shift resources among business units.

The management, compensation, and financial structures of the LBO Association square neatly with the rebirth of active investors. Institutional investors delegate the job of being active monitors to agents best qualified to play the role. The LBO partnerships bond their performance by investing their own resources and reputations in the transaction and taking the bulk of their compensation as a share in the companies' increased value.

To be sure, this delegation is not without its tensions. The fact that LBO partnerships and divisional managers control the LBO Association's small equity base but hold little of the debt creates incentives for them to take high-risk management gambles. If their gambles succeed, they reap large rewards by increasing their equity value; if their gambles fail, creditors bear much of the cost. But the reputational consequences of such reckless behavior can be large. As long as creditors behave rationally, an LBO partnership that tries to profit at the expense of its creditors or walks away from a deal gone sour will not be able to raise funds for future investments.

To date, the performance of LBO Associations has been remarkable. Indeed, it is difficult to find any systematic losers in these transactions, and almost all of the gains appear to come from real increases

> ## Wall Street allocates capital more effectively than public-company CEOs do.

in productivity. The best studies of LBO performance reach the following conclusions:

☐ LBOs create large gains for shareholders. Studies estimate that the average total premium to public shareholders ranges from 40% to 56%.[12] Kaplan finds that in buyouts that go public again or are otherwise sold (which occurs on average 2.7 years after the original transaction), total shareholder value increases by an average of 235%, or nearly 100% above market-adjusted returns over the same period.[13] These returns are distributed about equally between pre-buyout shareholders and the suppliers of debt and

LBO Partnerships Keep Staff Lean

LBO Partnership	Year Started	Number of Professionals	Number of Nonprofessionals	Number of Business Units	Combined Annual Revenues (In billions of dollars)
Berkshire Partners	1986	14	6	15	$ 1
Butler Capital	1979	8	14	33	2.3
Clayton & Dubilier	1976	10	11	8	4.8
Gibbons Green van Amerongen	1969	6	7	12	5.3
Kohlberg Kravis Roberts	1976	16	44	19	58.7
Thomas H. Lee Co.	1974	15	12	25	8
Odyssey Partners	1950	19	39	53	N.A.

equity to the transaction. Prebuyout shareholders earn average market-adjusted premiums of 38%, while the total return to capital (debt plus equity) for buyout investors is 42%. This return to buyout investors is measured on the total purchase price of the LBO, not the buyout equity. Because equity returns are almost a pure risk premium, and therefore independent of the amount invested, they are very high. The median market-adjusted return on buyout equity is 785%, or 125% per year.

□ Value gains do not come at the expense of other financial constituencies. Some critics argue that buyout investors, especially managers, earn excessive returns by using inside information to exploit public shareholders. Managers do face severe conflicts of interest in these transactions; they cannot simultaneously act as buyer and agent for the seller. But equity-owning managers who are not part of postbuyout management teams systematically sell their shares into LBOs. This would be foolish if the buyout were significantly underpriced in light of inside information, assuming that these nonparticipating insiders have the same inside information as the continuing management team. Moreover, LBO auctions are becoming common; underpriced buyout proposals (including those initiated by management) quickly generate competing bids.

No doubt some bondholders have lost value through going-private transactions. By my estimate, RJR Nabisco's prebuyout bondholders lost almost $300 million through the downgrading of their claims on the newly leveraged company. This is a small sum in comparison to the $12 billion in total gains the transaction produced. As yet, there is no evidence that bondholders lose on average from LBOs. Evidence on LBOs completed through 1986 does show that holders of convertible bonds and preferred stock gain a statistically significant amount and that straight bondholders suffer no significant gains or losses.[14]

New data may document losses for bondholders in recent transactions. But the expropriation of wealth from bondholders should not be a continuing problem. The financial community is perfecting many techniques, including poison puts and repurchase provisions, to protect bondholders in the event of substantial restructurings. In fact, versions of these loss-prevention techniques have been available for some time. In the past, bondholders such as Metropolitan Life, which sued RJR Nabisco over the declining value of the company's bonds, chose not to pay the premium for protection.

□ LBOs increase operating efficiency without massive layoffs or big cuts in research and development. Kaplan finds that average operating earnings increase by 42% from the year prior to the buyout to the third year after the buyout. Cash flows increase by 96% over this same period. Other studies document significant improvements in profit margins, sales per employee, working capital, inventories, and receivables.[15] Those who doubt these findings might take a moment to scan the business press, which has chronicled the impressive postbuyout performance of companies such as Levi Strauss, A.O. Scott, Safeway, and Weirton Steel.

Importantly, employment does not fall systematically after buyouts, although it does not grow as quickly as in comparable companies. Median employment for all companies in the Kaplan study, including those engaged in substantial divestitures, increased by nearly 1%. Companies without significant divestitures increased employment by 5%.

Moreover, the great concern about the effect of buyouts on R&D and capital investment is unwarranted. The low-growth companies that make the best candidates for LBOs don't invest heavily in R&D to begin with. Of the 76 companies in the Kaplan study, only 7 spent more than 1% of sales on R&D before the buyout. Another recent study shows

▌ LBO performance: dramatic gains in profit margins, cash flow, sales per employee, and working capital.

that R&D as a fraction of sales grows at the same rate in LBOs as in comparable public companies.[16] According to Kaplan's study, capital expenditures are 20% lower in LBOs than in comparable non-LBO companies. Because these cuts are taking place in low-growth or declining industries and are accompanied by a doubling of market-adjusted value, they appear to be coming from reductions in low-return projects rather than productive investments.

□ Taxpayers do not subsidize going-private transactions. Much has been made of the charge that large increases in debt virtually eliminate the tax obligations of an LBO. This argument overlooks five sources of additional tax revenues generated by buyouts: capital gains taxes paid by prebuyout shareholders; capital gains taxes paid on postbuyout asset sales; tax payments on the large increases in operating earnings generated by efficiency gains; tax payments by creditors who receive interest payments on the LBO debt; and taxes generated by more efficient use of the company's total capital.

Overall, the U.S. Treasury collects an estimated 230% more revenues in the year after a buyout than it would have otherwise and 61% more in long-term present value. The $12 billion gain associated with the RJR Nabisco buyout will generate net tax revenues of $3.3 billion in the first year of the buyout; the company paid $370 million in federal taxes in the year before the buyout. In the long term, the transaction will generate total taxes with an estimated present value of $3.8 billion.[17]

□ LBO sponsors do not have to take their companies public for them to succeed. Most LBO transactions are completed with a goal of returning the reconfigured company to the public market within three to five years. But recent evidence indicates that LBO sponsors are keeping their companies under private ownership. Huge efficiency gains and high-return asset sales produce enough cash to pay down debt and allow LBOs to generate handsome returns as going concerns. The very proliferation of these transactions has helped create a more efficient infrastructure and liquid market for buying and selling divisions and companies. Thus LBO investors can "cash out" in a secondary LBO or private sale without recourse to a public offering. One recent study

High debt creates incentives to avoid bankruptcy. Troubled companies are reorganized quickly.

finds that only 5% of the more than 1,300 LBOs between 1981 and 1986 have gone public again.[18]

Public companies can learn from LBO Associations and emulate many of their characteristics. But this requires major changes in corporate structure, philosophy, and focus. They can reduce the waste of free cash flow by borrowing to repurchase stock or pay large dividends. They can alter their charters to encourage large investors or experiment with alliances with active investors such as Lazard Frères' Corporate Partners fund. They can increase equity ownership by directors, managers, and employees. They can enhance incentives through pay-for-performance systems based on cash flow and value rather than accounting earnings. They can decentralize management by rethinking the role of corporate headquarters and shrinking their staffs.

Some corporations are experimenting with such changes—FMC, Holiday, and Owens-Corning—and the results have been impressive. But only a coordinated attack on the status quo will halt the eclipse of the public company. It is unlikely such an attack will proceed fast enough or go far enough.

Who can argue with a new model of enterprise that aligns the interests of owners and managers, improves efficiency and productivity, and unlocks hundreds of billions of dollars of shareholder value? Many people, it seems, mainly because these organizations rely so heavily on debt. As I've discussed, debt is crucial to management discipline and resolving the conflict over free cash flow. But critics, even some who concede the control function of debt, argue that the costs of leverage outweigh the benefits.

Wall Street economist Henry Kaufman, a prominent critic of the going-private trend, issued a typical warning earlier this year: "Any severe shock—a sharp increase in interest rates in response to Federal Reserve credit restraint, or an outright recession that makes the whole stock market vulnerable, or some breakdown in the ability of foreign firms to bid for pieces of U.S. companies—will drive debt-burdened companies to the government's doorstep to plead for special assistance."[19]

The relationship between debt and insolvency is perhaps the least understood aspect of this entire organizational evolution. New hedging techniques mean the risk associated with a given level of corporate debt is lower today than it was five years ago. Much of the bank debt associated with LBOs (which typically represents about half of the total debt) is done through floating-rate instruments. But few LBOs accept unlimited exposure to interest rate fluctuations. They purchase caps to set a ceiling on interest charges or use swaps to convert floating-rate debt into fixed-rate debt. In fact, most banks require such risk management techniques as a condition of lending.

Critics of leverage also fail to appreciate that insolvency in and of itself is not always something to avoid—and that the costs of becoming insolvent are likely to be much smaller in the new world of high leverage than in the old world of equity-dominated balance sheets. The proliferation of takeovers, LBOs, and other going-private transactions has inspired innovations in the reorganization and workout process. I refer to these innovations as "the privatization of bankruptcy." LBOs *do* get in financial trouble more frequently than public companies do. But few LBOs ever enter formal bankruptcy. They are reorganized quickly (a few months is common), often under new management, and at much lower costs than under a court-supervised process.

How can insolvency be less costly in a world of high leverage? Consider an oversimplified example. Companies A and B are identical in every respect except for their financial structures. Each has a going-concern value of $100 million (the discounted value of its expected future cash flows) and a liquidation or salvage value of $10 million. Company A has an equity-dominated balance sheet with a debt ratio of 20%, common for large public companies. Highly leveraged Company B has a debt ratio of 85%, common for LBOs. (See the illustration, "The Privatization of Bankruptcy.")

Now both companies experience business reversals. What happens? Company B will get in trouble with its creditors much sooner than Company A. After all, Company B's going-concern value doesn't have to shrink very much for it to be unable to meet its payments on $85 million of debt. But when it does run into trouble, its going-concern value will be nowhere near its liquidation value. If the going-concern value shrinks to $80 million, there remains $70 million of value to preserve by avoiding liquidation. So Company B's creditors have strong incentives to preserve the remaining value by quickly and efficiently reorganizing their claims outside the courtroom.

No such incentives operate on Company A. Its going-concern value can fall dramatically before creditors worry about their $20 million of debt. By the time creditors do intervene, Company A's going-concern value will have plummeted. And if Company A's value falls to under $20 million, it is much more likely than Company B to be worth less than its $10 million salvage value. Liquidation in this situation is the likely and rational outcome, with all its attendant conflicts, dislocations, and costs.

The evolving U.S. system of corporate governance and finance exhibits many characteristics of the postwar Japanese system. LBO partnerships act much like the main banks (the real power center) in Japan's *keiretsu* business groupings. The keiretsu make extensive use of leverage and intercorporate holdings of debt and equity. Banks commonly hold substantial equity in their client companies and have their own executives help them out of difficulty. (For years, Nissan has been run by an alumnus of the Industrial Bank of Japan, who became CEO as part of the bank's effort to keep the company out of bankruptcy.) Other personnel, including CFOs, move frequently between banks and companies as part of an ongoing relationship that involves training, consulting, and monitoring. Japanese banks allow companies to enter formal bankruptcy only when liquidation makes economic sense – that is, when a company is worth more dead than alive. Japanese corporate boards are composed almost exclusively of insiders.

Ironically, even as more U.S. companies come to resemble Japanese companies, Japan's public companies are becoming more like U.S. companies of 15 years ago. Japanese shareholders have seldom had any power. The banks' chief disciplinary tool, their power to withhold capital from high-growth, cash-starved companies, has been vastly reduced as a result of several factors. Japan's victories in world product markets have left its companies awash in profits. The development of domestic and international capital markets has created ready alternatives to bank loans, while deregulation has liberalized corporate access to these funds. Finally, new legal constraints prevent banks from holding more than 5% of the equity of any company, which reduces their incentive to engage in active monitoring.

Many of Japan's public companies are flooded with free cash flow far in excess of their opportunities to invest in profitable internal growth. In 1987, more than 40% of Japan's large public companies had no net bank borrowings – that is, cash balances larger than their short- and long-term borrowings. Toyota, with a cash hoard of $10.4 billion, more than 25% of its total assets, is commonly referred to as the Toyota Bank.[20]

In short, Japanese managers are increasingly unconstrained and unmonitored. They face no effective internal controls, little control from the product markets their companies already dominate, and fewer controls from the banking system because of self-financing, direct access to capital markets, and lower debt ratios. Unless shareholders and creditors discover ways to prohibit their managers from behaving like U.S. managers, Japanese companies will make uneconomic acquisitions and diversification moves, generate internal waste, and engage in other value-

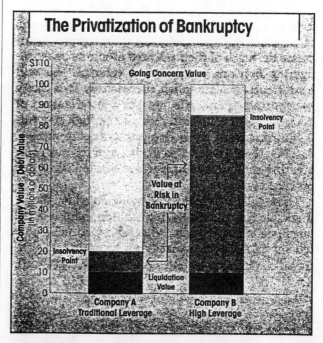

The Privatization of Bankruptcy

destroying activities. The long-term result will be the growth of bureaucracy and inefficiency and the demise of product quality and organizational responsiveness—until the waste becomes so severe it triggers a market for corporate control to remedy the excesses.

The Japanese remedy will reflect that country's unique legal system and cultural practices. But just as hostile takeovers, LBOs, and other control transactions went from unacceptable behavior in the United States to a driving force in corporate restructuring, so too will they take hold in Japan—once the potential returns outweigh the costs and risks of challenging the corporate status quo.

Meanwhile, in the United States, the organizational changes revitalizing the corporate sector will create more nimble enterprises and help reverse our losses in world product markets. As this profound innovation continues, however, people will make mistakes. To learn, we have to push new policies to the margin. It will be natural to see more failed deals.

There are already some worrisome structural issues. I look with discomfort on the dangerous tendency of LBO partnerships, bolstered by their success, to take more of their compensation in front-end fees rather than in back-end profits earned through increased equity value. As management fees and the fees for completing deals get larger, the incentives to do deals, rather than good deals, also increases. Institutional investors (and the economy as a whole) are best served when the LBO partnership is the last member of the LBO Association to get paid and when the LBO partnership gets paid as a fraction of the back-end value of the deals, including losses.

Moreover, we have yet to fully understand the limitations on the size of this new organizational form. LBO partnerships are understandably tempted to increase the reach of their talented monitors by reconfiguring divisions as acquisition vehicles. This will be difficult to accomplish successfully. It is likely to require bigger staffs, greater centralization of decision rights, and dilution of the high pay-for-performance sensitivity that is so crucial to success. As LBO Associations expand, they run the risk of recreating the bureaucratic waste of the diversified public corporation.

These and other problems should not cloud the remarkable benefits associated with the eclipse of the large public corporation. What surprises me is how few mistakes have occurred thus far in an organizational change as profound as any since World War II.

References

1. Equity values based on trends in the Wilshire Index. Private-placement data from IDD Information Services as published in Sarah Bartlett, "Private Market's Growing Edge," *New York Times*, June 20, 1989.

2. For more analysis of the oil industry, see my article, "The Takeover Controversy: Analysis and Evidence," in *Corporate Restructuring and Executive Compensation* (Cambridge, Mass: Ballinger, 1989).

3. Calculated from Standard & Poor's Compustat file.

4. Kevin J. Murphy, "Corporate Performance and Managerial Remuneration," *Journal of Accounting and Economics*, 1985, vol. 7, no. 1-3.

5. Federal Reserve Board, Balance Sheets of U.S. Economy.

6. G. Bennett Stewart III and David M. Glassman, "The Motives and Methods of Corporate Restructuring: Part II," *Journal of Applied Corporate Finance*, Summer 1988.

7. Stephen Phillips, "Revco: Anatomy of an LBO that Failed," *Business Week*, October 3, 1988.

8. "A Hollow Victory for Bob Mercer," *Industry Week*, February 23, 1987.

9. Jonathan P. Hicks, "The Importance of Being Biggest," *New York Times*, June 20, 1989.

10. Steven Kaplan, "Sources of Value in Management Buyouts," *Journal of Financial Economics*, forthcoming.

11. Michael C. Jensen and Kevin J. Murphy, "Performance Pay and Top Management Incentives," *Journal of Political Economy*, forthcoming.

12. Yakov Amihud, "Leveraged Management Buyouts and Shareholders' Wealth," in *Leveraged Management Buyouts: Causes and Consequences* (Homewood, Ill.: Dow Jones-Irwin, 1989).

13. That is, returns net of the returns that would normally be earned on these securities, given their level of systematic risk (beta) and general market returns.

14. L. Marais, K. Schipper, and A. Smith, "Wealth Effects of Going Private for Senior Securities," *Journal of Financial Economics*, 1989, vol. 23, no. 1.

15. In addition to Kaplan, see Abbie Smith, "Corporate Ownership Structure and Performance," unpublished paper, University of Chicago, 1989. See also Frank R. Lichtenberg and Donald Siegel, "The Effects of Leveraged Buyouts on Productivity and Related Aspects of Firm Behavior," *National Bureau of Economic Research*, 1989.

16. Lichtenberg and Siegel, NBER, 1989.

17. Michael C. Jensen, Robert Kaplan, and Laura Stiglin, "Effects of LBOs on Tax Revenues of the U.S. Treasury," *Tax Notes*, February 6, 1989.

18. Chris Muscarella and Michael Vetsuypens, "Efficiency and Organizational Structure: A Study of Reverse LBOs," unpublished paper, Southern Methodist University, April 1989.

19. Henry Kaufman, "Bush's First Priority: Stopping the Buyout Mania," *Washington Post*, January 1, 1989.

20. Average (book value) debt ratios fell from 77% in 1976 to 68% in 1987. Given the 390% increase in stock prices over this period, market-value debt ratios fell even more dramatically. Figures calculated from the NEEDS Nikkei Financials file for all companies on the First Section of the Tokyo Stock Exchange.

Article 3

Paying top executives "better" would eventually mean paying them more.

CEO Incentives – It's Not How Much You Pay, But How

by Michael C. Jensen and Kevin J. Murphy

The arrival of spring means yet another round in the national debate over executive compensation. Soon the business press will trumpet answers to the questions it asks every year: Who were the highest paid CEOs? How many executives made more than a million dollars? Who received the biggest raises? Political figures, union leaders, and consumer activists will issue now-familiar denunciations of executive salaries and urge that directors curb top-level pay in the interests of social equity and statesmanship.

The critics have it wrong. There are serious problems with CEO compensation, but "excessive" pay is not the biggest issue. The relentless focus on *how much* CEOs are paid diverts public attention from the real problem—*how* CEOs are paid. In most publicly held companies, the compensation of top executives is virtually independent of performance. On average, corporate America pays its most important

Michael C. Jensen is the Edsel Bryant Ford Professor of Business Administration at the Harvard Business School. His most recent HBR article, "Eclipse of the Public Corporation" (September-October 1989), won a McKinsey Award. Kevin J. Murphy is an associate professor at the University of Rochester's William E. Simon Graduate School of Business Administration. His earlier HBR article on executive compensation, "Top Executives Are Worth Every Nickel They Get," appeared in the March-April 1986 issue.

leaders like bureaucrats. Is it any wonder then that so many CEOs act like bureaucrats rather than the value-maximizing entrepreneurs companies need to enhance their standing in world markets?

We recently completed an in-depth statistical analysis of executive compensation. Our study incorporates data on thousands of CEOs spanning five decades. The base sample consists of information on salaries and bonuses for 2,505 CEOs in 1,400 publicly held companies from 1974 through 1988. We also collected data on stock options and stock ownership for

 Despite the headlines, top executives are not receiving record salaries and bonuses.

CEOs of the 430 largest publicly held companies in 1988. In addition, we drew on compensation data for executives at more than 700 public companies for the period 1934 through 1938.

Our analysis leads us to conclusions that are at odds with the prevailing wisdom on CEO compensation:

Despite the headlines, top executives are not receiving record salaries and bonuses. Salaries and bonuses have increased over the last 15 years, but

CEO pay levels are just now catching up to where they were 50 years ago. During the period 1934 through 1938, for example, the average salary and bonus for CEOs of leading companies on the New York Stock Exchange was $882,000 (in 1988 dollars). For the period 1982 through 1988, the average salary and bonus for CEOs of comparable companies was $843,000.

Annual changes in executive compensation do not reflect changes in corporate performance. Our statistical analysis posed a simple but important question: For every $1,000 change in the market value of a company, how much does the wealth of that company's CEO change? The answer varied widely across our 1,400-company sample. But for the median CEO in the 250 largest companies, a $1,000 change in corporate value corresponds to a change of just 6.7 cents in salary and bonus over two years. Accounting for all monetary sources of CEO incentives—salary and bonus, stock options, shares owned, and the changing likelihood of dismissal—a $1,000 change in corporate value corresponds to a change in CEO compensation of just $2.59.

Compensation for CEOs is no more variable than compensation for hourly and salaried employees. On average, CEOs receive about 50% of their base pay in the form of bonuses. Yet these "bonuses" don't generate big fluctuations in CEO compensation. A comparison of annual inflation-adjusted pay changes for CEOs from 1975 through 1988 and pay changes for 20,000 randomly selected hourly and salaried workers shows remarkably similar distributions. Moreover, a much lower percentage of CEOs took real pay cuts over this period than did production workers.

With respect to pay for performance, CEO compensation is getting worse rather than better. The most powerful link between shareholder wealth and executive wealth is direct stock ownership by the CEO. Yet CEO stock ownership for large public companies (measured as a percentage of total shares outstanding) was *ten times* greater in the 1930s than in the 1980s. Even over the last 15 years, CEO holdings as a percentage of corporate value have declined.

Compensation policy is one of the most important factors in an organization's success. Not only does it shape how top executives behave but it also helps determine what kinds of executives an organization attracts. This is what makes the vocal protests over CEO pay so damaging. By aiming their protests at compensation *levels*, uninvited but influential guests at the managerial bargaining table (the business press, labor unions, political figures) intimidate board members and constrain the types of contracts that are written between managers and shareholders. As a result of public pressure, directors become reluctant to reward CEOs with substantial (and therefore highly visible) financial gains for superior performance. Naturally, they also become reluctant to impose meaningful financial penalties for poor performance. The long-term effect of this risk-averse orientation is to erode the relation between pay and performance and entrench bureaucratic compensation systems.

Are we arguing that CEOs are underpaid? If by this we mean "Would average levels of CEO pay be higher if the relation between pay and performance were stronger?" the answer is yes. More aggressive pay-for-performance systems (and a higher probability of dismissal for poor performance) would produce sharply lower compensation for less talented managers. Over time, these managers would be replaced by more able and more highly motivated executives who would, on average, perform better and earn higher levels of pay. Existing managers would have greater incentives to find creative ways to enhance corporate performance, and their pay would rise as well.

These increases in compensation—driven by improved business performance—would not represent a transfer of wealth from shareholders to executives. Rather, they would reward managers for the increased success fostered by greater risk taking, effort, and ability. Paying CEOs "better" would eventually mean paying the average CEO more. Because the stakes are so high, the potential increase in corporate performance and the potential gains to shareholders are great.

How Compensation Measures Up

Shareholders rely on CEOs to adopt policies that maximize the value of their shares. Like other human beings, however, CEOs tend to engage in activities that increase their own well-being. One of the most critical roles of the board of directors is to create incentives that make it in the CEO's best interest to do what's in the shareholders' best interests. Conceptually this is not a difficult challenge. Some combination of three basic policies will create the right monetary incentives for CEOs to maximize the value of their companies:

1. Boards can require that CEOs become substantial owners of company stock.

2. Salaries, bonuses, and stock options can be structured so as to provide big rewards for superior performance and big penalties for poor performance.

3. The threat of dismissal for poor performance can be made real.

Unfortunately, as our study documents, the realities of executive compensation are at odds with these principles. Our statistical analysis departs from most studies of executive compensation. Unlike the annual surveys in the business press, for example, we do not focus on this year's levels of cash compensation or cash compensation plus stock options exercised. Instead, we apply regression analysis to 15 years' worth of data and estimate how changes in corporate performance affect CEO compensation and wealth over all relevant dimensions.

We ask the following questions: How does a change in performance affect current cash compensation, defined as changes in salary and bonus over two years? What is the "wealth effect" (the present value) of those changes in salary and bonus? How does a change in corporate performance affect the likelihood of the CEO being dismissed, and what is the financial impact of this new dismissal probability? Finally, how does a change in corporate performance affect the value of CEO stock options and shares, whether or not the CEO exercised the options or sold the shares? (For a discussion of our methodology, see the insert, "How We Estimate Pay for Performance.")

The table "The Weak State of Pay for Performance" provides a detailed review of our main findings for a subsample of CEOs in the 250 largest publicly held companies. Together, these CEOs run enterprises that generate revenues in excess of $2.2 trillion and employ more than 14 million people. The results are both striking and troubling. A $1,000 change in corporate market value (defined as share price appreciation plus dividends) corresponds to a two-year change in CEO salary and bonus of less than a dime; the long-term effects of that change add less than 45 cents to the CEO's wealth. A $1,000 change in corporate value translates into an estimated median change of a nickel in CEO wealth by affecting dismissal prospects. At the median, stock options add another 58 cents worth of incentives. Finally, the value of shares owned by the median CEO changes by 66 cents for every $1,000 increase in corporate value. All told, for the median executive in this subsample, a $1,000 change in corporate performance translates into a $2.59 change in CEO wealth. The table also reports estimates for CEOs at the lower and upper bounds of the middle two quartiles of the sample. (For an extensive review and comparison of the pay-for-performance relation for individual CEOs, see "A New Survey of Executive Compensation" that follows this article.)

This degree of pay-for-performance sensitivity for cash compensation does not create adequate incentives for executives to maximize corporate value. Consider a corporate leader whose creative strategic plan increases a company's market value by $100 million. Based on our study, the median CEO can expect a two-year increase in salary and bonus of $6,700—hardly a meaningful reward for such outstanding performance. His lifetime wealth would increase by $260,000—less than 4% of the present value of the median CEO's shareholdings and remaining lifetime salary and bonus payments.[1]

Or consider instead a CEO who makes a wasteful investment—new aircraft for the executive fleet, say, or a spanking addition to the headquarters building—that benefits him but diminishes the market value of the company by $10 million. The total wealth of this CEO, if he is representative of our sample, will decline by only $25,900 as a result of this misguided investment—not much of a disincentive for someone who earns on average $20,000 per week.

One way to explore the realities of CEO compensation is

The Weak State of Pay for Performance

A $1,000 Change in Shareholder Wealth Corresponds to . . .	Estimates for CEOs in the 250 Largest Companies	
	Median	Middle 50%
Change in this year's and next year's salary and bonus	$0.067	$0.01 to $0.18
Present value of the two-year change in salary and bonus	0.44	0.05 to 1.19
Change in the value of stock options	0.58	0.16 to 1.19
Wealth effect for change in likelihood of dismissal	0.05	0.02 to 0.14
Total change in all pay-related wealth	$1.29	$0.43 to $2.66
Change in value of direct stockholdings	0.66	0.25 to 1.98
Total change in CEO wealth	$2.59	$0.99 to $5.87

Note: The median individual components do not add to the median total change in CEO wealth since sums of medians do not in general equal the median of sums.

to compare current practices with the three principles that we outlined earlier. Let's address them one at a time.

CEOs should own substantial amounts of company stock. The most powerful link between shareholder wealth and executive wealth is direct ownership of shares by the CEO. Most commentators look at CEO stock ownership from one of two perspectives—the dollar value of the CEO's holdings or the value of his shares as a percentage of his annual cash compensation. But when trying to understand the incentive consequences of stock ownership, neither of these measures counts for much. What really matters is *the percentage of the company's outstanding shares the CEO owns.* By controlling a meaningful percentage of total corporate equity, senior managers experience a direct and powerful "feedback effect" from changes in market value.

Think again about the CEO adding jets to the corporate fleet. The stock-related "feedback effect" of this value-destroying investment—about $6,600—is small because this executive is typical of our sample, in which the median CEO controls only .066% of the company's outstanding shares. Moreover, this wealth loss (about two days' pay for the average CEO in a top-250 company) is the same whether the stockholdings represent a big or small fraction of the CEO's total wealth.

But what if this CEO held shares in the company comparable to, say, Warren Buffett's stake in the Berkshire Hathaway conglomerate? Buffett controls, directly and indirectly, about 45% of Berkshire Hathaway's equity. Under these circumstances, the stock-related feedback effect of a $10 million decline in market value is nearly $4.5 million—a much more powerful incentive to resist wasteful spending. '

Moreover, these differences in CEO compensation are associated with substantial differences in corporate performance. From 1970 through 1988, the average annual compound stock return on the 25 companies with the best CEO incentives (out of the largest 250 companies examined in our survey) was 14.5%, more than one-third higher than the average return on the 25 companies with the worst CEO incentives. A $100 investment in the top 25 companies in 1970 would have grown to $1,310 by 1988, as compared with $702 for a similar investment in the bottom 25 companies.

As a percentage of total corporate value, CEO share ownership has never been very high. The median CEO of one of the nation's 250 largest public companies owns shares worth just over $2.4 million—again, less than 0.07% of the company's market value. Also, 9 out of 10 CEOs own less than 1% of their company's stock, while fewer than 1 in 20 owns more than 5% of the company's outstanding shares.

It is unreasonable to expect all public-company CEOs to own as large a percentage of their company's equity as Warren Buffett's share of Berkshire Hathaway. Still, the basic lesson holds. The larger the share of company stock controlled by the CEO and senior management, the more substantial the linkage between shareholder wealth and executive wealth. A few companies have taken steps to increase the share of corporate equity owned by senior management. Employees of Morgan Stanley now own 55% of the firm's outstanding equity. Companies such as FMC and Holiday have used leveraged recapitalizations to reduce the amount of outstanding equity by repurchasing public shares, and thus allow their managers to control a bigger percentage of the company. After FMC adopted its recapitalization plan, for example, employee ownership increased from 12% to 40% of outstanding equity. These recapitalizations allow managers to own a bigger share of their company's equity without necessarily increasing their dollar investment.

Truly giant companies like IBM, General Motors, or General Electric will never be able to grant their senior executives a meaningful share of outstanding equity. These and other giant companies should understand that this limitation on executive incentives is a real cost associated with bigness.

Cash compensation should be structured to provide big rewards for outstanding performance and meaningful penalties for poor performance. A two-year cash reward of less than 7 cents for each $1,000 increase in corporate value (or, conversely, a two-year penalty of less than 7 cents for each $1,000 decline in corporate value) does not create effective managerial incentives to maximize value. In most large companies, cash compensation for CEOs is treated like an entitlement program.

There are some notable exceptions to this entitlement pattern. The cash compensation of Walt Disney CEO Michael Eisner, whose pay has generated such attention in recent years, is more than ten times more sensitive to corporate performance than the median CEO in our sample. Yet the small number of CEOs for whom cash compensation changes in any meaningful way in response to corporate performance shows how far corporate America must travel if pay is to become an effective incentive.

Creating better incentives for CEOs almost necessarily means increasing the financial risk CEOs face. In this respect, cash compensation has certain ad-

1. The median CEO in our sample holds stock worth $2.4 million. The average 1988 salary and bonus for the CEOs in our sample was roughly $1 million. At a real interest rate of 3%, the present value of the salary and bonus for the next five years to retirement (the average for the sample) is $4.6 million. Thus total lifetime wealth from the company is $7 million.

vantages over stock and stock options. Stock-based incentives subject CEOs to vagaries of the stock market that are clearly beyond their control. Compensation contracts based on company performance relative to comparable companies could provide sound incentives while insulating the CEO from factors such as the October 1987 crash. Although there is some evidence that directors make implicit adjustments for market trends when they set CEO pay, we are surprised that compensation plans based explicitly on relative performance are so rare.[2]

The generally weak link between cash compensation and corporate performance would be less troubling if CEOs owned a large percentage of corporate equity. In fact, it would make sense for CEOs with big chunks of equity to have their cash compensation less sensitive to performance than CEOs with small stockholdings. (For example, Warren Buffett's two-year cash compensation changes by only a penny for every $1,000 increase in market value.) In some cases, it might even make sense for pay to go up in bad years to serve as a financial "shock absorber" for losses the CEO is taking in the stock market. Yet our statistical analysis found no correlation between CEO stock ownership and pay-for-performance sensitivity in cash compensation. In other words, boards of directors ignore CEO stock ownership when structuring incentive compensation plans. We find this result surprising—and symptomatic of the ills afflicting compensation policy.

> Baseball managers often get fired after one losing season. CEOs stay on the job despite years of underperformance.

Make real the threat of dismissal. The prospect of being fired as a result of poor performance can provide powerful monetary and nonmonetary incentives for CEOs to maximize company value. Because much of an executive's "human capital" (and thus his or her value in the job market) is specific to the company, CEOs who are fired from their jobs are unlikely to find new jobs that pay as well. In addition, the public humiliation associated with a high-visibility dismissal should cause managers to carefully weigh the consequences of taking actions that increase the probability of being dismissed.

Here too, however, the evidence is clear: the CEO position is not a very risky job. Sports fans are accustomed to baseball managers being fired after one losing season. Few CEOs experience a similar fate after years of underperformance. There are many reasons

why we would expect CEOs to be treated differently from baseball managers. CEOs have greater organization-specific capital; it is harder for an outsider to come in and run a giant company than it is for a new manager to take over a ball club. There are differences in the lag between input and output. The measure of a baseball manager's success is the team's won-lost record this year; the measure of a corporate manager is the company's long-term competitiveness and value. For these and other reasons, it is not surprising that turnover rates are lower for CEOs than for baseball managers. It is surprising that the magnitude of the discrepancy is so large.

On average, CEOs in our base sample (2,505 executives) hold their jobs for more than ten years before stepping down, and most give up their title (but not their seat on the board) only after reaching normal retirement age. Two recent studies, spanning 20 years and more than 500 management changes, found only 20 cases where CEOs left their jobs because of poor performance.[3] To be sure, directors have little to gain from publicly announcing that a CEO is leaving because of failure—many underperforming CEOs leave amidst face-saving explanations and even public congratulations. But this culture of politeness does not explain why so few underperforming CEOs leave in the first place. University of Rochester's Michael Weisbach found that CEOs of companies that rank in the bottom 10% of the performance distribution (measured by stock returns) are roughly twice as likely to leave their jobs as CEOs whose companies rank in the top 10% of the performance distribution. Yet the differences that Weisbach quantifies—a 3% chance of getting fired for top performers versus a 6% chance of getting fired for laggards—are unlikely to have meaningful motivational consequences for CEOs.

Our own research confirms these and other findings. CEOs of large public companies are only slightly more likely to step down after very poor performance (which we define as company earnings 50% below market averages for two consecutive years) than after average performance. For the entire 1,400-company sample, our analysis estimates that the poor-performing CEOs are roughly 6% more likely to leave their jobs than CEOs of companies with average returns. Even assuming that a dismissed CEO never works again, the personal wealth consequences of this increased likelihood of dis-

2. See Robert Gibbons and Kevin J. Murphy, "Relative Performance Evaluation for Chief Executive Officers," *Industrial and Labor Relations Review*, February 1990, p. 30-S.

3. See Jerold B. Warner, Ross L. Watts, and Karen H. Wruck, "Stock Prices and Top Management Changes," *Journal of Financial Economics*, January-March 1988, p.461; and Michael S. Weisbach, "Outside Directors and CEO Turnover," *Journal of Financial Economics*, January-March 1988, p.431.

missal amounts to just 5 cents for every $1,000 loss of shareholder value.

With respect to pay for performance, there's no denying that the results of our study tell a bleak story. Then again, perhaps corporate directors are providing CEOs with substantial rewards and penalties based on performance, but they are measuring performance with metrics other than long-run stock market value. We tested this possibility and reached the same conclusion as in our original analysis. Whatever the metric, CEO compensation is independent of business performance.

For example, we tested whether companies rewarded CEOs on the basis of sales growth or accounting profits rather than on direct changes in shareholder wealth. We found that while more of the variation in CEO pay could be explained by changes in accounting profits than stock market value, the pay-for-performance sensitivity was economically just as insignificant as in our original model. Sales growth had little explanatory power once we controlled for accounting profits.[4]

Of course, incentives based on other measures will be captured by our methodology only to the extent that they ultimately correlate with changes in shareholder wealth. But if they don't – that is, if directors are rewarding CEOs based on variables other than those that affect corporate market value – why use such measures in the first place?

Moreover, if directors varied CEO compensation substantially from year to year based on performance measures not observable to us, this policy would show up as high raw variability in CEO compensation. But over the past 15 years, compensation for CEOs has been about as variable as cash compensation for a random sample of hourly and salaried workers – dramatic evidence of compensation's modest role in generating executive incentives.[5] "Common Variability: CEO and Worker Wages" compares the distribution of annual raises and pay

4. For more detail on these tests, see our article, "Performance Pay and Top-Management Incentives," *Journal of Political Economy*, April 1990.

5. Data on hourly and salaried workers come from the Michigan Panel Study on Income Dynamics. The sample includes 21,895 workers aged 21 to 65 reporting wages in consecutive periods. See Kenneth J. McLaughlin, "Rigid Wages?" University of Rochester Working Paper, 1989.

cuts of our CEO sample with national data on hourly and salaried workers from 1975 through 1986. A larger percentage of workers took real pay cuts at some time over this period than did CEOs. Overall, the standard deviation of annual changes in CEO pay was only slightly greater than for hourly and salaried employees (32.7% versus 29.7%).

Looking Backward: Pay for Performance in the 1930s

CEO compensation policies look especially unsatisfactory when compared with the situation 50 years ago. All told, CEO compensation in the 1980s was lower, less variable, and less sensitive to corporate performance than in the 1930s. To compare the current situation with the past, we constructed a longitudinal sample of executives from the 1930s using data collected by the Works Projects Administration. The WPA data, covering fiscal years 1934 through 1938, include salary and bonus for the highest paid executive (whom we designate as the CEO) in 748 large U.S. corporations in a wide range of industries. Nearly 400 of the WPA sample companies were listed on the New York Stock Exchange, and market values for these companies are available on the CRSP Monthly Stock Returns Tape. In order to compare

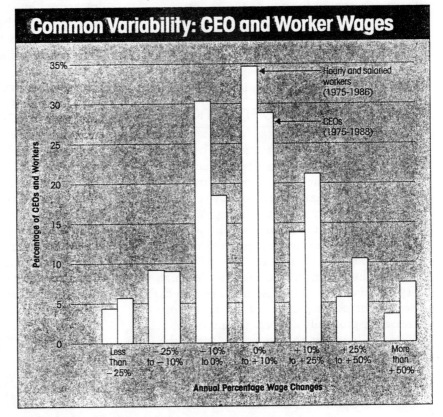

similar companies over the two time periods, we restricted our analysis to companies in the top 25% of the NYSE, ranked by market value. WPA compensation data are available for 60% of this top quartile group (averaging 112 companies per year), while data for more recent times are available for 90% of the top quartile companies (averaging 345 companies per year).

The results are striking. Measured in 1988 constant dollars, CEOs in top quartile public companies earned an average salary and bonus of $882,000 in the 1930s—more than the 1982 through 1988 average of $843,000 and significantly more than the 1974 through 1981 average of $642,000. Over this same time period, there has been a tripling (after inflation) of the market value of top quartile companies—from $1.7 billion in the 1930s to $5.9 billion in 1982 through 1988. Coupled with the decline in salaries, the ratio of CEO pay to total company value has fallen significantly—from 0.11% in the 1930s to 0.03% in the 1980s. Compensation was more variable in the 1930s as well. The average standard deviation of the annual pay changes—the best statistical measure of the year-to-year variability of compensation—was $504,000 in the 1930s compared with $263,500 in the 1980s.

The incentives generated by CEO stock ownership have also declined substantially over the past 50 years. To test this trend, we reviewed stock ownership data for CEOs in the 120 largest companies (ranked by market value) in 1938, 1974, and 1988. "Whatever Happened to CEO Stock Ownership?" reports our findings. The percentage of outstanding shares owned by CEOs (including shares held by family members) in the top 120 companies fell by a factor of nearly ten from 1938 to 1988. The trend is unmistakable: as a percentage of total market value, CEO stock ownership has declined substantially over the last 50 years and is continuing to fall.

The Costs of Disclosure

Why don't boards of directors link pay more closely to performance? Commentators offer many explanations, but nearly every analysis we've seen overlooks one powerful ingredient—the costs imposed by making executive salaries public. Government disclosure rules ensure that executive pay remains a visible and controversial topic. The benefits of disclosure are obvious; it provides safeguards against "looting" by managers in collusion with "captive" directors. The costs of disclosure are less well appreciated but may well exceed the benefits.

Managerial labor contracts are not a private matter between employers and employees. Third parties play an important role in the contracting process, and strong political forces operate inside and outside companies to shape executive pay. Moreover, authority over compensation decisions rests not with the shareholders but with compensation committees generally composed of outside directors. These committees are elected by shareholders but are not perfect agents for them. Public disclosure of "what the boss makes" gives ammunition to outside constituencies with their own special-interest agendas. Compensation committees typically react to the agitation over pay levels by capping—explicitly or implicitly—the amount of money the CEO earns.

How often do shareholder activists or union leaders denounce a corporate board for *under*paying the CEO? Not very often—and that's precisely the problem. Most critics of executive pay want it both ways. They want companies to link pay to performance, yet they also want to limit compensation to arbitrary amounts or some fuzzy sense of "what's fair." That won't work. Imposing a ceiling on salaries for outstanding performers inevitably means creating a floor for poor performers. Over time, by cutting off the upper and lower tails of the distribution, the entire pay-for-performance relation erodes. When mediocre outfielders earn a million dollars a year, and New York law partners earn about the same, influen-

Whatever Happened to CEO Stock Ownership?

CEO Inside Stock Ownership (as percentage of total outstanding stock)

Year	
1938	.3%
1974	.047%
1988	.037%

Note: Median stock ownership for CEOs in largest 120 companies, ranked by market value. Data were obtained from proxy statements and include not only shares held directly but also shares held by family members and related trusts.

CEO Incentives—It's Not How Much You Pay, But How—*Jensen and Murphy*   41

tial critics who begrudge comparable salaries to the men and women running billion-dollar enterprises help guarantee that these companies will attract mediocre leaders who turn in mediocre performances.

Admittedly, it is difficult to document the effect of public disclosure on executive pay. Yet there have been a few prominent examples. Bear, Stearns, the successful investment bank, went public in 1985 and had to submit to disclosure requirements for the first time. CEO Alan Greenberg's $2.9 million salary and bonus was the nation's fourth highest that year, and his ranking drew attention to the firm's compensation system. Under private ownership, compensation of the firm's managing directors was set at a modest $150,000 base plus a bonus pool tied to earnings—a tight link between pay and performance. Because the firm was so profitable in 1986, the bonus pool swelled to $80 million, an average of $842,000 for each of the firm's 95 managing directors. A public outcry ensued. Six months after going public, Bear, Stearns announced it was lowering the bonus pool from 40% to 25% of the firm's adjusted pretax earnings in excess of $200 million. According to one account, the firm's business success had "yielded an embarrassment of riches for top executives."[6]

More recently, we interviewed the president of a subsidiary of a thriving publicly traded conglomerate. This president is compensated with a straight fraction of his subsidiary's earnings above a minimum threshold, with no upper bound. Today he makes roughly five times what he made before his operation was acquired by the conglomerate, and corporate headquarters recognizes him as one of the company's outstanding executives. Why doesn't he want to be an officer of the conglomerate? For one, because his salary would have to be made public—a disclosure both he and the CEO consider a needless invitation to internal and external criticism.

We are not arguing for the elimination of salary disclosure. (Indeed, without disclosure we could not have conducted this study.) But it's time compensation committees stood up to outside criticism and stopped adopting policies that make their companies' incentive problem worse. The costs of negative publicity and political criticism are less severe than the costs to shareholder wealth created by misguided compensation systems.

Corporate Brain Drain

The level of pay has very little to do with whether or not CEOs have incentives to run companies in the shareholders' interests—incentives are a function of how pay, whatever the level, changes in response to corporate performance. But the level of pay does affect the quality of managers an organization can attract. Companies that are willing to pay more will, in general, attract more highly talented individuals.

> ## Are current levels of CEO compensation high enough to attract the best and the brightest? Probably not.

So if the critics insist on focusing on levels of executive pay, they should at least ask the right question: Are current levels of CEO compensation high enough to attract the best and brightest individuals to careers in corporate management? The answer is, probably not.

Who can disagree with these propositions?

☐ It is good when our most talented men and women are attracted to the organizations that produce the goods and deliver the services at the heart of the economy.

☐ People evaluate alternative careers at least in part on the basis of lifetime monetary rewards.

☐ People prefer to make more money than less, and talented, self-confident people prefer to be rewarded based on performance rather than independent of it.

☐ If some organizations pay more on average and offer stronger pay-for-performance systems than other organizations, talent will migrate to the higher paying organizations.

These simple propositions are at the heart of a phenomenon that has inspired much handwringing and despair over the last decade—the stream of talented, energetic, articulate young professionals into business law, investment banking, and consulting. Data on the career choices of Harvard Business School graduates document the trend that troubles so many pundits. Ten years ago, nearly 55% of newly graduated HBS students chose careers in the corporate sector, while less than 30% chose investment banking or consulting. By 1987, more than half of all HBS graduates entered investment banking or consulting, while under 30% chose careers in the corporate sector. Last year, just over one-third of all graduating HBS students chose corporate careers, while nearly 40% chose careers in investment banking or consulting. And Harvard Business School is not alone; we gathered data on other highly rated MBA programs and found similar trends.

We don't understand why commentators find this trend so mysterious. A highly sensitive pay-for-

6. *Wall Street Journal*, March 21, 1986.

How We Estimate Pay for Performance

Our analysis draws primarily on two sources of data: annual executive compensation surveys published in *Forbes* magazine from 1975 through 1988 and Standard & Poor's Compustat file. The base sample includes information on 2,505 CEOs from 1,400 companies. We estimated pay-for-performance sensitivities for each CEO using a variety of statistical techniques. The findings reported in the table "The Weak State of Pay for Performance" represent the median and "middle 50%" CEOs in a sample of the 250 largest companies.

Perhaps the best way to illustrate our methodology is to review pay-for-performance calculations for a single CEO – for example, David H. Murdock of Castle & Cooke, Inc., who tops our list of large-company CEOs with the best incentives. For each element of Mr. Murdock's compensation, we estimated answers to the same question: How does that compensation element change in response to a $1,000 change in corporate value, as measured by annual share price appreciation and dividends?

Two-Year Change in Salary and Bonus. We used least squares regression to calculate the relation between the dollar change in salary and bonus and the dollar change in shareholder wealth for all companies with at least seven years of pay-change data from 1975 through 1988. We estimate a single pay-for-performance sensitivity for each company, therefore our estimates for Castle & Cooke use data on both Murdock and his predecessor Donald Kirchhoff. We did not use data on three other former CEOs – Robert Cook, Ian Wilson, and Henry Clark, Jr. – because they each served as CEO for less than two years and we could therefore not calculate pay changes. The regression equation uses last year's performance in addition to this year's performance as explanatory variables. The result was:

(change in salary and bonus) = $32,300
+ .000986 (change in this year's shareholder wealth)
− .000219 (change in last year's shareholder wealth)

The pay-for-performance sensitivity is defined as the estimated slope coefficient in the regression equation. For this regression, the sum of the estimated coefficients implies that each $1,000 increase in the wealth of Castle & Cooke shareholders corresponds to an increase of 98.6 cents in this year's salary and bonus for Murdock, and a decrease of 21.9 cents in next year's salary and bonus.

Thus the total expected increase in salary and bonus over two years is 77 cents per $1,000 change in value.

We estimated 430 separate regressions like the one for Murdock, having eliminated 740 companies due to incomplete information and 230 companies that were no longer in the sample in 1988. The pattern of t-statistics for the individual regressions implies that the average pay-performance coefficients are positive and statistically different from zero at confidence levels exceeding 99%.

Pay-Related Wealth. The estimate of 77 cents is an accurate measure of how David Murdock's and Donald Kirchhoff's salary and bonus change due to a $1,000 change in shareholder value. But it underestimates the change in their wealth. Since part of the change is permanent, they will earn it for the rest of their careers. In addition, Murdock and Kirchhoff received "other" income as fringe benefits and payoffs from long-term performance plans. We measure the change in their total wealth as the discounted present value of the permanent component of the change in compensation plus other income for the year.

To estimate the wealth change, we make three assumptions: (1) all changes in salary and bonus are permanent, while other forms of pay are transitory; (2) the CEO receives the change in salary and bonus until age 66; and (3) the wage increase to age 66 is discounted at the real interest rate of 3%. The resulting regression equation for Castle & Cooke, based on these assumptions, is:

(other income + present value of change in salary and bonus) =
$150,000 + .00310 (change in this year's shareholder wealth)
+ .00060 (change in last year's shareholder wealth)

The sum of the estimated coefficients in this regression implies that Murdock's and Kirchhoff's wealth (as a result of changes in salary and bonus) changes an average of $3.70 for every $1,000 change in the market value of Castle & Cooke.

Stock Options. Stock options are an increasingly important component of executive compensation packages, and their value relates directly to changes in share price. However, holding a stock option does not provide the same incentives as owning a share of stock – a distinction sometimes overlooked by compensation practitioners. For example, stock ownership rewards both price appreciation and dividends, while options reward only appreciation.

Moreover, the value of an option changes by less than $1 when the stock price changes by $1. How much less depends on factors such as interest rates, dividend yields, and whether the option is in or out of the money. Our simulation results show that 60 cents is a good approximation for the value change of at-the-money options for a company with a (sample average) dividend yield of 5%. This holds for a reasonable range of maturities, variance of stock returns, and interest rates.

We collected data on total stock options held by each of the sample CEOs from the proxy statements issued in advance of the company's 1989 annual meeting. Unfortunately, outstanding options are not always reported on proxy statements. So we estimated Murdock's outstanding options as options granted in 1988 (50,000 shares) plus options exercisable within 60 days (300,000 shares). Castle & Cooke had 59.3 million shares outstanding. A $1,000 change in shareholder wealth corresponds to the following change in the value of Murdock's options:

$$\left(\frac{60\text{¢ change in value of option}}{\$1 \text{ change in stock price}} \right) \times \left(\frac{350{,}000 \text{ Options}}{59{,}250{,}000 \text{ Total Shares}} \right) \times \$1{,}000 = \$3.54$$

Thus Murdock's option-related wealth changes by $3.54 for every $1,000 change in shareholder wealth. This estimate understates the change in the value of his options to the extent that he holds options granted prior to 1988 that are not exercisable within 60 days. We also underestimate the option-value change if his outstanding options are in the money, while we overstate the value change of out-of-the-money options.

Dismissal Incentives. The threat of being fired for poor performance provides monetary as well as non-monetary incentives for CEOs to maximize value. We estimate the financial incentives associated with dismissal through a four-stage process. First, using nonlinear "logistic" regression techniques on our 1974 through 1988 sample of 2,505 CEOs, we estimate the probability that a CEO will leave the job as a function of industry, company size, CEO age, market-relative performance, and lagged market-relative performance. Second, we compute point estimates of the departure probabilities when the company earns the market rate of return for two years versus when the company realizes share-price returns 50% below the market in two consecutive

years. Third, we multiply the difference in these two "dismissal probabilities" by the discounted value of the CEO's potential lost wages, assuming that the CEO would have received the current salary until age 66, and, if dismissed, never works again. Fourth, we calculate the dismissal performance sensitivity by dividing the CEO's potential wealth loss by the shareholder loss associated with earning 50% below-market returns for two years.

In Murdock's case, the probability that a 65-year-old CEO in a smaller-than-median-size company leaves his job is 20.7% in years when the company earns the market return and 23.9% when his company earns 50% below the market return for two straight years. The probability that Murdock will be fired (or encouraged to leave) for poor performance is 3.2%. Murdock's dismissal-related loss is his $1.5 million 1988 pay multiplied by the turnover-probability difference, or about $48,000. (If Murdock had been younger than 65, we would have calculated the present value of his 1988 pay until he reached 66.) Castle & Cooke shareholders, on the other hand, would lose about $1.25 billion of their $1.67 billion equity from two straight years of 50% below-market performance. Thus Murdock's potential wealth loss is about 3.8 cents per $1,000 lost by shareholders.

It is important to note that while our estimates of other CEO incentive sources use data for the individual CEO's company, our estimates of CEO-dismissal performance sensitivities are based on the entire sample. It is generally impossible to make company-specific estimates of the wealth effects of dismissal threats.

Stock Ownership. The most important component of CEO incentives is also the easiest to measure. As of March 1989, Murdock held directly 13,203,932 shares of Castle & Cooke. In addition, his children hold 80,870 shares in trusts. All told, his family holds 13,284,802 shares, or 22.42% of Castle & Cooke's outstanding stock. His total stock-related incentives are roughly $224.24 per $1,000 change in market value.

Putting It All Together. David Murdock's total pay-for-performance sensitivity is simply the sum of the sensitivities of each compensation element, or $231.53 per $1,000 change in shareholder value. This makes Murdock the CEO with the best incentives in the 250 largest companies.

performance system will cause high-quality people to self-select into a company. Creative risk takers who perceive they will be in the upper tail of the performance and pay distribution are more likely to join companies who pay for performance. Low-ability and risk-averse candidates will be attracted to companies with bureaucratic compensation systems that ignore performance.

Compensation systems in professions like investment banking and consulting are heavily weighted toward the contributions made by individuals and the performance of their work groups and companies. Compensation systems in the corporate world are often independent of individual, group, or overall corporate performance. Moreover, average levels of top-executive compensation on Wall Street or in corporate law are considerably higher than in corporate America. Financially speaking, if you are a bright, eager 26-year-old with enough confidence to want to be paid based on your contribution, why would you choose a career at General Motors or Procter & Gamble over Morgan Stanley or McKinsey & Company?

Most careers, including corporate management, require lifetime investments. Individuals must choose their occupation long before their ultimate success or failure becomes a reality. For potential CEOs, this means that individuals seeking careers in corporate management must join their companies at an early age in entry-level jobs. The CEOs in our sample spent

Salaries for Top Lawyers Are High . . .

Rank	Firm	Average Income per Partner	Number of Partners
1	Cravath, Swaine, & Moore	$1,595,000	67
2	Cahill Gordon & Reindel	$1,420,000	57
3	Sullivan & Cromwell	$1,375,000	91
4	Wachtell, Lipton, Rosen & Katz	$1,350,000	46
5	Skadden, Arps, Slate, Meagher & Flom	$1,155,000	177

Source: *The American Lawyer*, July-August 1989, p. 34.

proprietors of their own businesses, or as CEOs of privately held companies. It is instructive, therefore, to compare levels of CEO compensation with the compensation of similarly skilled individuals who have reached leadership positions in other occupations.

The compensation of top-level partners in law firms is one relevant comparison. These numbers are closely guarded secrets, but some idea of the rewards to top partners can be gleaned from data on average partner income reported each year in a widely read industry survey. The table "Salaries for Top Lawyers Are High..." reports 1988 estimated average incomes earned by partners in the highest paying corporate law firms. These five firms paid their 438 partners *average* incomes ranging from $1.35 million to nearly $1.6 million. Partners at the very top of these firms earned substantially more. When comparing these results with corporate compensation, the appropriate question to ask is "How many public companies paid their top 67 or 177 executives average salaries of $1.6 million or $1.2 million in 1989?" The answer is, few or none. How surprising is it, then, that law school classes are bulging with some of the country's brightest students?

Compensation for the most successful corporate managers is also modest in comparison with compensation for the most successful Wall Street players. Here too it is difficult to get definitive numbers for a large sample of top executives. But the most recent annual survey, as reported in the table "...So Are Salaries on Wall Street," documents the kinds of rewards available to top investment bankers. At Goldman, Sachs, for example, 18 partners earned more than $3 million in 1988, and the average income for those partners was more than

. . . So Are Salaries on Wall Street

Firm	Number of Partners Earning More Than $3 Million in 1988	Average Earnings for Partners Earning More Than $3 Million in 1988
Drexel Burnham Lambert	20	$18,000,000
Goldman, Sachs	18	$ 9,100,000
Morgan Stanley	11	$ 4,300,000
Sterling Group	6	$36,700,000
Kohlberg Kravis Roberts	5	$59,000,000
Lazard Freres	5	$17,200,000
Salomon Brothers	5	$ 4,700,000
Neuberger & Berman	5	$ 4,700,000

Source: *Financial World*, July 11, 1989. Average earnings are based on *Financial World's* lower bound earnings estimate, p. 32.

an average of 16 years in their companies before assuming the top job. Of course, many people who reach the highest ranks of the corporate hierarchy could also expect to be successful in professional partnerships such as law or investment banking, as

$9 million. Only nine public-company CEOs had incomes in excess of $9 million in 1988 (mostly through exercising stock options), and no public company paid its top 18 executives more than $3 million each. The Wall Street surveys for 1989 are not yet available, but consistent with high pay-for-performance systems, they will likely show sharp declines in bonuses reflecting lower 1989 industry performance.

The compensation figures for law and investment banking look high because they reflect only the most highly paid individuals in each occupation. Average levels of compensation for lawyers or investment bankers may not be any higher than average pay levels for executives. But that's not the relevant comparison. The very best lawyers or investment bankers can earn substantially more than the very best corporate executives. Highly talented people who would succeed in any field are likely to shun the corporate sector, where pay and performance are weakly related, in favor of organizations where pay is more strongly related to performance – and the prospect of big financial rewards more favorable.

Money Isn't Everything

Some may object to our focus on monetary incentives as the central motivator of CEO behavior. Are there not important nonmonetary rewards associated with running a large organization? Benefits such as power, prestige, and public visibility certainly do affect the level of monetary compensation necessary to attract highly qualified people to the corporate sector. But unless nonmonetary rewards

vary positively with company value, they are no more effective than cash compensation in motivating CEOs to act in the shareholders' interests. Moreover, because nonmonetary benefits tend to be a function of position or rank, it is difficult to vary them from period to period based on performance.

 Money isn't everything, but nonmonetary rewards often create the wrong incentives for CEOs.

Indeed, nonmonetary rewards typically motivate top managers to take actions that *reduce* productivity and harm shareholders. Executives are invariably tempted to acquire other companies and expand the diversity of the empire, even though acquisitions often reduce shareholder wealth. As prominent members of their community, CEOs face pressures to keep open uneconomic factories, to keep the peace with labor unions despite the impact on competitiveness, and to satisfy intense special-interest pressures.

Monetary compensation and stock ownership remain the most effective tools for aligning executive and shareholder interests. Until directors recognize the importance of incentives – and adopt compensation systems that truly link pay and performance – large companies and their shareholders will continue to suffer from poor performance. ▱

Reprint 90308

"A New Survey of Executive Compensation," an extensive review and comparison of the pay-for-performance relation for individual CEOs, begins on the next page.

A New Survey of Executive Compensation

Routinely misused and abused, surveys contribute to the common ills of corporate compensation policy. Surveys that report average compensation across industries help inflate salaries, as everyone tries to be above average (but not in front of the pack). Surveys that relate pay to company sales encourage systems that tie compensation to size and growth, not performance and value. Surveys that rank the country's highest paid executives stir public outrage, raise legislative eyebrows, and provide emotional justification for increased demands in labor negotiations.

The basic problem with existing compensation surveys is that they focus exclusively on *how much* CEOs are paid instead of *how* they are paid. Our focus on incentives rather than levels leads naturally to a new and different kind of survey. Instead of reporting who's paid the most, our survey reports who's paid the best—that is, whose incentives are most closely aligned with the interests of their shareholders.

Our survey considers incentives from a variety of sources—including salary and bonus, stock options, stock ownership, and the threat of getting fired for poor performance. It includes only companies listed in the *Forbes* executive compensation surveys for at least eight years from 1975 through 1989, since we require at least seven years of pay change to estimate the relation between pay and performance. Our methodology is described in the insert "How We Estimate Pay for Performance."

Compensation surveys in the business press, such as those published by *Fortune* and *Business Week*, are really about levels of pay and not about pay for performance. Yet they often include an analysis or ranking of the appropriateness of a particular CEO's pay by relating it to company performance in some fashion. The methods adopted by *Fortune* and *Business Week* share a common flaw. CEOs earning low fixed salaries while delivering mediocre performance look like stars; on the flip side, CEOs with genuinely strong pay-for-per-

The 25 CEOs of Large Companies with the Best Incentives

			Total Effects (over Two Years) on CEO Wealth Corresponding to Each $1,000 Change in Shareholder Wealth		
Rank	Company	CEO	Change in All Pay-Related Wealth	Change in the Value of Stock Owned	Change in Total CEO Wealth
1	Castle & Cooke	David H. Murdock	$7.29	$224.24	$231.53
2	Amerada Hess	Leon Hess*	$0.02	$152.71	$152.73
3	Wang Laboratories	An Wang*	$0.84	$137.83	$138.68
4	Aon Corp.	Patrick G. Ryan	$0.76	$137.46	$138.22
5	Loews	Laurence A. Tisch	$0.00	$126.40	$126.40
6	Ethyl	Floyd D. Gottwald, Jr.	−$0.25	$90.73	$90.48
7	Marriott	J. Willard Marriott, Jr.*	$1.55	$72.58	$74.14
8	MCA	Lew R. Wasserman	$0.05	$70.10	$70.15
9	Paine Webber Group	Donald B. Marron	$55.59	$11.44	$67.03
10	Paccar	Charles M. Pigott	$2.25	$50.86	$53.12
11	Times Mirror	Robert F. Erburu	$3.29	$45.39	$48.67
12	Coastal Corp.	Oscar S. Wyatt, Jr.*	$0.43	$44.33	$44.75
13	Archer-Daniels-Midland	Dwayne O. Andreas	−$0.15	$41.23	$41.07
14	Carter Hawley Hale	Philip M. Hawley*	$23.36	$16.25	$39.60
15	McDonnell Douglas	John F. McDonnell*	$0.09	$33.79	$33.88
16	CBS	Laurence A. Tisch	$1.79	$31.58	$33.37
17	Humana	David A. Jones*	$1.34	$25.88	$27.22
18	Winn-Dixie Stores	A. Dano Davis	$2.72	$23.22	$25.95
19	Masco	Richard A. Manoogian	$8.78	$14.08	$22.86
20	American Int'l Group	Maurice R. Greenberg	$0.50	$21.72	$22.22
21	Digital Equipment	Kenneth H. Olsen*	$1.00	$19.06	$20.07
22	MCI Communications	William G. McGowan*	$1.77	$17.95	$19.73
23	Cummins Engine	Henry B. Schacht	$18.46	$0.87	$19.33
24	Walt Disney	Michael D. Eisner	$15.62	$2.88	$18.50
25	FMC	Robert H. Malott	$8.43	$7.04	$15.47

Note: Sample consists of CEOs in the 250 largest companies, ranked by 1988 sales. *Denotes founder or founding-family CEO.

formance practices rank poorly. For example, *Business Week*'s 1989 survey calculates the ratio of the change in shareholder wealth to the CEO's total compensation, both measured over three years. Executives with the highest ratios are labeled the "CEOs Who Gave the Most for Their Pay." Low-ratio CEOs purportedly gave shareholders the least. *Fortune*'s 1989 compensation issue uses a regression model to estimate how compensation varies with factors such as the CEO's age and tenure, company size, location, industry, and performance. Although the author cautions against taking the results too literally, CEOs earning more than predicted are implicitly designated as "overpaid," while those earning less than predicted are "underpaid."

Consider the case of Disney's Michael Eisner. By all accounts, Mr. Eisner's pay is wedded to company performance—in addition to loads of stock options, he gets 2% of all profits above an annually increasing threshold. Shareholders have prospered under Eisner, and few

have complained that his compensation is unreasonable in light of the $7 billion in shareholder wealth he has helped create since joining the company in 1984. But *Business Week* ranks Eisner second on the list of CEOs who gave their shareholders the least (right behind option-laden Lee Iacocca, who over the past decade helped create $6 billion in wealth for Chrysler shareholders), while *Fortune* flags Eisner as the nation's third most overpaid CEO. Surveys ranking Eisner and Iacocca low are clearly not measuring incentives. In contrast, our survey ranks Eisner and Iacocca as the nation's fourth and ninth respectively "best paid" CEOs measured on the basis of pay-related wealth alone.

We estimated the pay-for-performance relation for each of the 430 companies for which we have sufficient data. The results are summarized in the four nearby tables. Three of the tables include results for the 250 largest companies ranked by 1988 sales. The 25 CEOs with the best and worst overall incentives, as reflected by the rela-

The 25 CEOs of Large Companies with the Worst Incentives

			Total Effects (over Two Years) on CEO Wealth Corresponding to Each $1,000 Change in Shareholder Wealth		
Rank	Company	CEO	Change in All Pay-Related Wealth	Change in the Value of Stock Owned	Change in Total CEO Wealth
226	Central & South West	Merle L. Borchelt	$0.14	$0.32	$0.46
227	Campbell Soup	R. Gordon McGovern	$0.07	$0.38	$0.44
228	3M	Allen F. Jacobson	$0.28	$0.11	$0.39
229	Sears Roebuck	Edward A. Brennan	$0.17	$0.20	$0.37
230	AMP	Walter F. Raab	$0.03	$0.39	$0.36
231	Consolidated Edison	Arthur Hauspurg	$0.22	$0.12	$0.34
232	Detroit Edison	Walter J. McCarthy, Jr.	$0.24	$0.07	$0.31
233	Commonwealth Edison	James J. O'Connor	$0.24	$0.06	$0.30
234	Texas Utilities	Jerry S. Farrington	$0.23	$0.07	$0.29
235	Exxon	Lawrence G. Rawl	$0.14	$0.11	$0.25
236	AT&T	Robert E. Allen	$0.19	$0.04	$0.24
237	ARCO	Lodwrick M. Cook	–$0.10	$0.33	$0.23
238	IBM	John F. Akers	$0.13	$0.06	$0.19
239	Borden	Romeo J. Ventres	–$0.20	$0.38	$0.18
240	Eastman Kodak	Colby H. Chandler	$0.09	$0.08	$0.17
241	R.R. Donnelley & Sons	John R. Walter	–$0.18	$0.34	$0.16
242	Johnson & Johnson	Ralph S. Larsen	$0.11	$0.05	$0.15
243	Chevron Corp.	Kenneth T. Derr	–$0.04	$0.15	$0.11
244	GTE	James L. Johnson	$0.04	$0.07	$0.11
245	Pacific Gas & Electric	Richard A. Clarke	$0.06	$0.04	$0.10
246	Philadelphia Electric	Joseph F. Paquette, Jr.	$0.07	$0.01	$0.08
247	PacifiCorp	Al M. Gleason	–$0.04	$0.08	$0.04
248	Honeywell	James J. Renier	–$0.51	$0.40	–$0.10
249	Carolina Power & Light	Sherwood H. Smith, Jr.	–$0.61	$0.45	–$0.16
250	Navistar International	James C. Cotting	–$1.61	$0.20	–$1.41

Note: Sample consists of CEOs in the 250 largest companies, ranked by 1988 sales.

tion between their total compensation (composed of all pay-related wealth changes and the change in the value of stock owned), are summarized in the first two tables. Castle & Cooke, whose current CEO is David Murdock, ranks first with a total change in CEO wealth of $231.53 for every $1,000 change in shareholder wealth. His stockholdings contribute $224.24 of this amount, while the change in all pay-related wealth adds another $7.29.

With a few exceptions, it is clear that the best incentives are determined primarily by large CEO stockholdings. Donald Marron of Paine Webber is such an exception, with more than $55 of his total of $67 coming from changes in pay-related wealth. So too are Philip Hawley of Carter Hawley Hale, Henry Schacht of Cummins Engine, and Disney's Eisner.

The 25 companies providing their CEOs with the worst total incentives are led by Navistar International whose CEO James Cotting on average receives a $1.41 *increase* in wealth for every $1,000 *decrease* in shareholder value.

Carolina Power & Light's Sherwood Smith, Jr. receives a 16-cent increase for every $1,000 decrease in shareholder wealth. Other well-known corporations whose CEOs appear on the worst-incentives list include Chevron, Johnson & Johnson, Eastman Kodak, and IBM.

Although one has to recognize that there is statistical uncertainty surrounding our estimates of pay-related wealth sensitivity, no CEO with substantial equity holdings (measured as a fraction of the total outstanding equity) makes our list of low-incentive CEOs. As we point out in the accompanying article, an important disadvantage of corporate size is that it is extremely difficult for the CEO to hold a substantial fraction of corporate equity.

The inverse relation between size and stockholdings (and therefore the negative effect of size on incentives) is readily visible in the much higher sensitivities shown for the top 25 CEOs in smaller companies, those ranking from 251 to 430 in 1988 sales. (See the table "The Best of the Rest: CEO Incentives in Smaller Companies.") Warren

The Best of the Rest: CEO Incentives in Smaller Companies

			Total Effects (over Two Years) on CEO Wealth Corresponding to Each $1,000 Change in Shareholder Wealth		
Rank	Company	CEO	Change in All Pay-Related Wealth	Change in the Value of Stock Owned	Change in Total CEO Wealth
1	Berkshire Hathaway	Warren E. Buffett	$0.06	$446.77	$446.83
2	Williamette Industries	William Swindells, Jr.	$0.64	$427.10	$427.75
3	Riggs National	Joe L. Allbritton	$1.22	$358.19	$359.40
4	Hilton Hotels	Barron Hilton*	$0.85	$245.90	$246.75
5	Timken	William R. Timken, Jr.*	$5.20	$142.46	$147.66
6	United Missouri Bancshares	R. Crosby Kemper	$1.08	$118.65	$119.73
7	Zions Bancorporation	Roy W. Simmons	$2.76	$89.17	$91.93
8	First Empire State	Robert G. Wilmers	$18.72	$71.63	$90.36
9	Florida National Banks	John D. Uible	$1.85	$87.66	$89.51
10	Equimark	Alan S. Fellheimer	$15.53	$72.28	$87.81
11	W.W. Grainger	David W. Grainger*	$0.21	$79.13	$79.34
12	Fin'l Corp. of Santa Barbara	Philip R. Brinkerhoff	$54.68	$21.41	$76.09
13	Golden West Financial	Herbert M. Sandler*	$4.48	$67.36	$71.83
14	Merchants National	Otto N. Frenzel III	$9.59	$60.19	$69.79
15	First City Bancorp of Texas	A. Robert Abboud	–$0.21	$58.75	$58.54
16	First Security	Spencer F. Eccles	$2.63	$44.84	$47.47
17	Central Bancshares of the South	Harry B. Brock, Jr.*	$4.89	$38.25	$43.15
18	Fruehauf	T. Neal Combs	$16.20	$21.14	$37.34
19	Holiday	Michael D. Rose	$14.01	$20.94	$34.94
20	Cullen/Frost Bankers	Thomas C. Frost*	$8.90	$25.95	$34.85
21	Beneficial Corp.	Finn M.W. Caspersen	$3.37	$29.87	$33.23
22	Yellow Freight System	George E. Powell, Jr.	$0.86	$30.90	$31.76
23	Data General	Edson D. deCastro*	$1.89	$29.79	$31.68
24	Equitable Bancorporation	H. Grant Hathaway	$11.01	$17.23	$28.24
25	Imperial Corp. of America	Kenneth J. Thygerson	$24.98	$2.52	$27.51

Note: Sample consists of CEOs in companies ranked 251 to 430 by 1988 sales. *Denotes founder or founding-family CEO.

Buffett of Berkshire Hathaway leads this list with $446 per $1,000, followed by William Swindells, Jr. of Williamette Industries, Joe Allbritton of Riggs National, and Barron Hilton of Hilton Hotels. Again, the importance of large stockholdings is clear.

Indeed, one problem with current compensation practices is that boards often reward CEOs with substantial equity through stock options but then stand by to watch CEOs undo the incentives by unloading their stockholdings. Boards seldom provide contractual constraints or moral suasion that discourage the CEO from selling such shares to invest in a diversified portfolio of assets. One of the ironies of the situation is that the corporation itself often funds executive financial counseling by consultants whose common mantra is "sell and diversify, sell and diversify." While this can be personally advantageous to executives, it is not optimal for shareholders or society because it significantly reduces CEOs' incentives to run their companies efficiently.

Pay-related incentives are under the direct control of the compensation committee and the board. The table "Best Paid CEOs of Large Companies" lists the 25 companies that reward their CEOs in a way that provides the best incentives from pay-related wealth alone—changes in salary and bonus, long-term incentive plans, dismissal likelihood, and stock options. Each of these estimates is given in the table, along with the sum of the effects in the last column. The table makes clear that the major contributors to pay-related incentives are stock options and the present value of the change in salary and bonus.

Authors' note: The accompanying tables present estimates of pay-for-performance sensitivities for only a fraction of the CEOs in our full survey. Readers who would like a copy of the full 430-company survey, along with a detailed technical appendix fully describing our methodology, can write to Professor Kevin J. Murphy at the William E. Simon Graduate School of Business, University of Rochester, Rochester, NY 14627.

Best Paid CEOs of Large Companies

			Change in Pay-Related Wealth Corresponding to Each $1,000 Change in Shareholder Wealth				
Rank	Company	CEO	Change in Salary + Bonus over Two Years	Present Value of Pay Change	Change in Wealth due to Dismissal Likelihood	Change in Value of Stock Options	Change in All Pay-Related Wealth
1	Paine Webber Group	Donald B. Marron	$4.11	$46.91	$1.18	$7.51	$55.59
2	Carter Hawley Hale	Philip M. Hawley*	$0.03	$0.54	$0.98	$21.83	$23.36
3	Cummins Engine	Henry B. Schacht	$1.11	$18.29	$0.03	$0.14	$18.46
4	Walt Disney	Michael D. Eisner	$0.72	$11.35	$0.00	$4.27	$15.62
5	George A. Hormel	Richard L. Knowlton	$0.76	$7.47	$0.19	$4.70	$12.36
6	UAL	Stephen M. Wolf	$0.01	$0.45	$0.02	$11.57	$12.05
7	Fleet/Norstar	J. Terrence Murray	$0.72	$10.93	$0.03	$1.02	$11.98
8	Continental Bank	Thomas C. Theobald	$0.26	$2.01	$0.04	$9.40	$11.46
9	Chrysler Corp.	Lee A. Iacocca	$0.43	$5.38	$0.02	$4.74	$10.14
10	Zenith Electronics	Jerry K. Pearlman	$0.77	$7.44	$0.05	$2.27	$9.76
11	NCNB	Hugh L. McColl, Jr.	$0.76	$8.43	$0.01	$0.63	$9.07
12	Masco	Richard A. Manoogian	$0.01	$2.38	$0.16	$6.24	$8.78
13	FMC	Robert H. Malott	$0.01	$0.13	$0.47	$7.82	$8.43
14	Turner	Alfred T. McNeill	$2.01	$4.27	$0.27	$3.52	$8.06
15	B.F. Goodrich	John D. Ong	$0.51	$4.73	$0.14	$2.85	$7.72
16	Alco Standard	Ray B. Mundt	$0.88	$5.46	$0.88	$1.28	$7.61
17	Black & Decker	Nolan D. Archibald	$0.25	$3.89	$0.34	$3.30	$7.53
18	Castle & Cooke	David H. Murdock	$0.77	$3.70	$0.04	$3.54	$7.29
19	Brunswick Corp.	Jack F. Reichert	$0.40	$6.59	$0.26	$0.00	$6.85
20	Mellon Bank	Frank V. Cahouet	$0.42	$3.69	$0.65	$2.38	$6.72
21	Enron	Kenneth L. Lay	$0.46	$3.99	$0.05	$2.58	$6.62
22	Pan Am	Thomas G. Plaskett	$0.25	$0.77	$0.13	$5.55	$6.46
23	Toys "R" Us	Charles Lazarus*	-$0.13	$1.06	$0.11	$5.27	$6.45
24	Norwest	Lloyd P. Johnson	$0.22	$1.30	$0.10	$4.98	$6.37
25	First Union	Edward E. Crutchfield, Jr.	$0.48	$5.59	$0.03	$0.08	$5.71

Note: Sample consists of CEOs in the 250 largest companies, ranked by 1988 sales. *Denotes founder or founding-family CEO.

Article 4

The Business Economist at Work: Atlantic Richfield Company

By Anthony Finizza*

> *At Arco, the focus of the Economics Department is on the business aspects of the economic environment. Three levels of emphasis are bringing new views to executive management, strategic planning and support.*

JUST WHEN the world thought oil markets had calmed, Saddam Hussein threw the macroeconomy and the oil market into a cocked hat. Oil prices jumped out of the relatively narrow range that had characterized the market since the price crash of 1986. Senior management became increasingly uneasy, asking: Under what conditions will oil prices seek a new plateau? Will prices become more cyclical or will they settle down and return to another plateau below the range that we had envisioned? Does this event alter our long-term vision of oil markets? These questions are the types asked of the Economics group at Atlantic Richfield (Arco).

The Economics Department at Arco, formally called Economic and Environmental Analysis (EEA), is one of four segments of the Corporate Planning Division. Created in 1972, EEA was originally two departments, Environmental Analysis and Political Economics, which later were combined in 1982.

The EEA charter, largely unchanged in scope but honed over the past twenty years, has three levels of involvement in descending order of importance and difficulty:

*Anthony Finizza is Chief Economist, Atlantic Richfield Company, Los Angeles, CA.

See references at end of text.

1. *Visioning*
   Help Executive Management to learn things they don't know by:
   a. Challenging the firm's fundamental beliefs.
   b. Heightening management's awareness and understanding of leveraging, emerging issues that may affect the corporate portfolio.
   c. Testing and developing perceptions from outside sources to avoid inbred thinking.
2. *Strategic Planning*
   Manage the Environmental Analysis role in the Long Range Plan (LRP) process by:
   a. Suggesting new approaches and providing alternative views through scenario development.
   b. Testing and probing leveraging planning assumptions.
3. *Support*
   a. Provide economic support for Operating Companies and Corporate Staffs.

Note that the word "economics" does not appear in the charter. What the Economics Group brings to bear is an "economic way of thinking," along with other relevant disciplines (political science, etc.).

ROLE IN THE VISION FUNCTION

The first function is by far the most difficult to perform well and the most difficult to measure performance. Yet, there are a number of success stories.

The first example is of a mega-success. Analysis done in late 1984 for the 1985 long-range plan (LRP), suggested that oil prices would probably drop rapidly, a view developed more than one year in advance of the actual price drop. This competitive advantage allowed the company to undertake massive restructuring in advance of other companies. Although the energy scenarios had been suggesting a real price decline as early as the 1982 LRP (created in 1981), the new insight challenged basic company beliefs by calling for a price crash.

Second, the department's 1981 view of no increasing product prices, while inaccurate in detail, was directionally correct. It allowed the planning department to recommend sale of the Company's shale projects, which were predicated on rising real oil prices. This example points out the obvious fact that sometimes you only have to be somewhat differential from the competition to gain market advantage.

Third, insights from studies that the Economics Group undertook led to a restructuring of the firm's natural gas function.

Finally, the group developed insights about the Soviet Union, Eastern Europe, and the strength of the current environmental movement in advance of these becoming issues.

One forum for bringing in new views is the Business Environment Trends Team (BETT), chaired by the Chief Economist. The twelve-person team (three of whom are economists) has members from ten different corporate groups and an outside consulting service. The team's charter is to develop special insights that test management beliefs.

Another forum for identifying "surprises" is through a Rip Van Winkle process, an *ad hoc* method often used by the Economics Group. With this technique, one identifies a major assumption on which "one is betting the company." An example might be that of a real oil price rise by the year 2000. Because this major assumption may have gained status as a "sacred cow," planning can undertake little orthodox analysis. One has to step back, close one's eyes for twenty years (as Rip did) and wake up with prices, say, considerably lower than the reigning view. The point of the exercise is to identify the ways that this "discontinuity" could occur. The ways identified can help gauge the degree of certainty with which the Company should hold a price view as well as create an early warning system of variables for the group to monitor.

ROLE IN THE STRATEGIC PLANNING FUNCTION

Management of the environmental analysis role in the LRP process is part inspiration, but largely perspiration. The basic element of the Economic Group's contribution to the LRP process is providing international and domestic economic scenarios, energy supply and demand scenarios, and other elements of the future environment as planning cases for the LRP. The group develops, as appropriate, downside test cases to challenge project robustness.

The department's role is as provocateur: to identify and study critical issues, to make sure all aspects of the economic environment are considered, and to support the operating companies' economic group in division-specific studies.

The main guidance body for this role is the Strategic Planning Council, a committee chaired by the Vice President of Corporate Planning, with members including the eight divisional planning managers and the four corporate planning managers, one of whom is the Chief Economist.

Planning studies are identified and commissioned in the early stages of the annual LRP process at a company-wide meeting, the Environmental Analysis Forum, organized and chaired by the Chief Economist.

THE SUPPORT FUNCTION

The Economics Group provides economic support to various staffs. Interest-rate and exchange-rate forecasts are provided to the Treasury Department. The group provides support of litigation, economic advice for public advocacies, economic analysis of legislation for the Public Issues group, and input to Environmental Protection on economic aspects of pollution, global climate change, and various other topics.

Economists in the group sit on an interdivisional Tax Policy Council, making recommendation on the impact of alternative tax proposals on the Company. The group also provides monthly oil market perspectives to the Oil Pricing Committee. Most of these requests are routine, but the group does get frequent one-time only requests for economic analysis.

An important support area is political risk analysis. Before a Division can undertake a project in a foreign country, EEA has to pass on the political and business climate of that country.

The Economics Group developed and maintains a number of oil market models, one of which uses pathbreaking ideas from Artificial Intelligence.

The Chief Economist participates in a middle-management seminar six times a year where he presents the latest environmental outlook. The Economics Group also represents the Company on a number of industry committees (for example, the National Petroleum Council), trade associations (American Petroleum Institute), and professional organizations (for example, The International Association for Energy Economics).

HOW IS THE JOB DONE?

We provide information in oral or written form. Arco has a strong oral tradition, preferring presentations to long-winded memos. The economic staff uses a number of outside consultants, recognizing the need to provide nonparochial ideas. The large consulting budget, about 20-25 percent of the department's overall budget, includes outside economic and energy-modeling services, outside expert opinion, and special studies.

REPORTING RESPONSIBILITY

The Chief Economist supervises the economics function at Arco. He also serves as Manager, Economic and Environmental Analysis and reports to the Vice President of Corporate Planning, who in turn reports to the Chief Financial Officer. The Vice President of Corporate Planning is the agenda setter of the internal Management Group. This close tie insures that the Economics Group gets a hearing whenever it has a message to deliver.

There is another aspect of the reporting relationship that bears mentioning. At Arco, the Corporate Planning V.P. is the training ground for future leaders of the Corporation. Since it's inception, there have been ten Corporate Planning V.P.'s. In addition to the current V.P., the other nine include the current and past CEO, the current President, both Executive Vice-Presidents of Operating Company Groups, and three of the eight Operating Company Presidents. The tenth Executive Vice-President left the company but is now President of a set of assets that the company divested. This "success" story also explains the "preselling" of the importance and usefulness of the economics function.

STAFF

Including the Chief Economist, the Economics Group has five professional personnel: four economists and a political scientist. Two have the Ph.D. and three have training beyond the Master's degree. One person does international and domestic economic analysis, one performs country risk and political assessments, one addresses international energy issues, and one focuses on the domestic energy scene. The Chief Economist plays an oversight role as well as performs several of the support functions. While some economic departments at other companies have a number of junior analysts supporting the main staff, our principle is to have all members proficient in analytical techniques, all doing their own work. The time-honored premise is that we prefer to have people who are experts in their own right.

Prior to a significant downsizing of the corporation in 1985, the two departments from which the Economics Group was formed had ten professionals, while the political risk function had four people. The resultant combination was six. The widespread use of computers, a refocus on critical issues, and the deemphasis of monthly newsletters that were not perceived to have a strategic value helped in making the downsizing work.

The staff is encouraged to engage in outside professional activities. A number speak regularly in economic and energy issues to outside organizations. We must maintain a cachet both inside and outside the corporation.

The Corporate Planning philosophy is to have rapid turnover in its liaison groups, but less frequent movement in the specialized staffs. Members of the Economics Group have moved to other functions in the Company, but in general the positions do not lead to managerial positions.

SUMMARY

The Economics Group has changed emphasis over the past eight years, focusing on business aspects of the economic environment. The business economist at Arco is first and foremost an economist, but also a strategic planner, an idea generator, and hopefully, a sought-after resource.

REFERENCES

Finizza, A.J. "How the Rip Van Winkle Approach Helps Oil Executives Plan," *Long Range Planning*, Vol. 18, No. 1, pp. 59-63, 1985.

Levinson, M. "The Big Switch to Hands-On Economics," *Dun's Business Month*, August 1986, pp. 26-9.

Linden, D.W. "Dreary days in the dismal science," *Forbes*, January 21, 1991.

Wing, K.T. "What's An Economist To Do?," *Business Economics*, July 1987, pp. 34-7.

Section II
Demand Estimation and Other Applications of Econometrics

A basic tool of the managerial economist, namely econometrics, is the focus of this section. All economists should be familiar with basic econometric techniques, particularly regression analysis. This is true whether the economist has the role of producing econometric results, or interpreting the results produced by someone else. The articles here illustrate the use of econometrics in an applied setting. The first two articles illustrate the estimation of demand functions and demand elasticities.

The aggregate demand for beer in the United States is analyzed by Byunglak Lee and Victor J. Tremblay in "Advertising and the U.S. Market Demand for Beer." Factors that influence beer demand are found to be the price of beer as well as the prices of substitutes. Demographic factors are also found to influence beer demand. Advertising, however, does not seem to affect the aggregate demand for beer.

In "An Economic Analysis of the Demand for Abortions," Marshall H. Medoff estimates an abortion demand equation. Using cross–sectional data for U.S. states, he finds that the demand for abortions is affected negatively by price, and positively by income. The proportion of unmarried women in a state, the proportion of women in the labor force in a state, and the availability of Medicaid funding for abortions were found to have a positive and significant affect on abortions per pregnancy.

In "Search Costs and Apartment Rents," John D. Benjamin and Kenneth M. Lusht use regression analysis to examine the factors that affect apartment rents in State College, Pennsylvania. Their model includes variables to capture the effect of the physical characteristics of the apartment unit, and also the location, vacancy, tenants, management characteristics of the apartment, and the search costs of renters. This approach, which allows for the estimation of the implicit prices of characteristics of apartments, is often referred to as hedonic price function estimation.

The factors that affect the sale price of homes in metropolitan Philadelphia is the subject of "Price Concessions, Time on the Market, and the Actual Sale of Price of Homes," by Paul K. Asabere and Forrest E. Huffman. The authors use regression analysis to examine the effect of location and physical characteristics of homes on the sale prices of homes. Of particular concern are the effect of the price concession, which is the difference between the list price and the ultimate sale price, and the effect of the time the house was on the market on the sale price. As the authors expected, other things equal, the sale price of homes is negatively related to the price concession and positively related to the time on the market.

Article 5

Advertising and the US market demand for beer

BYUNGLAK LEE* and VICTOR J. TREMBLAY ‡

*First Economic Research Institute, Seoul, Korea and ‡Department of Economics,
Oregon State University, Ballard Extension Hall 303, Corvallis, OR 97331-3612, USA

The US per capita market demand for beer is empirically estimated to determine the
effect of advertising on the demand for beer. The empirical results indicate that the
most important determinants of demand are the price of beer, the price of substitutes,
demographic factors, and a light beer dummy variable. The positive effects of income
and lagged consumption appear to be small. Although many have argued that
advertising promotes beer consumption, the empirical results of this study do not
support this hypothesis.

I. INTRODUCTION

Because alcoholic beverage consumption can be addictive,
the effect of beer advertising on consumer demand is an
important social concern. If, for example, advertising increases demand by helping create false needs and promoting
alcohol abuse, then a ban on beer advertising may promote
social welfare.[1]

There has been much debate concerning the effect of
advertising on the market demand for beer. Brewers and
advertisers deny any link between advertising and total beer
consumption. For example, Donald B. Shae, President of the
US Brewers Association, argues that advertising affects firm
but not market demand and that the best prevention of
alcohol abuse is education.[2] Alternatively, members of a
coalition of PTA (Parent-Teacher Association) and consumer groups united under Project SMART (Stop Marketing Alcohol on Radio and Television) have claimed that
beer advertising misleads and promotes alcohol abuse. In
1985 this group petitioned the Federal Trade Commission
to restrict the advertising of alcoholic beverages. Although
this petition was rejected by the Federal Trade Commission,

the decision was not based on solid empirical evidence using
US data.[3]

To determine the effect of advertising on beer consumption the US market demand for beer will be estimated. There
have been several previous studies that have estimated the
demand for beer, but they each suffer from a number of
weaknesses. For example, Horowitz and Horowitz (1965)
omit price as an explicit variable. Hogarty and Elzinga
(1972) ignore several important determinants of beer
consumption (i.e., demographic factors and the price of
substitutes), and, according to Nelson (1988), the work by
Ornstein and Hanssens (1985) suffers from a serious multicollinearity problem.

The results of this analysis will also be used to answer a
number of other questions concerning the demand for beer.
First, the price and income elasticities of beer demand can be
estimated. Some studies have found beer to be a normal
good and others an inferior good, and elasticity estimates
from this study can shed light on this controversy. In
addition, this study can determine the importance of demographics and analyse the effect of the introduction of light
beer on the demand for beer.

---

[1] A ban on advertising also raises the issue of free speech. In *Central Hudson and Gas Corp. v. Public Service Commission* (447 U.S. 557, 1980),
the US Supreme Court held that commercial speech can be restricted if there is a substantial social gain from the restriction and the
restriction is not more extensive than needed to fulfil its goal. Thus, an advertising ban on addictive commodities would be legal if and only
if it substantially reduces market demand.
[2] This discussion can be found in McAvoy (1985).
[3] The most reliable evidence indicating that advertising has little effect on the demand for alcoholic beverages uses Canadian data. However,
Duffy (1983) found that advertising had a small positive and significant effect on the demand for beer in the United Kingdom. For a
summary of the evidence see Wilcox *et al.* (1986).

II. EMPIRICAL MODEL

The model of beer demand is based on Lancaster's (1966, 1971, 1979) characteristics approach to consumer theory and Stigler and Becker's (1977) theory of taste formation. According to Lancaster the consumer is assumed to gain utility from the characteristics that a commodity possesses and not directly from the commodity itself. Stigler and Becker argue that tastes are determined by the consumer's consumption capital, which is formed by the consumer's experience in the marketplace. These extensions of consumer demand theory imply the following individual demand function:

$$q = q(\mathbf{P}, Y, \mathbf{Z}, \mathbf{T})$$

where q equals quantity demanded, $\mathbf{P}$ is a vector of commodity prices, Y is consumer money income, $\mathbf{Z}$ is a vector of important commodity characteristics, and $\mathbf{T}$ is a vector of taste-influencing variables.

Economic theory suggests that the important prices are a commodity's own price and the prices of substitutes and complements. It is assumed that beer has no complements and that whiskey and cola-drinks are substitutes for beer.[4]

When going from an individual's demand function to the market demand, Varian (1984) shows that money income, Y, must be replaced by the individual income levels of all potential consumers, $\mathbf{Y}$. For empirical applications the question is how to parsimoniously capture the effect of $\mathbf{Y}$. Barten (1977) shows that under rather restrictive assumptions one can consider both demand and income per capita.[5] This is the procedure that will be adopted in this study. It assumes that a representative consumer's demand function can be modelled and that income distribution has little effect on beer demand.

The effect of income on the demand for beer is still unresolved. For example, Hogarty and Elzinga (1973) and Clements and Johnson (1983) found beer to be a normal good. McGuinness (1980) and Ornstein and Hanssens (1985) found that income had no effect on the demand for beer, and Niskanen (1962), Lynk (1984), and Tremblay (1985b) found evidence that beer is an inferior good. In any case, they all found that changes in income had a small effect on demand.

The characteristics of the typical American brand of beer have changed little since World War II. The only major change came with the introduction of light beer, a beer with approximately one-third less alcohol and calories than regular beer. It is the only successful new product introduced by the brewing industry in the last century.[6] The impact of this new product will be captured by a light beer dummy variable, which equals one from 1975 (the first year light beer was marketed nationally) through the present and zero otherwise. If this product provides consumers with a more desirable set of characteristics, then demand will rise with its introduction. Alternatively, demand may fall if this dummy variable actually captures a taste for moderation as the health risks of alcohol consumption became more apparent in the 1970s and 1980s.

Several variables may influence a consumer's consumption capital for beer. First, because some consumers may become addicted to alcohol, current and past consumption may be complements. Thus, a 'habit formation model', where current consumption is a positive function of past consumption, should be used.[7] This requires the addition of lagged per capita consumption to create a dynamic model of demand. Second, since health concerns and information about the adverse affects of drinking alcoholic beverages increase with age, fewer people drink beer as they grow older. For example, 61% of consumers 18–24 years old drink beer whereas only 24% of those over 65 years old drink beer.[8] To control for the effect of changes in demographics, the percentage of the population (18 years of age and older) that drink beer is added to the demand function.

Finally, advertising may change tastes and persuade consumers to buy more beer.[9] The main problem with the advertising variable is that it is difficult to measure. Schmalensee (1972) and Baye (1981) argue that advertising must be

---

[4]Because of data limitations the price of wine, another possible substitute for beer, is ignored. Studies by Horowitz and Horowitz (1965) for the US and Johnson and Oksanen (1977) and Clements and Johnson (1983) for Canada find that the price of wine has no significant impact on the demand for beer, however.

[5]This is the procedure adopted by numerous single equation demand studies including: Kao and Tremblay (1988), Porter (1986), Baltagi and Levin (1986), and Schneider et al. (1981) for cigarettes, Hogarty and Elzinga (1972) for beer, and Chang (1977) for meat.

[6]Light beer was first introduced by the Rheingold Brewing Co. under the Gablinger brand in 1967 and later that same year by the Meister Brau Brewing Company. Both products were unsuccessful, primarily because they were marketed as diet beers. In 1972 the Miller Brewing Company purchased Meister Brau and was able successfully to market its Miller Lite version of Meister Brau Lite at the national level, beginning in 1975. This success is attributed to its 'less filling and tastes great' marketing theme, which was designed to attract the heavy beer drinker. After the success of Miller Lite, many other brewing firms introduced their own brands of light beer. See, *Advertising Age*, 9 January, 1967 and 10 November, 1975 for a more complete discussion.

[7]See Pollak and Wales (1969) for a discussion of this model and Becker and Murphy (1988) for a more recent discussion of a rational model of addiction.

[8]*Advertising Age* (16 January, 1984). Other age group figures are as follows: 61% of the 18–24-year-old population drink beer, 58% of the 25–34-year-old population, 44% of the 35–49-year-old population, 26% of the 50–64-year-old population, and 24% of those 65 years and over.

[9]Nelson (1974) argues that advertising may also increase demand by informing customers of a commodity's existence. This effect is expected to be negligible, however, for a mature industry like brewing.

measured in terms of physical quantity and not advertising expenditures when time series data are used, because pure inflation will affect expenditures but not quantities, *ceteris paribus*. Another issue is whether or not to deflate advertising by population. Tremblay (1985b) argues that advertising has a public quality and should not be deflated by population. Comanor and Wilson (1974, p. 71) point out that not all advertising has a public quality (e.g., in printed media) and suggest that advertising should be deflated by population.

In addition, both current and previous advertising messages may influence current demand. Following Nerlove and Arrow (1962) the stock of advertising is defined as total advertising minus depreciation. Grabowski (1977–1978) found that the effect of beer advertising depreciates very rapidly and that this year's stock of advertising equals the advertising level of the current year. Peles (1971), however, found that the impact of beer advertising depreciates at 40–50% per year, implying that the stock of current advertising depends on both current and past advertising levels.

Given these measurement problems, the work by Leamer (1983), and the central role of advertising in this study, several measures of advertising are used. They are: the physical quantity of current advertising, the stock of the physical quantity of advertising (with an assumed 45% depreciation rate), the physical quantity of current advertising per capita, and the stock of the physical quantity of advertising per capita (with a 45% depreciation rate).

Two functional forms are utilized. First, because it is widely used, the following double-logarithmic functional form is adopted.

$$\ln Q = \alpha_0 + \alpha_1 \ln P_b + \alpha_2 \ln P_w + \alpha_3 \ln P_c + \alpha_4 \ln M$$
$$+ \alpha_5 \ln ADV + \alpha_6 \ln POP_r + \alpha_7 D_{75} + \alpha_8 \ln Q_{t-1} \quad (1)$$

where Q is the per capita consumption of beer, P_b is the real price of beer, P_w is the real price of whiskey, P_c is the real price of cola-drinks, M is the real disposal income per capita,

ADV is an advertising variable: ADV_q is a physical quantity of advertising; ADV_k is the stock of advertising capital; ADV_{qpc} is the physical quantity of advertising per capita; ADV_{kpc} is the stock of advertising capital per capita in brewing industry; POP_r is ratio of total beer drinkers (18 years old and over) to total population, D_{75} is a light beer dummy variable and Q_{t-1} is one-year lagged per capita consumption of beer

A more complete description of the variables, the data, and their sources can be found in the Data Appendix.

This specification may be incorrect for beer, however, because it constrains both the price and income elasticities to be constant. It is likely that there is a saturation level or an upper limit on consumption. That is, as price falls or as income rises (assuming a normal good) consumption may increase at a decreasing rate. To allow the income elasticity to vary with income and the price elasticity to vary with price, the following saturation model will also be used.

$$\ln Q = \beta_0 + \beta_1 P_b + \beta_2 \ln P_w + \beta_3 \ln P_c + \beta_4 (-1/M)$$
$$+ \beta_5 \ln ADV + \beta_6 \ln POP_r + \beta_7 D_{75} + \beta_8 \ln Q_{t-1}{}^{10} \quad (2)$$

These specifications are estimated using annual observations from 1953 to 1983.

This sample and these specifications suggest three potential empirical problems. First, because the price of beer is an endogenous variable, consistent parameter estimates of Equations 1 and 2 cannot be obtained from the method of ordinary least squares. Further, the work by Greer (1981) and Tremblay (1985a, b) indicates that brewing firms are not price takers, and a market supply function cannot be unambiguously defined for an imperfectly competitive industry. Following Rohlfs (1974), an instrumental variable technique (with corrected standard errors) is used to correct for this endogeneity problem.[11] Second, advertising may also be an endogenous variable.[12] A Hausman (1978) specification test performed on these data rejects this hypothesis.

---

[10]This function is semi-log in the price of beer and log-reciprocal in income. In this specification the price elasticity of demand equals the absolute value of β_1 times P_b. As P_b falls, demand becomes relatively more inelastic. The income elasticity equals β_4 divided by M. As M increases (assuming beer is a normal good), the income elasticity of demand falls. See Phlips (1974, pp. 109–12) for a more complete description of this specification.

[11]This procedure assumes that the equilibrium price is a function of demand (or more accurately, marginal revenue) and marginal cost conditions. Thus, the instruments include all predetermined demand, cost, and important market structure variables. The following variables are used as instruments: the price of whiskey, the price of cola drinks, per capita disposable income, the physical quantity of advertising, the percentage of the population that drink beer, a light-beer dummy variable, lagged per-capita beer consumption, the total cost of materials, the number of beer drinkers, the average wages of production workers in the brewing industry, a price index of the price of advertising, the production capacity of the industry, a technology variable that measures the cost savings due to technological change, the average state excise taxes per barrel, the Herfindahl–Hirschman index of industry concentration, and the market share of beer imports. Data sources are listed in the Data Appendix. The demand function is identified because there are several predetermined variables in the system that are not included in the demand function. Kao and Tremblay (1988), Tremblay (1987), and Friedlaender *et al.* (1983) give other applications of this technique to concentrated industries.

[12]Grabowski (1976) concludes that the level of sales can be a strong explanatory variable of advertising outlays. See also Bass (1969), Schmalensee (1972), Comanor and Wilson (1974), Martin (1979), and McGuinness (1980).

however.[13] Thus, advertising is assumed to be predetermined. Finally, because time series data are used, serial correlation may be a problem. Unless there is strong evidence from the Durbin–Watson d and the Durbin h tests that autocorrelation is not present, empirical results with autocorrelation corrections are also calculated.[14]

III. THE EMPIRICAL RESULTS

The empirical results are reported in Tables 1 and 2. The light beer dummy variable and lagged consumption are added sequentially to analyse the sensitivity of the advertising variable parameter estimate.[15] Because the results are

Table 1. *Beer demand regression coefficients: double-log model*[a]

Independent variables	Without autocorrelation corrections			With autocorrelation corrections	
	1.1	1.2	1.3	1.4	1.5
Intercept	1.074	1.767**	0.793	0.251	0.925
	(1.293)	(2.235)	(0.969)	(0.305)	(1.168)
$\ln P_b$	−0.976*	−0.896*	−0.613**	−0.725**	−0.615**
	(−3.296)	(−3.371)	(−2.275)	(−2.117)	(−2.169)
$\ln P_w$	0.541*	0.453*	0.311**	0.387**	0.294***
	(3.282)	(3.000)	(2.042)	(2.065)	(1.835)
$\ln P_c$	0.334*	0.447*	0.358*	0.293*	0.409*
	(3.577)	(4.715)	(3.701)	(3.204)	(4.764)
$\ln M$	0.139	0.054	0.080	0.205***	0.125
	(1.401)	(0.567)	(0.879)	(1.864)	(0.125)
$\ln ADV_q$	0.012	0.022	0.022	0.005	0.018
	(0.482)	(0.973)	(1.101)	(0.232)	(0.905)
$\ln POP_r$	2.341*	2.502*	1.786*	2.058*	2.262*
	(7.849)	(9.148)	(3.843)	(6.140)	(8.258)
D_{75}		−0.039**	−0.036**		−0.042*
		(−2.488)	(−2.379)		(−2.920)
$\ln Q_{t-1}$			0.244		
			(1.369)		
R^2	0.996	0.997	0.998	0.995	0.997
Durbin–Watson d	1.566	1.862			
Durbin h			0.017[b]		

[a]The sample period is 1953–1983, and the figures in parentheses are t-ratios.
[b]No significant autocorrelation at the 1% level.
*Significant at the 1% level.
**Significant at the 5% level.
***Significant at the 10% level.

[13]With this technique, advertising is regressed on all exogenous demand, cost, and other advertising determining variables: the real price of whiskey, the real price of cola drinks, per-capita disposable income, the percentage of the population that drinks beer, the light beer dummy variable, the market share of imported beer, the total cost of materials, the average wage rate of production workers in the brewing industry, a price index of the price of advertising, the production capacity of the beer industry, a technology variable that incorporates cost savings due to technological change, the percentage of packaged sales, the Herfindahl–Hirschman index of concentration. The predicted value of advertising from this regression is then added to the beer demand regression (i.e., per capita beer consumption is regressed on the real price of beer, the price of substitutes, per capita income, the demographic variable, lagged per capita beer consumption, the light beer dummy variable, advertising, and predicted advertising). The null hypothesis that predicted advertising has no significant impact on demand (that advertising is an exogenous variable) is not rejected at reasonable significance levels. In addition, a Granger (1969) causality test (with two, four, and eight year lags) indicates that consumption does not cause advertising. These results support McGuinness and Cowling (1975) who argue that the simultaneous nature of advertising and sales is broken down when advertising is measured in terms of physical quantity rather than total expenditures.
[14]The Durbin–Watson d test for autocorrelation turns out to be inconclusive in many equations. Nakamura and Nakamura (1978) argue that when the null hypothesis of no autocorrelation is in doubt, however, the hypothesis should be rejected.
[15]The sign on the light-beer dummy variable is always negative, and insignificant coefficient estimates on lagged consumption indicate that beer consumption is unlikely to be very addictive for most consumers.

Table 2. *Beer demand regression coefficients: saturation model*[a]

Independent variables	Without autocorrelation corrections			With autocorrelation corrections	
	2.1	2.2	2.3	2.4	2.5
Intercept	3.027*	2.888*	1.920*	1.969*	2.266*
	(10.062)	(10.342)	(3.494)	(6.404)	(7.694)
$\ln P_b$	−0.643**	−0.587**	−0.490**	−0.703*	−0.646*
	(−2.471)	(−2.477)	(−2.131)	(−2.773)	(−2.931)
$\ln P_w$	0.321**	0.244***	0.207***	0.310**	0.255**
	(2.415)	(2.000)	(1.747)	(2.353)	(2.176)
$\ln P_c$	0.230*	0.362*	0.314*	0.253*	0.368*
	(2.848)	(4.160)	(3.450)	(3.398)	(4.720)
$-1/M$	576.777*	323.315	247.236	514.336**	299.337
	(2.375)	(1.369)	(1.116)	(2.138)	(1.385)
$\ln ADV_q$	0.002	0.014	0.021	0.006	0.019
	(0.089)	(0.607)	(1.060)	(0.268)	(0.927)
$\ln POP_t$	2.184*	2.342*	1.698	2.055*	2.258*
	(8.329)	(9.704)	(3.739)	(7.015)	(9.245)
D_{75}		−0.042*	−0.037**		−0.039**
		(−2.716)	(−2.441)		(−2.629)
$\ln Q_{t-1}$			0.264		
			(1.480)		
R^2	0.996	0.997	0.998	0.994	0.997
Durbin–Watson d	1.344	1.564			
Durbin h			0.292[b]		

[a]The sample period is 1953–1983, and the figures in parentheses are t-ratios.
[b]No significant autocorrelation at the 1% level.
*Significant at the 1% level.
**Significant at the 5% level.
***Significant at the 10% level.

found to be insensitive to the specifications discussed above, only ten of the 44 specifications that were estimated are reported here.[16]

In most cases the empirical results are as expected. In every specification the price of beer has a significant negative effect on the demand for beer. Estimates of the price elasticity of demand, which equal the parameter estimates on price in the double-log specification and are reported in Table 3 for the saturation model, indicate that the demand for beer is relatively inelastic. In addition, the estimates from the dynamic models indicate that the long-run price elasticities exceed the short-run elasticities, as economic theory would predict, because adjustment to the desired level of consumption is not instantaneous.[17] These results can be found in Table 4.

Whiskey and cola drinks are found to be gross substitutes for beer. Cross-price elasticity estimates between beer and whiskey range from 0.207 to 0.541 and are always significantly different from zero at traditional levels.[18] The cross-price elasticity estimates between beer and cola drinks range from 0.230 to 0.447 and are all significant.

In support of the results found by McGuinness (1980) and Ornstein and Hanssens (1985), income appears to have little effect on the demand for beer. All of the income elasticity estimates are positive, but few are significantly different from zero. The results in Table 2 provide some evidence of saturation, however. The income elasticity of demand is positive but declines as income rises.[19] Although the estimates are close to zero, results from the dynamic model indicate that the long-run income elasticities exceed the

[16]Three versions of each functional form (double-log and saturation) are estimated (one with all variables, one without lagged beer consumption, and one without lagged consumption and the light beer dummy variable). Each of these specifications is estimated with the four different measures of advertising (the physical quantity of advertising, the stock of the physical quantity of advertising, the physical quantity of advertising per capita, and the stock of the physical quantity of advertising per capita). Finally, autocorrelation corrections are also made when required. This results in 44 specifications. The empirical results from all specifications are available from the authors upon request.
[17]Estimates of the long-run price elasticity equal the short-run price elasticity divided by one minus the coefficient on lagged consumption.
[18]In six of the other 34 specifications, this variable is not significant at conventional levels.
[19]For example, the mean income elasticity falls from 0.189 in 1953 to 0.105 by 1983.

short-run elasticities because the adjustment to the desired level of consumption takes time.[20] These estimates can be found in Table 4.

As expected, the fraction of the population that drinks beer is a very important factor in determining beer consumption. The parameter estimate is positive and significant in all specifications.

The light-beer dummy variable parameter estimates are always negative and significant. It is likely that this dummy variable captures a growing concern for moderation[21] as the health risks of alcohol consumption became more apparent in the 1970s and 1980s.[22]

The effect of lagged consumption is generally small and insignificant.[23] This suggests that beer is not a very addictive commodity, at least for the average consumer.

Finally, there is no support for the hypothesis that advertising has a significant positive effect on market demand. In every specification, regardless of how advertising is measured, the advertising parameter estimate is never significantly different from zero. Furthermore, the point estimates of the advertising elasticity of demand are very small,

ranging from 0.002 to 0.022.[24] Although advertising is likely to influence firm market shares, these results indicate that advertising has no significant effect on the US market demand for beer.

IV. CONCLUDING REMARKS

The main purpose of this research has been to determine the effect of advertising on the US market demand for beer. To test this hypothesis the US per capita market demand for beer is estimated. The empirical results indicate that the most important determinants of demand are the price of beer, the prices of substitutes (whiskey and cola drinks), demographic factors and the light-beer dummy variable. Demand appears to have increased slightly but at a decreasing rate with rising income, and the effect of lagged consumption is generally small and insignificant.

Although many respectable groups have argued that advertising promotes beer consumption, the empirical results of this study do not support this hypothesis. If social welfare is best served by reducing alcoholic beverage consumption, policies other than a restriction on advertising should be sought.[25] Given the results of this study, higher excise taxes and a policy designed to keep the public well informed of the health risks associated with heavy drinking would be most effective in reducing the demand for beer.

DATA APPENDIX

The data consist of 31 annual observations from 1953 to 1983. This period is chosen because the price indices for beer,

Table 3. *Elasticities of demand: saturation model*

Regression model	Price elasticities	Income elasticities
(2.1)	−0.618	0.199
(2.2)	−0.556	0.112
(2.3)	−0.464	0.085
(2.4)	−0.666	0.178
(2.5)	−0.612	0.103
Mean	−0.583	0.135

Table 4. *Short-run and long-run elasticities of demand*

Regression model	Price elasticities		Income elasticities	
	Short-run	Long-run	Short-run	Long-run
(1.3)	−0.613	−0.811	0.080	0.106
(2.3)	−0.464	−0.630	0.085	0.115
Mean	−0.539	−0.721	0.083	0.111

[20]Estimates of the long-run income elasticity equal the short-run price elasticity divided by one minus the coefficient on lagged consumption.

[21]This is reflected, for example, in the rise in the minimum legal drinking age. According to Wagenaar (1983) 19 states raised the minimum drinking age from 18 to 19, 20 or 21 years of age from 1976 to 1983.

[22]This result is contrary to intent of the Miller Lite's 'tastes great and less filling' advertising claim that more light beer can be consumed at a time. The possibility of growing moderation suggests that a time trend beginning at 1975 may be more appropriate than a dummy variable. The advertising parameter estimates are still insignificant with this specification, however.

[23]This variable is positive and significant in five of the 34 other specifications that are not listed.

[24]Its maximum value in other specifications is 0.043.

[25]Advertising restrictions may still be justifiable if, for example, advertising is socially excessive. See Nichols (1985) for a recent discussion of this concern.

whiskey, and soft drinks are unavailable before 1953. The 1953 cutoff also avoids the impact of the federal excise tax increase in 1951 and the effects of World War II on beer consumption. The dependent variable is measured as annual beer consumption in 31 gallon barrels and is obtained from *Brewers Almanac* (various issues).

Measurement procedures and data sources for the independent variables are as follows. The price of beer is measured by a price index taken from the *Handbook of Labor Statistics* (1978) for the period 1953–1977 and *Modern Brewery Age Blue Book* (1986) for 1978–1983. The prices of whiskey and cola drinks are measured by price indexes from the *Handbook of Labor Statistics* (1978) for 1952–1977 and *CPI Detailed Report* for 1978–1983. Per capita income is defined as disposable income, obtained from the *Survey of Current Business*, divided by total US population, obtained from *Current Population Reports: Population Estimates and Projections* (various issues). The age group figures on the percentage of the population (18 years of age and older) that drinks beer, used to derive the fraction of the population that drinks beer, are obtained from *Advertising Age* (16 January, 1984). The physical quantity of advertising is obtained by dividing total advertising expenditures, obtained from *Brewers Almanac* (various issues), by a weighted average price index of advertising (network and spot television, network and spot radio, magazines, and newspapers), obtained from Schmalensee (1972) for 1953–1966, Sterling and Haight (1978) for 1967–1969, and *Broadcasting* (6 February, 1978 and 24 March 1986) for 1970–1983.

Instrumental variable data are obtained as follows. Brewing industry capacity (measured in millions of barrels), the average state excise tax figures per barrel, the market share of imports, the total cost of materials, the average wages of production workers in the brewing industry, and the percentage of packaged sales (bottles and cans) to total taxpaid withdrawals of beer are obtained from *Brewers Almanac* (various issues). The technology variable is measured as the annual change in the natural log of total beer costs for a representative beer producer when output and input prices are held fixed at their mean values. This estimate is obtained from a translog cost function that was estimated for US beer producers by Tremblay (1987). Data sources for the Herfindahl–Hirschman index are listed in Tremblay and Tremblay (1988).

All money figures are in 1967 dollars. Consumer goods are deflated by the Consumer Price Index, and producer goods are deflated by the Producer Price Index. Both indexes are obtained from the US Department of Commerce, Bureau of the Census.

ACKNOWLEDGEMENTS

The authors wish to thank Yang-Ming Chang, Allen Featherstone, Mark McNulty, Carol Horton Tremblay, and an anonymous referee for helpful comments on earlier versions of this paper. The authors are responsible for all remaining errors.

REFERENCES

Advertising Age (1967) Rheingold unit markets Gablinger's beer, containing no carbohydrates, 9 January, p. 3.

Advertising Age (1975) Miller wants competitors to shed light, 10 November, p. 93.

Advertising Age (1984) Beer marketing, 16 January, p. 10.

Advertising Age (1985) Whole world is watching U.S. alcohol ad debate, 11 February, p. 70.

Baltagi, B. H. and Levin, D. (1986) Estimating dynamic demand for cigarettes using panel data: the effects of bootlegging, taxation and advertising reconsidered, *Review of Economics and Statistics*, **68**, 148–55.

Barten, A. P. (1977) The systems of consumer demand functions approach: a review, *Econometrica*, **45**, 23–51.

Bass, F. M. (1969) A simultaneous equation regression study of advertising and sales of cigarettes, *Journal of Marketing Research*, **6**, 291–300.

Baye, M. R. (1981) Optimal adjustments to changes in the price of advertising, *Journal of Industrial Economics*, **30**, 95–103.

Becker, G. S. and Murphy, K. M. (1988) A theory of rational addiction, *Journal of Political Economy*, **96**, 675–700.

Brewers Almanac, US Brewers Association Inc., Washington DC. various issues.

Brewers Digest (1985) Tide may have turned on beer–wine issue. February, pp. 18–23.

Broadcasting, (various issues).

Central Hudson and Gas Corp. v. Public Service Commission (1980) 447 U.S. 557.

Chang, H-S. (1977) Functional forms and the demand for meat in the United States, *Review of Economics and Statistics*, **59**, 355–9.

Clements, K. W. and Johnson, L. W. (1983) The demand for beer, wine, and spirits: a systemwide analysis, *Journal of Business*, **56**, 273–304.

Comanor, W. S. and Wilson, T. A. (1974) *Advertising and Market Power*, Harvard University Press, Cambridge, MA.

Duffy, M. (1983) The demand for alcoholic drink in the United Kingdom, 1963–78, *Applied Economics*, **15**, 125–40.

Elzinga, K. G. (1986) The beer industry, in *The Structure of American Industry*, Adams, W. (ed.), Macmillan, New York.

Friedlaender, A. F., Winston, C. and Wang, K. (1983) Cost, technology, and productivity in the U.S. automobile industry. *Bell Journal of Economics*, **14**, 1–20.

Grabowski, H. G. (1976) The effects of advertising on the inter-industry distribution of demand, *Explorations in Economic Research*, Winter, 21–75.

Grabowski, H. G. (1977–78) The effects of advertising on intra-industry shifts in demand. *Explorations in Economic Research*, Winter, 675–701.

Granger, C. W. J. (1969) Investigating causal relations by econometric models and cross-spectral methods, *Econometrica*, **37**, 424–38.

Greer, D. F. (1971) Product differentiation and concentration in the brewing industry, *Journal of Industrial Economics*, **19**, 201–19.

Hausman, J. A. (1978) Specification tests in econometrics, *Econometrica*, **46**, 1251–71.

Hogarty, T. F. and Elzinga, K. G. (1972) The demand for beer, *Review of Economics and Statistics*, **54**, 195–8.

Horowitz, I. and Horowitz, A. R. (1965) Firms in a declining market: the brewing case, *Journal of Industrial Economics*, **13**, 129–53.

Johnson, J. A. and Oksanen, E. H. (1977) Estimation of demand for alcoholic beverages in Canada from pooled time series and cross sections, *Review of Economics and Statistics*, **59**, 113–18.

Johnston, J. (1984) *Econometric Methods*, McGraw-Hill, New York.

Judge, G. G., Griffiths, W. E., Hill, R. C., Lee, T-C. (1980) *The Theory and Practice of Econometrics*, Wiley, New York.

Kao, K. and Tremblay, V. J. (1988) Cigarette 'health scare', excise taxes, and advertising ban: comment, *Southern Economic Journal*, **54**, 770–6.

Kmenta, J. (1986) *Elements of Econometrics*, Macmillan, New York.

Lancaster, K. J. (1966) A new approach to consumer theory, *Journal of Political Economy*, **74**, 132–57.

Lancaster, K. J. (1971) *Consumer Demand: A New Approach*, Columbia University Press, New York.

Lancaster, K. J. (1979) *Variety, Equity and Efficiency*, Columbia University Press, New York.

Leamer, E. E. (1983) Let's take the con out of econometrics, *American Economic Review*, **73**, 31–43.

Lynk, W. (1984) Interpreting rising concentration: the case of beer, *Journal of Business*, **57**, 43–55.

Marris, R. (1968) Galbraith, Solow and the truth about corporations, *The Public Interest*, **11**, 37–46.

Martin, S. (1979) Advertising, concentration and profitability: the simultaneity problem, *Bell Journal of Economics*, **10**, 639–47.

McAvoy, K. (1985) Tide may have turned on beer–wine issues, *Brewers Digest*, February, 18–23.

McGuinness, T. (1980) An econometric analysis of total demand for alcohol beverages in the UK, 1956–75, *Journal of Industrial Economics*, **29**, 85–109.

McGuinness, T. and Cowling, K. (1975) Advertising and the aggregate demand for cigarettes, *European Economic Review*, **6**, 311–28.

Modern Brewing Age Blue Book, Norwalk, CT (various issues).

Nakamura, A. and Nakamura, M. (1978) On the impact of the tests for serial correlation upon the test of significance for the regression coefficient, *Journal of Econometrics*, **7**, 199–210.

Nelson, J. P. (1988) Economic and legal determinants of alcoholic beverage consumption: a Bayesian approach, *Pennsylvania State University Working Paper*, January.

Nelson, P. (1974) Advertising as information, *Journal of Political Economy*, **82**, 729–54.

Nerlove, M. and Arrow, K. J. (1962) Optimal advertising policy under dynamic conditions, *Economica*, **29**, 129–42.

Nichols, L. M. (1985) Advertising and economic welfare, *American Economic Review*, **75**, 213–18.

Niskanen, W. A. (1962) The demand for alcoholic beverages, Unpublished PhD Dissertation, University of Chicago.

Ornstein, S. I. and Hanssens, D. M. (1985) Alcohol control laws and the consumption of distilled spirits and beer, *Journal of Consumer Research*, **12**, 200–13.

Peles, Y. (1971) Rates of amortization of advertising expenditures, *Journal of Political Economy*, **79**, 1032–58.

Phlips, L. (1974) *Applied Consumer Analysis*, North-Holland, Amsterdam.

Pollak, R. H. and Wales, T. J. (1969) Estimation of the linear expenditure system, *Econometrica*, **37**, 611–28.

Porter, R. H. (1986) The impact of government policy on the U.S. cigarette industry, in *Empirical Approaches to Consumer Protection Economics*, Ippolito, P. M. and Scheffman, D. T. (eds), Federal Trade Commission, Washington, DC, pp. 447–81.

Rohlfs, J. (1974) Econometric analysis of supply in concentrated markets, *International Economic Review*, **15**, 69–74.

Schmalensee, R. (1972) *The Economics of Advertising*, North-Holland, Amsterdam-London.

Schneider, L., Klein, B. and Murphy, D. M. (1981) Governmental regulation of cigarette health information, *Journal of Law and Economics*, **24**, 575–612.

Sterling, C. H. and Haight, T. R. (1978) *The Mass Media: Aspen Institute Guide to Communication Industry Trends*, Praeger, New York.

Stigler, G. J. and Becker, G. S. (1977) De gustibus non est disputandum, *American Economic Review*, **67**, 76–90.

Tremblay, V. J. (1985a) A reappraisal of interpreting rising concentration: the case of beer, *Journal of Business*, **58**, 419–31.

Tremblay, V. J. (1985b) Strategic groups and the demand for beer, *Journal of Industrial Economics*, **34**, 183–98.

Tremblay, V. J. (1987) Scale economies, technological change and firm-cost asymmetries in the U.S. brewing industry, *Quarterly Review of Economics and Business*, **27**, 71–86.

Tremblay, V. J. and Tremblay, C. H. (1988) The determinants of horizontal acquisitions: evidence from the U.S. brewing industry, *Journal of Industrial Economics*, **37**, 21–45.

US Department of Commerce (Bureau of the Census), *Current Population Reports: Population Estimates and Projections*, (various issues).

US Department of Commerce (Bureau of the Census) (1987) *Statistical Abstract of the United States*.

US Department of Commerce (Bureau of Economic Analysis) (1987) *Survey of Current Business*, **67**.

US Department of Labor (Bureau of Labor Statistics) (1978) *Handbook of Labor Statistics*.

US Department of Labor (Bureau of Labor Statistics), *CPI Detailed Report*, (various issues).

Varian, R. (1984) *Microeconomic Analysis*, W. W. Norton, New York.

Wagenaar, A. C. (1983) *Alcohol, Young Drivers, and Traffic Accidents*, D. E. Heath, Lexington, MA.

Wilcox, G. B., Shea, D. and Hovland, R. (1986) Alcoholic beverage advertising and the electronic media, *Communications and the Law*, February, 31–41.

Article 6

AN ECONOMIC ANALYSIS OF THE
DEMAND FOR ABORTIONS

MARSHALL H. MEDOFF*

This study uses an economic model of fertility control to estimate the demand for abortions. The results show that the fundamental law of demand holds for abortions, with the price elasticity of demand equal to − .81. Abortions are a normal good with an income elasticity of demand equal to .79. The demand for abortions is also positively related to the labor force participation of women and to being unmarried. Catholic religion, education and the poverty status of women were found to have no statistically significant impact on the demand for abortions.

I. INTRODUCTION

On 22 January 1973, the United States Supreme Court ruled in *Roe v. Wade* that states could not prohibit a woman from having an abortion, as long as it was done in the first three months of pregnancy. States could regulate, but not prohibit, second-trimester abortions and could prohibit abortions during the third trimester only.[1]

The focus on abortions since the Supreme Court's decision has been primarily on moral and ethical issues. Research on the issue consists principally of numerical tabulations according to selected demographic characteristics (age, race, weeks of gestation, etc.) of the women obtaining abortions.[2] Absent are socioeconomic considerations explaining the demand for abortions.

This study empirically estimates the demand for abortions using the economic model of fertility control developed by Michael [1973]. The effect of many of the socioeconomic factors discussed by Michael should also be relevant in explaining the demand for abortions. Section II outlines the abortion demand model in terms of the general theory of fertility control. The third section examines the empirical results and the last section discusses the policy implications of the results.

* Professor, Department of Economics, California State University, Long Beach. I would like to thank Stanley K. Henshaw, Deputy Director of Research of the Alan Guttmacher Institute, for providing me data from the 1981–82 Abortion Provider Survey. Funding for this research was provided by California State University, Long Beach through the Scholarly and Creative Activity Committee Assigned Time Program.

1. During the second trimester many states required all abortions to be performed in a hospital. In June 1983, the U.S. Supreme Court ruled that such state regulations did not advance maternal health and, therefore, were illegal.

2. Two exceptions are Deyak and Smith [1976] who estimated the benefits for women seeking abortions as a result of the 1973 Supreme Court ruling, and Coelen and McIntyre [1978] who analyzed the pronatalist and abortion policies in Hungary.

Michael [1973, S132] argues that fertility control behavior can be explained within a household choice-theoretic framework in terms of a household production model. Michael's model suggests that a household's fertility control decision is based on a comparison of the costs and benefits associated with an additional child over time. The net cost simply represents a household's effective excess demand for children given prices, income level, level of production of complements and substitutes, etc. If the net cost is positive, a woman will engage in fertility control by purchasing and using goods and time inputs to reduce the probability of conception. One such good reducing the probability of conception to zero is abortion.

Household choices on abortions thus arise from the interaction of income, prices, and preferences. Abortion is a posterior decision—the decision by a woman who is pregnant not to have the child. Since abortion can be considered a method of contraception, the demand for abortions is modeled in terms of the explicit and opportunity costs at the time of the abortion decision [Coelen and McIntyre 1978].

The abortion demand equation to be estimated is[3]

$$A_i = b_0 + b_1 P_i + b_2 Y_i + b_3 SNGL_i + b_4 LFP_i \\ + b_5 CATH_i + b_6 W + b_7 M. \qquad (1)$$

The dependent variable is the abortion rate (the number of abortions per thousand pregnancies) of women of childbearing age fifteen to forty-four in state i during the 1980 calendar year.[4]

The price of abortions (P) is the average cost of an abortion using a local anesthesia in nonhospital facilities performed the first twelve weeks in each state.[5] Since abortions are not fundamentally different from other conventional goods and services one would expect the fundamental law of demand to hold.[6] Income Y is the average income of women fifteen to forty-four years old and reflects the budget constraint.

Also relevant in an abortion decision is a woman's marital status. Unmarried women may have a greater demand for abortions since their outlays for an

3. The linear specification is preferable to the log-linear form since the linear form is a first-order approximation of an arbitrary demand function and it allows the elasticities of demand to vary along the demand curve rather than restricting them to a constant value. Equation (1) was estimated using the log-linear specification and the empirical results, which are available upon request, were qualitatively the same as those reported.

4. About 3 percent of all women of childbearing age obtained an abortion in 1980 [Alan Guttmacher Institute 1985].

5. Ninety-two percent of all abortions are done in the first trimester and 78 percent of all abortions are performed in a nonhospital facility [Alan Guttmacher Institute 1985].

6. Abortion rates and prices were obtained from the Alan Guttmacher Institute [1985], which is a research foundation affiliated with Planned Parenthood. Each year the Guttmacher Institute does a national survey of abortion providers and the services they offer. The survey produces the most complete available information about abortions in the U.S. and in each state, and the results are summarized by the U.S. Department of Commerce in the *Statistical Abstract of the United States*.

additional child are higher than married women.[7] Married women (spouse present) are more likely to have lower outlays for childbearing and childrearing (due to shared household responsibilities, and because of economies of scale, as well as greater productivity of time and information with additional children) than unmarried women.[7] The variable *SNGL* is the percentage of women fifteen to forty-four who are unmarried and its predicted effect is positive.

Women in the labor force, regardless of marital status, have a greater opportunity cost of an additional child than women not in the labor force and should have a greater demand for abortions. This may reflect, in part, a greater aspiration for material goods or longer time horizon (i.e., a greater weight attached to a future unwanted outcome) as well as a greater value of time. The predicted effect of *LFP*, the labor force participation rate of women fifteen to forty-four, is positive.[8]

An additional determinant of the demand for abortions is demographic differences in tastes or preferences. One such taste factor is religion. Religious faith and affiliation are powerful forces in influencing household choices. The Roman Catholic Church strongly disapproves of abortion and imposes severe psychological sanctions against women having an abortion. The Church's disapproval likely increases the subjective costs of abortions for Catholics and lowers their demand for them. The variable *CATH* is the percentage of Catholic population in each state.[9]

Most fertility studies typically assume constant cross-section tastes across groups or populations. While it is likely that tastes change slowly over time, such an assumption appears doubtful when cross-section differences across women in different states are of particular interest. Hamermesh and Soss [1974] argue that the degree of social stability, social ties, and social norms of states in the far West is substantially different from that in other regions. Some anomie in western states might foster a greater tendency by households to have abortions. To control for the possibility of differential tastes, a dummy variable equal to one for states in the far West (California, Oregon, Washington, Nevada, Arizona and Hawaii) is included.

In 1980, the use of federal funds to provide abortions for indigent women under the Medicaid program was severely restricted. However, fourteen states continued to provide Medicaid abortions at their own expense. As a conse-

7. In 1980, 50.5 percent of all married women (spouse present) had at least one child, versus 14.2 percent for unmarried women [U.S. Bureau of the Census 1983].

8. The variables in equation (1) are restricted to women since the production of children is done exclusively by women and, as noted by De Tray [1973], methods of fertility regulation are generally controlled by women. One might argue that the independent variables should be the characteristics of pregnant women, not all fertile women. Since abortion is a quasi-method of contraception there is no bias in the estimated coefficients; the explicit and opportunity costs at the time of the abortion decision are the same for fertile and for pregnant women.

9. The data on all economic variables were obtained from the U.S. Bureau of the Census, State Reports, Detailed Characteristics [1983]. The data on Catholic membership by state are from Churches and Church Membership in the United States, a census commissioned by the National Council of Churches [Johnson, Picard and Quinn 1974].

quence one would expect the demand for abortions to be greater in these states since cost is not a consideration in the utilization of abortion services. The variable M is a dummy variable equal to one for the fourteen states that continued Medicaid funding.[10]

III. EMPIRICAL RESULTS

Since the price of abortions is determined simultaneously with the abortion rate, equation (1) was estimated using two-stage least squares.[11] The variables exogenous to equation (1) are the average hospital cost per day, number of hospitals, number of abortion clinics and number of physicians per 100,000 population in each state.[12] The two-stage least-squares regression results of equation (1) (absolute value of t-statistics in parentheses) are

$$A = -207.780 - .942P + .031Y + 4.194SNGL + 4.456LFP$$
$$\quad (1.42) \quad (3.22) \quad (3.31) \quad (1.74) \quad (2.57)$$

$$+ 18.287W + 1.207CATH + 43.775M, \quad R^2 = .77. \quad (2)$$
$$\quad (1.74) \quad (1.50) \quad (2.12)$$

The empirical results provide substantial support for the a priori expectations of the abortion demand model.[13] The price of abortions is negative and significantly different from zero at the .05 level of significance. The significant inverse relationship between the price of abortions and the abortion rate confirms that the fundamental law of demand is applicable to abortions. Income is positive and statistically significantly different from zero at the .01 level of significance, which suggests that abortions are normal goods with respect to income.[14] Both $SNGL$ and LFP are significantly positive which is consistent with the hypothesis that women in the labor force and unmarried

10. Alaska, California, Colorado, Georgia, Hawaii, Maryland, Michigan, New Jersey, New York, North Carolina, Oregon, Pennsylvania, Washington, and West Virginia.

11. In order to test the possibility that the residual variance decreased with the size of a state's female population, a Goldfeld-Quandt [1965] procedure was utilized on equation (1). The result showed that the calculated F-value did not exceed the critical F-value at the .05 level of significance and hence the null hypothesis of homoscedasticity could not be rejected.

12. These variables were incorporated in the two-stage least-squares estimates of the supply equation (absolute value of t-statistics in parentheses):

$$P = 196.963 + .137A + .475COST - .164HOSP$$
$$\quad (5.54) \quad (1.65) \quad (4.19) \quad (1.85)$$

$$+ .095CLINIC - .776PHY - 58.403W + 9.465M.$$
$$\quad (.79) \quad (2.24) \quad (2.69) \quad (.64)$$

13. Equation (1) was also estimated with the number of abortions per thousand live births and the number of abortions per thousand women of childbearing age fifteen to forty-four. The empirical results were qualitatively the same as those reported in the text. Also adding the percentage of nonwhite women fifteen to forty-four to equation (1) found the regression coefficient on race was not significantly different from zero and the estimated coefficients of the other variables in equation (1) remained virtually identical to the estimates presented. The complete empirical results are available upon request.

14. These latter results are consistent with Deyak and Smith [1976] who found that the abortion rate was inversely related to travel costs (a proxy for the price of abortion services) and the percentage of women with incomes under $3000. They also found neither age or education had a statistically significant effect on the abortion rate.

women, due to the greater explicit and implicit cost of childbearing, have a greater demand for abortions. Women have eighteen more abortions per thousand pregnancies in western states and forty-four more abortions per thousand pregnancies in Medicaid states.

A somewhat surprising result is that the percentage of a state's Catholic population does not have a statistically significant influence on the demand for abortions. One possible explanation is that Catholic women do not uniformly support the official position of the Catholic Church against abortions. The Harris and Gallup Opinion polls in 1979 found that 74 percent of those surveyed believe that a woman who is no more than three months pregnant should have the right to decide whether or not she wants to have an abortion [Alan Guttmacher Institute 1985]. Assuming these surveys are representative, the results suggest that Catholic women do not necessarily view abortion as an unacceptable means of fertility control merely because of the Catholic Church's opposition.

Michael [1973, S137–41] argues that education operating through several different channels may have an influence on a household's fertility control decision. Education may reduce the demand for abortions by increasing the knowledge about effective contraceptive techniques. On the other hand, education may also increase the demand for abortions since it raises the opportunity cost of a household's time and, if children are time-intensive relative to other goods purchased, increases the relative price of an additional child [Becker 1965; Willis 1973]. To provide additional evidence on the effect of education, equation (1) was re-estimated with the percentage of women in each state aged fifteen to forty-four who have completed twelve years of school added to equation (1). The effect of education was negative but not statistically significantly different from zero. The estimated coefficients of all the other variables remained virtually identical to the previous estimates reported.[15]

Bernstam and Swan [1986] contend that the Aid to Families with Dependent Children (AFDC) subsidy is an incentive for poor women to have children. If their contention is correct then the estimated coefficient of income in equation (1) would be biased upwards since the AFDC subsidy is income related. Poor women are subsidized relative to rich women, which increases the number of abortions of high income women relative to low income women. In order to test for this possibility equation (1) was re-estimated with the percentage of women in each state aged fifteen to forty-four in poverty added to equation (1). The empirical results showed that the percentage of women in poverty was not statistically significantly different from zero. The estimated coefficients of all the other variables remained virtually identical to the previous estimates presented.[16] Thus the empirical results remain robust with respect to the adjustment for education and for the presence of women in poverty.

An important practical question to economists is how sensitive the demand

15. The complete empirical results are available upon request.
16. The complete empirical results are available upon request.

for abortions is to changes in any of the economic variables in the demand function. The estimated elasticities are computed at the sample mean.[17] The price elasticity of demand for abortions is −.81, which is consistent with other studies that have found that the price elasticity of demand for health services is inelastic [Klarman 1965]. The positive elasticity with respect to income is .79 and shows the abortion is a normal good.[18] The labor force elasticity of demand is 1.10, while the unmarried women elasticity of demand is .57.

IV. POLICY IMPLICATIONS

Many opponents of abortion have attempted, through the political process, to limit or prohibit legal abortions. The estimated demand equation provides the likely impact of such actions.

One policy proposal has been to prohibit all Medicaid-financed abortions. The results suggest that forbidding all Medicaid-financed abortions would, everything else constant, have resulted in a reduction of forty-four abortions per thousand pregnancies or equivalently a 17.5 percent drop in the 1980 abortion rate. In 1980 there were approximately 1.5 million abortions performed. This would imply that prohibiting all Medicaid financed abortions would result in 262,500 less abortions being consumed.

A second proposal is to prohibit all abortions constitutionally. This would not eliminate all abortions since a possible alternative to a legal abortion is an illegally obtained abortion. Making abortions illegal, however, would raise the total price. Assuming that the illegal price was 50 percent higher than the prevailing 1980 market price and using the estimated price elasticity of demand of −.81 suggests that, ceteris paribus, the abortion rate would decrease by 40.5 percent. Applying this latter figure to the 1980 total of 1.5 million abortions performed implies that making abortions illegal would have reduced the number of abortions consumed by 607,500. If the illegal price were 75 percent higher than the 1980 market price, the reduction in the number of abortions consumed would be 911,250; if the illegal price were 100 percent higher, the drop in the number of abortions consumed would be 1,215,500.

Future trends in the abortion rate will be determined by changes in many factors not discussed in this study, such as sexual behavior patterns, availability of contraceptive services, and the perceived risks of contraceptive methods. However, the projected secular increase in the income and labor force participation of women combined with a decline in marriage rates and increase in divorce rates suggests, based on the empirical results, an increase in abortion rates in the United States. The annual increases in the abortion rate are likely to be small but persistent.

17. The mean and standard deviation (in parentheses) for the dependent variable and explanatory variables in equation (1) are A: 250.898 (87.847); P: 213.64 (43.15); Y: 6407.3 (936.338); $SNGL$: 34.158 (3.056); LFP: 61.99 (4.602); $CATH$: 20.022 (13.806); W: .12 (.3249); M: .28 (.0448).

18. These results cannot be compared with those of Deyak and Smith [1976] or Coelen and McIntyre [1978] since neither study provided sample means for their price or income variables.

REFERENCES

Alan Guttmacher Institute. *Abortion Services in the United States, Each State and Metropolitan Area, 1981–1982*. New York: The Alan Guttmacher Institute, 1985.

Becker, Gary S. "A Theory of the Allocation of Time." *Economic Journal*, September 1965, 493–517.

Bernstam, Mikhail and Peter Swan. "In Production of Children as Claims on the State: A Comprehensive Labor Market Approach to Illegitimacy in the United States, 1960–1980." Hoover Institution, 1986.

Coelen, Stephen P. and Robert J. McIntyre. "An Econometric Model of Pronatalist and Abortion Policies." *Journal of Political Economy*, December 1978, 1077–1101.

De Tray, Dennis. "Child Quality and the Demand for Children." *Journal of Political Economy*, March/April 1973, S70–95.

Deyak, Timothy A. and V. Kerry Smith. "The Economic Value of Statute Reform: The Case of Liberalized Abortion." *Journal of Political Economy*, February 1976, 83–99.

Goldfeld, Steven M. and Richard E. Quandt. "Some Tests for Homoscedasticity." *Journal of the American Statistical Association*, September 1965, 539–47.

Hamermesh, Daniel S. and Neal M. Soss. "An Economic Theory of Suicide." *Journal of Political Economy*, January/February 1974, 83–98.

Johnson, Douglas W., Paul R. Picard, and Bernard Quinn. *Churches and Church Membership in the United States*. Washington, D.C.: Glenmary Research Center, 1974.

Klarman, Herbert E. *The Economics of Health*. New York: Columbia University Press, 1965.

Michael, Robert T. "Education and the Derived Demand for Children." *Journal of Political Economy*, March/April 1973, S128–64.

U.S. Bureau of the Census. *State Reports, Detailed Characteristics: 1980*. Washington, D.C.: Government Printing Office, 1983.

Willis, Robert J. "A New Approach to the Economic Theory of Fertility Behavior." *Journal of Political Economy*, March/April 1973, S14–64.

Article 7

Search Costs and Apartment Rents

JOHN D. BENJAMIN
Department of Finance and Real Estate, Kogod College of Business Administration, The American University, 4400 Massachusetts Avenue, N.W., Washington, DC 20016

KENNETH M. LUSHT
Department of Insurance and Real Estate, Smeal College of Business Administration, The Pennsylvania State University, University Park, PA 16802

Abstract

Differences in apartment rents are explained with a hedonic equation that includes property management variables omitted in prior studies. Our joint hypotheses are that differences in contributions to rent exist among property managers as a function of their ability to reduce search costs to renters and that the manager's fee for providing search-cost-reducing information is reflected in the amount of rent paid. Two proxies for the level of search costs are found to be positively and significantly related to the rent level.

Key Words: Apartment rents, property management, search costs

Following Rosen's (1974) theoretical framework for revealing the implicit prices of the component characteristics of differentiated goods, empirical work produces somewhat standard lists of characteristics which are used to explain house prices and apartment rents. Traditionally, these lists include matrices of physical, locational, and quality characteristics (Blomquist and Worley, 1981), with more recent work extending the hedonic function to arguments associated with a sale of property rights (Marks, 1984). Developers, property managers, and appraisers use these lists of characteristics to predict market rents and values for income-producing residential properties.

Less frequently seen are hedonic functions that include variables which reflect the contributions of property management, despite evidence that rents may be significantly affected by the mere presence of a "resident caretaker" (Kain and Quigley, 1970), and that quality-related characteristics may explain almost as much variation in rents as physical characteristics do (Jaffe and Bussa, 1977).

The notion that the property manager matters is extended in this article to include the likelihood that in markets where the search for information is costly, as in the market for apartment rentals, managers able to reduce search costs will be in a position to extract higher rents. After summarizing the literature with respect to search costs and prices in section 1, we describe our data sources and empirical methodology in section 2. Section 3 presents our results and section 4 concludes the article.

1. Background

Analyses of price formation often make the convenient assumption of perfect information. In practice, that assumption is likely to be disappointed, and when it is relaxed to allow imperfect information and resulting search costs, a variety of interesting outcomes may occur. Introductory texts routinely refer to the relationship between information and the prices of goods such as used cars (Akerlof, 1970) and eyeglasses (Benham, 1972). Recently, an emerging literature which compares the outcomes of auctions versus private negotiations focuses on the significance of information sharing and information costs (for example, McAfee and McMillan, 1987).

The seminal insight was Stigler's (1961), who demonstrated that in markets with costly searches, prices reflect the tradeoff between the expected costs and benefits of the search. Because buyers with high costs of search will be prepared to pay higher prices than those with lower costs, price dispersion in equilibrium is likely.

How search costs affect prices is of particular interest in real estate markets, which tend to be populated by relatively uniformed buyers and sellers negotiating for relatively high-priced assets. For example, the frequently analyzed relationship between the selling prices of houses and their times on the market is largely a function of the informational content of a sale not occurring (Kaserman, Trimble, and Johnson, 1989). In a test of the search-cost/selling-price tradeoff, Miller (1977) found that out-of-town (high-search-cost) buyers paid a statistically significant price premium of about 3 percent over in-town buyers.

Information producing agents such as appraisers and brokers flourish in markets such as real estate, and an answer to the question of whether any portion of the commission or fee for providing search-cost reducing information is captialized into prices paid is essential to understanding how markets behave. When properties are sold, commissions are nominally paid by sellers, but there are reasons to speculate that at least part of the costs of information gathering are borne by buyers through the extraction of higher prices. Compared to a sale-by-owner, a broker listing attracts a larger number of interested shoppers, and the information provided by a broker's records may assist in setting reservation prices. The larger the broker, the greater the advantage. In turn, the availability of a multiple listing service (MLS) provides the same kind of advantage for MLS members over individual brokers. From a buyer's perspective, paying more for an equivalent property is unattractive unless the price premium is offset by reduced costs of search. Because brokers, and particularly multiple listing brokers, offer more choices than individual owners do, expected search costs will be reduced. This helps explain why buyers use agents employed by sellers (Bagnoli and Khanna, 1991).

Given the potential gains to both sellers and buyers from the use of brokers' information, the expectation is that the costs of that information will be shared. Frew and Jud's (1987) study of Charlotte house markets shows that about one-third to one-half of commissions were shifted to buyers through higher prices. Assuming that commissions average 6 percent, their findings indicate a 2 to 3 percent premium. Under a plausible set of marketing assumptions, Salant's (1991) simulations produces a similar 2.9 percent increase in the optimal asking price when a broker is retained after an unsuccessful attempt to sell by the owner.

We test whether information-cost sharing also occurs in the market for apartment rentals: specifically, whether any or all of the property management fee is shifted to student renters in a college town. Renters face a large number of choices, and because their tenure tends to be relatively short-term, the search process is regularly repeated. Thus, over time, search costs for renters are likely to be substantial. The student rental market in particular seems a good place in which to search for a relationship between information costs and prices. The likelihood that students have relatively low opportunity costs is offset by the facts that they tend to be relatively uninformed, have a short time frame available to conduct a search, often lack private transportation, and in the sample market have no apartment locator service available. If a sharing of information costs cannot be found in this environment, it is less likely to be found elsewhere.

Like buyers, renters tend to search for housing either through agents (property managers) or directly through owners. Though there are no multiple listing services for rentals (though some communities have apartment locator services), search cost economies can be obtained through the use of property management firms which offer centralized, accessible rental offices and through the use of management firms that are relatively large.

The advantages of a centralized and accessible rental office need not be belabored, except to note its particular importance in markets such as this one, characterized by short search times, a relative lack of information, and a lack of private transportation. The advantage of size is also straightforward: large property managers offer more choices. Search costs are reduced by providing a greater selection of apartment-unit types and by offering increased information through heavier advertising and a larger rental operations staff.

In a student market, other search-cost-reducing services associated with relatively large management firms are longer lists of prospective roommates, the availability of videotapes of properties and units, and a better chance of solving the downtown tenant's parking problem. Downtown parking spaces are in limited supply, and all renters are not guaranteed on-site space. Larger management firms are more likely to solve the parking search problem because when a space is not available at the rented unit, it will more likely be available at a managed property nearby. Thus, larger firms are in a better position to solve the joint shelter/parking problem in one stop.

Because larger management firms offer more alternatives than smaller firms, there is an increased likelihood of making a renter match. This marketing advantage parallels the advantage of larger brokers, or MLS members, which Yinger (1981) has associated with reduced search times for buyers.

2. Data and methodology

Our model is estimated based on the 1988–1989 and 1989–1990 rents, and on the physical, locational, and quality-related characteristics of 721 observations from 156 apartment complexes that house primarily university students in State College, Pennsylvania. The State College housing market is affected by Penn State University and is typical of a college town. Students comprise about half of the local area population but make up a majority of the apartment occupants. Limiting our sample to this single, demographically homogeneous submarket avoids the identification problems associated with market segmentation.

The sample is further limited to units that are professionally managed. This controls for any difference in rents extracted by professional versus owner-managers. Prior studies in student markets have found such differences, which have been attributed largely to the monopoly power of the professional firms (Ipcar, 1974; Gray, 1979; Appelbaum and Glasser, 1982; a review is found in Gilberbloom and Appelbaum, 1987). There are 34 management firms represented in our sample.

Data were obtained from a university housing office that collects data on the local housing market and from individual property management firms. To determine the extent to which certain physical, locational, vacancy, search cost, tenant mix, and property management differences influence rent, we utilized the following model:

$$Rent_i = f\,(P_{ij},\; L_i,\; V_i,\; Y_i,\; U_{ij},\; PM_{uj},\; T_{ij}) \qquad \begin{aligned} i &= 1, \ldots, n \\ j &= 1, \ldots, n \end{aligned} \qquad (1)$$

where

$Rent_i$ = the observed monthly rent on the ith apartment unit;

P_{ij} = a set of j characteristics for the ith apartment including:
   (a) the number of bedrooms (efficiency, one, two, three, or four bedrooms),
   (b) 0-1 dummy variable for a furnished apartment,
   (c) 0-1 dummy for a modern kitchen (includes garbage disposal, modern appliances, etc),
   (d) 0-1 dummy for all utilities paid, and
   (e) 0-1 dummy variable for parking available;

L_i = a location variable indicating distance from campus for the ith apartment, measured as minutes of walking time to the campus center;

V_i = 0-1 dummy variable showing the existence of vacant space on the first day of the fall semester;

Y_i = 0-1 dummy variable that captures changes in rent from schools years 1988–1989 to 1989–1990;

U_{ij} = a set of j search costs proxies for the ith apartment including:
   (a) 0-1 dummy variable for apartment unit property manager with or without centralized rental office, without regard to location, and
   (b) 0-1 dummy variable for apartment unit property manager with or without centralized rental office located near the university campus (i.e., downtown), and
   (c) the number of apartment-unit types managed by the property manager;

PM_{ij} = a set of j property management proxies for the ith apartment including:
   (a) 0-1 dummy variable for the presence of a resident manager in the apartment complex where the ith apartment is located, and
   (b) 0-1 dummy variable for the availability of 24-hour emergency maintenace service; and

T_{ij} = a set of j tenant proxies for the ith apartment including:
   (a) 0-1 dummy variable for graduate students and professional persons as the only residents in the apartment complex where the ith apartment is located, and
   (b) 0-1 dummy variable for undergraduate students as the only residents in the apartment complex where the ith apartment is located.

Summary statistics for the sample are presented in table 1. The variables and their expected signs, shown in table 2, are for the most part familiar.

Three variables are used as proxies for the level of search costs: (1) whether the managing firm has a centralized rental office that serves all units, (2) whether the centralized rental office is downtown (proximate to the university campus), and (3) the number of unit types managed. It is expected that search costs will be reduced by the availability of a centralized rental office and further reduced if the office is proximate to campus. These savings should produce rent premiums.

The third proxy for search costs is the number of apartment-unit types offered by the managing firm. Unit types differ from each other by differences in number of bedrooms, being furnished or unfurnished, location, and so on. Thus, an apartment complex may have one or more observations depending on the number of unit types within the complex. The average number of unit types managed by a firm is 31, with a range of 2 to 97. Tenants should be willing to pay additional rent as compensation for providing more one-stop options.

Two variables are used as proxies for on-site services to tenants: (1) whether there is a resident manager in the complex where the unit is located, and (2) whether the management firm offers 24-hour emergency maintenance service. Although our discussions with students, managers, and owners indicate that some tend to associate the presence of a resident manager more with a policing function than with providing services, on balance the perception is that a resident manager is viewed positively by student tenants. This is consistent with results from other markets (Kain and Quigley, 1970). We also expect the availability of 24-hour maintenance service to be valued by tenants.

Table 1. Summary statistics for apartment market ($n = 721$).

Variable	Mean	Standard Deviation	Minimum Value	Maximum Value
Rent	486.90	171.37	150.00	1200.00
Bedroom	1.53	0.82	0.50	4.00
Furnished	0.41	0.49	0.00	1.00
Modern kitchen	0.53	0.50	0.00	1.00
Utilities paid	0.18	0.38	0.00	1.00
Parking availability	0.82	0.38	0.00	1.00
Walk time in minutes	19.20	9.09	5.00	30.00
Vacancy	0.85	0.36	0.00	1.00
1989–1990 (year 2)	0.56	0.50	0.00	1.00
Centralized rental office	.91	.28	0.00	1.00
Rental office downtown	.50	.50	0.00	1.00
Unit types managed	40.29	28.47	2.00	97.00
Resident manager	.26	.44	0.00	1.00
24-hour maintenance service	.93	.25	0.00	1.00
Graduate/Professional residents only	.23	.42	0.00	1.00
Undergraduate residents only	.05	.21	0.00	1.00

Table 2. Dependent variable = monthly rent per unit (*n* = 721).

Variable	Expected Sign	Linear Coefficient (t-value)	Semi-Log Coefficient (t-value)
Intercept		119.79 (4.36)	5.38 (102.45)
Bedroom	+	134.68 (27.51)*	0.27 (28.97)*
Furnished	+	72.15 (7.69)*	0.12 (6.78)*
Modern kitchen	+	93.46 (9.95)*	0.17 (9.73)*
Utilities paid	+	85.62 (7.20)*	0.18 (8.05)*
Parking availability	+	41.58 (3.78)*	0.10 (4.92)*
Walk time in minutes	−	−3.30 (−5.16)*	−0.01 (−4.39)*
Vacancy	+	−6.86 (−.55)	0.01 (.52)
1989–1990	+	24.33 (3.01)*	0.04 (2.33)*
Centralized rental office	+	−14.17 (−.79)	−0.05 (−1.50)
Rental office downtown	+	25.65 (2.13)**	0.06 (2.48)*
Unit types managed	+	0.33 (1.75)**	0.01 (2.60)*
Resident manager	+	15.98 (1.69)**	0.05 (2.78)*
24-Hour maintenance service	+	69.87 (4.07)*	0.12 (3.80)*
Graduate/Professional residents only	+	10.12 (.90)	0.04 (1.60)
Undergraduate residents only	+	78.66 (3.22)*	0.12 (2.64)*
		$\bar{R}^2$ = .64	$\bar{R}$ = .66
		F = 88.12	F = 94.26

*Significant at 1 percent level (one-tailed test).
**Significant at 5 percent level (one-tailed test).

Complexes inhabited by only graduate students and professionals, or by only undergraduate students, may be preferred by tenants with different utility functions with respect to behaviors associated with social and academic priorities. Finally, a relatively standard apartment lease is employed for student renters. Lease provisions such as no children and/or pets allowed, lease term, and so on, do not show much variation across sample properties and are not included in the model.

3. Results

Table 2 shows the results for the regression estimates using the linear and semilog forms. The model is well behaved, with proper signs and coefficients of plausible size. The size of the unit is the primary pricing factor, and two of the proxies for a reduced level of search costs, a downtown rental office and the number of unit types managed, are positive and significant.

The following discussion refers to the linear form. Each bedroom increases rent by $135 per month, and furnished partments command $72 more than those unfurnished. Modern kitchens, utilities paid, and parking availability also positively affect rent, contributing $93, $86, and $42 per month, respectively. All of these coefficients are significant at the 1 percent level.

The variable for minutes required to walk to the campus center has the expected significant (1 percent level) negative sign. For each extra minute of walking time, rent decreases by approximately $3.

Vacancy is negatively related to rent but is insignificant. This relationship was not expected because higher rent results in lower demand and, therefore, higher vacancy. Thus, vacant space on the first day of the fall semester (the date of highest demand for apartment space by the student population) should reflect above-market rent. One explanation is that owners had lowered rents to reflect occupancy conditions.

The 1989–1990 coefficient of $24 indicates a 5 percent annual increase in rents, evaluated at the 1989 mean of $463. This percentage increase matches closely the estimates of owners and managers, and is significant at the 1 percent level.

Of primary interest are the three search cost proxies: a centralized rental office, a downtown rental office, and the number of unit types managed. If the property manager has a downtown office, rent increases by $26 per month with the coefficient significant at the 2 percent level. Each unit type managed increases rent per unit by $0.33, with the coefficient significant at the 5 percent level. Thus, a manager offering a downtown rental office and a selection of, say, 70 unit types is able to extract monthly rent that is about $39 higher than is a manager without a downtown office who offers 30 unit types. The rent elasticity with respect to having a downtown office is 0.264, while the rent elasticity with respect to the number of unit types managed is 0.275. These results support the hypothesized connection between rent levels and tenant search costs.

The coefficient on the centralized office variable is incorrectly signed but insignificant. This variable is collinear with the downtown office variable, and the fact it is insignificant while the downtown office variable is significant indicates that it is necessary but not sufficient to have a centralized office. To have a nontrivial effect on search costs and in turn rents, the office must be proximate to the student market.

The two on-site service variables have coefficients that are positive and significant. The presence of a resident manager raises rent by $16 with the coefficient significant at the 5 percent level. The availability of 24-hour emergency maintenance service is priced at $70, with the coefficient significant at the 1 percent level.

4. Conclusions and implications

This study is the first to link search costs and prices in a rental market. We test the joint hypotheses that search costs for apartment renters are affected by the availability and accessibility of a centralized rental office and by the number of apartment unit types offered by a property management firm, and that part of the savings is captured in the form of higher rents. The model includes variables for physical characteristics, location, the vacancy rate, the quality of on-site services, the tenant mix, and three proxies for the level of tenant search costs. Differences in contributions to rent are found to exist among property managers as a function of both a downtown location of the rental office and the number of apartment-unit types managed.

We did not have data on the incremental costs of providing added on-site services and reduced search. Given our esitmates of the rent premiums that these services produce, however, a firm's cost/benefit tradeoff could be modeled rather simply (as in Sirmans, Sirmans, and Benjamin, 1989). It is worth noting that we could find no systematic association between a management firm's fee structure and its apparent contribution to rent levels.

Our sample was restricted to professionally managed units. If the relationship between professional management firms and owner-managers is similar to the relationships among management firms with respect to the quality of services offered and the search-cost burdens imposed on tenants, our results suggest that the ability of professional firms to extract higher rents than owner-managers may be better explained by the offering of lower search costs and a higher level of on-site services than it is by the alternative appeal to their monopoly power.

Acknowledgments

We acknowledge the helpful comments of Don Jud and two anonymous reviewers. Graduate students Mukul Sinha, Michael Dunne, Janette Deihl, and Eric Pellegrin, and the Office for Town Independent Students (OTIS) at The Pennsylvania State University assisted in the collection and analysis of the data.

Notes

1. The double log form produced similar results, as did the results from estimating separate equations for the individual years 1988–1989 and 1989–1990. Regressions were also estimated by replacing the number of unit types managed with 0-1 variables which indicated whether the manager is "large" (one of the four largest) or "small" (others). We tried two variations. In the first, the 0-1 variable took a value of 1 if the manager was one of the four with the greatest number of unit types and 0 otherwise. In the second, the four largest managers were lumped together with the dummy variable indicating whether the manager was in the large category or not. In the first regression, three of the four large managers had significantly positive coefficients, while the coefficient for the fourth was insignificant. In the second regression, the four largest management firms exracted rents which were $37 per month higher than those extracted by smaller firms, a difference significant at the 1 percent level. This represents about a 7 percent premium and also indicates that much of the typical management fee is being shifted to the renter. The directions and magnitudes of the other coefficients in both regressions were similar to those shown in table 2. In none of the regressions was serious

multicollinearity indicated, based on SAS variation inflation, eigenvalue, and condition index indicators. Autocorrelation and heteroscedasticity were not found to be strongly present by standard tests and residual plots. The error term appears to be normally distributed.

References

Akerlof, G. "The Market for Lemons: Qualitiative Uncertainty and the Market Mechanism." *Quarterly Journal of Economics* (August 1970), 488–500.

Appelbaum, R. and Glasser, T. "Concentration of Ownership in Isla Vista, California." University of California, Santa Barbara Housing Office, 1982.

Bagnoli, M. and Khanna, N. "Buyers' and Sellers' Agents in the Housing Market." *Journal of Real Estate Finance and Economics* (June 1991), 147–156.

Benham, L. "The Effect of Advertising on the Price of Eyeglasses." *Journal of Law and Economics* 15 (October 1972), 337–352.

Blomquist, G. and Worley, L. "Hedonic Prices, Demands for Urban Amenities, and Benefit Estimates." *Journal of Urban Economics* 9 (1981), 212–221.

Frew, J. and Jud, D. "Who Pays the Real Estate Broker's Commission?" *Research in Law and Economics* 10 (1987), 177–188.

Gilderbloom, J. and Appelbaum, R. "Toward a Sociology of Rent: Are Rental Housing Markets Competitive?" *Social Problems* 34 (June 1987), 261–276.

Gray, T. "Student Housing and Discrimination." Working paper, University of California at Santa Barbara, 1979.

Ipcar, C. "The Student Ghetto Housing Market." Working paper, Lansing College, 1974.

Jaffe, A.J. and Bussa, R.G. "Using a Simple Model to Estimate Market Rents: A Case Study." *The Appraisal Journal* (January–February 1977), 7–13.

Kain, J.F. and Quigley, J.M. "Explaining Metropolitan Housing Quality." *Journal of the American Statistical Association* 65 (1970), 532–548.

Kaserman, D., Trimble, J. and Johnson, R. "Equilibration in a Negotiated Market: Evidence from Housing." *Journal of Urban Economics* (July 1989), 30–42.

Marks, D. "The Effect of Rental Control on the Price of Rental Housing: A Hedonic Approach." *Land Economics* (February 1984), 81–94.

McAfee, R. and McMillan, J. "Auctions and Bidding." *Journal of Economic Literature* (June 1987), 699–738.

Miller, N. "The Impact of Market Transaction Phenomena on Residential Property Value." Unpublishes doctoral dissertation, Ohio State University, 1977.

Rosen, S. "Hedonic Prices and Implicit Markets: Product Differentiation in Price Competition." *Journal of Political Economy* 82 (January–February 1974), 33–55.

Salant, S. "For Sale by Owner: When to Use a Broker and How to Price the House." *Journal of Real Estate Finance and Economics* (June 1991), 157–174.

Sirmans, G.S., Sirmans, C.F. and Benjamin, J.D. "Determining Apartment Rent: The Value of Amenities, Services, and External Factors." *The Journal of Real Estate Research* (Summer 1989), 33–43.

Stigler, G. "The Economics of Information." *Journal of Political Economy* (June 1961), 213–225.

Yinger, J. "A Search Model of Real Estate Broker Behavior." *American Economic Review* 71 (1981), 591–605.

Article 8

Price Concessions, Time on the Market, and the Actual Sale Price of Homes

PAUL K. ASABERE
Professor of Real Estate, School of Business and Management, Temple University, Philadelphia, PA 19122

FORREST E. HUFFMAN
Associate Professor of Real Estate, School of Business and Management, Temple University, Philadelphia, PA 19122

Abstract

This article examines the relationships between listing price concessions, time on the market, and the actual sale price of homes. The principal hypothesis that significant listing price concessions, usually the result of overpricing, can lead to real discounts on the final sale price is proven by our empirical results. We also found that the longer the time on the market, the higher the sale price, ceteris paribus. This finding is consistent with the theory that the longer a property remains on the market, the higher the probability is that a relatively superior selling price can be realized.

Key words: Concessions, stigmatized, lingering, discounting

The real estate broker/seller faces the problem of trading off selling price and the time required to sell the property. As Trippi (1977) and Miller (1978) point out, the broker/seller faces two conflicting objectives: maximizing selling price while minimizing time on the market. Therefore, brokers and sellers must consider carefully the impacts on potential sales price and time on the market in establishing listing prices for property for sale. By determining the optimal listing price, the broker/seller maximizes sales price and minimizes time on the market and in doing so, maximizes the present value of the net selling price based on his/her opportunity cost of time (Miller and Sklarz, 1988).

Several empirical studies have examined the relationships between selling price and time on the market. Most of these studies show varying relationships between time on the market and selling price. Trippi (1977) finds a positive relationship between price and time on the market. Miller (1978) also finds a significant, positive relationship between time on the market and inflation-adjusted selling price. He concludes that the positive relationship is likely due to differential selling (search) costs. However, Cubbins (1974) finds an inverse relationship and concludes that a house can be sold faster the higher the price is attached to it. Allen, Shilling, and Sirmans (1987) find no statistically significant relationship between time on the market and selling price. Several other empirical studies have found that the ratio of selling price to list price is negatively related to time on the market (Belkin, Hempel, and McLeavey, 1976; Miller 1977). In essence, the longer the property remains on the market, ceteris paribus, the greater is the concession from price (Larsen and Park,

1989). Haurin (1988) examines the effect of atypical housing features on time on the market. The author assumes that the greater the atypicality, the greater the variance of offers and thus the longer the time on the market. He finds that unusual houses take longer to sell. These findings are consistent with the trade-off pricing behavior suggested by Miller and Sklarz (1988) discussed above.

The conflicting results of prior studies may be largely due to the existence of differing market environments. An examination of the relationship between selling price and time on the market must carefully identify the market environment being studied. A complete examination of the relationship between selling price and time on the market should also include an analysis of broker/seller pricing decisions. In this study we examine the relationships between sales prices, time on the market, and an aspect of broker/seller pricing (concessions on listing price by seller) with special reference to a buyers' market. The balance of the article is organized in the following manner: section 1 presents the hypotheses and the empirical framework; section 2 discusses the data and the results of the empirical analysis, and section 3 gives the summary and conclusions of the study.

1. The hypotheses and the empirical framework

Our primary assumption is that home sellers trade off selling price and time on the market. Miller (1978) assets that owners with high selling costs must select a price that is immediately attractive to potential buyers. The pricing behavior of these owners may preclude the highest bid because their opportunity costs may be so high that a low bid achieved quickly will have a higher present value than a higher price secured after a long period of time. According to Miller (1978), owners with no immediate urgency to sell have the oppportunity cost to select higher asking prices and wait for an acceptable bid. Thus, as Miller and Sklarz (1988) explain, the seller is seeking to maximize the present value of the net selling price based on his/her opportunity cost of time. The listing price that theoretically maximizes the present value of the selling price would be equal to the true market value of the property.

One view is that if the true market value were known in advance, then the seller would list at that price. A seller who lists a property at a price greater than the true market value is either misinformed about the market or is seeking to capture a price greater than market value. In either case, it is possible to price oneself out of the market (Ferreira and Sirmans, 1989). In fact, conventional practice is to attempt to realize the real net benefits of setting listing price equal to market value by employing the services of real estate appraisers.

Another view is that sellers prefer to err on the high side of any transaction so as not to preclude realizing the highest possible bid. As a result, sellers systematically establish higher initial asking prices. However, in a competitive market, this should result in a longer time on the market (Zerbst and Bruggeman, 1977; Ferreira and Sirmans, 1989) and significant price concessions (list price minus sale price).

In summary, two seller pricing strategies exist at the extreme. One is to price near perceived market value in order to attract the maximum number of buyers and potential bids, but then only make small price concessions. The other is to drastically overprice, hope for price reliance effects, and make large concessions as necessary to bidding buyers (Miller and Sklarz, 1987). A pricing behavior that systematically establishes higher list prices, however, can lead to sales prices that are suboptimal. Rising carry costs due to lengthening time on the market would lead to higher opportunity costs. A seller suddenly faced with rising opportunity cost may choose to offer significant price concessions which can result in real price discounts.

There is a reason why carrying costs would increase over time significantly enough to create rapid real discounting behavior on the part of sellers. Homes priced close enough to true market value will, in the "initial" period of being placed on the market, attract sufficient numbers of buyers to have a strong probability of sale. But if they are priced too high and do not sell early, they miss their chance during critical early exposure and thus become "stigmatized." The result is that, after lingering on the market, substantial price declines are necessary to induce renewed buyer search behavior. There is also the issue of potential influence of broker on seller. For a broker, there is an incentive to minimize the time devoted to a given transaction so as to increase volume transacted per period. In a bargaining environment, it is expected that obtaining agreement relatively quickly by making significant price concessions would be consistent with broker interest. Of course, the magnitude of the concessions and whether real price discounts might result would depend on the nature of the market environment.

To state formally, let:

$$P_L = \text{list price,}$$

$$P_T = \text{true market price (theoretical),}$$

$$P_A = \text{actual sale price.}$$

Therefore,

$$(P_L - P_A) = \text{selling price concession,}$$

$$(P_L - P_T) = \text{overpricing cushion (buffer),}$$

$$P_L \geq P_A: \text{restriction.}$$

If $(P_L - P_A) = (P_L - P_T)$,

then $P_A = P_T$.

This scenario produces no significant price differences. The situation occurs in a competitve market environment where market forces result in equilibrium prices at true market values.

If $(P_L - P_A) < (P_L - P_T)$,

then $P_A > P_T$.

This scenario results in significant premium effects. This situation would occur, for example, in a sellers' market environment where sellers can take advantage of the market.

If $(P_L - P_A) > (P_L - P_T)$,

then $P_A < P_T$.

This scenario produces suboptimal or discount prices. This situation would occur, for example, in a buyers' market environment where price concessions are dictated by the market.

Our principal hypothesis of this study is that there will be a negative relationship between sales prices and price concessions for our study period, a period that falls under the scenario of a buyers' market. Our second hypothesis is that there will be a positive relationship between time on the market and sales price. This would be consistent with the theory that the longer a property stays on the market, the higher the probability that a relatively superior selling price can be captured (see Miller, 1978). To obtain evidence on the partial effects of price concessions and time on the market on home prices, we employ a hedonic equation of the standard form, as in Rosen (1974), Crether and Mieszkowski (1974), King (1973).

$$\operatorname{Log}\hat{P}_A = \operatorname{Log}\beta_0 + \beta_1[(P_L - P_A)/P_L] + \beta_2(TOM) + \sum_{j=3}^{n} \beta_j X_j + \epsilon \qquad (1)$$

$\operatorname{Log}\hat{P}$ = the natural logarithm of deflated sale price of the home (i.e., inflation adjusted):

P_L = list price;

P_A = actual sale price;

$[(P_L - P_A)/P_L]$ = proportional concession on listing price by the seller;

TOM = time on the market;

X_{js} = controls for market characteristics, locational characteristics, neighborhood characteristics, and physical characteristics (these are defined in table 1);

$\operatorname{Log}\beta$ = constant term;

ϵ = an error term of the ordinary sort.

The coefficient β_1 in equation (1) is expected to be significantly negative ($\beta_1 < 0$) while the coefficient β_2 is expected to be significantly positive ($\beta_2 > 0$). These would support the hypotheses of our article. There are obvious reasons why the specific functional form represented by equation (1) is adopted. First, we are principally interested in measuring the percentage price discounts (or premium) associated with unit changes in our key variables (price concessions and time on the market). Second, the relationships between sales price and several property characteristics have been found to be chronically nonlinear (see, for example, Kowalski and Colwell, 1986; and Colwell and Sirmans, 1978). Section 2 presents the results of the empirical analysis.

2. The data and the empirical results

We use 337 residiential sales over the time period of December 1986 to June 1990 obtained from multiple listing services (MLS) covering the Pennsylvania counties of Philadelphia, Montgomery, and Chester. One hundred twenty-five sales were drawn from the city of Philadelphia, 100 in outlying suburbs of Montgomery County, and the remaining 112 in rural areas of Chester County. We use dummy variables to represent these urban, suburban, and rural locational characteristics. Additional information collected from the MLS included lot size, number of bedrooms and baths, sales price, date of sale, listing price, and days on the market. We use three proxies to control for specific neighborhood conditions. These are median home value, median household income, and average monthly rent of the census tract as derived from 1980 census reports. We control for macro-economic effects by including standard macro-variables. These are: monthly, seasonally adjusted unemployment rates compiled by the U.S. Department of Labor; the average monthly mortgage contract rate as reported by the Federal Reserve System; a time-of-sale variable; and the monthly Consumer Price Index as compiled by the U.S. Department of Commerce. The Consumer Price Index is used to deflate our dependent variable sale price. Descriptive statistics for all relevant variables and their definitions are reported in table 1.

The results of our empirical analysis as shown in table 2 are very interesting. The adjusted coefficient of determination (R^2) for the two equations is approximately 0.72. This figure is quite impressive for explaining prices across large cities and metropolitan areas.

Table 1. Summary statistics for relevant variables.

Variable	Definition	Mean	Standard Deviation
P_A (S)	Actual sales price of the home	181,441.28	129,437.26
P_L (S)	List price	193,562.05	140,096.41
$[(P_L - P_A)/P_L]$	Proportional concession on listing price	0.05	0.07
TOM (days)	Time on the market	125.04	81.63
RATE (%)	Rate of interest on conventional, 30-year mortgage	9.62	0.36
UNPLY (%)	Unemployment rate	5.35	0.25
URBAN (%)	(1, 0) Dummy variable for urban location	0.37	0.48
SUBURB (%)	(1, 0) Dummy variable for suburban location	0.30	0.46
RURAL (%)	(1, 0) Dummy variable for rural location	0.33	0.47
INCOME (S)	Median household income of census tract (1980)	21,333.36	5,648.52
RENT (%)	Median gross rent of census trace (1980)	243.73	67.39
VALUE (S)	Median value of improvements in census tract (1980)	61,413.06	29,893.40
BEDR	Number of bedrooms	3.45	0.97
BATH	Number of bathrooms	2.05	0.89
SQFT	Lot size	45,916.25	99,766.96
CMONTH	Continuous month-of-sale variable	55.66	12.67

Table 2. The regression results (dependent variable is log of deflated sales price).

Variables	Equation¹	Equation²
$[(P_L - P_A)/P_L]$	−0.89	−0.89
	(−3.84)*	(−3.81)*
TOM	0.0005	—
	(2.14)*	
LogTOM	—	0.06
		(2.59)*
RATE	0.07	—
	(1.25)	
UNPLY	−0.09	−0.12
	(−1.06)	(−1.31)
LogRATE	—	0.69
		(1.17)
URBAN	−0.21	−0.22
	(−3.21)*	(−3.40)*
SUBURB	−0.14	−0.15
	(−1.94)*	(−2.06)*
INCOME	0.000013	0.000013
	(2.84)*	(2.75)*
RENT	0.0023	0.0023
	(3.90)*	(3.82)*
VALUE	0.000005	0.000005
	(4.30)*	(4.43)*
BEDR	0.08	0.08
	(3.87)*	3.79)*
BATH	0.22	0.22
	(8.33)*	(8.25)*
SQFT	0.0000014	0.0000013
	(7.12)*	(6.97)*
CMONTH	—	−0.0004
		(−0.24)
CONST	10.09	9.21
	(12.20)	(6.26)*
$\bar{R}^2$	.072	.073

Note: t-ratios are shown in parentheses below regression coefficients.
*Significantly different from zero at the 95 percent level of confidence.

The control variables for macro-economy (RATE and UNPLY) produced insignificant results in both equations. It should be noted, however, that our study period was a time of relatively low and stable unemployment and interest rates. As indicated in table 1, the mean unemployment rate was 5.35 with a standard deviation of 0.25. The mean and standard deviation for interest rates were 9.62 and 0.36, respectively.

The control variables for urban (URBAN), suburban (SUBURB), and rural (RURAL) locations produced unique but interesting results. The estimated coefficients on both URBAN and SUBURB are significantly negative in the two equations. These results imply that, on average, homes within the city of Philadelphia (URBAN) sell at a 19 percent discount while homes within the suburban (SUBURB) Montgomery county sell at a 13 percent price discount. All are relative to home sales within rural Chester County (RURAL). While these results appear rather paradoxical, anecdotal evidence suggests that this may well be the case. In the case of the city of Philadelphia it may be partly explained by unpopular city policies such as high transfer taxes, wage taxes, and other city policies that drive out residents. For suburban Montgomery County, which has been expanding rapidly in recent years in terms of construction of new homes, these results seem to suggest possible oversupply.

All three control variables for neighborhood (INCOME, RENT, and VALUE) worked as expected. The estimated coefficients on INCOME, RENT and VALUE are significantly positive at the 95 percent level of confidence, as expected. These results imply that the high-income, high-rent, and prestigious neighborhoods lead to premium prices. These are consistent with theory.

All the three control variables for property characteristics (BEDR, BATH, and SQFT) also behaved as expected. Their estimated coefficients are significantly positive at the 95 percent level of confidence. Apart from the estimated coefficient on BATH which has an unusually large magnitude (0.22), all the magnitudes of the other coefficients appear to make sense. In the case of BATH the huge coefficient may be due to the fact that we may be capturing some of the effects due to building size and systems quality. Unfortunately, our data do not allow us to include a building size variable. The time of sale variable (CMONTH), however, proved to be insignificant as shown in equation (2). Other specifications for time in trial runs also proved to be insignificant at conventional levels. Homes did not appreciate in value significantly in our study period, a result consistent with our buyers' market presumption.

Our variable for price concessions $[(P_L - P_A)/P_L]$ produced significant results. The estimated coefficients are significantly different from zero at the 99 percent level of confidence in both equations. The sign on the variable is negative as hypothesized. The magnitude of the estimated coefficient is -0.89 in both equations. This means tht every concession point (.01) is associated with an 0.89 percent discount in actual sales price. The time on the market variable (TOM) also behaved as hypothesized. It was significantly differently from zero at the 95 percent level of confidence in both equations. The sign is positive as hypothesized. Based on equation (2), for example, a 1 percent increase in TOM would lead to a 6 percent increase in actual sale price of the home.

3. Summary and conclusions

The hypothesized relationships between sales price and price concessions is borne out by the results of our empirical analysis. The estimated coefficient β_1 on our price concessions variable $[(P_L - P_A)/P_L]$ is significantly negative at conventional levels. It appears that when homes are priced too high and do not sell early, they miss their chance during critical early exposure and thus become stigmatized. The result is that when they linger on the market, substantial price declines are necessary to induce renewed buyer search behavior. Such rapid real discounting behavior on the part of sellers would likely prevail in a buyers' market environment when supply greatly exceeds demand, thereby enabling purchasers to bargain for lower prices and get them, which results in falling values (Dasso and Ring, 1989, p. 321).

The hypothesized relationship between sales price and time on the market (TOM) is also supported by the results of our empirical analysis. The estimated coefficient β_2 on time on TOM is significantly positive at conventional levels. This is consistent with the theory that the longer a property remains on the market, the higher the probability is that a relatively superior selling price can be captured (Trippi, 1977, Miller, 1978).

Acknowledgments

The authors would like to acknowledge the financial support of the Pennsylvania Association of Realtors' education foundation. Our special thanks also go to an anonymous reviewer whose helpful comments helped to improve the quality of this article. The usual caveat applies.

References

Allen, P.R., Shilling, J.D. and Sirmans, C.F. "Contracting, Contingencies and Single-Family House Prices." *Economic Inquiry* 25 (January 1987), 159–164.

Belkin, J., Hempel, D.J. and McLeavey, D.W. "An Empirical Study of Time on Market Using Multidimensional Segmentation of Housing Markets." *AREUEA Journal* 4 (Fall 1976), 57–75.

Colwell, P.F. and Sirmans, C.F. "Area, Time, Centrality and the Value of Urban Land" *Land Economics* 54 (1978), 514–519.

Crether, D.M. and Mieszkowski, P. "Determinants of Real Estate Values." *Journal of Urban Economics* (April 1974), 127–146.

Cubbins, J.S. "Price, Quality and Selling Time in the Housing Market." *Applied Economics* 6 (1974), 171–187.

Dasso J. and Ring, A.A. *Real Estate Principles and Practices*. 11th ed. Englewood Cliffs, NJ: Prentice Hall, 1989.

Ferreira, E.J. and Sirmans, G.S. "Selling Price, Financing Premiums and Days on the Market." *The Journal of Real Estate Finance and Economics* 2 (September 1989), 209–222.

Haurin, D. "The Duration of Marketing Time of Residential Housing." *AREUEA Journal* 16 (4) (1988), 396–410.

King, A.T. *Property Taxes, Amenities, and Residential Land Values*. Cambridge, MA: Ballinger Publishing Co., 1973.

Kowalski, J.G. and Colwell, P.F. "Market Versus Assessed Values of Industrial Land." *AREUEA Journal* 14 (1986), 361–373.

Larsen, J.E. and Park, W.J. "Non-Uniform Percentage Brokerage Commissions and Real Estate Market Performance." *AREUEA Journal* 17 (4) (1989), 423–438.

Miller, N.G. "The Influence of Market Transaction Phenomena on Residential Property Values." Unpublished doctoral dissertation, The Ohio State University, 1977.

Miller, N.G. "Time on the Market and Selling Price." *AREUEA Journal* 6 (Summer 1978), 164–174.

Miller, N.G. and Sklarz, M.A. "Pricing Strategies and Residential Property Selling Prices." *The Journal of Real Estate Research* 2 (1) (1987), 31–40.

Rosen, S. "Hedonic Prices and Implicit Markets: Product Differentiation in Pure Competition." *Journal of Political Economy* (January–February 1974), 35–55.

Trippi, R.R. "Estimating the Relationship Between Price and Time of Sale for Investment Property." *Management Science* 23 (April 1977), 838–842.

Section III
Forecasting

Managers frequently make and evaluate forecasts. Forecasting issues, techniques, and illustrations are the focus of this section. In the first article, "Economic Forecasting in the Private and Public Sectors," Alan Greenspan provides an overview of economic forecasting. He discusses the similarities and differences between the use of econometric models and judgmental forecasting. Also, he describes the difference in the role of the forecaster for a private sector organization, such as a firm, versus the role of a forecaster for a public sector organization that sets policy.

Nada R. Sanders discusses the results of his survey of forecasting managers of U.S. companies in his article "Corporate Forecasting Practices in the Manufacturing Industry." He reports that the survey respondents are familiar with both judgmental and quantitative forecasting techniques. Generally, judgmental techniques are more commonly used than are quantitative techniques. Of the quantitative techniques, the moving average is the most popular for forecast horizons of less than one year; regression analysis is the most popular for forecast horizons that exceed one year.

In "Predicting Interest Rates: A Comparison of Professional and Market–Based Forecasts," Michael T. Belongia examines the reliability of three–month Treasury bill interest rate forecasts by economists. Forecasts of the economists are compared to a naive forecast of no change in the interest rate, and a forecast implicit in the T–bill futures market. Based on three evaluation criteria—the mean absolute error, the mean error, and the root mean squared error—the forecast accuracy of the economists does not clearly dominate the two alternatives.

Article 9

Economic Forecasting in the Private and Public Sectors

By Alan Greenspan*

The similarities and differences between public and private forecasting are highlighted in this article. The advantages and limitations of economic models and judgmental forecasts are reviewed, and a process that incorporates features of both is recommended. Forecasting is also complicated by difficulties in determining where we are at the present time as well as an increasingly elusive and complex economic structure.

OVER THE YEARS, I have been involved with economic forecasting from a variety of perspectives — as producer and consumer, both inside and outside government. I would like to take this opportunity to reflect on some of the similarities and differences between economic forecasting in the private and public sectors. The broad approaches taken and the conceptual difficulties faced by forecasters are quite similar in both sectors. The principal differences surround the context and focus of the forecasts and the ends that they serve.

Let me begin by highlighting what I see as the chief similarities between private and public sector forecasting. This group is, of course, more aware

*Alan Greenspan is Chairman of the Board of Governors of the Federal Reserve System, Washington, DC. He is a Fellow and former President of NABE. This article was presented at the 32nd Annual Meeting of the National Association of Business Economists, September 23-27, 1990, Washington, DC.

than most that I address of the opportunities, challenges, and limitations presented by economic forecasting. The same cannot often be said of the constituency served by the forecaster. In both the private and public sectors, a large gap commonly exists between the expectations of consumers of forecasts and the abilities of the forecaster. In some cases the forecaster must overcome considerable skepticism that economic projections are of any value. In other cases, expectations reach far beyond the abilities of the practitioner. In either situation, the clarity with which the forecaster can communicate the key conditioning assumptions and the uncertainties surrounding a forecast can be as important as the predictions themselves.

Whether employed by the government or by private firms, it is vital that forecasters have a clear understanding of what economic events they are attempting to anticipate and over what time periods. Success in this effort requires a thorough knowledge of how the focus of the forecast relates to the objectives of the decisionmaker and reflects the critical features of the economic environment in which he or she must operate. Too often one observes forecasts that seem to focus on a set of economic statistics because they are readily available or the traditional object of analysis, rather than because of their immediate relevance to the decisionmaker. The adept forecaster is capable of drawing the distinction.

MODELS VS. JUDGMENTAL FORECASTING

Over the years, one recurring theme in discussions of forecasting — both within and outside government — has been the debate over the relative merits of economic models and so-called "intuitive" or judgmental approaches. This is a distinction with little meaning or practical relevance. With a few exceptions, it is rare to find pure practitioners from either camp. Most of us are involved in some combination of these efforts. To be sure, there is considerable variation in how economists achieve this melding of models and judgment, and in the weights implicitly assigned to each approach. But the mix is almost always present, and this is appropriate.

I would even take the argument a step further and suggest that, in some respects, it is difficult to distinguish models from judgments. At their core, the two approaches can be quite similar, frequently being based on the same economic theories and similar bodies of empirical evidence. Of course, the intuitive forecaster generally does not have a thousand equations ready to execute at a moment's notice. More often, he or she relies on a handful of key economic relationships, with the relative importance of these key relationships shifting as the economic landscape changes. Much the same is true, in a sense, of model-based forecasters. For a given economic episode, usually only a few key equations in an econometric model drive the forecast produced by the model. A skillful forecaster of either persuasion recognizes and exploits the critical economic relationships in play at any point in time.

I do not mean to imply that there are no meaningful differences between the use of economic models and methods that rely primarily on judgment. Both approaches have their particular strengths and weaknesses. Forecasters, regardless of their preferred *modus operandi*, should be aware of these differences and should be looking for ways to take advantage of the complementarities offered by the approaches.

ADVANTAGES AND LIMITATIONS OF MODELS

Perhaps the greatest advantage of a fully articulated model is that it helps the forecaster keep track of the interrelationships among the primary variables of interest. I have in mind two kinds of relationships. The first type is the simple accounting identity, such as the one that links government budget deficits, the current account balance, and the excess of domestic saving over investment. These identities play a much larger role that is generally recognized. They enforce a common discipline on forecasters that is unrelated to their theoretical predispositions. Regardless of how formal or informal the model, these identities serve as a powerful check on the internal logic of any forecast.

The second type of relationship reflects behavioral interdependencies. These relationships usually are subject to substantial uncertainty and, as a result, tend to be the focus of greater controversy.

Taken together, identities and behavioral equations can aid the forecaster in tracing out a sequence of complicated interactions. For example, it would be difficult without a model to quantify the net impact on domestic interest rates of a change in the fiscal deficit, because it may involve simultaneous links among domestic demand, international capital flows, domestic and foreign monetary policy responses, exchange rates, and so on.

Another advantage of the econometric approach, if it is based on appropriate statistical methods, is that it permits the forecaster to assess systematically the historical accuracy of economic relationships, providing information over time on which have been most and least reliable. These historical measures can be used, in turn, to quantify the uncertainty surrounding the forecaster's assessment of the future.

There are limits, however, to the apparent power of the econometric model as a forecasting tool. In spite of significant progress toward accommodating more sophisticated — and we hope more realistic — formal models, it is still fair to say that, on the whole, our econometric models are at best very crude approximations of the true economy. The economy we are attempting to model is exceedingly complex, best characterized by continually evolving institutions and economic relationships. The widespread use of addfactors in most model-based projections is the clearest manifestation of the difficulty that our large-scale models have in representing a complicated reality. At this stage in their development, statistical models still require large doses of judgment if they are to be useful to decision-makers.

Another set of limitations of econometric models might fall under the general label of "model uncertainty." By this I mean simply that we cannot be sure that our characterizations of the fundamental relationships incorporated in our models are accurate representations of the underlying economic processes. For example, econometric models in the 1950s and 1960s did not devote much attention to the determinants of inflation and its role in the course of macroeconomic adjustment. The failure to recognize fully the role of inflation expectations led initially, at least, to the generally poor record of the profession on forecasting inflation in the 1970s.

Another facet of model uncertainty surrounds the standard econometric practice of estimating fixed economic relationships under the assumption that the structure of the economy is unchanging. If the structure of the economy is more like a moving target than a sitting duck, we will rarely accumulate enough observations from any given structure to estimate accurately the parameters for our models. Tests for structural change have been developed, but these tests work best when a reasonable number of observations from *both* structures have been collected so that a change may be reliably detected. If the change is occurring now, standard statistical tests may not discover it until one, two, or five years from now.

Developments in financial markets provide a prime example of these difficulties. Twenty years ago we did not anticipate the degree to which financial innovation and deregulation would make the prediction of money demand difficult, with its corresponding consequences for defining a monetary aggregate that could be monitored usefully by policymakers. Looking ahead, it seems reasonable to assume that similar events will occur that will alter our understanding of some of the fundamental relationships in the economy.

A final source of uncertainty may be attributed to the functional form of our models. Most models are essentially linear, in part because historical data are not rich enough to distinguish among the myriad nonlinear forms that might be entertained. The linear approximation is convenient, and no doubt reasonably accurate, for many historical periods. However, it seems possible that the linear approximation may break down during critical economic episodes. For example, the gradual expansion and steep contraction of the business cycle may not be represented well by a linear model.

Moreover, the precision of the estimated parameters in our models if often overstated. The large t statistics that are supposed to represent our confidence in parameter estimates can be quite misleading, because they are frequently the product of an extensive "data-mining" process during which hundreds of alternative equations are estimated and discarded. As a consequence of this biased procedure, our confidence that such relationships represent true economic structure, rather than random chance, must be considerably less than that implied by the reported statistics.

ADVANTAGES AND LIMITATIONS OF JUDGMENTAL FORECASTING

Some of the weak points of the intuitive forecasting approach are simply mirror images of the strengths of the model-based approach. For example, in the intuitive approach, it may be difficult, if not impossible, to keep track of the numerous interactions and simultaneities that exist among the variables of interest. Moreover, it can be exceptionally difficult for consumers of these forecasts to

identify the critical underlying assumptions and gauge the sensitivity of the forecast to changes in these assumptions.

For the most part, the strengths of intuitive forecasting complement the weaknesses of model-based prediction. The flexibility of the intuitive approach may allow its practitioner to adjust more quickly to shifts in key parameters or to perceived changes in the economic structure. At times of rapid change, such as at business cycle turning points, intuitive forecasters may be able to pick up on and react to the nonlinear response of the economy better than those who are relying solely on conventional econometric models. Moreover, intuitive forecasters may catch important developments early on by recognizing the signals or anomalies in weekly or monthly data as they are received. While some work has been done to formalize this process in statistical models, at present the judgmental forecaster seems to have the edge on this front.

Given the strengths and weaknesses of these approaches, it seems obvious that the best forecasting strategy will incorporate features of both model-based and intuitive forecasting.

Indeed, a healthy mix of the two techniques is used in economic forecasting at the Federal Reserve. Model-based results often provide a useful starting point for framing the overall outlook. They also help us to gauge quickly the likely influence of incoming information on the outlook and to estimate the sensitivity of forecasts to key conditioning assumptions. However, in spite of the usefulness of models, the role of judgment remains substantial. For example, a significant degree of judgment must be used when reconciling results from a variety of formal, econometric equations, all of which have some degree of plausibility as representations of economic behavior. Moreover, incorporating anecdotal evidence, which may reveal important economic changes before they are reflected in any data, can only be accomplished judgmentally. In that regard, the Federal Reserve benefits substantially from the timely information reported by the District Banks from their extensive contacts with businesses within their regions. Given the tremendous quantity of data with which we are faced — much of it of an idiosyncratic nature — and given the changing economic environment and institutions, the Federal Reserve relies heavily on judgment in evaluating economic prospects.

PRIVATE VS. PUBLIC POLICY FORECASTING

As I have suggested, private and public forecasters share many of the same basic concerns and face similar analytical issues regarding forecast methodology. Nonetheless, some important distinctions can be made between the activities of private and public forecasters.

Because a firm's or industry's ultimate measure of success or failure is its profitability, the most valued private forecasters will be those who accurately anticipate factors that influence the bottom line. These include factors that characterize the demand for the firm's product, such as market share, relative prices, and developments in competing markets. They also include components of the firm's cost structure, such as its cost of raising capital, its energy mix and intensity, and conditions in the specific labor markets from which it hires. For the most part, forecasts of the aggregate economy are required as a backdrop for critical industry-specific developments. To be sure, for some industries, such as durable goods, the macro backdrop looms relatively large. However, for many other industries, macroeconomic considerations are dominated by the influences of changing technologies, tastes, and other developments in closely related markets. It will almost always be the case that the private forecaster *must* perform well on the firm- or industry-specific variables. Thus, it is reasonable that private forecasters devote more resources to forecasting in much greater detail a more narrow set of microeconomic variables than does the economist in the public sector.

The policy forecaster, on the other hand, necessarily focuses on those aspects of the economy that policy most directly influences. For example, it is generally agreed that monetary policy affects the general price level in the long run, and aggregate output and employment in the short run. These are the variables by which the success of monetary policy most often is judged. Consequently, they are the variables of primary interest to the policy forecaster. Changes in monetary and fiscal policies may alter the relative price of cold rolled sheet steel and the cost of capital for farm machinery producers as well. And, because firm-specific data often provide important clues to the macroeconomic puzzle, the policy forecaster must retain some grasp of industry-specific details in forming his or her macro projections. But understanding all of the microeconomic ramifications of macroeconomic policy is beyond the scope of public-sector forecasters, who must concentrate their resources on the effort to predict aggregate outcomes and the consequences of policy actions.

Let me conclude with a final observation that I believe holds in both the public and private sectors, and whether one emphasizes formal models or more intuitive approaches. Economic forecasting is really the art of identifying tensions or imbalances in the economic process and understanding in what manner they will be resolved over the short to intermediate term. For example, at the microeconomic level, consider the dynamic relationships among production, prices, inventories, and consumption. An unexpected change in consumption creates a tension or imbalance at the firm or in the industry. It may lead to a change in prices, production schedules, or inventories, with corresponding implications for subsequent output. There may be substantial uncertainty about how important each channel will be in resolving the tension, and the exact sequence in which each channel will come to the forefront of the resolution process. But we can be sure that the initial tension in the system will be resolved over time.

A macroeconomic example might be the tensions created when growth in nominal income exceeds the real growth potential of the economy. In the long run, such a discrepancy is reflected in the pace of inflation. But in the short run, the tensions created by outsized nominal income growth can result in changes in real output, changes in inflation, or both. The timing and composition of the responses of production and inflation to this tension are the focus of much macroeconomic attention.

Clearly, detecting key imbalances is a crucial element in the forecast process and is one reason why determining where the economy is at any particular moment is so important in assessing where it may be headed. Much of a forecaster's success in predicting the future clearly depends on how well he or she can determine *existing* conditions. Given the difficulties we face in determining where we are at present, we should have only modest expectations for our ability to predict the future. While our forecasting tools have improved considerably over the postwar period, our forecast accuracy has not. This observation suggests that we are engaged in a continual struggle in which the benefits of improved techniques are eroded by an increasingly elusive and complex economic structure. Since inevitably the structure will become increasingly more complex in the years ahead, forecasters in both the private and public sectors face a constant challenge to develop more reliable forecast procedures that combine the flexibility of the intuitive approach with the systematic discipline of the model-based approach.

Article 10

CORPORATE FORECASTING PRACTICES IN THE MANUFACTURING INDUSTRY

NADA R. SANDERS

Department of Management Science, Wright State University, Dayton, OH 45435

Organizational forecasting is one of the most critical business functions since it serves as an input to all other business decisions. These decisions can only be as good as the quality of the forecast upon which they are based. Forecasts are used in organizations to set production schedules, budget capital, and allocate resources. Research in the field of forecasting has developed numerous quantitative forecasting procedures which range in level of complexity, ease of use, and expertise required [6]. However, surveys reporting on the status of forecasting in business find that managers use judgmental forecasting methods far more than quantitative ones [3, 7, 8, 9]. This can create problems for organizations, as research has consistently shown quantitative methods to be superior to judgmental methods, both in terms of accuracy and timeliness [1, 2, 5]. Further, there is a large literature base that points to many biases inherent in judgmental forecasting, including lack of consistency, tendency to overforecast, and wishful thinking [4].

Given the importance of accurate forecasting, organizations need to increase the acceptance and use of quantitative forecasting procedures among managers. The first step in this process is to understand the reasons for current management practices. As the management of manufacturing organizations is in many ways different from management of service organizations, forecasting practices in manufacturing firms may also be different. Past forecasting surveys have focused on all industry segments combined. The purpose of this article is to provide an understanding of forecasting practices in the manufacturing industry and, where appropriate, provide a comparison with the service industry.

One question of interest to manufacturing managers is whether forecasting practices differ in the manufacturing industry. Second, what are the unique forecasting problems facing manufacturing managers given the characteristics of their environment. The answers to these questions lead to possible solutions addressing forecasting problems related to the manufacturing industry and, consequently, a greater use of formal forecasting. In this article, the results of a forecasting survey designed to answer the above questions will be reported.

METHODOLOGY

A copy of the forecasting survey was mailed to 500 U.S. companies. The cover letter was addressed by name to the company's highest ranking officer (president, vice president or CEO) with instructions for the survey to be passed on to the manager primarily responsible for forecasting. The respondents were mainly executives with forecasting responsibility, which was confirmed through an analysis of job descriptions.

Of the responses received, 82 questionnaires were fully usable. This represents an overall response rate of 16.4%, comparable to past surveys. Confidential information about the identities of the respondents suggested that the sample was representative with regard to size, age, and type of firm.

The survey asked respondents to identify their industry segment as either manufacturing or service. Out of the responses received, 57% came from manufacturing organizations. The analysis in this study focuses on responses from these firms. The study compares their responses to the responses provided by service organizations.

FAMILIARITY WITH FORECASTING METHODS AND LEVEL OF USAGE

The initial goal of the survey was to establish the level of familiarity managers have with various forecasting methods. These results are summarized in Table 1.

The first observation is that manufacturing managers appear to be more familiar with quantitative methods than managers in service firms (average of 81.3% vs. 69.8%). Also, the number of manufacturing managers not at all familiar with quantitative methods is less than for service firms (average of 12.3% vs. 20.5%). Second, both categories of managers appear equally familiar with the simpler quantitative techniques. The difference in their familiarity appears to

TABLE 1: Percentage of Respondents Familiar with Forecasting Techniques

	Manufacturing/Service		
	Very Familiar	Somewhat Familiar	Unfamiliar
Judgmental Forecasting Techniques			
Manager's opinion	82/73	17/22	1/5
Jury of executive opinion	68/74	25/23	7/3
Sales force composite	65/72	30/26	5/2
Quantitative Forecasting Techniques			
Naive	86/80	10/6	4/14
Moving average	94/99	2/0	4/1
Exponential smoothing	89/74*	7/13	4/13
Straight line projection	96/87	0/6	4/7
Regression	86/81	9/11	5/8
Simulation	82/68*	6/12	12/20
Classical decomposition	62/54	8/7	30/39
Box-Jenkins time series	55/13*	9/22*	36/64'

* Denotes significant differences at the 5 percent level based on a test for proportions.

be with the more complex techniques such as simulation, classical decomposition, and the Box-Jenkins method. This is a positive sign for manufacturing organizations and may indicate that manufacturing managers have an overall better preparedness for formal forecasting than service managers. Finally, as expected, managers in both types of organizations are highly familiar with judgmental forecasting methods, with an average familiarity of 71.7% for manufacturing and 72.3% for service.

A question directly related to familiarity is the education level of the managers preparing organizational forecasts. Forecasting managers in manufacturing firms appear to have an overall higher education level than in service firms; this may be part of the reason for the difference in familiarity. The percentages of respondents for both types of firms are as follows:

	Manufacturing	Service
High school	0	7
Associate degree	5	13
Bachelor's degree	41	44
Master's degree	45	31
PhD	9	5

The degree to which manufacturing managers actually utilize different forecasting techniques was evaluated for different time horizons and compared to service managers. These results are shown in Table 2. Results confirm past findings that judgmental methods are used far more than quantitative methods by all firms. Overall, the most popular forecasting technique among manufacturing managers was manager's opinion.

Differences between manufacturing and service firms appear with regard to the level of usage of quantitative methods. These results show that quantitative methods have an overall greater usage level among manufacturing managers. Again, the greatest disparity between manufacturing and service firms is with use of the more sophisticated techniques. Further, the only quantitative technique that does not have a high level of usage among manufacturing managers is the naive method. The most popular short-range forecasting technique among manufacturing managers was the moving average. For long range, it was regression analysis.

FINDINGS ON USAGE OF JUDGMENTAL FORECASTING METHODS

In order to evaluate the degree of usage of judgmental methods, respondents were asked to indicate the frequency of use. Over half of all the respondents stated that they always use judgmental methods. When asked to provide reasons for using judgmental methods, the following were the top responses provided by manufacturing managers:

- Accuracy (27%)
- Difficulty in obtaining data (26%)
- Ease of use (20%).

Respondents were further asked to indicate the frequency with which forecasts generated by quantitative methods were judgmentally adjusted prior to use. The majority of the respondents in both types of firms stated that they always or frequently adjust quantitative forecasts. Incorporating knowledge of their environment was the major reason cited for the adjustment.

FORECASTING PROBLEMS AND NEEDS OF PRACTITIONERS

One goal of the survey was to develop a better understanding of the needs of manufacturing managers. The survey asked respondents what advancements in the field of forecasting they would most like to see. Responses included: better guidelines for using current techniques (24%), availability of more accurate tech-

TABLE 2: Percentage of Respondents Using Different Techniques for Different Time Horizons

| | Forecast Period Manufacturing/Service | | | |
	Immediate < 1 mo.	Short 1–6 mo.	Medium 6 mo–1 year	Long > year
Judgmental Forecasting Techniques				
Manager's opinion	28/27	42/37	36/37	9/7
Jury of executive opinion	16/17	30/29	41/38	27/24
Sales force composite	29/28	18/16	31/35	7/10
Quantitative Forecasting Techniques				
Naive	12/19	16/20	14/15	0/0
Moving average	21/12	37/27	29/28	7/9
Exponential smoothing	14/6	22/14	21/9*	6/0
Straight line projection	9/7	13/12	13/10	10/4
Regression	16/9	35/9*	33/14*	23/4*
Simulation	5/0	13/1*	14/6	10/5
Classical decomposition	0/0	10/4	15/6	10/7
Box-Jenkins time series	4/1	5/0	6/1	5/0

* Denotes significant differences at the 5 percent level based on a test for proportions.

niques (21%), and guidelines for using judgmental forecasting methods.

The survey further asked respondents to indicate what advancements they would most like to see in their particular organization. The following are top responses by manufacturing firms:

- Better data (37%)
- Greater management support (26%)
- Better training (22%).

These responses indicate that, overall, managers need more support from their organizations.

Finally, respondents were asked to indicate how significant forecasting accuracy is to their organization and provide reasons for their response. The overwhelming majority of manufacturing firms stated that forecast accuracy was highly significant. Some of the reasons provided include:

- Can lead to inventory/production and scheduling problems and can adversely affect pricing decisions
- Customer service failure
- Inventory cost
- Flexibility to react to the plan is as important as the forecast.

DISCUSSION

The results of this survey support past findings that judgmental methods are the dominant forecasting procedure used in all industries. However, findings show that manufacturing managers appear ahead in familiarity and usage of quantitative procedures. One explanation for this, revealed by the survey, may be a higher education level of manufacturing versus service managers responsible for forecasting.

The second major finding relates to the level of usage of judgmental forecasting methods and the reasons provided for this practice. The results of this survey reveal that a factor which may contribute to the low usage level of quantitative methods is lack of relevant data, cited by manufacturing managers as one of the major reasons for using judgmental forecasting methods. Also, the need for better data was cited as the improvement managers would most like to see in their organizations. This finding indicates that organizations need to provide greater support in terms of data procurement and handling, as well as data processing.

Not only does the overwhelming majority of manufacturing managers regularly use judgment, quantitatively derived forecasts are routinely judgmentally adjusted. This practice reflects management's lack of confidence in the forecasting process. One way of addressing this is through the regular monitoring of forecast accuracy in order for management to gain confidence in quantitatively derived forecasts [6].

The last finding from this survey relates to the advancements managers would most like to see. Manufacturing managers expressed a strong interest in better guidelines for using currently available techniques. This has also been recognized as an important issue by APICS, which has made an effort to address the issue in the forecasting chapters of the APICS handbook. Organizations can assist with this by providing better training to forecast managers. At the same time, the teaching of forecasting should center as much on guidelines for usage as forecasting theory.

CONCLUSION

Results of this survey provide some new and interesting information about forecasting practices in the manufacturing industry. However, the difficulty with a survey of this type is that it asks more questions than it answers. There are a number of issues that emerged that should be investigated in future research. These issues include questions on sources practitioners use to learn forecasting methods, types of computer tools used in practice, the use of outside consultants, and the role the production and inventory management function plays in forecasting. These results are important to practitioners in order to be informed of current practices. This information is also important to academicians in understanding gaps between forecasting theory and the needs of forecasters in practice.

REFERENCES

1. Armstrong, J. S. *Long Range Forecasting: From Crystal Ball to Computer.* New York: John Wiley & Sons, 1985.
2. ———— "Research on Forecasting: A Quarter-Century Review, 1960–1984." *Interfaces* (1986): 89–103.
3. Dalrymple, D. J. "Sales Forecasting Practices—Results from a United States Survey." *International Journal of Forecasting* (Summer 1987): 379–391.
4. Hogarth, R. M. *Judgment and Choice.* New York: John Wiley & Sons, 1987.
5. ———— and S. Makridakis. "Forecasting and Planning: An Evaluation." *Management Science* (June 1981): 115–138.
6. Makridakis, S., S. Wheelwright, and V. McGee. "Forecasting: Methods and Applications." New York: John Wiley & Sons, 1983.
7. Mentzer, J. and J. Cox. "Familiarity, Application and Performance of Sales Forecasting Techniques." *Journal of Forecasting* (Summer 1984): 27–36.
8. Sparkes, J. R. and A. K. McHugh. "Awareness and Use of Forecasting Techniques in British Industry." *Journal of Forecasting* (Summer 1984): 37–42.
9. Wheelwright, S. C. and D. G. Clarke. "Corporate Forecasting: Promise and Reality." *Harvard Business Review* (1976): 40–42.

About the Author—

NADA R. SANDERS is associate professor of operations management and logistics at Wright State University. Dr. Sanders holds an MBA and a PhD in operations management from the Ohio State University. Her research interests include inventory management and demand forecasting, JIT, and DSS. Dr. Sanders is a member of APICS, DSI, TIMS, and the International Institute of Forecasters. Her research has appeared in a number of journals, including Decision Sciences *and* Omega.

Article 11

Predicting Interest Rates: A Comparison of Professional and Market-Based Forecasts

Michael T. Belongia

Interest rates have varied substantially in recent years. Since 1981, for example, the monthly average three-month Treasury bill rate has ranged between 5.18 percent and 16.30 percent while the Baa corporate bond rate ranged between 9.61 percent and 17.18 percent; the prime rate during this time reached a high of 20.5 percent and fell to a low of 7.5 percent. Interest rate movements are important, of course, because they affect the present value of streams of future payments, that is, wealth. Moreover, the risk of interest rate changes is related directly to the level of interest rates.[1] During the 1980s, therefore, firms and individuals have faced substantial exposure to interest rate risk.

There are at least two approaches that can be taken to reduce the magnitude of this problem. The first is to hedge interest rate risk, which has been discussed at length in this *Review* and elsewhere.[2] The second is to forecast the likely course of interest rates. This article investigates the reliability of such forecasts in general and assesses the specific usefulness of forecasts by professional economists.

Michael T. Belongia is a senior economist at the Federal Reserve Bank of St. Louis. Paul Crosby provided research assistance.

[1]Interest rate risk, for a firm whose portfolio is composed of streams of future receipts and payments, is measured by the interest elasticity of the portfolio; for a single asset, this can be expressed as $-n(i/1+i)$, where n is the term to maturity. A more general expression for a portfolio of assets and liabilities is derived in Belongia and Santoni (1987). In either case, the level of interest rate risk rises with the interest rate.

[2]See Belongia and Santoni (1984, 1985).

INTEREST RATE FORECASTS: THEORY AND EVIDENCE

Given the popular attention that such forecasts command, it is surprising to note what economic theory says about them: they are unlikely to provide accurate insights about the future. This argument is stated clearly by Zarnowitz:

> It might be argued that these are *forecasts* of people who study the economy (experts), which are quite unlike the *expectations* of those who act in the economy (agents). On the one hand, the experts are usually credited with more knowledge of the economy at large than the agents have. On the other hand, the experts are often charged with being less strongly motivated to predict optimally than the agents who are seen as having more at stake. [3]

Economists, at least on one level, lack sufficient incentives to make forecasts that are more accurate than information already available in the marketplace. Moreover, previous studies have shown there is little systematic difference among professional forecasts, at least partly because they "use to a large extent the same data, receive the same news, interact, and draw upon a common pool of knowledge and techniques."[4]

The key issue, however, really is not whether experts have more (or better) information than the public, but whether individuals who consistently can fore-

---

[3]See Zarnowitz (1983), p. 2.

[4]See Zarnowitz (1986), p. 6, and the references cited therein.

cast interest rates more accurately than the market are likely to make their forecasts public. The reason has to do with individual self-interest. Quite simply, why would anyone reveal valuable insight about the future when he could increase his wealth directly by appropriately trading in financial markets using this information?

If, for example, a person *knew* that the three-month Treasury bill rate would be 6.50 percent in December, while the futures market currently priced it at 7.00 percent, the forecaster's wealth gain would be limited only by his ability to buy December Treasury bill futures; in this example, he would make a profit of $1,250 on every contract he could buy.[5] Certainly, he has no incentive to make the same forecast public without appropriate compensation, at least until he had taken as large a position in the market as he could. Of course, forecasters may have incentives to sell forecasts that are of no value to their wealth; it is not clear, however, why other individuals would pay for such predictions.

As a general rule, the accuracy of economic forecasts varies widely across variables. Previous research has found that predictions of the three-month Treasury bill rate six months into the future by major commercial forecasters are within two percentage points of the actual rate only 67 percent of the time.[6] Thus, if in June, the three-month Treasury bill rate was forecast to be 7 percent in December, there is only a 0.67 probability that the actual December rate would be somewhere between 5 percent and 9 percent. Other studies have shown that error statistics often double in size when the forecast horizon is extended as little as from one to two quarters ahead.[7]

The Efficient Markets Hypothesis and Interest Rate Forecasts

A model of interest rate determination demonstrates why individuals are unable (as opposed to unwilling) to forecast interest rates more accurately, on average, than the forecasts already implied by current spot rates or prices in the interest rate futures markets. This model, known as the efficient markets model, states that the *expected* interest rate at some specified future point in time, given all information presently available, is equal to the current interest rate plus whatever change in the interest rate is suggested by currently available information.[8]

The driving force behind the efficient markets model is the information available to traders in the market and the incentives they have to use this information. Current market rates and expectations of future rates are influenced by changes in information that affect expectations about the future. Because new information is unknown until it actually is released, success in predicting future interest rates depends upon predicting both future changes in the information *and* the market's reaction to such "news."

An Illustration of the Efficient Markets Model

One illustration of the efficient markets model applied to actual data is the change in interest rates that follows the weekly Federal Reserve M1 announcement that usually occurs at 4:30 p.m. [EST] each Thursday. The assumption is that the interest rate at 3:30 p.m., just prior to the announcement, fully reflects all currently available information relevant to the Treasury bill rate, including various forecasts of the Fed's yet-to-be-announced change in M1; thus, the available information at 3:30 p.m. includes both actual and predicted data.

When the Fed announces the M1 change at 4:30 p.m., the market's information set is revised with the actual M1 change replacing its predicted value. If no other significant information is released until rates are observed again at 5 p.m., the change in the Treasury bill rate from 3:30 to 5 p.m. reflects the market's reaction to the news in the M1 announcement. If the actual and predicted M1 values are different, the efficient markets model predicts that interest rates will react to the new information in the Fed's M1 announcement; many studies have found this result empirically.[9]

---

[5]Treasury bill futures are priced by subtracting the Treasury bill interest rate from 100. Thus, interest rates of 7.00 and 6.50 percent imply contract prices of 93.00 and 93.50, respectively. Moreover, each basis-point change in the interest rate is worth $25 on the value of a contract. Buying one contract at 93.00 and selling at 93.50 would show a simple profit of 50 basis points × $25 = $1,250, abstracting from commission and other costs.

[6]McNees, p. 11.

[7]Typically, the criterion is root-mean-squared error (RMSE); see McNees (1986). Also, see Zarnowitz (1983).

[8]The efficient markets model applied to interest rate determination can be expressed as:
$$E(i_{t+1} | \Omega_t) = i_t(1 + E(i_{t+1} - i_t | \Omega_t)),$$
where E is the expectations operator and Ω_t is the information available to agents at the time forecasts are made. For more detail on this model, see Fama and Miller (1972) or Mishkin (1983).

[9]See Sheehan (1985) and Belongia and Sheehan (1987) for a survey and critique of these studies.

This example demonstrates the major point of the efficient markets model: changes in interest rates depend on changes in information. A forecast that interest rates will be higher six months from now than what already is implied by the underlying term structure really is a forecast that new information will be revealed which will cause market participants to raise the rate of interest. Such forecasts are potentially useful only if the forecasters consistently have better information, on average, than the other market participants generally possess. Or, to state the proposition differently, a useful forecast is not simply an accurate one; it also must tell something about the future that is not already reflected in current market interest rates.

A COMPARISON OF INTEREST RATE FORECASTS

A comparison of alternative interest rate forecasts is essentially a comparison of information sets that forecasters possess. The futures market, as well as forecasts that simply assume the future will resemble the present, provide useful alternatives to forecasts produced by specialized forecasting services. If all forecasts have similar accuracy, it would suggest that market participants use essentially the same information.

Survey Forecasts

The information content of economists' forecasts is intriguing for a variety of reasons. Presumably, their specialized training gives them insight to the workings of financial markets. In return for their services, the economists involved earn relatively large salaries; moreover, some command considerable public attention. The latter group should include those whose forecasts are among the best of competing alternatives.

Market Forecasts

The futures market offers an interesting perspective on forecasts. At a given point in time, individuals may enter into agreements to buy or sell interest-sensitive assets, such as Treasury bills, at a date as much as two years into the future. The collective actions of investors betting that interest rates will rise from today's level (who will sell Treasury bill futures short) and investors betting that interest rates will fall (who will buy, or go long in, Treasury bill futures) determine, at each moment in time, the "market's" expectation of what interest rates will be at a specified future date. Such forecasts are interesting for two reasons: they reflect all available information held by market partici-

pants and these participants have a compelling reason to forecast accurately. If they are wrong, the money lost is their own!

A naive or no-change model is an interesting third alternative because, as previously noted, predicting interest rates really involves predicting changes in information and the market's reaction to this news. If one believes it is impossible to predict actions by OPEC, changes in macroeconomic policy, revisions in economic data and other factors that affect expectations of future interest rates, the best strategy would be to predict no change in information and, hence, no change in interest rates. Certainly, as the length of the forecast horizon grows shorter, the probability of large changes in information (and interest rates) declines as well.

Sources of Forecasts: Professional and Market Data

The six-month-ahead forecasts of the three-month Treasury bill rate by nine economists surveyed regularly by the Wall Street Journal were collected over the period December 1981 through June 1986. These forecasts, which are published on or about each January 1 and July 1, yielded 10 forecast periods and 90 predictions to be evaluated. Each forecast was assumed to be made the day before publication.[10]

Comparable forecasts from the futures market were derived by observing on June 30 the three-month Treasury bill rate implied by the December Treasury bill futures contract and on December 31 the rate implied by the June contract. A larger sample to be used later also employed observations on the March futures contract from the previous September 30 and on the September contract from March 31. These data were compared with actual Treasury bill rates on the day the relevant futures contract ceased trading.[11] The procedure yielded 40 observations, of which 10 coincided with dates of the economists' forecasts. The naive or no-change forecast was obtained by observing the spot Treasury bill rates on the last business days of March, June, September and December and predicting that same rate would exist on the last day of the month six months hence. Again there are 40 observa-

---

[10]The full Wall Street Journal survey includes many more economists, but only nine individuals have responded consistently since the initial survey in December 1981.

[11]Treasury bill futures contracts usually are liquidated in the third week of their terminal months, not the last day of the month as with the economist forecasts.

Chart 1

Treasury Bill Rates: Actual and Predicted

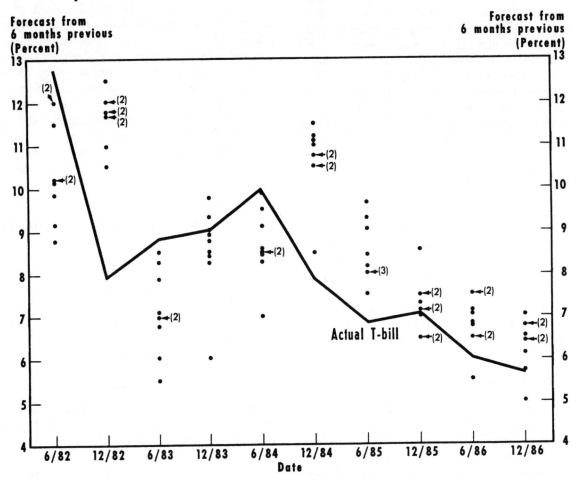

Forecast from 6 months previous (Percent)

Forecast from 6 months previous (Percent)

Actual T-bill

Date

6/82 12/82 6/83 12/83 6/84 12/84 6/85 12/85 6/86 12/86

---

tions over the 1977–86 interval with 10 coinciding with dates of the economist survey. Although this sample of market-based forecasts includes only 10 observations that coincide with the economists' forecasts, it serves as the basis for the first comparison. Subsequent analysis uses the entire sample back to 1977 for a stronger test of forecast accuracy.

Forecasts of Direction of Change

A first assessment about the accuracy of the professional forecasts was made against a relatively weak criterion, the predicted *direction* of change. That is, if rates were forecast to increase (or decrease), did they? The individual forecasts relative to subsequent actual values are plotted in chart 1.

The 90 individual expert predictions correctly forecast the *direction* of change on 38 occasions, or 42 percent of the time. If interest rate movements are random, a 50 percent record of accuracy would be expected.[12] Only one of the nine forecasters guessed

---

[12]This type of performance — the strategies of professional investors yielding returns inferior to those of simple rules — is common. For example, the mean equity fund managed by professional institutional money managers rose 16.7 percent in 1986 compared with an 18.7 percent rise in the S&P 500 index. Moreover, more than 67 percent of the money managers produced returns in 1986 smaller than the general increase in market values, as measured by the S&P 500; see Wallace (1987). For a more extensive discussion of this result and a similar finding of inferior performance by mutual fund managers over time, see Malkiel (1985), pp. 147–82, and the references to his chapter 7.

Table 1
Summary Statistics for Errors from Alternative Forecasts: June 1982-December 1986

	MAE	Mean error	RMSE	n
Economist individual forecasts	1.625	−0.406	2.056	90
Economist mean forecast	1.550	−0.406	1.889	10
Futures market forecast	1.466	−1.132	2.253	10
Naive forecast	1.321	−0.543	1.859	10

the direction of change correctly more than one-half of the time; he was correct on six of 10 occasions. Three others guessed the correct direction of change on five of 10 occasions. The worst individual performance was two correct predictions.

For the 40 quarterly predictions derived from futures market observations, 22, or nearly 55 percent, correctly forecast the direction of change. Over the shorter 1982–86 sample, five of 10 directions of change were predicted correctly by the futures market. On the simple criterion of direction of change, the futures market outperforms the economists surveyed.[13]

Point Forecasts

A different criterion by which to evaluate forecasts is a comparison of the point estimates of the predicted changes in interest rates with the actual changes. These comparisons were analyzed several ways. First, forecasts by the nine experts provided 90 individual predictions of the Treasury bill rate. These individual predictions also could be aggregated to form a consensus, or average, prediction for the nine economists at a specific moment in time. The performance of the experts relative to the futures market and naive forecasts first was judged over the short 1982–86 sample that coincided with the economist survey. Differences between actual Treasury bill rates and, respectively, the economist, futures market and naive forecasts were calculated to generate values for forecast errors. All errors were calculated as actual minus predicted values. Table 1 shows the summary statistics for these errors.

The entries in table 1 represent the mean absolute error (MAE), mean error and root-mean-squared error (RMSE) from forecasts for the three-month Treasury bill rate six months into the future. The first two rows are associated with the individual and consensus forecasts from the survey of experts. The third row is based on the differences between the actual Treasury bill rate and the futures market prediction. The fourth row is based on the naive predictions, the differences between current and previous actual rates.

The most interesting aspect of these summary statistics is their remarkable similarity. Of course, this result was predicted by the earlier theoretical discussion, which emphasized that all available information would be reflected in current market rates. The mean errors for all forecasts are negative, indicating that these methods tended to overestimate the interest rate; the futures market, however, tended to be the most bearish forecaster on this account by overpredicting the Treasury bill rate an average of 1.132 percentage points. MAE statistics also are similar, with a range of about 30 basis points between the best (naive) and worst (individual economist). The RMSE statistic, which is a measure of the dispersion of forecast errors, shows the naive and economist consensus to perform best.[14]

---

[13]There is no meaningful way to construct a direction-of-change criterion for the naive forecast.

[14]The likely explanation for the futures prediction having the highest RMSE is the method of calculation. The RMSE will tend to be lower for forecasts that made many errors of a similar size relative to forecasts that had smaller errors, on average, but had several very large errors. This result occurs, of course, because calculating the RMSE involves squaring the forecast errors. The effects of random variation in small samples also is a potential source of distortion. Thus, two very large futures market errors offset a record of generally accurate forecasts as indicated by other statistics.

Table 2
Market-Based Forecasts Over a Longer Horizon: March 31, 1977 - December 31, 1986

	MAE	Mean Error	RMSE	n
Futures market forecast				
Daily data	1.676	−0.163	2.589	40
Weekly averages	1.702	−0.141	2.634	40
Naive forecast				
Daily data	1.740	0.035	2.578	40
Weekly averages	1.788	0.027	2.695	40

Longer Sample Results for Market-Based Forecasts

Error statistics from the longer 10-year sample of quarterly observations described earlier are reported in table 2. Because daily interest rate changes are volatile and a large, one-day change could affect the results, forecasts for a specific date also were compared with the average Treasury bill rate for the week in which that date occurred.

Relative to the previous results, the futures market average errors declined substantially to near 15 basis points, compared with the shorter sample mean error of about 113 basis points. MAE and RMSE values increased slightly, however, for the longer sample. The forecast errors do not appear to vary with the use of daily or weekly average values for the terminal period spot rate. The naive forecast also shows slight increases in MAE and RMSE values but its mean error falls about 50 basis points to near zero. Again, while these statistics are not directly comparable with the economist forecasts because of the different sample periods, nothing in them suggests superior performance by the economists.

Market Reaction to Forecasts

As a final check on the information content of the expert forecasts, daily Treasury bill rates were divided into two groups: those for days when the experts' forecasts were published and those for other trading days. (Recall that the forecasts are useful to the market only if they add to the existing pool of market information.) To test whether this is true, equation (1) was estimated:

$$(1)\ TB_t = 0.015 + 0.998\ TB_{t-1} + 0.049\ \text{ANNOUNCEMENT} + e_t,$$
$$\ (1.02)\ (657.2)\phantom{TB_{t-1}}\ (0.95)$$
$$\bar{R}^2 = 0.99 \qquad DW = 1.77$$

where the daily value of the Treasury bill rate (TB_t) is regressed on the previous day's value (TB_{t-1}) and a dummy variable (ANNOUNCEMENT) that takes a value of one on the 11 days that the expert forecasts were released.[15] If the expert forecasts add to the market's information, the coefficient for the ANNOUNCEMENT variable should be significantly different from zero; as the t-statistic of 0.95 reveals, however, we cannot reject the hypothesis that the forecast announcements have no effect on Treasury bill rates. Apparently, the Treasury bill market had already incorporated the information underlying these forecasts prior to their public release.

SUMMARY

Interest rate risk has been substantial in the 1980s, and, by no coincidence, the demand for interest rate forecasts has increased. There are strong theoretical reasons to believe, however, that such forecasts are subject to large errors. Moreover, anyone who could predict interest rates more accurately, on average, than other market participants would have no reason to make his forecasts publicly. Comparisons of interest rate forecast errors support the notion that several market-based forecasts, using information easily accessible to the general public, predict the Treasury bill rate six months into the future as well as a panel of prominent forecasters.

Why, then, do economists make public forecasts of interest rates and seemingly earn large salaries for doing so? Several explanations related to other primary functions of corporate economists seem plausible. First, economists may serve an advertising function for their firms: they are paid, in part, to get the

---

[15]It is possible to use the January 3, 1987, survey for this estimation.

firm's name mentioned in the press often, and forecasting interest rates is one way to achieve this end. Second, economists may provide a managerial insurance function. If a business decision has the potential to cause large losses, managers who have relied on the input of economists cannot be held negligent, in the sense of acting without seeking "the best information available at the time." Finally, forecasting interest rates may be a trivial portion of an economist's overall function; his compensation may be based primarily on analytical performance in other areas. It is unlikely, however, that economists are employed primarily for their ability to predict interest rates more accurately than the market.

REFERENCES

Belongia, Michael T., and Gary J. Santoni. "Hedging Interest Rate Risk with Financial Futures: Some Basic Principles," this *Review* (October 1984), pp. 15–25.

_____. "Cash Flow or Present Value: What's Lurking Behind That Hedge?" this *Review* (January 1985), pp. 5–13.

_____. "Interest Rate Risk, Market Value, and Hedging Financial Portfolios," *Journal of Financial Research* (Spring 1987), pp. 47–55.

Belongia, Michael T., and Richard G. Sheehan. "The Informational Efficiency of Weekly Money Announcements: An Econometric Critique," *Journal of Business and Economic Statistics* (forthcoming).

Fama, Eugene F., and Merton H. Miller. *The Theory of Finance*, (Holt, Rinehart and Winston, Inc., 1972).

Granger, C. W. J. "Comment," *Journal of Business & Economic Statistics* (January 1986), pp. 16–17.

Litterman, Robert B. "A Statistical Approach to Economic Forecasting," *Journal of Business & Economic Statistics* (January 1986), pp. 1–4.

Malkiel, Burton G. *A Random Walk Down Wall Street*, 4th edition, (W. W. Norton and Company, Inc., 1985).

McNees, Stephen K. "Forecasting Accuracy of Alternative Techniques: A Comparison of U.S. Macroeconomic Forecasts," *Journal of Business & Statistics* (January 1986), pp. 5–15.

Mishkin, Frederic S. *A Rational Expectations Approach to Macroeconometrics: Testing Policy Ineffectiveness and Efficient-Markets Models* (University of Chicago Press, 1983).

Sheehan, Richard G. "Weekly Money Announcements: New Information and Its Effects," this *Review* (August/September 1985), pp. 25–34.

Wallace, Anise C. "Funds That Put The Pros to Shame," *New York Times*, February 8, 1987.

Zarnowitz, Victor. "Rational Expectations and Macroeconomic Forecasts," NBER Working Paper No. 1070 (January 1983).

_____. "The Record and Improvability of Economic Forecasting," NBER Working Paper No. 2099, Cambridge, MA (December 1986).

Section IV

Production, Cost, and Related Topics

Core topics of microeconomics include production and cost analysis. The production function shows the output of a good or service as a function of the inputs used to produce it. The cost function shows the cost of producing various levels of output given the prices of the inputs. Managers should be familiar with both the theoretical and empirical aspects of production and cost theory. This section begins with articles that illustrate regression analyses of production and cost functions. This is followed by an article in which the marginal revenue product of professional baseball players is estimated. The two remaining articles are concerned with concepts related to production and cost. One discusses the learning or experience curve. The other shows an application of linear programming.

The estimation of production functions for education is the subject of "Educational Cost Factors and Student Achievement in Grades 3 and 6: Some New Evidence," by David Stern. In his production relationship, student achievement is the output. This is measured with the average student performance on achievement tests in reading, mathematics, and writing by third and sixth grade students in California school districts. The inputs into the production of student achievement include the expenditure on teachers' salaries per student and measures of the socioeconomic background of the students. Stern finds that there is a consistent positive relationship between student achievement and student socioeconomic background. The teacher salary input, however, does not exhibit a consistent positive relationship with student achievement.

The estimation of average cost functions for nursing homes is the subject of "The Effect of Chain Ownership on Nursing Home Costs," by Niccie L. McKay. The hypothesis of interest is whether nursing homes that are part of a chain of nursing homes have lower average costs than do independent nursing homes once other factors that affect cost are held constant. The output measure for nursing homes is patient days. Using data from Texas nursing homes, the author finds that chain nursing homes do have lower average cost per patient day at intermediate and high levels of patient days than do the independent nursing homes.

The estimation of average cost functions for secondary and elementary schools is the subject of "Scale Economies, Capacity Utilization, and School

Costs: A Comparative Analysis of Secondary and Elementary Schools," by John Riew. Per pupil operating cost at each school in the sample is regressed on school enrollment, school capacity utilization, and school quality measures. Riew finds evidence that scale economies do exist for both types of schools. Also, capacity utilization is found to influence per pupil operating cost.

The labor market for professional major league baseball players is analyzed by Thomas H. Bruggink and David R. Rose, Jr., in "Financial Restraint in the Free Agent Labor Market for Major League Baseball: Players Look at Strike Three." The marginal revenue product (MRP) of both hitters and pitchers is estimated with a two–stage process. The effect of team hitting performance and team pitching performance on team winning percentage is first estimated with regression analysis. Regression analysis is again used to estimate the effect of team winning percentage and other factors on team revenue. These equations can then be used to estimate the contribution to team revenue of an individual player (his marginal revenue product) based on his performance. The authors find that the average actual salary/MRP ratio for their sample of players was less than one in 1984, and was lower in 1985 and 1986 than in 1984. This evidence supports the view that baseball owners colluded to pay free agent players less in 1985 and 1986.

As more output is produced by an organization, the average cost of producing each unit of output tends to decrease at a decreasing rate. The learning curve or experience curve is the label attached to this empirical regularity. In "Learning Curves in Manufacturing," Linda Argote and Dennis Epple summarize the research concerning the learning curve phenomenon in a number of settings. The effects of other factors on the learning curve, such as the depreciation of acquired knowledge, employee turnover, and the transfer of knowledge to other goods or organizations, are also discussed.

Linear programming is a technique that is used to maximize or minimize an objective function subject to constraints. In "A Classroom Exercise Using Linear Programming in the Construction of Duration–Matched Dedicated Portfolios," Robert A. Strong and Kent D. Carter provide an illustration of the linear programming technique. Their example shows the way one would arrange a bond portfolio that will have a required present value and given duration. Duration refers to the weighted average of the time that cash flows occur. The objective function is to minimize the number of bonds purchased to minimize commission costs. The constraints will ensure the proper duration of the portfolio, the appropriate present value of the bond portfolio, and that the portfolio is diversified.

Article 12

Educational Cost Factors and Student Achievement in Grades 3 and 6: Some New Evidence

DAVID STERN

School of Education, University of California, Berkeley, CA 94720, U.S.A.

Abstract — Per pupil spending on teachers' salaries, which is the largest component of instructional cost, is itself the product of four factors: the teacher/pupil ratio, the level of starting salaries, the steepness of the salary schedule above the minimum, and the actual placement of incumbent teachers on the salary schedule. Using California data on grades 3 and 6, this paper finds that using per pupil expenditure on teachers' salaries to predict student achievement gives very different results than by using these four factors. This implies that previous production function studies may have failed to discover relationships that existed in the data they analyzed. Results of these studies in the aggregate will not be clear until they are done in a common format which systematically accounts for the factors of instructional cost.

INTRODUCTION

ECONOMISTS AND other researchers have spent considerable effort trying to estimate "production functions" which relate students' learning to costly educational inputs (for reviews of this literature see Averch *et al.*, 1972; Benson, 1978; Cohn, 1979; Lau, 1979; Hanushek, 1986). Many of the studies have failed to show strong, consistent relationships between school outputs and inputs such as teachers' salaries or the teacher/student ratio. It has been especially difficult to demonstrate a direct connection between achievement and the amount of money spent per pupil, when students' socioeconomic background is statistically controlled (Childs and Shakeshaft, 1987; Walberg and Fowler, 1987). These negative findings have led to the conclusion, as stated by Hanushek (1986, p. 1166), that "schools are *economically inefficient*, because they pay for attributes that are not systematically related to achievement" (emphasis in original).

However, most previous studies have not made systematic use of the simple fact that per pupil expenditure on teachers' salaries, which is the largest single component of instructional cost, is the product of four independent factors. The four factors are the teacher/pupil ratio, the level of starting salaries on the local salary schedule, the amounts by which the salary schedule rewards teachers for seniority and further education, and the levels of seniority and further education that incumbent teachers have actually acquired. Each of these factors can be influenced by local school authorities through collective bargaining and personnel policies. Furthermore, each of these factors may have a different influence on the achievement of students. A model that uses only some of these factors, or only their product, will not give a complete account of how per pupil expenditure on teachers' salaries is associated with student achievement. The purpose of this paper is to measure and compare the joint and separate association of these four factors with student achievement, using data from grades 3 and 6 in Californian public schools.

METHOD

The procedure here focuses on the amount of money spent for teachers' salaries. This is the largest single item in school budgets. The following alge-

[Manuscript received 15 July 1987; revision accepted for publication 13 July 1988.]

braic identity gives salary expenditure per pupil as a product of four factors:

$$S = N \times L \times (H/L) \times (M/H),$$

where S = per pupil expenditure for teachers' salaries,
N = teacher/pupil ratio,
L = lowest posted salary for a full-time teacher,
H = highest posted salary for a full-time teacher,
M = mean salary of incumbent full-time teachers.

In the empirical work reported here, the unit of observation is a particular grade level (3 or 6) in an individual school. Expenditure for teachers' salaries is computed from the actual salaries paid to teachers for teaching at that grade level in that school. If a teacher is assigned only part-time to third grade (or to sixth grade), then that teacher's time and salary are prorated accordingly. L and H, the lowest and highest salaries that may be paid to a full-time teacher, are taken from the district salary schedule, but M, the mean salary of incumbent teachers, is measured for teachers in grade 3 or 6 at the individual school. H/L therefore measures how much the district salary schedule offers to reward teachers for seniority and additional formal education, while M/H reflects the amount of seniority and additional education that have actually been acquired by incumbent teachers at a particular school and grade level. The ratio M/H is the result of local hiring policies, enrollment trends, and the pattern of teacher attrition.

The number of pupils at a particular school and grade level is measured in terms of "daily student class hours" (DSCH). One student supervised by a teacher for 1 hr/day is one DSCH. Thirty students in class for 5 hr/day are $5 \times 30 = 150$ DSCH. A concept like DSCH had to be invented, instead of using a conventional measure like average daily attendance (ADA), because the procedure here matches classroom-level data on number of students with salary information for the teacher in that classroom. Data on ADA are generally not available by classroom, though in theory they might be. DSCH does have the theoretical advantage of reflecting any differences among districts in length of the local school day; ADA does not reflect such differences.

For an illustration of how these salary factors interact, consider the following numbers which are close to the mean values in the data used for 1985–1986. Suppose L, the lowest posted salary on the local district salary schedule, is $20,000/year, and H, the posted maximum, is $36,000. Then H/L, the index of potential reward for seniority and additional education, is 1.80 in this district. In a particular school and grade level, suppose salary for incumbent full-time teachers, M, is $30,000. Then the ratio M/H, or 0.833, is a measure of how far up on the salary ladder, on average, these teachers are positioned, given their seniority and education. Suppose further that teachers in this school are each responsible, on average, for 150 DSCH, so the number of teachers/DSCH is 1:150. Then the product of these four factors, $20,000 \times 1.80 \times 0.833 \times (1:150) = 200, is the annual cost of teachers' salaries/DSCH in this example.

These four components of teachers' salary/DSCH were used as predictors of students' achievement in grades 3 and 6 in Californian public schools. Using weighted least-squares regression, separate equations were estimated to predict school mean achievement in mathematics, reading and writing at each of the two grade levels. In addition to the four components of salary/DSCH, predictors in the regressions included the proportion of students in the school receiving AFDC, the proportion identified as limited or non-English speaking, an index of occupational status of students' parents as estimated by teachers, and the square root of the number of students at the particular grade level in each school.

DATA AND FINDINGS

The California State Department of Education annually gives achievement tests as part of the California Assessment Program (CAP). This produces data on school mean achievement in various subjects at several grade levels, along with the measures of students' socioeconomic background listed in the last paragraph. Since 1982, the Department has also conducted an annual census of students and teachers at the classroom level for the California Basic Educational Data System (CBEDS). The availability of data on students and teachers at the classroom level now makes it possible to measure the association between student achievement and instructional cost for specific grade levels in individual schools; previous studies correlating CAP achievement scores and costs data have had to be done at the level of the school district (e.g. Sebold and Dato, 1981).

The CBEDS data are collected in October; CAP testing for grades 3 and 6 takes place in the spring. For the analysis reported here, CAP achievement and socioeconomic data from spring, 1984 were merged with the CBEDS enrollment and salary data from October 1983. In addition, 1986 CAP data were merged with the October 1985 CBEDS. The analysis was thus performed for two separate years, 1983–1984 and 1985–1986.

For the 1985–1986 analysis, data on minimum and maximum salaries were taken from district salary schedules, which were compiled by the State Department of Education. However, the Department did not compile this information before 1985, and the resources available for this research effort were not sufficient to collect the 1983–1984 salary

schedules from all of California's 1034 school districts. Therefore, the 1983–1984 analysis used self-reported salaries from the CBEDS survey to measure the highest and lowest salary paid to a full-time teacher in each district.

Unweighted means and standard deviations of all variables used in the regression analysis are displayed in Tables 1 and 2. The numbers of schools shown are those for which CAP data are available. CBEDS data on district minimum and maximum salaries were not available for almost half the schools in 1983–1984.

Tables 3–6 show results of the regression analysis. Each table shows three different regressions for school mean achievement in each of three subjects: mathematics, reading and written language. The first regression uses only the socioeconomic variables and the number of students in the relevant grade as predictors. The second regression adds

Table 1. Means and standard deviations by school, 1983–1984

	Grade 3 ($N = 3653$)		Grade 6 ($N = 3093$)	
	Mean	SD	Mean	SD
School percent AFDC	15.47	14.03	15.68	14.72
School percent limited, non-English	11.66	15.78	7.02	9.87
Parent occupation index of students in grade	2.05	0.43	2.05	0.41
Number of students in grade	68.01	29.33	72.72	39.52
Teacher salary/student hr	204.07	43.55	179.49	40.11
District minimum teacher salary	14,158.10	2,938.34	14,056.40	3,020.66
District max./min. teacher salary	2.39	0.63	2.42	0.65
School mean/district max. teacher salary	0.78	0.13	0.78	0.13
Teacher FTE/student hr	0.0083	0.0015	0.0072	0.0013
Mathematics achievement scaled score	277.14	42.23	262.46	36.10
Reading achievement scaled score	272.36	45.68	251.25	39.16
Writing achievement scaled score	276.06	43.75	261.28	32.58

Table 2. Means and standard deviations by school, 1985–1986

	Grade 3 ($N = 3133$)		Grade 6 ($N = 2452$)	
	Mean	SD	Mean	SD
School percent AFDC	15.94	15.09	15.80	14.66
School percent limited, non-English	13.62	17.39	8.40	11.23
Parent occupation index of students in grade	2.03	0.42	2.02	0.41
Number of students in grade	79.31	38.39	76.78	41.00
Teacher salary/student hr	229.71	45.84	204.82	43.27
District minimum teacher salary	19,552.40	1,496.08	19,536.50	1,504.60
District max./min. teacher salary	1.87	0.18	1.88	0.18
School mean/district max. teacher salary	0.82	0.10	0.81	0.11
Teacher FTE/student hr	0.0078	0.0012	0.0069	0.0011
Mathematics achievement scaled score	286.04	44.05	271.50	37.42
Reading achievement scaled score	282.78	46.30	263.40	39.55
Writing achievement scaled score	288.22	44.80	274.31	34.84

Table 3. Regressions for grade 3 achievement, 1983–1984 (t-statistics in parentheses)

	Mathematics			Reading			Writing		
School percent AFDC	-0.696 (-14.63)	-0.725 (-11.93)	-0.642 (-10.40)	-0.730 (-16.19)	-0.755 (-13.17)	-0.638 (-11.09)	-0.666 (-15.25)	-0.650 (-11.82)	-0.560 (-10.05)
School percent limited, non-English	-0.171 (-4.35)	-0.236 (-4.48)	-0.124 (-2.24)	-0.472 (-12.64)	-0.568 (-11.41)	-0.409 (-7.92)	-0.459 (-12.71)	-0.532 (-11.16)	-0.410 (-8.20)
Parent occupation index in grade	40.408 (22.28)	38.630 (15.11)	40.831 (15.94)	49.099 (28.55)	46.886 (19.43)	49.731 (20.84)	46.978 (28.23)	44.684 (19.31)	46.851 (20.29)
Square root of number of students in grade	-2.668 (-8.75)	-2.294 (-5.51)		-2.746 (-9.50)	-2.303 (-5.86)		-2.648 (-9.47)	-2.358 (-6.25)	
Teacher salary/student hr		0.0429 (2.40)			0.0502 (2.97)			0.0503 (3.11)	
District min. teacher salary			0.000468 (0.91)			0.000652 (1.37)			0.000631 (1.37)
District max./min. teacher salary			-4.310 (-1.86)			-5.756 (-2.66)			-3.570 (-1.71)
School mean/district max. teacher salary			13.922 (2.08)			21.452 (3.45)			19.977 (3.32)
Teacher FTE/student hr			587.865 (1.17)			547.422 (1.17)			375.448 (0.83)
Intercept	228.625 (44.72)	220.056 (27.35)	207.417 (12.40)	210.735 (43.46)	201.763 (26.56)	182.469 (11.71)	216.867 (46.23)	208.019 (28.56)	189.682 (12.57)
R^2	0.440	0.472	0.482	0.578	0.613	0.630	0.569	0.599	0.610
N	3619	1897	1897	3619	1897	1897	3619	1897	1897
F	709.15	337.43	219.80	1238.88	598.03	402.54	1191.51	564.78	369.71

Table 4. Regressions for grade 6 achievement, 1983–1984 (t-statistics in parentheses)

	Mathematics			Reading			Writing	
School percent AFDC	−0.690 (−18.13)	−0.750 (−15.86)	−0.693 (−14.39)	−0.733 (−19.44)	−0.774 (−16.38)	−0.685 (−14.40)	−0.619 (−15.63)	−0.535 (−13.50)
School percent limited, non-English	−0.238 (−4.71)	−0.288 (−4.32)	−0.254 (−3.80)	−0.525 (−10.50)	−0.596 (−8.94)	−0.535 (−8.11)	−0.546 (−9.76)	−0.490 (−8.92)
Parent occupation index in grade	42.761 (29.09)	42.962 (21.64)	42.064 (21.25)	48.409 (33.23)	48.126 (24.27)	47.066 (24.07)	38.648 (23.24)	37.464 (23.02)
Square root of number of students in grade	−1.598 (−8.09)	−1.407 (−5.11)	−1.278 (−4.57)	−1.547 (−7.91)	−1.470 (−5.35)	−1.239 (−4.48)	−1.195 (−5.18)	−1.080 (−4.70)
Teacher salary/student hr		−0.00950 (−0.60)			−0.0351 (−2.24)		−0.0468 (−3.56)	
District min. teacher salary			0.000602 (1.38)			0.000786 (1.83)		0.000116 (3.26)
District max./min. teacher salary			0.246 (0.13)			−2.557 (−1.37)		−0.519 (−0.33)
School mean/district max. teacher salary			14.999 (2.76)			11.400 (2.13)		6.886 (1.54)
Teacher FTE/student hr			−1136.957 (−2.27)			−1307.955 (−2.65)		−2156.221 (−5.25)
Intercept	200.787 (51.02)	200.679 (32.49)	186.416 (14.11)	180.193 (46.20)	186.539 (30.24)	175.226 (13.44)	212.373 (41.04)	199.653 (18.39)
R^2	0.539	0.575	0.582	0.616	0.640	0.654	0.623	0.647
N	3055	1694	1694	3055	1694	1694	1694	1694
F	890.83	456.53	293.43	1225.38	599.75	397.87	566.64	385.72

Table 5. Regressions for grade 3 achievement, 1985–1986 (t-statistics in parentheses)

	Mathematics			Reading			Writing		
School percent AFDC	-0.742 (-15.23)	-0.737 (-14.87)	-0.726 (-14.68)	-0.678 (-15.04)	-0.671 (-14.66)	-0.660 (-14.46)	-0.663 (-14.97)	-0.664 (-14.73)	-0.652 (-14.52)
School percent limited non-English	-0.093 (-2.28)	-0.066 (-1.56)	-0.054 (-1.24)	-0.316 (-8.34)	-0.295 (-7.50)	-0.260 (-6.50)	-0.357 (-9.59)	-0.335 (-8.65)	-0.311 (-7.88)
Parent occupation index in grade	41.918 (20.46)	42.826 (20.29)	42.069 (19.81)	52.982 (27.98)	53.720 (27.54)	53.399 (27.28)	48.252 (25.91)	48.749 (25.39)	48.035 (24.95)
Square root of number of students in grade	-2.407 (-7.91)	-2.621 (-8.19)	-2.673 (-8.16)	-2.009 (-7.15)	-2.217 (-7.49)	-2.118 (-7.02)	-2.040 (-7.38)	-2.237 (-7.68)	-2.221 (-7.48)
Teacher salary/ student hr		-0.0211 (-1.55)			-0.0088 (-0.70)			-0.0050 (-0.40)	
District min. teacher salary			-0.00008 (-0.13)			-0.00111 (-1.97)			-0.00040 (-0.72)
District max./ min. teacher salary			9.444 (1.90)			1.707 (0.37)			9.560 (2.12)
School mean/district max. teacher salary			9.476 (1.55)			19.704 (3.50)			19.992 (3.61)
Teacher FTE/ student hr			-1893.568 (-3.62)			-1698.253 (-3.52)			-1690.706 (-3.57)
Intercept	235.027 (42.30)	239.375 (37.75)	226.951 (10.56)	207.901 (40.48)	209.841 (35.81)	225.517 (11.23)	223.547 (44.25)	225.081 (39.02)	211.413 (10.85)
R^2	0.453	0.456	0.460	0.583	0.586	0.591	0.570	0.572	0.578
N	3132	3023	3023	3132	3023	3023	3132	3023	3023
F	648.09	505.62	320.87	1094.40	854.06	544.05	1037.14	807.55	516.27

Table 6. Regressions for grade 6 achievement, 1985–1986 (t-statistics in parentheses)

	Mathematics			Reading			Writing		
School percent AFDC	−0.652 (−15.04)	−0.656 (−14.73)	−0.626 (−14.01)	−0.669 (−16.24)	−0.670 (−15.85)	−0.643 (−15.15)	−0.599 (−15.29)	−0.610 (−15.18)	−0.576 (−14.35)
School percent limited non-English	−0.271 (−5.16)	−0.266 (−4.87)	−0.274 (−4.99)	−0.564 (−11.29)	−0.555 (−10.72)	−0.557 (−10.68)	−0.462 (−9.70)	−0.443 (−9.00)	−0.457 (−9.26)
Parent occupation index in grade	43.277 (24.93)	43.212 (24.27)	42.113 (23.64)	47.706 (28.92)	47.643 (28.23)	46.809 (27.67)	39.100 (24.90)	38.935 (24.26)	37.760 (23.59)
Square root of number of students in grade	−2.172 (−9.42)	−2.202 (−9.18)	−2.362 (−9.67)	−2.201 (−10.05)	−2.250 (−9.89)	−2.327 (−10.03)	−2.137 (−10.25)	−2.187 (−10.11)	−2.311 (−10.54)
Teacher salary/student hr		0.0075 (0.60)			−0.0057 (−0.48)			−0.0322 (−2.84)	
District min. teacher salary			0.00171 (3.24)			0.00074 (1.47)			0.00075 (1.59)
District max./min. teacher salary			16.039 (3.73)			10.437 (2.56)			15.329 (3.97)
School mean/district max. teacher salary			19.000 (3.63)			14.371 (2.89)			8.339 (1.77)
Teacher FTE/student hr			−1571.497 (−3.18)			−1624.726 (−3.46)			−2594.275 (−5.84)
Intercept	215.216 (46.37)	214.157 (39.75)	150.668 (8.14)	201.032 (45.59)	202.789 (39.70)	169.073 (9.61)	226.877 (54.05)	234.227 (48.23)	198.269 (11.92)
R^2	0.542	0.541	0.547	0.632	0.631	0.635	0.576	0.576	0.585
N	2442	2360	2360	2442	2360	2360	2442	2360	2360
F	721.31	554.33	355.26	1046.43	804.04	510.64	826.15	638.67	413.52

expenditure/DSCH on teachers' salaries. The third equation, instead of using teacher salary expenditure/DSCH, uses the four components of it: level of the salary schedule as indicated by minimum full-time salary paid in the district, ratio of maximum to minimum salary in the district, school mean salary at grade 3 or 6 divided by district maximum salary, and the number of full-time equivalent teachers/DSCH in the school at grade 3 or 6. The whole analysis was done by generalized least-squares, with all data weighted by the square root of the number of students in the relevant grade level at the school.

Students' socioeconomic characteristics, along with the number of students in the school at grade 3 or 6, account for approximately half the inter-school variance in mean achievement. Student achievement is consistently and significantly higher in schools with higher socioeconomic status and smaller numbers of students. These predictors account for less of the variance in mathematics scores than in reading and written language. In particular, the percentage of limited-English-speaking students is more strongly associated with (lower) reading and writing scores than with mathematics achievement.

When expenditure/DSCH on teachers' salaries is added to the equation, the results are mixed. In three of the 12 equations using this predictor, the coefficient was positive and statistically significant at the 0.05 level, but in three other equations it was negative and significant. In the remaining six equations, the coefficient was not statistically significant. If these were the only results we had, we would conclude, as did Hanushek (1986), that differences in per pupil spending for teachers' salaries are not associated in a consistently and significantly positive direction with students' achievement.

However, when per pupil spending on teachers' salaries is replaced by its four components, the results are quite different. The ratio of the mean salary of incumbent teachers at the school in grade 3 or 6 to the district maximum salary — which reflects the amount of seniority and further education these teachers have acquired — has a positive and statistically significant coefficient in nine of the 12 equations. The ratio of district maximum to minimum salary, which measures the potential monetary reward for seniority and further education, has a positive and significant coefficient in four equations and a significantly negative coef-

ficient in one equation. The minimum salary level in the district is significantly positive twice and significantly negative once. The number of full-time teachers/DSCH is negative and significant in nine of 12 equations. Excluding schools in Los Angeles County, which contains the state's largest school district, yielded a very similar pattern of results.

DISCUSSION

The main finding here is that per pupil expenditure for teachers' salaries appears to have no consistent and significant association with student achievement in grades 3 and 6, but when per pupil expenditure on teachers' salaries is replaced by its four component factors, a very different pattern emerges. The index of teachers' seniority and education does have a positive and statistically significant association with achievement, but the teacher/pupil ratio has a negative association with achievement. These two effects offset each other, leaving no consistent association between student achievement and per pupil spending on teachers' salaries.

The generally positive association of student achievement with the index of teachers' education and seniority may indicate that more highly educated and experienced teachers are in fact more effective. After all, that is the rationale for structuring teachers' salary schedules to pay more for experience and further education. Even Hanushek (1986), who is skeptical about the effect of school resources on students' learning, concludes that teachers' experience is fairly consistently associated with achievement (see also Murnane and Phillips, 1981). However, this association does not necessarily mean that more experienced or highly educated teachers are more effective. It could instead reflect the fact that teachers with more seniority sometimes prefer, and are able, to get themselves assigned to schools where the high-achieving students are present.

The minimum salary level in a district would be positively associated with student achievement if a higher starting salary enabled the district to recruit more effective teachers. Similarly, given the starting salary level, the district might be able to recruit and retain better teachers if it offers larger salary increments as teachers gain seniority and further education. Although the association of these two factors with student achievement is usually positive in Tables 3–6, it is not usually significant and sometimes it is negative. Despite evidence from other studies that higher salaries do attract more and better qualified teachers (see Manski, 1987; Stern, 1986), the effect on student achievement is not strongly evident here.

The final component of teacher cost, namely the number of teachers/student hr, does not appear to be positively associated with student achievement in our California school data. Although many practitioners and policy makers strongly maintain that reducing class size would be beneficial, our result is consistent with most previous research, which finds that differences in class size, within the range of ordinary practice, are not usually associated with students' achievement (see Hanushek, 1986; Robinson and Wittebols, 1986).

It is interesting to note that the number of students enrolled in grade 3 or 6 at a given school does have a strong and consistently negative association with the mean achievement of those students. This seems to indicate that the size of the group itself affects students' learning, apart from the teacher/pupil ratio.

The fact that several of our estimated coefficients suggest a negative relationship between the teacher/pupil ratio and student achievement may be attributable to circumstances resulting from declining student enrollment. In California public elementary schools, enrollment fell nearly 9% between 1974–1980, and as of 1984, enrollment had recovered to only 94% of its 1974 level (California State Department of Education, 1986). Since public school revenues are tied to enrollment, districts with declining enrollment face severe budget problems, which necessitate cutting back programs, closing schools and reducing the number of teachers by attrition, early retirement, or layoffs. All this is bad for morale. Yet, because districts are usually reluctant to lay off teachers, the number of teachers usually does not decline as fast as the number of students. Consequently, when student enrollment declines, the teacher/pupil ratio typically increases. Therefore, districts where student enrollment has declined most sharply may have suffered more disruption of programs, deterioration of morale, and consequent negative effects on student achievement — but at the same time, they have higher teacher/pupil ratios. This historical explanation may account for the finding in Tables 3–6 of a negative relationship between student achievement and the number of teachers/student hr.

In addition to what these findings reveal about this particular population of schools in these particular years, there is an important general implication for other research studies of this kind. Using per pupil expenditure on teachers' salaries to predict student achievement gives very different results than using its component factors. Using the component factors is preferable because each of these factors is subject to some degree of independent control by local school authorities, and each may, in theory, have a different effect on student achievement. Until the separate research studies relating educational costs to student achievement use a similar procedure to factor the components of instructional cost, it will not be at all clear what this body of research has really found.

Acknowledgements — The author wishes to thank Terry Emmett for bibliographic assistance and Phyllis Cohen for meticulous preparation of the data files.

REFERENCES

Averch, H.A., Carroll, S.J., Donaldson, T.S., Kiesling, H.J. and Pincus, J. (1972) *How Effective is Schooling? A Critical Review and Synthesis of Research Findings.* Santa Monica, CA: Rand Corporation.

Benson, C.S. (1979) *The Economics of Public Education*, 3rd edn, Chap. 7. Boston: Houghton-Mifflin.

California State Department of Education (1986) *1984–85 Selected Education Statistics.* Sacramento, CA.

Childs, T.S. and Shakeshaft, C. (1987) A meta-analysis of research on the relationship between educational expenditures and student achievement. Paper presented to the *Ann. Mtg American Educational Research Association*, Washington, D.C.

Cohn, E. (1979) *The Economics of Education*, revised edn, Chap. 8. Cambridge, MA: Ballinger.

Hanushek, E.A. (1986) The economics of schooling. *J. Econ. Lit.* **24**, 1141–1177.

Kiesling, H.J. (1984) Assignment practices and the relationship of instructional time to the reading performance of elementary school children. *Econ. Educ. Rev.* **3**, 341–350.

LAU, L.J. (1979) Educational production functions. In *Economic Dimensions of Education* (Edited by WINDHAM, D.M.). Washington, D.C.: National Academy of Education.

MANSKI, C.F. (1987) Academic ability, earnings, and the decision to become a teacher: evidence from the National Longitudinal Study of the High School Class of 1972. In *Public Sector Payrolls* (Edited by WISE, D.A.). Chicago: Univ. of Chicago Press.

MURNANE, R.J. and PHILLIPS, B.R. (1981) Learning by doing, vintage, and selection: three pieces of the puzzle relating teaching experience and teaching performance. *Econ. Educ. Rev.* **1**, 453–465.

ROBINSON, G.E. and WITTEBOLS, J.H. (1986) *Class Size Research: A Related Cluster Analysis for Decision Making*. Arlington, VA: Educational Research Service.

SEBOLD, F.D. and DATO, W. (1981) School funding and student achievement: an empirical analysis. *Public Finance Q.* **9**, 91–105.

STERN, D. (1986) Compensation for teachers. *Rev. Res. Educ.* **13**, 285–317.

TURNER, R., CAMILLI, G., KROC, R. and HOOVER, J. (1986) Policy strategies, teacher salary incentive, and student achievement: an explanatory model. *Educ. Researcher* **15**, 5–11.

WALBERG, H.J. and FOWLER, W.J. JR. (1987) Expenditure and size efficiencies of public school districts. *Educ. Researcher* **16**, 5–13.

Article 13

The Effect of Chain Ownership on Nursing Home Costs

Niccie L. McKay

Although it is commonly assumed that chain ownership will result in lower costs due to economies of scale, the empirical evidence with respect to the effect of chain ownership on nursing home costs is mixed. Chain for-profit nursing homes will have a cost advantage over independent for-profit homes only if there are firm-level (multiple-home) economies of scale. For the study population of Texas nursing homes in 1983, cost structures differed sufficiently across ownership types to warrant estimating separate cost functions by ownership type. The results indicate that, when other factors affecting cost are held constant, chain homes have lower average costs than independent homes at intermediate and high levels of output, but higher average costs at low and very high levels of output. The results highlight the importance of considering whether or not to pool data across ownership categories when estimating nursing home cost functions.

The cost of nursing home care is an important policy issue because government programs pay for almost half of total expenditures on nursing home care. In 1986, for example, public funding accounted for 48 percent of the $38.1 billion spent on nursing home care (*Health Care Financing Review* 1987). An understanding of the determinants of nursing home costs and of the effects of different types of ownership on these costs can aid policymakers in the search for reimbursement methods that will control costs and provide an acceptable level of quality for publicly funded nursing home care.

Address correspondence and requests for reprints to Niccie L. McKay, Ph.D., Assistant Professor, Department of Health Care Administration, Box 58, Trinity University, 715 Stadium Drive, San Antonio, TX 78212. This article was received on October 10, 1988, went through two revisions, and was accepted for publication on June 8, 1990.

Several studies have examined the effect of ownership type on nursing home costs. These studies have consistently shown that average costs are higher for nonprofit and government providers than for for-profit homes.[1] The evidence with respect to the effect of chain ownership on nursing home costs, on the other hand, is not nearly as clear-cut.

The public perception seems to be that chain providers automatically have an advantage over independently owned homes. An article in the *Wall Street Journal*, for example, observed that "the long-term need for nursing homes seems to favor big operators . . ." (February 4, 1988). It is commonly assumed that chain ownership will result in lower costs due to economies of scale from centralized purchasing and administration. The empirical evidence on this question is rather mixed, however. One recent study (Arling, Nordquist, and Capitman 1987) concluded that average costs were lower for chain homes than for other providers, while three other studies (Birnbaum et al. 1981; Meiners 1982; Schlenker and Shaughnessy 1984) found that chain ownership did not significantly affect cost.

This study provides a new and more detailed analysis of the effect of chain ownership on nursing home costs. After reviewing previous research, the article begins by discussing the conceptual framework for assessing how chain ownership affects cost. The empirical portion of the study uses 1983 data for nursing homes in Texas to estimate both a common regression with a dummy variable for ownership type (that is, using pooled data) and separate cost functions by ownership type. The results from the separate regressions (the appropriate estimation procedure for this data set) indicate that cost differences between chain and independent for-profit homes depend on the level of output (i.e., the number of patient days). More specifically, average cost is lower for chain homes than for independent homes at intermediate and high levels of output, but higher at low and very high levels of output. The final section of the article compares the results to those of other studies and discusses the policy implications of the findings.

PREVIOUS RESEARCH

Only a few previous studies have investigated the effect of chain ownership on nursing home costs. Three studies examined the effects of chain ownership tangentially in the course of analyzing the various determinants of nursing home costs. Birnbaum et al. (1981) and

Meiners (1982) both used the 1973/1974 National Nursing Home Survey to estimate a general nursing home cost function; both found that the coefficient of a dummy variable for chain ownership was not statistically significant. Schlenker and Shaughnessy (1984) reached the same conclusion using data for Colorado nursing homes in 1980.

Arling, Nordquist, and Capitman (1987), the previous study that looked most closely at chain ownership, used three ownership categories—public/nonprofit, individual for-profit, and chain—to examine costs for Virginia nursing homes in 1985. Regression analysis using pooled data (that is, including dummy variables for chain and individual for-profit ownership) indicated that chain homes in the sample had significantly lower costs than public/nonprofit providers, as did individual for-profit homes. (The article did not report whether or not there was a statistically significant difference between the costs of chain and individual for-profit homes.)

The study also estimated separate regression equations for each ownership category and concluded that, in general, chain homes "appear to provide a standard, relatively low-cost level of care that is concentrated on the Medicaid market" (p. 265). Unfortunately, the authors did not use statistical techniques to determine whether it was more appropriate to estimate a common regression equation or separate equations by ownership category, nor did they compare the results of the two estimation techniques.

CONCEPTUAL FRAMEWORK

Economic theory provides a framework for analyzing nursing home costs (see Scanlon 1980, and Palmer and Vogel 1985). For-profit nursing homes are assumed to make choices that will minimize cost and maximize profit, subject to various regulatory constraints. Nonprofit providers, on the other hand, by definition have objectives other than profit. A common assumption, for example, is that nonprofit nursing homes desire to maximize their size, subject to quality and break-even constraints (Scanlon 1980). All else equal, one would thus expect nonprofit providers to have higher average costs than for-profit homes, a prediction confirmed by numerous empirical cost studies.[2]

In the for-profit sector, both chain and independent homes seek to minimize cost, and therefore economies of scale are the key to assessing the effect of chain ownership on nursing home costs. Economies of scale, which exist when long-run average cost declines as output increases,[3] can result from pecuniary or real savings. Pecuniary savings are due to a decrease in input prices as output increases, usually resulting from greater bargaining power on the part of a larger firm. Real savings are due to the increased productivity of inputs at larger levels of output. Real savings, generally the result of specialization or indivisibilities, mean that each unit of output can be produced using fewer inputs as output increases.

Economic theory would suggest that whether or not chain ownership will affect nursing home costs will depend on whether or not there are economies of scale at the firm level, as opposed to the plant level. Plant-level economies of scale refer to decreases in long-run average cost as output at a given plant (nursing home) increases; both chain and nonchain providers would benefit from plant-level economies of scale.[4] Multiple-plant (chain) ownership will confer a cost advantage only if there are firm-level cost savings, that is, only if average cost is lower for chain homes than for nonchain homes at any given level of output.

Multiple-plant economies of scale could result from real savings due to a more specialized central staff, or from pecuniary savings due to lower input prices. Capital costs, in particular, could be lower if multiple-plant firms could obtain funds at a lower cost. Capital-raising economies of scale could be a combination of real savings, due to spreading the nearly fixed transactions costs of issuing common stock or borrowing funds over larger levels of output, and pecuniary savings, stemming from the ability of larger firms to negotiate lower interest rates.

In the case of nursing homes, multiple-home economies of scale could result from joint purchasing arrangements that lead to lower prices for inputs such as food, medical and household supplies, and furnishings. Or, chains might lower labor costs by sharing various types of consultants (e.g., for nursing, physical therapy, or social work) among homes. Other possible sources of multiple-home economies of scale are capital savings, due to lower interest expenditures on building and equipment, or lower average costs of centralized management.

The effect of chain ownership on average cost is an empirical question, because there is no theoretical basis for assuming that chain ownership leads to firm-level economies of scale. If firm-level economies of scale do *not* exist, either firm size does not affect average cost or average cost increases as firm size increases. The latter case, firm-level diseconomies of scale, is usually attributable to coordination problems and limits to management.

Table 1: Descriptive Statistics: Texas Nursing Homes in 1983
($N = 826$)

Variable	Mean or Percent (Standard Deviation)	
Average cost	$29.09	($6.89)
Total patient days	30,018.4	(15,115.3)
Beds	100.5	(48.6)
Occupancy rate	82.8%	(13.9%)
Private patient days as percent of total patient days	28.0%	(15.1%)
Ownership		
For-profit ($N = 722$)	87.4%	
Chain ($N = 469$)	56.8%	
Independent ($N = 253$)	30.6%	
Nonprofit ($N = 88$)	10.7%	
Government ($N = 16$)	1.9%	
Certification		
Skilled nursing facility (SNF) only ($N = 48$)	5.8%	
Intermediate care facility (ICF) only ($N = 666$)	80.6%	
Both SNF and ICF ($N = 112$)	13.6%	

DATA

The Texas Department of Human Resources requires an annual cost report from all nursing homes receiving Medicaid reimbursement. This study used data obtained from the 1983 cost reports, which covered 955 of the 1,001 nursing homes in Texas. Of the 955 homes that received at least some payment from the Medicaid program, 129 operated for less than 12 months in 1983. Because nursing home costs may be unusually high in a year of entry into or exit from the market, the final data set included only the 826 nursing homes that operated for the entire year.[5]

The Texas Department of Human Resources cost report provided detailed information on facility characteristics, revenues, and costs. Table 1 presents descriptive statistics for Texas nursing homes in 1983. The average nursing home had about 100 beds and provided approximately 30,000 patient days of care per year, with private patients accounting for 28 percent of total patient days. The Texas nursing home market is dominated by for-profit providers: 87 percent of all homes were for-profit operations, 11 percent were nonprofit, and 2 percent were operated by a government agency. And chain ownership is widespread — 57 percent of all providers were chain-owned for-profit nursing homes.

Because Medicaid patients account for such a large proportion of total payments for nursing home care, the Medicaid reimbursement method has a great influence on a nursing home's incentive to control (minimize) costs. Although there are a variety of rate-setting methods, most states use average cost either to determine a fixed reimbursement rate or to set ceilings for rates based on each home's cost (Bishop 1980). In 1983, Texas used a prospective, fixed-rate reimbursement method in which the costs of all nursing homes participating in the Medicaid program were used to calculate the median cost of a given level of care (i.e., skilled nursing facility — SNF — or intermediate care facility — ICF). The median cost, adjusted for projected inflation, then determined the reimbursement rate for a given level of care, and all homes received the same reimbursement rate (Texas Department of Human Resources). Because nursing homes in Texas were allowed to retain any difference between the fixed reimbursement rate and actual cost, the reimbursement method should not have altered cost-minimizing behavior by the for-profit homes in the study population.

RESULTS

The first step in assessing the effect of chain ownership on nursing home costs was to examine whether or not average cost varied with type of ownership. Nursing homes were classified into three groups on the basis of ownership: chain for-profit ($N = 469$), independent for-profit ($N = 253$), and nonprofit/government ($N = 104$). Two-sample t-tests were used to test the null hypothesis that the mean average costs (i.e., the mean costs per patient day) were equal between any two ownership groups.

As shown in Table 2, the mean cost per patient day for nonprofit/government providers was significantly greater than that for chain and independent for-profit homes. As noted, numerous nursing home cost studies have come to the same conclusion (see Palmer 1985 for a survey). The surprising result was that the mean cost per patient day for chain-owned homes was statistically greater than for independent for-profit homes ($t = 2.15$). This result is inconsistent with the conventional wisdom that chain ownership leads to a lower average cost for nursing home care.

The above results are interesting, but preliminary. Average cost did vary by type of ownership, but other factors affecting cost also

Table 2:   Two-Sample *t*-Tests by Ownership Type

| | Mean Values | | |
Variable	Chain For-Profit (N = 469)	Independent For-Profit (N = 253)	Nonprofit/ Government (N = 104)
Average Cost	$28.11*†	$27.53*‡	$37.28†‡
As percent of total patient days			
SNF days	3.3%*†	4.5%*	5.8%†
ICF days	71.7%*†	68.0%*‡	51.6%†‡
Private days	25.0%*†	27.6%*‡	42.7%†‡
Beds	106.9*	88.3*‡	101.4‡
Total patient days	30,307	28,247‡	33,027‡
Occupancy rate	78.5%*†	87.9%*	90.0%†

*Difference between chain and independent group means is statistically significant at the .05 confidence level.

†Difference between chain and nonprofit/government group means is statistically significant at the .05 confidence level.

‡Difference between independent and nonprofit/government group means is statistically significant at the .05 confidence level.

varied among homes. Regression analysis was used to examine the effect of chain ownership on nursing home average cost, holding constant other important determinants of nursing home costs.

In order to be consistent with previous work, this study first estimated a typical nursing home cost function using the data set for all Texas nursing homes in 1983 (see Palmer 1985 for a survey of nursing home cost studies):

$$AC = f(Y, YSQ, OCCR, PRIV, OWN, CERTIF, HSA)$$

The dependent variable is average cost (*AC*). The continuous independent variables are the total number of patient days (*Y*), the square of the total number of patient days (YSQ),[6] the occupancy rate (*OCCR*), and the percent of total patient days accounted for by private patients (*PRIV*). The remaining independent variables, ownership (*OWN*), certification (*CERTIF*), and region (*HSA*), are categorical variables. Ownership categories are chain for-profit (*CHAIN*) and nonprofit/government (*NONPGOVT*), with independent for-profit as the base. Certification categories are SNF only (*SNF*) and both SNF and ICF (*BOTH*), with ICF only being the reference group. Regional differences were taken into account by assigning a dummy variable to each of the 12 health service areas in Texas (HSA1, Amarillo, is the reference area).

Direct measures of two important determinants of nursing home costs—case mix and quality—were not available. The cost function does, however, include the certification variable, a crude proxy for case-mix differences, and the proportion of private patients, a measure found to be associated with quality differences (see Walsh 1979, and Ruchlin and Levey 1972). Moreover, other nursing home cost studies found that cost differences among ownership types persisted even after controlling for case mix and quality (see, for example, Birnbaum et al. 1981, and Arling, Nordquist, and Capitman 1987). Nonetheless, the analysis is limited by the absence of more accurate measures of case mix and quality.

Table 3 presents the estimation results both for a common regression with a dummy variable for ownership type (the usual specification in nursing home cost studies) and for separate regressions by ownership type. Estimating a common regression presumes that the intercept varies but the slope coefficients are the same across ownership categories. The F-statistic for a test of the null hypothesis that the slope coefficients are equal across ownership categories is 155.4, more than sufficient to reject the null hypothesis at the 1 percent confidence level.[7] (Using for-profit homes only, the conclusion is also to estimate separate regressions for chain and independent homes.)[8] For this data set, the appropriate technique thus is to estimate a separate regression for each ownership category.[9]

Although the magnitudes of the coefficients vary, the different specifications give similar results for the effects of the occupancy rate, the percentage of private patients, and the type of certification on average cost. As was true in other cost studies, average cost decreased as the occupancy rate increased and increased as the percentage of private patients increased. Homes certified as SNF-only had higher average costs than ICF-only homes, as did homes with both SNF and ICF patients.

It is with regard to scale effects that the choice of specification will influence conclusions about the effect of ownership on nursing home costs. The coefficients of the number of patient days (Y) and patient days squared (YSQ) are statistically different from zero at the 1 percent confidence level in the separate regression results for chain homes and in the common regression equation. In the initial separate regression equations for independent and nonprofit/government providers, however, the coefficients of patient days and patient days squared were not statistically distinguishable from zero. The cost functions for indepen-

Table 3: Parameter Estimates of Nursing Home Cost Functions

	Separate Regressions			Common Regression (N = 826)
Variable	Chain For-Profit (N = 469)	Independent For-Profit (N = 253)	Nonprofit/ Government (N = 104)	
INTERCEPT	37.89**	32.83**	80.95**	41.02**
Y	−.00016**	—	—	−.0002**
YSQ	1.37×10^{-9}**	—	—	2.33×10^{-9}**
OCCR	−9.60**	−8.07**	−55.70**	−13.40**
PRIV	6.08**	6.82**	17.61**	11.52**
SNF	4.25**	4.07**	14.62**	6.65**
BOTH	4.43**	3.05**	6.56*	3.92**
CHAIN	—	—	—	−0.17
NONPGOVT	—	—	—	7.33**
REGION†				
HSA 2	−0.79	−1.34	−8.53	−3.82**
HSA 3	1.21	−3.03	−4.06	−1.06
HSA 4	−1.81*	0.40	0.31	−1.91
HSA 5	−0.62	−1.20	−4.97	−1.53
HSA 6	−1.63*	−0.94	−6.14	−2.62*
HSA 7	−1.00	−0.15	−4.48	−1.03
HSA 8	−1.43	−0.22	−7.64	−2.36*
HSA 9	−1.68	−1.14	−11.65*	−3.55**
HSA10	−2.17*	−1.21	−8.31	−2.83*
HSA11	−1.03	0.03	2.25	−0.97
HSA12	−0.29	−0.15	26.46*	1.62
F-ratio	18.79	8.42	5.83	32.73
Adjusted R^2	.39	.31	.41	.42

*Statistically significant at the .05 confidence level.

**Statistically significant at the .01 confidence level.

†HSA2 = Lubbock; HSA3 = El Paso; HSA4 = Abilene; HSA5 = Dallas-Fort Worth; HSA6 = Austin; HSA7 = Paris; HSA8 = Edinburg; HSA9 = San Antonio; HSA10 = Beaumont; HSA11 = Houston; HSA12 = Midland.

dent and nonprofit/government providers were therefore reestimated without the patient-day variables, and those results are reported in Table 3.[10] The estimation results based on the common regression show that all homes appear to have U-shaped average cost curves, but, when estimated separately, average cost is U-shaped only for chain homes.

The choice of specification becomes especially important when examining how chain ownership affects nursing home costs. In the common regression, the dummy variable for chain ownership is not statistically different from zero, suggesting that, all else equal, average cost was approximately the same for chain and independent for-profit homes.

A different picture emerges from the separate regressions, however. Because the slope coefficients are unequal, a comparison of average cost between chain and independent homes depends on the level of output (that is, the number of patient days). Graphs of chain and independent homes' average cost functions were prepared for each of the 36 certification/region categories. The graphs show how chain and independent average costs change over the relevant range of output (5,000 to 100,000 patient days), based on the parameter estimates from the separate regressions by ownership type and evaluated at the mean occupancy rate and percentage-of-private-patients values for all for-profit homes. In other words, the graphs compare chain and independent homes' average cost curves, holding constant all other factors affecting cost.

Figure 1 presents the average cost curves for chain and independent for-profit homes in the Austin health service area (HSA6) that provide only ICF care. In this certification/region category, accounting for about 12 percent of all Texas for-profit homes, chain average cost was higher than independent average cost at low and very high levels of output, but lower at intermediate and high levels of output. This pattern was typical: 95 percent of the for-profit homes were in a certification/region category that exhibited a similar set of average cost curves.[11]

The range of output over which chain homes had lower average costs than independent homes varied, depending on the certification/region category. Calculating the intersections of the chain and independent homes' average cost functions for each certification/region category and then weighting the intersections by the proportion of homes in that category, the weighted average range over which chain homes had lower average costs than independent homes was approximately 26,000–90,000 patient days.

In the common regression, with only the intercept varying, cost differences at low, intermediate, and high levels of output cancelled out, resulting in an insignificant coefficient on the dummy variable for chain ownership. The separate regressions, which allow both intercept and slope coefficients to vary, indicate that, although there are cost differences between chain and independent homes, those differences depend on the scale of operation. In most cases, chain homes do have a cost advantage over independent homes, but only at intermediate and high levels of output.

A final issue to be considered in this investigation of nursing home

Figure 1: Average Cost Curves for Chain and Independent For-Profit Nursing Homes in HSA6 That Provide Only Intermediate Care*

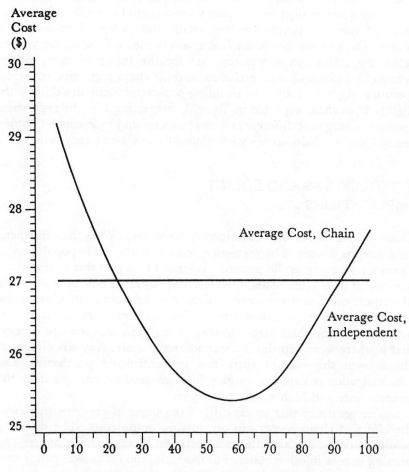

Total Number of Patient Days, in Thousands

*Average cost is evaluated at the mean occupancy rate and percent of private patients for all for-profit homes.

costs is the role of occupancy rates in explaining ownership cost differences. For Texas nursing homes in 1983, the average occupancy rate for chain homes was significantly less than for independent homes (see Table 2, t = 9.03). And this difference in average occupancy rates appears to have been an important determinant of the actual cost differences between the two types of homes.

Although regression analysis holds the occupancy rate constant when measuring ownership cost differences, it is possible that chain homes with unusually low occupancy rates could be responsible for the reported cost differences between chain and independent for-profit homes. To examine this possibility, chain homes with occupancy rates below the minimum occupancy rate for the group of independent homes (52.5 percent) were excluded, and the chain regression equation reestimated ($N = 440$). The resulting parameter estimates differ only slightly from those reported in Table 3, suggesting that the regression results showing cost differences between chain and independent homes are not due to chain homes with unusually low occupancy rates.

CONCLUSIONS AND POLICY IMPLICATIONS

Chain providers are often assumed to have lower costs than independent nursing homes. The regression results for the study population of Texas nursing homes did provide evidence to support this assumption, but only at intermediate and high levels of output. Thus, at those levels of output, there was evidence of firm-level economies of scale in the production of nursing home care. At low and very high levels of output, chain homes had higher average costs than independent homes, that is, there were firm-level diseconomies of scale. Any advantages of chain ownership—lower costs due to centralized purchasing and administration or capital savings—thus appeared to operate only in the intermediate and high ranges of output.

The results of this article differ from those of previous studies of the effect of chain ownership on nursing home costs. The differing results could be due to differences between Texas nursing homes and nursing homes in other states. For example, the mean occupancy rate of Texas nursing homes is well below the national average occupancy rate.[12] Or the differing results could stem from the fact that case mix was not thoroughly considered in this study. Another possibility is that differing methods of analysis were responsible for the differing results.

In the case of the three studies that found no effect of chain ownership on nursing home cost (Birnbaum et al. 1981; Meiners 1982; Schlenker and Shaughnessy 1984), the differences could be due to the fact that this study estimates separate regressions by ownership type rather than a common regression with a dummy variable for chain ownership. Estimating a common regression using the data for Texas nursing homes yielded the same result as the previous studies: the dummy variable for chain ownership was not statistically significant. But a test of whether or not to pool the data concluded that the appropriate technique was to estimate separate regressions for each ownership category. And that approach resulted in a different conclusion, namely, that chain ownership does affect nursing home cost, with the nature of the effect depending on the level of output.

Although the study by Arling, Nordquist, and Capitman (1987) did present results both for a common regression and for separate regressions by ownership category, the authors did not report the results of a pooling test to determine which was the appropriate estimation technique. Furthermore, the separate regressions in that study did not include a measure of output (utilization or capacity) as one of the independent variables, and thus it was not possible to compare average costs at a given level of output across ownership categories.

Reporting the results of a test of whether or not it is appropriate to pool nursing homes across ownership types when estimating a cost function therefore distinguishes this work from previous studies in this area. It is notable that the choice of estimation technique also influences conclusions about the extent of *plant-level* economies of scale. That is, in the common regression, all homes appear to have U-shaped average cost curves, while the separate regressions indicate that only chain homes exhibit plant-level economies of scale.

These results are important because they suggest that the pooling decision must be explicitly considered in attempts to describe and predict changes in nursing home costs. Researchers must determine whether or not pooling is appropriate in order to characterize accurately the nature and extent of nursing home cost differences across ownership types.

The question of whether or not to pool can also affect public reimbursement policy. Cost analysis is an important tool available to policymakers who set reimbursement rates for public patients. As Birnbaum et al. (1981) suggest, cost analysis can aid "regulatory agencies [that] wish to negotiate the lowest possible prices for nursing home services consistent with agency goals" (p. 5). This policy prescription assumes, however, that the cost analyses available for regulatory purposes accurately represent nursing home costs. Using cost estimations based on pooled data when it is not appropriate to pool could lead to reimbursement rates that have unintended, and perhaps undesirable, consequences.

When nursing home cost structures do differ significantly across ownership categories, one approach is to set different reimbursement rates for different ownership categories. In general, regulatory agencies want to obtain a given amount and quality of nursing home services for public patients at the lowest possible cost. Because nursing homes of different ownership types have different objectives and face different incentives, policymakers may set reimbursement rates according to ownership type in their effort to control costs while maintaining quality. Cost analysis can provide an accurate and systematic basis for setting differential reimbursement rates.

A different regulatory approach is to argue that reimbursement rates should not take into account differences in ownership type. For example, Birnbaum et al. (1981) found that nonprofit homes had higher costs than for-profit homes. But they argued that setting different reimbursement rates on the basis of ownership "creates incentives for either inefficiency or increased production of amenities" (p. 167). Even in this case, however, policymakers need accurate information about costs in order to predict the effects of changes in reimbursement policy on nursing homes.

For the study population of Texas nursing homes, the fact that the extent of differences in costs depends on the level of output means that the choice of Medicaid reimbursement method probably will not greatly affect the overall relative performance of chain and independent for-profit nursing homes. That is, gains for chain homes of a given size will tend to be counterbalanced by losses for chain homes of other sizes, and the net effect most likely will be no change in the overall extent of chain ownership.

The cost function parameter estimates presented in this article must be viewed in the context of a data set that covers one state in one year. A consensus about the effect of chain ownership on nursing home costs must await further research using data for other states in other years. In addition to the empirical results, however, this study has demonstrated the importance of explicitly considering whether or not to pool the data when examining the effect of ownership type on nursing home costs. Although estimating a common regression may well be appropriate for other data sets, testing for pooling before estimating a nursing home cost function would appear to be well worth the small amount of effort involved, especially given the possibility that conclusions about nursing home cost structures may depend on the choice of estimation technique.

ACKNOWLEDGMENTS

I would like to thank S. Charles Maurice, John A. Coventry, Mary E. Deily, and an anonymous reviewer for helpful comments. I am also grateful to the Texas Department of Human Resources for supplying data on nursing homes in Texas.

NOTES

1. See Arling, Nordquist, and Capitman (1987); Birnbaum et al. (1981); Bishop (1980); Meiners (1982); Palmer (1985); Ruchlin and Levey (1972); and Schlenker and Shaughnessy (1984).
2. See Note 1.
3. Changes in long-run average cost as capacity changes do not measure true economies of scale. In the case of nursing homes, therefore, economies of scale should be measured with respect to changes in output (patient days) rather than with respect to changes in capacity (beds).
4. The empirical evidence on plant-level economies of scale is somewhat mixed. The consensus, however, is that the extent of scale economies, measured with respect to changes in the number of beds, is small (see Palmer 1985).
5. Using the data set with all 955 observations would not have altered the study's conclusions.
6. Both the total number of patient days and the square of the total number of patient days are included in order to allow the average cost curve to be U-shaped with respect to output (patient days). The results change very little if the number of beds and the square of the number of beds are used instead.
7. The calculated F is $F = [(S2 - S1)/(N - 1)]/[S1/(T - 2N)]$, where $S1$ = unrestricted sum of squares (from separate regressions by ownership type); $S2$ = restricted sum of squares (from common regression with dummy variable for ownership type); N = number of ownership categories; and T = number of nursing homes (see Maddala 1977). The critical value of F (degrees of freedom are 2,820) is 4.61 at the 1 percent confidence level.
8. Using for-profit homes only, the calculated F is 29.24, and the critical value of F (degrees of freedom are 1,718) is 6.63 at the 1 percent confidence level.
9. Estimation of a common regression with ownership interaction terms for all variables, which allows both intercept and slope coefficients to vary across ownership types, yields coefficients identical to the results of the separate regressions by ownership category. The statistical significance of the coefficients varies between the common regression with interaction terms and the separate regressions, however, due to differences in degrees of freedom and, more importantly for this data set, due to high correlations among the interaction terms. The separate regressions sidestep the multicollinearity problem associated with the numerous interaction terms and thus give a clearer picture of how cost behavior varies by ownership type.
10. The results of the separate regression equations including patient days and

patient days squared for independent and nonprofit/government providers are quite similar to the results presented in Table 3.

11. The other 5 percent of for-profit homes were in certification/region categories for which chain homes had higher average costs than independent homes at all levels of output.

12. The mean occupancy rate for the study population of Texas nursing homes in 1983 was 83 percent (see Table 1). In 1982, the national average occupancy rate was 91 percent (*Vital and Health Statistics* 1986).

REFERENCES

Arling, G., R. H. Nordquist, and J. A. Capitman. "Nursing Home Cost and Ownership Type: Evidence of Interaction Effects." *Health Services Research* 22, no. 2 (June 1987):255–69.

Birnbaum, H., A. J. Lee, C. Bishop, and G. Jensen. *Public Pricing of Nursing Home Care*. Cambridge, MA: Abt Books, 1981.

Bishop, C. E. "Nursing Home Cost Studies and Reimbursement Issues." *Health Care Financing Review* 1, no. 3 (Spring 1980): 47–64.

Health Care Financing Review. "National Health Expenditures, 1986–2000." Vol. 8, no. 4 (Summer 1987): 1–36.

Maddala, G. S. *Econometrics*. New York: McGraw-Hill Book Co., 1977.

Meiners, M. R. "An Econometric Analysis of the Major Determinants of Nursing Home Costs in the United States." *Social Science and Medicine* 16, no. 8 (1982): 887–98.

Palmer, H. C. "Studies of Nursing Home Costs." In *Long-Term Care: Perspectives from Research and Demonstrations*. Edited by R. J. Vogel and H. C. Palmer. Rockville, MD: Aspen Systems Corp., 1985, pp. 665–721.

Palmer, H. C., and R. J. Vogel. "Models of the Nursing Home." *In R. J. Vogel and H. C. Palmer (eds.)* In *Long-Term CAre: Perspectives from Research and Demonstrations*. Edited by R. J. Vogel and H. C. Palmer. Rockville, MD: Aspen Systems Corp., 1985, pp. 537–78.

Ruchlin, H. S., and S. Levey. "Nursing Home Cost Analysis: A Case Study." *Inquiry* 9, no. 3 (September 1972): 3–15.

Scanlon, W. J. "A Theory of the Nursing Home Market." *Inquiry* 17, no. 1 (Spring 1980): 25–41.

Schlenker, R. E., and P. W. Shaughnessy. "Case Mix, Quality, and Cost Relationships in Colorado Nursing Homes." *Health Care Financing Review* 6, no. 2 (Winter 1984): 61–71.

Texas Department of Human Resources. "Reimbursement Methodology for Skilled Nursing Facility and Intermediate Care Facilities." Mimeograph.

Vital and Health Statistics. "Nursing and Related Care Homes as Reported from the 1982 National Master Facility Inventory Survey." Series 14, No. 32 (September 1986).

Walsh, T. J. "Patient-Related Reimbursement for Long-Term Care." In *Reform and Regulation in Long-Term Care*. Edited by V. LaPorte and J. Rubin. New York: Praeger 1979, pp. 153–67.

Article 14

Scale Economies, Capacity Utilization, and School Costs: A Comparative Analysis of Secondary and Elementary Schools

JOHN RIEW

INTRODUCTION

PAST studies of scale economies in public schools typically use the school district, rather than the individual school, as the unit of observation because various pertinent school data are more readily available for the district. In the few cases where analyses have appropriately dealt with individual schools, the focus of attention has been at the secondary level.[1] Most of the published cost analyses, moreover, relate to the sixties and the early seventies during which time schools were operating generally, at full capacity. Thus, they understandably exhibit little concern over cost implications of school under–utilization. Enrollment decline with its impact on school costs is currently a subject that commands intense interest. The present study, using a school level data base recently developed by the Montgomery County (Maryland) Public Schools, analyzes school costs under conditions of declining enrollment. Specifically, it examines separating the effects of changing school size and of capacity under–utilization on school operating costs for secondary schools and separately for elementary schools.

THE APPROACH

A cost function is sought to examine to what extent, if any, the scale and the utilization rate in school operation influence school costs. Variables considered pertinent to such a function include those which represent service quality, S, quantity or enrollment, Q, degree of school capacity utilization, U, prices of input factors, P, and environmental conditions affecting input requirements, E. Given the sets of these variables, the generalized school cost function is given by

John Riew is Professor of Economics, The Pennsylvania State University.

1. John Riew, "Economies of Scale in High School Operation," *Review of Economics and Statistics* 48 (August, 1966): 280–287; *See* also Elchanon Cohn, "Economies of Scale in Iowa High School Operations," *Journal of Human Resources* 3 (Fall, 1968): 422–434.

$$C = f (S, Q, U, P, E, e)$$

where e is a random disturbance term. The present study relies basically on an ordinary least squares regression model designed to explain the variation in the average per pupil cost as a function of the two critical variables, Q and U.

Changes in enrollment can influence the average cost per pupil through dual effects: the effects attributable to scale economies (or diseconomies) and the effects attributable to changes in capacity utilization. Much of the schools' resource inputs are in fixed physical assets and their under–utilization would result in higher overhead costs associated with these assets as well as with their maintenance and operation. This relationship between school under–utilization and costs exists regardless of whether the school is large or small. In so far as changing enrollment brings about changes in capacity utilization and in the size of school operations, the cost impact of changing enrollment ought to be analyzed in the context of changes in both the utilization rate and the operational scale.

Economies of scale may be achieved through teacher specialization (which a larger enrollment permits) and resulting improvements in instructional efficiency. Also, more economic meshing of the personnel assignments (classroom teachers, professional support staff, administrators, and clerical, custodial, and others) can be achieved more readily with a larger enrollment.[2] Such advantages also will apply to uses of various instructional equipment. Furthermore, with larger schools, the cost of procurement and maintenance of larger capacity equipment is proportionately less than for smaller capacity equipment. Similar advantages also apply to the cost of purchasing and handling larger quantities of supplies.

Basically, when we speak of economies or optimal school size, we envisage an average cost curve in a long run in which all inputs are variable (the optimal size being its minimum point). When we refer to the utilization rate and its relationship to cost,

---

2. Assume that a school counselor of Type A typically handles 300 pupils and that a counselor of type B can serve 450 pupils. An increase in enrollment from 600 to 900 will lower the average per pupil cost by enabling full utilization of each counselor employed. The larger the enrollment the lesser would be the likely under–utilization of school resources. This illustration points to an interesting point; whether a given cost saving should be attributed to scale economies or to a change in utilization rates is not always apparent. The cost saving in the above case comes from *full utilization* of Type B counselor as a result of enrollment increase, a *rise in the scale of operation*. This confusion can be resolved by relating economies of scale to a long run context in which all inputs are variable, while referring economies of full utilization to a short run in which some inputs, such as classrooms, gymnasiums, and laboratories are fixed.

we think of a school with a given enrollment capacity and consider the utilization rate cost relationship in a short run context. A severe under–utilization of facilities, such as school buildings that are fixed in the short run, can cause the short run average costs to lie substantially above the long run average cost.

The school quality variables may include such items as teacher qualifications, the breadth of school curriculum, and the professional support staff. What we refer to as the environmental variables may include such factors as population density or rural/urban differences expected to affect the cost of pupil transportation, local living costs that may influence factor prices, such as staff salaries, or certain socio–demographic aspects that could have a bearing on the level of remedial programs and other special education activities. The larger and the more heterogeneous the area under study, the greater will be the need for a more thorough examination of educational quality and other cost relevant variables.

The separate analyses of elementary and secondary schools become necessary because these two levels of schools operate differently with respect to instructional specialization, the level of facilities, and the nature and breadth of curriculum. Hence, they should be treated as two distinct enterprises; their combined treatment will result in possible mixing of two dissimilar tendencies.

DATA AND VARIABLES

Mainly for reasons of data availability, the Montgomery County Public Schools (MCPS) of Maryland have been chosen for empirical analysis. A wide range of data for individual schools, secondary as well as elementary, are available on school facilities, staff and student characteristics, and on various components of operating costs. In the academic year 1978–79, the period covering these data, enrollment decline already had become a serious problem for elementary and junior high schools while senior high schools remained relatively unaffected. The demographic bulge associated with the children of parents who were part of the World War II "baby boom" was yet to pass through the senior high level of the public school system. Since the present interest is in analyzing school costs under conditions of declining enrollment, attention is focused on the elementary and middle level (junior high, grades 7–9, and middle, grades 6–8) schools.

As of September 1978, there were twenty–nine middle level schools with enrollments ranging from 561 to 1,306, with a median of 825 (Table 1). The utilization rates among these schools ranged from 49 percent to 108 percent.[3] Thirteen schools, or nearly half the total, were operating at less than 75 percent of capacity enrollment.

By contrast, elementary schools were generally smaller with enrollments varying from 142 to 720 and operating at generally lower utilization rates ranging from 35 percent to 95 percent. Of 126 elementary schools, more than two thirds were operating at less than 75 percent of capacity. As many as thirtysix schools were operating at less than 60 percent of capacity.

The regression analysis that follows was undertaken for the twenty–nine middle level schools and separately for the 126 elementary schools. School expenditure figures used here refer to operating items only; capital outlays that vary widely over the years are not included. The operating items include: (1) salaries for classroom teachers, professional support staff (reading specialists, counselors, resource teachers, language specialists, librarians), and instructional aides; and (2) costs of administration, operations (utilities including fuel, electricity, water and telephone) and maintenance (mainly staff salaries for maintenance of property and equipment). For the public schools as a whole, these items in 1978–79 comprised 77.4 percent of total operating expenditures.[4]

Educational standards and rules governing such matters as curriculum and pupil/teacher ratio are fairly uniform among schools at each level in the county.[5] Under the circumstances, the importance of controlling for quality differences among schools becomes less critical. This was especially true for middle level schools among which only moderate variations were observed in such areas as teacher qualifications as measured by training and experience. Among elementary schools, the more notable differences existed in the provision of services of professional support staff and teacher aides. Montgomery County is a relatively small area with only minor variations in socio–economic background,

---

3. The utilization ratio is derived by dividing actual enrollment by capacity enrollment, the latter as determined by the Planning Department of MCPS based primarily on classroom capacities.

4. *Operating Budget Request*, vol. II, Fiscal Year Ending June 30, 1980, Montgomery County Public Schools, December 14, 1978, pp. C1–C14 and pp. D1–D4.

5. The pupil/teacher ratios (teachers defined as regular classroom teachers only) are mandated by the school district for middle level schools as well as elementary schools. These district mandated pupil/teacher ratios are strictly adhered to and there is little variation in such ratios, among individual schools. Under the circumstances, inclusion of the pupil/teacher ratio as a school quality variable becomes largely meaningless.

TABLE 1

STATISTICS OF ENROLLMENT AND THE UTILIZATION RATES AMONG MIDDLE LEVEL AND ELEMENTARY SCHOOLS IN MONTGOMERY COUNTY PUBLIC SCHOOLS, 1978–79.

| | No. of Schools (1) | ENROLLMENT | | | UTILIZATION (in percent) | | |
		Range (2)	Mean (Median) (3)	Standard Deviation (4)	Range (5)	Mean (Median) (6)	Standard Deviation (7)
Junior High, Middle Schools	29	561–1,306	846 (825)	167	49–108	79.4 (79.9)	15.7
Elementary Schools	126	142–720	394 (385)	128	35–93	68.7 (69.2)	14.0

Sources: Computed from the data available in *Statistical Profiles*, 1978–79, Department of Educational Accountability, Montgomery County Public Schools, Rockville, Maryland, April 1979 and from the statistical files of MCPS.

and this fact tended to minimize the difference in exogenous influences on educational input requirement. Upon examination of various factors considered pertinent to school costs, regression models were developed to estimate the per pupil operating costs in the elementary and the secondary (the middle level) schools. The variables which enter into the regression equations include:

C_p = Operating expenditures per pupil, measured in dollars.

ENR = Enrollment (number of pupils enrolled as of September 1978).

UTL = Utilization rate, the actual enrollment as ratio of the capacity enrollment measured in percentage points.

TR = Teacher training, measured by teachers with masters degree plus thirty or more credits as percent of total classroom teachers.

EXP = Teacher experience, measured by number of teachers with seven years or more of classroom experiences as percent of all classroom teachers.

PROF = Professional support staff, expressed as ratio of the number of support staff to the number of regular classroom teachers.

AIDE = Teacher aides, expressed as ratio of the number of aides to the number of regular classroom teachers.

By regressing C_p on the explanatory variables under alternative formulations, the relationship between each of the chosen variables and the behavior of school costs could be examined.

EMPIRICAL RESULTS

THE SECONDARY LEVEL

For the secondary schools, a parabolic relationship was assumed between per pupil cost and enrollment in view of the similar results indicated by earlier studies for senior high schools.[6]

---

6. The term, per pupil cost, henceforth, will be used interchangeably with per pupil expenditures. Some may object to this, arguing that the data used in the regression equations do not reflect technically efficient conditions (Michaelson 1972). However, the idea that the cost that enters into a cost function should not be the actual cost, but some idealized version thereof under truly efficient management, is dubious and non–operational. The "relevant" cost is the one actual producers come out with, not some engineering device that ignores the human dimension. Thus, what we are interested in is the cost relationship that prevails under the existing production processes exhibited by actual

The relationships between the cost and other variables were all assumed linear. The interaction term (ENR•UTL) included in our regression equations was, in all instances, shown to be statistically not significant and was eliminated as an explanatory variable. The most preferred estimation equation, shown in column 1, Table 2, has an adjusted R^2 of .418 and is highly significant at a probability level of .01. Thus, about 42 percent of the variation in average per pupil expenditures among the twenty–nine middle level schools in 1978–79 was accounted for by the four independent variables of which enrollment and utilization rate were statistically significant at the .05 and .20 levels, respectively (the marginal significance level for the UTL variable is .12, two–tailed test). The parabolic relationship between cost and enrollment is consistent with the findings of previous studies of individual high schools.[7]

The regression equation suggests that an enrollment increase of one pupil, holding the other variables constant, lowers average per pupil operating expenditures by [2.243 − 2(.001095 ENR)] dollars at a given level of ENR until ENR finally reaches 1,024.[8] The U–shaped average cost curve implied here reflects the use of a parabola in the estimation equation. Thus, a school with 600 pupils, for instance, if it behaves in "average fashion," will see its per pupil operating expenditures falling by 92.9 cents by having one more pupil. For a school with 800 pupils, adding one pupil reduces per pupil expenditures by 49.1 cents and for one with 900 pupils, 27.1 cents. That there are scale diseconomies beyond the enrollment of 1,024, implicit in the parabolic specification for the ENR variable, seemed somewhat questionable when a rectangular hyperbola replacing the parabola also gave a good fit to the date (equation 2, Table 2), yielding high t ratio (showing statistical significance at the .05 level) and R^2 of .396 (only moderately below the .418 obtained with the parabolic function). This suggests that the basis for specifying an upper limit to the optimal school size is not so strong within the range of the MCPS data.

Based on equation 1, Table 2, preferred over equation 2 in view of its higher R^2, an increase in enrollment of a school from

---

educational planners. What happens to the cost relationship when educational administrators adopt new policies or practices for political, pedagogic, or economic reasons is another matter; *see* Stephen Michelson, "Equal School Resource Allocation," *Journal of Human Resources* 7 (Summer, 1972): 283–306.

7. *See* Riew *op. cit.* and Cohn *op. cit.*

8. From equation 1, Table 2, $\partial C_p/\partial(ENR) = -2.243 + 2[.001095(ENR)]$. Thus, when $\partial C_p/\partial(ENR) = 0$, (ENR) = 2.243/.00219 = 1024.2.

TABLE 2
REGRESSION RESULTS OF SCHOOL COST EQUATIONS.

Explanatory Variables	Per Pupil Operating Costs					
	Middle Level Schools			Elementary Schools		
	(1)	(2)	(3)	(4)	(5)	(6)
Constant	2904.332	1398.30	2493.49	801.075	1217.956	1179.028
ENR	−2.243		−2.162			−.488
	(2.51)		(2.375)			(2.887)
$(ENR)^2$	.001095		.001025			
	(2.22)		(2.059)			
$\dfrac{1}{ENR}$		276292.6		69272.12	70644.79	
		(2.436)		(3.313)	(3.297)	
UTL	−2.770	−1.965			−3.043	
	(1.56)	(1.149)			(2.016)	
$\dfrac{1}{UTL}$			125.22	14510.77		14352.17
			(1.419)	(2.427)		(2.318)
TR	−2.227	−1.924	−1.911	.994	1.070	1.238
	(.61)	(.515)	(.517)	(.541)	(.577)	(.668)
EXP	3.208	3.476	3.159	.212	.189	.248
	(1.19)	(1.271)	(1.161)	(.255)	(.226)	(.295)
PROF				5.765	6.237	5.572
				(4.082)	(4.522)	(3.910)
AIDE				3.591	3.582	3.859
				(3.662)	(3.623)	(3.954)
R^2	.418	.396	.408	.517	.510	.507
F	5.820	5.589	4.862	23.340	22.719	22.463

(t values in parentheses)

600 to 800, with the other independent variables held constant, would allow the school a savings of \$142 in the average per pupil operating expenditures.[9] In addition, if this increase in enrollment also meant a rise in the utilization rate, say, from 60 percent to 80 percent (assuming that the school's capacity enrollment is 1,000), there will be a further reduction in the per pupil expenditures of \$55.40 (= −2.770(80−60) from equation 1, Table 2) for this school; thus, adding 200 pupils to its enrollment will bring about a reduction in per pupil operating expenditures by a combined sum of \$197.

As for teacher training or teacher experience, neither variable is shown to have a statistically significant relationship with the cost. This is not surprising in view of the fairly uniform standards on teacher qualifications which apply to all schools within the district.

---

9. $\Delta C_p = [-2.243(800) + .001095(800^2)] - [-2.243(600)] + .001095(600^2)] = 142.00$

Examining the elementary level cost functions, we note that the results are considerably different from those of the secondary schools. In the school size/cost relationship as well as in the utilization rate/cost relationship, a hyperbolic function gave the best fit to the data among all alternative functions (equation 4–6, Table 2). As for the other variables, a linear function was found to be appropriate. The interaction term (ENR•UTL) included in the regression equations, as was the case for the secondary schools, was shown to be statistically not significant. Thus, equation 4, the preferred estimation equation, has an R^2 of .57, highly significant at the .01 level. Of the six explanatory variables, both enrollment and utilization rate are statistically significant at the .01 level. It should be noted, also, that the professional support staff and teacher aide variables are very significant cost factors in the elementary school system. Among the secondary schools, neither of these variables were found to influence per pupil costs.

At the elementary level, according to equation 4, Table 2, an enrollment increase of one pupil, holding other variables constant, could be expected to lower the average per pupil operating expenditure by 69272.12 $(ENR)^{-2}$ at any given level of ENR.[10] Thus, for an elementary school with 200 pupils, for instance, the marginal addition to enrollment will bring about a reduction of per pupil expenditures by $1.73. For a larger school with 300 pupils, adding one pupil will reduce per pupil expenditures by 77.0 cents, and for schools with 400 and 600 pupils the expected fall in the average expenditures will be 43.3 and 19.2 cents, respectively (Table 3). The smaller the enrollment of a school, the greater the cost advantage per unit increase in enrollment. This is an important aspect of scale economies which applies to both elementary and secondary schools. An increase in elementary school enrollment from 300 to 500, with all other independent variables held constant, would mean a savings of $92 in per pupil costs;[11] if the enrollment rises by the same number at a higher level of enrollment, say, from 400 to 600, the fall in per pupil costs would be substantially less, $57.

Again, when a school with a given enrollment capacity experiences a change in enrollment, this also entails a change in the utilization rate. Thus, if, for a school that has a capacity of 600

---

10. From equation 4, Table 2. $\partial C_p / \partial (ENR) = -69272.12 \, (ENR)^{-2}$.
11. From equation 4, Table 2. $\Delta C_p = 69272.12 \, (1/300 - 1/500) = 92.34$.

TABLE 3

SCALE ECONOMIES EFFECTS OF MARGINAL ENROLLMENT INCREASES

Current Enrollment	Changes in Per Pupil and Total Operating Costs			
	Middle Level Schools		Elementary Schools	
	Per Pupil (1)	Total[a] (2)	Per Pupil (3)	Total[a] (4)
200			−$1.73	$346
300			−.77	−231
400			−.43	−172
500			−.28	−140
600	−$.93	−$558	−.19	−114
700	−.71	−497	−.14	−98
800	−.49	−432		
900	−.27	−243		
1000	−.05	−50		

[a]The figures are derived by multiplying the per pupil cost changes into current enrollment at each enrollment level.

Source: Computed from Equations 1 and 4 of Table 2.

pupils, the enrollment rises from 300 to 500, with the resulting increase in the utilization rate from 50 percent to 83.3 percent, this will engender the combination of the scale effect ($92) and the effect of the rise in utilization rate ($116), leading to a reduction in per pupil operating expenditure by a total sum of $208.[12]

THE COMPARISON

Examination of Table 3 reveals that the levels of enrollment over which scale economies take effect are higher for secondary schools than for elementary schools. While, as was noted, scale economies are more significant at lower levels of enrollment, becoming increasingly less important as enrollment rises, it is not until secondary school enrollment reaches the high level of 900 that the decrease in per pupil costs from marginal enrollment increases becomes a low 27.0 cents (column 3, Table 3). For elementary schools, the per pupil costs reduction of such trivial amount occurs at the much lower enrollment of 500. At the secondary level, the greatest cost saving from scale economies, as measured by reduction in per pupil costs from marginal enrollment increases, occurs over the enrollment range of 600–800. By contrast, the corresponding range at the elementary level is 200–

12. From equation 4, Table 2. ΔC_p = 14510.77/50 − 14510.77/83.3 = 116.02.

400. Measured more appropriately by the total cost effect of marginal enrollment increases (columns 2 and 4, Table 3), the greatest scale economies exist over the enrollment range of 600–900 for secondary schools and over the lower and narrower range of 200–300 for elementary schools. To explain such differences, consider that for secondary schools, with their more specialized instructional staff, other professional support personnel, and the more varied programs, the efficient operation would require a larger pool of students.[13]

The data presented in Table 3 reveal still another important aspect of scale economies. The magnitudes of the expected cost savings from increases in the operational scale are significantly larger for secondary schools than for elementary schools over most of the relevant enrollment ranges. With the marginal addition to enrollment in secondary schools of 600, 700, and 800, for instance, the expected costs reductions will be $558, $497, and $432, respectively, whereas for elementary schools of 200, 300, and 400, the cost effects of the marginal enrollment increase will be, respectively, $346, $271 and $172 (columns 2 and 4, Table 3). Alternatively, a small elementary school with current enrollment of 200, with an enrollment increase of 100, can expect a reduction in per pupil cost of $113.79 and, thus, a total cost reduction of $22,758 for the 200 pupils currently enrolled. By comparison, a relatively small secondary school of 600 pupils, by adding 100 to its enrollment, can expect a much larger costs saving of $49,170 (= 87.96 × 600) for their 600 pupils. The net costs involving the incoming 100 pupils in each case will, of course, depend on the cost structure(s) of the schools(s) from which they come, relative to the cost structure of the receiving school(s).

Increases in enrollment are cost saving over most of the enrollment ranges for both the secondary and elementary schools. But, the cost saving, as it relates to the secondary schools, comes more significantly from the effect of scale economies than from the effect of increases in utilization rates. If enrollment rises by 200 from 600 to 800 for a secondary school with enrollment capacity of 1,000, the expected fall in per pupil cost from the scale effect (from equation 1, Table 2) is $145; this compares with a much smaller $55 attributable to the rise in utilization rates. If enroll-

---

13. Had senior high schools been included in this analysis, scale economies most likely would have been shown to occur over even higher ranges of enrollment than for the middle level schools since among senior high schools the degrees of specialization in instruction and other professional support programs are even greater; see Riew *op. cit.* and Cohn, *op. cit.*

ment increase occurs at a higher level, from 700 to 900, the corresponding reductions in per pupil cost will be \$98 and \$55, respectively, the scale effect still exceeding the effect of capacity utilization. It should be noted that the UTL–cost relationship specified in a hyperbola (equation 3, Table 2) does not fit the data as well as in a linear specification (of equation 1, Table 2), but is statistically significant at the .20 level.[14] This seems to suggest that over higher ranges of utilization rates, the actual cost saving from an increase in the utilization rate is smaller than indicated in the linear specification.[15]

The cost savings from scale economies are significant at the elementary level also, but here the effects of capacity utilization are larger than the scale effects. If enrollment rises by 200, from 300 to 500, for an elementary school with a capacity enrollment of 600, the per pupil cost will fall by \$116, attributable to the change in utilization rate, and by a smaller amount of \$92 through scale economies. If, instead, the enrollment rises from 400 to 600, the corresponding reductions in per pupil costs will be \$77 and \$57, respectively, the capacity utilization effect still exceeding the scale effect. As was with scale economies, it is important to note that at the elementary level the cost savings from changes in capacity utilization are the greater the lower the existing rates of utilization.

A NOTE ON DATA

The precise nature of the utilization rate/cost relationship should be examined in the context of how school capacity is defined and what is included in the cost. As for the former, the MCPS definition was followed, whereby the capacity is tied closely to classroom capacities. In addition to classrooms, one could argue, such other facilities as gymnasiums, laboratories, and workshops should also be considered as determinants of school capacity. It is assumed that their provisions vary generally in proportion to classroom capacities. Costs in this study do not include

---

14. That the utilization rate/cost relationship at the secondary level is shown to be generally precarious (as seen by lower t statistics in equation 1 – 3, Table 2) is difficult to understand intuitively; it may be explained in part by the fact that as of the late seventies (the period covered by the data) the severity of under–utilization was not so great among secondary schools as among elementary schools and perhaps, also by the relatively small number of secondary schools included in this analysis.

15. Thus, with the enrollment increase from 700 to 900 for the secondary school cited above, the actual difference between its scale effect and capacity use effect may be larger than indicated by the figures presented (\$98 vs. \$55).

capital outlays, which vary widely over the years, although the associated personnel costs (for upkeep, repairs, operation, security, etc., of the physical facilities) and utilities costs (for fuel, electricity, water, etc.,) are all included. The greater the under–utilization of the schools' physical facilities, the larger would be the overhead of these associated costs. Had capital outlays been included in the costs, the observed utilization rate/cost relationship would have been more pronounced.

Inclusion of capital outlays would have similarly enhanced the observed size/cost relationship, i.e., the scale effect. The physical education program and the library, for instance, require many provisions for a school of any size. The same can be said, especially at the secondary level, of various provisions for science laboratories, language, music, and vocational training. For these items, larger schools would incur lower overhead costs.

The failure to include transportation costs, on the other hand, would entail a bias toward overstating scale economies. Such a bias, however, is likely to be relatively small in view of the fact that Montgomery County is largely a residential suburb and differences in the distance traveled by school bus are relatively small among schools of different sizes. Whereas in sparsely populated rural districts, school transportation costs are more substantial, these costs will have to be taken into account more explicitly in an overall cost–efficiency analysis.

SUMMARY AND CONCLUSION

The massive enrollment decline witnessed during the seventies and continuing into the eighties adds a new element to concern over school costs. Decline in school population and under–utilization of school resources have been relatively new experiences for America's public schools and the precise nature of their cost implications are yet to be fully understood.

Rational school planning, as it relates to costs, requires a clear understanding of scale economies and, in the present context, a knowledge of the cost impact of capacity under–utilization. An accurate picture of the long run average cost curve, the essence of scale economies, can be obtained when we can ascertain the short run influences of the deepening under use of school resources.

The present paper attempts to provide separate accounts of scale and capacity utilization effects, by level of schools. The study suggests that significant scale economies exist at elementary as well as at secondary levels. It suggest further that: (1) the ranges of enrollment over which scale economies occur differ greatly between school levels, the economies extending over higher and wider ranges of enrollment for the secondary schools; (2) within the relevant ranges of enrollment larger scale economies occur over the lower portion of the ranges, this being the case at both levels of schools; and (3) scale economies, in terms of saved costs per unit increase in school size, generally are much larger at the secondary level than at the elementary level.

Unit costs in capital outlays and associated operating expenses rise as the schools' fixed facilities are subject to under–utilization. This is intuitively apparent and, indeed, at the elementary level, the cost effect of changes in capacity utilization is shown to exceed the scale effect. At the secondary level, the utilization rate/cost relationship does not exhibit the robustness observed at the elementary level; yet, it appears that at this level also the capacity utilization effect is substantial, though far outweighed by the scale effect. The efficient operation of secondary schools, with their specialized instructional staff, other professional support personnel, and their more varied programs, may require a larger pool of students. And this may explain the dominance of the scale economies effect over the capacity utilization effect at the secondary level.

Presence of scale economies and cost advantages of higher capacity use point to the merits of minimizing enrollment loss to the schools that remain in operation. Advantages of keeping enrollment losses to minimum, this study suggests, are especially important for secondary schools. Thus, in pursuit of cost efficiency, certain school reorganization including changes in grade configuration among levels of schools, or school consolidation must become part of the viable options. In this connection, moving from the traditional three year senior high school to a four year high school (the action already taken by some school jurisdictions) with, perhaps, simultaneous transfer of the sixth graders from elementary to junior high schools, may be one way to help achieve the cost efficiency objective. Granted that these changes, especially those involving school closures, may adversely affect some members of the communities, however, the costs of inaction certainly seem significant enough and ought to be made known among the taxpayer-voters and the school authorities.

Article 15

Financial Restraint in the Free Agent Labor Market for Major League Baseball: Players Look at Strike Three*

THOMAS H. BRUGGINK
Lafayette College
Easton, Pennsylvania

DAVID R. ROSE, JR.
Manufacturers Hanover Trust
New York City

Professional baseball has provided economists with a wealth of issues and data over the years. Research in this area has been particularly productive because the pay and marginal revenue products of the players are easily measured. The principal issues have been salaries, the player pension fund, and the negotiating opportunities of players who are classified as free agents. In this study we examine the salary consequences of the baseball owners' boycott of the free agents market for players following the 1985 and 1986 seasons.

In 1987 baseball arbitrator Thomas Roberts ruled that baseball team owners had violated baseball's Basic Agreement by colluding in the free agent market for baseball players. The owners, in an effort to exercise financial restraint, did not bid on eligible free agents after the 1985 season (unless the former team was no longer interested in the player). In 1988 baseball arbitrator George Nicolau ruled that the owners once again boycotted the free agent market following the 1986 season.

These historic decisions raise more questions than they answer. What were the salary consequences for the involved players? What remedies should be forthcoming? What does this decision do to the status of owner-player negotiations in view of the fact that there have already been two player strikes in the past decade? This study will attempt to shed light on the first question. In particular, the salary consequences for affected free agents will be measured in an effort to estimate the economic consequences associated with the owners' financial restraint. The financial restraint hypothesis is that owners paid free agents lower salaries during the two collusion years than the players would have earned in the absence of collusion.

Following a very short discussion on the free agent market in section I, we introduce the Scully two equation model [14] in section II to measure marginal revenue products (MRP) of players. In section III we provide the regression results and the salary/MRP comparisons before and after the alleged collusion. Our conclusions are presented in section IV.

*The authors thank the following persons for the helpful comments made on earlier versions of this manuscript: Robert Higgs, Michael Connell, and Alan Childs of Lafayette College, and an anonymous referee of this journal.

I. Background Issues

For decades major league baseball owner negotiations with their players were guided by the reserve clause. Under this clause in the Basic Agreement, players could not move freely from team to team. Movement of players occurred only if they were traded for one or more players from another team or their contracts were purchased by the receiving club. With players having very little bargaining power over their salaries, owners had a profit incentive to pay players less than their economic contributions to team revenue. This monopsonistic exploitation, statistically measured by several economists [14; 9; 13], was made possible by the exclusive rights that the teams had on their players.

In 1975 the reserve clause was overturned by a baseball arbitrator, and the era of free agency began with star players Andy Messersmith and Jim "Catfish" Hunter. A free agent is a player who has at least six years of experience and is not currently under contract with a team. He declares himself a free agent during the off-season and all teams may competitively bid for his services (including his old team). Free agents include premier players who feel they are being grossly underpaid, ordinary players hoping to enhance their salaries, and players in the twilight of their career who are resisting the lowering of their once lofty salaries.

As the result of the auction bidding mechanism used in the free agent market, the free agents were able to obtain salaries *in excess* of their marginal revenue products, [3; 12]. Furthermore, the players who were eligible for free agency but did not declare also saw their salaries go up because their bargaining positions were strengthened by the high salaries of comparable free agents [17; 12; 6]. However, the non-free agent players, even after the negotiating power provided indirectly by free agency and salary arbitration, still continued to receive less then their economic value to the team, although the rate of monopsonistic exploitation had decreased [8].

With the advent of free agency, salaries of *all* baseball players rose dramatically, from an average of $51,501 in 1976 to $143,765 in 1980, and up to $438,779 in 1988 according to Major League Baseball Player Association statistics [18]. As salaries were rising, the reported profits of the baseball clubs fell. A collective loss of $43 million was announced in 1983 [18]. In 1984, twenty-one of the twenty-six teams claimed they were losing money [6]. In an effort to improve the baseball clubs' financial conditions, Peter Uberroth, the newly appointed baseball commissioner, admonished the owners for participating in the free agent market and urged them to strengthen their teams by developing new players from the minor leagues.

In response, the owners largely abstained from the free agent market following the 1985 and 1986 seasons. This led to a grievance filing by the Major League Baseball Players Association. On September 21, 1987, arbitrator Thomas Roberts ruled that the major league owners had colluded in the free agent market by not bidding for the free agents. This violated Article XVIII of the Basic Agreements (negotiated by both parties in 1976), which prohibits clubs from acting in concert with other clubs.[1] A ruling on a similar grievance filed on behalf of the 1986 group was reached on August 31, 1988, also in favor of the players.

In summary, it is apparent that before free agency, players received salaries substantially

---

1. Article XVIII of the basic agreements establishes a system of free agency to eligible members of the bargaining unit. Paragraph H reads:

The utilization or non-utilization of rights under this Article XVIII is an individual matter to be determined solely by each Player and each Club for his or its own benefit. Players shall not act in concert with other Players and Clubs shall not act in concert with other Clubs.

below their net contribution to team revenues. Since the advent of free agency, however, free agent players received salaries at or above their economic value while players not eligible for free agency continued to be exploited, albeit to a lesser degree. The remaining issue now is whether the recent efforts by team management to refrain from bidding for free agents has resulted in a lowering of free agents' salaries compared to their respective contribution to team revenues.

II. Methodology

This study will estimate the marginal revenue product of free agents in 1984, the last season before the owners' alleged collusion, and in 1985 and 1986, the two years in which the Major League Baseball Players Association filed grievances on behalf of the free agents. If the owners exercised financial restraint, the salary/MRP ratios for the 1985–86 groups will be lower than that of the 1984 group. A lower average ratio in 1985–86 is consistent with the financial restraint hypothesis and the charges of collusion.

Measurement of marginal revenue products for free agent players will be based on the standard work in this area: the Scully model. In his classic study on monopsony exploitation before the free agency era, Gerald Scully developed the first methodology that estimated marginal revenue products for various skill levels of players [14]. In particular, he formulated a two-equation regression model from which individual player MRP's can be derived.

The first equation related a team's winning percentage to a variety of hitting and pitching performance variables. The second equation relates team revenue to the team's winning percentage and to the specific characteristics of the team's market area. A player's estimated MRP is derived from the results of these two equations.

There are a few limitations to this model, however. First, the underlying assumption of this model is that fans go to baseball games to see *teams* play, not to see specific players play. Second, Scully's choice of player performance variables is somewhat arbitrary. Third, he assumes that team performance is merely the summation of individual performances. Despite these problems, his methodology nevertheless has become *the* standard model for all subsequent works on the measurement of MRP [19; 13; 3; 17; 12; 6].

The first equation is a team production function with its output being the team's winning percentage. This is regressed upon a number of different team inputs. The first set of inputs is hitting and pitching performance indicators. There are many measures of hitting and pitching performance that could have been used. For hitting, indicators that could have been used include batting average, slugging percentage (total bases divided by at bats), and total runs scored. For pitching, earned run average and the strikeout-to-walk ratio provide good measures of performance.[2] Following Scully's model, team slugging percentage and team strikeout-to-walk ratio were chosen as the performance indicators. Team slugging average is found by dividing the team's total bases for the season by the team at bats. The team strikeout-to-walk ratio is measured by dividing total

2. Team slugging percentage is chosen as the principal performance indicator for hitting and team strikeout to walk ratio is chosen as the principal performance indicator for pitching. Both are based on an earlier study [15] and affirmed by our own preliminary work. It is not surprising that these variables work well. Although team batting averages, doubles, triples, and homeruns are recorded weekly by the newspapers, the slugging average takes all of these into account with one statistic. With the strikeout to walk ratio the pitcher's ability to dominate the hitters is balanced against his control over the strike zone. The strikeout to walk ratio is therefore independent of the team's on-the-field performance, and thus it does the best in uniquely measuring pitching ability.

strikeouts by the pitching staff for the season by the number of walks. These team measures are divided by their respective league averages in order to yield a more relative measure of hitting and pitching performance for each team.

Performance variables measuring speed and defense have been found in other studies to be insignificant predictors of winning percentage [15]. Therefore, variables measuring these attributes will not be included in the first equation. On the other hand, measures of team intensity have been found to be instrumental in the determination of winning percentage. The variables *CONT* and *OUT* are used to capture the intensity or lack of intensity that would be expected at the end of the season when it is still in contention or out of the pennant race. The dummy variable *CONT* is equal to one of a team finishes the season as champion of its division or five or less games out of first place. *OUT* is equal to one if a team is twenty games or more out of first place at the end of the season.[3] Teams in contention would be expected to play with more intensity via greater baserunning and defensive efforts, and are more active in the acquisition of experienced players who can fill specialized roles such as pinchhitting or relief pitching. Teams in contention will acquire these players even if late season roster deadlines for playoff eligibility prevent these players from participating in the playoffs. Teams out of contention would be expected to play with lesser intensity when they bring up minor league players, give starts to inexperienced pitchers, and let players experiment at different field positions.

Therefore, the specification of the winning percentage equation is:

$$PCTWIN = a_1 + a_2TSA + a_3TSW + a_4CONT + a_5OUT + e_1 \qquad (1)$$

where

$PCTWIN$ = Team winning percentage
TSA = Team slugging average divided by league slugging average
TSW = Team strikeout-to-walk ratio divided by league strikeout-to-walk ratio
$CONT$ = Contention dummy variable = 1 if team is less than 6 games out of 1st place; 0 otherwise
OUT = Out of contention dummy variable = 1 if team is 20 or more out of 1st place; 0 otherwise
e_1 = random disturbance term.

The second equation relates team revenue to a number of market characteristics as well as the team's won-loss percentage. Revenue will be defined as attendance revenue (home attendance multiplied by the team's average ticket price, split 80%/20% between home and visiting teams), plus broadcasting revenue (local rights plus the national rights, which are divided equally among all 26 teams), plus concession revenue (home attendance multiplied by estimated per-capita concession sales).

Besides winning percentage, there are many other variables that can explain the magnitude of a team's revenue, namely those determining a team's attendance and consequently its revenue. Therefore, a variable is included that measures the population of each metropolitan statistical area

3. It has been observed by others using the Scully model that these two dummy variables appear to be disguised versions of the dependent variable [17]. However, the correlation coefficient between *PCTWIN* and *CONT* is .67 and between *PCTWIN* and *OUT* is −.65. These moderately sized correlations suggest that they are not exactly disguised versions of *PCTWIN* in this study.

(MSA) where a major league ball club is located. Because Scully argued that baseball fans would rather go to see a game in a new ball park than in an older stadium, a dummy variable for stadiums built before World War II and not renovated since then is also included. Scully also included a variable in his second equation that measured the difference in the intensity of fan interest. This variable had almost a negligible effect upon team revenue and will not be included in this regression. However, a dummy variable will be included that identifies the four metropolitan areas that have *two* major league teams. Having a second team present in the same metropolitan area will decrease the revenues of both teams, *ceteris paribus*.

Therefore, the specification of the revenue equation is:

$$REVENUE = b_1 + b_2PCTWIN + b_3SMSA + b_4STD + b_5TWOTM + e_2 \qquad (2)$$

where

$REVENUE =$ Team revenue from attendance (attendance × average ticket price), broadcasting and concessions (attendance × per-capita concession revenue)

$PCTWIN =$ Team winning percentage

$SMSA =$ Size of the metropolitan area

$STD =$ Old stadium dummy variable

$TWOTM =$ Two teams in metropolitan area dummy variable

$e_2 =$ Random disturbance term.

Estimation of an individual hitter's MRP is calculated by taking his own slugging average, multiplying it by his percentage of the team's at bats, dividing that product by the league average for team slugging, and then multiplying that result by the appropriate coefficients in equations (1) and (2). The individual hitter's MRP is:

$$MRP_{hitter} = (a_2 \times \text{Individual } SA \times \text{Individual \% of team at bats} \times b_2)/\text{league } TSA \qquad (3)$$

where Individual SA = slugging average (total bases/at bats) of a particular player, and at bats includes walks.

Estimation of an individual pitcher's MRP is calculated by multiplying his individual strikeout-to-walk ratio by his share of team innings pitched, dividing that total by the league TSW, and then multiplying that result by the appropriate coefficients in equations (1) and (2). The figures that are calculated are to be treated as gross MRP estimates. The individual pitcher's MRP is:

$$MRP_{pitcher} = (a_3 \times \text{Individual } SW \times \text{Individual \% of teams innings pitched}$$
$$\times b_2)/\text{league } TSW \qquad (4)$$

where Individual SW = strikeout-to-walk ratio of a particular pitcher.

In order to estimate *net* MRP's for players, it would be necessary to subtract player development costs from the gross MRP players. However, player costs are difficult to obtain and in earlier studies were arbitrarily estimated as a *constant* for all players. Due to these data limitations, Somers and Quinton did not subtract player costs from their MRP estimates when they were studying the performance of the first group of free agents [17]. In this study, the financial

Table I: Winning Percentage Equation

Y = *PCTWIN* = Team winning percentage (100% = 1000)
X_2 = *TSA* = Team slugging average divided by league slugging average
X_3 = *TSW* = Team strikeout-to-walk ratio divided by league strikeout-to-walk ratio
X_4 = *CONT* = In contention dummy variable
X_5 = *OUT* = Out of contention dummy variable
e_1 = Random disturbance term

(t-ratios in parentheses)

$$PCTWIN = 3.30 + 426.19TSA + 72.47TSW + 63.54CONT - 50.10OUT + e_1$$
$$\quad\;\; (0.04) \quad (4.80) \qquad (2.20) \qquad (6.10) \qquad (-5.42)$$

standard error = 34.04   (Mean of *PCTWIN* = 500)
Adjusted R^2 = 72.8%
F-statistic = 52.43
DF = 73

restraint hypothesis will be tested using gross MRP's since the test statistic relies on difference on the salary/MRP ratios, and not the magnitude of the MRP estimates.

The next step will be to obtain salaries for all free agents in the year after their free agency. Salaries will be defined as including all incentive bonuses paid out to the free agents as well as their salaries. Free agents who participated in less than *one* percent of their team's at bats or innings pitched will be disqualified from their sample group (most of these players were injured for part of the season or were released from the team roster during the season), as well as those free agents who did not play at all in the year following their free agency. Individual salary/MRP ratios will then be calculated by dividing each free agent's salary by his MRP for the corresponding year he was a free agent.

For the purpose of measuring the effects of financial restraint, the free agents were divided into groups representing the 1984 free agents (the year before the collusion ruling) and the 1985–86 free agents (the two years of alleged collusion). An average salary/MRP ratio was calculated from the individual salary/MRP ratios of each group and a two-sample, one tail test was performed to test the statistical significance of the difference between the average salary/MRP ratios for the two groups.

III. Data and Results

Regression 1 (Winning Percentage Equation)

Winning percentage (*PCTWIN*) is normally based on 1.000, but it was decided to use a base of 1000 instead for ease of interpretation. Team slugging average (*TSA*), as well as team strikeout-to-walk ratio (*TSW*), were gathered from various sources [18; 16]. Both the *TSA* and *TSW* variables are relative; they are based on league averages. If a team has a *TSA* of 1.05, it would mean that this team's slugging average is five percent better than the league average.

The regression results for the winning percentage equation are given in Table I. The signs on all the coefficients met prior expectations and all were statistically significant at 1% levels except for *TSW*, whose coefficient is statistically significant at a 1.5% level. A correlation matrix and a test for heteroscedasticity are provided in Appendices I and II.

Regression 2 (Revenue Equation)

Attendance for each team during the season was obtained from that team's respective league [1; 17], while average ticket prices were obtained from the Commissioner's office [14]. Broadcasting revenues came from the annual baseball broadcasting issue of *Broadcasting* magazine [2].

Concession figures, the third element of team revenue, were the most difficult component of *REV* to obtain. Only three clubs were willing to give out per-capita concession sales figures. At the point, the concession component of revenue could have been dropped. However, it was felt that concessions were of too much importance in the measurement of revenue. Consequently, a method was developed to forecast concession sales figures for the other teams.

The first step in this method was to divide one of the three actual per-capita sales figures by that team's average ticket price to yield a "concession factor." This was done for each year in the study. Next, this concession factor was divided into all of the other teams' average ticket prices to give a per-capita concession sales figure for each team in each specific year.

Average ticket price was used as a proxy for per-capita concessions because average ticket price reflects many team-specific characteristics (such as cost-of-living in a specific metropolitan area, management decisions, etc.) that concession sales figures would also encompass.

After three sets of concession figures were calculated for each team, each set being based on one of the actual per-capita concession sales figures, one set was chosen to use in the measurement of the concession aspect of revenue. This set was chosen because its concession factor was in the middle of the concession factors of the other two scenarios. As with average ticket price, all concession figures for the Canadian baseball clubs (Toronto and Montreal) were converted to American dollars using exchange rates found in *International Financial Statistics* [7].

Data for the population variable (*SMSA*) were obtained from the *Statistical Abstract of the United States* [20]. The population used for each city was the largest metropolitan classification available that included the identified city: for example, Chicago was identified as being in a Consolidated Metropolitan Statistical Area (CMSA) while Kansas City was identified as being in a Metropolitan Statistical Area (MSA). The population figures for the Canadian teams were obtained via a telephone interview with Statistics Canada [19]. All population figures are estimates done after the last actual census in each country, which was 1980 in the U.S. and 1981 or 1986 in Canada. The *TWOTM* variable is self-explanatory; the criterion for a yes response was that two teams shared a CMSA. Finally, for the old stadium variable (*STD*), the only stadiums that fit the requirements were Wrigley Field and Comiskey Park in Chicago, Fenway Park in Boston, Tiger Stadium in Detroit, and Cleveland Municipal Stadium.

The regression results for the second equation are in Table II. If the winning percentage of a team increases by 1 unit (0.1%), its revenue will increase by $53,071 on average, holding all of the other variables constant. If a team's metropolitan area size grows by 1 million people, its revenue will increase by $1,469,440. A team that plays in an old stadium will make $1,322,698 more in revenue than a team that does not play in an old stadium. Finally, if there are two teams in one metropolitan area, each team's revenue will be lower by $7,376,298, on average.

The positive sign of the stadium coefficient can perhaps be explained by looking at the fact that three of the teams that play in old stadiums (the Chicago Cubs, the Boston Red Sox, and the

Table II: Revenue Regression

Y = REV = Team revenue from attendance, broadcasting and concessions ($)
X_2 = $PCTWIN$ = Team winning percentage; based on 1000
X_3 = $SMSA$ = Size of the metropolitan area (millions)
X_4 = STD = Old stadium dummy variable
X_5 = $TWOTM$ = Two teams in metropolitan area dummy variable
e_2 = Random disturbance term

(t-ratios in parentheses)

$$REV = -1,522,481.5 + 53070.5(PCTWIN) + 1469440.2(SMSA)$$
$$(-1.17) \qquad (5.84) \qquad\qquad (6.29)$$

$$+ 1322698.6(STD) - 7376297.6(TWOTM) + e_2$$
$$(0.97) \qquad\qquad (-3.27)$$

standard error = 4,712,291   (mean of REV is 30,935,231)
Adjusted R^2 = 68.2%
F-statistic = 42.2
DF = 73

Detroit Tigers) won divisional titles during the three year period of this study. No team playing in an old stadium won a divisional crown during the years studied by previous authors. (The coefficient was negative in those studies). Another explanation is that fans actually prefer the friendly confines of old stadiums.[4] However, the coefficient is not statistically significant.

All other coefficients were of the correct sign and were statistically significant at the 1% level. A correlation matrix and a test for heteroscedasticity are provided in Appendices I and II.

Salary/MRP Ratios

All salary data were obtained from *USA Today* and its annual baseball salary issues [21]. Salary data are available from other sources, but for the sake of consistency, this was the only source of salary data used (the data only went back to 1984). If the salary for a free agent could not be found in the year after his free agency, he was disqualified from the sample group, even if he did play in that year.

The total number of players who filed for free agency after each of the three years was 79 in 1986, 62 in 1985, and 58 in 1984. By removing all of the free agents who did not meet the criteria specified and whose salaries were not obtainable, the size of the 1984 sample group was reduced to 34. For the 1985–86 combined sample group, there were 69 free agents who met all of the requirements and whose salaries were obtainable.

The test of the difference between the two sample groups involves the computation of the ratio of each free agent's salary to his MRP (MRP and salary figures for each player are given in Appendix III). As discussed earlier, the salary/MRP ratios use gross MRP figures because the costs of player development are not subtracted from the measured MRPs. The reported salary/MRP ratios are thus lower than what they would be if net MRP values were used. These ratios

---

4. The authors wish to thank the referee for this observation.

Table III: Mean Ratios of Salaries to Gross Marginal Revenue Products (Standard Errors in Parentheses)

	Salary/MRP 1984	Salary/MRP 1985–6	Difference
Unweighted Average	0.961 (0.204)	(0.693) (0.110)	0.268
Weighted Average	1.217 (0.327)	0.750 (0.110)	0.467
Sample size	34	69	

are then averaged for each group of free agents: 1984 (year before the collusion ruling) and 1985–86 (the two years of alleged collusion). These averages are then compared to each other, and the difference is determined. For the 1984 sample group, the average ratio of salary to gross MRP was 0.961. (All figures are in Table III). For the 1985–86 agent group, the average ratio of salary to gross MRP was only .693. This yields a fairly large difference of 0.268, which is a 28% drop in the mean salary/MRP during the two years of alleged collusion. This is consistent with the hypothesis that baseball owners exercised financial restraint in bidding for the available free agents in the 1985 and 1986 seasons.

The second ratio calculated was a weighted average ratio. Each free agent's salary was divided by mean salary of his sample group to obtain a weight for this player. This quotient was then used to weight this player's ratio. This procedure gives more weight to the salary/MRP ratios of high-salaried players. The mean salary/MRP for the weighted ratios is 1.217 in 1984, while the weighted ratio for the 1985–86 group of free agents is 0.750, which gives a difference of 0.467. This difference is a 38% drop in the mean salary/MRP ratios for free agents during the two years of alleged collusion.

The standard hypothesis tests on the difference between two population means can be performed to establish whether the observed differences in the sample means reflect true differences. The standard test requires an assumption that the unknown population variances are equal. When a pooled variance is used, the t-ratios for the difference between the mean salary/MRP ratios are 1.58 for the unweighted means and 1.69 for the weighted means. The probability-values are 6% and 5% respectively. The support for the hypothesis of no difference in the mean ratios is small, and the hypothesis can be rejected at the 10% level (one-tail) for both tests.

The t-test permits the assumption of equal population variances to be violated somewhat without invalidating the t-test. However, because of the large differences in the sample variances in this case, the assumption of equal population variances is doubtful. If the sample variances are not pooled, the distribution of the test statistic is uncertain [8]. In such cases the t-distribution is used as an approximation provided the sample sizes are large. With this change, the t-ratios for the difference between the mean salary/MRP ratios are 1.25 for the unweighted means and 1.35 for the weighted means. The probability-values are 11% and 9%, respectively. The support for the hypothesis of no difference is still small, but the hypothesis can be rejected at the 10% level only for the weighted means.[5]

5. What is not reflected in these tests is the high proportion of the population that is included in each sample. All free agents were included for the three years except those players who were disqualified because they had less than 1% of the team at bats or innings pitched, were not signed by any team, or did not have their salaries published in *USA Today* [21]. The samples were roughly half of the size of the population. Sample differences thus reflect true differences more strongly than what is indicated by the usual t-tests.

In conclusion, the mean salary/MRP ratios for free agents in 1985–6 were 28% smaller for unweighted means and 38% smaller for weighted means than those found in 1984. This is consistent with the hypothesis of financial restraint in the free agent market by club owners. Free agent players received lower salaries in 1985–6 than what they would have received if competitive bidding took place as it did in 1984 and earlier years. There is little reason to doubt that this group of free agents suffered the economic consequences associated with the club owners' nonparticipation in the bidding process.

When free agents receive less in salary than their economic worth to the club, this does not mean that their salaries are necessarily lower in the "collusion years" than they were earlier. A player whose performance is improving can find his salary going up as well as the gap between his salary and his worth to the team. But by limiting the salary increases paid to free agents (who are forced to resign with their old team), club owners save on salary expenditures not only for the free agents but for all players on the team as non-free agents compare their performances and salary with those of free agents.

It is interesting to note that the average salary for baseball players in 1987 declined slightly. The player association reported an average salary of $412,454, down from $412,520 in 1986 (the owners reported an average salary of $402,579 [11]). This is the first decline since the player association started keeping records in 1967. Financial restraint in the free agent market appears to have set the tone for salaries generally.

IV. Conclusion

Two baseball arbitrators have recently ruled that the club owners colluded after the 1985 and 1986 baseball seasons by not bidding on the available free agents. This study suggests that a testable hypothesis is whether there were salary consequences associated with the owners' alleged collusion in 1985–86. The results showed that there is a large difference between the salary/MRP ratios of the 1984 free agent group and those of the 1985–86 free agent group. The mean ratios were 28% lower for the unweighted ratios and 38% lower for the weighted ratios. This outcome suggests that the free agents in 1985 and 1986 did suffer economic consequences compared to the 1984 group. This finding is consistent with the financial restraint hypothesis. Although financial restraint is the natural economic consequence of collusion, these results do not empirically establish that collusion occurred, since financial restraint could have been due to the independent decisions of the 26 baseball clubs.

The nonparticipation by club owners in the 1985 and 1986 free agent markets did result in collusion rulings. In 1989, baseball arbitrator Thomas Roberts assessed a $10 million penalty on the owners. Additional rulings on the appropriate remedies are still forthcoming. Suggested remedies by the players association have included new free agency opportunities for the affected players as well as punitive damages from the owners [11]. Our results suggest that the salary consequences of financial restraint can be estimated, at least on the average, for the affected players. A remedy to the players in the form of lost compensation can be based on the estimated net MRP compared to the actual salaries received. The difference between the estimated market value and the actual salary would be the economic damage deserving compensation. This gap could be increased by a factor of 3 to reflect the type of punitive damages that are awarded for violating in this nation's antitrust laws. Although baseball is exempt from our antitrust laws, there is no reason why an arbitrator should avoid use of the treble damage remedy.

Punitive damages are difficult to determine and pose problems in assigning the guilty parties. If a claim of $10 million is awarded to the free agents, not only does this sum have to be allocated in an equitable fashion, it must also be collected equitably. It is not clear whether all teams should contribute, or contribute equally, to pay for any assessed fine.

Although bringing the 1985–86 free agent players up to market value may not be sufficient to deter owners from further nonparticipation, in the short run, it may not be necessary to worry about future collusion. Industrial organization theory suggests that the large number of baseball clubs will make it nearly impossible for the owners to resist the temptation to cheat on any agreement to refrain from bidding for free agents. This is especially likely in baseball because of the considerable overcapacity in most baseball-stadiums and the widely varying population markets. A "star" player can fill many of those empty seats. Since the owners have no mechanism to punish those who sign free agents, competitive bidding will most likely re-emerge over time.

Such a long term solution is not likely to placate the players. The present Basic Agreement expires on December 31, 1989. Before then, the owners and players must work out some compromises on the free agency system to prevent a third strike by the players.

Appendix I.

	Simple Correlation Matrix for Equation (1)				
	PCTWIN	*TSA*	*TSW*	*CONT*	*OUT*
PCTWIN	1.00	0.48	0.38	0.67	−0.65
TSA	—	1.00	0.14	0.26	−0.38
TSW	—	—	1.00	0.38	−0.22
CONT	—	—	—	1.00	−0.39
OUT	—	—	—	—	1.00

	Simple Correlation Matrix for Equation (2)				
	REV	*PCTWIN*	*SMSA*	*STAD*	*TWOTM*
REV	1.00	0.69	0.65	0.06	0.33
PCTWIN	—	1.00	0.39	0.06	0.14
SMSA	—	—	1.00	0.01	0.81
STAD	—	—	—	1.00	0.10
TWOTM	—	—	—	—	1.00

Appendix II

Park Test for Heteroscedasticity

A Park test was used to test for heteroscedasticity in each of the regressions. It is performed by regressing the logarithm of the squared residual error terms of the regression on the logarithm of each of the explanatory variables. This test is only performed on the quantitative variables in each regression.

The results of Park tests performed on both of the regression show that there was no heteroscedasticity present in either equation.

Park Tests for Equation (1): (t-ratios in parentheses)

$LE2$ = Logarithm of squared residual errors in equation (1)
$LPCYWIN$ = Logarithm of winning percentage

$LSMSA =$ Logarithm of the size of the metropolitan area

$LE2 = 24.73 + 0.75(LPCTWI)$
$\qquad (1.80) \qquad (0.34)$

$LE2 = 28.70 + 0.48(LSMSA)$
$\qquad (46.24) \qquad (1.22)$

Park Tests for Equation (2): (t-ratios on parentheses)

$LE2 =$ Logarithm of squared residual errors in equation 2

$LTSA =$ Logarithm of team slugging average

$LTSW =$ Logarithm of team strikeout-to-walk ratio

$LE2 = 6.11 - 1.62(LTSW)$
$\qquad (27.41) \qquad (-0.32)$

$LE2 = 6.11 - 0.61(LTSW)$
$\qquad (27.41) \qquad (-0.34)$

Appendix III

The following list shows: 1) the players in each of the three years, 2) their salary, and 3) their gross marginal revenue product, as estimated by the two-step statistical procedure used on this paper. It is important to remember that the MRP's are overstated because the costs of player development have not been subtracted out.

Player	Pitcher/Batter	Salary ($)	Gross MRP ($)
		1984	
Sutter, B.	P	1,354,167	642,031
Sutcliffe, R.	P	1,260,000	1,007,038
Thornton, A.	B	1,100,000	2,867,745
Lynn, F.	B	1,090,000	2,551,949
Kingman, D.	B	1,087,500	2,894,351
Fingers, R.	P	1,065,000	236,913
Whitson, E.	P	800,000	683,937
Eckersley, D.	P	750,000	610,118
Lacy, L.	B	725,000	2,262,839
Gantner, J.	B	687,500	2,179,340
Johnson, C.	B	683,333	1,822,633
Trout, S.	P	640,000	439,280
Hooton, B.	P	565,000	234,285
Stoddard, T.	P	556,250	237,358
Aase, D.	P	525,000	94,812
Russell, B.	B	450,000	951,694
Lezcano, S.	B	425,000	1,338,002
Jones, R.	B	390,000	1,120,048
Kison, B.	P	320,000	255,947
Royster, J.	B	325,000	755,591
Pryor, G.	B	316,667	987,736
Rozema, D.	P	310,000	458,587
Wohlford, J.	B	308,333	1,080,720
Ayala, B.	B	303,333	447,937
Ruhle, V.	P	295,000	278,641
Wilfong, P.	B	266,667	1,157,000
Almon, B.	B	255,000	824,602
Grubb, J.	B	250,000	767,892

Perez, T.	B	225,000	522,088
Reuschel, B.	P	200,000	291,316
Dilone, M.	B	175,000	697,713
Bumbry, A.	B	160,000	1,209,574
Henderson, S.	B	150,000	1,470,329
Nicosia, S.	B	105,000	660,858

1985

Gibson, K.	B	1,200,000	2,992,193
Moore, D.	P	1,000,000	590,288
Sutton, D.	P	890,000	683,346
Fisk, C.	B	875,000	2,706,241
Wynegar, B.	B	733,333	1,011,495
McRae H.	B	650,000	1,462,624
Darwin, D.	P	610,000	708,050
Thon, D.	B	600,000	964,037
Bernazard T.	B	580,000	2,041,866
Bochte, B.	B	572,500	1,311,503
Grich, B.	B	500,000	1,828,197
Beniquez, J.	B	450,000	1,762,465
Blue, V.	P	450,000	252,247
Yeager, S.	B	412,809	340,599
Dwyer, J.	B	400,000	940,335
Easterly, J.	P	350,000	184,135
Brookens, T.	B	325,000	1,821,998
Niekro, P.	P	300,000	460,905
Perez, T.	B	275,000	957,874
Lopez, A.	P	223,272	190,603
Iorg, D.	B	210,000	436,252
Jones, Lynn	B	185,000	396,132
Washington, U.L.	B	180,000	755,704
Quirk, J.	B	150,000	808,147
Sakata, L.	B	75,000	344,998
Ruhle V.	P	60,000	385,572
Spilman, H.	B	60,000	140,582

1986

Morris, J.	P	1,850,000	1,137,796
Raines, T.	B	1,666,333	2,983,349
DeCinces, D.	B	1,050,000	2,193,271
Parrish, L.	B	1,000,000	1,587,793
Downing, B.	B	900,000	2,365,389
Randolph, W.	B	900,000	1,693,671
Boone, B.	B	883,000	1,376,311
Guidry, R.	P	850,000	1,109,779
Clancy, J.	P	850,000	672,368
Gedman, R.	B	772,504	1,653,103
Whitt, E.	B	750,000	1,716,122
Forsch, B.	P	750,000	518,683
Palmer, D.	P	725,000	531,143
Alexander, D.	P	650,000	774,469
Ward, G.	B	633,000	1,542,425
Knight, R.	B	600,000	2,205,698
Jackson, R.	B	525,000	1,743,840

Smith, L.	B	500,000	2,082,477
Washington, C.	B	480,000	546,012
Garner, P.	B	450,000	1,420,315
Lopes, D.	B	450,000	1,172,441
Dempsey, R.	B	400,000	1,243,807
Roenicke, G.	B	380,000	497,771
Sambito, J.	P	360,000	132,700
John, T.	P	350,000	207,298
Concepcion, D.	B	320,000	1,150,704
Dwyer, J.	B	307,500	784,531
Heep, D.	B	300,000	879,545
LaCoss, M.	P	300,000	371,801
Andersen, L.	P	300,000	185,865
Speier, C.	B	275,000	758,676
Royster, J.	B	260,000	1,004,068
Porter, D.	B	260,000	830,432
Moore, C.	B	256,000	891,522
Cerone, R.	B	250,000	834,201
Herndon, L.	B	225,000	1,094,889
Quirk, J.	B	200,000	193,408
Spilman, H.	B	175,000	433,585
Stewart, S.	P	175,000	98,661
Martinez, T.	P	162,500	324,748
Price, J.	P	100,000	82,866
Noles, D.	P	75,000	91,503

References

1. American League of Professional Baseball Clubs. Correspondence.

2. *Broadcasting* magazine. Various issues.

3. Cassing, James and Richard W. Douglas, "Implications of the Auction Mechanism in Baseball's Free Agent Draft." *Southern Economic Journal*, July 1980, 110–21.

4. Commissioner's Office, Major League Baseball. Correspondence.

5. *Easton Express* newspaper. 8 June 1988.

6. Hill, James Richard, "The Threat of Free Agency and Exploitation in Professional Baseball: 1976–79," *Quarterly Review of Economics and Business*, Winter 1985, 68–82.

7. International Monetary Fund, "Canada." *International Financial Statistics*, September 1987, 147.

8. Keller, Gerald, Brian Warrack and Henry Bartel. *Statistics for Management and Economics*. Belmont, Calf.: Wadsworth Publishing Co., 1988.

9. Medoff, Marshall H. "On Monopsonistic Exploitation in Professional Baseball." *Quarterly Review of Economics and Business*, Summer 1976, 113–21.

10. National League of Professional Baseball Clubs. Correspondence.

11. *The New York Times*. 4 December 1984, 18 July 1985, 28 September 1987, 8 November 1987, 6 April 1989.

12. Raimondo, Henry J., "Free Agents' Impact on the Labor Market for Baseball Players." *Journal of Labor Research*, Spring 1983, 183–93.

13. Scoville, James. "Wage Determination and the Development of Collective Bargaining in Baseball," in *Proceedings of the 29th Annual Meeting of the Industrial Relations Research Association*. 1976, pp. 317–23.

14. Scully, Gerald W., "Pay and Performance in Major League Baseball," *American Economic Review*, December 1974, 915–30.

15. ———. "The Economics of Discrimination in Professional Sports: The Case of Baseball," in *Government and the Sports Business*, edited by Roger G. Noll. Washington: Brookings Institution, 1974.

16. Siwoff, Seymour, Steve Hirdt and Peter Hirdt. *The 1985 Elias Baseball Analyst*. New York: Macmillan Publishing Company; Collier Books, 1985.

17. Sommers, Paul M. and Noel Quinton, "Pay and Performance in Major League Baseball: The Case of the First Family of Free Agents." *The Journal of Human Resources*, Summer 1982, 426–36.

18. *The Sporting News*. Various issues.

19. Statistics Canada. Telephone interview.

20. United States Department of Commerce. Bureau of the Census. *Statistical Abstract of the United States*. 1987 and 1986.

21. *USA Today*. Various issues.

Article 16

Learning Curves in Manufacturing

LINDA ARGOTE AND DENNIS EPPLE

Large increases in productivity are typically realized as organizations gain experience in production. These "learning curves" have been found in many organizations. Organizations vary considerably in the rates at which they learn. Some organizations show remarkable productivity gains, whereas others show little or no learning. Reasons for the variation observed in organizational learning curves include organizational "forgetting," employee turnover, transfer of knowledge from other products and other organizations, and economies of scale.

AS ORGANIZATIONS PRODUCE MORE OF A PRODUCT, THE unit cost of production typically decreases at a decreasing rate. This phenomenon is referred to as a learning curve, a progress curve, an experience curve, or learning by doing. A learning curve for the production of an advanced military jet built in the 1970s and 1980s (Fig. 1) illustrates the two salient properties of learning. The number of direct labor hours required to assemble an aircraft decreased significantly as experience was gained in production, and the rate of reduction of assembly hours declined with rising cumulative output.

Learning curves have been documented in many organizations, in both the manufacturing and service sectors. The unit costs of producing aircraft (1, 2), ships (3), refined petroleum products (4), and power plants (5, 6) have been shown to follow the characteristic learning-curve pattern. Learning curves have also been found to characterize outcomes as diverse as success rates of new surgical procedures (7), productivity in kibbutz farming (8), and nuclear plant operating reliability (9).

The productivity gains associated with organizational learning curves are often quite large. For example, during the first year of production of Liberty ships during World War II, the average number of hours of labor required to produce a ship decreased by 45%, and the average time it took to build a ship decreased by 75% (10). A recent study of a truck plant reported a remarkable growth in productivity of approximately 190% over the first year of the plant's operation (11).

Organizations vary considerably in the rates at which they learn (12–14). Whereas some organizations show extraordinary rates of productivity growth as cumulative output increases, others fail to show expected productivity gains from learning. Lockheed's production of the L-1011 Tri-Star in the 1970s is an example of a program with little evidence of learning (15, 16). Lockheed lost over $1 billion on the Tri-Star program in the 1970s (16).

Why did little or no productivity growth occur in production of the Lockheed Tri-Star while the truck plant mentioned earlier showed impressive growth in productivity? For U.S. manufacturing and other organizations to compete effectively, we need to understand why some organizations show rapid rates of learning and others fail to learn. Thus, we need to identify factors affecting organizational learning curves and use this knowledge to improve manufacturing performance.

Understanding factors affecting learning can enable managers to improve the performance of a firm in many areas. Applications include formulating manufacturing strategy (17), production scheduling (12), pricing and marketing (18), training (19), subcontracting production (20), and predicting competitors' costs (21). The rate and transfer of learning are also important issues for antitrust policy (22) and trade policy (23).

We examine evidence from several disciplines on organizational learning curves, particularly in manufacturing. Our focus is primarily on empirical studies that analyzed organizations or work groups. We show that organizations vary considerably in the rate at which they learn and identify factors responsible for the variation.

Research on Organizational Learning Curves

The first documentation of an organizational learning curve was published in 1936 by Wright (1), who reported that unit labor costs in air-frame production declined with cumulative output (24). Further interest in learning was stimulated by Alchian's 1948 study of learning in 22 aircraft production programs (2).

The conventional form of the learning curve is a power function:

$$y = ax^{-b} \qquad (1)$$

where y is the number of direct labor hours required to produce the xth unit; a is the number of direct labor hours required to produce the first unit; x is the cumulative number of units produced; and b is a parameter measuring the rate labor hours are reduced as cumulative output increases.

As this expression shows, the standard measure of organizational experience in the learning-curve formulation is the cumulative number of units produced, a proxy variable for knowledge acquired through production. If unit costs decrease as a function of this knowledge, other variables being equal, organizational learning is said to occur.

Learning curves are often characterized in terms of a progress ratio, p. With the learning curve in Eq. 1, each doubling of cumulative output leads to a reduction in unit cost to a percentage, p, of its former value (25). Thus, an 80% progress ratio means that each doubling of cumulative output leads to a 20% reduction in unit cost.

Before the discovery of learning curves in organizations, the learning-curve pattern had been found to characterize the perform-

L. Argote is associate professor of industrial administration and D. Epple is professor of economics at the Graduate School of Industrial Administration, Carnegie Mellon University, Pittsburgh, PA 15213.

ance of individual subjects as they gained experience with a task (26). For example, an early study of individual learning curves focused on the number of errors individual students made as they progressed through a typing course (27). Organizational learning curves, by contrast, focus on the performance of entire organizations or organizational subunits (for example, manufacturing plants). Although the productivity of an organization may be affected by individuals learning how to perform their jobs better, it is also affected by many additional factors such as technological developments and improved coordination of the production process. Thus, organizational learning involves more than individuals becoming better at their particular jobs.

Much of the work on organizational learning curves has focused on specifying the functional form of the relation between unit costs and cumulative output and on studying the phenomenon in different industries (12, 13). Several new trends in research on organizational learning curves are apparent. The set of outcome measures has been broadened to include, for example, industrial accidents per unit of output (28) and defects or complaints to quality control per unit of output (29). The transfer of productivity gains acquired through learning by doing across organizations is also being studied (5, 6, 30). Increasing attention is being given to disentangling the various factors that contribute to organizational learning (30, 31).

Variation in Organizational Learning Rates

The frequency distribution of progress ratios found in more than 100 studies in different industries is presented in Fig. 2 (13). Note that the progress ratios vary a great deal, reflecting the variation in the rate productivity grows with increasing cumulative output. Also, the modal progress ratio falls at 81 to 82%—giving rise to the general assumption of an "80% learning curve" (32).

Understanding the reasons why learning rates vary is a major challenge for research. The different rates of learning (Fig. 2) are not simply a function of the different products studied, although differences in products are, of course, a source of variation. There is often more variation across organizations or organizational units producing the same product than within organizations producing different products. For example, productivity gains varied more within shipbuilding production programs than between production programs during World War II (10). Similarly, Hayes and Clark (14) found considerable variation in the rate of learning across plants in the same firm producing the same product with similar equipment and materials.

Different plants producing the same product that have different rates of learning are shown in Fig. 3. The data are from three truck plants producing the same product within the same company. The cumulative number of trucks produced is plotted against the number of direct labor hours required to assemble each truck. Although each plant shows the characteristic learning-curve pattern, the pattern is different for each plant. Thus, there is considerable variation in productivity among these plants that is not explained by the conventional learning-curve model (33).

This variation in the rate that organizations learn may be due to organizational "forgetting," employee turnover, transfer of knowledge, and the failure to control for other factors, such as economies of scale, when estimating learning curves.

Organizational forgetting. When production is resumed after an interruption such as a strike, unit cost is often higher than the level achieved before the interruption (34). Similarly, there is evidence that knowledge acquired through learning by doing depreciates: recent output rates may be a more important predictor of current production than cumulative output (30). Theoretical research and simulation results have also indicated that forgetting has implications for planning and scheduling (35).

Organizational forgetting may explain why Lockheed's costs for the L-1011 Tri-Star did not follow the learning-curve pattern. The production of the L-1011 Tri-Star was characterized by wide variations in the rate of output (Table 1). Lockheed estimated that its production costs would fall below price in mid-1974 (36). The conventional learning-curve formulation applied to the Tri-Star yielded a prediction that costs would fall below price about the time the 50th plane was built, sometime in 1973 (37). In November 1975, Lockheed reported that unit costs at that time were less than the price at which planes were being sold (38). Planes were sold for

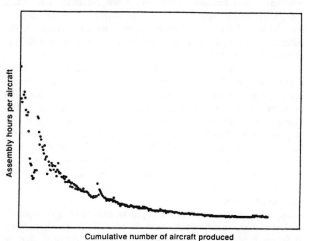

Fig. 1. Relation between assembly hours per aircraft and cumulative number produced. Units omitted.

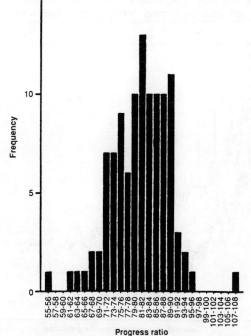

Fig. 2. Distribution of progress ratios observed in 22 field studies (n = 108) (13).

$20 million in 1975. Cuts in production occurred in late 1975. Costs rose to exceed price and, apparently, remained above price for the rest of the production program (*39*). In 1982, the L-1011 was sold for $50 to $60 million per plane. This corresponds to $29 to $35 million in 1975 dollars. Thus, production cost per plane was less than $20 million in real terms in 1975 but greater than $29 million in real terms in 1982.

In the conventional learning-curve model, unit costs decrease as a function of cumulative output. This model does not explain the Lockheed data, however, since costs rose as cumulative output continued to increase. A model in which knowledge depreciates and recent output is more important than cumulative output in predicting costs can explain the Lockheed data. Lockheed's costs rose when production was cut and recent output was relatively low. Even though a detailed analysis of the L-1011 data would be required to test the hypothesis that depreciation of knowledge occurred, the pattern of costs reported by Lockheed is consistent with the depreciation hypothesis.

Why might knowledge acquired through learning by doing depreciate? Knowledge could depreciate because individual employees forget how to perform their tasks or because individuals leave the organization and are replaced by others with less experience. For example, it would not be surprising if many managerial and line employees who worked on the L-1011 during its early period of high annual output (1973 to 1975) were no longer on the project when the company resumed comparatively high output levels later in the program (1979 to 1980). Depreciation could also be due to changes in products or processes that make previously acquired knowledge obsolete.

Depreciation can also result if organizational records or routines are lost or become difficult to access. An example, recently described in *Science*, is provided by the difficulty in accessing data collected by Landsat, an earth surveillance program. It is estimated that 90% of the data collected before 1979 is inaccessible because the data were recorded by equipment that no longer exists or cannot be operated and "bleeding" of magnetic images occurred over time (*40*).

Thus, forgetting or depreciation of organizational knowledge can cause organizational learning rates to vary. When depreciation

Table 1. Lockheed's production of the L-1011 Tri-Star (*15, 38, 53*).

| Year | L-1011 production | |
	Annual units	Cumulative units
1972	17	17
1973	39	56
1974	41	97
1975	25	122
1976	16	138
1977	6	144
1978	8	152
1979	24	176
1980	25	201
1981	18	219

occurs and the conventional learning curve is used, two organizations that have achieved the same level of cumulative output will be at different points on the learning curve if the recent output level of one is different from that of the other. Such differences in recent output levels may arise for a host of reasons including strikes, materials shortages, and fluctuations in product demand that lead to temporary shutdown of some plants but not others. A method for extending the analysis of learning to encompass depreciation is provided in Argote, Beckman, and Epple (*30*).

Turnover. When organizational knowledge is possessed by individual employees, employee turnover can be expected to have an impact on learning and forgetting in organizations. Thus, differing rates of turnover across organizations could explain the differences observed in organizational learning curves.

Does turnover affect the rate of learning and forgetting in firms? Research indicates that turnover of direct production workers did not have a significant effect on the rate of learning or forgetting in World War II shipyards (*30*). This result is striking, given that turnover in these organizations averaged more than 10% per month. The result is consistent, however, with results from several laboratory studies that found increases in the performance of groups over successive trials in the face of turnover (*41*).

Why did turnover not matter in these production environments? The jobs of production workers in the shipyards were standardized and designed so that a new employee could become proficient with minimal training (*42*). Procedures existed for training and transmitting knowledge to new members.

Many production environments today also experience considerable turnover. For example, the corporate office required one plant that we studied to accept, over a 2-month period, more than 300 employees from a neighboring plant that closed. When these new employees arrived, more than 300 employees left the plant and another 150 moved to different jobs within the plant. Thus, at the end of the second month, 15% of employees at the plant were either new to the plant or at different jobs within the plant than at the beginning of this 2-month period. Plant managers at this corporation recognize that high turnover may occur and attempt to design their operations to mitigate its effects.

Although results to date do not suggest that turnover affects the rate of organizational learning, in the limit, turnover would surely affect learning and forgetting in firms (*43*). Moreover, organizations confronted with high rates of turnover may insulate themselves from its effects by routinizing jobs and procedures. The consequence may be a lower rate of learning than is achieved by organizations not confronted with such turnover. Turnover may matter more in organizations where jobs are not standardized and procedures do not exist for transmitting knowledge to new members. Turnover of managers and technical support staff, such as engineers, may also

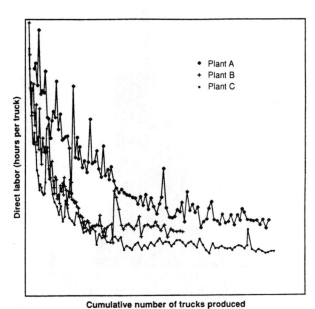

Fig. 3. Relation between direct labor hours per truck and cumulative number produced for three truck plants. Units omitted.

matter more than turnover of direct production workers (*44*).

Transfer of productivity gains. Another possible reason for different rates of organizational learning is the transfer of knowledge across products or across organizations. Experience gained in the production of one product can be transferred to the production of related products (*45*). For example, suppose two organizations produce the same product. The first organization produces only one product while the second organization produces a related product using some of the same operations as were used to make the first product. The second organization should benefit from the additional cumulative output generated by the second product and have lower costs on the shared operations. Thus, if the two organizations have similar cumulative output levels for the product they both produce, the second organization should have lower costs and be farther down the learning curve than the first because of the transfer of knowledge from the related product.

Similarly, an organization that produced a related product in the past may be able to transfer knowledge to the manufacture of a product currently in production. Thus, an organization with previous experience producing a related product may appear to have a faster rate of learning than an organization without prior experience, even though their cumulative output levels for the product currently in production are the same.

Transfer of knowledge across organizations might also occur (*46*). Transfer might occur through personnel movement, communication, participation in meetings and conferences, training, improved supplies, modifications in technology, or "reverse-engineering" of products. Knowledge transferred from outside the firm is difficult to measure. One approach to measuring this knowledge involves aggregating cumulative output across all firms in the industry. This measure of industry experience has been found to have a significant effect on unit costs in some industries (*5*) but not in others (*6*). Organizations coming on line later have been found to begin with higher productivity levels than their counterparts with early start dates (*30*). Once organizations began production, however, they did not benefit from knowledge acquired from other organizations.

Another approach to measuring knowledge acquired outside the firm is to assume that calendar time is an adequate proxy variable for knowledge acquired in the general environment. Several studies in which this approach was used have found that calendar time is not as good a predictor of an organization's productivity growth as is its own cumulative output (*3, 11, 31*). Kelsey *et al.* (*7*) found that calendar time was a significant predictor of surgical success rates only for the first 20 operations performed. For later operations, calendar time was not significant but experience was. The researchers suggested that surgeons were more likely to learn from the experience of others when they first begin to perform the procedure but not later. Thus, there is evidence that transfer may occur across organizations, and it seems particularly likely to occur in the early phases of production.

If transfer occurs for one organization but not another, the organizations will appear to have different rates of learning, even if their "internal" rates of learning from their own past production experience are the same. For example, consider two plants operated by the same company. One plant leads by beginning production first. The corporation invests in transferring knowledge acquired by the lead plant to the second plant. If transfer occurs, the second plant will have higher productivity than the first plant for the same level of cumulative output; the learning curve of the second plant will lie below that of the first.

Differences in learning rates across plants can also arise from incomplete transfer across shifts within plants (*11*). Managers at one plant we studied were disappointed that incomplete transfer occurred from the first shift to the second when the second shift was introduced at the plant. They speculated that the incomplete transfer was due to inadequate documentation of lessons learned from the first shift.

As an example of how incomplete transfer can cause differences in learning rates, consider two plants producing the same product. One plant operates with one shift per day while the other operates with two shifts (not an unusual occurrence). If the rate of learning per shift is the same in both plants but incomplete transfer occurs across shifts, the learning curves at the two plants will be different. When unit cost is plotted versus cumulative output from plant data, the plant operating with one shift per day will exhibit greater learning than the plant operating with two shifts per day. For example, suppose that unit costs for the two plants are compared at the point where both have produced 10,000 units. For the plant operating with two shifts per day, the cumulative output per shift will be only 5,000, that is, half the cumulative output per shift of the plant operating with only one shift. Thus, if there is no transfer across shifts, the plant operating with two shifts per day will have the productivity at a cumulative output of 10,000 units that the plant operating with one shift per day had at a cumulative output of 5,000 units.

Other factors affecting learning rates. An investigator should control for other variables that affect production because exclusion of such variables may bias the estimated rate of learning. For example, suppose economies of scale are present, so that a given increase in inputs results in a more than proportionate increase in output. If the scale of operation is gradually increased over time, productivity will rise because of increasing exploitation of economies of scale. If one estimates the rate of learning without controlling for the changing scale of operation, this increasing exploitation of scale economies will result in an overestimate of the amount of learning.

Womer (*47*) has cogently argued for the importance of integrating estimation of learning with production function estimation as a vehicle for controlling for the effects of factors other than learning. A production function is a relation specifying output per period as a function of inputs that period, the state of technical knowledge, and other variables that may affect output. Symbolically, this may be written:

$$q = F(n, k, z) \qquad (2)$$

where n denotes productive inputs, k denotes measures of the state of technical knowledge, and z denotes other variables that may affect production (*48*).

In general, issues that must be addressed in estimating a production function are selection of a functional form; choice of the variables n, k, and z; specification of the properties of random factors affecting the production process; and choice of an appropriate method of estimating the parameters of interest. There is some evidence that a plateau occurs, especially in machine-intensive industries (*49*). The choice of functional form should be flexible enough to accommodate this leveling out of the learning curve. It is also important to correct for problems that may arise if data are collected on a per period basis when several periods are required to produce each unit (*50*). Other issues in choice of functional form, specification of error structures, and estimation methods are addressed by others (*51*).

The choice of variables to be included in the model varies according to the production process being studied. For example, in a single plant with unchanging physical facilities, labor hours may be the only input that varies over time. In studying multiple plants, it may be appropriate to include measures of capital investment and other inputs that differ across plants, and such measures would also be needed if the facilities in a given plant change over time. An early example of empirical work on organizational learning that controlled for additional factors in the analysis was done by Rapping (3). He found both economies of scale and learning to be present in his study of productivity gains in shipbuilding.

Although cumulative output is typically used as the measure of knowledge acquired through learning by doing, measures that place relatively greater weight on recent output than on output in the distant past are appropriate if depreciation occurs (30). When production occurs at several plants, additional variables such as cumulative output aggregated across plants may be included in addition to a plant's own cumulative output as measures of the transfer of knowledge. If the plant has the potential to benefit from improvements in technical knowledge in the larger environment, proxies for the pace of such improvements are appropriate. One such proxy is calendar time (52). Finally, it may be necessary to control for factors such as labor turnover, product mix, and adjustment costs associated with changing inputs.

Conclusion

Although learning curves have been found in many organizations, there is great variation in the rate at which organizations learn, ranging from production programs with little or no learning to those with impressive productivity growth. We identified reasons why organizational learning rates vary. These include organizational forgetting, employee turnover, transfer of knowledge across products and across organizations, incomplete transfer within organizations, and economies of scale. Learning is a powerful source of productivity growth, and better understanding of learning can enhance manufacturing performance.

REFERENCES AND NOTES

1. T. P. Wright, *J. Aeronaut. Sci.* **3**, 122 (1936).
2. A. Alchian, *Econometrica* **31**, 679 (1963).
3. L. Rapping, *Rev. Econ. Stat.* **47**, 81 (1965).
4. W. B. Hirschmann, *Harvard Bus. Rev.* **42**, 125 (1964).
5. M. B. Zimmerman, *Bell J. Econ.* **13**, 297 (1982).
6. P. L. Joskow and N. L. Rose, *Rand J. Econ.* **16**, 1 (1985).
7. S. F. Kelsey *et al.*, *Am. J. Cardiol.* **53**, 56C (1984).
8. H. Barkai and D. Levhari, *Rev. Econ. Stat.* **55**, 56 (1973).
9. P. L. Joskow and G. A. Rozanski, *ibid.* **61**, 161 (1979).
10. A. D. Searle and C. S. Gody, *Mon. Labor Rev.* **61**, 1132 (1945).
11. D. Epple, L. Argote, R. Devadas, Graduate School of Industrial Administration (GSIA), Carnegie Mellon University, Working Paper, in preparation.
12. L. E. Yelle, *Decis. Sci.* **10**, 302 (1979).
13. J. M. Dutton and A. Thomas, *Acad. Manage. Rev.* **9**, 235 (1984).
14. R. H. Hayes and K. B. Clark, *Harvard Bus. Rev.* **64**, 66 (1986).
15. "Tri-Star production costs," *Aviat. Week Space Technol.*, 15 October 1979, p. 32.
16. "Tri-Star's trail of red ink," *Bus. Week*, 28 July 1980, pp. 88 and 90.
17. R. H. Hayes and S. C. Wheelwright, *Restoring Our Competitive Edge: Competing Through Manufacturing* (Wiley, New York, 1984).
18. R. J. Dolan and A. P. Jeuland, *J. Mark.* **45**, 52 (1981).
19. F. K. Levy, *Manage. Sci.* **11**, B136 (1965).
20. J. V. Jucker, *AIIE Trans.* **9**, 321 (1977).
21. B. D. Henderson, *J. Bus. Strategy* **4**, 3 (1984).
22. A. M. Spence, *Bell J. Econ.* **12**, 49 (1981).
23. H. K. Gruenspecht, *J. Int. Econ.* **12**, 225 (1988).
24. Empirical evidence of learning inspired theoretical work to reconcile the phenomenon with economic production theory [J. Hirshleifer, *J. Bus.* **35**, 235 (1962) and W. Y. Oi, *Econ. J.* **77**, 579 (1967)]. Implications of learning by doing for both competitive and noncompetitive markets have also been investigated [K. J. Arrow, *Rev. Econ. Stud.* **29**, 155 (1962); D. Fudenberg and J. Tirole, *Bell J. Econ.* **14**, 522 (1983); S. Rosen, *Q. J. Econ.* **86**, 366 (1972); R. H. Smiley and S. A. Ravid, *ibid.* **98**, 353 (1983); A. M. Spence, *Econometrica* **52**, 101 (1984)].
25. The parameter, *b*, in Eq. 1 is related to the progress ratio, *p*, by the expression: $p = 2^{-b}$. Thus, an 80% learning curve would be indicated by a value for *b* in Eq. 1 of approximately 0.322.
26. Early studies of individual learning and forgetting were performed by H. Ebbinghaus [*Memory: A Contribution to Experimental Psychology* (Dover, New York, 1885)] and E. L. Thorndike [*Psychol. Rev. Ser. Monogr. Suppl.* **2**, 1 (1898)]. Recent syntheses of the literature on individual learning can be found in M. K. Johnson and L. Hasher, *Annu. Rev. Psych.* **38**, 631 (1987); W. A. Wickelgren, *ibid.* **32**, 21 (1981); Y. Anzai and H. A. Simon *Psychol. Rev.* **86**, 124 (1979); J. E. Mazur and R. Hastie, *Psychol. Bull.* **85**, 1256 (1978); and J. R. Anderson, *Cognitive Psychology and Its Implications* (Freeman, New York, 1985). Many researchers of individual learning fit their data to an exponential rather than to a power function. There is some evidence, however, that power functions may fit individual learning data better than exponential functions [A. Newell and P. S. Rosenbloom, in *Cognitive Skills and Their Acquisition*, J. R. Anderson, Ed. (Erlbaum, Hillsdale, NJ, 1981), pp. 1–55].
27. L. L. Thurstone, *Psychol. Monogr.* **26**, 1 (1919).
28. L. Greenberg, *Min. Eng.* **23**, 51 (1971).
29. L. Argote, GSIA Working Paper, in preparation.
30. L. Argote, S. L. Beckman, D. Epple, *Manage. Sci.*, in press.
31. M. B. Lieberman, *Rand J. Econ.* **15**, 213 (1984).
32. P. Conley, *IEEE Spectrum* **7**, 63 (1970).
33. Progress has been made on a theory of organizational learning [B. Levitt and J. G. March, *Annu. Rev. Sociol.* **14**, 319 (1988) and J. F. Muth, *Manage. Sci.* **32**, 948 (1986)]. The theory, however, does not explain why learning rates differ across production programs.
34. W. Z. Hirsch, *Rev. Econ. Stat.* **34**, 143 (1952); N. Baloff, *IEEE Trans.* EM-17, 132 (1970).
35. D. R. Sule, *Int. J. Prod. Res.* **21**, 771 (1983); T. L. Smunt and T. E. Morton, *IEE Trans.* **17**, 33 (1985); T. L. Smunt, *Int. J. Prod. Res.* **25**, 689 (1987).
36. T. E. Fandell, *Wall Street Journal*, 3 June 1974, p. 1.
37. U. E. Reinhardt, *J. Financ.* **28**, 821 (1973).
38. S. J. Sansweet, *Wall Street Journal*, 7 November 1975, p. 1.
39. "Lockheed loses hope," *ibid.*, 14 May 1980, p. 12; R. J. Harris, *ibid.*, 20 April 1982, p. 7.
40. E. Marshall, "Early data: Losing our memory," *Science* **244**, 1250 (1989).
41. C. A. Insko *et al.*, *J. Pers. Soc. Psychol.* **39**, 431 (1980); C. A. Insko *et al.*, *J. Exp. Soc. Psychol.* **18**, 557 (1982).
42. F. C. Lane, *Ships for Victory: A History of Shipbuilding Under the U.S. Maritime Commission in World War II* (Johns Hopkins Univ. Press, Baltimore, MD, 1951).
43. Reviews of the literature on the effects of turnover on groups and organizations can be found in R. L. Moreland and J. M. Levine [in *Psychology of Group Influence*, P. Paulus, Ed. (Erlbaum, Hillsdale, NJ, 1989), pp. 143–186) and D. R. Dalton and W. D. Tudor [*Acad. Manage. Rev.* **4**, 225 (1979)].
44. For discussions of the effect of managerial turnover on firm performance see O. Grusky, *Am. J. Soc.* **69**, 21 (1963); D. Helmich, *Acad. Manage. Rev.* **2**, 252 (1977); D. L. Worrell, W. N. Davidson, P. R. Chandy, S. L. Garrison, *Acad. Manage. J.* **29**, 674 (1986); J. Pfeffer and A. Davis-Blake, *ibid.*, p. 72.
45. G. S. Day and D. B. Montgomery, *J. Mark.* **47**, 44 (1983).
46. W. Cohen and D. Levinthal, *Econ. J.* **99**, 569 (1989).
47. N. K. Womer, *Manage. Sci.* **25**, 312 (1979).
48. The conventional learning curve in Eq. 1 can be expressed as a production function. The left-hand variable in Eq. 1 is labor hours per output ($y = h/q$). Thus, Eq. 1 can be rewritten in the form: $q = a^{-1}hx^b$. Thus, the production function implicit in the conventional learning curve has a single input, labor hours, and a single measure of the state of technical knowledge, *x*, cumulative output. This formulation also imposes the assumption of proportionality between output and hours.
49. R. Conway and A. Schultz, *J. Ind. Eng.* **10**, 39 (1959); N. Baloff, *ibid.* **17**, 25 (1966); N. Baloff, *Oper. Res. Q.* **22**, 329 (1971).
50. N. K. Womer, *Manage. Sci.* **30**, 982 (1984).
51. E. R. Berndt and M. S. Khaled, *J. Polit. Econ.* **87**, 1220 (1979); L. R. Christensen and W. H. Greene, *ibid.* **84**, 655 (1976); M. B. McElroy, *ibid.* **95**, 737 (1987); M. Fuss, D. McFadden, Y. Mundlak, in *Production Economics: A Dual Approach to Theory and Applications*, M. Fuss and D. McFadden, Eds. (North-Holland, Amsterdam, 1978), pp. 217–268; A. Zellner, J. Kmenta, J. Dreze, *Econometrica* **34**, 784 (1966); W. E. Diewert, *J. Polit. Econ.* **79**, 481 (1971).
52. R. Solow, *Rev. Econ. Stat.* **39**, 312 (1957).
53. Lockheed Aircraft Corporation, *Lockheed Annual Report* (Corporate Publications, Burbank, CA, 1972), p. 1; *ibid.* (Corporate Publications, Burbank, CA, 1974), p. 8; S. J. Sansweet, *Wall Street Journal*, 31 March 1976, p. 2; *ibid.*, 16 March 1977, p. 11; "Lockheed Corp. says losses on Tri-Star spurted in period," *ibid.*, 20 June 1980, p. 21; R. J. Harris, *ibid.*, 1 July 1981, p. 10; *ibid.*, 8 December 1981, p. 3; *ibid.*, 9 December 1981, p. 22.
54. We gratefully acknowledge the support of the National Science Foundation's Decision, Risk, and Management Science Program and Economics Program (grant number SES-8808711) and of the Center for the Management of Technology and Information in Organizations at Carnegie Mellon University. We thank E. Bailey, P. S. Goodman, R. S. Kaplan, L. Lave, T. McGuire, R. L. Moreland, T. Morton, and G. Salancik for their helpful comments.

Article 17

A CLASSROOM EXERCISE USING LINEAR PROGRAMMING IN THE CONSTRUCTION OF DURATION-MATCHED DEDICATED PORTFOLIOS

by

Robert A. Strong
and
Kent D. Carter

This paper shows how linear programming can be used as a timesaving managerial aid in discovering a feasible solution to a multi-security duration-matching problem. A classroom exercise which does so provides a forum for reviewing (1) the linear programming procedure, (2) theoretical issues regarding portfolio duration, and (3) the motivation for portfolio dedication.

Robert A. Strong is an Associate Professor of Finance
Kent D. Carteris an Assistant Professor of Management
University of Maine
College of Business Administration
Orono, ME 04469
(207) 581-1986

INTRODUCTION

This paper shows how using linear programming to solve a classroom duration matching problem accomplishes three tasks:

1. It provides review of the utility of linear programming and illustrates an unusual financial application of the technique;
2. It provides a framework for the discussion of the duration-matching form of portfolio dedication;
3. It provides a good way to discuss certain theoretical issues regarding the meaning of duration when applied to a portfolio of assets.

THE CONCEPT OF DURATION MATCHING

Portfolio dedication involves managing an asset portfolio such that it services the requirements of a corresponding liability or portfolio of liabilities. Portfolio dedication is a form of immunization which, if done properly, ensures the asset portfolio will not suffer from the effects of reinvestment rate risk or interest rate risk.

There are two keys to duration matching. First, an asset portfolio must be constructed such that its duration matches that of the liabilities it will service, and second, the market value of the asset portfolio must equal the present value of the liability cash flows.

CONCEPTUAL ISSUES WITH LINEAR PROGRAMMING AND DURATION

Duration is a useful concept with many applications in portfolio and cash management. When applied to a single security, the calculation is quick. Duration is the weighted average of time until the security's cashflows occur, where the weights reflect the time value of money. Cashflows are discounted using the yield to maturity of the security. See equation 1.

$$D = \sum_{all\ t}^{n} \frac{C_t * t}{(1 + R)^t} \times \frac{1}{P_0} \tag{1}$$

where C_t = cash flow at time
         R = yield to maturity
         P_0 = current price of the bond

Duration can be more conveniently calculated using the "closed form" equation shown in Chua's 1984 *Financial Analysts Journal* article. This alternative method of calculation is not shown in all textbooks, and because the article is only three pages long, it can be a useful part of classroom discussion by itself. This method is shown in equation 2.

$$D = \frac{C \left| \frac{(1+R)^{M+1} - (1+R) - RM}{R^2 (1+R)^M} \right| + \frac{FM}{(1+R)^M}}{P_0} \tag{2}$$

where M = periods until maturity
         F = face value of the bond
         C = periodic coupon payment

and other variables are as described above.

Conceptual issues sometimes arise when it is necessary to calculate the duration of a portfolio. Consider the case of a bond portfolio containing 100 different issues. On the one hand, the portfolio's yield to maturity can be calculated by assuming that the portfolio is a single security, and finding the discount rate which equates the current value of the portfolio with the future cashflows associated with it. This discount rate can then be used to calculate the portfolio duration.

On the other hand, the bond manager might know the individual yields to maturity of the 100 portfolio components, and use these to determine the duration of each of the 100 components. The portfolio yield and portfolio duration can then be calculated as a weighted average, with the weights reflecting the dollar investment in each component relative to the entire portfolio value. See equation 3.

$$D = \sum_{i=1}^{n} \frac{x_i}{x} * D_i \tag{3}$$

where x_i = total value of investment in security i
X = total value of the investment
D_i = duration of security i

and

$$\sum_{i=1}^{n} x_i = 1.0$$

The two methods will yield slightly different values because duration is not a linear function of the yield to maturity, or, stated another way, because of the effects of convexity.

In some cases, calculating duration via the "single security" approach is virtually intractable. With twelve months in the year and bonds paying interest on either the first of fifteenth of the month, there may be as many as twenty-four different cash flows each year. The valuation equation for a long-term bond portfolio, therefore, could conceivably contain over 500 terms. Finding the yield to maturity of such an income stream requires substantial computer time and perhaps considerable managerial aggravation.

For most applications, the difference in the portfolio durations calculated via these two methods is probably immaterial. Also, it is not uncommon for the bid/ask spread on a corporate bond to be over 1% of par value. If a large portfolio must be assembled on the open market, the uncertainty associated with the spread can cause the final portfolio duration to differ from the target figure by a few months or more.

The use of linear programming requires that portfolio duration be calculated via the "individual components" method. This is the simplest method, and the technique used by most fund managers. Its advantages usually outweigh any theoretical concerns about the "true" meaning of duration.

AN EXAMPLE

Suppose two philanthropists endow their alma mater with grant money for scholarships to paid over the next twelve years. Every six months, ten students will be selected to receive $2,000 each. This means the "liability" is a series of outflows of $20,000 each, paid every six months, with a total of twenty-four payments.

The benefactor will provide an initial sum which is sufficient to finance these future payments. Perhaps the university endowment office uses a 10% annual discount rate for calculations of this sort. The cost to the benefactor, then, is the present value of a stream of twenty-four payments of $20,000 each, paid every six months, using a 10% annual discount rate. This amount is $275,973.

The duration of these payments is simply the weighted average of time until cashflows occur, and for this liability stream the duration is 5.19 years. The task is the assembly of a basket of bonds such that the basket has a market value of $275,973 and a duration of 5.19.

The Linear Program

Linear programming is normally used to optimize some function, either by maximizing benefits or by minimizing costs subject to a set of constraints. The technique can also be useful in finding a feasible solution to an otherwise unwieldy problem. When there is a large universe of eligible securities, numerous combinations of bonds satisfy both the cost and duration requirements. Finding any combination, however, can take considerable management time if it is necessary to use a trial-and-error approach to solving the problem.

For the sake of this example, assume the portfolio manager must choose bonds from the selection in Table 1.

Two of the constraints are relatively obvious. The total investment in bonds must equal the present value of the liability cash flows ($275,973), and the duration of the selected bond portfolio must equal 5.19 years.

TABLE 1 Bonds for Dedicated Scholarship Portfolio			
Bond	Price	YTM	Duration
Exxon Pipeline 8 1/4s01	87 5/8	10.05%	7.53
Duke power 8 1/2s00	88 5/8	9.98%	7.15
Chesapeke & Potomac Telephone 8 3/4s10	88 3/4	10.05%	9.34
Texas Electric Service 7 5/8s99	79 3/4	11.02%	6.79
Manfacturers Hanover 8 1/8s04	78 1/2	11.10%	8.13
90-day T-bills	98.02	8.02%	0.25

The portfolio manager may also choose to add constraints such that some degree of diversification is achieved. Otherwise, the linear programming algorithm might select a single bond plus Treasury bills as its solution. Treasury bills will be necessary here because all of the eligible bonds have durations greater than the target figure of 5.19. These bonds must be mixed with the short-duration T-bills to reduce the overall portfolio duration. Assume the manager decides that at least $30,000 par value should be purchased of each of the bonds in Table 1. The objective function for the linear program can simply be a minimization of the number of bonds used. This makes sense if commission costs are material to the duration-matching decision. Table 2 presents this linear program. It will minimize the number of bonds purchased, while ensuring that the correct dollar amount is spent, that the portfolio duration is correct, and that there is diversification across all the available bonds.

Non-integer solutions.

The initial run of the linear program may yield a solution which seeks to purchase fractional bonds, and that is exactly what happens in this particular case. The initial run of the linear program prescribes a portfolio with $80,132 par value of the Chesapeake and Potomac Telephone bonds. If this happens, it is necessary to round the bond quantities chosen by the linear program down to the nearest integer, and change constraints three through seven into equalities, requiring the selection of an integer number of bonds. Rounding down ensures that funds will be available to buy enough T-bills to satisfy the duration constraint. This technique is quick, and simply causes a slight adjustment in the quantity of T-bills purchased.

TABLE 2
Linear Program for Duration Matching

$$\text{Minimize } N_1 + N_2 + N_3 + N_4 + N_5$$

Subject to

CONSTRAINT ONE: Ensure market value of bonds equals present value of liability cash flows

$$\$876.25N_1 + \$886.25N_2 + \$887.25N_3 + \$797.50N_4 + \$785N_5 + \$9802N_6 = \$275,973$$

CONSTRAINT TWO: Ensure duration of asset portfolio equals duration of liability cash flows

$$\frac{\$876.25 \times 7.54N_1}{\$275,973} + \frac{\$886.25 \times 7.15N_2}{\$275,973} + \frac{\$887.50 \times 9.34N_3}{\$275,973} +$$

$$\frac{\$797.5 \times 6.79N_4}{\$275,973} + \frac{\$785 \times 8.13N_5}{\$275,973} + \frac{9820 \times 0.25N_6}{\$275,973} = 5.19$$

CONSTRAINTS THREE
  THRU SEVEN: Ensure at least $30,000 par value is bought of each bond

  (3) $876.25 x N1 = at least $26,287.50

  (4) $886.25 x N2 = at least $26,587.50

  (5) $887.50 x N3 = at least $26,625.00

  (6) $797.50 x N4 = at least $23,925.00

  (7) $785.00 x N5 = at least $23,550.00

N1, N2, etc. is the quantity of each bond purchased

If you prefer not to use fractional quantities of Treasury bills, you can include a non interest-rate-sensitive cash equivalent asset in the list of eligible securities. By definition, non interest-rate-sensitive securities have a duration of zero.

Integer programming would eliminate the need to worry about whole quantities of bonds. This is another dimension that can be added to the example if you wish.

The Solution.

Table 3 presents the solution to the duration-matching problem. This portfolio has a duration equal to the duration of its associated liabilities, and its market value is within a dollar of the present value of the liability cash flow stream. Linear programming quickly solves a problem that would be tedious even with only five eligible bonds. Students appreciate the usefulness of this new application. With a universe of hundreds to choose from, a mathematical aid is clearly a help.

TABLE 3
Bonds for Duration-Matched Portfolio

Bond	Price	Value	Duration	Value-Weighted Duration
$30,000 Exxon Pipeline 8 1/4s01	87 5/8	$26,287.5	7.53	0.72
$30,000 Duke power 8 1/2s00	88 5/8	26,587.5	7.15	0.69
$30,000 Chesapeke & Potomac Telephone 8 3/4s10	88 3/4	71,000	9.34	2.40
$30,000 Texas Electric Service 7 5/8s99	79 3/4	23,925	6.79	0.59
$30,000 Manfacturers Hanover8 1/8s04	78 1/2	23,550	8.13	0.69
90-day T-bills	98.02	104,623	0.25	0.10
TOTALS		$275,973		D = 5.19

REFERENCES

1. Bodie, Z., A. Kane, and A. Marcus. *Investments*. Homewood, IL: Richard D. Irwin, 1989.

2. Chua, Jess H. "A Closed-Form Formula for Calculating Bond Duration," *Financial Analysts Journal*, May/Jun 1984, pp. 76-78.

3. Francis, J. *Management of Investments*. New York: McGraw Hill, 1988.

4. Hopewell, M. and G. Kaufman. "Bond Price Volatility and Years to Maturity," *American Economic Review*, September 1973, pp. 749-753.

5. Jacob, N. and R. Pettit. *Investments*. Homewood, IL: Richard D. Irwin, 1988.

6. Kolb, R. *Principles of Finance*. Glenview, IL: Scott, Foresman, 1988.

7. Macaulay, F. R. *Some Theoretical Problems Suggested by the Movement of Interest Rates, Bond Yields, and Stock Prices in the United States Since 1856*, National Bureau of Economic Research (New York: Columbia, 1938).

8. Redington, F. M. "Review of the Principles of Life Office Valuation, "*Journal of the Institute of Actuaries*, 1952, pp. 286-340.

9. Samuelson, P. A. "The Effect of Interest Rate Increases on the Banking System," *American Economic Review*, March 1945, pp. 16-27.

Section V
Market Structure, Pricing, and Related Topics

The extent of competition in a market, or market structure, and its effect on price is a concern of both economists and managers. In this section the articles focus on matters of market structure and price.

The degree of competitiveness of the airline industry and its effect on air fares is the topic of "The Determinants of Direct Air Fares to Cleveland: How Competitive?" by Paul W. Bauer and Thomas J. Zlatoper. The authors use regression analysis to determine the factors, including the extent of competition, that affect first class, coach, and discount air fares to Cleveland, Ohio. These factors include the number of carriers on the route, the mileage from the city of origin, and the number of stops on the flight. The evidence supports the view that, as more carriers service a route, the air fares are lower.

The effect of competition on cable television prices is addressed in "Cable Television and Competition: Theory, Evidence and Policy," by Stanford L. Levin and John B. Meisel. A comparison of cable television markets with and without competition reveals that, other things equal, competitive markets have a monthly basic cable rate that is about three dollars lower. This is consistent with theoretical expectations.

Jeffrey D. Karrenbrock examines the relationship between the wholesale and retail price of gasoline in "The Behavior of Retail Gasoline Prices: Symmetric or Not?" The process by which oil is refined into gasoline and ultimately reaches the gasoline retail market is described. The article then turns to the empirical question of whether increases in wholesale gasoline prices are more fully and quickly passed through to retail prices than are decreases in wholesale prices. Data from January 1983 through December 1990 were examined. This represents a period of both increases and decreases in wholesale and retail gasoline prices. The magnitude of increases and decreases in retail gasoline prices in response to increases and decreases in wholesale prices are not significantly different in magnitude. Wholesale price increases, however, are reflected in retail prices more quickly than are wholesale price decreases.

The causes and consequences of recent corporate takeovers is the subject of "The Takeover Wave of the 1980s," by Andrei Shleifer and Robert W. Vishny. They state that the 1980s represented a period of deconglomeration. Many of the acquired firms were diversified conglomerates, and their business lines were subsequently sold off to different buyers. Acquirers also bought firms in their lines of business. The leveraged buyouts and hostile takeovers that attracted much public attention were part of this process. Increased corporate cash reserves and reduced antitrust enforcement are offered as explanations for the takeover wave of the 1980s. The authors believe that the claims of reductions in competition, employment, and research and development due to takeovers have been exaggerated.

Article 18

The Determinants of Direct Air Fares to Cleveland: How Competitive?

by Paul W. Bauer
and Thomas J. Zlatoper

Paul W. Bauer is an economist at the Federal Reserve Bank of Cleveland. Thomas J. Zlatoper is a professor at John Carroll University and a research associate at the Center for Regional Economic Issues at Case Western Reserve University. The authors would like to thank John R. Swinton and Paula J. Loboda for their expert research assistance, and thank Randall W. Eberts for his comments.

Introduction

Eleven years ago, Congress decided in the form of the Airline Deregulation Act of 1978 that the operational decisions of airlines—where planes can fly and what fares can be charged—would be better left to the airlines than to the regulators.

This decision has caused numerous changes in the industry: discount fares have become widespread and traffic has boomed, new carriers have come and gone, hub-and-spoke networks have emerged, and frequent-flier plans have become the rage. As long as the industry remains competitive, many analysts assert that travelers have little to fear from these continuing changes, since competition ensures that fares are held close to cost and that economically viable service is provided.

With the consolidation of the airline industry that started in 1986, many analysts have begun to wonder about its competitiveness, both now and in the future. The wave of mergers has resulted in an increase in the number of airlines that offer nationwide service, but this comes in the form of "fortress hubs." At such airports, the dominant carrier typically offers about three-quarters of the airport's flights. In addition, the national carriers now face less competition from regional and

local service carriers, many of whom have been purchased by or signed operating agreements with the national carriers. The impact of these developments (and of possible future consolidations) on fares depends on the competitiveness of the markets for air travel.

To gain insight into the competitiveness of the airline industry, this paper examines the determinants of air fares for first-class, coach, and discount service to a particular destination: Cleveland, Ohio. We begin by examining two of the market models that have been proposed for the airline industry. The first is the traditional view that market competitiveness is determined by the number and concentration of firms in the market. The second is the theory of contestable markets, in which the number of actual competitors in the market plays only a small role. According to this theory, it is the number of carriers that could potentially enter the market that constrains fares.

We then discuss the implications for appropriate public policy. A reduced-form equation for air fares is constructed, and the data that were collected to estimate its parameters are described. Finally, we present and analyze the empirical results and discuss the implications for public policy.

Our results suggest that these markets (the airline routes) are not perfectly contestable. The number of actual competitors does influence the fares charged by the airlines, other things being equal. Thus, policymakers should act where possible to ease entry barriers in the industry in order to preserve and enhance competition.

I. Economic Models of Airline Competition

The traditional method of determining the amount of competition in a market is to examine the market shares of the largest firms operating in that market. This measure is relevant because, until recently, most economists thought that competitiveness was determined by the number and concentration of the actual participants in the market.

The U.S. Department of Justice uses a Hirschman-Herfindahl Index (HHI: the sum of the squares of all of the firms' market shares) as an aid in assessing the impact of proposed mergers on market competition. This index ranges from close to zero in the case of a perfectly competitive market to 10,000 (100^2) in the case of a monopoly.[1] The Department of Justice guidelines recommend rejecting mergers that result in markets with an HHI greater than 1,800 unless the resulting increase in the HHI is less than 50 or there are some other special considerations. The rationale is that fewer competitors reduce the competitiveness of the market, since there will be less pressure to hold down prices and costs and since the firms will find it easier to collude.

The airline industry appears to be very uncompetitive when one examines the HHIs of various airline routes. According to a recent Congressional Budget Office study, on a typical route only 2.5 carriers offer service. Even if these carriers each had an equal share of the market, this would result in an HHI of over 4,000.

The U.S. Department of Transportation—the agency charged with oversight of the airline industry—has taken a different approach than the Justice Department. Over the last few years, it has allowed mergers to occur between carriers even when many of their routes overlapped. For example, TWA and Ozark competed on many routes involving their joint hub of St. Louis, and their merger in 1986 resulted in a large increase in concentration on these routes. In 1983, the HHI was about 3,100; just after the merger, the

HHI was about 5,800; and in 1988 the HHI had risen to about 6,800, with TWA offering about 82 percent of the flights out of St. Louis. The TWA-Ozark merger was clearly outside the Department of Justice's guidelines discussed above (however, there was the special consideration that Ozark was in financial difficulty and might have failed unless it was taken over).

In approving mergers such as this one, the Department of Transportation relied heavily on the relatively new theory of contestable markets developed primarily by Baumol, Panzar, and Willig (1982).[2] This theory states that under certain conditions, it is not necessary to have a large number of firms actually operating in a market in order for prices and output in that market to approximate the ideal outcome of a perfectly competitive market. If entry barriers into the market are low, and if there are no irrecoverable costs to exiting the market, then even markets with only a few firms will be constrained to follow the same marginal-cost pricing that perfect competition with many firms would. If the firms in the market tried to raise prices above marginal cost (the extra cost of producing an additional unit of output), then entrepreneurs could enter the market and charge a slightly lower price than the incumbent firms (taking away those firms' customers) and could earn an above-average profit. The ease of entry and exit from a perfectly contestable industry means that potential competitors also exercise competitive pressure on the firms in the industry.

There were several reasons to believe that the airline industry might approximate a perfectly contestable market after the Civil Aeronautics Board stopped regulating routes and fares, a process phased in over several years starting in the late 1970s. Planes now can quickly be shifted from one route to another, and many of the airlines rent a significant proportion of their aircraft fleets. In addition, there is a ready secondary market for used aircraft, so a major component of an airline's capital stock is much easier to acquire and dispose of than in most other industries.

Working against the idea that the airline industry is perfectly contestable are the current congestion problems in the air traffic control network. Also, new entrants find it difficult to acquire gate space and slots for takeoffs and landings at the more congested airports. Computer reservation systems, travel agent commissions, frequent-flier plans, and hub-and-spoke

■ **1** Since the market shares are squared before summing, the market shares of the largest firms will influence the index the most.

■ **2** The theory of contestable markets has been applied to a number of other industries. Whalen (1988) finds evidence that the banking industry is perfectly contestable.

networks are also cited as characteristics of providing air service that make entry into new markets difficult. Borenstein (1988) provides a more detailed investigation of these issues.

If the market for air fares approximates a perfectly competitive market, then there is very little need for government oversight of the economic conditions in the airline industry, although there still would be a role in the regulation of air safety. Actual and potential competitors force the airlines serving a market to provide the service that passengers want at the lowest possible fares. If the market is not perfectly contestable, then the government can ensure that entry into the market is as free as possible, and should enforce existing antitrust laws to protect consumers by preserving as much competition in the market as possible.

II. Empirical Model and Data

Although other researchers (for example, Bailey, Graham, and Kaplan [1985], Borenstein [1988], Butler and Huston [1987], and Call and Keeler [1985]) have explored the extent of competition in the airline industry by using models similar to the one we develop, none of these studies employs data as recent as ours (April 1987). Thus, not only are our data further away from the beginning of deregulation, but they also follow the latest wave of mergers that occurred in 1986.

The following observations will be useful in constructing the testable hypotheses. If the market were perfectly contestable, then the number of carriers serving a route would have no relationship to passenger fares. If potential competitors constrain the fare-setting abilities of existing carriers, then the market is imperfectly contestable and the effect of the number of carriers serving a route should have a significant, although small, effect on the fares charged. Lastly, if entry is so blocked that existing carriers have little to fear from new entrants, then the degree of competition on a route will be determined by the number of carriers currently serving the route, and the effect of an additional carrier on the route could cause a significant reduction in fares. This is the more traditional view of the relationship between the degree of competition and the number of competitors.

In comparing the fares charged with the number of carriers on the route across routes, one must allow for other factors that influence fares. In essence, we are estimating a reduced-form equation for air fares, so that anything that influences the demand for, or the cost of, air travel

should be taken into account. The most important of these factors are the length of the route, the volume of traffic on the route, and whether one or both of the airports involved are hubs or are restricted in takeoff and landing slots.

The characteristics of a particular flight on a given route can also influence both the supply and the demand for the flight. The most important of these are the number of stops on a particular flight, whether a meal is provided, and the particular carrier offering the flight. Finally, the demand for air service on a particular route will depend in part on characteristics of the flight's origin and destination cities, such as their average per capita incomes and whether they are business or tourist centers.

We estimate the following model using ordinary least squares (OLS):

$$
\begin{aligned}
(1) \quad FARE = \; & a_0 + a_1 \text{ CARRIERS} \\
& + a_2 \text{ CARRIERS}^2 + a_3 \text{ PASS} \\
& + a_4 \text{ MILES} + a_5 \text{ MILES}^2 \\
& + a_6 \text{ POP} + a_7 \text{ INC} + a_8 \text{ CORP} \\
& + a_9 \text{ SLOT} + a_{10} \text{ STOP} \\
& + a_{11} \text{ MEAL} + a_{12} \text{ HUB} \\
& + a_{13} \text{ EA} + a_{14} \text{ CO} + \text{error},
\end{aligned}
$$

where

FARE = one-way air fare;

CARRIERS = number of carriers;

CARRIERS^2 = number of carriers squared;

PASS = total number of passengers flown on route (all carriers);

MILES = mileage from the origin city to Cleveland;

MILES^2 = the number of miles squared;

POP = population of the origin city;

INC = per capita income of the origin city;

CORP = proxy for potential business traffic from the origin city;

SLOT = dummy variable equaling 1 if the origin city has a slot-restricted airport, 0 otherwise;

STOP = number of on-flight stops;

MEAL = dummy variable equaling 1 if a meal is served, 0 otherwise;

HUB = dummy variable equaling 1 if the origin city has a hub airline, 0 otherwise;

EA = dummy variable equaling 1 if the carrier is Eastern Airlines, 0 otherwise;

CO = dummy variable equaling 1 if the carrier is Continental Airlines, 0 otherwise.

This model is estimated separately for each of three classes of fares: first class, coach, and restricted discount.

The data to estimate this model were combined from a number of sources. The *Official Airline Guide* (April 1987) was the source of the fare information and the data on the flight characteristics, such as CARRIERS, STOP, SLOT, MEAL, EA, and CO. All of the data pertain to direct domestic flights terminating in Cleveland. Unfortunately, fares for connecting flights could not be analyzed here because only direct fares are reported in the *Official Airline Guide*. In future research, we hope to obtain such data.

generated by each city. Information on whether an origin city was considered to have a hub airline (HUB) was obtained from 1985 Department of Transportation statistics. For each of the three fare classes, summary statistics on the variables used in the analysis are provided in table 1.

III. Estimation Results

Tables 2, 3, and 4 report OLS estimates of equation (1) for first-class, coach, and discount fares. The amount of variation in fares explained in each estimated equation (the adjusted R-square statistics in tables 2 through 4) is generally high, and is higher for the first-class and coach categories than for the discount category. This is probably the result of the discount fares being less homogeneous than the other fare classes. For our discount fare, we always selected the least expensive restricted-discount fare reported in the

TABLE 1

Summary Statistics of the Variables

Variable	First-Class Fares		Coach Fares		Discount Fares	
	Mean	Standard Deviation	Mean	Standard Deviation	Mean	Standard Deviation
FARE	330.17	123.63	201.78	89.60	62.65	29.85
CARRIERS	2.77	1.33	2.89	1.25	2.88	1.25
PASSENGERS	18,458.00	22,802.00	15,260.00	21,414.00	15,273.00	21,406.00
MILES	744.19	535.18	537.27	465.43	541.25	466.32
INCOME	13,996.00	1,766.00	13,709.00	1,643.60	13,727.00	1,656.10
CORP	10.63	16.67	8.76	15.17	8.75	15.17
SLOT	0.22	0.42	0.19	0.39	0.19	0.39
STOP	0.46	0.60	0.41	0.63	0.42	0.63
MEAL	0.60	0.49	0.44	0.50	0.44	0.50
HUB	0.71	0.46	0.66	0.47	0.66	0.47
CO	0.16	0.37	0.08	0.27	0.08	0.27
EA	0.16	0.37	0.07	0.26	0.08	0.27
POP	4,046.30	4,668.20	3,497.60	4,184.90	3,493.40	4,187.80

SOURCE: Authors' calculations.

Data on passengers (PASS) and nonstop mileage from origin to destination (MILES) were taken from the U.S. Department of Transportation's *Origin and Destination City Pair Summary*. Data on per capita income (INC) of the origin cities were obtained from the *Survey of Current Business* (April 1986 issue). The number of Standard & Poor's companies headquartered in each origin city (CORP) was compiled to be used as a proxy for the business traffic likely to be

Official Airline Guide, and these fares were not always subject to exactly the same restrictions.[3]

In interpreting these results, recall that only direct flights to Cleveland were included in the data. Also note that since more than 90 percent of passengers travel on some type of discount fare,

■ 3 It was not possible to select one particular type of discount fare for all of the routes because no type of discount fares were reported for all routes.

TABLE 2

First-Class Fare Estimates

Variable	Estimated Coefficient	Standard Error	T-Ratio
CARRIERS	-19.50	22.20	-0.878
CARRIERS^2	2.79	4.42	0.632
MILES	0.233	0.455E-1	5.13
MILES^2	-0.974E-5	0.197E-4	-0.495
POP	-0.598E-2	0.357E-2	-1.67
INC	-0.195E-2	0.285E-2	-0.686
CORP	3.62	1.05	3.45
PASS	-0.818E-3	0.106E-2	-0.771
STOP	12.50	9.18	1.36
SLOT	7.13	23.90	0.299
HUB	11.30	12.60	0.900
MEAL	11.20	10.50	1.07
EA	-18.30	11.40	-1.60
CO	-66.40	11.60	-5.72
CONSTANT	212.00	40.60	5.21

NOTE: All values are authors' calculations. Number of observations = 163; R-squared = 0.863.

according to the Air Transport Association, this class of service is probably the most important for evaluating the competitiveness of the industry.[4]

The first issue is the effect of the number of carriers on fares. The estimated values for CARRIERS and CARRIERS^2 have the expected signs

TABLE 3

Coach Fare Estimates

Variable	Estimated Coefficient	Standard Error	T-Ratio
CARRIERS	-23.00	11.60	-1.99
CARRIERS^2	4.00	2.19	1.83
MILES	0.277	0.231E-1	12.00
MILES^2	-0.520E-4	0.104E-4	-4.98
POP	-0.114E-2	0.200E-2	-0.570
INC	-0.178E-2	0.168E-2	-1.06
CORP	1.22	0.487	2.51
PASS	-0.275E-3	0.522E-3	-0.527
STOP	7.64	3.59	2.13
SLOT	-0.746	11.20	-0.667E-1
HUB	4.18	5.16	0.810
MEAL	0.945	5.35	0.177
EA	5.80	7.48	0.775
CO	-56.50	7.42	-7.61
CONSTANT	126.00	22.00	5.75

NOTE: All values are authors' calculations. Number of observations = 323; R-squared = 0.871.

for all three classes of fares. These results suggest that as additional carriers begin service on a route, fares are lowered, since CARRIERS is negative. But because the coefficient of CARRIERS^2 is positive, each additional carrier lowers fares on the route less than the one before. After three or four carriers are serving a route, fares no longer appear to be affected by the number of carriers.

These coefficients are statistically significant for coach and discount fares, but are not significant for first-class fares. For discount fares, the addition of one carrier to a monopoly route would lower fares by about $11, other things being equal. Adding a third carrier to the route would again lower fares, but by only about $6.50. With a fourth carrier, fares drop even less, by about $2. Fares do not appear to fall any more once about four carriers are serving the route. At this point, discount fares are about $20 less than they would be if only one carrier served the route. Extrapolation beyond this point is not warranted since the maximum number of carriers on any route in our sample is only five.

The above result for first-class fares does not mean that these fares are perfectly contestable, however. If we estimate the same model as equation (1), but replace CARRIERS and CARRIERS^2 with a dummy variable equal to one if there is more than one carrier on the route and zero otherwise, we find that the coefficient of this variable is significant and negative for first-class fares. First-class fares are about $21 lower on routes with more than one carrier, other things being equal. In other words, since fares are cheaper on routes with more than one carrier, these results do not support the notion that these routes are perfectly contestable.

Earlier studies that investigated whether the market for air fares was perfectly contestable also found little support for perfect contestability. As mentioned above, their data generally came from the early 1980s and thus may have been estimated too soon after deregulation for the airlines to have adjusted to their new environment. Because our study employs fare data from April 1987, it is unlikely that the lack of contestability is a result of the airlines' having insufficient time to adjust to the deregulated environment. This data set also has the advantage of being gathered about a year after the merger wave that peaked in 1986.

Not surprisingly, MILES has a positive and significant estimated coefficient for each class of fares. Coach and discount fares have a significant amount of "fare taper": as the flight distance increases, the cost per mile falls. First-class fares

■ 4 Cited in Kahn (1988).

do not exhibit this property to a significant extent. For a flight of average length, first-class and coach fares increase about $0.22 per mile and discount fares increase about $0.06 per mile.

The PASS, SLOT, and HUB variables all measure possible capacity constraints facing the airlines serving a given route.[5] HUB is not statistically significant at the 5 percent level for any type of fares. The density of traffic on a route as measured by the PASS variable significantly increases discount fares. Only discount-fare passengers pay the expected premium for flying into slot-restricted airports. Flying into a slot-restricted airport increases the one-way fare by about $18 for these passengers.

TABLE 4

Discount Fare Estimates

Variable	Estimated Coefficient	Standard Error	T-Ratio
CARRIERS	-17.50	4.76	-3.67
CARRIERS^2	2.19	0.905	2.42
MILES	0.791E-1	0.961E-2	8.24
MILES^2	-0.140E-4	0.434E-5	-3.23
POP	-0.868E-3	0.829E-3	-1.05
INC	-0.411E-2	0.679E-3	-6.05
CORP	-1.06	0.203	-5.22
PASS	0.853	0.217E-3	3.93
STOP	-3.85	1.48	-2.60
SLOT	17.70	4.63	3.82
HUB	-3.50	2.16	-1.62
MEAL	1.80	2.21	0.813
EA	-10.60	3.04	-3.49
CO	-4.17	3.09	-1.35
CONSTANT	113.00	9.10	12.40

NOTE: All values are authors' calculations. Number of observations = 323; R-squared = 0.799.

Flight characteristics, such as the number of intermediate stops on the flight, influence coach and discount fares, but not first-class fares. Coach passengers pay about $7.60 for each stop, whereas discount-fare passengers actually get compensated about $3.85 for each stop. The fare charged does not seem to depend on whether the flight includes a meal.

The characteristics of the cities involved influence the fare charged to the various classes of passengers. The larger the population of the origin city, the lower the fare for all three classes of service, although this result is statistically significant at the 5 percent level only for first-class fares. The per-capita income variable seems to affect only discount fares significantly. Discount fares fall as incomes rise, indicating that higher-income passengers expect compensation in the form of lower fares for flying with discount tickets, other things being equal. The more important the city is as a business center (as measured by CORP), the higher the first-class and coach fares tend to be. Discount fares, on the other hand, are lower.

Continental charges significantly less than other carriers for first-class and coach service, other things being equal. Conversely, Eastern charges significantly less for discount service than other airlines, other things being equal.[6] Texas Air may own both of these carriers, but they appear to follow different criteria in setting fares. Keep in mind that these carrier-based fare differentials reflect differing cost and demand characteristics, including quality of service.

IV. Conclusion

An understanding of forces setting fares and the level of competition in the airline industry is crucial in order to formulate effective public policies for the industry. Some analysts have suggested that the ease of entry into most airline markets after deregulation increased the competitiveness of fares, even though the actual number of carriers is relatively small. We found that the number of airlines serving a route does influence the fares charged for all classes of service. Thus, the airline industry is not perfectly contestable even when very recent data are employed.

The benefits to passengers of adding an additional carrier on a typical route are still sizable, with fares declining until about four carriers are serving the route. This result is the strongest for discount fares. Fares on routes with four to five carriers are about $20 less than fares on routes with only one carrier, other things being equal. This is about a third of the average one-way discount fare.

■ **5** It is reasonable to consider whether both the number of carriers and the number of passengers on a route should be treated as endogenous variables in equation (1). Hausman specification tests were performed and indicate that in setting the fare on a given route, these variables can be treated as exogenous variables.

■ **6** We only report results that controlled for Continental and Eastern Airlines, because only these two carriers appeared to behave differently from the other carriers in setting fares.

Since deregulation, the airlines' clear goal has been to maximize their profits. Thus, they charge the highest fare possible on all their routes, with competition among existing carriers and the ease of entry of new carriers limiting how high those fares can be on a particular route. It is important that policymakers look at both the actual number of competitors and the ease of entry for a particular route. Since the number of carriers serving the typical route has risen since 1983—even if one allows for the recent merger wave—this suggests that the market for air fares remains fairly competitive, but that public policies to ease the entry of more carriers per route could lead to increased benefits for consumers.

In short, these findings suggest that the traditional concepts of market concentration, such as the number of competitors, are still relevant in assessing the amount of competition on a given route, even in the deregulated environment. Consequently, the antitrust laws that are applied to other industries are pertinent to the airline industry.

References

Bailey, Elizabeth E., Graham, David R., and Kaplan, Daniel P., *Deregulating the Airlines*, Cambridge, MA: The MIT Press, 1985.

Baumol, William J., Panzar, John C., and Willig, Robert D., *Contestable Markets and the Theory of Industry Structure*, New York: Harcourt Brace Jovanovich, Inc., 1982.

Borenstein, Severin, "Hubs and High Fares: Airport Dominance and Market Power in the U.S. Airline Industry," Institute of Public Policy Studies Discussion Paper No. 278, University of Michigan, March 1988.

Butler, Richard V. and Huston, John H., "Actual Competition, Potential Competition, and the Impact of Airline Mergers on Fares," paper presented at the Western Economic Association Meetings, Vancouver, British Columbia, July 1987.

Call, Gregory D. and Keeler, Theodore E., "Airline Deregulation, Fares, and Market Behavior: Some Empirical Evidence," in Andrew F. Daughety, ed., *Analytical Studies in Transport Economics*, New York: Cambridge University Press, 1985.

Congressional Budget Office, "Policies for the Deregulated Airline Industry," July 1988.

Hausman, J.A., "Specification Tests in Econometrics," *Econometrica*, November 1978, *46*, 1251-71.

Kahn, Alfred E., "I Would Do It Again," *Regulation*, 1988, *2*.

Morrison, Steven and Winston, Clifford, "Empirical Implications and Tests of the Contestability Hypothesis," *The Journal of Law and Economics*, April 1987, *30*, 53-66.

Official Airline Guides, *Official Airline Guide: North American Edition*, April 1, 1987, *13*.

Standard & Poor's Corporation, *Statistical Service: Security Price Index Record*, 1986 Edition.

U.S. Department of Commerce, Bureau of the Census, *State and Area Data Handbook*, 1984.

U.S. Department of Commerce, Regional Economic Measurement Division, "County and Metropolitan Area Personal Income, 1982-84," *Survey of Current Business,* April 1986.

U.S. Department of Transportation, Center for Transportation Information, *Origin and Destination City Pair Summary,* Data Bank 6, Computer Files.

Whalen, Gary, "Actual Competition, Potential Competition, and Bank Profitability in Rural Markets," *Economic Review,* Federal Reserve Bank of Cleveland, Quarter 3, 1988, 14–20.

Article 19

Cable television and competition

Theory, evidence and policy

Stanford L. Levin and John B. Meisel

There is currently widespread discussion in the USA of the merits of amending legislation to allow competition in the cable television market, notably from the telecommunications companies. This article explores what economic theory can contribute to this debate, and adduces empirical evidence on the effects of competition in the cable market where it presently exists. The authors conclude that blocking entry into cable, and indeed into telecommunications markets, is likely to be poor policy, and that increased competition would foster the development of an efficient modern broadband network.

Stanford L. Levin is Chairman and Professor of Economics, and John B. Meisel is Professor of Economics, in the Department of Economics, Southern Illinois University at Edwardsville, Edwardsville, IL 62026-1102, USA (Tel: +1-618-692 2592; Fax: +1-618-692 3047).

Cable television companies and local exchange telecommunications companies in the USA are currently engaged in a heated debate over competition in the cable television market and, by inference, in the local exchange telecommunications market. Cable companies would like to preserve their current monopolies, once again submitting, if necessary, to limited local regulation in order to do so. Local exchange carriers, on the other hand, would like to be allowed to enter into the cable markets, either with new entry or by buying existing cable companies. Other versions of this debate are taking place in many other countries around the world.

In the USA the discussion is taking place in Congress, at the National Telecommunications and Information Administration (NTIA) and at the Federal Communications Commission (FCC). Congress is considering legislation to reregulate cable and legislation to repeal the cable/telco cross-ownership ban. The NTIA is also considering revising its recent policy statement on a video dial tone in favour of more competition in the cable market. The FCC is reconsidering its statutory definition of what constitutes competition in cable, and hence when the cable companies can be free from regulation, and how cable companies should be regulated, as well as the cable/telco cross-ownership ban.

This article explores what economic theory can contribute to this debate. The article then compares cable companies operating in a non-monopoly environment with those which do not to see if the expected benefits of additional suppliers are present. The article concludes by using economic theory and empirical evidence to make policy recommendations on cable television and telecommunications competition and on the cross-ownership issue.

Cable and broadband

No discussion of cable television and telecommunications can take place without reference to broadband. Cable companies, telecommunications companies and their other competitors are all likely to be thinking about broadband, and each would like to control the underlying broadband network. Explorations of the theory and policy of cable must take place in this context.

Broadband services delivered over fibre-optic networks are likely to change the entire telecommunications industry fundamentally. Not only may existing services, including telecommunications and television, be delivered differently, but new services not yet evisaged may become common. To date, much of what has been written about broadband has concerned technology only, but the policy response to broadband will undoubtedly be important. The broadband infrastructure that results will affect the nature, availability and pricing of telecommunications and related services in the coming years.

One of the most contentious issues surrounding broadband is who will provide the broadband delivery system. The answer depends on both economics and regulation. There may or may not be more than one broadband delivery system, depending on ultimate costs, economies of scale, local market characteristics and customer preferences. Similarly, there may or may not be private networks supplementing all or part of the public broadband network. Larger markets are more likely to have more than one system, particularly if absolute costs are relatively low, while smaller markets may have only one system.

Both telecommunications companies and cable TV companies, along with others, are positioning themselves to provide the broadband network. Local exchange companies are interested because of their current services and because they see the need to consolidate all revenues to cover total costs. They believe that the cost of a broadband network requires current telco revenues, cable transmission revenues and perhaps other revenues from new services or from programming in order to make the broadband network investment feasible. Cable companies are interested because they currently supply television/video services and because they see the telcos as a threat to their current business. Cable facilities are wearing out and need to be replaced, and telcos are considering replacing or upgrading local loops, sometimes with fibre. This is bringing the ownership issue to a head, as the resolution of this issue will help to determine who will do the replacement and with what technology.

Both telcos and cable are viable competitors and broadband network providers. Telephone penetration rates are over 90%, and virtually everyone, with some rural exceptions, has telephone lines passing by his or her residence. Cable had a 54% penetration rate at the end of 1989, but, more importantly, 80% of residences were passed by cable,[1] and this latter figure should continue to increase.

The FCC is currently investigating the cable/telco cross-ownership ban, and a recommendation could be made at any time. The NTIA is also considering the cross-ownership ban.[2] The NTIA previously recommended that the cross-ownership ban be left intact but that telcos be encouraged to provide distribution services as a common carrier. It is now reconsidering these issues and is investigating whether the cross-ownership ban is retarding development of the telecommunications infrastructure. The NTIA is also soliciting comments on whether telcos need the ability to engage in programming in order to have sufficient incentive to deploy a broadband distribution system. Janice Obuchowski, the new Administrator of the NTIA, states that 'NTIA pioneered the concept of "video dial tone," in which telephone companies could provide the "conduit" to the home for competitive video programming.

[1]Federal Communications Commission, 'Notice of Inquiry: In the Matter of Competition, Rate Deregulation and the Commission's Policies Relating to the Provision of Cable Television Service', December 1989, p 24.
[2]National Telecommunications and Information Administration, Comprehensive Study on the Domestic Telecommunications Infrastructure, Department of Commerce, Washington, DC, January 1990, pp 656–660.

In the coming year, NTIA will be looking beyond that concept in the continuing cable–telco cross-ownership debate to determine whether all companies, including local exchange telephone companies, should be able to enter the video programming market.'[3]

It is becoming increasingly clear that telcos are interested in entering the cable business. Although they are barred from doing so within their service areas at this time, Pacific Telesis is attempting to buy cable companies outside its service territory, and all of the regional Bell holding companies are involved in telecommunications abroad, often in cable ownership.[4] These overseas activities seem to expand daily. The companies have all shown their willingness to invest abroad to gain cable experience; certainly they are hoping to have the opportunity to use this experience in the USA. For example, 'Investing in foreign cable systems allows the regional companies to gain experience in combining cable and telephone services. The cable contracts in Britain allow companies to provide telephone and television services over the same networks. And the Baby Bells plan to install fiber-optic cable, which can carry both telephone and video signals, in some European homes.'[5]

Raymond Smith, Chairman and CEO of Bell Atlantic, presents a position that is generally representative of the Bell portion of the local exchange telecommunications industry.[6] He wants Bell Atlantic to be the company that builds the fibre-based broadband system in its service territory. Under this scenario, Bell Atlantic would provide broadband transport services to all 'legitimate' users on a 'non-discriminatory price-list basis'.[7] While Bell Atlantic would like to form joint ventures with programmers, they do not appear interested in entering the programming business. In exchange, Bell Atlantic is willing to allow any user of the broadband network to provide telecommunication services in competition with it.

This Bell Atlantic view is similar to the NTIA's proposal for a video dial tone:

The NTIA 'video dial tone' proposal entails: (1) expanding the common carrier regulatory model applicable to video transport (but not allowing such common carriers to supply program content) and (2) facilitating local telephone company provision of such transport to others (regardless of whether they have a local cable franchise). According to NTIA, the public interest benefits of the regime would be: (1) its immediate competitive effect on existing cable systems, causing them to be more responsive to consumers in terms of quality of service, and programming choices; and (2) further enhancements to exchange telephone facilities made in order to deliver video signals.[8]

Cable companies, on the other hand, seem interested in protecting their monopoly both from entry and from acquisition by telcos. While they are also opposed to any reregulation of the industry, they would probably prefer that to losing their franchise as a result of entry.

Entry and mergers

Cable television markets have historically been regulated, franchised monopolies. As a result of the 1984 Cable Communications Policy Act municipal governments can no longer regulate basic cable rates in markets in which there are three or more off-the-air signals.[9] In addition, it is now more difficult for a municipality to deny renewal of a franchise to a cable company. In essence, then, many cable companies are unregulated, legally protected monopolies.

[3]Janice Obuchowski, 'The state of the Union in telecommunications regulation', *Telecommunications*, January 1990, p 25.
[4]See, for example, Calvin Sims, 'The Baby Bells scramble for Europe', *New York Times*, 10 December 1989, Sec 3, pp 1ff; and Paul Travis, 'Bell South joins French CATV firm', *Telephony*, 22 January 1990, p 3.
[5]Sims, *ibid*.
[6]Doug Halonen, 'Ringing in a new era', *Electronic Media*, 11 December 1989.
[7]*Ibid*.
[8]*Op cit*, Ref 1, p 14.
[9]The FCC will probably change this standard. It has recently begun this process by issuing a rulemaking to alter its standard for what constitutes effective competition. See 'FCC effective-competition rule could amount to "price cap" for cable', *Communications Daily*, Vol 10, No 237, 10 December 1990, pp 1–2.

Alfred Sikes, Chairman of the FCC, has stated, however, that 'The FCC has an interest in ensuring a video service marketplace which is effectively competitive, because that has proven to be the most efficient means of safeguarding the public's interest in an economically robust and diversified media market.'[10] It is in this context that the FCC continues to investigate cable television regulation and cable/telco cross-ownership issues. Sikes discusses the importance of entry, and also states that 'Any price regulation, of course, should be applied only to the extent that competitive marketplace forces are demonstrably inadequate to safeguard customers' interest. If price regulation is to be reimposed, as a number of interest groups have urged, it is important at the same time to take steps aimed at engendering the kind of pro-entry, procompetitive policies which, over time, will facilitate phasing out any such regulation.'[11]

There is no economic reason to block competitive entry, resulting in more than one broadband network, and there may even be reasons to allow mergers between telcos and cable companies. Telcos and cable companies each bring something to a prospective merger. Cable companies have customers and the right to a market for TV-type services. Telcos have large size (as do some cable companies), access to capital, better customer relations and technological expertise. Cable systems wearing out and telcos considering replacement of local loops will help achieve a resolution to the merger issue.

While allowing potential competitors to merge is not usually good public policy, in this case it could remove an important impediment to broadband deployment. The structural conflicts make achieving a broadband network difficult, and the alternative may be not two networks but none. The question may be how to get the best single network. At the same time it may be possible to replace a cable monopoly with a better alternative, particularly if there are no barriers for any service provider who wishes to use the new broadband network.

Any evaluation of competition must also make the distinction between a competitive market structure and competitive behaviour, and in this case competitive behaviour can be preserved. The owner may be required to operate the network as a common carrier. This may happen automatically, with pressure to sell the substantial excess network capacity. The owner's economic interest in exclusion should be low, and antitrust may provide a sufficiently effective enforcement threat and remedy. If these financial pressures are not sufficient, however, regulation can always be used to ensure access to the broadband network.

Currently, telcos are prevented by the Modified Final Judgment (MFJ) from originating information or video services. They can, however, probably control a small proportion of the total number of channels without any adverse effect on competitive behaviour; indeed, they are an important source of potential competition. Developing open network architecture experience may suggest how to resell the network and network services and how to get competitive behaviour with one underlying network.

Even so, some regulation may be needed. The need for this regulation will be greater if there is only one broadband network. This regulation will have to address how Bell operating companies and independent telcos involved in broadband and cable/telco cross-ownership should be treated. For example, they may or may not be allowed to originate programming. Regulation may also have to deter-

[10]Alfred Sikes, 'Statement on Federal Communications Commission cable television policies, recommendations, and initiatives', Subcommittee on Communications, Committee on Commerce, Science and Transportation, United States Senate, 17 November 1989, p 8.
[11]*Ibid*, p 11.

mine whether the broadband network provider should formally be required to adhere to common-carrier status or whether there are sufficient market forces to make such regulation unnecessary.

Recently, however, telcos have not upheld the concept of common carriage. Under federal and state regulatory pressure many quickly caved in on dial-a-porn and related issues. Some telcos have refused to carry certain services they deemed inappropriate, have agreed to carry certain services only on separate exchanges or with pre-subscription, and have provided selective billing arrangements depending on the nature of the service. While less regulation is, in general, preferable, actions to date weaken the argument for no regulation unless telcos are more willing to demonstrate that they can behave as true common carriers.

Relaxing the ban on cable/telco cross-ownership can prevent unjustified competing systems, while providing maximum choice, better service and lower prices to customers. Such accommodations are particularly likely to result as existing cable systems reach the end of their useful life; the opportunity will be excellent for a cable/telco combination to install a new multipurpose fibre-based broadband delivery system. At the same time, if the market will support more than one broadband system, that, too, will be allowed to develop.

Empirical analysis

Economic theory is clear as to the benefits of competition.[12] Most importantly, competition should result in lower prices. In addition, competition should result in improved service quality or more diverse price–quality choices from the customer's point of view, although this is more difficult to measure objectively.

Since there are a small number of jurisdictions with competing cable television systems, it is possible to measure whether customers in these areas with competition receive the expected benefits.[13] If they do benefit, these results will confirm the predictions of economic theory and will support procompetitive cable television policy recommendations.

The methodology for such a study is to compare areas with competitive and non-competitive cable companies. The objective is to identify jurisdictions which are similar in most respects except for the presence or absence of competition. Then, controlling for other influences, it is possible to measure the extent to which, for example, price is lower for the cable systems with competition than for those cable systems without competition.[14]

Table 1 lists the matched cities and cable companies for the competitive and non-competitive sample. There is a larger sample of 47 firms in 19 pairs of markets and a smaller sample of 35 firms in 14 pairs of markets. The smaller sample is useful as a check on the larger sample; some of the firms in the larger sample operate in both competitive and non-competitive areas in a locality, and it is difficult to obtain reliable data, other than price data, specific to each area. The smaller sample eliminates these firms and markets where the data may not be sufficiently reliable.[15]

In addition to competition having an effect on price, cost considerations and the quality of the service may also affect price. An older system and a greater density of customers may both result in lower costs

[12]For a description of the industry and some theoretical analyses, see for example Thomas W. Hazlett, 'Duopolistic competition in cable television: implications for public policy', *Yale Journal on Regulation*, Vol 7, pp 65–148 (including a response by Albert K. Smiley and reply by Hazlett; and Harry M. Shooshan III, 'Cable television: promoting a competitive industry structure', in Paula R. Newberg, ed, *New Directions in Telecommunications Policy*, Duke University Press, Durham, NC, 1989.

[13]Hazlett suggests that only in about 1–3% of all US markets does a cable firm face competition from another cable firm or from a multichannel microwave competitor. See Thomas W. Hazlett, 'Should telephone companies provide cable TV?', *Regulation*, Winter 1990, p 77.

[14]Primeaux, for example, uses such an approach to study electricity prices. See Walter J. Primeaux, Jr, 'Estimate of the price effect of competition: the case of electricity', *Resources and Energy*, Vol 7, 1985, pp 325–340.

[15]This sample is the group of firms from 'Cable rates in competitive and non-competitive markets', *Consumers' Research*, May 1990, p 10, for which data are available for all the variables in the study.

Table 1. List of cable companies.

Competitive	Non-competitive
1 Chula Vista, CA Cox Cable Ultronics	1 Chula Vista, CA Cox Cable
2 Sacramento, CA Pacific Select TV	2 Sacramento, CA Viacom Cablevision
3 Orange County, FL Cablevision Ind	3 Orange County, FL Cablevision of Central Florida Cablevision Ind
4 Orlando, FL Cablevision of Central Florida	4 Ft Lauderdale, FL Selkirk Communications
5 Vidalia, GA TCI Southland	5 Louisville, GA TelleScripps
6 Warner Robbins AFB, GA Cox Cable	6 Macon, GA Cox Cable
7 Boone County, KY Storer	7 Covington, KY Storer
8 Frankfort, KY Community Cablevision	8 Lexington, KY TeleCable
9 Glasgow, KY TeleScripps Glasgow EPB	9 Bowling Green, KY Storer
10 Monroe, MI Toledo Blade	10 Adrian, MI Westmarc
11 Omaha, NE Cox Cable	11 Lincoln, NE Cablevision
12 Hillsboro, NC Cablevision Industries	12 Carrboro, NC Albert Cable
13 Paramus, NJ Cablevision UA Cablesystems	13 Palisades Park, NJ Vision Cable TV
14 Cleveland, OH North Coast TBA	14 Akron, OH Warner Amex Cable
15 Allentown, PA Twin-County Trans Video Service Electric	15 Reading, PA Berks Cable
16 Pottsville, PA Warner Wire Teleview	16 Lebanon, PA Valley Video Service
17 Henderson, TN Multivision	17 Jackson, TN Tribune Cable
18 Carollton, TX Storer	18 Addison, TX Storer
19 Sandy, UT TCI Insight Cablevision	19 Ogden, UT Community TV of Utah

Notes: 19-market sample: 27 competitive, 20 non-competitive.
14-market sample: 21 competitive, 14 non-competitive.
The 14-market sample omits markets 1, 3, 6, 7 and 18 from the 19-market sample.

and prices. The number and quality of channels provided by the cable system should also affect the price that the cable company is able to charge.

The following regression model can be used to estimate these relationships.

$$\text{PRICE} = F \text{ (COMP, DENSITY, AGE, SATCHAN/TOTCHAN/MAJCHAN)} \tag{1}$$

where:

PRICE = monthly basic cable price[16] for the most comprehensive service that does not include pay movie channels;

COMP = 1 if competitive, 0 otherwise;

DENSITY = homes passed per mile of cable;

AGE = age of the system in months;

SATCHAN = the number of satellite channels included in basic service;

[16]From *ibid.*

Table 2. Regression results, 19-market sample.

Variable	Dependent variable		
	PRICE	*PRICE*	*PRICE*
COMP	−3.28[a]	−3.33[a]	−3.24[a]
DENSITY	−0.0000418	−0.0000525	−0.0000327
LDENSITY			
AGE	−0.0000776	−0.0000881	−0.0000666
LAGE			
SATCHAN	0.0651		
LSATCHAN			
TOTCHAN		0.0664	
LTOTCHAN			
MAJCHAN			0.22445[c]
LMAJCHAN			
CONSTANT	16.56[a]	16.02[a]	13.88[a]
Adj R²	0.243	0.250	0.247
F-stat	4.69[a]	4.84[a]	4.60[a]
	LPRICE	*LPRICE*	*LPRICE*
COMP	−0.248[a]	−0.259[a]	−0.255[a]
DENSITY			
LDENSITY	0.0370	0.0339	0.0373
AGE			
LAGE	−0.0101	−0.0092	−0.0079
SATCHAN			
LSATCHAN	0.0516		
TOTCHAN			
LTOTCHAN		0.1462	
MAJCHAN			
LMAJCHAN			0.2712[b]
CONSTANT	2.62[a]	2.29[a]	2.01[a]
Adj R²	0.203	0.241	0.255
F-stat	3.90[a]	4.65[a]	4.77[a]

[a]Significant at the 1% level or better.
[b]Significant at the 5% level or better.
[c]Significant at the 10% level or better.

[17]Data on DENSITY, AGE, SATCHAN and TOTCHAN from *Factbook, The Networks for the Nineties, Cable 1990, Part I*, Warren Publishing, Washington, DC, 1990.
[18]The density hypothesis is that marginal cost will be lower in more dense systems, resulting in lower prices. This may result from shorter distances from the cable to residences, for example. On the other hand, more dense systems may have lower average costs, which would not necessarily result in lower prices.
[19]The following empirical evidence meets Smiley's call for an empirical demonstration that actual competition in cable markets 'effectively constrains rates'. See Hazlett, *op cit*, Ref 12, p 122.

TOTCHAN = the number of total channels included in basic service;[17]

MAJCHAN = the number of major satellite channels included in basic service; major channels are those satellite channels received on at least half of the cable systems in the study.

LPRICE, LDENSITY, LAGE, LSATCHAN, LTOTCHAN and LMAJCHAN are logarithms of the respective variables. The sign on the coefficient of the competition variable should be negative, as should the signs on the coefficients of the cost variables (density[18] and age). The sign on the coefficients on the variables for the number of channels (satellite and total) and for the number of quality channels (major channels) should be positive.

The regression model is estimated with a linear and logarithmic specification. The results of the regressions are presented in Table 2 for the larger sample and in Table 3 for the smaller sample.[19] All the regressions are significant, and the significant coefficients are robust across both samples and all of the alternative specifications.

The linear estimation suggests that customers of competitive cable companies pay between $2.94 and $3.33 per month less for service, and this basic service typically includes more channels. The logarithmic estimation suggests elasticities between −0.22 and −0.30. The cost variables are not significant in any regression. This may suggest that costs are a relatively unimportant factor in setting cable prices, within limits. It also suggests that cable companies are charging what they can in the market, given customers' demands, and that relatively small differences in cost will not affect the market price.

Customers do pay more for more channels received as part of their

Table 3. Regression results, 14-market sample.

Variable	Dependent variable		
	PRICE	PRICE	PRICE
COMP	−3.01[a]	−3.08[a]	−2.94[a]
DENSITY	−0.00011	−0.000088	−0.000089
LDENSITY			
AGE	−0.000077	−0.00012	−0.00012
LAGE			
SATCHAN	0.1114[c]		
LSATCHAN			
TOTCHAN		0.0869[c]	
LTOTCHAN			
MAJCHAN			0.2102[c]
LMAJCHAN			
CONSTANT	15.77[b]	15.73[a]	14.79[b]
Adj R²	0.303	0.230	0.250
F-stat	4.81[a]	4.74[a]	3.75[a]
	LPRICE	LPRICE	LPRICE
COMP	−0.222[a]	−0.298[a]	−0.233[a]
DENSITY			
LDENSITY	0.0316	0.0429	0.0317
AGE			
LAGE	−0.0215	−0.0485	−0.0285
SATCHAN			
LSATCHAN	0.0760		
TOTCHAN			
LTOTCHAN		0.3229[b]	
MAJCHAN			
LMAJCHAN			0.2505[b]
CONSTANT	2.68[a]	1.97[a]	2.27[a]
Adj R²	0.202	0.290	0.250
F-stat	3.15[b]	4.58[a]	3.75[a]

[a]Significant at the 1% level or better.
[b]Significant at the 5% level or better.
[c]Significant at the 10% level or better.

basic service, although the evidence on this issue is less forceful. The evidence does suggest that the major channels are more important to customers (they are more willing to pay for them) than are the total number of channels or the number of satellite channels. Customers of these cable companies, all else equal, pay just over $0.20 extra per major channel each month.

The evidence here supports Hazlett's earlier findings regarding the effect of competition on cable television prices.[20] Hazlett found a significantly lower price for basic service and for the Home Box Office pay channel in jurisdictions in which city governments franchised more than one cable firm as compared to those jurisdictions in which a single monopoly franchise was awarded. A statistically significant estimate of $1.82 was reported as the marginal effect of competition on a broader group of services than was used in this study.

Recently, two other studies have considered the issue of cable competition, although they have not looked directly at the relationship between competing cable companies and the price paid by customers for cable service. For example, Dertouzos and Wildman analysed 340 cable systems and found that five or more off-air broadcast signals provided sufficient competition for cable.[21] They found that per-channel prices were 16% lower in markets with five or more off-air broadcast signals. Crandall analysed 2752 cable systems and found that each incremental off-air broadcast signals lowered basic cable prices until five broadcast signals were available, at which point there was no incremental effect on basic cable prices.[22] These two studies found that the number of off-air signals affected the price of basic cable service, while the study reported here finds that the presence of competing cable systems affects the price of basic cable service.

[20]See Thomas W. Hazlett, 'Competition v franchise monopoly in cable television', Contemporary Policy Issues, Vol 80, 1986.
[21]James N. Dertouzos and Steven S. Wildman, 'Competitive effects of broadcast signals on cable', paper prepared for the National Cable Television Association, 22 February 1990.
[22]Robert Crandall, 'Regulation, competition and cable performance', paper prepared for Tele-Communications, Inc, 6 April 1990.

Conclusions

The analysis presented here is consistent with competitive hypotheses: competition results in lower prices. This also suggests that the most effective restraint on cable prices will come from competition and not from various regulatory schemes which may not reduce prices and in the past have restricted service offerings.

The cable bill recently passed in the US House of Representatives,[23] for example, does not allow for truly competing cable systems which could restrain, and probably reduce, prices, although there is some mandatory resale of programming. In addition, the price regulation which it authorizes for off-air, public broadcasting and community access channels probably does not cover the services which are driving cable television value (and price) in the eyes of customers. The analysis here suggests that what cable customers may care about are the major satellite channels, and to the extent that there are cable complaints[24] the House legislation is not likely to address them. At the same time it is hard to be enthusiastic about extending the concept of basic telecommunications, with all of its difficulties, to the cable industry. This will surely lead to endless discussion of the public interest, the proper definition of basic services and fears of cross-subsidization.

Competition in cable television may lead to more than one broadband system. While a cursory analysis might suggest that there should be only one broadband provider, perhaps leasing space to information or programming services, a closer look calls this conclusion into question. For example, each of three long-distance telephone companies has enough capacity to serve all of the market, yet the benefits of competition are sufficiently great that this market structure is not questioned. Broadband may, in fact, develop in the same manner. Policy should be designed to ensure that competition is allowed and that the market functions to answer the market structure question efficiently. Competition and markets should be viewed as a discovery process, ultimately determining how many broadband providers there will be. While there is still a role for policy and regulation, it should be implemented within this market context.

Circumstances in the telecommunications and cable industries are creating the need for a resolution of various cable/telco issues. With increasing competition, old facilities and customers demanding services that cannot be provided with current equipment, policy must be clarified. Protecting a monopoly, no matter how or of what type, is usually poor policy, designed to serve not customers but owners of a monopoly service or franchise. Policy makers should be particularly wary of arguments that such restrictions to competition will result in good service, low prices or infrastructure development. There is little evidence to suggest that this is the case, and much to suggest that it is not.

In this context, blocking entry into telecommunications or into cable is likely to be poor policy. The cable/telco cross-ownership ban should probably be repealed, additional entry should be allowed into cable, mergers between cable companies and telcos may be advantageous, and entry into telecommunications is desirable. This position is becoming increasingly widely held.[25] There are many examples of the type of services which may eventually be available.[26] A combination of demand by customers coupled with advances by suppliers will allow the market to determine the level of broadband services and network deployment

[23]Mary Lu Carnevale, 'House passes bill to limit cable-TV fees', *Wall Street Journal*, 11 September 1990, p A4.
[24]United States General Accounting Office, *Telecommunications: Follow-Up National Survey of Cable Television Rates*, GAO/RCED-90-199, Government Printing Office, Washington, DC, June 1990.
[25]See for example Hazlett, *op cit*, Ref 13, and 'US conference of mayors back telco entry into cable TV with safeguards, franchise', *Telecommunications Reports*, 26 June 1989, p 35, as well as the FCC and NTIA.
[26]See for example John Markoff, 'Here comes the fiber-optic home', *New York Times*, 3 November 1989, p F1.

that is appropriate for the USA. International developments will provide additional information to suppliers and customers which will help them determine their desires.

Regulatory barriers have little or no place in these developments. Entry can often be used as an alternative to regulation, as in the case of cable companies. Both the FCC and NTIA appear to be giving strong consideration to the benefits of increased competition and reduced regulatory restrictions. Such policies, if implemented, could allow the USA to continue to provide superior telecommunications and video services efficiently over a modern broadband network.

Article 20

Jeffrey D. Karrenbrock

Jeffrey D. Karrenbrock was an economist at the Federal Reserve Bank of St. Louis when this paper was written. David H. Kelly provided research assistance.

The Behavior of Retail Gasoline Prices: Symmetric or Not?

SINCE DEREGULATION in the early 1980s, crude oil prices have been allowed to move freely with market conditions. Because of oil supply shocks and seasonal movements in gasoline demand, retail gasoline prices often fluctuate more widely than consumer prices in general. Some analysts and politicians have criticized these retail gasoline price movements, alleging that they do not respond symmetrically to price changes at earlier stages of the marketing chain. In particular, they believe that retail gasoline prices do not reflect decreases in oil and wholesale gasoline prices as rapidly and fully as they do price increases. The shaded insert on page 20 contains comments typical of this line of criticism. The perceived asymmetry in retail gasoline price movements is of special concern to consumers who believe that they are being "gouged" by the oil industry.

Much of the perception of possible asymmetry focuses on the relationship between the price of oil and the retail price of gasoline. This suggests that oil producers or refineries are principally responsible for the asymmetry. In fact, a survey undertaken by the American Petroleum Institute concluded that 80 percent of Americans believed that *oil companies* artificially raised the price of gasoline after Iraq's invasion of Kuwait on August 2, 1990.[1] This statistic suggests that many Americans believe retail gasoline stations are owned and operated by the oil refiners. In some cases this is true, but much of the gasoline sold at the retail level is sold through outlets that are not owned by the oil producers and refiners. The fact that many retail outlets are "independent" suggests that they have some autonomy in setting the retail price. The role these retailers play in the perceived asymmetry is largely ignored, even though they are as much a possible source of such an asymmetry as are the oil producers and refiners.[2] This article analyzes the role that retailers may play in the perceived asymmetric movement of retail gasoline prices. Specifically, we test whether

---

[1] McKenzie (1991).

[2] An article by Solomon (1990), however, does point out the potential role of retail outlets. See "Gasoline Prices Resist Crude Behavior."

What Goes Up Need Not Come Down?

"Those who are doing the gouging will hear from the president." —Treasury Secretary Nicholas Brady. *The Wall Street Journal*, (Shribman and McQueen) August 9, 1990.

"Retail (gasoline) prices go up much faster than they come down." —a spokesman for the Automobile Association of America. *The Wall Street Journal*, (Solomon) August 9, 1990.

"Pump prices are fast to respond to rising prices but slower to fall when crude prices fall." —Antonio Szabo, oil consultant with Bonner & Moore. *The Wall Street Journal*, (Business Bulletin) August 3, 1989.

"Whenever oil prices fall, there is always this stickiness in gasoline prices on the way down. You never see this stickiness on the way up." —Ed Rothschild, energy expert at Citizen Action. *New York Times*, (Wald) July 2, 1990.

"When crude prices go up, product prices tend to rise with crude prices. But when crude prices go down, product prices tend to lag—they go down slowly." —John Hilton, oil industry analyst for Argus Research Corp. *St. Louis Post-Dispatch*, (Crudele) June 19, 1990.

wholesale gasoline price increases are passed along to the retail customer more fully and rapidly than are wholesale gasoline price decreases.

GASOLINE DISTRIBUTION, PRICING AND MARGINS

The purchase of gasoline at the retail pump is the end of a long and complicated marketing chain. A simplified illustration of how oil, after undergoing refining, reaches the consumer as gasoline is shown in figure 1. From the oil fields, oil is moved to the refineries either by tanker, pipeline, or a combination of the two. The refinery receiving the oil may be owned by the company that produced the oil or may be independent. On January 1, 1990, 205 U.S. refineries, owned by over 100 companies, were in operation.

At the refinery, oil is distilled into a variety of products including gasoline, home heating oil, diesel oil, jet fuels, asphalt, kerosene and lubricants. One barrel of oil (42 U.S. gallons) yields about 43 percent gasoline.[3] Gasoline is transported from the refinery by truck, pipeline, tanker or barge. Some is moved directly from the refinery to retail outlets; some is moved from the refinery to terminal storage areas closer to final consumption. From these storage areas, the gasoline is generally moved to the point of final sale by truck. Once the gasoline reaches its final destination before purchase, it is usually stored in large underground tanks.

Refiners may sell gasoline directly to "end users" such as large trucking firms, industrial manufacturers and utilities. They may also sell directly to retail gasoline outlets. Retail gasoline stations owned by the refining company are classified as "end users." Retail gasoline stations not owned by refining companies are known as "independents." As figure 1 shows, sales to end users accounted for about 19 percent of refiners' gasoline sales, by volume, in 1988, with 17 percent of the sales to company outlets and 2 percent to other end users.

The other 81 percent of refiners' gasoline sales are made to either "jobbers" or independent retail outlets. Jobbers purchase gasoline from the refiners which they in turn sell and distribute to retail stations and large users. Gasoline sales made by refiners to the non-company-owned retail outlets and to jobbers are referred to as "sales for resale."

Several different entities are involved in the pricing of gasoline as it is moved from the oil field to the retail gasoline outlet. When oil is sold to the refinery, the price for this transaction is called the producer price. The price charged for gasoline by the refiner or jobber to

---

[3]See Anderson (1984, p. 216).

Figure 1
Oil and Gasoline Distribution Channels

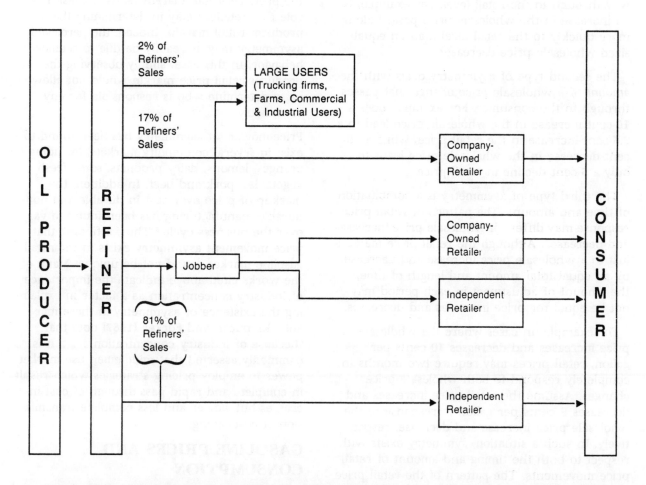

1. Based, in part, on information provided in Dougher and Jones (1990), p. 7.

the retail gasoline station is called the wholesale price.[4] The price the gasoline station charges the consumer is called the retail price. The differences between prices at various levels in the marketing chain are called "margins." The difference between the retail and wholesale price is called the wholesale-retail margin. The difference between the wholesale price and producer price is called the producer-wholesale margin. The overall difference is called the producer-retail margin.

[4]The price that the jobber pays the refiner is included in the "sales for resale" price series used in this study.

DEFINITIONS OF ASYMMETRIC GASOLINE PRICE MOVEMENTS

Retail price movements are defined as asymmetric if an increase in the wholesale price affects the retail price differently than an equal-sized decrease. Three types of asymmetry are defined. The first deals with the length of *time* in which a wholesale price change works its way through to the retail level. For example, is an increase in the wholesale price passed along more quickly to the retail level than an equal-sized wholesale price decrease?

The second type of asymmetry deals with the *amount* of a wholesale price change that passes through to the consumer. For example, does a 10-cent increase in the wholesale price lead to a 7.5-cent increase in the retail price, while a 10-cent decrease in the wholesale price leads to only a 5-cent decline in retail price?

The third type of asymmetry is a combination of time and amount. The pattern of retail price response may differ for wholesale price increases and decreases. Although the retail price may adjust to a wholesale price increase and decrease by an equal total amount and length of time, the amount of adjustment in each period may not be equal for price increases and decreases.

For example, in cases where the wholesale price increases and decreases 10 cents per gallon, retail prices may require two months to completely respond to both wholesale price changes. Assume the retail price increases and decreases 9 cents per gallon in response to the wholesale price increase and decrease, respectively. In such a situation, symmetry exists with respect to both the timing and amount of retail price movements. The pattern of the retail price response might be to increase (decrease) 7 cents in the initial month and increase (decrease) 2 cents in the month following a wholesale price increase (decrease). This pattern is symmetric. However, the pattern could be such that the retail price rises 7 cents and 2 cents in the first two months for a wholesale price increase, while the retail price falls only 3 cents in the initial month and 6 cents in the second month in response to a wholesale price decrease. This pattern is not symmetric.

Since producers, wholesalers and retailers all play a role in the determination of the retail price of gasoline, the perceived asymmetric price movements in the industry could be occurring between the producer and wholesale level or the wholesale and retail level. As noted earlier, many discussions of the perceived price asymmetry in the gasoline industry focus on the producer-retail price margin. Such a focus on the producer-retail margin tends to mask the role that retailers play in determining the producer-retail margin. Indeed, the perceived asymmetry may as readily be due to retailer behavior. In this case, simply observing the producer-retail price margin would not allow us to determine who is responsible for any asymmetry.

Price-movement asymmetry has been found to exist in several commodity markets, including oranges, lemons, dairy products, some fresh vegetables, pork and beef. In addition, the markup of price over cost in durable and non-durable manufacturing has been found to vary over the business cycle.[5] Thus, a finding that price movement asymmetry exists in the retail gasoline market would not be unique. Many of the works cited above indicate the importance of industry concentration as a factor in explaining the existence of asymmetry in these markets. Kinnucan and Forker (1987) note that "because of industry concentration . . ., it is commonly asserted that middlemen use market power to employ pricing strategies which result in complete and rapid pass-through of cost increases but slower and less complete transmission of cost savings."

GASOLINE PRICES AND CONSUMPTION

The U.S. average retail and wholesale prices of gasoline are shown in figure 2 for the period examined (January 1983 to December 1990). Several intervals of relatively large and rapid wholesale price changes are shown in the figure. In early 1986, following the collapse of oil prices, wholesale gasoline prices dropped sharply. In the spring of 1989, gasoline prices rose sharply due "in part because of the temporary closing of the port of Valdez, Alaska, at the terminus of the Trans-Alaska pipeline, after the

---

[5]Pick et al (1990), Kinnucan and Forker (1987), Ward (1982), Heien (1980) and Hahn (1990) all find asymmetry in the agricultural markets. Domowitz et al (1988), Bils (1987) and Morrison (1988) find asymmetric markups in the manufacturing sector.

Figure 2
U.S. Average Retail and Wholesale Gasoline Prices[1]

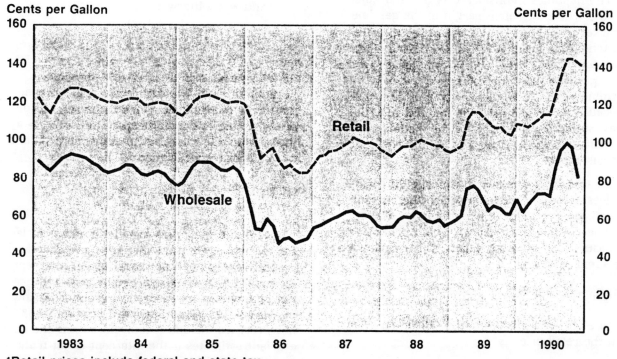

Cents per Gallon   Cents per Gallon

[1]Retail prices include federal and state tax.

Exxon Valdez oil spill in March."[6] The jump and subsequent decline in prices in late 1990 are associated with an OPEC oil price increase prompted by Iraq in late July 1990, the subsequent Iraqi invasion of Kuwait and the world embargo of Iraq-Kuwait oil. In all instances, the retail price appears to parallel the wholesale price quite closely. A more detailed and systematic analysis is necessary to determine if there is indeed a symmetric response in retail prices to a wholesale price increase and decrease. Although not shown in figure 2, the wholesale and retail prices of different grades of gasoline (premium, unleaded regular and leaded regular) also

exhibit similar parallel movements with wholesale price changes.

Since the analysis below examines asymmetry for different gasoline grades, it is useful to note the relative importance of these fuels. The mix of different grades of gasoline has changed substantially during the last 30 years. Prior to 1975, leaded gasoline accounted for over 50 percent of all motor gasoline fuel sales. Leaded gasoline's market share began to decline, however, after the enactment of environmental laws that required automobiles to burn unleaded gasoline and refiners to reduce the lead content of their

[6]See Wald (1990).

gasoline. Today, leaded gasoline accounts for only about 17 percent of total motor gasoline consumption, while unleaded regular and premium gasoline account for 59 percent and 24 percent, respectively.[7]

TESTING THE WHOLESALE-RETAIL MARGIN FOR SYMMETRY

The hypothesis considered is that movement in the wholesale-retail margin in the gasoline market is symmetric. We test to see if decreases in wholesale gasoline prices are passed along to consumers as rapidly and as fully as are wholesale gasoline price increases. We test only for symmetry in the wholesale-retail price margin because the model used for this test may be best suited for this margin. The model assumes a markup method is used to set the retail price of gasoline.[8]

To test for symmetric movements in retail prices, we use a model in which the current retail gasoline price (R_t) is a function of the wholesale gasoline price (W_t); both prices are measured in cents per gallon. This relationship is summarized as

$$(1) \quad R_t = a_0 + a_1 W_t.$$

The effect of a change in the wholesale price on the retail price is

$$(2) \quad R_t - R_{t-1} = a_1(W_t - W_{t-1}).$$

In order to examine how the affect of a wholesale price increase differs from that of a decrease, periods of wholesale price increases and decreases must be separated.

Following an approach similar to that developed by Wolfram (1971), this segmentation can be achieved using the model

$$(3) \quad \Delta R_t = a_1 WI_t + a_2 WD_t + e_t,$$

where

$$\Delta R_t = R_t - R_{t-1},$$
$$WI_t = W_t - W_{t-1}, \text{ if } (W_t - W_{t-1}) > 0,$$
$$\text{and} = 0 \text{ otherwise},$$
$$WD_t = W_t - W_{t-1}, \text{ if } (W_t - W_{t-1}) < 0,$$
$$\text{and} = 0 \text{ otherwise},$$
$$e_t = \text{a random error term.}[9]$$

All WI_t are positive or zero and all WD_t are negative or zero. If retail prices respond symmetrically to wholesale price increases and decreases, then one would expect to find $a_1 = a_2$. In order to allow for lags in adjustment time, a more general specification is

$$(4) \quad \Delta R_t = a_0' + \sum_{i=0}^{p} a_{1,i} WI_{t-i} + \sum_{i=0}^{q} a_{2,i} WD_{t-i} + e_t$$

where p and q are the specified number of lags for the wholesale price increases and decreases, respectively (p need not equal q). An intercept, a_0', could be positive, negative or zero and need not be included on theoretical grounds. Following Heien (1980) and Boyd and Brorsen (1988), however, we include it to avoid biasing the coefficient estimates if the intercept is not truly zero. This variable captures the average influence of all other factors besides raw material price changes that influence the retail price.[10]

Differences in the *timing* of price pass-through would be indicated by differences in the number of lags for increases (p) and decreases (q). The test of interest for the *amount* of pass-through now becomes testing the equality $\sum_{i=0}^{p} a_{1,i} = \sum_{i=0}^{q} a_{2,i}$. In other words, is the cumulative

---

[7]Based on volumes of first sales of motor gasoline in the *Petroleum Marketing Annual* [U.S. Department of Energy, (1988)], p. 216.

[8]This approach seems to more accurately represent the pricing behavior of retail outlets than oil refiners. Refiners with several oil products are perhaps more likely to employ a more sophisticated pricing mechanism than the retailer with a narrower range of oil products. One could make the argument, however, that retail outlets also have a multi-product pricing function, especially if the station is associated with a convenience store. Dougher and Jones (1990) note suggestions that low margins on gasoline may be offset by higher margins on convenience foods.

[9]Wolfram's procedure uses the level of the dependent variable, while we use the first difference of the dependent

variable. The model was also run for unleaded gasoline using the natural logs of all variables. The results are similar to those using the first-difference data.

[10]In some studies, a variable to measure changes in other major marketing margin cost components, such as labor, transportation and packaging materials, has been included in equation 4. Preliminary estimates for this study that included transportation wages and/or service station wages showed that neither variable was statistically significant.

effect of a wholesale price increase equivalent to that of a wholesale price decrease? If wholesale price changes are fully reflected in the retail price, we would expect to see $\sum_{i=0}^{p} a_{1,i} = 1$ and $\sum_{i=0}^{q} a_{2,i} = 1$. Symmetry in the pattern of retail price response cannot be rejected if p equal q and all $a_{1,i} = a_{2,i}$.

DATA AND ESTIMATION PROCEDURE

January 1983 through December 1990, a period of relatively little government intervention in the gasoline market, was chosen as the period of analysis. Honeycutt (1985) notes that a ". . . factor that influenced gasoline marketing, beginning in August 1971 and continuing to January 1981, was extensive federal intervention in the marketplace."[11] Furthermore, he notes that "statements by several major refiners that any changes in gasoline marketing would be phased in gradually suggest that not all important responses to decontrol had occurred by September 1981."[12] In order to allow time for these "important responses" to have little or no effect on the results, the period studied here starts in January 1983. During the period analyzed, the number of months with price increases and decreases for retail and wholesale prices was roughly equal across all grades of gasoline.

The retail prices used are tax-adjusted U.S. City Average Retail Prices of Motor Gasoline.[13] The prices used were reduced by the sum of the federal gasoline tax and a simple average of the 50 states' gasoline tax.[14] No attempt was made to interpolate tax rates between months where tax rates were actually observed. The most current reported tax rates were used until new tax data became available.[15]

Wholesale prices are those from data referred to as "Sales for Resale."[16] These are sales of refined petroleum products to purchasers who are "other-than-ultimate consumers." This series does not include refined petroleum product sales made directly to end users, such as agriculture, industry and utility consumers or sales made by refiners to company-operated retail outlets. Wholesale prices are reported exclusive of taxes.

RESULTS

Equation 4 was estimated for premium, unleaded regular and leaded regular gasoline. Preliminary estimates of lag lengths were selected using Akaike's (1970) Final Prediction Error (FPE) criterion.[17] The FPE procedure used to estimate the "best" lag length requires the user to specify a maximum lag length. For our data, the lag lengths selected by the FPE procedure were sensitive to alternative maximum lag lengths.[18]

---

[11]Honeycutt (1985), p. 108.

[12]Ibid., p. 113.

[13]The unadjusted data are calculated by the U.S. Bureau of Labor Statistics and reported in the U.S. Energy Information Agency's *Monthly Energy Review*. These prices include all federal, state and local taxes paid at the time of sale. For the period 1978 forward, prices were collected from a sample of service stations in 85 urban areas selected to represent all urban consumers—about 80 percent of the total U.S. population. Service stations are selected initially, and on a replacement basis, in such a way that they represent the purchasing habits of the Consumer Price Index population. Service stations in the current sample include those providing all types of service (i.e., full, mini and self-serve). See *Monthly Energy Review*, February 1989, p. 106. Retail prices are collected at different stations during the month of estimation.

[14]Taxes were removed from the retail price using information provided in the U.S. Department of Energy's *Petroleum Marketing Monthly*. Federal and state motor fuel taxes are reported by the agency about twice a year (generally those effective on January 1 and July 1).

[15]Handling the tax rate changes in this manner could bias the results because tax rate changes that occur between reported tax rate changes are not accounted for until the next reporting month.

[16]See the U.S. Department of Energy's *Petroleum Marketing Annual* and the *Petroleum Marketing Monthly*. This price series is based on information provided to the Energy

Information Agency by firms responding to two separate surveys. The first survey, EIA-782A, "Refiners'/Gas Plant Operators' Monthly Petroleum Product Sales Report," is sent to a census of about 200 refiners and gas plant operators. The second survey, EIA-782B, "Reseller/Retailers' Monthly Petroleum Product Sales Report," is sent to about 3,000 resellers and retailers. Some of the firms in this survey are replaced on an annual basis. In both surveys, firms are surveyed on a monthly basis and are asked to report prices on a monthly volume-weighted basis.

[17]Batten and Thornton (1984) note that the FPE criterion attempts to balance the "risk" due to bias when shorter lag lengths are selected against the "risk" due to the increase in variance when longer lag lengths are chosen. Thornton and Batten (1985) point out that the FPE procedure gives relatively more importance to a lack of bias than efficiency. They argue that the procedure is asymptotically inefficient in that, on the average, it selects lags that are too long in large samples.

[18]Maximum lag lengths of six, nine and 12 months were specified in the FPE procedure. Results for the six-month and nine-month maximum were identical, although the 12-month maximum model chose longer WI lags (10 months) for premium and unleaded regular gasoline. Lag lengths suggested by the six- and nine-month maximum lag length models were used in estimating equation 4.

Table 1

Symmetry Tests For Different Grades of Gasoline from January 1983-December 1990

Type of gasoline	Number of months lagged WI	WD	Price parameter estimates Increase $\Sigma a_{1,i} = 0$	Decrease $\Sigma a_{2,i} = 0$	t-value for test of $\Sigma a_{1,i} = \Sigma a_{2,i}$	t-value for test of $\Sigma a_{1,i} = 1$	$\Sigma a_{2,i} = 1$	R^2	D.W.
Premium	1	1	.98* (18.28)	.90* (16.98)	.88	.34	1.79	.91	1.94
Unleaded regular	1	1	1.03* (18.64)	.99* (17.64)	.46	.53	.22	.92	2.15
Leaded regular	1	2	1.10* (19.58)	1.05* (16.93)	.49	1.70	.80	.92	2.29

Note: Numbers in parentheses are the absolute values of the t-statistics.

*Indicates statistical significance at the 5 percent level.

After estimating the model with the lag lengths suggested by the FPE procedure, F-tests and t-tests were performed to see if any of the lags (incrementally or as a group) could be eliminated as statistically insignificant. Only the significant lags are reported below.[19] Significant first-order autocorrelation was not present in any of the estimated equations.

Timing Symmetry

The ordinary least squares estimates for equation 4 are summarized in table 1. Lag lengths used for periods of wholesale price increases were the same across all grades of gasoline; lag lengths used for periods of wholesale price decreases were the same for premium and unleaded regular. Leaded regular gasoline had a slightly longer lag length for wholesale price decreases. These models suggest that wholesale price increases affect retail prices for two months (the initial month plus a lagged month). Similarly, wholesale price decreases affect the retail price of premium and unleaded regular gasoline for two months. For leaded regular gas-oline, however, wholesale price decreases affect the retail price for three months. Thus, the hypothesis that the length of time in which retail prices completely respond to a wholesale price change is symmetric cannot be rejected for premium and unleaded regular gasoline but can be for leaded regular gasoline.

Amount Symmetry

Since the impact of the wholesale price change on the retail price is distributed over more than one month, the test for symmetry in the amount of pass-through examines whether the total response to a wholesale price increase is equal to the total response to a wholesale price decrease. In other words, is $\sum_{i=0}^{p} a_{1,i} = \sum_{i=0}^{q} a_{2,i}$? The results of this test are shown in table 1. For all grades of gasoline, the cumulative response of retail prices to a wholesale price increase is no different from that to a wholesale price decrease. In addition, the hypotheses that $\sum_{i=0}^{p} a_{1,i} = 1$ and $\sum_{i=0}^{q} a_{2,i} = 1$ cannot be rejected for any grade of gasoline. This implies that wholesale price decreases are fully passed along to

---

[19]The reported lag lengths are those suggested by the FPE criterion except for premium's WI (for which the FPE procedure suggested a lag length of three months), and unleaded's WD (for which the FPE procedure suggested a lag length of two months).

Table 2
The Pattern of Retail Gasoline Price Response

Equation 4 Parameter Estimates

	Wholesale increases		Wholesale decreases			
	$a_{1,0}$	$a_{1,1}$	$a_{2,0}$	$a_{2,1}$	$a_{2,2}$	a_0'
Premium	.64* (14.39)	.34* (7.62)	.29* (6.43)	.62* (11.57)	—	−.16 (1.02)
Unleaded regular	.68* (14.97)	.35* (7.71)	.30* (6.41)	.69* (12.65)	—	−.08 (.50)
Leaded regular	.76* (17.21)	.34* (7.69)	.23* (5.13)	.68* (12.85)	.14* (3.05)	−.07 (0.41)

Note: Numbers in parentheses are the absolute values of the t-statistics.
*Indicates statistical significance at the 5 percent level.

consumers, as are wholesale price increases. In short, the hypothesis that the amount of pass-through in the retail gasoline market is symmetric cannot be rejected for the period of investigation.

Pattern Symmetry

Even though the time it takes retail prices to respond fully to wholesale price changes and the total amount that retail prices respond to wholesale price changes are symmetrical, there is a difference in the pattern of response to wholesale price increases and decreases. The coefficient estimates for equation 4 are graphically shown, by grade of gasoline, in figure 3. For wholesale price increases, the largest retail response occurs in the current month for all grades of gasoline. But, for wholesale price declines, retail prices respond relatively little in the first month, and make their largest adjustment in the month following the wholesale price decline.

Using the premium gasoline model as an example, a direct interpretation of the coefficients, as reported in table 2, is as follows: a 10-cent increase in the wholesale price leads to a 6.4-cent increase in the retail price during the initial month, while a 10-cent wholesale price decline leads to a 2.9-cent decline in the initial period. For premium gasoline, there is about a 3.5-cent per gallon difference in the amount that the retail price responds to a 10-cent wholesale price increase and decrease during the initial month. For unleaded regular and leaded regular, the difference is about 3.8 cents and 5.3 cents per gallon for every 10 cent change in the wholesale price, respectively. Indeed, a test for equality of the $a_{1,0}$ and $a_{2,0}$ coefficients is rejected for all grades of gasoline, indicating asymmetry in the amount of price response during the initial month of the wholesale price change. Wholesale gasoline price increases are passed along more fully in the initial month than are wholesale price decreases. The amount of the total retail adjustment occurring in the initial month ranges from 65 percent to 69 percent for wholesale price increases, and from 22 percent to 32 percent for wholesale price decreases.[20]

During the second month, between 31 percent and 35 percent of the total retail adjustment occurs for wholesale price increases, and between

[20] The initial month percent response for a wholesale price increase was calculated as $[a_{1,0}/(\sum_{i=0} |a_{1,i}|)] \cdot 100$.

Figure 3
Asymmetry in the Pattern of Retail Price Response
(Estimated Coefficients for Equation 4)

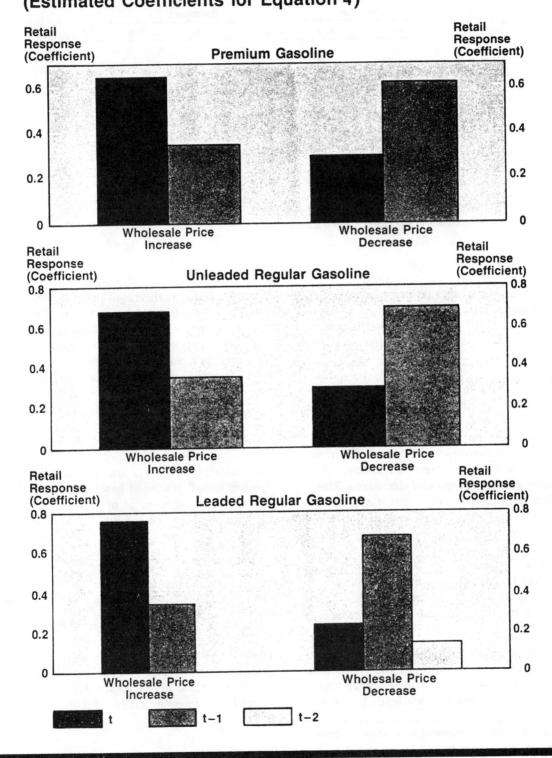

65 percent and 70 percent for wholesale price decreases. The hypothesis that $a_{1,1} = a_{2,1}$ is rejected for all grades of gasoline, indicating asymmetry in the amount of price response during the month following a wholesale price change. For leaded gasoline, a third month is needed before the impact of a wholesale price decline is fully reflected in the retail price.

CONCLUSION

This paper has tested for symmetric retail gasoline price responses to changes in wholesale gasoline prices. The results show that the length of time in which a wholesale price increase is fully reflected in the retail gasoline price is the same as that of a wholesale price decrease for premium and unleaded regular gasoline. Wholesale gasoline price increases for leaded regular gasoline are passed along to the consumer more quickly than price decreases. Although the time in which retail prices fully respond to increases and decreases in wholesale prices is the same for both premium and unleaded gasoline, the pattern of retail price adjustment is such that consumers will experience the bulk of a wholesale price change sooner for price increases than they do for decreases. However, contrary to the popular belief that consumers do not benefit from wholesale gasoline price decreases, wholesale gasoline price decreases are eventually passed along to consumers as fully as are wholesale gasoline price increases.

REFERENCES

Akaike, Hirotugu. "Statistical Predictor Identification," *Annals of the Institute of Statistical Mathematics* (1970), pp. 203-17.

Anderson, Robert O. *Fundamentals of the Petroleum Industry* (University of Oklahoma Press, 1984).

Batten, Dallas S., and Daniel L. Thornton. "How Robust Are the Policy Conclusions of the St. Louis Equation?: Some Further Evidence," this *Review* (June/July 1984), pp. 26-32.

Bils, Mark. "The Cyclical Behavior of Marginal Cost and Price," *The American Economic Review* (December 1987), pp. 838-55.

Boyd, Milton S., and B. Wade Brorsen. "Price Asymmetry in the U.S. Pork Marketing Channel," *North Central Journal of Agricultural Economics* (1988), pp. 103-09.

"Business Bulletin," *The Wall Street Journal*, August 3, 1989.

Crudele, John. "Gasoline Up, Oil Down in Price Paradox," *St. Louis Post-Dispatch*, June 19, 1990.

Domowitz, Ian, R. Glenn Hubbard, and Bruce C. Petersen. "Market Structure and Cyclical Fluctuations in U.S. Manufacturing," *The Review of Economics and Statistics* (February 1988), pp. 55-66.

Dougher, Rayola S., and Russell O. Jones. *Gasoline Distribution and Service Station Margins: An Assessment of EPA Assumptions and Implications for Methanol* (American Petroleum Institute, September 1990).

Fraser, R.W. "Uncertainty and the Theory of Mark-up Pricing," *Bulletin of Economic Research* (1985), pp. 55-64.

Hahn, William F. "Price Transmission Asymmetry in Pork and Beef Markets," *The Journal of Agricultural Economics Research* (1990), pp. 21-30.

Heien, Dale M. "Markup Pricing in a Dynamic Model of the Food Industry," *American Journal of Agricultural Economics* (1980), pp. 11-18.

Honeycutt, T. Crawford. "Competition in Controlled and Uncontrolled Gasoline Markets," *Contemporary Policy Issues* (Spring 1985), pp. 105-18.

Kinnucan, Henry W., and Olan D. Forker. "Asymmetry in Farm-Retail Price Transmission for Major Dairy Products," *American Journal of Agricultural Economics* (1987), pp. 285-92.

McKenzie, Richard B. "Did 'Big Oil' Gouge Prices?" *The Journal of Commerce*, March 6, 1991, p. 8A.

Morrison, Catherine J. "Markups in U.S. and Japanese Manufacturing: A Short Run Econometric Analysis," Working Paper Series No. 2799, National Bureau of Economic Research, Inc. (1988).

Pick, Daniel H., Jeffrey D. Karrenbrock, and Hoy F. Carman. "Price Asymmetry and Marketing Margin Behavior: An Example for California-Arizona Citrus," *Agribusiness*, Vol. 6, No. 1, (1990), pp. 75-84.

Shribman, David, and Michel McQueen. "Office-Seekers Revive 1970s Campaign Strategy of Bashing Oil Companies Over Spike in Prices," *The Wall Street Journal*, August 9, 1990.

Solomon, Caleb. "Gasoline Prices Resist Crude Behavior," *The Wall Street Journal*, May 2, 1990.

_____. "Oil Companies Bend in Wake of Public Outcry," *The Wall Street Journal*, August 9, 1990.

Thornton, Daniel L., and Dallas S. Batten. "Lag-Length Selection and Tests of Granger Causality Between Money and Income," *Journal of Money, Credit, and Banking* (May 1985), pp. 164-78.

U.S. Department of Energy, Energy Information Agency. *Monthly Energy Review*, Washington, D.C., various issues.

_____. *Petroleum Marketing Annual*, Washington D.C., various issues.

_____. *Petroleum Marketing Monthly*, Washington D.C., various issues.

Wald, Matthew L. "Prices of Gasoline Fail to Reflect Drop in Cost of Crude Oil," *New York Times*, July 2, 1990.

Ward, Ronald W. "Asymmetry in Retail, Wholesale, and Shipping Point Pricing for Fresh Vegetables," *American Journal of Agricultural Economics* (1982), pp. 205-12.

Wolfram, Rudolph. "Positivistic Measures of Aggregate Supply Elasticities: Some New Approaches—Some Critical Notes," *American Journal of Agricultural Economics* (May 1971), pp. 356-59.

Article 21

The Takeover Wave of the 1980s

Andrei Shleifer and Robert W. Vishny

The takeover wave of the 1980s moved large enterprises toward specialization and away from the diversification of the 1960s. The easy availability of funds made acquisitions affordable, while the hands-off antitrust policy allowed mergers between two firms in the same industry. Hostile takeovers and leveraged buyouts fostered the break up of conglomerates and the sell-off of divisions to buyers in the same industry; they helped speed the economy-wide move toward specialization. The poor performance of conglomerates indicates that this trend toward specialization is likely to make U.S. industry more competitive. Current state antitakeover laws are probably the result of intense lobbying by managers trying to entrench themselves; these laws do not promote competitiveness of U.S. industry. In contrast, the current accommodating federal antitrust stance encourages specialization.

TAKEOVERS DRAMATICALLY ALTERED THE U.S. ECONOMY IN the 1980s. The total value of assets changing hands in this period was $1.3 trillion. Of the 500 largest industrial corporations in the United States in 1980 (Fortune 500), at least 143 or 28% had been acquired by 1989. The majority of takeovers have been friendly, carried out with the consent of the management of the target firm. But in many other so-called "hostile" takeovers, the target firm's management fought the bid. The period also saw the rise of management buyouts, in which managers used borrowed funds to buy the company they run.

Hostile takeovers and management buyouts have sparked enormous public controversy as well as calls for and enactment of antitakeover laws. Takeovers are blamed for layoffs, decimation of communities, cuts in investment and R&D, short horizons of U.S. managers, increased instability resulting from higher debt, as well as the decline of U.S. competitiveness. Many new state laws all but ban hostile takeovers, and Congress periodically considers federal antitakeover legislation. In 1988, a presidential candidate promised that his Justice Department would block mergers between large firms in the same industry to protect consumers from monopoly.

In this article, we summarize what we and others have learned about the 1980s takeover wave. The evidence suggests that takeovers in the 1980s represent a comeback to specialized, focused firms after years of diversification. In the 1980s, most acquirers bought other firms in their own lines of business. In addition, many diversified firms (conglomerates) were taken over, and their various business lines were sold off to different buyers in the same line of business. To a significant extent, takeovers in the 1980s reflect the

The authors are professors of finance at the University of Chicago Graduate School of Business, Chicago, IL 60637.

deconglomeration of American business. Hostile takeovers and leveraged buyouts, which have attracted much public scrutiny, facilitated this process of deconglomeration. We show below that some of the common objections to takeovers, such as reduction of competition, cuts in employment, investment, and R&D, are not supported by the data. Although there is no evidence on the long-run post takeover performance of the 1980s acquisitions, the past failures of conglomerates suggest that performance is likely to improve.

We begin with a historical perspective on the 1980s takeover wave, then address some common concerns about takeovers, and finally discuss public policy.

Takeovers in the 1980s in Historical Perspective

There have been four takeover waves in the 20th century. The largest of them occurred around the turn of the century. The Sherman Antitrust Act of 1890 precluded collusive agreements between firms but allowed the creation of near monopolies with 50 to 90% market shares. In response to this law and with the help of new stock issues during the booming market, many industries merged into near monopolies overnight (1). The U.S. Steel Corporation was formed in this period and controlled 65% of steel-making capacity. American Tobacco had a 90% market share. (However, General Motors could not find financing to buy Ford for $3 million!) The wave ended in 1904 when the Northern Securities decision of the Supreme Court greatly expanded the interpretation of the Sherman act. Congress firmed up this case law by prohibiting monopolization through merger in the Clayton Antitrust Act of 1914.

The second merger wave came in the late 1920s, again coincident with a buoyant stock market receptive to new securities issued to finance the takeovers. As in the first wave, most deals were mergers of firms in the same industry. Now the courts did not allow monopoly, but still permitted formation of oligopolies—concentrated industries dominated by a few firms. Allied Chemical and Bethlehem Steel are products of this wave. This merger wave was stopped by the Great Depression and the collapse of the stock market, rather than by regulation.

The third wave is the conglomerate mergers of the late 1960s. Like the previous waves, it came during a stock market boom, which enabled buyers whom the stock market rewarded with high price/earnings ratios to finance their acquisitions with equity at attractive terms. Unlike those in the previous merger waves, a typical 1960s merger brought together two firms from completely different industries, leading to the formation of the so-called conglomerates. ITT and Teledyne are famous products of this era. The most likely reason for diversification was the antitrust policy which turned fiercely against mergers between firms in the same industry when the Celler-Kefauver Act passed in 1950. Unable to acquire businesses related to their own, flush with cash, and facing a favorable market for equity issues, acquirers bought companies outside their industries.

At the time conglomerates were formed, several theories were advanced to explain how they would improve the efficiency of U.S. businesses. One idea was that control of businesses changed from self-taught, unsophisticated entrepreneurs who started their own firms to experienced professional managers of conglomerates. Another idea was that conglomerates were an efficient way to monitor individual businesses by subjecting them to regular quantitative evaluations by the central office. Perhaps the most widely accepted rationale for conglomerates was the view that the central office reallocated investment funds from slowly growing subsidiaries, which generated cash, such as insurance and finance, to fast growing high technology businesses, which required investment funds. In this way, each conglomerate created an internal capital market, which could allocate investment funds more cheaply and efficiently than the banks or the stock and the bond markets.

The alleged superior efficiency of conglomerates is probably not what drove their creation. As in all other waves, it was more likely the case that firms wanted to grow and had access to cheap internal and external funds. But they could not continue to grow in their own lines of business because of aggressive antitrust enforcement. As a second best alternative from the point of view of growth-oriented managers, firms diversified. From the point of view of the shareholders, it might well have been best just to pay out the 1960s profits as dividends.

Recent evidence shows that conglomerate acquisitions typically failed. Although the buyers paid a premium to acquire the businesses, earnings of these businesses did not rise when they were acquired by conglomerates. In fact, some studies find that their earnings performance deteriorated (2). Equally telling are the massive divestitures of assets acquired by conglomerates during the 1960s and 1970s. According to one estimate, 60% of the unrelated acquisitions taking place between 1970 and 1982 had been divested by 1989 (3).

Why have conglomerates failed, despite all the efficiency arguments advanced in their favor? Perhaps the most important reason is that conglomerate builders ignored Adam Smith's principle that specialization raises productivity. In conglomerates, managers running central offices often knew little about the operations of the subsidiaries and could not allocate funds nearly as well as experts could. Nor could they rely on the managers of the subsidiaries to give them honest and accurate information, since each manager lobbied for his own business, and had little incentive to give up resources for the benefit of the other parts of the conglomerate. As a result, the crucial business decisions were made by nonspecialists with only limited information who had to divide their attention and resources between multiple businesses. Some divisions were neglected; others were probably overfed. For example, the Eveready battery division of Kraft is alleged to have been ignored as cheese took priority, and the cosmetics business of Revlon suffered as the company dedicated its scarce capital to expanding its health care subsidiaries. In addition, conglomerates lost many divisional top managers, who left to run their own shows at smaller specialized firms. The inefficiency of decision-making by nonspecialists offset the potential benefits of conglomerates.

In their attempt to monitor the divisions, conglomerates developed large and expensive central offices. But these central office controls often proved much less effective than the market discipline that stand-alone businesses are subjected to. Such businesses face competition in product markets, competition for capital in capital markets, and managerial competition. To a large extent, divisions of conglomerates are insulated from these forces, because they can afford to lose money and can be subsidized by other divisions, do not have to raise external capital, and face weaker managerial competition. In some respects, conglomerates resembled state ministries in centrally planned economies, where centralized control and transfer pricing replaced market forces. As this happened, many divisions of conglomerates became weaker competitors and often performed very poorly—as measured by low earnings and the high rate of divestitures. Below we argue that the takeover wave of the 1980s was to a large extent a response to the disappointment with conglomerates.

As did all merger waves, the 1980s saw rising stock prices and rising corporate cash reserves stimulating the usual demand for expansion through acquisitions. However, in the 1980s the Reagan Administration consciously eased up on antitrust enforcement in an effort to leave the market alone. As a consequence, intraindustry acquisitions became possible on a large scale for the first time in 30 years. The easy availability of internal and external funds for investment coupled with the negative experience with the diversification of the 1960s and the first laissez-faire antitrust policy in decades shaped the takeover wave of the 1980s.

The return to expansion in core businesses is evident in the prevalence of two types of deals in the 1980s. In the first type, a large firm with most of its assets in a particular industry bought another large firm in the same industry. Some peripheral businesses were divested, but most of the acquired assets were kept. Such deals were common in gas pipelines, food, banking, airlines, and oil. In the second type of deal, a "bustup," the acquired firm was typically a conglomerate. Placing its assets in specialists' hands required a sale of many divisions to separate buyers. Our data indicate that in 62 hostile takeover contests between 1984 and 1986, 30% of the assets were on average sold off within 3 years (4). In 17 cases more than half the assets were sold. Roughly 70% of the selloffs were to buyers in the same line of business.

In the face of the hostile pressure to divest, some managers realized that they themselves could profit from bustups, by taking the company private and then selling peripheral business to specialized acquirers. This realization explains a significant number of leveraged buyouts of the 1980s followed by large-scale divestitures. For leveraged buyouts in our 1984 to 1986 sample, selloffs are even higher than for takeovers as a whole, amounting to 44% of total assets.

In the 1980s takeover wave, the so-called "corporate raiders" and many leveraged buyout (LBO) specialists played the critical role of brokers. They acquired conglomerates, busted them up, and sold off most business segments to large corporations in the same businesses. Michael Jensen has argued that takeovers by raiders and by leveraged buyout funds move us toward a new incentive-infused organizational form that will permanently deliver shareholders from the wasteful ways of public corporations (5). The evidence does not support his view. First, most takeovers do not involve raiders or LBO funds. Second, many raider and LBO-controlled firms are temporary organizations designed to last only as long as it takes to sell off the pieces of the acquired firm to other public corporations. The remaining pieces are often reoffered to the public, especially when their value has been enhanced by some operating changes.

A takeover that illustrates some of the features of the 1980s wave is the acquisition of cosmetics giant Revlon by the raider Ronald Perelman. This fiercely hostile takeover took place in 1985, at the price of $2.3 billion. Before the takeover, Revlon acquired many businesses outside cosmetics, particularly in health care. The top management of Revlon thought that health care offered better growth opportunities than cosmetics, and so reduced the investment and advertising budget of cosmetics to support the growth of the health care business. After the takeover, Perelman sold off $2.06 billion of Revlon's health care and other noncosmetics businesses. Perelman had an offer to sell the cosmetics business for $905 million (which, combined with $2.06 billion, shows how profitable this bustup was), but turned it down. About 60% of asset selloffs were to other companies in the health care field, but some were to management buyout groups. After the selloffs, Revlon substantially revamped the cosmetics business and tripled its advertising budget. ("Some of the most beautiful women in the world wear Revlon.") Headquarters staff was also reduced, although there is no evidence of blue-collar layoffs or of investment cuts. Revlon's profits increased substantially.

Table 1 summarizes more systematically the eventual allocation of assets induced by the hostile takeovers of 1984 to 1986. Combining direct acquisition of related assets with acquisitions of divested assets, we find that 72% of all assets that changed hands as a result of hostile takeovers were sold to public corporations in closely related businesses within 3 years. Only 15% of the assets ended up in private firms, such as those formed when management and leveraged buyout specialists take divisions private (MBOs). And only 4.5% of the assets was bought by public corporations acquiring outside of their core businesses. This last number clearly illustrates the move away from conglomerates.

Has deconglomeration and expansion in core businesses raised efficiency and U.S. competitiveness? Some economists have taken the increase in stock prices of the acquired firms—which is not nearly offset by the modest stock price declines of acquiring firms—to be by itself incontrovertible evidence that efficiency must have improved. We do not take this position, since much evidence shows that the stock market can make large valuation mistakes (6). The possibility that the stock market is overly enthusiastic about the takeovers of the 1980s should not be dismissed. After all, the market greeted the conglomerate mergers of the 1960s with share price increases, and most of these mergers failed. Nonetheless, there are reasons to expect the takeovers of the 1980s to raise long-term efficiency.

The fact that many takeovers dismantle conglomerates and allocate divisions to specialists creates a presumption that performance should improve. There is, in fact, evidence that divisions are more productive when they are part of less diversified companies, although this evidence does not establish the link specifically for divested divisions (7). There is also evidence that acquired firms are less profitable than the firms buying them (8). This suggests that more assets in an industry are being allocated to the organizations that can better manage them. Overall, the evidence recommends cautious optimism about the efficiency of takeovers in the 1980s.

Some Objections to Takeovers

The takeover wave of the 1980s aroused much public concern about reduced competition, employment cuts, and reductions in investment, especially in research and development. These concerns are largely unsupported by the data.

Since most of the mergers in the 1980s have been between firms that compete in product markets, the obvious question is whether these takeovers decrease competition and lead to price increases. After all, mergers from the first two waves of this century had the explicit goal of raising prices. Some takeovers in the 1980s could potentially reduce competition and raise prices, particularly among airlines, gas pipelines, and supermarkets where markets are regional rather than national, and so, easier to dominate. However, gaining

Table 1. The movement of assets, 1984 to 1986.

Type of asset	Millions of dollars	Per-cent
Assets that changed hands	68,743	100
Assets that went to strategic buyers	49,660	72
Strategic acquisitions net of selloffs	26,010	38
Selloffs to strategic buyers	23,650	34
Assets that went to MBOs	10,234	15
Direct MBOs net of selloffs	4,834	7
Selloffs to MBOs	5,400	8
Assets that stayed with initial nonstrategic bidders	3,810	5.5
Assets that went to unrelated acquisitions	3,154	4.5
Direct unrelated bidders	373	0.5
Selloffs to unrelated bidders	2,781	4
Selloffs of headquarters, stocks	667	1
Not identified selloffs	1,219	2
Assets that did not change hands (nondivested assets of targets remaining independent)	39,716	
Total value of offers in the sample	108,459	

significant market power through takeovers in the 1980s seems to be the exception rather than the rule. First, in most cases the market share of the combined companies remains too small for effective market dominance: much smaller than that of 1920s oligopolies let alone the turn of the century trusts. Second, the share price behavior of nonmerging firms in the industry suggests that large profits from decreased competition are not the driving force behind most mergers. Oligopoly theory predicts that when an anticompetitive merger takes place, all firms in the industry should experience a rise in their profits and share prices since they all benefit from industry price increases. Conversely, when an anticompetitive merger is blocked by the antitrust authorities the share prices of all firms in the industry should decline along with those of the merging firms. The evidence, in contrast, shows that share prices of most nonmerging firms in an industry actually rise when a merger is challenged, inconsistent with the importance of decreased competition (9). While the evidence is not conclusive, decreased competition and higher consumer prices from takeovers are probably not important in the 1980s.

The second major concern is the effect of hostile takeovers on employment. It has been argued that hostile takeovers represent a breach of employees' trust and transfer wealth from employees to shareholders through wage reductions and employment cuts (10). Recent research sheds substantial light on this issue. First, except in isolated episodes, there is no evidence of substantial wage cuts following hostile takeovers (11). Second, removal of excess pension assets from pension plans does accelerate after takeovers, which probably means a reduction in expected pensions. On average, however, these removals are small (12). Third, layoffs rise after hostile takeovers. Among the 62 targets of hostile takeovers between 1984 and 1986, the total post takeover layoffs were about 26,000 people, which amounts to about 2.5% of the labor force of an average target firm. These layoffs are noticeable for the target firm, but small in the context of the national economy. By comparison, General Electric cut its work force by over 100,000 between 1981 and 1987.

Post takeover layoffs are disproportionately targeted at high-level white collar workers as hostile takeovers lead to reduction of headquarters employment, consolidation of headquarters, and other corporate staff reductions (4). When incumbent managers are reluctant to lay off redundant headquarters employees without external pressure, hostile acquirers do the dirty job for them. It is hard to worry too much about these layoffs, since unemployment among educated white collar workers barely exists in the United States.

In sum, transfers from employees clearly do take place after hostile takeovers, but their magnitude is small relative to the wealth gains of the shareholders.

Perhaps the greatest public concern about takeovers is that they reduce investment in physical capital and particularly in R&D. Insufficient investment in physical capital and in R&D is often held responsible for declining U.S. competitiveness, as outdated products come out of outdated plants. An opposing view holds that the trouble with U.S. industry is excessive investment in businesses and technologies that should rationally be abandoned to lower cost foreign rivals (13). Such investment only sucks up capital from high-tech industries and high-tech manufacturing where the United States should take the lead. This view makes investment cuts in basic industries a primary source of post takeover efficiency gains. Takeovers are needed because managers in declining industries are reluctant to shrink operations and distribute cash to shareholders.

Investment cuts that follow hostile takeovers have been large in some basic industries, especially the oil industry, where exploration was arguably excessive in the early and mid-1980s. One can also point to sporadic examples of investment cuts in other industries. On the other hand, our own evidence on hostile takeovers 1984 to 1986 suggests that investment cuts are neither the reason for, nor an important consequence of, most hostile takeovers. Of the 62 takeover contests that we study, investment cuts play a central role in at most 12 cases.

Investment is more often reduced after highly leveraged acquisitions, such as leveraged buyouts. In the struggle to meet interest payments after a buyout, good projects as well as bad ones may be abandoned. But these deals represent at most 15 to 20% of the takeover activity during this period (14). Not having yet seen a post takeover recession, it is difficult to evaluate the difficulties that these highly leveraged deals will experience. It is important to notice, however, that selloffs usually enable firms to pay off a substantial share of their debt within a few years. In fact, many debt contracts have provisions requiring firms to sell off assets and reduce the debt. On the whole, with the exception of highly leveraged acquisitions there is not much evidence that takeovers result in large capital spending cuts.

With respect to R&D cuts, the evidence is clear. Targets of takeovers are not R&D-intensive companies (15). On the contrary, they tend to be companies in mature, capital-intensive industries that are performing poorly and are not at the cutting edge of technology. Because takeover targets do little R&D to begin with, there are no noticeable R&D cuts after takeovers. It is a mistake to believe that R&D cuts are an important motive for or even an important consequence of takeovers.

The concern over debt and over R&D and investment cuts are part of the broader concern, which does not pertain to takeovers alone, that managers of U.S. corporations have short horizons. This concern has been expressed in particular in an influential MIT study, which argues that the economy of the United States is losing its competitiveness because the pressures of debt and of financial markets prevent managers from undertaking long-term projects (16).

Although there may be important differences between the United States and Japan in terms of planning horizon and willingness to invest, these differences appear to run much deeper. Part of the difference may stem from higher savings rates in Japan and more bullish stock market investors, and the rest may be due to a relatively greater emphasis by Japanese managers on growth and market share than on profitability. Takeovers are a minor factor by comparison to these considerations.

In sum, the evidence suggests that the three common concerns about hostile takeovers are exaggerated. The fact that takeovers of the 1980s have helped move assets out of conglomerates and toward more specialized users creates a presumption in their favor.

Public Policy Toward Takeovers

Public policy toward takeovers has taken several forms, including antitrust enforcement, state antitakeover legislation, and changes in tax policy particularly with respect to tax deductibility of interest payments on debt. We consider these policies briefly.

Federal antitrust policy has been quite important for takeovers. The hands off policy in the 1980s permitted the wave of related acquisitions. In a few cases, such as airlines, enforcement should probably have been tighter. However, a return to the antitrust stringency of the 1950s and 1960s, where an acquisition that raised a firm's market share from 5 to 7% could be disallowed, would be a mistake. The failed conglomerate wave was a direct consequence of this policy. In many cases, it might well be best if the firm did not make any acquisitions at all, and simply returned its excess earnings to shareholders. But as long as corporations are committed to survival and growth, and so continue to make acquisitions, the bias toward diversification induced by aggressive antitrust is damaging. For this reason, we would like to see antitrust policy remain largely as it is.

Much more damaging interventions are currently coming from state antitakeover laws, which aim to completely stop hostile takeovers. The usual justification of such laws is that, first, they enable managers to focus on the long term without the pressure of takeovers and, second, they prevent large-scale layoffs. These arguments, although theoretically appealing, do not have a large amount of empirical support; there is certainly little support for the view that large cuts in employment take place. The real reason for the state laws probably has little to do with these two arguments. Rather, these laws reflect the desire of target firms' managers to keep their jobs and their ability to influence legislators. The politics of the state laws are simple: managers and employees are voters as well as contributors, whereas shareholders typically reside out of state and are therefore neither.

State antitakeover laws entrench managers and allow conglomerates to survive. The best alternative to these laws is probably a federal law that subsumes them.

Last, tax policy has had a large effect on takeovers. Of the tax provisions that subsidize takeovers, the most important is tax deductibility of interest payments. If a company pays out $1 of its profit as interest, it can reduce its corporate profits tax base, whereas if it pays out the same $1 as dividends, it cannot have the deduction. This asymmetry allows firms to raise their values through increased use of debt. In this way, tax law subsidizes debt-financed acquisitions.

The extent of this subsidy is not as great as one might think, for several reasons. First, the target firm can itself borrow and buy back its own shares and so keep the gains from increased debt from accruing to the acquirer. Presumably, the acquiring firm can only profit to the extent that it can tolerate more debt, perhaps because it can cut some of the spending or divest divisions. Second, much of the debt is temporary, which greatly limits the value of the tax shield. As we pointed out earlier, divestitures usually lead to rapid reductions in debt.

Despite these limits on the value of the debt subsidy, there is no reason to subsidize debt at all. Accordingly, a limitation on tax deductibility of interest, or alternatively making dividend payments tax deductible as well, would reduce the distortion. An increase in the basic tax rate on corporate profits could keep the latter reform from increasing the budget deficit.

The Takeover Wave of the 1980s—*Shleifer and Vishny*   211

Conclusion

The takeovers of the 1980s, like those of the previous merger waves, partly reflect the desired expansion of large corporations in times of easy access to funds. With the current antitrust stance, this expansion has taken place within the areas of expertise of the acquiring firms and has made corporations more focused. Although the jury is still out on this takeover wave, the disappointing experience with conglomerates suggests that these takeovers are likely to raise efficiency as corporations realize the gains from specialization.

REFERENCES AND NOTES

1. G. S. Stigler, *Am. Econ. Rev.* **40**, 23 (1950).
2. D. C. Mueller's "The Effects of Conglomerate Mergers" [*J. Bank. Financ.* **1**, 315 (1977)] is a survey of these studies. D. J. Ravenscraft and F. M. Scherer's *Mergers, Sell-Offs, and Economic Efficiency* (Brookings Institution, Washington, DC, 1987) is the most recent and detailed study.
3. S. N. Kaplan and M. Weisbach, "Acquisitions and Divestitures: What Is Divested and How Much Does the Market Anticipate?" University of Chicago, mimeo, 1990.
4. S. Bhagat, A. Shleifer, R. W. Vishny, "Hostile Takeovers in the 1980s: The Return to Corporate Specialization," *Brookings Pap. Econ. Act. Microecon.* (1990), p. 1.
5. M. C. Jensen, *Har. Bus. Rev.* **67**, 61 (1989).
6. For a review of this evidence, see A. Shleifer and L. H. Summers, "The Noise Trader Approach to Finance" [*J. Econ. Perspect.* **4**, 19 (1990)].
7. F. R. Lichtenberg, "Industrial De-Diversification and Its Consequences for Productivity," Columbia University, manuscript, 1990.
8. H. Servaes, "Tobin's Q, Agency Costs, and Corporate Control," University of Chicago, mimeo, 1989.
9. R. Stillman, *J. Finan. Econ.* **11**, 225 (1983).
10. A. Shleifer and L. H. Summers, "Breach of Trust in Hostile Takeovers," in *Corporate Takeovers: Causes and Consequences*, A. J. Auerbach, Ed. (Univ. of Chicago Press, Chicago, 1988), pp. 33–68.
11. J. Rosett, "Do Union Wealth Concessions Explain Takeover Premiums? The Evidence on Contract Wages" (NBER Working Paper 3187, National Bureau of Economic Research, Cambridge, MA, November, 1989).
12. J. Pontiff, A. Shleifer, M. Weisbach, "Excess Pension Fund Reversions After Takeovers," University of Rochester, mimeo, 1989.
13. M. C. Jensen, *Am. Econ. Rev.* **76**, 323 (1986).
14. S. N. Kaplan, "The Effects of Management Buyouts on Operating Performance and Value," *J. Finan. Econ.* **24**, 217 (1989).
15. B. H. Hall, "The Impact of Corporate Restructuring on Industrial Research and Development," *Brookings Pap. Econ. Act. Microecon.*, p. 85 (1990).
16. M. L. Dertouzos, R. K. Lester, R. M. Solow, *Made in America* (MIT Press, Cambridge, MA, 1989).

Section VI
Regulation

Government involvement of some sort is apparent in all aspects of the economy. Because of this, managers must make decisions that consider the regulatory environment in which they operate. The articles in this section illustrate the nature of the scope of government regulation.

Environmental regulation is, and promises to continue to be, a major area of government regulation. In "Economic Incentives and the Containment of Global Warming," Wallace E. Oates and Paul R. Portney provide a primer on the policy instruments to control pollution that environmental economists suggest. The article goes on to discuss the control of carbon emissions to contain global warming. The authors emphasize the importance of international cooperation in setting policies concerning this matter, and the difficulties surrounding achievement of policy cooperation.

The regulation of electric utility firms is the topic of "What Can Regulators Regulate? The Case of Electric Utility Rates of Return," by Walter J. Primeaux, Jr. Time–series regression analysis is used to see if the introduction of regulation affected the profit–to–sales ratio of a sample of electric utilities in Florida, Iowa, and Mississippi. A reduction in this profit measure is expected with the introduction of rate of return regulation. Most, but not all, of the firms in the sample did experience a decline in the profit–to–sales ratio upon introduction of regulation.

The negative health effects caused by lead in paint have resulted in regulations regarding abatement of leaded paint in housing. In "The Effect of Lead Paint Abatement Laws on Rental Property Values," Deborah Ann Ford and Michele Gilligan examine empirically the question of whether the risk of costly abatement is reflected in the market value of rental property. They report that properties at risk of needing abatement have a market price of nearly $4,000 less per rental housing unit than less risky units. Because the authors estimate that the cost of abatement is less than their estimated discounted market price, abandonment of rental properties by investors if abatement were required would not be expected.

Empirical estimates of the extent to which an increase in gasoline taxes would decrease traffic fatalities is the topic of "The Effect of Gasoline Taxes on Highway Fatalities," by J. Paul Leigh and James T. Wilkinson. They estimate a cross–sectional regression equation that explains differences in state traffic fatalities as a function of driver characteristics and the gasoline tax in each state. Other things equal, higher gasoline taxes are associated with reduced traffic fatalities. A 10 percent increase in the gasoline tax is estimated to reduce highway fatalities by 2 percent.

Article 22

ECONOMIC INCENTIVES AND THE CONTAINMENT OF GLOBAL WARMING

Wallace E. Oates
University of Maryland
and
Resources for the Future

and

Paul R. Portney
Resources for the Future

INTRODUCTION

It is hard to imagine a policy problem more daunting than global warming. To begin with, we are not sure what we are up against. The problem is shrouded in uncertainties of the most difficult sort. Actions today to reduce emissions of greenhouse gases will have their effects on global climate many years down the road, and the magnitude and timing of these effects are the subject of much dispute. Point estimates of possible changes in temperature, rainfall, and other dimensions of global climate come with large confidence intervals, and the estimates are themselves often based on relatively simplistic extrapolations that do not allow for potentially frightening changes in climate should we set off some nonlinear, self-reinforcing processes of which we are currently unaware. Our imperfect knowledge has led to sharply contrasting policy positions: at one extreme are those suggesting that we wait until we have a firmer understanding of the global warming process before adopting costly preventive measures; at the other are those urging rapid action to forestall some possibly catastrophic outcomes.

But uncertainty is not the only aspect of global warming that makes it so difficult to address in the policy arena. Effective policies to reduce emissions of greenhouse gases are likely to be very expensive. William Nordhaus [1991], for example, estimates that the cost of cutting greenhouse gas emissions in half, *if* done efficiently on a worldwide scale, would be on the order of 1 percent of world output, and could easily cost more. We could find ourselves in the United States spending as much on such policies as we spend on all other efforts to control pollution combined! Broad support for such costly policies will be hard to find.[1]

Moreover, global warming is an international public good. Emissions from one country are essentially a perfect substitute for emissions elsewhere. The issue then is one of total planetary emissions of these gases. And no one country is of sufficient size to "go it alone." It has been estimated, for example, that even if the OECD countries (the source of most of the world's *current* emissions of greenhouse gases) were to eliminate all such discharges over the next 15 years, the effect would be insufficient to obtain a 20 percent reduction in total world emissions by 2005 if the USSR and Eastern Europe only stabilize their emissions at current levels and if the developing countries undertake no measures to control their emissions of these gases. Effective policies to address global warming will have to be international in scope--they must enlist widespread participa-

Eastern Economic Journal, Vol. 18, No. 1, Winter 1992

tion if there is to be any hope of success. We are all-too-familiar with the various public-goods or free-rider problems that put obstacles in the path of such cooperation.

These obstacles might not seem so formidable if we could assume a broad similarity in the positions and views of different countries. But this is emphatically not the case. Global warming is projected to have dramatically different effects on the well-being of populations in different areas. Some countries are likely to be net beneficiaries from global warming, as their present cold climates become milder. Others will suffer from changes that promise agricultural ruin. In addition to differences in projected effects, there are widely differing *perceptions* of the seriousness of the problem. There are important North-South differences here. The push for policies to contain global climate change is coming largely from the wealthier, industrialized countries. Many developing countries, in contrast, have what they see as more pressing issues of economic growth. They are slow, quite understandably, to consider seriously policies that would impede development efforts. It thus appears that the industrialized countries are going to be asked to *assist* the developing countries with programs to control emissions of green-house gases if their participation is to be expected. A consensus on global policy is not going to come easily!

Our purpose in this paper is not to present a blueprint for policy, or even to advocate a general policy approach. Indeed, the issues here are so formidable and complicated that we are far from clear in our own minds about the appropriate policy response. But a wide ranging and heated debate is underway. More than this, some countries are taking the lead in introducing policy measures unilaterally as a spur to more widespread participation. Sweden, Finland, and the Netherlands, for example, have already introduced "Green Taxes" to reduce emissions of carbon dioxide.

Our more modest aim is to try to sort out some of the policy issues in a systematic way. We begin in the early sections of the paper by returning to the basic literature in environmental economics and reviewing what we have learned about the properties and use of various policy instruments in a domestic context. With this as background, we then venture into a global setting and explore how we must restructure the analysis to incorporate the additional complexities that "openness" introduces for the design and implementation of effective policy. Our primary objective is to provide an overview of the policy debate that will help both to channel the debate in constructive directions and to suggest a research agenda that poses the questions that we must answer to make sensible policy decisions.[2]

A REVIEW OF POLICY INSTRUMENTS

The literature in environmental economics has drawn a sharp distinction between the so-called "command-and-control" (CAC) approach to environmental regulation and the use of economic incentives, or incentive-based (IB) approaches, to pollution control. Under the CAC rubric are policies where the environmental authority specifies, often in great detail, the regulations for each of a very large number of sources or group of sources. These regulations typically go well beyond establishing discharge limits for individual sources: they often specify the form of pollution-control technology that the source must employ, the pollutant content of the fuels to be used, certain features of the products to be produced, and so on. Such measures are characterized by their inflexibility: they typically allow little latitude for innovative responses on the part of sources.

Incentive-based approaches, in contrast, establish a set of penalties for emissions (or rewards for reductions in discharges) but allow the source wide scope for choosing both the form and magnitude of its response. A central theme in this literature is the large cost-saving potential of IB as compared to CAC. At a theoretical level, it is straightforward to show that various economic-incentive instruments have the capacity to achieve *any* desired level of environmental quality at the least cost to society [Baumol and Oates, 1971]. Moreover, there now exists a substantial body of empirical work that produces estimates of the magnitude of these cost-savings, estimates that range from roughly 50 to over 90 percent relative to CAC outcomes.[3]

In addition to these potentially large savings based on the more efficient deployment of existing control technologies in the short run, the literature emphasizes the longer-term savings that IB approaches provide through continued research and development of new control technologies. In short, environmental economists have established a powerful case for the use of economic incentives to achieve our environmental objectives at much lower cost than the more widely used CAC measures.

From the perspective of the containment of global warming, the cost-saving properties of the IB approach to environmental regulation take on real significance, for (as we noted in the introductory section) it could be a very expensive enterprise. With this in mind, we turn first to a consideration of the two major economic instruments emerging from the literature on environmental regulation: emissions taxes and systems of transferable emissions permits.

Emissions Taxes

Under the tax approach, the environmental authority would levy a fee on each pound of carbon (or other greenhouse gas) discharged, and the source would have a tax liability equal to the fee times the number of pounds of carbon that it chooses to emit. Since carbon emissions are equally damaging irrespective of the particular place where they are emitted, there is no need to tailor the tax rate geographically. A single tax rate applicable to all sources is what is needed. And, if the environmental authority is committed to the attainment of some target level of aggregate reductions in carbon discharges, it can adjust the tax rate until this target is achieved. Cost-minimizing behavior by individual sources will ensure that marginal abatement cost is equated across all sources so that the aggregate reduction is achieved at minimum overall cost. Decentralized decisions in the presence of the tax lead to the least-cost outcome.[4]

Transferable Emission Permits

The basic alternative to the tax approach is a system of transferable emissions permits. In a simplified setting, it is easy to show that the two are, in a fundamental sense, equivalent. Under the tax approach, the environmental authority raises the tax to the level needed to achieve the target level of emissions reductions. Under the permit approach, the agency simply issues permits that, in total, equal the target level of emissions. Sources are then free to buy and sell these permits. In the first case, the authority sets "price" and the sources respond by choosing quantities of emissions; in the second case, the agency sets quantity directly and sources bid the price of permits up to their market-clearing level.

While this basic equivalence exists in principle, these two approaches have some important differences in a policy setting. Three of these differences appear to have disposed regulators in the United States to the permit, rather than the fee, approach. They explain to some extent why regulators in the U.S. have chosen the transferable-permit approach under the Emissions Trading Program rather than a system of effluent charges, and also why the 1991 Clean Air Act Amendments included such a permit system to achieve the mandated reductions in national sulfur-dioxide emissions to address the acid-rain problem.

First, the permit approach gives the environmental regulator direct control over the quantity of emissions. This is a very important advantage since environmental goals are typically formulated in quantity terms, e.g., in terms of specified levels of emissions or pollutant concentrations. The new amendments to the Clean Air Act, for example, call for a 10 million ton (roughly a 50 percent) reduction in annual sulfur emissions by the end of the next decade. A regulator will thus prefer having direct control over the quantity of emissions through the issue of permits, rather than indirect (and uncertain) control through the manipulation of the tax rate. In contrast, and especially in a changing world, a regulator would find it necessary periodically to adjust the rate of an effluent tax to prevent emissions of pollutants from rising with a growing economy. No such problem of adjustment exists under permits in the sense that quantity will remain fixed. The price of permits will simply rise to clear the market in the face of increased demand from new sources wishing to discharge the pollutant.

Second, the permit approach offers a way around some of the political opposition that has blocked the introduction of emissions taxes. It is true, of course, that permits *could* be issued through an auction so that sources would have to pay directly for all their emissions, much as they do under a system of effluent charges. But there is another way to set a permit system in motion. The regulator can simply distribute the permits free of charge to existing sources who can then trade among themselves or sell them to new sources. The granting of a valuable asset will obviously encounter much less resistance from polluting firms than will the levying of a tax. This is, in fact, what has been done under the Emissions Trading Program in the United States for the control of air pollution.

And third, the permit approach promises much more ready acceptance simply on the grounds of familiarity. Regulators have experience and are comfortable with the permit instrument. It seems a much less radical move to make permits transferable than to replace an existing permit system with a scheme of emission taxes.

Transferable permits, for all these reasons, have real appeal. They appear to share all the desirable properties of a system of effluent fees, but to avoid certain administrative and distributive problems that have made fee systems unattractive to environmental regulators. The experience over the past decade with Emissions Trading does, however, raise one potentially serious problem with the permit approach: the operation of permit markets. As we have indicated, it is easy to show in theory that a competitive equilibrium in the permit market has all the nice economic properties, including aggregate cost minimization, that we wish for our system of emissions control. The difficulty is that, in practice, markets for air pollution permits haven't worked as smoothly as envisioned. In particular, these markets have been quite thin, especially on the supply side. Robert Hahn [1989] contends that this has been largely the result of unfortunate restrictions on trading that have clouded definitions of property rights and raised serious uncertainties about the ability to obtain these rights in the marketplace when needed. Even so, the number of potential participants in these markets is often small with certain large sources in a position to exercise monopolistic price-setting powers [Hahn, 1984]. The thinness of these markets and infrequency of transactions suggest that sources may not observe a clear, well defined price signal to indicate the opportunity cost of their emissions. The absence of such a clear price signal is likely to impair the functioning of the permit system, unlike a regime of emission taxes where the tax itself gives a clear and clean measure of the cost of emissions.

While market thinness has been a real problem under Emissions Trading, it seems unlikely that this would be a significant problem in a market for carbon emissions. The markets for Emissions Trading relate to specific air pollutants in particular areas. The markets are highly localized, and this limits the number of potential participants. In contrast, the market for carbon emissions would presumably be national or international in scope. In such a setting, there should be plenty of active buyers and sellers so that competitive conditions would prevail.

POLICY CHOICE IN AN UNCERTAIN WORLD

The formal equivalence of systems of emission taxes and transferable permits exists in a world of perfect information. We find in the more realistic setting of imperfect knowledge that there are some important asymmetries between these two policy instruments. If we are uncertain about the benefits and costs of emission control, then, in hindsight we will tend to make errors in our choices of values for tax rates or quantities of permits. And, as Martin Weitzman [1974] and others have shown, the errors can be of very different magnitude depending on the policy instrument in use. If we are going to make mistakes (and we surely will), we want these mistakes to involve as little damage as possible.

The Weitzman theorem shows that it is the *relative* steepness of the marginal benefit and marginal abatement cost curves that determines which of the two policy instruments, pollution taxes or a system of transferable permits, promises the larger expected welfare gain. The basic idea is straightforward. Suppose that the marginal benefit curve associated with pollution control is quite steep while marginal abatement costs are relatively constant over the relevant range. This would represent a case where the benefits from changes in environmental quality vary dramatically with changes in pollution levels. Such a case might involve crucial threshold effects, where, if pollutant concentrations exceed some critical level, disastrous consequences take place. Under these circumstances, we want to be sure that we have reliable and precise control over the quantity of polluting waste emissions. It is clear that in a setting of uncertainty concerning true levels of abatement costs and, perhaps, benefits, we would use the tax instrument at our peril. If the environmental authority were to set the tax too low (which could easily happen where we are uncertain of the response of sources to a particular level of the tax rate), then emissions would turn out to be higher than planned. Were they to exceed the critical level, an environmental catastrophe would result. It is best in such instances to employ a permit system under which the regulator has direct control over the quantity of emissions and can avoid the threat associated with too low a tax rate. In Weitzman's words, "Our intuitive feeling, which is confirmed by the formal analysis, is that it doesn't pay to 'fool around' with prices in such situations" [1974, 489].

In contrast, under other circumstances, the marginal damages from additional polluting emissions may not vary significantly. The effects from more emissions will, in such cases, be fairly constant. There will not exist any serious threshold effects over the relevant range of emissions. However, it may be that the marginal costs of control vary dramatically. There exist, in fact, many careful estimates of the marginal costs of emission control which indicate that, after a relatively constant range, marginal costs begin to increase sharply. In this setting, the more pressing danger from a policy-making perspective is one of excessive costs. If, for example, the regulator were to set too tough a standard for emissions reductions, he might impose enormous costs on sources. The danger in this case is greater under the permit instrument, for if the supply of permits is set too low, excessive control costs will be forced upon sources. Under a fee regime, this danger is avoided, since sources can always opt to pay the fee and avoid the more costly control activities.

Uncertainty and imperfect information thus introduce another set of quite important considerations in the selection of the preferred policy instrument. In which direction is this argument likely to cut in the case of carbon emissions and the problem of global warming? The answer is not entirely clear, but it is worth some thought.

Is the problem of global warming characterized by critical threshold concentrations of greenhouse gases, the violation of which sets off a catastrophic reaction? Most projections of the process of global warming involve a gradual, continuous process, but this is because that is the way in which the problem has been modelled. There are fears that significant *non-linearities* might be present in the processes of global change - that at some point the process of global warming could suddenly become self-reinforcing and take off [Peck and Teisberg, 1991; Chao, 1991]. But, at this point, such fears are no more than conjectures about the range of possible courses that global warming might conceivably take. In truth, we don't know if there are significant threshold effects, and, if there are, we don't know what the critical levels of carbon-dioxide concentrations are. We are thus not in a position to build our policies around avoiding certain critical concentrations of atmospheric greenhouse gases.

On the cost side, there are good reasons to believe that the costs of additional increments of emissions reductions will rise, and probably quite rapidly, after some point. There are certain measures that can be undertaken relatively inexpensively to reduce carbon emissions. After these measures are taken, we will have to turn to more expensive options. *If* existing studies of abatement cost functions are a guide, we should expect these rising costs to set in quite sharply as we attempt to decrease carbon emissions yet more dramatically [Jorgenson and Wilcoxen, forthcoming; Nordhaus, 1991, forthcoming]. This suggests that there is a real danger in setting purely quantitative targets for emissions reductions; such targets could involve enormous costs, much higher than those envisioned at the outset.

This danger could be avoided by selecting a price rather than a quantity instrument, that is, by using emissions taxes instead of a system of transferable permits. Taxes could be set at the level which will call forth those control activities that we can *reasonably afford*. Note that such a policy choice implies uncertainty as to just how much emission reductions we would get. But in return for this uncertainty, we would protect ourselves against the potentially large costs that could be incurred to get some (perhaps quite small) additional reductions in carbon discharges.

For the case of global warming, the uncertainty argument would thus seem to favor the use of emissions taxes over transferable permits. But there are some important qualifications. First, if, as our scientific knowledge concerning global warming expands, we find that there are, in fact, some critical threshold values of carbon concentrations that we must not violate, then the case would swing back to support the policy instrument that gives us a firmer control over levels of emissions, namely, a permit system. Second, the force of this particular argument for taxes should be seen in the proper perspective. In the use of a permit system, if it were found that the supply of permits had been restricted to excessively stringent levels with unjustifiable cost implications, adjustments could be made over time to increase the supply of permits and alleviate somewhat the cost pressures. However, such adjustments take time, are not always accommodated easily in a regulatory system, and involve other costs of their own. But it is important to recognize that these policy instruments, be they transferable permits or tax rates on carbon emissions, can be adjusted over time to produce more satisfactory results. There is, in short, some room for the correction of "mistakes." But we would do well to try to avoid the larger mistakes at the outset.

POLICY DESIGN IN A GLOBAL SETTING

Although we have examined briefly certain general aspects of the major policy instruments for the control of global carbon emissions, we turn now explicitly to the issue of policy choice and design in a global environment. The existing literature on environmental regulation presumes that there is a central environmental authority that is empowered to introduce and enforce policy measures. In a global setting, things become more complicated. Most important, there typically does not exist an international agency with the authority to introduce and ensure compliance with global policies. Such an agency can only come into being upon the agreement of all the countries involved, and even then its powers are likely to be significantly more circumscribed than those of a national or regional authority.[5]

As we discussed earlier, problems of international coordination loom large for the containment of global warming because of the widely differing positions and perspectives of various countries. The examination of policy alternatives must be seen in this context.

Economic Incentives for the Containment of Global Warming

The discussion in this paper has focused on two primary incentive-based policy measures: emission taxes and transferable permits. In view of their tremendous cost-saving potential, they are strong candidates to play a central role in containing global warming and deserve careful consideration.

The debate over the relative merits of these two policy instruments for the control of carbon emissions is already underway. Several thoughtful studies have addressed the issue and, interestingly, reach quite different conclusions. Darius Gaskins and Bruce Stram [1990], for example, contend that carbon taxes are the more promising approach, while Michael Grubb [1989] and Joshua Epstein and Raj Gupta [1990] opt for systems of transferable permits.

The central issues in this choice do not revolve around the basic economic properties of the two policy instruments, but around their feasibility and effectiveness in the existing international setting. In order to achieve the least-cost allocation of abatement efforts under the tax approach, cost-minimizing sources must all face a *single* tax rate per unit of carbon emissions. This will result in the requisite equating of marginal abatement cost across all sources. This would require, in a strict sense, that every source of carbon emissions on the planet face the *same* tax per unit of emissions.

Designing, instituting, and managing such a regime is a tall order to put it mildly. The problems of determining the rate and administering the tax are formidable. Would a single international agency manage the system and collect the revenues? This would seem highly unlikely: the potential revenues from such taxes are enormous, and as Thomas Schelling has observed [1991], no country is likely to give over control of such a major revenue source to an international agency. Moreover, there are other tricky issues to be resolved: How would tax rates be adjusted over time in response to changing exchange rates? Should the taxes be levied at the point of production or consumption of fossil fuels? Do all countries have the "administrative capacity" to operate such a tax system effectively? Finally, there is the troublesome issue of widespread distortions in existing price structures in many countries, notably the developing countries, such that a single, uniform carbon tax would not, in fact, result in equating the true marginal abatement costs across nations. We will return to these last two issues shortly.

The obstacles to the introduction of a "pure" global emissions tax may well be insurmountable. But this certainly does not mean that the tax approach should be abandoned at this point. There are various compromises that deserve careful study. The use of carbon taxes that are designed and administered by each of many countries (perhaps with some coordination) has real appeal. While such a system admittedly would forgo some of the cost-saving potential of the tax approach in terms of intercountry pollution "quotas," it would promote a cost-effective pattern of abatement within individual countries and would provide a powerful incentive for R&D efforts to find new ways to reduce carbon discharges. As James Poterba [1991] finds, such taxes are likely to be regressive in their pattern of incidence, but this regressivity can, if desired, be offset by adjustments in the rest of the tax system and/or with transfers. We need to investigate carefully the ways in which such taxes could be introduced on a national scale with, perhaps, some degree of coordination across countries. Such studies are already underway in many countries, e.g., for the United States, the study by the Congressional Budget Office [1990].

One potential peril in the design of such tax measures and their management concerns their enormous revenue potential. Not only can they be a source of considerable macroeconomic disturbance [Jorgenson and Wilcoxen, 1990; Poterba, 1991], but it will be easy to lose sight of their primary objective of environmental regulation: as they become a significant element in the revenue system, there will be pressures to use them for other purposes such as reducing the federal deficit. Interestingly, it is unclear whether an attempt to maximize revenues from this source would involve higher or lower tax rates than would be appropriate for purposes of environmental management. This depends on the elasticity of the carbon tax base [Oates, 1991]. But what is clear is that the attempt to achieve two objectives - regulating carbon emissions and raising additional tax revenues - with a single policy instrument can pose conflicts. The revenues from carbon taxes can provide a welcome addition to the public treasury, one that can be used to replace revenues from other distorting taxes that impair the functioning of the economy [Terkla, 1984]. But these revenues are best regarded as a kind of *bonus,* a serendipitous inflow into the treasury, whose level is determined independently by the need to control emissions of greenhouse gases.[6]

The use of transferable permits for the containment of global warming must also involve compromises relative to a *pure* system that would have sources around the globe trading entitlements to carbon emissions in a single international market. There are various ways that this could work [Grubb, 1989; Epstein and Gupta, 1990]. At one level, permits could be used basically as a mechanism to allocate entitlements across countries with trading limited to transactions between national governments. Countries which found abatement (at the margin) especially difficult and expensive could then negotiate for purchases of permits from other countries for whom abatement efforts come more easily and cheaply. Within each country, national authorities would institute systems to keep carbon emissions within the national allowance. Such national systems could make use of transferable permits but need not.

Instituting a transferable permit system requires agreement on an initial allocation of permits among countries, potentially a very contentious matter. Grubb [1989] and Epstein and Gupta [1990] suggest that some kind of per-capita allocation (perhaps modified by population age structure) could serve as a reasonable and acceptable basis for this allocation. With the initial allocation in place, countries could proceed with trading.

Epstein and Gupta regard the explicit quantity restriction associated with a permit system as a compelling advantage over a tax regime; taxes, they fear, could have little effect on levels of emissions, resulting in "toying with basic parameters of a complex system whose sensitivities are not fully understood" [1991, 17]. While this is a danger, we remain uneasy with the potential cost "errors" under a permit system. Jorgenson and Wilcoxen [forthcoming], along with others, find that, after some point, marginal abatement costs for controlling carbon emissions rise quite rapidly. This makes the selection of a particular quantity target a delicate matter. Too stringent a target could prove very costly and disruptive.

Gaskins and Stram [1990] raise important issues related to the visibility and flexibility of the regulatory instrument. They contend that the tax approach has important advantages on these counts. Once permits are issued and traded, they argue, the cost of curtailing carbon emissions becomes hidden in product prices and is less apparent to the public and its representatives than a tax that is paid over and over again. Moreover, entitlements tend to create vested interests, making adjustments in the supply of permits difficult to bring about. For example, if after some time we learned that the atmosphere could accommodate significantly more greenhouse gases than earlier had been believed, we would want to increase the number of permits. But existing permit holders (like those owning taxi medallions in New York City) would object since this would devalue their permits for which they may have paid a sizeable sum. For these reasons, Gaskins and Stram contend that "political-economy" considerations favor the tax regime. While there may well be some force to their contention, we point out that it is not always that easy to change tax rates either!

Abatement Versus Adaptation

The literature in environmental economics demonstrates that the optimal response to a "detrimental externality" is a unit tax on the source of the externality, equal to marginal social damage, accompanied by *no* payments (compensation) to victims of the damaging activity [Baumol and Oates, 1988, chs. 3 and 4]. The latter part of this prescription addresses the need for appropriate levels of *defensive activities*. Victims of pollution often have at their disposal various kinds of defensive measures through which they can alleviate to some degree the damages they suffer. They may, for example, be able to locate away from the sources of the pollution or alter their daily pattern of activities to avoid harm. If, however, victims are compensated for whatever damages they absorb, they will not have the proper inducement to engage in such defensive activities. Compensation of victims thus results in distortions: too little in the way of defensive activities by victims and too much in the way of abatement by sources. This analysis, we stress, assumes that all defensive activities are private in nature. They provide benefits only to the individual that undertakes them. In such a setting the damages that victims experience provide precisely the correct incentive to engage in defensive activities. No additional incentives in the form of payments or taxes are appropriate.

It is important in finding the least-cost response to environmental externalities to get the appropriate balance of abatement and defensive efforts. In the context of global warming, these defensive efforts, or "adaptation" as they are called in the emerging literature, are likely to play an important role in addressing the global warming problem [Rosenberg et al., 1989]. Many forms of adaptive response are private in nature, involving relocation decisions or changing patterns of tillage, irrigation, and crop selection. For them, we can presumably rely on individual decisions over time to make the appropriate adjustments.

But there are potential forms of adaptation to global warming that do not involve purely private benefits. To cite only a few:

1) The construction of sea walls to prevent inundation with rising levels of the sea;

2) The protection of natural ecosystems;

3) Agricultural research to identify, for instance, new plant cultivars suitable for expected alterations in climate.

Adaptation to global warming thus involves some important activities that have dimensions of *publicness* and will presumably require public programs. It is important that such forms of adaptation be identified and provided for.

Administrative Capacity and Distorted Prices

The cost-saving properties of the two IB policy measures considered above depend in fundamental ways on the presence of two conditions: the "administrative capacity" of governments to introduce and manage these policy measures effectively, and the operation of reasonably competitive markets that are not characterized by serious price distortions. If the latter condition is not satisfied, then existing prices obviously will not provide accurate signals to users of the true opportunity costs of resources.

While the assumption of *roughly* efficient markets may be a reasonable one for the advanced industrialized economies, it is far from clear that it is legitimate for many of the developing countries. Quite pervasive and sizeable price distortions appear to exist in many developing economies, and they are frequently present in the energy sector where prices are often maintained at well below free-market levels. Kosmo [1989], for example, cites petroleum and natural gas prices in Egypt of, respectively, one-third and from ten to twenty percent of world levels. In China, a two-tiered structure of prices for coal exists with "in-plan" coal in Beijing selling for about $50 per ton in the late 1980s, while the "out-plan," or negotiated, coal price was over double this figure [Wang, 1988]. More generally, the developing countries tend to make much wider use of excise taxes and subsidies that distort prices across broad classes of commodities.

Even if price distortions were not such a widespread phenomenon, it is not clear that the administrative capacity always exists in the developing countries to operate a system of effluent taxes or transferable permits. Such policy regimes require a substantial level of regulatory sophistication and experience. (Of course, most forms of CAC regulation also require some administrative sophistication for both their design and effective enforcement.) Our concern here is that certain *institutional* realities must be faced up to in the design of global policy measures. And the problems of price distortions and administrative capacity are important ones that will require careful study in the analysis of the international response to global warming.[7]

Recognition of these kinds of constraints on feasible policy suggests a somewhat broader frame of reference in terms of the most effective *mix* of policies on a global scale. This is admittedly a formidable problem of the "second-best." But it may well be that the most effective global policy strategy will be one that involves the introduction of some fairly sophisticated IB policies in the industrialized countries alongside the use of various more *blunt* measures in some of the developing countries.

This leads to one further observation. We noted in the introduction the sharp distinction that the environmental economics literature makes between economic incentives and CAC policies. While useful, perhaps, for certain pedagogical purposes, this lumping of all "other" policies into the CAC class is quite misleading. In fact, it is sometimes unclear just where this dividing line is. A program under which the regulator specifies precisely what treatment technology is to be used clearly falls in the CAC class. But what about a program under which the regulator assigns an overall emissions limitation, but leaves the source to find the most effective method of compliance? Such flexibility clearly allows some scope for cost-saving efforts on the part of the polluter. Moreover, some studies have found that cost-sensitive CAC measures can stack up reasonably well relative to their IB counterparts [Oates, Portney, and McGartland, 1989].

This is not to suggest that IB policies will not have a central role to play in an efficient system for the containment of global warming. They surely will. But at the same time, we must be sensitive to the wide array of potential policy instruments and the existing constraints on their use if we are to fashion a policy *mix* that addresses the problem in an effective way.

On the Need for Global Participation

We stressed in the introduction the need for widespread participation in global efforts to reduce emissions of greenhouse gases. This reflects largely the simple fact that in the future no country (or even select group of countries) will account for the vast bulk of carbon emissions. Nations in all parts of the world and in varying stages of development must become partners in this effort if we are to have any realistic hope of effectively controlling emissions of these gases.

Grubb [1989] and others have argued that in the absence of an effective global agreement, much can still be done through regional or select group (e.g., OECD) agreements, or even through unilateral action. Such efforts can provide leadership, create a co-operative environment conducive to broader participation at a later time, and set in motion efforts to develop substitute technologies. While there is surely some merit to these arguments, it is important to recognize their limitations. One especially serious issue arises. Suppose, for example, that the OECD countries were to form an effective alliance to reduce carbon emissions. One result of such an effort is likely to be a dramatic decrease in the world demand for fossil fuels with a consequent fall in fuel prices. This fall in price would *encourage* other countries to increase their consumption of fossil fuels. To some extent, then, the efforts of the co-operating countries would be offset by natural market responses elsewhere. The extent of this "displacement" would depend on the relative price elasticities of demand, but it could be a substantial offsetting effect. This is a troublesome obstacle to effective action by a limited number of countries. And how to avoid it is not entirely clear. Perhaps the co-operating countries could use some of the revenues from their emission taxes to bolster the demand for fossil fuels and simply build up reserves of these fuels. This issue requires further attention [Bohm, 1991].

A COMPREHENSIVE APPROACH TO REGULATION OF GREENHOUSE GASES

The discussion throughout the paper has run primarily in terms of the control of carbon emissions. Carbon dioxide, however, is but one, albeit the most important, of several greenhouse gases. Others include chlorofluorocarbons (CFCs), methane, nitrous oxides, and ozone. The control of carbon dioxide will likely be the centerpiece of any policy to regulate greenhouse gas emissions, but the other gases are far from insignificant. As Richard Stewart and Jonathan Wiener [1990] emphasize, a comprehensive program to address global warming must incorporate the whole class of greenhouse gases.

The extension of the basic IB instruments to encompass these other gases does not, *in principle*, create any serious problems [Morgenstern, 1991]. The contribution to global warming of the different greenhouse gases varies quite dramatically. Methane, for example, is estimated to have twenty-one times the "radiative-forcing" effect (i.e., capacity to trap heat in the atmosphere) of an equivalent amount of carbon dioxide. The Intergovernmental Panel on Climate Change [1990] has estimated the global warming potential for numerous gases, and from these estimates we can express the warming effects of different gases in terms of a common metric: "carbon equivalents."

Systems of effluent taxes or transferable permits can address this issue by tailoring tax rates or trading ratios to reflect the carbon equivalents of the various gases. The tax, for instance, per unit of methane emissions would, under this approach, be twenty-one times that on discharges of carbon dioxide. This is admittedly a further complication in such systems, but it will be important to build these distinctions into any IB policy measures.

To conclude, we return to the theme of identifying regulatory instruments that can achieve our global environmental objectives in a cost-effective way. To this end, we should look to policies that allow wide flexibility on the part of sources to seek out and adopt the most inexpensive means of reducing their greenhouse gas emissions. Incentive-based measures are obviously strong candidates, and ways of structuring them to function effectively in the global arena rank high on the policy-research agenda. But where we find it necessary to turn to the command-and-control class of policy instruments, it is essential to keep this theme before us. As we emphasized, there exists a wide range of CAC approaches to regulation, and some are much superior to others. In particular, regulatory approaches that involve government officials specifying the precise ways in which sources are to comply with emissions limitations are likely to be extremely inefficient. They provide no flexibility in the short run to adopt less expensive means of compliance and little incentive over the longer haul for research and development activities for new and less costly technologies. A sensible mix of policies should allow wide flexibility in the response of sources and provide incentives for the development of improved methods for controlling emissions.

We are grateful to Lee Friedman, James Kahn, and Jonathan Wiener for helpful comments on earlier drafts of the paper and to the National Science Foundation for its support of this work.

NOTES

1. There is, incidentally, some controversy over the likely costs of reducing emissions of greenhouse gases. Some studies find that the costs cited above are greatly exaggerated. For an excellent survey and assessment of these cost studies, see Joel Darmstadter [1991].
2. For a useful treatment of greenhouse warming, including both a description of the process and its effects and analyses of the various economic aspects of the problem, see Rosenberg et al. [1989].
3. See Tietenberg [1985, ch. 3] for a useful survey of these empirical studies.
4. The literature has also explored unit subsidies for emissions reductions as an alternative to taxes. While such subsidies can establish the same incentives for pollution control by individual sources as unit taxes, they have the serious problem of encouraging entry into polluting industries by making these industries more, rather than less, profitable. Subsidies thus distort the entry-exit decisions of polluting firms. On this, see, for example, Baumol and Oates [1988, ch. 14].
5. The United Nations occasionally tries to play this role, and did so with some success for the Protocol leading to the phasing-out of CFC use among the signatories. Likewise, the European Community has some powers to enforce environmental and other agreements in the member countries. But the many-nation character of these programs makes them much more complex and delicate than national measures for environmental management.
6. In principle, under an optimal-taxation approach, we can determine a second-best tax rate on waste emissions that optimizes the tradeoff between environmental gains and the gains from an improved tax system that places reduced reliance on distorting taxes [Lee and Misiolek, 1986]. While such a result may be unimpeachable in principle, it makes enormous demands in terms of information *and* in terms of institutions. It would require a public decision-maker who is not only informed but is in a position to transcend competing environmental and revenue needs and reach the proper compromise. The dangers here, since there are many other tax bases available, would seem to lie largely on the side of reduced effectiveness in environmental regulation. For this reason, it seems to us that the determination and management of taxes on polluting waste emissions should fall under the aegis of an environmental regulator, rather than the tax authority [Oates, 1991].
7. We do not mean to imply that regulatory structures for environmental management are absent in developing countries. China, for example, has an extensive and fairly sophisticated system for administering its environmental laws (even including economic incentive mechanisms).

REFERENCES

Baumol, W. J., and Oates W. E. The Use of Standards and Prices for Protection of the Environment. *Swedish Journal of Economics*, March 1971, 42-54.

———. *The Theory of Environmental Policy*, 2nd ed. Cambridge: Cambridge University Press, 1988.

Bohm, P. Incomplete International Cooperation to Reduce CO_2 Emissions: Alternative Policies, unpublished paper, 1991.

Chao, H. Managing the Risk of Global Climate Change. Electric Power Research Institute, unpublished paper, 1991.

Darmstadter, J. The Economic Cost of CO_2 Mitigation: A Review of Estimates for Selected World Regions. *Resources for the Future Discussion Paper ENR91-06*, 1991.

Epstein, J. M., and Gupta, R. Controlling the Greenhouse Effect:Five Global Regimes Compared. *Brookings Occasional Papers.* Washington: The Brookings Institution, 1990.

Gaskins, D., and Stram, B. A Meta Plan: A Policy Response to Global Warming. Vienna Workshop for Cooperative Research on Climate Change, unpublished paper, 1990.

Grubb, M. *The Greenhouse Effect: Negotiating Targets.* London: Royal Institute of International Affairs, 1989.

Hahn, R. Market Power and Transferable Property Rights. *Quarterly Journal of Economics*, November 1984, 753-65.

_____. Economic Prescriptions for Environmental Problems: How the Patient Followed the Doctor's Orders. *Journal of Economic Perspectives*, Spring 1989, 95-114.

Intergovernmental Panel on Climate Change. *Climate Change: The IPCC Scientific Assessment.* Cambridge: Cambridge University Press, 1990.

Jorgenson, D. W., and Wilcoxen, P. J. Global Change, Energy Prices, and U.S. Economic Growth. *Harvard Institute of Economic Research Discussion Paper No. 1511*, August 1990.

_____. Reducing U.S. Carbon Dioxide Emissions: The Cost of Different Goals, in *Advances in the Economics of Energy and Natural Resources*, edited by J. R. Moroney. Greenwich, CT: JAI Press, forthcoming.

Kosmo, M. Economic Incentives and Industrial Pollution in Developing Countries. *Policy and Research Division Working Paper #1989-2,* Washington: Environmental Department, The World Bank, 1989.

Lee, D. R., and Misiolek, W. S. Substituting Pollution Taxation for General Taxation: Some Implications for Efficiency in Pollution Taxation. *Journal of Environmental Economics and Management*, December 1986, 338-47.

Morgenstern, R. D. Towards a Comprehensive Approach to Global Climate Change Mitigation. *American Economic Review*, May 1991, 140-45.

Nordhaus, W. D. A Sketch of the Economics of the Greenhouse Effect. *American Economic Review*, May 1991, 146-50.

_____. The Cost of Slowing Climate Change: A Survey. *The Energy Journal,* forthcoming.

Oates, W. E. Pollution Charges as a Source of Public Revenues, unpublished paper, 1991.

Oates, W.E., Portney, P. R., and McGartland, A. M. The *Net* Benefits of Incentive-Based Regulation: A Case Study of Environmental Standard Setting. *American Economic Review*, December 1989, 1233-42.

Peck, S., and Teisberg, T. Exploring Optimal Intertemporal CO_2 Control Paths. Electric Power Research Institute, unpublished paper, 1991.

Poterba, J. M. Tax Policy to Combat Global Warming: On Designing a Carbon Tax. *National Bureau of Economic Research Working Paper No. 3649,* 1991.

Rosenberg, N. J., et al., eds. *Greenhouse Warming: Abatement and Adaptation.* Washington: Resources for the Future, 1989.

Schelling, T. C. Economic Responses to Global Warming: Prospects for Comparative Approaches, in *Global Warming: Economic Policy Responses,* edited by R. Dornbusch and J. Poterba. Cambridge: MIT Press, 1991, 197-221.

Stewart, R. B., and Wiener, J. B. A Comprehensive Approach to Climate Change. *The American Enterprise*, November/December 1990, 75-80.

Tietenberg, T. H. *Emissions Trading: An Exercise in Reforming Pollution Policy.* Washington: Resources for the Future, 1985.

Terkla, D. The Efficiency Value of Effluent Tax Revenues. *Journal of Environmental Economics and Management*, June 1984, 107-23.

U.S. Congressional Budget Office. *Carbon Charges as a Response to Global Warming: The Effects of Taxing Fossil Fuels.* Washington: Congressional Budget Office, 1990.

Wang, Y. Coal Prices in Beijing, unpublished paper. Washington: The World Bank, 1988.

Weitzman, M. Prices vs. Quantities. *Review of Economic Studies*, October 1974, 477-91.

Article 23

What Can Regulators Regulate?
The Case of Electric Utility Rates of
Return

WALTER J. PRIMEAUX JR

IBE Distinguished Professor of Business Administration, University of Illinois, Champaign, IL, USA

The efficacy of electric utility regulation has not been finally determined. This study assesses the impact of commission regulation on the level of earnings realized by electric power utility firms. Time series data for the individual electric firms operating in Florida, Iowa and Mississippi were used in this analysis. These are the only three states regulated since World War II and it was possible to compare profit rates for the individual firms *before* and *after* commission regulation was instituted. The results show that regulation has lowered profits in some cases. However, there appears to be significant randomness in the process.

INTRODUCTION

Criticism of utility regulation may now be at a peak; however, the efficacy of the process has been the subject of considerable skepticism through the years.[1] The purpose of this study is to assess the impact of the imposition of commission regulation on earnings realized by electric utility firms. Kahn (1970, p. 31) has said that regulated profits are the most obvious and comforting evidence that regulation can be 'effective'. Indeed, he asserts that accounting profits are the target of most regulators.

The results of this investigation show that state regulation has caused mixed results; in some cases it has lowered profits, but in others they were either higher or unchanged after state regulation was imposed.

PREVIOUS STUDIES

In a landmark study Stigler and Friedland (1962) found that regulation of electric utility firms, as indicated by the presence of a state regulatory commission, added nothing to the explanation of interstate rate differences. The authors conclude that pure monopoly profits would not occur in the absence of regulation. Moore (1970) found that regulation has not reduced prices more than 5% and probably less than that. Moore (1975) concludes that regulation had a perverse effect because it actually caused higher prices. Jackson (1969) discovered that regulation did not succeed in reducing residential rates in 1940 and 1950 but was significant in 1960.

Although these are four important empirical studies by competent economists they have not determined once and for all the impact of regulation on the economic performance of electric utility firms. Also, the previous studies were restricted to examining the price effects of regulation and, except for the indirect examination by Stigler and Friedland, the effects of regulation on rates of return were not examined. Moreover, Kahn (1970) explains that there is little convincing evidence that the performance of regulated industries differs significantly from what it would be in the absence of regulation; therefore further study of regulation is very important.

THE THEORY

Unregulated monopolies, according to theory, would charge a price above average cost and earn an economic profit. The notion is that in the absence of the market mechanism, where price competition would drive prices down to lower levels, the unregulated monopolist would exact a higher price and earn higher profits than if it faced competition or if it were regulated.[2] Kahn (1970, p. 31) explains that the regulatory process has focused primarily on profits as the control target because

> ... these are politically the most visible—excessive profits the most obvious danger and sign of consumer exploitation, in the absence of effective competition, regulated profits the most obvious and comforting evidence that regulation can be 'effective'.

Kahn's argument is a good one.[3] Even though regulators may scrutinize prices very closely, as suggested by Joskow (1973), there is an ultimate effect on profits.

The above discussion indicates that effective regulation would be expected to reduce the profit levels of electric utility monopolists.

The residential natural gas price faced by an electric utility monopolist would also affect its profit level. Since gas is a substitute for some important electric utility applications, such as heating and clothes drying, one would expect a direct relationship between profit rates and natural gas prices. As residential prices of a competitive gas company increase, profitability of the electric monopoly would increase as customers covert to using electricity where feasible.[4]

Profitability of an electric utility monopolist would be affected by the general regulatory climate and economic trends throughout the country. Utility commissions do not operate in a vacuum. They observe what is happening in other jurisdictions and react accordingly. This is not to say that they all react in the same way, but that they are all influenced to some extent by the overall economic and social environment in which regulated utility firms exist. This tendency is enhanced by the National Association of Regulatory Utility Commissioners, which publishes statistics and engages in other matters of interest to regulators and students of regulation.[5] Because of these influences, one would expect profitability of individual firms in this business to parallel that of the industry as a whole.

Sales growth is another important influence on profitability of the firm; however, the net effect cannot be determined unambiguously. The fact is, sales growth would probably cause a firm's total profit to increase but profitability per unit sold may rise or decline, depending on the operating conditions of the particular firm involved. Profitability per unit sold would increase as sales increase if the firm is operating with excess capacity. Even if excess capacity does not exist, if regulatory lag is minimized and higher consumer prices are quickly approved as costs rise when new customer load is added, profits per unit may increase. On the other hand, sales growth could cause lower per unit profitability if the firm's average costs are rising and if the firm faces long regulatory lags before higher rates are approved to offset the rising costs incurred as new customers are added. So two effects are reflected by sales growth; these are capacity utilization and regulatory lag.

Electric utility regulation is based on 'cost-plus-profit' procedure (Shepherd, 1967, p. 30; Pegrum, 1965, pp. 664–82). Under this form of regulation the utility firm is permitted to *recover* all costs of operation. Earnings are generated by the firm being allowed to earn a fair return on its investment. Consequently, all taxes, operating expenses, and depreciation are recoverable by the utility firm, then a fair return on investment is added as compensation to investors.[6] To the extent that consumer rates are established on a previous test year basis, future expected costs are those involved in the rate-determination procedures, not costs actually incurred by the firm during the relevant operating year.

As mentioned above, utility regulation is essentially a 'cost-plus-profit' procedure. Since utility firms are allowed to recover all costs of operation one would not expect per unit profitability to be affected by production expenses. If regulation is effective, the firm would be just compensated for its production costs; yet, rising or falling production costs would not affect profitability because they merely represent recovered expenses. However, even the most avid champion of regulation would not argue that regulators or regulation are perfect; consequently, it is possible that the regulatory procedures could cause a firm to be under- or overcompensated for its cost outlays, and if this happens this would affect the firm's profitability. These kinds of overcompensation would occur because regulators are unable to establish the appropriate price configuration which will just generate sufficient revenue to permit the firm to cover all of its costs and generate the appropriate return on investment. The cost-estimating errors might occur from joint cost allocations; or from cost economies which the firm is able to implement once rates are set; or from errors in the costs forecasts made by the regulatory commission.

The next section presents the procedure followed to assess the impact of implementation of state utility regulation on rates of return.

PROCEDURE

Following the above statement by Kahn (1970), this study examines rates of return (profits) as evidence of the efficacy of electric utility regulation.[7]

Previous studies have largely relied upon price data which were generated during the very early days of utility regulation and some have depended on cross-section analyses, aggregating firms controlled by diverse state regulatory regimes.

The method employed here was designed to avoid some of the problems previously mentioned. If, indeed, utility regulation across the country is applied in a very 'uneven' manner, as suggested by Primeaux (1978), cross-section comparisons may be affected by problems which are very difficult to isolate. Moreover, regulators are expected to accomplish efficient outcomes because automatic markets are not permitted to operate. Their task is very difficult, and there is no certainty that the effects of regulation will fall upon firms in a consistent manner (Primeaux, 1978). In a cross-section study, aggregation of data makes it very difficult to assess the impact of commission regulation on an individual firm.

Time series data for the *individual electric firms* operating in Florida, Iowa and Mississippi were used in the statistical analyses. These states were used because they are the only ones in which commission regulation has been implemented since 1948,[8] and it was possible to compare profit rates for individual firms before and after commission regulation was installed and make an assessment of the effect of the

Table 1. All Class A and B Electric Utilities in Florida, Iowa and Mississippi (firms constituting the sample of the study)

Florida	Iowa	Mississippi
Florida Power Corp.	Iowa Illinois Gas & Electric Co.*	Mississippi Power Co.
Florida Power & Light Co.	Iowa Southern Utilities Co.	Mississippi Power & Light
Tampa Electric Co.	Iowa Public Service Co.*	
Gulf Power Co.	Iowa Power and Light Co.	
Florida Public Utilities Co.	Interstate Power Co.*	
	Iowa Electric Light & Power Co.	

*Serves both Iowa and Illinois. Iowa sales were 64.64% of total kWh sales in 1979.
*Serves Iowa and South Dakota. Iowa sales were 99.1% of total kWh sales in 1979.
*Serves Illinois, Iowa and Minnesota. Iowa sales were 79.6% of total sales in 1979.
Proportions of sales in Iowa were provided through Mr Robert Latham of the Iowa Commerce Commission in a telephone conversation

change in each case. The earliest data are from 1948 because of concern that the World War II or depression periods would affect the validity of the results.

Each firm was examined individually by ordinary least squares regressions, employing time series data from 1948 through 1976.[9] This procedure made it possible to isolate the specific impact of commission regulation on each firm's rate of return.

Commission regulation was implemented in Florida in 1951, in Iowa in 1963 and in Mississippi in 1956. Table 1 lists *all* of the class A and B privately owned electric utility firms in the three states being examined; there are thirteen firms involved. Publicly (municipally) owned firms were not included in the sample, because they are generally not regulated by the state regulatory commission.[10]

One might assert that the firms were not entirely free from some sort of regulation prior to the date that the state commission was established; therefore a comparison of before and after performance would not really reveal how effective regulation is.[11] However, the central issue in all of the previous studies, as well as this examination is in fact how effective is state commission regulation in affecting economic performance. This is really the important question, since this form of regulation dominates all others.[12]

THE REGRESSION MODEL

As mentioned earlier, ordinary least squares linear regression analysis was used to determine the effects of Commission regulation on the rates of return of firms in the sample.

Our analytical framework suggests the following functional form:

Profit = f(regulation, natural gas price, industry profits, demand growth, production expenses)

The OLS multiple regression equation includes the following variables:

Π/S = Profit-to-sales ratio: realized net income in dollars per 1000 kWh sold. (Dependent variable.)

R = A regulatory dummy variable, taking a value of 1 for years when the firm was regulated by a state commission, a zero for years before.

P_G = Residential average natural gas price, in thousands of dollars per trillion BTUs.

Π/S_1 = Net income as a percentage of operating revenue for all class A and B utilities in the United States (an index or trend variable indicating national movements in profitability or rates of return).

GR = A demand growth variable, in percentage change of kWh sold. A proxy for capacity utilization and regulatory lag.

ER = Production expense in dollars per 1000 kWh.

In short, the equation to be tested is

$$\Pi/S = b_0 + b_1 R + b_2 P_G + b_3 \Pi/S_1 + b_4 GR + b_5 ER$$

Expected relationships between the profit-to-sales ratio and the explanatory variables are as follows:

$$\frac{\partial \Pi}{S} \bigg/ \partial P_G > 0, \quad \frac{\partial \Pi}{S} \bigg/ \frac{\partial \Pi}{S_1} > 0, \quad \frac{\partial \Pi}{S} \bigg/ \partial GR < 0,$$

$$\frac{\partial \Pi}{S} \bigg/ \partial ER = 0$$

All financial data were deflated by the GNP implicit price deflator and separate time series equations were run for each firm. These data reflect firm performance for the years 1948–76. The regulation variable (R) was lagged to conform to the Stigler and Friedland (1962) study, where regulation was said to have taken place three years after the State commission was established.

The Π/S variable (net income in dollars per 1000 kWh sold) is proxy for the rate of return earned by the electric utility firm. This specification was used as the dependent variable because of the desire to assess the effect of commission regulation on firms' profits. Plant or assets were not considered to be the appropriate units to use to standardize earnings for comparison purposes. Utility firms add plant capacity in discrete units and plants additions always create excess capacity. This condition would cause large increases in the denominator without comparable increases in the numerator. Moreover, all plant is not necessarily of the same vintage. Consequently, questions are raised concerning the appropriate *real* value of assets. The decision

Table 2. OLS Estimates of profit functions—Florida Companies

Florida company	Constants	R	P_G	Π/S_t	GR	ER	DF	R^2	Dw
Tampa Electric Co.	−4.41174	−0.59838ᶜ (−1.78752)	0.00009 (1.44796)	0.52123ᵃ (3.16918)	0.89976 (.5648)	0.20908ᵇ (2.37430)	21	0.642	1.692'
Florida Power Corp.	−0.12579	−1.57940 (−1.20767)	0.00012 (1.02904)	0.83056ᵃ (3.03493)	−1.77620 (−1.26293)	0.10026 (1.17550)	20	0.347	1.744'
Florida Public Utilities Co.*	−2.57334	−3.56660ᵃ (−5.57107)	0.00031ᵇ (2.33873)	0.75306ᵇ (2.76553)	−3.62349 (−1.61043)	−0.00114 (−0.01148)	20	0.778	2.192'
Gulf Power Co.	−7.3127	−4.72870ᵃ (−9.99847)	0.00022ᶜ (1.71849)	0.86956ᵃ (4.33614)	−3.11441 (−1.44155)	0.36669ᵃ (3.86421)	22	0.888	1.908
Florida Power & Light Co.	−0.48954	0.8864 (0.5809)	−0.00003 (−0.2898)	0.3777 (1.0490)	0.6183 (0.2841)	0.0630 (0.3851)	18	0.191	1.65'

ᵃSignificant at 1% level (two-tailed test).
ᵇSignificant at 5% level (two-tailed test).
ᶜSignificant at 10% level (two-tailed test).
*Combination company—sells both gas and electricity.
'Adjusted for autocorrelation.
t-values appear in parentheses beneath the corresponding coefficients.

was made to use sales units (kWh) as the denominator because this measure is clearly and consistently defined throughout the whole time series period. Moreover, since time series data are used, the necessary distinction between per unit profitability and total profitability does not create serious problems.

If regulators just allow cost recovery the ER variable would be expected to be insignificant and unrelated to profit. Since this variable is a proxy for total costs, one would not expect that it would affect profitability unless regulatory commissions allow excessive or insufficient estimates of costs in the procedure of rate determination.[13]

The sign of the coefficient of the regulation dummy variable (R) is the crucial one for determining whether or not regulation is effective; a negative sign would indicate that regulation has lowered accounting profits and would support the proposition that state regulation has been effective.

REGRESSION RESULTS

Both OLS and seemingly unrelated regression equations were run but the results were quite similar, so only the OLS results are presented. Only linear equations are presented; log specifications were also run but they did not increase the level of explained variance.

In addition to the variables mentioned above, an OPEC dummy variable was included to attempt to isolate the effect of the energy shortage on rates of return earned by electric utility firms included in the sample. This variable was not statistically significant, and it showed a high degree of multicollinearity with other independent variables. Consequently, it was omitted. Interaction variables were statistically

insignificant and regression coefficients were unaffected when they were removed.

The Cochrane–Orcutt iterative technique was employed to develop a model which would be free of significant autocorrelation. The equations adjusted by this procedure are indicated on the tables which present the final regressions (Cochrane and Orcutt, 1949).

The overall results show some support for the notion that commission regulation has reduced accounting profits in the electric utility industry, but the results are mixed.

Florida

Table 2 presents equations for the five firms from Florida. The P_G variable reveals that some consumers did react to higher gas prices by switching to electricity for some purposes. The table shows positive signs on the P_G variable in four of the five equations. Only in the equations for Florida Public Utilities Co. and Gulf Power Co. is the P_G variable significant at the 10% level or better, showing that higher natural gas prices actually caused higher per unit profits for these firms.

The Π/S_t variable is positive in all equations and statistically significant at the 5% level or better in four of the five cases. The positive sign indicates that the Florida firms were all allowed to increase their profitability as the profitability of electric utility firms across the country increased. This is probably some indication that the Florida public utility commission attempted to be responsive to the needs of the regulated firms with respect to profit requirements.

The G variable is statistically insignificant in all cases, so profits per unit for the Florida firms did not change as sales growth occurred. This result can be

Table 3. OLS Estimates of Profit Functions—Iowa Companies

Iowa company	Constant	R	P_G	Π/S_i	GR	ER	DF	R^2	Dw
Iowa Illinois Gas Electric Co.*	-1.44904	-1.71169[b] (-2.62874)	-0.00000 (-0.61245)	0.48061[b] (2.21322)	1.52631 (0.50887)	0.40767[b] (2.55049)	19	0.68	1.720[f]
Interstate Power Co.*	-9.81659	-1.18522[b] (-2.28945)	-0.00002[a] (-4.77232)	0.95723[a] (5.54275)	-1.82396 (-1.23434)	0.71873[a] (7.34623)	19	0.889	1.958[f]
Iowa Public Service Co.*	-2.30377	-1.54372[a] (-3.65634)	-0.00001[f] (-2.67048)	0.56910[a] (4.06307)	-7.19481[a] (-2.91498)	0.26934[a] (4.47373)	20	0.890	1.966
Iowa Southern Utilities Co.*	-3.01474	0.59078 (1.66241)	-0.00000[b] (-2.29551)	0.53269[a] (5.44760)	-0.15969 (-0.09492)	0.22267[a] (5.25954)	19	0.789	1.69[f]
Iowa Electric Light & Power Co.*	-7.46769	-0.93935[a] (-2.90121)	-0.00001[a] (-4.41385)	0.83597[b] (8.04852)	-0.82313 (-0.60161)	0.54953[a] (9.52610)	19	0.939	1.893[f]
Iowa Power & Light Co.*	-0.60528	-0.03450 (-0.09510)	0.00440[b] (2.02921)	0.17439 (1.12843)	-2.06567 (-1.44625)	-0.02699 (-0.51561)	17	0.442	1.713[f]

[a]Significant at 1% level (two-tailed test).
[b]Significant at 5% level (two-tailed test).
[c]Significant in 10% level (two-tailed test).
*Combination company—sells both gas and electricity.
[f]Adjusted for autocorrelation.
t-values appear in parentheses beneath the corresponding coefficients.

explained in terms of production capability which allowed these firms to sell additional units of electricity without relying on less efficient generating facilities.

The ER variable is significant at the 5% level or better in two of the five regressions in Table 2, and the coefficient is consistently positive. This set of coefficients shows that profits increased as costs increased, reflecting a tendency for the Florida commission to overcompensate firms for the cost incurred in operating the business.

The coefficient on the R variable indicates that regulation has caused lower profits in three of the five Florida firms. Florida Power & Light Co. has experienced a tendency toward higher profits since regulation and Florida Power Corp. a tendency toward lower ones since regulation, but both effects are statistically insignificant. The coefficients on the R variable for Tampa Electric Co., Florida Public Utilities Co. and Gulf Power Co. reflect significantly lower profits after state regulation was established.

After state commission regulation, Tampa Electric Co.'s profits were lower by $.598 per 1000 kWh sold; Florida Public Utilities Co.'s profits were lower by $3.566 per 1000 kWh sold; and Gulf Power Co's profits were lower by $4.728 per 1000 Wh sold.

Iowa

Table 3 presents the equations for the six firms from the state of Iowa. As indicated in the table, every firm from the state of Iowa is a combination firm, selling both natural gas and electricity. The table also shows that the coefficient on the P_G variable is negative in every case and statistically significant at the 5% level or better in five of the six equations. These results mean that consumers do react to higher natural gas prices and do generally switch to electricity for some uses as the price of natural gas rises. The results also show that this substitution caused lower profits for the six public electric utility monopolists who also sell natural gas. These results seem to indicate that the

regulatory commission in Iowa has allowed combination firms to earn higher profits from natural gas than from equivalent electric services.

The Π/S_i variable is positive in all cases and statistically significant in five of the six equations at the 5% level or better. As with the Florida firms, this indicates that the Iowa commission attempted to allow firms to increase their profitability as the profitabilty of firms across the country increased. This is some indicator of the responsiveness of the Iowa commission to the needs of regulated firms in that state.

The GR variable is negative in five of the six equations for the Iowa firms. However, the variable is statistically significant in only one equation. The significant coefficient indicates that Iowa Public Service Co. incurred decreases in profits per unit sold as its sales increased. These results probably reflect that, as sales growth took place, this firm used less efficient plants to produce the additional output, reducing profit per unit. They may also indicate that this firm was not as aggressive and successful in seeking rate adjustments when sales were growing and costs were increasing. Consequently, profits were adversely affected by regulatory lag. Of course, both of these explanations are likely and they may apply concurrently.

The ER variable is positive and significant at the 5% level or better in five of the six equations in Table 3. These results reflect a strong tendency of the Iowa commission to overcompensate firms for the projected cost component in their electric rate computation. The results mean that profits are higher for these firms as costs increase.

The coefficient of the R variable reveals that commission regulation has caused lower profits for four of the six Iowa firms included in the sample. Table 3 reveals that the coefficient on the R variable is significant at the 5% level or better for all Iowa firms, except Iowa Sourthern Utilities Co. and Iowa Power & Light Co.

Table 4. OLS Estimates of Profit Functions—Mississippi Companies

Mississippi company	Constant	R	P_G	Π/S_1	GR	ER	DF	R²	Dw
Mississippi Power Co.	0.35908	−0.58550[b]	0.00742[a]	−0.24847[b]	−2.36444[b]	−0.19733[a]	21	0.677	1.680[f]
		(−1.86285)	(5.31785)	(−2.18973)	(−2.44406)	(−4.01406)			
Mississippi Power & Light	0.24682	−0.24682	0.00329[b]	0.09202	−2.13357	1.34864	20	0.384	1.819[f]
		(−0.6943)	(2.31943)	(0.74598)	(−1.64900)	(0.43424)			

[a]Significant at 1% level (two-tailed test).
[b]Significant at 5% level (two-tailed test).
[c]Significant at 10% level (two-tailed test).
[f]Adjusted for autocorrelation.
t-values appear in parentheses beneath the corresponding coefficients.

The equations in Table 3 reveal that the profit reductions from commission regulation ranged from a low of $.939 per 1000 kWh sold for Iowa Electric Light & Power Co. to a high of $1.711 per 1000 kWh sold for Iowa Illinois Gas Electric Co. Intermediate reductions per 1000 kWh sold were Interstate Power Co. ($1.185) and Iowa Public Service Co. ($1.543).

Mississippi

Table 4 presents the equations for the two firms in the sample from the state of Mississippi. The sign on the P_G variable is in the expected direction, indicating that higher natural gas prices cause profits of the electric utilities to increase. These firms are electric monopolies but they do not sell natural gas, as in the case of the firms from Iowa. Consumers substituting electricity for natural gas when gas prices rise would increase the profitability of electric firms. The P_G coefficients in the equations were significant at the 5% level or better.

The Π/S_1 for Mississippi Power & Light is positive but insignificant at the 10% level. However, the coefficient on this variable in the Mississippi Power Co. equation is negative and statistically significant. These results show that the Mississippi regulatory commission, in contrast to both the Florida and Iowa commissions, does not seem to be so responsive to the overall regulatory environment in permitting firms in that state to increase profits. This may also indicate a lack of responsiveness of the Mississippi Public Service Commission to the needs of the regulated firms in that state.

The GR variable is negative for both firms but only significant for Mississippi Power Co., which has possibly faced extensive regulatory lag in obtaining rate increases in the face of rising costs per kWh sold. Profits per unit sold are unaffected as sales growth takes place for Mississippi Power & Light.

The ER variable is significant in the equation at the 5% level for Mississippi Power Co. but not for Mississippi Power & Light. These results indicate that the Mississippi commission is just allowing Mississippi Power & Light to recover costs as they increase, so profit per unit is unaffected. In Mississippi Power Co.'s situation, however, the commission undercompensates the firm and profits per unit fall as production expenses increase.

The negative coefficients on the R variable reveals that commission regulation has tended to lower profit per kWh sold for both firms in Mississippi. Only in Mississipi Power Co.'s case, however, is the reduction statistically significant. Mississippi Power Co.'s profits have been lowered by $.585 per 1000 kWh sold.

CONCLUSIONS

Commission regulation has lowered rates of return earned by firms included in this study. Table 5 presents the mean value of the dependent variable for each firm in the sample and the regulatory effect for comparison purposes.

Of the five firms operating in Florida, three experienced statistically significant lower rates of return after regulation. The lower profits developed from this analysis ranged from $.598 per 1000 kWh sold to $4.728 per 1000 kWh sold.

Only two of the six firms operating in the state of Iowa did not experience statistically significant lower rates of return after commission regulation. The reductions experienced by the four firms which were affected ranged from a low of $.939 to a high of $1.711 per 1000 kWh sold.

One of the two firms operating in Mississippi experienced lower profits after regulation. The reduction amounted to $.585 per 1000 kWh sold.

Table 5 reveals that the Iowa firms showed the highest average profitability at $4.119 per 1000 kWh sold, the Florida firms averaged $2.948 and the Mississippi firms averaged $1.020 per 1000 kWh sold. The table also shows that the regulatory commission of Florida has reduced profits by the greatest average magnitude, $2.964 per 1000 kWh sold. The Mississippi commission reduced profits by the smallest amount, $.585 per 1000 kWh sold and the Iowa commission reduced profits by $1.344 per 1000 kWh sold. These data give some indication of the relative impact of commission regulation in the three states.

One conclusion is that some firms fared better under regulation than others. These kinds of differences are obscured in more aggregated studies and they do show the merit of time series approaches to assessing the impact of regulation.

Although regulation seemed to lower profits of the firms in this study, care must be taken not to attribute this result to overall effectiveness of the regulatory process. That is, more evidence must be developed to assure that these results are not merely chance

Table 5. Summary of Mean Values for Dependent Variable Compared with Values for Dummy Variable (Firms in the Sample)

	Regulatory effect Dummy variable[a]	Mean value Dependent variable[b]
Florida		
Florida Power Corp.	−$1.579*	$1.249
Florida Power & Light Co.	+0.8864*	$0.906
Tampa Electric Co.	−$0.598	$2.891
Gulf Power Co.	−$4.728	$5.066
Florida Public Utilities Co.	−$3.566	$4.630
Mean of Florida firms[c]	−$2.964	$2.948
Iowa		
Iowa Illinois Gas & Electric Co.	−$1.711	$4.067
Iowa Southern Utilities Co.	+$0.590*	$4.252
Iowa Public Service Co.	−$1.543	$7.244
Iowa Power and Light Co.	−0.034*	$0.991
Interstate Power Co.	−$1.185	$4.512
Iowa Electric Light and Power	−$0.939	$3.648
Mean of Iowa firms[c]	−$1.344	$4.119
Mississippi		
Mississippi Power Co.	−$0.585	$1.244
Mississippi Power and Light	−$0.246*	$0.796
Mean of Mississippi firms[c]	−$0.585	$1.020

*Statistically insignificant.
[a]Measured in terms of dollars per 1000 kWh sold.
[c]Mean of statistically significant effects only ten percent level or better.

outcomes of regulation. The point is that, even though regulation seemed to be working as it should in a number of cases examined, several signs of randomness seems to be present in the statistical results.[14] These indications of randomness will be presented in the discussion below.

The first concern about regulation which emerges from these data involve the fact that in some cases commissions tended to overcompensate *some* utility firms for the higher costs incurred from higher input prices; however, commissions were somewhat inconsistent, and other firms were just compensated for these cost increases. This outcome suggests that utility firms are subjected to the will and fancy of a regulatory body which *may* be unable or unwilling to make critical adjustments to the returns they earn. Moreover, in contrast to the impersonal markets which effectively regulate other types of businesses, utility firms are controlled by regulators who make judgements which raise serious questions of equity.

The second concern involves the fact that some firms' profits were lowered after regulation while others were unchanged, even within the same state jurisdiction. This fact, too, provides additional evidence of the randomness within the regulatory process and raises additional questions of equity.

Finally, although regulation has reduced rates of return in some cases examined here, from public policy point of view it is still not clear that regulation is cost effective. Moreover, regulation is also charged with responsibilities other than financial control, and we are unable to determine whether performance in those areas is effective. These are all important matters which require additional rigorous research.

Acknowledgements

Mark Hirschey, Paul Newbold, Kimio Morimune, Jon Nelson, David Ciscel, Robert Rasche, Dan Hollas, John Mikesell, Patrick Mann, Julian Simon and Randy Nelson provided useful criticism of an earlier version. This study was assisted by research grants from the Investors in Business Education, DOE, and the Office of Energy Research at the University of Illinois.

NOTES

1. See, for example, Primeaux (1986), Stigler and Friedland (1962, pp. 1–16), Moore (1970, pp. 365–75), Moore (1975), Primeaux (1979) and Primeaux (1975, pp. 175–6).
2. The regulatory process is discussed in Primeaux (1978).
3. Although Kahn (1970) explains that excessive profits are the main concern of regulators, these bodies also review utility operations for the following possible abuses: (1) inclusion of improper operating expenses in the cost of service used for rate making; (2) price discrimination among customers; (3) poor customer service. An assessment of price discrimination among customer classes is presented in Primeaux and Nelson (1980).
4. This relationship would not necessarily hold in a gas–electric combination company. In this situation the firm is a monopolist both for gas and for electricity, and sells both services in a given city. Consequently, a consumer facing a higher price for natural gas may change to electricity but the same firm would continue to earn profit from selling the substitute energy to him. The net effect on profitability in this case, depends upon both how the regulatory commission discriminates between gas and electric prices and the extent of consumer responses to price changes.
5. Phillips (1969, p. 96) explains that this body has also established for its members an annual regulatory development

course which covers regulatory principles and their applications. This reflects their influence on commission thinking and attitudes. The importance of the regulatory climate is discussed in Benjamin (1966, p. 19).

6. The rate-making procedure is quite complex, and it will not be discussed here. A case study of rate making and a discussion of costs of service is presented in Garfield and Lovejoy (1964, pp. 249–59).

7. The important problem of how to manipulate rates of return to induce efficiency is not addressed here. For discussions of this problem see Kahn (1970, p. 53) and Iulo (1961).

8. Actually, Minnesota and Texas have also implemented commission regulation since World War II but it was not possible to include them in this study. Commission regulation has jurisdiction in Texas only where it has been requested by the public, and data are insufficient in Minnesota's case because it was only recently regulated.

9. Data are from *Statistics of Privately Owned Electric Utilities in the United States* (various years) and *Gas Facts* (various years).

10. Profitability of publicly owned electric firms is discussed in Mann (1970, pp. 478–84).

11. The question examined is how effective is regulation, not how effective is effective regulation.

12. The usual arrangement was that firms were regulated at the local level by some sort of city commission prior to state commission regulation. One study found local regulation even less effective than state commission regulation (see Sampson (1958).

Some concern may arise because the behavior of regulated utilities with respect to accounting conventions may be different from unregulated utilities. This difference in behavior could occur if regulated utilities attempted to adopt accounting conventions which would conceal excess profitability in the face of regulation. This possibility is probably not a problem in this analysis, however, because the Federal Power Commission and the US Department of Energy prescribed uniform systems of accounts for utilities in the data used here, even if firms were unregulated at the state level. This requirement is not part of a regulatory procedure.

13. As mentioned earlier, the electric utility regulatory procedure allows a recovery of all expenses and costs only, plus a rate of return on investment. (see Shepherd, 1967). A discussion of how consumer prices must be compatible with the *allowed* rate of return is presented in Somers (1971, p. 44). Consumer prices, of course, translate the regulated or allowed return into the amount which companies will realize from sales of services and ultimately net profit. The regulated and allowed rates of return are discussed in Roberts *et al.* (1978).

14. Randomness of the regulatory process is also mentioned in Primeaux (1978).

REFERENCES

American Gas Association (various years). *Gas Facts*, Arlington.

R. N. Benjamin (1966). Economic and regulatory problems of electric utilities. In *The Economics of Regulation of Public Utilities*, Evanston: Northwestern University.

D. Cochrane and G. H. Orcutt (1949). Application of least squares regression to relationships containing autocorrelated error terms. *Journal of the American Statistical Association* 44, March, 32–61.

P. J. Garfield and W. F. Lovejoy (1964). *Public Utility Economics*, Englewood Cliffs, NJ: Prentice-Hall.

W. Iulo (1961). *Electric Utilities—Cost and Performance: A Study of Inter Utility Differences in the Unit Electric Cost of Privately Owned Electric Utilities*, Pullman: Washington State University.

R. Jackson (1969). Regulation and electric utility rate levels. *Land Economics* 45, August, 372–76.

P. L. Joskow (1973). Pricing decisions of regulated firms: A behavioral approach. *Bell Journal of Economics* 4, Spring, 118–40.

A. E. Kahn (1970). *The Economics of Regulation*, New York: John Wiley.

P. Mann (1970). Publicly owned electric utility profits and resource allocation. *Land Economics* 46, November, 478–84.

C. G. Moore (1975). Has electricity regulation resulted in higher prices? An econometric evaluation using a calibrated regulatory input variable. *Economic Inquiry* 13, June, 207–36.

T. G. Moore (1970). The effectiveness of regulation of electric utility prices. *Southern Economic Journal* 36, April, 365–75.

D. F. Pegrum (1965). *Public Regulation of Business*, Homewood, IL: Irwin.

C. F. Phillips (1969). *The Economics of Regulation*, Homewood, IL: Irwin.

W. J. Primeaux, Jr (1975). A reexamination of the monopoly market structure for electric utilities. In A. Phillips (ed.), *Promoting Competition in Regulated Markets*, Washington: The Brookings Institution, pp. 175–200.

W. J. Primeaux, Jr (1978). Rate base methods and realized rates of return, **16**, January, 95–107.

W. J. Primeaux, Jr (1979). Some problems with natural monopoly. *The Antitrust Bulletin* 24, Spring, 63–85.

W. J. Primeaux, Jr (1986). *Direct Electric Utility Competition: The Natural Monopoly Myth*, New York: Praeger.

W. J. Primeaux, Jr and R. A. Nelson (1980). An examination of price discrimination and internal subsidization by electric utilities. *Southern Economic Journal* 46, July, 84–99.

R. B. Roberts *et al.* (1978). Determinants of the requested rate of return and the rate of return granted in a formal regulatory process. *Bell Journal of Economics* 9, Autumn, 611–21.

R. J. Sampson (1958). Comparative performance of electric utilities under state and under local rate regulation. *Land Economics* 34, May, 174–7.

W. G. Shepherd (1967). Utility growth and profits under regulation. In W. G. Shepherd and T. G. Gies (eds) *Utility Regulation New Directions in Theory and Policy*, New York: Random House.

H. Somers (1971). Rate of return and misallocation of resources. In J. E. Haring and J. F. Humphrey (eds), *Utility Regulation During inflation*, Los Angeles: Occidental College.

Statistics of Privately Owned Electric Utilities in the United States (various years). Washington: Federal Power Commission/DOE.

G. Stigler and C. Friedland (1962). What can regulators regulate? The case of electricity. *The Journal of Law and Economics 5*, No. 1, 1–16.

Article 24

The Effect of Lead Paint Abatement Laws on Rental Property Values

Deborah Ann Ford* and Michele Gilligan**

Lead paint is a source of childhood lead poisoning, a vicious disease with high costs to both the victims and society. Treatment of the disease requires placing the victim in a lead-free environment. Laws have been enacted by many localities, which would require removal of lead from residential property. However, property owners have resisted the enforcement of these laws with threats of abandonment. Theory suggests that abandonment will occur only if the value of the rental property after removal of the paint is less than the cost of removal. This paper shows that these costs have already been discounted into property values. Data from Baltimore, Maryland indicates that the market has placed a value of approximately $15,250 per structure or $3,813 per rental unit on expected abatement costs. This value in most cases is less than the value of the rental property. Thus abandonment should occur infrequently.

LEAD-BASED PAINT AND HOUSING

Lead paint in housing is a problem when it is accessible to children under the age of six. When housing is not maintained, paint can chip and peel; children can breathe lead dust, teethe on surfaces covered with lead paint, and eat paint chips (Chisolm 1971). While exposure to lead in the air, food, water, and soil is prevalent in all urban areas, lead paint is the most concentrated source of lead exposure. Studies

*Department of Economics and Finance, School of Business, University of Baltimore, Baltimore, Maryland 21201.
**School of Law, University of Baltimore, Baltimore.
Date Received: February 9, 1987; Revised: June 24, 1987.
[1]The term abatement has never been defined precisely. Removal of all lead paint particles and dust would be almost impossible. Abatement is used to refer to the process of making lead paint and dust inaccessible, by covering it or removing it with one of several techniques.

show a clear relationship between housing quality and blood lead levels in children (Farfel 1985).

Lead poisoning in children, if not treated, can lead to persistent, forceful vomiting, convulsions, coma or death. Other effects are diminished intelligence, poor motor nerve response, behavioral problems, mental retardation and a shorter expected life span (W. Nelson 1983). Such terrible consequences led public health officials, parents, and others to demand that lead paint be removed from America's housing stock.

Lead was used as an additive to most paints in the 1930s and 1940s to produce durability and brightness. By the early 1950s most interior paint no longer contained high concentrations of lead. The removal from the market of paint with a high content of lead did not eliminate lead in housing, however. One third of the housing units in the United States were built before 1940. One half of the housing units were built before 1960, prior to federal regulation, state regulation, and most local regulation of the lead content in paint (U.S. Department of Commerce, Bureau of the Census, *Statistical Abstract of the United States*, 101st edition).

In 1971, the U.S. Congress passed the Lead-Based Paint Poisoning Prevention Act. This Act, requiring federal regulation of the lead content in paint, provided funding for local screening programs to find and treat children at risk and for local abatement programs.[1] Nonetheless, government funding has been used only for secondary prevention, i.e., finding children at risk and treating them, rather than primary prevention, i.e., finding and abating properties with impermissible concentrations of lead paint before a child becomes seriously ill. The secondary approach, frequently referred to as the health approach, does not prevent childhood lead poisoning because the harm has been done to at least one child. If abatement is performed correctly, however, future tenants will not be harmed. The primary approach, known as the housing approach, would require systematic abatement of all residential structures, regardless of whether a child was already ill. We know of no instances where such an approach has been used.[2]

Fifteen years after the passage of the Lead-Based Paint Poisoning Prevention Act, lead poisoning of children is still a major problem in older cities. In fiscal year 1986, 649 children in the City of Baltimore were found to have elevated blood lead levels. Of these, 101 were hospitalized for treatment. Philadelphia, Scranton, Louisville, and Memphis all have city-operated abatement teams because of the large number

[2]For a full discussion of present abatement laws see Michele Gilligan and Deborah Ann Ford, "Investor Response to Lead-Based Paint Abatement Laws: Legal and Economic Considerations," *Columbia Journal of Environmental Law*, 12: 401–48, 1987.

of sick children. In the 1980s, lawsuits against public housing authorities have been filed in the District of Columbia, Philadelphia, and Wilmington by representatives of children poisoned by lead paint in public housing. Similar private tort actions against property owners have been filed in Baltimore, New York, Boston, St. Louis, and other cities. Plaintiffs have been awarded substantial damages in many of these cases. Nevertheless, property owners have resisted enforcement of abatement laws with threats of abandonment of large numbers of low-cost rental units.

The prospect of lead paint creates a great deal of financial uncertainty for an owner. There may be uncertainty as to whether it even exists in a particular dwelling. If the paint is present, abatement will be required only if a child becomes ill, and the cost of abatement will depend on the amount and location of the paint. The possibility of successful legal action on behalf of the victim also increases the uncertainty. Owners are facing increasing difficulty in finding insurance companies willing to cover lead paint liabilities because sympathetic jurors may award substantial damages.

The present study was designed to determine whether lead paint abatement costs both direct and indirect were being discounted into the prices of high-risk property in Baltimore in 1984. One would expect all of these potential costs to be reflected in property prices.

RENTAL PROPERTY VALUE WITHIN URBAN AREAS

In recent years, most property value studies have followed the basic theory set forth by Dildine and Massey (1974). They showed that the value of all residential real property is equal to the present value of its gross rental price. This price is determined by (1) the physical characteristics of the property itself, such as age, structure type, physical dimensions, and condition, and (2) neighborhood conditions such as parks, crime rate, racial composition, neighborhood income levels, school reputations, and distance from the central business district. For owner-occupied housing this bundle of housing services has an imputed rent that is not observable. Observed transaction prices are the present value of this unobserved bundle of services. For rental properties, the gross rental price is observable and may be assumed to reflect all property and neighborhood characteristics.

Most of the research on rental properties has centered on the incentives for maintenance. Dildine and Massey showed that optimal maintenance levels would occur where marginal costs equal marginal benefits. More precisely, optimal maintenance would occur where the present value of expenditures equals the present value of current and future changes in rentals, either market or imputed.

Elliott, et al. (1985) and Quinn, et al. (1980) studied data in St. Louis and found that Dildine and Massey were correct for stable neighborhoods but not in places of declining demand. The St. Louis data showed that often landlords were increasing maintenance expenditures as rent levels were falling. The conclusion seems to be that in a case of neighborhood filtering, vandalism may be the cause of high maintenance. Owners not willing to abandon must increase upkeep in order to maintain a positive cash flow. All of this research defines maintenance as expenditures necessary to maintain, but not increase, value. In the Elliott and Quinn studies no reference is made to value as such.

The neighborhoods to be analyzed in this paper are low income and predominantly minority. Sternlieb (1966 and 1973) and Stegman (1972) did extensive survey work on the slums of Newark and Baltimore respectively in the early 1970s. The economic incentives for property owners in slum areas are no different from those of owners in other areas. They require a rate of return commensurate with the risk of their investment. Sternlieb and Stegman both found high operating costs in the slums. Vacancy rates and nonpayment of rent were both high; maintenance because of vandalism, large families, and poor tenants was substantially above other areas; property taxes as a percentage of gross income was extremely high. The latter happens because assessment values in the slums are often higher than market values. Since reassessment occurs only periodically, if market values are falling, assessment will lag behind.

Stegman found in 1970 that of 247 rental units in Baltimore, taxes accounted for 19% of gross rents, interest 15%, and maintenance 22%. Such high operating costs led to very low gross rent multipliers. Market values were difficult to determine in these studies but Stegman estimated gross rent multipliers of 2-3 and Sternlieb of 3-4. Our own analysis of 1984 Baltimore data found similar patterns.

No economic analysis of lead paint abatement has appeared in the literature. Abatement is not maintenance in that it does not preserve property value. Abatement may more properly be viewed as code enforcement. Quinn, et al. maintain that enforcing housing codes in a declining market will only encourage abandonment. However, our study indicates that abandonment due to forced lead paint abatement should occur only in extreme cases of very marginal property.

MODEL

In the absence of lead paint, we can assume that rental property can be valued as the present value of the rent stream. Following Dildine and Massey, neighborhood and property characteristics other than lead paint are assumed reflected in rental prices.

Let:

$$P = Rk^{-1} \tag{1}$$

where

P = value or price

R = annual gross rents

k = required rate of return

Real estate market values are often determined by some gross rent multiplier. Equation (1) can be rewritten as:

$$P = \alpha R$$

where $\alpha = k^{-1}$ (2)

= gross rent multiplier

The multiplier α need not be identical for all rental properties in an urban area but is usually constant within a neighborhood. In slum areas the multiplier may be expected to be 2-4 whereas in middle income areas, it might be 8-11. Clearly the property is valued less per dollar of expected gross rent in a slum than in a middle income area.

Now assume that a purchaser knows with certainty that he must abate lead paint at some future time. His offering price, or the value of the property, will be:

$$P = Rk^{-1} - C(1+k)^{-N} \tag{3}$$

where

C = cost of abatement

N = year in which abatement will take place

Under most state and local laws, abatement is not required unless a child who resides in the structure is found to have an elevated blood lead level. An investor may estimate that such an occurrence is not likely for several years. If so, abatement can be postponed.

In fact, neither the timing nor the necessity for abatement is known with certainty. All investment properties do not contain lead paint. Even if a property contains the paint, abatement will be required only when ordered by a government agency or a court.

Because the necessity for abatement is uncertain, let

P_1 = probability that lead paint exists

P_2 = probability that lead paint will have to be abated

then

$$P = Rk^{-1} - P_1 \int_0^z P_2(t)C\,e^{-kt} \tag{4}$$

Equation 4 assumes that P_1 and P_2 are conditional, i.e., that the existence of lead paint and its necessary abatement are related. For the investor, estimating P_1, the existence of lead paint, depends on the age of the structure, its past maintenance, and the number of lead poisoning cases in the immediately surrounding neighborhood.

$P_2(t)$ is the probability of being required to abate in any year t. Estimating P_2 for any year is complicated since, given the health approach of the laws, abatement depends on a child living in the property and becoming ill. In any case, lead paint needs to be abated only if it exists. Therefore, P_2 is conditional upon P_1 being greater than 0. Many investors may simply estimate the probability of necessary abatement without actually separating P_1 and P_2. However, for analytical purposes, the two probabilities should be identified as independent estimates.

The cost of abatement, C, is also uncertain. Public statements by property owners seem to indicate that expectations are skewed upwards. They fear very high abatement costs. However the fear of liability may be a component of expected lead paint costs to property owners. This paper will not make any assumptions with regard to the distribution of C. Instead a hedonic index will be used to estimate the term:

$$P_1 \int_0^x P_2(t) C \, e^{-kt}$$

DATA AND EMPIRICAL TEST

Data for this study was obtained from three sources. Transaction data was obtained from the Greater Baltimore Board of Realtors Multiple List Service (MLS). Listed prices of property coded as residential rental in 1984 were used as a basic database. The data included information on number of units per structure, rent per unit, structure size, and structure age. The price was the listing price, not the actual transaction price. However, an assumption can be made that differences between listing and selling price are random, not systematic, and will have no effect on statistical tests.[3]

Neighborhood characteristics were obtained from the 1980 Baltimore City Census Profile. Neighborhood characteristics included, but were not limited to, average income, percentage of population which

---

[3] A hypothesis could be made that if the differences are biased, the ratio of listed prices to transaction prices in the risky neighborhoods would be larger than in non-risky areas. Sellers might be forced to search longer for investors willing to purchase properties with possible lead problems. In this case the results of this study will understate the discounting of lead risk into property value.

was black, average rent levels and age of structure data.

The Baltimore City Childhood Lead Poisoning Prevention Program provided data on census tracts from which children had been hospitalized for lead poisoning within recent years. They considered these tracts as risky areas for the disease. If some residences have already been proven to have the paint, structures nearby, built at approximately the same time period, would be likely candidates for abatement. Of 207 census tracts within the City of Baltimore, 44 were identified as risky to potential victims of lead paint and property owners. At least one child had been hospitalized from each risky tract and, in some cases, many more. Data limitations precluded further divisions into moderate and high risk.

Risky tracts may differ from non-risky tracts in many ways unrelated to lead paint. As mentioned previously, other studies have shown gross rent multipliers substantially lower for slum areas than for middle income areas. Table 1 presents summary statistics regarding neighborhood and property characteristics for risky versus non-risky census tracts in Baltimore.

Risky neighborhoods not only had lower values for higher rental incomes, but also a higher than average number of blacks and significantly lower incomes than non-risky neighborhoods. These findings are consistent with those of the National Center for Health Statistics developed in a survey conducted between 1976 and 1980. The survey results estimated that 18.5% of all black children from households with an income less than $7,500 had elevated blood lead levels. For black households with income over $15,000, the percentage of children at risk is 2.8%. For white children from low-income families, 5.9% had elevated blood levels as opposed to .7% from high-income families.[4]

TABLE 1

Neighborhood & Property Characteristics

	Risky Census Tracts	Non-Risky Census Tracts
Average income[1]	$9,900	$13,512
Average percent black[1]	73.4%	43.2%
Average age of structure[1]	41.6 years	36.8 years
Average listed price[2]	$48,444	$75,679
Average rental income of listed properties[2]	$12,312	$11,018

[1]Census Profile, Baltimore City, 1980
[2]All observations from MLS properties coded Residential Rental in 1984

[4]*Vital and Health Statistics of the National Center for Health Statistics*, No. 79 (May 12, 1982).

Whatever the causes of these statistics, the implication is that lead paint poisoning is clearly corrolated with race and with income.

The average age of structures was slightly higher in the risky census tracts. However, given the age of Baltimore's housing stock, even the non-risky areas are old enough to contain lead paint. Therefore age would not seem to be a factor in price difference.

Clearly property value differences in this sample could be attributed to factors other than lead paint. For that reason, we decided to test only neighborhoods, defined as census tracts, with below-average incomes for the city and with populations consisting of more than 50% black. There were nine risky and eight non-risky census tracts that had these qualifications. There were thirty-one sales observations in these census tracts, fourteen in the risky tracts and seventeen in the non-risky tracts. The benefit from the selection of observations from homogeneous census tracts seemed to outweigh the loss in numbers of observations.

From equation 4, if a risky census tract (RCT) is a proxy for

$$P_1 \int_0^x P_2(t) C\, e^{-kt},$$

then a reasonable test for the effect of lead paint risk would be:

$$Price_i = \beta_0 + \beta_1\, Rent_i + \beta_2\, Risky\ Census\ Tract_i + e. \qquad (5)$$

Since rent is a function of neighborhood and property characteristics, a two-stage least squares procedure was used. Rent was estimated in the first stage, and the predicted value then used to explain market value in stage two. The first stage was calculated as

$$Annual\ Rent_i = \begin{array}{l} 651 \quad + \quad 1726\ Total\ Rooms_i - 28.30\ Percent\ Blacks_i \\ (0.69) + (26.60) \qquad\qquad\quad (3.55) \qquad\qquad\qquad (6) \\ -871.22\ RCT_i + \ .008\ Household\ Income_i + e \\ \quad (1.17) \qquad\qquad (0.17) \end{array}$$

$$R^2 = .82$$

$$F = 187.8$$

$$N = 159$$

(Values in parenthesis are t statistics)

Clearly rent is determined primarily by the amount of rental space. Total rooms was computed by adding the number of efficiencies, one-bedroom, two-bedroom, and three-bedroom units for rent. The only other significant affect on rent was the percentage of blacks in the neighborhood. Risky census tract was insignificant in explaining the rent level for a building as was average household income.

Such a conclusion is not unreasonable, given the education level of the renters. Ignorance, lack of mobility, income restrictions, and other causes of market inefficiencies could cause lead paint to be a nonsignificant factor to renters but not property owners (Ackerman 1971).

When equation 5 was tested in the second stage using estimated rent for the 31 relevant observations, the results were:

$$Price_i = 24453 + 2.6\ Rent_i - 15250\ RCT_i + e$$
$$\quad\quad\quad (4.33)\quad\quad (7.51)\quad\quad\quad (2.34)$$
$$R^2 = .70$$
$$F = 32.48$$

The value for β_2 indicates that properties in risky neighborhoods sold for \$15,250 less in 1984 than did properties with the same gross rents in similar non-risky neighborhoods. The average number of units per structure was four. Therefore the discount per unit was \$3,813. We conclude that by 1984, the market was aware of the lead paint problem, and potential costs were being discounted into prices.[5]

Property owners have frequently threatened to abandon their properties rather than spend money on abatement, and local governments are naturally concerned at the prospect of mass abandonment of low-cost housing. In fact, if property owners are forced to abate, their properties will increase in value because uncertain future abatement costs will no longer exist. Thus, the expenditure is not an unrecoupable loss.

Investors will abandon only if:

$$Price_i = \beta_0 + \beta_1 Rent_i - P_1 P_2 Cost(1+i)^N < 0 \quad\quad (7)$$

If abatement is required immediately, equation 7 can be rewritten.

$$Price_i = \beta_0 + \beta_1 Rent_i - Cost < 0 \quad\quad (8)$$
$$\text{or}\quad \beta_0 + \beta_1 R_i < C$$

Abandonment will occur only if the cost of abatement is greater than the discounted value of the rent stream.[6] If C is less than $\beta_0 + \beta_1 R_i$, the property can be sold for a positive amount even if the seller takes a capital loss.

A recent study by the Subcommittee on Lead Paint Abatement Methodologies of the Baltimore City Task Force on Lead Paint Prevention supports the findings in this paper. Using different types of procedures, they abated three houses. Each house contained six rooms:

---

[5]Equation 5 was estimated in a log-linear form, as well as linear-log and log-log for rent. The effect was insignificant on all coefficients. Since the model is conceptually linear, there seemed to be no reason to experiment with nonlinear functional forms.
[6]Actually abandonment will occur only if equation 7 holds and the value of the cleared land is less than the cost of demolishing the present structure. If land values in the neighborhood are high, a new building may replace the old.

3 bedrooms, a living-room, dining room, kitchen and bath. The total cost ranged between $2,466 and $3,264 per unit or $2.75 to $3.65 per square foot.[7] The total cost for an apartment unit would usually be less than those for a house because of the smaller overall size. The figures from the subcommittee study are well within any estimates of discounted costs in this paper, especially if investors are discounting possible legal costs as well as actual abatement costs. Figures from both studies are also substantially less than average property values in the risky census tracts.

During 1984 and 1985, the Baltimore City Health Department established a City Operated Lead Abatement Program. Regulations were developed that required abatement to begin within three days of notification of an ill child's presence in the unit. An extension of three days was allowed for noncompliance. At the end of that time, if abatement had not begun, city work crews performed the abatement, and the property owner was billed for the cost.

This program is no longer in existence. However, according to a departmental report in June, 1985, "The threat of abatement by city crews for noncompliance resulted in a dramatic behavior change by the property owners. Some 98 percent of the property owners started the work on the specified date."[8] No cases of abandonment in the face of required abatement were reported.

Such short-term data does not prove that abandonment would never result from enforced abatement. However, abandonment did not occur in that year in Baltimore. We believe that abatement costs were less than the value of the property. Thus, abandonment is not a rational decision for investors.

SUMMARY

Expectations of lead paint abatement have been discounted into property values in Baltimore. As evidence has shown, forced abatement did not result in property abandonment. If widespread forced abatement were to occur, most owners would either comply or sell their properties. The cost of abatement would need to be greater than the discounted value of future rent streams for the property to be removed from the rental market.

Given the low prices that property owners have paid in recent years, they anticipated the lead paint expenditures and will not abandon if abatement is enforced. The aggregate costs of mandatory abatement

---

[7]The crews abated all surfaces including floors, which is generally not necessary. However no profit margins or clean-up costs were included. Only direct labor and material was costed.
[8]Jobs Bill, City Operated Abatement Program Progress Report and Plan for Fiscal Year 1985.

will be high, but the costs of non-abatement to victims is also high. Baltimore and other cities should begin mandatory abatement immediately.

The authors would like to thank the Greater Baltimore Board of Realtors and the Baltimore Childhood Lead Poisoning Prevention Program of the Baltimore City Public Health Department for data and information that made this study possible. The project was partially funded by a summer research grant from the University of Baltimore Educational Foundation. An anonymous referee was extremely helpful.

REFERENCES

[1] Samuel B. Abbott. Housing Policy, Housing Codes and Tenant Remedies: An Integration. *Boston University Law Review* 56: 1–146, 1976.

[2] Bruce A. Ackerman. Regulating Slum Housing Markets on Behalf of the Poor: Of Housing Codes, Housing Subsidies and Income Redistribution Policy. *Yale Law Journal* 80: 1093–1197, 1971.

[3] J. Julian Chisolm, Jr. Lead Poisoning. *Scientific America* : 224, February 1971.

[4] Larry L. Dildine and Fred A. Massey. Dynamic Model of Private Incentives to Housing Maintenance. *Southern Economic Journal* 40: 631–39, April 1974.

[5] Karen M. Eisenstadt. *Factors Affecting Maintenance and Operating Costs in Private Rental Housing.* The New York City Rand Institute, 1972.

[6] Donald S. Elliott, Jr., Michael A. Quinn and Robert E. Mendelson. Maintenance Behavior of Large-Scale Landlords and Theories of Neighborhood Succession. *American Real Estate and Urban Economics Association Journal* 13: 425–45, Winter 1985.

[7] Mark R. Farfel. Reducing Lead Exposure in Children. *Annual Review of Public Health* 6: 333–60, 1985.

[8] Michele Gilligan and Deborah Ann Ford. Investor Response to Lead-Based Paint Abatement Laws: Legal and Economic Considerations. *Columbia Journal of Environment Law* 12: 401–48, 1987.

[9] Edwin S. Mills and Bruce W. Hamilton. *Urban Economics.* Scott, Foresman & Co., third edition 1984.

[10] Waldo E. Nelson. *Textbook of Pediatrics.* Saunders Co., twelfth edition, 1983.

[11] David M. O'Hara. Social Factors in the Recurrence of Increased Lead Absorption in Children. In J. Julian Chisolm, Jr. and David M. O'Hara, *Lead Absorption in Children: Management, Clinical and Environmental Aspects.* Urban & Schwarzenberg, 1982.

[12] Michael A. Quinn. Maintenance Effort and the Professional Landlord: An Empirical Critique of Theories of Neighborhood Decline. *American Real Estate and Urban Economics Association Journal* 8: 345–69, Winter 1980.

[13] Michael A. Stegman. *Housing Investment in the Inner City: The Dynamics of Decline: A Study of Baltimore, Maryland, 1968–1970.* MIT Press, 1972.

[14] George Sternlieb. *The Tenement Landlord.* Urban Studies Center, Rutgers University, 1966.

[15] _____ and Robert W. Burchell. *Residential Abandonment: The Tenement Landlord Revisited.* Center for Urban Policy Research, Rutgers University, 1973.

Article 25

THE EFFECT OF GASOLINE TAXES ON HIGHWAY FATALITIES

J. Paul Leigh and James T. Wilkinson

In recent years, between 44,000 and 52,000 Americans died annually in road and highway accidents [Baker et al., 1984]. Because many of the victims are young, the total number of life-years lost in vehicle accidents is nearly as great as the number lost to heart disease. Yet, the research devoted to traffic deaths is paltry compared to that on heart disease [Foege, 1985, p. 14]. Economists have analyzed a number of policy alternatives for reducing the death and injury toll of road and highway accidents, but largely ignored gasoline taxes [Leigh and Frank, 1987]. This article examines the use of higher gasoline taxes to reduce fatalities. The benefit of lower fatalities would be in addition to the frequently cited gains associated with reduced air pollution and congestion, decreased dependence on foreign energy sources, and a reduced federal deficit.

We first describe the market failures associated with the consumption of gasoline. Second, we develop a simple model in which changes in gas taxes affect fatalities indirectly through reduced speeds and fewer miles driven. Next we present the results from estimating a reduced form of the model. These results support the hypothesis that an increase in gasoline taxes will lead to a reduction in automotive fatalities. Arguments and evidence are summarized in the closing section.

Is There a Market Failure?

Market failures provide a potential justification for government intervention to increase gasoline taxes. There are three areas where externalities may be generated by the consumption of gasoline. The first involves pollution and congestion, the second involves dependence on imported oil, and the third involves accidents, injuries, and fatalities. Congestion and pollution externalites have been studied extensively. For example, French [1988] found that the social benefits of reduced pollution and congestion resulting from a 15-cent-per-gallon increase in the gas tax would exceed social costs. The pollution and congestion literature does not address the possible effects of an increase in the gas tax on accidents, injuries, and fatalities. To the extent that a tax increase reduces fatalities, social benefits will be even larger.

A large percentage of the oil we consume is imported, and a disruption of oil imports would adversely affect the U.S. economy. Externalities arise when these potential costs are not reflected in petroleum and gasoline prices. Yucel and Dahl [1990] show that a gas tax may be effective in reducing dependence on foreign oil.

There will be additional externalities if drivers underestimate the social costs associated with automobile accidents. This may be the case if young, inexperienced drivers and drugged or drunk drivers underestimate accident risk, if drivers in general underestimate accident risk, or if courts send signals that underestimate accident costs.

Young drivers are likely to underestimate accident risk because the ability to assess such risks depends, in part, on driving experience.[1] Drug and alcohol consumption can reduce both the ability to assess risk and the ability to drive safely. Stricter laws or more rigorous enforcement of laws governing the minimum legal driving age and drinking age and drunk driving laws are one response to these problems [Cook and Tauchen, 1984; Saffer and Grossman, 1987; Wilkinson, 1987]. Although a higher tax would affect all drivers, it would be an additional response to these externalities.[2]

There is a psychological literature which suggests that all drivers may systematically underestimate accident risk [Fischoff, Furby, and Gregory, 1987; Groeger and Brown, 1989; Slovic, Fischoff, and Lichenstein, 1980; De Joy, 1989]. Most surveys reveal that the majority of drivers believe themselves to be "better than average"; as a matter of logic, however, this cannot be. Also, psychologists note that people's perception of risk is greatly influenced by their perception of control. Most people believe, erroneously, that travel by bus, train, or airplane is more dangerous than travel in their own cars, in part because they are in control of their cars [Slovic, Fischoff, and Lichenstein, 1980; Allman, 1985]. Thus, "better-than-average" drivers in control of their own vehicles may systematically underestimate accident risk.

Critics such as Lave [1987] point out that these arguments imply that drivers are irrational (a heretical proposition for most economists). Drivers who systematically underestimate accident risks would perceive insurance (which is priced according to true accident risks) to be systematically overpriced. Thriving auto insurance markets suggest that this is not the case.[3]

Current legal arrangements may fail to deter excessive risk-taking. For

[1] Furthermore, young drivers are likely to prefer a higher level of risk [Rubin and Paul, 1979], which would impose costs on other, more risk-averse drivers.

[2] Enforcing laws governing underaged or drunk driving can be expensive. While a gas tax imposes costs broadly on all drivers, the implementation and enforcement costs of this policy are minimal.

[3] However, drivers may still be willing to pay for "overpriced" insurance if they are sufficiently risk averse.

example, court judgments in fatal accident cases may be less than the true social cost. Using a theoretically superior willingness-to-pay measure of costs, Garen [1988] and Moore and Viscusi [1988] find value-of-life estimates that are four times greater than estimates used in court. Thus, the courts signal that accident costs are below true social costs. In addition, White [1988] argues that the incentives to avoid accidents are weaker under current liability rules than would be economically efficient.

A higher gasoline tax may be justified on pollution and congestion grounds alone. That this policy can reduce fatalities as well makes it more attractive. There may be cases in which drivers do not face the true social costs of accidents. In these situations, the number of accidents may exceed the social optimum. A higher gasoline tax is one policy alternative that can reduce the number of accidents.

Modeling Traffic Deaths

In this section, we develop an econometric model that will be used to estimate the effects of changes in gasoline taxes on automotive fatalities. The model is composed of a fatalities "production function" and a demand curve for gasoline. As described below, fatalities are a function of gasoline consumption and other variables. Gasoline taxes affect fatalities indirectly through their effect on gasoline consumption. An increase in the gasoline tax causes people to drive fewer miles or drive in a more fuel-efficient manner (e.g., more slowly). Both changes will reduce fatalities.

Following Wilkinson [1987], the number of fatalities in a state (F) is assumed to be determined by the quantity of gas consumed (Q), driving behavior (B), and characteristics of drivers and their automobiles (C).[4]

$$F = f(Q, B, C) \tag{1}$$

Driving behavior is measured by average vehicle speed ($AVGSPEED$) and the standard deviation of vehicle speeds ($STDSPEED$). Higher average speeds and greater variance in speeds should lead to more fatalities. The most important characteristics of a state's drivers are the percentage of young male drivers ($YMALES$) and the percentage of drunk drivers. The percentage of drunk drivers is measured indirectly with an alcoholic-beverage-consumption variable ($ALCOHOL$). Vehicle characteristics are captured by variables measuring average vehicle weight ($AVGWT$) and the percentage of new vehicle registrations ($PCTNEW$). Heavier cars are presumably safer than lighter cars. Newer cars incorporate the latest safety technologies, and older cars may have safety-related defects because of inadequate maintenance. However, to improve fuel efficiency, the average weight of new cars has been declining [Crandall and Graham, 1989]. Thus, the effect of vehicle age on fatalities must be determined empirically.

From standard economic theory, demand for a commodity depends upon prices (P), income (I), and tastes and preferences (X).[5]

---

[4] Wilkinson (1987) also included drunk driving deterrence policies in the fatalities production function. In this paper, the effects of these policies are assumed to enter through the alcohol-consumption variable.

[5] We ignore prices of substitutes and complements. There are very few good substitutes for gasoline. Most complementary goods (tires, cars) are purchased infrequently.

Table 1. Variable descriptions and sources.

Variable	Source	Description
Fatalities	1	Annual fatalities per 1,000 persons over age 15
Gas price	2	Real price of gasoline excluding state gasoline taxes
Gas tax	4	Real state per gallon tax on gas
Real income	3	Real per capita income
Average speed	4	Average vehicle speed weighted by vehicle-miles traveled
Stand. dev. speed	4	Average standard deviation of vehicle speed weighted by vehicle-miles traveled
Pct. young males	4	Percentage of licensed drivers who are males under age 24
Alcohol consump.	5,6	Annual apparent consumption of ethanol in gallons per person over age 15
Pct. new car reg.	7	Number of new car registrations as percentage of all car registrations
Avg. car weight	8	National average car weight in pounds

Sources:
[1] U.S. Department of Transportation, *Fatal Accident Reporting System*.
[2] U.S. Department of Energy, Office of Scientific and Technical Information, *A Facsimile Report: State Energy Price System*, Oak Ridge, TN, November 1982.
[3] U.S. Department of Commerce, *U.S. Statistical Abstract*.
[4] U.S. Department of Transportation, *Highway Statistics*.
[5] Distilled Spirits Council, *Annual Statistical Abstract*.
[6] U.S. Brewers Association, *Brewers Almanac*.
[7] *Ward's Automotive Yearbook*, 1981.
[8] U.S. Department of Commerce, *U.S. Motor Vehicle and Equipment Industry Since 1958*, May 1985.

$$Q = q(P, I, X) \tag{2}$$

The quantity of gasoline demanded will fall as the price of gasoline rises. To determine the effect of changing gas taxes, retail gas prices are separated into an untaxed price per gallon (*PRICE*) and the per gallon tax (*GASTAX*). If gasoline is a normal good, more gasoline will be consumed at higher incomes. Differences in tastes and preferences across states are captured using a random effects error structure in the estimation process.

The effects of a change in gasoline taxes are estimated using a reduced form equation. In the reduced form equation, fatalities are a function of the price of gas, the gas tax, income, the mean and standard deviation of vehicle speeds, the percentage of young male drivers, alcohol consumption, the percentage of new cars, and average vehicle weight (see equation [3]). Table 1 presents variable names and descriptions.

$$
\begin{aligned}
F_{i,j} = {} & \beta_0 + \beta_1 * PRICE_{i,j} + \beta_2 * GASTAX_{i,j} + \beta_3 * INCOME_{i,j} \\
& + \beta_4 * AVGSPEED_{i,j} + \beta_5 * STDSPEED_{i,j} + \beta_6 * YMALES_{i,j} \\
& + \beta_7 * ALCOHOL_{i,j} + \beta_8 * PCTNEW_{i,j} \\
& + \beta_9 * AVGWT_j + \mu_j + \varepsilon_{i,j}
\end{aligned}
\tag{3}
$$

where i = state index and j = time index.

Table 2. Regression results.

Variables	Coefficient (Std. error)	Coefficient (Std. error)
Intercept	−3.949**	−5.454**
	(1.862)	(1.088)
Price	−.014	.020
	(.054)	(.039)
Gas tax	−.177**	−.204**
	(.082)	(.078)
Income	.109	.141
	(.152)	(.144)
Average speed	.504*	.526**
	(.268)	(.267)
Std. dev. speed	.284**	.244*
	(.143)	(.136)
Pct. young males	8.640**	8.748**
	(1.375)	(1.359)
Alcohol	.031	.026
	(.105)	(.103)
Pct. new cars	.077	.076
	(.063)	(.063)
Average weight	−.159	
	(.168)	
R-squares	.351	.356

** Significant at 5 percent or better in a 2-tailed test.
 * Significant at 10 percent or better in a 2-tailed test.

Equation (3) is similar to most of the traffic fatality equations reviewed in Zlatoper [1989] except it includes gas-price and tax variables instead of miles-traveled or gas-consumption variables.[6] Equation (3) is estimated using data from all 50 states and the District of Columbia for the years 1976 to 1980. There are 255 observations. All variables are entered as logarithms. The random effects error structure is used to capture differences across states.[7]

Results

Regression results are presented in Table 2. Two specifications were estimated, the second of which does not include the average-vehicle-weight variable.[8]

As expected, higher gasoline taxes lead to lower fatalities. Our findings

[6] The effects of gasoline consumption are measured indirectly through the demand equation variables. Because gasoline prices directly affect gas consumption and miles traveled, a miles-traveled variable is not included.

[7] A fixed effects error structure was also considered. However, both a Hausman test and a Lagrange multiplier test supported the use of the random effects specification.

[8] The vehicle-weight variable was not included because of possible interactions with the new-car-percentage variable. The vehicle-weight variable was dropped (instead of the new-car variable) because it does not vary by state.

Table 3. Estimates of fatality reductions.

	Estimates of lives saved annually from a 10 percent increase in gas taxes	
	Specification 1	Specification 2
Lower limit	80	255
Mean estimate	885	1020
Upper limit	1690	1785

Note: Table values based on confidence intervals and mean estimates of gas-tax coefficients from Table 2 and a base of 50,000 fatalities per year. An alternative interpretation of the results is that the table values represent lives saved from a 10 percent change in retail prices. See note 9 in the text.

indicate that a 10 percent increase in the gasoline tax reduces fatalities by 1.8 to 2.0 percent. The price of gasoline, net of state taxes, does not affect the fatality rate. This is not completely unexpected, because differences in tax levels account for much of the variation in total retail gas prices across states.[9]

Variation in the percentage of young male drivers had the largest impact on fatalities. A state where the proportion of young male drivers is 1 percentage point above its neighboring state can expect to have a fatality rate that is almost 9 percent higher. Driving behavior variables also had significant effects. Both higher speeds and speed variances were associated with higher fatality rates. Income levels, alcohol consumption, vehicle weight, and vehicle age were not significantly related to fatalities in these regressions.

Table 3 provides estimates of the likely decrease in the annual number of fatalities that would result from a 10 percent increase in gasoline taxes. The table uses confidence intervals for the gas-tax coefficients from Table 2 and assumes an annual base of 50,000 fatalities. Table 3 indicates that the decline in fatalities would be between 80 and 1785. The mean estimates indicate reductions of from 885 to 1020 fatalities.

Conclusions

Traffic fatalities are a leading cause of accidental deaths in the United States. Externalities associated with driving may cause the number of fatalities to exceed the socially optimal level. This paper demonstrates that a higher tax on gasoline is an additional tool policy makers can use to reduce fatalities. A 10 percent increase in gasoline taxes was shown to lower fatalities by 1.8 to 2.0 percent. These estimates imply a reduction of between 885 to 1020 fatalities a year.

The higher gas tax reduces fatalities because people are induced to drive fewer miles or to drive more slowly. However, over a long period, people may also be induced to switch to smaller, more fuel-efficient, but less crashworthy cars. While this effect does not appear to be important in this study, these

[9] A 10 percent change in gas taxes would change retail prices only a few cents. The gas tax coefficient indicates that this would have a large impact on fatalities. An alternative interpretation of the tax and price coefficients is that a 10 percent change in total retail prices would reduce fatalities by 1.8 to 2.0 percent.

long-run effects would imply that the actual decline in fatalities may be smaller than the results found here.

The results shown here do not automatically support an increase in gasoline taxes. Higher taxes impose greater costs on all drivers—costs that could exceed the benefits of lower fatalities. However, the results do show that if policy makers are concerned about reducing automotive fatalities, higher gasoline taxes may be a useful tool for achieving that goal.

We would like to thank Harold Waldon for excellent programming and Pamela Davis for editing. Mark French offered a number of helpful comments; however, we claim responsibility for any remaining errors. The views expressed here do not necessarily represent those of the Federal Reserve System. Part of Leigh's effort was financed by grant number R01 OH02586 from the National Institute of Occupational Safety and Health. The listing of authors is alphabetical; our contributions to the paper were equal.

J. PAUL LEIGH is with the Department of Economics at San Jose State University and the Department of Medicine at the Stanford University Medical Center.

JAMES T. WILKINSON is an Economist with the Federal Reserve Bank of Kansas City.

REFERENCES

Allman, W. F. (1985), "Staying Alive in the 20th Century," *Science 85* 8 (5), pp. 30–41.

Baker, Susan P., Brian O'Neill, and Ronald S. Karpf (1984), *The Injury Fact Book* (Lexington, MA: Lexington Books).

Cook, P. J. and George Tauchen (1984), "The Effect of Minimum Drinking Age Legislation on Youthful Auto Fatalities, 1970–1977," *Journal of Legal Studies* 13, pp. 169–190.

Crandall, R. W. and J. D. Graham (1989), "The Effects of Fuel Economy Standards on Automobile Safety," *Journal of Law and Economics* 32 (1), pp. 97–118.

Crandall, R. W., H. E. Gruenspecht, T. E. Keeler, and L. B. Lave (1986), *Regulating the Automobile* (Washington, DC: The Brookings Institution).

De Joy, David M. (1989), "The Optimism Bias and Traffic Accident Risk Perception," *Accident Analysis and Prevention* 21 (4), pp. 333–340.

Fischhoff, B., L. Furby, and R. Gregory (1987), "Evaluating Voluntary Risks of Injury," *Accident Analysis and Prevention* 19 (1), pp. 67–82.

Foege, Walter and the Committee on Trauma Research (1985), *Injury in America* (Washington, DC: National Academy Press).

French, Mark (1988), "Efficiency and Equity of a Gasoline Tax Increase," Finance and Economics Discussion Series, No. 33, Federal Reserve Board, Washington, DC.

Garen, John E. (1988), "Compensating Wage Differentials and the Endogeneity of Job Riskiness," *Review of Economics and Statistics* 70 (1), pp. 9–16.

Groeger, J. A. and I. D. Brown (1989), "Assessing One's Own Risk and Others' Driving Ability: Influences of Sex, Age and Experience," *Accident Analysis and Prevention* 21 (2), pp. 195–168.

Lave, Charles A. (1987), "Injury as an Externality," *Accident Analysis and Prevention* 19 (1), pp. 29–37.

Leigh, J. P. and A. L. Frank (1987), "Tax Gasoline to Save Lives," *New England Journal of Medicine* 316 (1), pp. 54.

Moore, M. J. and W. K. Viscusi (1988), "Doubling the Estimated Values of Life," *Journal of Policy Analysis and Management* 7 (3), pp. 476–490.

Rubin, P. H. and C. W. Paul (1979), "An Evolutionary Model of Tastes for Risk," *Economic Inquiry* 17 (4), pp. 585–596.

Saffer, Henry and Michael Grossman (1987), "Beer Taxes, the Legal Drinking Age, and Youth Motor Vehicle Fatalities," *Economic Inquiry* 25 (3), pp. 403–418.

Slovic, Paul, Barry Fischhoff, and S. Lichenstein (1980), "Facts and Fears: Understanding Perceived Risk," in R. Schwing and W. A. Albers, Jr. (eds.), *Societal Risk Assessment: How Safe is Safe Enough?* (New York: Plenum).

White, Michelle J. (1988), "An Empirical Test of the Efficiency of Liability Rules in Accident Law." Unpublished manuscript, University of Michigan.

Wilkinson, James T. (1987), "Reducing Drunken Driving: Which Policies Are Most Effective?" *Southern Economic Journal* 54 (2), pp. 322–334.

Yucel, Mine K. and Carol Dahl (1990), "Reducing U.S. Oil-Import Dependence: A Tariff, Subsidy, or Gasoline Tax?" *Economic Review* (May) (Federal Reserve Bank of Dallas), pp. 17–25.

Zlatoper, T. J. (1989), "Models Explaining Motor Vehicle Death Rates in the United States," *Accident Analysis and Prevention* 21 (2), pp. 125–154.

Section VII

Investment Decisions and Benefit–Cost Analysis

Long–term investment decisions are a major determinant of firm profitability. The articles in this section examine issues related to long–term investment decisions, or what are often referred to as capital budgeting decisions. In addition, articles concerned with benefit–cost analysis, the public sector analog of private sector investment analysis, are included in this section. The first article is "The Capital Budgeting Process: Theory and Practice," by Tarun K. Mukherjee and Glenn V. Henderson. The authors review numerous surveys of practitioners conducted by analysts of capital budgeting. The discussion is organized around the four stages of capital budgeting: investment opportunity identification, development of the specific project proposal, project selection, and the assessment of selected projects. The authors evaluate and attempt to explain some of the divergences between the capital budgeting procedures expounded by academics in textbooks and those procedures used by practitioners.

Stephen W. Pruitt and Lawrence J. Gitman present their survey results in "Capital Budgeting Forecast Biases: Evidence from the *Fortune 500*." The authors conducted a survey of the highest ranking financial officers from the *Fortune 500* firms to elicit responses that would reveal the extent of biases in project revenue and project cost estimates. They report that nearly 80 percent of respondents believe that revenue forecasts are overstated. Belief that cost estimates are understated is reported by 43 percent of the respondents.

In "Stock Market Reaction to Strategic Investment Decisions," J. Randall Woolridge and Charles C. Snow examine the way that the stock market prices of corporations react to announcements of corporate investment decisions. The authors use the event study methodology popular in financial economics to examine abnormal stock price returns of corporations around the time of announcements of joint ventures, R&D projects, capital expenditures, and product/market diversification. Positive average abnormal returns are associated with all four announcement types, with R&D projects and joint venture announcements having the largest average response.

The returns to research and development (R&D) expenditures on 100 new pharmaceutical products is the subject of "A New Look at the Returns and Risks to Pharmaceutical R&D," by Henry Grabowski and John Vernon. They report that the average drug has a discounted payback period of 23 years. This corresponds to an annual return of approximately 9 percent, which is about the same as the authors' estimate of the cost of capital for the pharmaceutical industry.

A benefit–cost analysis case study is presented in W. Steven Barnett's article "Benefit–Cost Analysis of the Perry Preschool Program and Its Policy Implications." The Perry Preschool Project was conducted in Ypsilanti, Michigan. Children with low socioeconomic status and low IQ scores were assigned to either the program or the control group. Upon estimation of the cost of the program, and estimation of benefits attributable to the program from reduced delinquency, earnings increases, and reduced welfare costs, Barnett concludes that the program had a positive net present value. This implies that the Perry Preschool Program was an appropriate government investment.

Whether the city of Fort Wayne, Indiana would benefit from a minor league baseball franchise is addressed by Mark S. Rosentraub and David Swindell in " 'Just Say No?' The Economic and Political Realities of a Small City's Investment in Minor League Baseball." The authors outline the calculations necessary to estimate the economic impact of new spending by fans and visiting teams, capital infrastructure, new jobs, tax revenue, and psychological gains to the city. Based on their analysis, the authors conclude that the city of Fort Wayne made the correct decision in not subsidizing a baseball franchise.

John P. Blair's article, "Benefits From a Baseball Franchise: An Alternative Methodology," is a response to the analysis in the Rosentraub and Swindell article. He believes that Rosentraub and Swindell incorrectly use a fiscal impact study instead of a benefit–cost study. Blair performs a benefit–cost analysis and concludes that the city of Fort Wayne should have subsidized the stadium to attract the baseball franchise.

In "Hammers and Their Use: Some Issues Involved in the Selection of Appropriate Tools for Public Policy Analysis," David Swindell and Mark S. Rosentraub reply to John Blair. They argue that Blair's benefit–cost analysis does not consider the opportunity cost of alternative public investments by the city, and does not consider the distribution of the benefits. Because of these limitations they conclude that their original fiscal impact study is the more appropriate tool to use to assess the value of the baseball franchise to the city.

Article 26

The Capital Budgeting Process: Theory and Practice

TARUN K. MUKHERJEE

Department of Economics and Finance
University of New Orleans
New Orleans, Louisiana 70148

GLENN V. HENDERSON

Department of Finance, Insurance, Real Estate,
and Law
University of Cincinnati
Cincinnati, Ohio 45221

Survey evidence in a four-stage framework for the capital budgeting process reveals that many capital budgeting practices differ from what the relevant theory prescribes. Much of the gap, however, can be explained by deficiencies in the theory itself, suggesting new directions for ongoing capital budgeting research.

It is generally assumed that management's primary goal is to maximize the wealth of the firm's shareholders. Capital budgeting theory prescribes decision rules in keeping with this objective. To what extent are these rules followed in practice? To answer this question we first reviewed the bulk of existing surveys in this area in a four-stage framework of the capital budgeting process.

Review of Surveys

Pinches [1982] applied the Mintzberg, Raisinghini, and Theoret [1976] four-stage model to capital budgeting. These stages are

(1) Identification of an investment opportunity,

(2) Development of an initial idea into a specific proposal,

(3) Selection of a project, and

(4) Control, including postaudit, to assess forecast accuracy.

Each stage has aspects of interest. In the case of identification, for example, it would be helpful to know where proposals come from, the process by which they are forwarded for consideration, and whether this process is continual or periodic.

We need to know if proposals are pre-screened during development, at what organization level, and the nature of the screening process. Are cash-flow (rather than profit) estimates used as theory mandates? How are these estimates derived, and who is responsible for project budgets?

In the selection stage, topics of interest include
— Preselection classification of projects and any impact of classification on selection,
— Personnel (or departments) with selection authority,

— Techniques of analysis,
— Methods of risk assessment,
— The extent of capital rationing, its origin, and its impact on project analysis,
— The use of cost of capital measures, and
— The personnel with authority to approve capital investments.

Postadoption procedures also are important. Questions of interest include the extent to which accepted projects are monitored after adoption, how the post-

The Capital Budgeting Process

Year Surveyed	Identification			Development				Selection									Control				Authors, (Publications)
	Source	Process	Timing	Screening Level	Screening Process	Budget Responsibility	Cash-Flow Estimation	Project Classification	Responsible Personnel	Techniques Used	Risk Assessment	Capital Rationing	Origin of Rationing	Analysis of Rationing	Cost of Capital	Approved Authority	Postaudit	Audit Process	Performance Measures	Performance Incentives	
1959	X	X	X	X	X	X	X	X		X						X		X	X		X	Istvan 1961
1960									X									X	X			Miller 1960
1959, 1964									X	X												Klammer 1972
1964								X								X						Christy 1966
1969	X					X			X	X												Mao 1970
1969							X		X	X						X	X	X			X	Williams 1970
1971								X		X	X	X	X	X								Fremgen 1975
NR	X					X		X	X	X						X						Petty, Scott & Bird 1975
1976									X	X	X	X	X									Gitman & Forrester 1977
NR						X				X	X					X						Schall, Sundem & Geijsbeck 1978
1975, 1979										X	X											Kim & Farragher 1981
1979										X	X					X						Oblak & Helm 1980
1980								X													X	Rosenblatt 1980
1980								X	X	X	X	X	X	X	X	X						Gitman & Mercurio 1982
1965, 1970, 1975, 1980								X	X	X	X					X	X					Klammer & Walker 1984

NR = Not Reported

Table 1: Chronological listing of capital budgeting surveys classified by stages.

audit process works, what measures of performance are used, and whether success is rewarded or failure is punished.

In Table 1, we list some often cited capital budgeting surveys, indicating which elements of the four-stage process they consider. The emphasis of past surveys has been on the selection stage — whether, for example, firms calculate net

---

It is generally assumed that management's primary goal is to maximize the wealth of the firm's shareholders.

---

present values or use the cost of capital, and how they adjust for risk. Our discussion of the other three stages of capital budgeting is, consequently, less complete.

We recognize the difficulties in drawing inferences from a number of surveys done over a 30-year period. Problems include the possible presence of unrecognized biases of respondents or interviewers, nonresponse bias, and sampling bias. These problems aside, examining the surveys as a whole provides a perspective that no one survey alone can. Further, the cumulative evidence allows consideration of all four stages of capital budgeting in a way that no single survey does.

Identification

Istvan [1961] found that only one of the 48 firms he interviewed made any special effort to stimulate capital investment ideas. Klammer's [1972] findings are at odds with Istvan's; 82 percent of Klammer's firms had investment search procedures in 1959, and by 1970, this had

grown to 94 percent.

Surveys indicate that ideas for new projects come from lower levels in the managerial organization. This finding is consistent over time. Sixty percent of Istvan's 1961 proposals were originated by operating personnel, not top management. Mao's [1970] interviews indicated that financial executives were not project originators; packaged plans were forwarded from departments to financial managers for evaluation. Petty, Scott, and Bird [1975] reported that "[N]ew proposals generally flow from the lower managerial level" (p. 170).

Istvan [1961] reported three timing patterns for proposal submission. Fourteen percent of his respondents used periodic submissions. Thirty-seven percent allowed continuous submission for projects previously included in an overall capital budget. Forty-nine percent allowed submission of proposals at any time.

No evidence was provided as to strategic planning of this aspect of firm growth. None of the surveys addressed the issue of rewards for valuable ideas.

Development

Existing evidence indicates that ideas are screened before full-blown proposals are developed. Istvan [1961] identified four approaches to screening: (1) originator to decision maker (seven percent), (2) review by a nonspecialist before forwarding to decision maker (55 percent), (3) review by a specialist or team (27 percent), and (4) a combination of 2 and 3 (11 percent). Petty, Scott, and Bird [1975] found "some dominance of the division level and plant level over the central office level in the screening process" (p. 162).

Prescreening may explain high reported acceptance rates (for example, see Gitman and Forrester [1977], and Oblak and Helm [1980]).

The nature of the prescreening process has not been thoroughly investigated. However, evidence suggests that some screening takes place during proposal budget development. Williams [1970] identified departments responsible for the budget: 39 percent of the budgets were prepared by engineering, 33 percent by accounting, 17 percent by finance or budget committees, while 11 percent were considered divisional responsibilities. It may be inferred from this finding that engineers and accountants are more involved in prescreening than personnel in finance are.

An important analytical issue is the estimation of cost-benefit data. Schall, Sundem, and Geijsbeck [1978] report that the majority of firms (62 percent) use cash flow as the relevant data, with the most commonly used definition of cash flow being net income plus depreciation. The details of cash-flow computation are not known, but Istvan's [1961] results suggest that firms were omitting some important components from these estimates in 1959. Of the 48 firms interviewed, 16 did not consider incremental overhead, and 19 did not consider incremental selling and administrative costs; more than half did not consider permanent increases in working capital.

Mao [1970] reports that many financial executives have misgivings about cash-flow estimates. Experience with a project's sponsor, the project initiator's previous track record, and interdepartmental

politics all affect the credibility of cash-flow predictions. Carter [1971] refers to such subjective assessments as *threshold values.*

Selection

Selection is the aspect of capital budgeting that has received the most attention; indeed, every capital budgeting survey has inquired about this phase.

Firms classify projects by type and allow some classifications to be exempt from financial justification. Almost all (97 percent) of Fremgen's [1975] respondents approved investments that were not quantifiably profitable; the most frequent justifications were public and employee

---

Ideas for new projects come from lower levels in the managerial organization.

---

safety. Rosenblatt [1980] found that firms typically classified projects and used acceptance and selection criteria that depended upon the classification. Klammer and Walker [1984] reported that required documentation can vary with the classification; for instance, standard forms are waived for urgent projects.

Just who is making capital budgeting decisions is unclear. Weaker proposals apparently are eliminated in prescreening during development. Generally, finance is not responsible for the budget development during screening [Williams 1970; and Mao 1970]. Finance, however, appears to control selection [Gitman and Forrester 1977, p. 68].

The most frequently investigated aspects of capital budgeting are the techniques used, risk assessment, capital rationing, and the use of cost of capital measures. The evidence is abundant and, by and large, shows considerable consensus.

Techniques Used

Firms have adopted sophisticated (discounted cash flow, DCF) techniques [Klammer 1972; Petty, Scott, and Bird 1975; Gitman and Forrester 1977; Schall, Sundem, and Geijsbeck 1978; Oblak and Helm 1980; Kim and Farragher 1981; Klammer and Walker 1984], and DCF analysis is becoming a standard practice. The internal rate of return is the favored DCF technique, with net present value being a distant second choice [Fremgen 1975; and Klammer and Walker 1984]. Most firms use non-DCF techniques as a secondary form of analysis. The most frequently used are payback period and accounting rate of return.

Risk Analysis

Most firms explicitly consider risk in analysis of capital investments [Gitman and Forrester 1977; Petty, Scott, and Bird 1985; Klammer and Walter 1984]. Again the proportion of firms using such analysis has increased over time. The more popular risk-adjustment techniques were applying risk-adjusted discount rates (or required rates of return), and adjusting the required payback period. Sensitivity analysis, omitted as a choice in earlier surveys, has gained in popularity [Petry 1975; Kim and Farragher 1981; Gitman and Mercurio 1982; Klammer and Walker 1984], and may now be the most widely used risk-analysis technique.

Capital Rationing

It appears that capital rationing is com-monplace. Gitman and Forrester [1977] found the cause is "a limit placed on borrowing by internal management" (p. 69). The same reason was reported by Fremgen [1975], who noted further that "the capital limitation was not a single, fixed dollar amount but was a somewhat inexact amount within a recognized range" (p. 23).

Exactly how firms deal with rationing is unclear. The theoretical prescription for the problem, linear programming (LP), is used infrequently [Fremgen 1975; Gitman and Forrester 1977; Klammer and Walker 1984] (between four and 13 percent). Gitman and Mercurio [1982, p. 27] report markedly higher use of LP, but their survey does not make it clear how their respondents are using this technique. Such applications could be in areas other than capital rationing such as production scheduling and inventory management.

Hurdle Rate

Surveys suggest that the use of the weighted average cost of capital (WACC) as a hurdle rate has increased dramatically over the years, especially since the late 1970s. Christy [1966], Williams [1970], and Petty, Scott, and Bird [1975] found less than 30 percent of the firms using the WACC. Later studies [Schall, Sundem, and Geijsbeck 1978; Oblak and Helm 1980; and Gitman and Mercurio 1982] show a substantial increase in the use of WACC (up to 83 percent).

Although the use of cost of capital has increased, there is considerable variation on how it is determined and when it is applied. Gitman and Mercurio [1982] provide the most detailed analysis of this aspect of capital budgeting. They note that, although a vast majority of firms follow procedures recommended in textbooks for computing as well as applying cost of capital, a significant minority do not. Their findings include (1) nearly 17 percent of respondents employed the cost of specific source of funds as a cutoff rate (almost 90 percent of these firms were in Fortune's second 500); (2) in determining costs of debt and preferred stock, 66 percent used current costs of similar obligations, while the remaining 34 percent used historical contractual cost; (3) only about 16 percent differentiated between

---

Firms classify projects by type and allow some classifications to be exempt from financial justification.

---

the cost of retained earnings and that of new common stock; (4) although the majority of respondents measured the cost of equity as the return required by investors, over 17 percent used either dividend yield or earnings to price ratio; (5) nearly all firms were using the cost of capital for making new project decisions, but many of these firms were also using the same discount rate in lease-purchase and bond refunding decisions.

Project Approval

Gitman and Mercurio [1982] provided the most recent and most specific information on project approval. Sixty-five percent of their firms required formal committee approval. For 70 percent, the approval of the responsible manager was necessary, and 83 percent required approval depending on project cost.

It appears, however, that for all intents and purposes, all submitted proposals are already approved. Two-thirds of Gitman and Forrester's [1977] respondents accepted over 75 percent of formally analyzed projects; and over a third accepted more than 90 percent. Oblak and Helm [1980] reported similar results for multinationals. Luck, Morgan, Farmer, and Stringer [1971] noted in their survey that even if submitted projects were turned down, they were recycled and eventually accepted. Thus, even though final approval is formal and may require committee or manager approval, disapproval can be informal (or unintentional) and can occur long before selection.

Control

Evidence indicates that a vast majority of firms have adopted postaudits. According to Miller [1960], 78 percent of firms had postaudits. Williams [1970] found 81 percent of firms using postaudits. Klammer and Walker's [1984] results documented an increasing use of such audits — 67 percent in 1970, 75 percent in 1975, and 90 percent in 1980.

Istvan [1961] is detailed on this aspect of capital budgeting. Half of the 48 firms he interviewed had follow-up procedures. The type of projects subject to postaudits varied. Most firms concentrated on larger projects, some audited all implemented projects, some checked expansions, and others audited only replacements. Firms that rejected postaudits cited the expense and the futility of reviewing commitments already made. Firms that did conduct postaudits said that the primary reason was to establish error patterns as a measure for judging future proposals from the same originators. Istvan also reported that, in the majority of the cases, the personnel performing audits were either project originators or members of the screening committee that approved the project.

Evidence suggests that project success is measured in terms of short-run accounting profitability measures. Miller [1960] reported the use of return on assets (or return on investment, ROI) as a criterion for judging project success. Williams [1970] reported that, of the firms which used postaudits, the majority employed ROI to evaluate performance. Rosenblatt's evidence [1980] on incentives reinforces these results. Of 21 firms interviewed, 15 had bonus systems. For those 15, the most frequently mentioned success criteria were accounting measures: return on assets, concurrence between expected and actual results, and profit and loss.

The Pertinent Theory

To what extent do these practices conform to capital budgeting theory? A quick overview of the pertinent theory might give us a better perspective.

According to theory, the firm's goal should be to maximize the wealth of its shareholders. Theory has formulated selection rules consistent with this goal. Wealth maximization, however, has implications for other stages as well. In the identification stage, theory implicitly assumes that all projects are evaluated based on economic merit. In the development stage, an implication is that all feasible ideas are developed into full-blown proposals, and none is accepted (or rejected) for noneconomic reasons. Theory

considers incremental after-tax cash flow as the correct definition of benefits for capital budgeting analysis. Proper estimation of cash flow requires quantifying of all project ramifications including impact on sales of other company products, working capital requirements, and reactions from competitors.

In selection, theory suggests the use of discounted cash flow (DCF) techniques and, more specifically, use of net present value (NPV) analysis. The NPV approach assumes that a firm correctly estimates incremental cash flow from each of the available projects, discounts cash flow of each project using a discount rate that corresponds to the risk associated with each project, and accepts all projects with positive NPV.

Another DCF technique is internal rate of return (IRR). The IRR is that discount rate which equates the NPV of a project to zero. Although NPV and IRR are both effective, NPV is considered superior because (1) it conforms to the value-additivity principle, (2) its assumed reinvestment rate is consistent with valuation theory and uniform across projects, and (3) it avoids multiple answers for a single project which sometimes result from using IRR. Most textbooks on managerial finance elaborate on these points (for example, Brigham [1985]).

Theoretically, capital rationing (rejection of positive NPV projects that are not displaced by directly competing, mutually exclusive alternatives) should not exist in efficient capital markets. In such a market, funds should be available for any project that promises returns in excess of an appropriate risk-adjusted, required-return rate. (If a firm faces a capital shortage, it encounters a rising cost of capital — not capital rationing.) Theory, therefore, requires a publicly held firm to continue investing as long as the expected rate of return from a project is higher than its required rate. Holding back on otherwise positive NPV projects runs counter to the wealth-maximizing objective.

Theory implies that methods used to review investment decisions (in the control phase) should be consistent with those used for selection. If DCF methods are theoretically correct for selection, methods which consider the time value of money should be used to monitor implemented projects and to evaluate managerial performance.

Gaps Between Theory and Practice

Contrasting capital budgeting practices with theory reveals a number of differences. This is most apparent in selection, which has been a primary focus of financial theory and is the most closely examined aspect of business practice. Differences exist but are less closely examined at the other stages as well. Thus, in contrast to theoretical assumptions, many projects are rejected during the preselection stages apparently for noneconomic considerations (for example, personalities, and interdepartmental politics). Also, since finance's role at this stage is minor, it is possible, given the problems firms have with incremental costing, that some projects are mistakenly rejected (accepted) because of misallocated costs. Evidence also suggests that firms may not always use cash flows and when they do, they overlook some components in

developing those flows [Istvan 1961].

In selection, where the evidence is most complete, contradictions are most evident. These include the following:

(1) The use of discounted cash flow techniques is now the rule rather than the exception, but it is internal rate of return, not the theoretically preferable net present value technique, that business has chosen as its method.

(2) Despite many years of disparagement, payback period is still widely used.

(3) Capital rationing is commonplace. Such a condition is at odds with the financial market equilibrium theories. The theoretical prescription for optimization under capital constraints, linear programming, is infrequently used.

(4) Firms use the cost of capital. However, a significant minority do not use it exactly as it is suggested by theory.

(5) Risk analysis models are yet to be accepted universally. Many firms simply change the required payback period to adjust for risk.

The majority of firms appear to conduct postaudits. However, ROI-type measures are the most frequently reported basis of performance measurement. Such procedures are inconsistent with the use of DCF techniques for selection. They may encourage managers to concentrate on short-run profitability at the expense of the long-term goals of the firm and are likely, therefore, to be dysfunctional [Kaplan 1984].

Deficiences of the Relevant Theory

Why do differences between theory and practice persist? Our review of the related literature leads us to believe that much of the gap can be attributed to deficiencies in the theory itself.

It would be impossible to review all the articles relating the shortcomings of capital budgeting theory. Covering only a few articles raises serious questions about the theoretical foundations of normative capital budgeting models, their applicability to the corporate environment, and their effectiveness when they are used. The limitations of the theoretical models include

— An inability to capture the role of organizational structure and behavior in corporate decision making,
— A failure to incorporate management behavior toward risk,
— Difficulties in application due especially to unrealistic assumptions about data availability, and
— Inability to incorporate strategic considerations in decisions made by the firm.

These limitations help explain many of the differences between theory and practice noted in the previous section.

Existing theory assumes that capital budgeting decisions are based solely on economic analysis. However, in an organizational environment, other factors (such as politics, intuition, business structure, and lack of effective communication) play important roles. For example, the popularity of the payback period method may partly be attributed to its being an easily understood common denominator in a complex setup in which people from all parts of the firm participate.

Organizational behavior may partly explain why the IRR method is more popular to practitioners than the NPV. Bower

and Lessard [1973] support such a summary measure as IRR on the ground that "financial decisions are made by executives who work best with measures that can be simply interpreted on the basis of intuition and experience" (p. 323). Similarly, divisionalized structure of a large business firm may explain why capital rationing is widely practiced. Brealey and Myers [1984] argue that in most cases a budget limit exists not necessarily because the firm cannot raise new funds,

---

Just who is making capital budgeting decisions is unclear.

---

but rather as a means of discouraging biased cash-flow forecasts. They comment, "Some ambitious divisional managers habitually overstate their investment opportunities. Rather than trying to determine which projects really are worthwhile, headquarters may find it simpler to impose an upper limit on divisional expenditures and thereby force the division to set their own priorities" (p. 106).

Capital budgeting theory assumes that the management is unselfish; when there is a conflict between the shareholders' interest and management's, shareholders' interests take precedence. However, the personal stake of a manager may be far more important than assumed by theory. Such a concern about management's interests may explain management's definition of risk. Theoretical models assume symmetric risk preferences. But negative variations may be more important to managers; a project with a large downside risk is unlikely to be accepted, regardless of a large expected NPV.

According to Crum, Laughhunn, and Payne [1981], and Blatt [1979], a utility function that correctly depicts the management attitude toward risk may very well imply a two-step risk evaluation process. The first step eliminates projects with a chance of ruinous losses. In the second step, the remaining projects are evaluated on the basis of their risk/return trade-off. Blatt argues that the first step may be achieved by setting up a maximum payback period. Such an explanation provides a rationale for the continued popularity of payback as a selection criterion. Such a risk preference may also explain the popularity of changing the payback period as a risk-adjustment tool.

The capital budgeting models require accurate data. Often such data are expensive, and the cost of obtaining additional information may not be justified by the benefits accrued. Hoskins and Mumey [1979] argue: "The superiority of net present value lies in its use of additional information but this superiority may or may not be worth its hire" (p. 64). The payback method on the other hand, as Weingartner [1969] puts it, "reduces the information search by focusing on that time at which the firm expects to "be made whole again" (p. B-606).

The requirement of a large amount of data as well as high data-processing efficiency may also be responsible for a relatively low use of risk analysis models (see observations made by McInnes and Carleton [1982] regarding the probability distribution approach). Infrequent use of linear programming models also can be attributed to similar problems.

Finally, the DCF techniques fail to consider the strategic environment in which corporate decisions are made. Considering the capital budgeting process as part of overall company operations requires that the models consider a firm's strategic needs to grow and innovate. In keeping with these needs, the firm makes many investment decisions today to create investment opportunities for tomorrow. Such decisions include investments in R&D or in a negative NPV project now to establish a foothold in a market with strong growth potential in the future. Myers [1984] points out limitations of the DCF approach for making strategic decisions which involve "time series links between projects." He suggests applying option pricing theory instead.

Summary and Implications

The survey evidence on capital budgeting practices relating to the four stages of capital budgeting — identification, development, selection, and control — indicates several inconsistencies between the pertinent theory and practice. Since the major concern of both the surveys and the theory has been the selection stage, such gaps are most evident at this stage. Deficiencies of the theory itself are, to a large extent, responsible for the continuing gaps.

Current capital budgeting models presume that managers work to maximize the value of the firm and perceive risk in some consistent quantifiable manner and that requisite data is available — uncontaminated by corporate personalities and politics. The models implicitly assume all projects are evaluated — that none are killed prematurely in prescreening and none are classified as exempt because of corporate procedures or executive privilege. They assume good projects are accepted with little regard for capital constraints and only limited consideration of project riskiness. Existing evidence makes each of these assumptions suspect.

It appears that future work in capital budgeting should consider organizational behavior theory. The capital budgeting process entails more than calculating the cost of capital and project net present values. To understand what businesses do in capital budgeting, we must better understand the dynamics of corporate interactions. Efforts in integrating finance models with decision models (for example, the models proposed by Emshoff [1978]) would be welcome. It is also important that capital budgeting models appreciate and incorporate management behavior toward risk. A fruitful course may result from the integration of financial and psychometrics models (as suggested by Slovic [1972]). Agency theory provides research opportunities in the area of capital budgeting. Some efforts have already been made (see Statman [1982] on agency theory and payback method, and Logue and Tapley [1985] on agency theory and performance monitoring). Incorporating option theory might also help with the firm's strategic decisions.

What role can future surveys play in bridging the gap? Past surveys overemphasized selection. Pinches [1982] appears justified in characterizing such an emphasis as myopic. Future surveys need to include all four stages of capital bud-

geting. Further, surveys in the future need to broaden the scope of their inquiries and explore why businesses behave the way they do. Capital budgeting models to date have been essentially economics models, utilizing simplifying assumptions to take advantage of the power of mathematics. The extent to which business employs the models testifies to their usefulness. Business has

---

The theoretical prescription for the problem, linear programming, is used infrequently.

---

learned from academia. Now it appears time for academia to learn from business. Proposed theory has been modified in practice. If we can learn why, it would serve to make future theories even more valuable, for business and academia alike.

Acknowledgments

The inventory of articles we reviewed in this paper has taken us a few years to build. Aggarwal's [1980] list of surveys acted as our starting point. Since the Aggarwal article, many new surveys have appeared in the literature. We incorporated as many surveys as we came across when we first started writing this article. We are certain that we have missed some good ones, but we had to stop at some point. However, we do not believe that our conclusions would have been significantly different even if we included all the available surveys. The Pinches paper [1982] provides an excellent list of capital-budgeting related survey and nonsurvey articles. These articles' references led us to more. We circulated earlier drafts of this paper among our colleagues and added a few more to our inventory based on their suggestions. We are particularly thankful to Professor George E. Pinches for the most valuable suggestions we received on a separate draft on the same topic.

References

Aggarwal, R. 1980, "Corporate use of sophisticated capital budgeting techniques: A strategic perspective and a critique of survey results," *Interfaces*, Vol. 10, No. 2 (April), pp. 31–34.

Blatt, J. M. 1979, "Investment evaluation under uncertainty," *Financial Management*, Vol. 8, No. 2 (Summer), pp. 66–76.

Bower, J. L. 1970, *Managing the Resource Allocation Process*, Richard D. Irwin, Homewood, Illinois.

Bower, R. S. and Lessard, D. R. 1973, "An operational approach to risk screening," *Journal of Finance*, Vol. 28, No. 2 (May), pp. 321–337.

Brealey, R. and Myers, S. 1984, *Principles of Corporate Finance*, McGraw-Hill, New York.

Brigham, E. F. 1975, "Hurdle rates for screening capital budgeting practices: A survey," *Financial Management*, Vol. 4, No. 3 (Autumn), pp. 17–26.

Brigham, E. F. 1985, *Financial Management: Theory and Practice*, Dryden Press, New York.

Carter, E. E. 1971, "The behavioral theory of the firm and top-level corporate decisions," *Administrative Science Quarterly*, Vol. 16, No. 4 (December), pp. 413–428.

Christy, G. A. 1966, *Capital Budgeting: Current Practices and Their Efficiency*, University of Oregon, Eugene.

Crum, R. A.; Laughhunn, D. J.; and Payne, J. W. 1981, "Risk-seeking behavior and its implications for financial models," *Financial Management*, Vol. 10, No. 4 (Winter), pp. 20–27.

Crum, R. A. and Derkinderen, F. G. J. 1981, *Epilogue*, in *Capital Budgeting Under Conditions of Uncertainty*, R. A. Crum and F. G. J. Derkinderen, eds., Martinus Nijhoff Publishing, Boston.

Emshoff, J. R. 1978, "Experience-generalized decision making: The next generation of management models," *Interfaces*, Vol. 8, No. 4 (August), pp. 40–48.

Fremgen, J. M. 1975, "Capital budgeting practices: A survey," *Management Accounting*, Vol. 54, No. 11 (May), pp. 19–25.

Gitman, L. J. and Forrester, J. R. 1977, "A survey of capital budgeting techniques used by major US firms," *Financial Management*, Vol. 6, No. 3 (Fall), pp. 66–71.

Gitman, L. J. and Mercurio, V. A. 1982, "Cost of capital techniques used by major US firms: Survey and analysis of Fortune's 1000," *Financial Management*, Vol. 11, No. 4 (Winter), pp. 21–29.

Gordon, L. A. and Pinches, G. E. 1982, *Effective Capital Budgeting: A Decision Support System Perspective*, Addison-Wesley, Reading, Massachusetts.

Haka, S. F.; Gordon, L. A.; and Pinches, G. E. 1985, "Sophisticated capital budgeting selection techniques and firm performance," *Accounting Review*, Vol. 60, No. 4, pp. 651–669.

Hastie, K. L. 1974, "One businessman's view of capital budgeting," *Financial Management*, Vol. 3, No. 4 (Winter), pp. 27–35.

Hoskins, C. G. and Mumey, G. A. 1979, "Payback: A maligned method of asset ranking," *Engineering Economist*, Vol. 25, No. 1 (Fall), pp. 53–65.

Istvan, D. F. 1961, *Capital Expenditure Decisions: How They Are Made in Large Corporations*, Bureau of Business Research, Indiana University, Bloomington.

Kaplan, R. S. 1984, "The evolution of management accounting," *Accounting Review*, Vol. 59, No. 3 (July), pp. 390–418.

Kim, S. H. and Farragher, E. J. 1981, "Current capital budgeting practices," *Management Accounting*, Vol. 62, No. 12 (June), pp. 26–30.

Klammer, T. 1972, "Empirical evidence of the adoption of sophisticated capital budgeting techniques," *Journal of Business*, Vol. 45, No. 3 (July), pp. 387–397.

Klammer, T. and Walker, M. C. 1984, "The continuing increase in the use of sophisticated capital budgeting techniques," *California Management Review*, Vol. 27, No. 1 (Fall), pp. 137–148.

Logue, D. E. and Tapley, T. C. 1985, "Performance monitoring and the timing of cash flows," *Financial Management*, Vol. 14, No. 3

(Autumn), pp. 34–39.

Luck, G. M.; Morgan, J. R.; Farmer, P. J.; and Stringer, J. 1971, "The management of capital investment," *Journal of Royal Statistical Society*, Vol. 134, Part 4, pp. 485–533.

McInnes, J. M. and Carleton, W. J. 1982, "Theory, models and implementations in financial management," *Management Science*, Vol. 28, No. 9 (September), pp. 957–978.

Mao, J. C. T. 1970, "Survey of capital budgeting: Theory and practice," *Journal of Finance*, Vol. 25, No. 2 (May), pp. 349–360.

Miller, J. H. 1960, "A glimpse at practice in calculating and using return on investment," *National Association of Accountants Bulletin*, Vol. 41 (June), pp. 65–76.

Mintzberg, H.; Raisinghini, D.; and Theoret, A. 1976, "The structure of unstructured decision process," *Administrative Science Quarterly*, Vol. 21, No. 2 (June), pp. 246–275.

Myers, S. C. 1984, "Finance theory and finance strategy," *Interfaces*, Vol. 14, No. 1 (January-February), pp. 126–137.

Oblak, D. J. and Helm, R. J. 1980, "Survey and analysis of capital budgeting methods used by multinationals," *Financial Management*, Vol. 9, No. 4, (Winter), pp. 37–41.

Petry, G. H. 1975, "Effective use of capital budgeting tools," *Business Horizons*, Vol. 8, No. 5 (October), pp. 57–65.

Petty, J. W.; Scott, D. F.; and Bird, M. R. 1975, "The capital expenditure decision-making process of large corporations," *The Engineering Economist*, Vol. 20, No. 3 (Spring), pp. 159–172.

Pinches, G. E. 1982, "Myopia, capital budgeting and decision making," *Financial Management*, Vol. 11, No. 3 (Autumn), pp. 6–19.

Pinches, G. E. 1984, "Effective use of capital budgeting techniques," *Chemical Engineering Progress*, Vol. 80, No. 11 (November), pp. 15–19.

Rosenblatt, M. J. 1980, "A survey and analysis of capital budgeting decision processes in multi-division firms," *The Engineering Economist*, Vol. 25, No. 4 (Summer), pp. 259–273.

Roth, H. P. and Brown, R. M. 1982, "Post-auditing capital investments using IRR and NPV Models," *Management Accounting*, Vol. 63, No. 8 (February), pp. 29–33.

Schall, L. D. and Sundem, G. L. 1980, "Capital budgeting methods and risk: A further analysis," *Financial Management*, Vol. 9, No. 1 (Spring), pp. 7–11.

Scott, D. F. and Petty, J. W. 1984, "Capital budgeting practices in large American firms: A retrospective analysis and synthesis," *Financial Review*, (March), pp. 111–123.

Schall, L. D.; Sundem; G. L.; and Geijsbeck, W. R. 1978, "Survey and analysis of capital budgeting methods," *Journal of Finance*, Vol. 33, No. 1 (March), pp. 281–287.

Slovic, P. 1972, "Psychological study of human judgment: Implications for investment-decision making," *Journal of Finance*, Vol. 27, No. 4 (September), pp. 779–799.

Statman, M. 1982, "The persistence of the payback method: A principal-agent perspective," *The Engineering Economist*, Vol. 27, No. 2 (Winter), pp. 95–100.

Weingartner, H. M. 1969, "Some new views on the payback period and capital budgeting decisions," *Management Science*, Vol. 15, No. 12 (August), pp. B594–607.

Williams, R. W. 1970, "Industry practice in allocating capital resources," *Managerial Planning*, Vol. 18, No. 6, (May-June), pp. 15–22.

Article 27

Capital Budgeting Forecast Biases: Evidence from the *Fortune* 500

Stephen W. Pruitt and Lawrence J. Gitman

Stephen W. Pruitt is Assistant Professor of Finance in the Department of Economics and Finance at the School of Business Administration, University of Mississippi, University, Mississippi. Lawrence J. Gitman is Professor of Finance in the Department of Finance at the College of Business Administration, Wright State University, Dayton, Ohio.

I. Introduction

Despite the obvious importance of revenue and cost forecasts in the development of accurate capital budgeting proposals, little empirical research has been directed toward whether these forecasts are typically biased and, if so, how the bias arises and is handled by decisionmakers. In two theoretical papers, Brown [2, 3] suggests that capital budgeting proposals could appear to be biased when they are not simply because of the manner in which projects are selected for implementation. Basically, Brown's model implies that a project is more likely to be accepted if the estimated net present value of the project is overstated due to the understatement of project costs and/or the overstate-

ment of project revenues. Miller [9, 10] extended Brown's work by noting that this effect implies that investors will be disappointed if they act on textbook project decision rules and suggested the implementation of a Bayesian statistical adjustment to correct for this upward project profitability inflation.

In a recent *Financial Management* article, Statman and Tyebjee [15] present the results of a behavioral experiment. These results provide significant evidence in support of Miller's [9] hypothesis that capital budgeting forecasts are perceived by people with work experience to be optimistically biased and that these individuals tend to adjust project profitability estimates downward in an effort to compensate for this bias. However, their research leaves unanswered a wide range of additional questions concerning capital budgeting forecast biases in industry. This article provides insights and answers to a variety of these questions based on responses to a comprehensive mail survey of the financial managers of some of the largest corporations in the United States.

The authors give special thanks to Dean Edward A. Moses and the College of Business Administration at the University of North Florida for partial support of this research. Additional thanks is due Dean Waldemar M. Goulet and the College of Business and Administration at Wright State University for its support. The authors also are grateful to Meir Statman, Edward Miller, Robert Taggart, and two anonymous referees for helpful comments on an earlier draft of this article.

Section II describes the survey methodology and provides a brief profile of the respondents. The following section presents and analyzes the actual survey results and, where appropriate, compares and contrasts our findings with earlier work on capital budgeting forecast biases. The final section discusses and summarizes the major findings of the current research.

II. Survey Methodology and Respondent Profile

A. Survey Methodology

On May 23, 1986 a questionnaire[1] accompanied by a cover letter briefly explaining the purpose of the survey was mailed to the highest ranking financial officer (either the Vice President of Finance or the Treasurer [14]) of each of the 500 largest industrial firms appearing in the 1986 *Fortune* listing [4]. Because respondents were guaranteed complete anonymity, identification of the responding individuals or firms was not possible. However, several respondents who identified themselves by requesting a copy of the completed study were later contacted in an effort to gain further insight into the issues under study.

A substantial majority (22 of 26 items) of the survey statements were concerned with capital budgeting forecast biases. A seven-point semantic differential scale was used to allow the respondents to indicate their degree of "disagreement" or "agreement" with each of the statements. The other four items sought to profile (i) the respondent and (ii) the general outcomes of the capital budgeting projects implemented by their firm. In all cases, survey respondents were specifically asked to provide *their opinion* about their firm's activities and not the opinion of managerial personnel in general. Only "closed-ended" questions were included to streamline the response time and thereby enhance the response rate.

A total of 121 usable responses (a 24.2% response rate) were received. Although there were occasional instances of missing or incomplete information, none of the independent survey items was answered by fewer than 118 respondents and the "no answer" response rate was fairly evenly distributed throughout the survey instrument.[2] Forty-nine respondents voluntarily provided identifying information.

---

[1]Space limitations prohibit the inclusion of the questionnaire. Interested readers may obtain a copy of the survey instrument directly from the authors.
[2]Respondents were asked to complete only six of the survey questions if they indicated either agreement or disagreement with two previous questions.

B. Respondent Profile

Although precise identification of the majority of respondents was impossible, an examination of the self-reported titles on the completed surveys indicated a significant degree of top-management participation. Indeed, 40.8% of the respondents identified themselves by top-management titles, such as "Chief Financial Officer" or "Vice President of Finance." In contrast, only 6.7% of the surveys apparently were completed by lower-level managerial personnel, such as "Senior Financial Analyst" or "Assistant Director of Planning and Control." Mid-to-upper-level personnel, such as "Controller," "Manager of Financial Planning and Analysis," and "Director of Financial Planning," accounted for 52.5% of the completed survey instruments. The respondent's 18.4-year mean level of work experience further suggests that a high level of managerial responsibilities typifies survey participants. Over 59% of the respondents indicated the attainment of an M.B.A. or other master's-level degree, just over 36% indicated the achievement of a bachelor's degree, and five respondents (4.2%) reported earning a doctoral degree in at least one field.

III. Survey Results

Exhibit 1 summarizes the responses to each of the 22 statements concerning capital budgeting forecast biases.

A. Revenue Forecast Biases

As is evident from the results of statement 1, nearly 80% of the respondents felt that revenue forecasts of capital budgeting proposals (not necessarily accepted projects) are typically overstated. This supports Miller's [9] hypothesis and Statman and Tyebjee's [15] experimental results. Interestingly, statements 2 and 3, which were designed to uncover potential reasons for any forecast biases, provided almost as many questions as they did answers. Thirty-seven percent of the respondents felt that biases were intentionally introduced by forecasters and 36.4% felt that at least some portion of the bias was due to a lack of experience. However, a survey-by-survey analysis indicates that, although 68.6% of the respondents identified the optimistic bias as being due to *either* intentional overstatement or a lack of experience, or both, fully 31.4% were unable to ascribe the bias to either of these two possibilities.

In an effort to clarify these results, a number of voluntarily self-identified survey participants who reported that revenue forecasts were optimistically bi-

Exhibit 1. Summary of Survey Participant Responses to Capital Budgeting Forecast Bias Statements

Survey Statement	Percent Generally Disagree 1 2 3	Percent Neither Disagree Nor Agree 4	Percent Generally Agree 5 6 7
1. Revenue forecasts of capital budgeting proposals (not necessarily accepted projects) are typically overstated.	12.4 Mean: 5.12	9.1	78.5 Std. Dev: 1.16
2. The above-mentioned overstatement bias (if any) of revenue forecasts is intentionally introduced by forecasters.	45.5 Mean: 3.42	17.2	37.3 Std. Dev: 1.74
3. The above-mentioned overstatement (if any) of revenue forecasts is due to the lack of experience of the forecaster.	34.5 Mean: 3.48	29.1	36.4 Std. Dev: 1.70
4. Revenue forecasts tend to deviate more from actual outcomes when the proposed project represents a significant departure from established corporate operations.	8.3 Mean: 5.46	10.7	81.0 Std. Dev: 1.35
5. Cost forecasts of capital budgeting proposals (not necessarily accepted projects) are typically understated.	38.0 Mean: 3.99	19.0	43.0 Std. Dev: 1.41
6. The understatement bias mentioned above (if any) of cost forecasts is intentionally introduced by forecasters.	54.2 Mean: 2.64	18.7	27.1 Std. Dev: 1.90
7. The understatement bias mentioned above (if any) of cost forecasts is due to the lack of experience of the forecaster.	33.3 Mean: 3.03	31.3	35.4 Std. Dev: 1.96
8. Cost (and/or R&D) forecasts tend to deviate more from actual outcomes when the proposed project represents significant advances in production and/or research technology.	5.9 Mean: 5.33	12.6	81.5 Std. Dev: 1.36
9. Research and development costs are typically underestimated.	11.8 Mean: 4.67	26.3	61.9 Std. Dev: 1.39
10. Research and development people typically underestimate R&D costs.	12.6 Mean: 4.61	32.8	54.6 Std. Dev: 1.23
11. Marketing people typically overestimate sales.	9.1 Mean: 5.45	4.1	86.8 Std. Dev: 1.88
12. Your company typically assigns the responsibility for project proposal preparation and project acceptance to the same individual or group.	71.9 Mean: 2.73	5.8	22.3 Std. Dev: 1.88
13. The decisionmakers for capital budgeting projects tend to have more experience than the forecasters who provide them with data.	14.8 Mean: 4.95	17.4	67.8 Std. Dev: 1.44
14. In general, decisionmakers who evaluate forecasts consider them to be optimistic in their estimates and adjust forecasts to correct them.	20.0 Mean: 4.48	20.8	59.2 Std. Dev: 1.39
15. Post-audit studies of projects show a marked tendency for forecasts to be more optimistic than actual values.	11.7 Mean: 5.06	12.5	75.8 Std. Dev: 1.38
16. Of projects that are implemented, those that top management feels are unsuccessful are more likely to be post-audited.	34.7 Mean: 3.97	22.3	43.0 Std. Dev: 1.91
17. Initial profitability estimates of accepted projects are maintained as the benchmark for actual performance even if these numbers are later revised as part of the decision-making process.	33.9 Mean: 4.17	18.2	47.9 Std. Dev: 1.87
18. The overall profitability of projects deemed essential by upper management is often inflated to help insure project acceptance.	47.1 Mean: 3.59	22.3	30.6 Std. Dev: 1.52
19. By inflating the profitability estimates of capital budgeting projects the chance of acceptance is improved.	15.7 Mean: 5.12	5.8	78.5 Std. Dev: 1.42
20. The actual profitability (after the fact) of accepted projects is typically higher than forecast.	61.2 Mean: 3.12	31.4	7.4 Std. Dev: 1.11
21. Actual profitability of accepted projects is likely to end up very close to proposal projections.	57.9 Mean: 3.46	21.5	20.6 Std. Dev: 1.18
22. Generally, management has a great deal of confidence in the overall profitability projections of most capital budgeting proposals.	37.2 Mean: 4.19	12.4	50.4 Std. Dev: 1.27

ased but who did *not* report intentional manipulation or lack of experience as the cause were contacted by telephone and asked their opinions about the source of the bias. Almost universally, their responses fell in one of two categories.

One group suggested that the optimistic bias resulted primarily from a sort of "myopic euphoria" in which the individuals responsible for the preparation of the forecasts were simply too involved with the projects to be totally objective. According to those who suggested this view, the lack of complete objectivity was neither intentional nor due to a lack of experience, but rather was due to a "mass psychology" phenomenon in which each individual's positive opinion of the project reinforced and magnified that held by each of the other members of the group. This resulted in overstatement of the positive qualities of the proposed project and understatement of its potential problems. This phenomenon, known in social psychology as the "risky-shift" or "group polarization effect" is perhaps the most widely supported finding in that field, having been documented empirically in over 300 separate research investigations.[3]

Another closely related "psychological explanation" for the perception that revenue estimates are biased concerns "salesmen's optimism." Clearly, many revenue estimates are prepared in marketing organizations. These groups are often composed of a large proportion of ex-salespersons who have come up through the ranks, and the practical psychology of successful selling requires that one first sell oneself on the merits of the products in question. To the extent that the optimistic bias in forecasts is due to these psychological or similar "non-rational" phenomena, the design and creation of effective "bias purging" mechanisms may prove extremely difficult.

A second group of respondents felt that the optimistic bias resulted from erroneous initial information provided to forecasting staff members by *upper-level* managerial personnel. This was done, the group felt, in an effort to improve the likelihood that a given manager's or division's "pet project" would be accepted. This hypothesis supports Pinches' [13] comments that at least a portion of the optimistic bias in capital budgeting proposals may stem from capital rationing and inappropriate reward and punishment structures in many corporations.

Statement 4 asked whether revenue forecasts tend to deviate more from actual outcomes when the proposed project represents a significant departure from established corporate operations (*i.e.*, new products or distribution schemes). The results support Mansfield, Rapoport, Schnee, Wagner, and Hamburger's [6] findings that the degree of project innovation and *ex post* forecast error are positively related.

B. Cost Forecast Biases

Statements 5 through 8 essentially repeat statements 1 through 4, but from the standpoint of cost, as opposed to revenue, forecasts. Interestingly, whereas almost 80% of the survey respondents felt that revenue forecasts were optimistically biased, only 43% of these same individuals felt that cost forecasts were typically understated. It may be, for example, that the capital budgeting projects reviewed by the survey respondents

---

[3]Myers and Lamm [11] provide a concise summary of 156 references on the subject.

Exhibit 2. Summary of Ratio of Actual-to-Forecast Cost Levels of Implemented Capital Budgeting Projects Reported by Survey Participants

Survey Statement: Which of the following ratios of *actual costs to forecast costs* best describes the average outcomes on capital budgeting projects implemented by your firm? (Note: A ratio of 1.00 would indicate that the actual cost equaled the forecast cost.)

Ratio of actual cost to forecast cost	Percent of Respondents
Less than 0.50	1.7
0.50 to 0.99	15.4
about 1.00	43.6
1.01 to 2.00	39.3
2.01 to 3.00	0.0
Greater than 3.01	0.0
Weighted Average Response:	1.15

typically involve replacement decisions (in which costs are relatively easy to estimate) rather than product development proposals. In that event, the combined revenue and cost results support the implication of Miller's [9] model that there should be a positive relationship between the degree of difficulty in estimating a project's overall benefits and the degree of forecast bias.

In an attempt to gain insight into the actual-to-forecast cost ratio of the typical capital budgeting project implemented in their respective firms, participants were asked to select from six possible ranges the one outcome that most closely approximated their opinion. Although their responses, reproduced in Exhibit 2, do present evidence of cost understatement bias (an average ratio of actual-to-forecast cost of 1.15), a significant percentage (43.6%) of the survey participants indicated that the average cost forecasts for the capital budgeting proposals implemented by their firms were relatively free from bias.

Whereas the survey respondents did not, in general, feel that cost forecasts were typically understated, they were almost unanimous in their agreement that cost forecasts were more likely to deviate from actual outcomes when the proposed project represented significant advances in production and research technology. This finding is strongly supportive of results of Marshall and Meckling [7], Peck and Scherer [12].

Statement 9 pertained specifically to biases in research and development costs and not just to cost forecasts in general. Strongly supporting the previous firm-specific work by Meadows [8] and Allen and Norris [1] and the experimental results of Statman and

Tyebjee [15], nearly 62% of the survey respondents suggested that R&D costs are typically understated, a finding which further suggests that the overstatement bias discovered by Mansfield and Brandenburg [5] may have been specific to the firm investigated.

C. Verification of the Results of Statman and Tyebjee

Statements 10 and 11 were exact restatements of questions previously asked of subjects in the experimental work of Statman and Tyebjee [15]. These were included to ascertain whether their findings could be extended to a more generalized sample composed of full-time corporate employees. The general implications of the results clearly support Statman and Tyebjee's experimental work, including their finding that forecasts provided by marketing people are considered more biased than those provided by research and development employees. However, the standard errors of the responses were far larger than those registered by the experimental subjects, indicating less universal agreement than that uncovered in their experimental research.

In an attempt to extend Statman and Tyebjee's finding that the degree of perceived forecast bias is positively related to the decisionmaker's years of full-time work experience, the respondents' reported years of work experience were regressed against their responses to statements 10 and 11, respectively. The results failed to support the hypothesis, as the t-statistics for the slope coefficients of the two regressions (0.48 and 1.15) were not significant at the 10% level.[4]

D. Other Reasons for the Optimistic Bias

Statements 12 through 19 were designed to further explore the apparent generally optimistic bias in capital budgeting forecasts and how firms attempt to deal with it. Responses to statement 12 support Miller's [9] hypothesis that it is common practice for corporations to assign project forecast preparation and project acceptance to separate individuals. The results of statement 13 suggest that this may well stem from the fact that the decisionmakers typically possess more corporate experience than the forecasters who provide them with data, while the results of statement 14 suggest

that, in general, these decisionmakers attempt to correct for optimistic biases by adjusting submitted forecasts downward.

Statements 15 and 16 were designed to see if the survey respondents may have learned of the presence of the optimistic bias in capital budgeting proposals through their experiences with project post-audits in their respective firms. A substantial majority of the survey participants suggested that project post-audits show a marked tendency for forecasts to be more optimistic than actual values (a fact that supports most empirical studies on post-audit bias), and over 40% of the respondents indicated that the projects that top management feels are unsuccessful are more likely to be post-audited. Combined, these facts support Miller's conjecture [9, 10] and Statman and Tyebjee's [15] experimental results suggesting that real-world experiences, rather than textbook knowledge, lead managers to the belief that forecasts are optimistically biased.

Statement 17 provides a measure of support for Statman and Tyebjee's [15] suggestion that, while decisionmakers adjust forecasts to correct for optimistic bias, the project's original forecast is maintained as a benchmark for determining post-audit performance. Indeed, it would appear that in just under 50% of the companies surveyed, this procedure may be the rule.

Statements 18 and 19 present evidence on the probability that intentional overstatement of profitability increases a given project's chance of acceptance. While only 30% of survey respondents felt that *upper* management was responsible for intentionally biasing project forecasts, over 75% of the participants felt that profitability inflation improved the chance that a given project would eventually be accepted and implemented by the firm. Clearly, additional research targeted at uncovering the extent to which non-upper-level managers intentionally bias project profitability estimates is warranted.

E. Management's Degree of Confidence

Statements 20, 21, and 22 concern top management's degree of confidence in the final profitability forecasts of the capital budgeting proposals eventually implemented by their firms. Statements 20 and 21 provide additional evidence that capital budgeting forecasts are considered optimistically biased.[5] From statement 22, only 50% of the survey participants indicated that they had a great deal of confidence in the overall

---

[4]Given that Statman and Tyebjee's results suggested that the relationship between the degree of perceived forecast bias and work experience was not significant beyond two years of experience and the fact that, here, only three survey respondents reported work experience below this level, the negative results discussed in the current research should *not* be construed as contradicting Statman and Tyebjee's earlier work.

---

[5]Statements 21 and 22 were intentionally worded similarly and document the high degree of consistency in the responses to the survey.

profitability projections of the average capital budgeting proposal in their respective firms. Further, when the respondents' self-reported years of full-time corporate work experience were regressed against their answers to this final question, the test statistic was negative and significant at the 5% level (t = -2.08). Perhaps more than any other result, this suggests that upper-level managers consider capital budgeting forecasts to be inadequate.

IV. Summary and Future Research Directions

Using 121 responses to a 26-question mail questionnaire sent in May 1986 to the highest ranking financial officer in each of the 500 firms included in the 1986 *Fortune* 500 listing, this article evaluates various aspects of bias in capital budgeting forecasts. The results support both Miller's [9, 10] hypothesis that capital budgeting forecasts are optimistically biased by people with work experience and that these individuals tend to adjust downward profitability estimates of projects in an effort to compensate for this bias and Statman and Tyebjee's [15] experimental results providing significant evidence in support of Miller's hypothesis.

The specific findings of the research have important implications for both corporate managers and the collegiate academic community. Turning first to corporate managers, the results of the study suggest that greater attention be paid to eliminating the incentives for project profitability overstatement by *all* corporate employees. Further, since managers clearly adjust profitability estimates downward on an informal basis, there may be considerable gains from the adoption of more formal and precise adjustment procedures, such as those advocated by Miller [10].

For the collegiate academic community, the survey results presented here exemplify the lack of confidence that corporate managers place in the profitability estimates provided by textbook capital budgeting decision rules. If academics are serious about providing solutions to real-world problems, better attention must be paid to the development of capital budgeting selection criteria that explicitly acknowledge decisionmaking in a competitive and informationally imperfect environment.

References

1. J. M. Allen and K. P. Norris, "Project Estimates and Outcomes in Electricity Generation Research," *Journal of Management Studies* (October 1970), pp. 271–287.
2. K. C. Brown, "A Note on the Apparent Bias of Net Revenue Estimates for Capital Investment Projects," *Journal of Finance* (September 1974), pp. 1215–1227.
3. ———"The Rate of Return of Selected Investment Projects," *Journal of Finance* (September 1978), pp. 1250–1253.
4. "The Fortune 500," *Fortune* (April 28, 1986), pp. 175–201.
5. E. Mansfield and R. Brandenburg, "The Allocation, Characteristics, and Outcome of the Firm's Research and Development Portfolio: A Case Study," *Journal of Business* (October 1966), pp. 447–464.
6. E. Mansfield, J. Rapoport, J. Schnee, S. Wagner, and M. Hamburger, *Research and Innovation in the Modern Corporation*, New York, Norton, 1971, Chapter 5.
7. A. Marshall and W. Meckling, "Predictability of the Costs, Time, and Success of Development," in National Bureau of Economic Research (ed.), *The Rate and Direction of Inventive Activity: Economic and Social Factors*, Princeton, NJ, Princeton University Press, 1962.
8. D. L. Meadows, "Estimate Accuracy and Project Selection Model in Industrial Research," *Industrial Management Review* (Spring 1968), pp. 105–119.
9. E. M. Miller, "Uncertainty Induced Bias in Capital Budgeting," *Financial Management* (Autumn 1978), pp. 12–18.
10. ———"The Competitive Market Assumption and Capital Budgeting Criteria," presented to the Financial Management Association, October 1986, New York.
11. D. G. Myers and H. Lamm, "The Group Polarization Phenomenon," *Psychological Bulletin* (July 1976), pp. 602–627.
12. M. J. Peck and F. M. Scherer, *The Weapons Acquisition Process: An Economic Analysis*, Cambridge, MA, Harvard University Press, 1962.
13. G. E. Pinches, "Myopia, Capital Budgeting and Decision Making," *Financial Management* (Autumn 1982), pp. 6–19.
14. *Standard and Poor's Register of Corporations, Directors, and Executives,"* New York, Standard and Poor's Corporation, 1986.
15. M. Statman and T. Tyebjee, "Optimistic Capital Budgeting Forecasts: An Experiment," *Financial Management* (Autumn 1985), pp. 27–33.

Article 28

STOCK MARKET REACTION TO STRATEGIC INVESTMENT DECISIONS

J. RANDALL WOOLRIDGE and CHARLES C. SNOW

College of Business Administration, The Pennsylvania State University, University Park, Pennsylvania, U.S.A.

This study examines the stock market's reaction to public announcements of corporate strategic investment decisions. It includes a wide variety of strategic decisions: formation of joint ventures, research and development projects, major capital expenditures, and diversification into new products and/or markets. Three alternative hypotheses concerning the stock market's reaction to announcements of these decisions are tested. The Shareholder Value Maximization hypothesis predicts a positive reaction to corporate investments because the stock market rewards managers for developing strategies that increase shareholder wealth. The Rational Expectations hypothesis predicts no stock price reaction because investors expect managers to undertake periodic investments in order to maintain their firms' competitive fitness. The Institutional Investors hypothesis predicts a negative reaction to announcements of corporate investments. The U.S. capital markets are dominated by institutional investors who, in pursuit of superior quarterly performance, may disdain long-term investments because they reduce short-term earnings. Analysis of 767 strategic investment decisions announced by 248 companies in 102 industries indicates that the stock market's reaction to strategic investments conforms most closely to the predictions of the Shareholder Value Maximization hypothesis. This overall finding holds for investments of varying size and duration. The implications of a positive reaction by the stock market to investment announcements are drawn for corporate strategy research and management practice.

For over a decade, American managers have been urged to make investment decisions that improve the long-run competitiveness of their firms (e.g. Hayes and Abernathy, 1980). Advocates of this view frequently point to examples of Japanese managers deliberately sacrificing short-run profits in order to gain substantial market shares for their companies. Many American managers, however, argue that it is difficult to adopt a long-run perspective in today's business environment. The biggest obstacle to long-run or strategic decision-making, they claim, is the stock market. For example, in a survey of 100 chief executive officers of major corporations, 89 agreed that America's competitive edge has been 'dulled' by failure to emphasize long-term investment. Ninety-two percent of this group believed that Wall Street's preoccupation with

quarterly earnings was the cause (*Wall Street Journal*, 1986).

Are American managers forced to manage for the short-term in order to meet the demands of Wall Street? In other words, do they make long-term investments that increase the satisfaction of all their firms' stakeholders, or do they merely take actions that result in short-run profitability in order to please securities analysts? This distinction has been drawn very clearly in the business press. Some writers have claimed that the stock market forces managers to take a short-run view in their decision-making (e.g. *Business Week*, 1984; Drucker, 1986; Pennar, 1986). Conversely, others have maintained that managers can develop long-run strategies for their companies that will be rewarded by the stock market (e.g. Hector, 1988). However, to date, neither view has been solidly grounded in empirical research. The present study attempts to provide such evidence by examining the stock market's reaction to the announcements of a wide variety of strategic decisions.

THEORETICAL BACKGROUND

Strategic investments and competitive advantage

In perfectly competitive factor and product markets, strategic investment projects with positive (or negative) net present values are nonexistent. If a strategic investment is perceived to have a positive net present value, then it instantly attracts new entrants to the industry. This in turn increases factor prices and capacity and drives product prices down. Higher factor prices and lower product prices reduce returns to all firms, forcing the weaker ones to leave the industry. With fewer competitors, factor prices decline and product prices rebound, increasing returns for the surviving firms until once again actual and required returns are equal. Therefore, strategic investment decisions with positive net present values have no sustainable competitive advantage.

The ability of strategic investment decisions to generate positive net present values rests on imperfections in product and factor markets that permit a firm to gain a competitive advantage over other firms in the industry. A firm can gain competitive advantage, for example, by becoming the low-cost producer, differentiating its product or service, and/or situating itself as a profitable link in an industry's value chain (Porter, 1980, 1985). Competitive advantages form barriers to potential entrants and result in an imperfectly competitive industry in which strategic investment decisions with positive net present values are possible (Shapiro, 1985).

Strategic investments and stock valuation

According to traditional valuation theory, the market value of the firm is the sum of (a) the discounted value of future cash flows expected to be generated from assets in place and (b) the net present value of expected cash flows from investment opportunities that are expected to be available to and undertaken by the firm in the future (Brealey and Myers, 1988). The value of a firm changes as the stock market receives general or firm-specific information that changes the market's expectations about the cash returns from current and future assets.

The pricing efficiency of the stock market has been one of the most studied topics in corporate finance. The vast majority of the empirical research supports the belief that the market is informationally efficient with respect to publicly available information (Brealey and Myers, 1988). This means that stock prices reflect all public information and respond rapidly to releases of new information that may affect the risk and return of securities. This phenomenon is normally examined by assessing the reaction of stock prices to corporate events. For example, many studies have shown that stock prices adjust upward (downward) to increases (decreases) in dividend payments on the day of the announcement and fluctuate in a random fashion thereafter (Brealey and Myers, 1988), indicating that the information in the dividend announcement is fully reflected in the stock price on the day of the announcement.

Thus, in an informationally efficient market, stock price responses to corporate announcements represent the market's evaluation of corporate decisions. However, to isolate the effect of a particular firm's announcement, its security return must be adjusted for the expected return on the stock. The actual return, minus the expected return, is called the 'abnormal' or 'excess' return.

Recent financial theory posits that managers are compelled by capital market forces to make investment decisions aimed at maximizing firm value (Fama and Jensen, 1985; Rappaport, 1986; Reimann, 1987). According to this view, accounting-based performance measures such as earnings per share, return on investment, and return on equity do not properly measure the value of managers' investment decisions. The true test of the long-run value of an investment decision is whether it creates economic value for shareholders as measured by abnormal stock returns (Rappaport, 1986). Therefore, the *Shareholder Value Maximization* hypothesis predicts that the stock market will react positively to corporate announcements of strategic investment decisions. Such decisions increase a firm's market value by enhancing its ability to generate future cash flows.

An alternative hypothesis, which we call the *Institutional Investors* hypothesis, makes exactly the opposite prediction from that of the Shareholder Value Maximization hypothesis. It has been argued that U.S. investors—especially large, powerful financial institutions—focus primarily on quarterly earnings and thereby discourage managers from pursuing strategies aimed at long-term competitive advantage (Ellsworth, 1985). According to this view, much of the short-term orientation of the stock market comes from professional money managers such as pension and investment-fund managers and bank trust departments. Their short-run orientation is presumably derived from their own requirements to make successful quarterly investment decisions in order to retain their current customers and attract new ones. Increased trading volume on the exchanges and higher turnover rates for institutional investment portfolios usually are cited as evidence in support of the short-run orientation. Managers who do not maintain quarterly earnings to satisfy institutional investors will see their companies' stock prices decline. They may then face the threat of hostile takeover offers from corporate raiders. Therefore, the Institutional Investors hypothesis predicts that announcements of corporate investment decisions with long-term, uncertain payoffs (such as research and development projects) will be associated with negative stock returns.[1]

A third hypothesis, derived from the economic theory of perfect competition, might be called the *Rational Expectations* hypothesis. It predicts that the stock market will not react quickly or strongly to corporate announcements of strategic investment decisions. The logic of the Rational Expectations hypothesis is that across a variety of industries, companies, and strategic decisions, competitive advantages are at best temporary. If corporate investment announcements produced insignificant stock returns, then it would appear that investments serve to maintain competitive

fitness rather than generate competitive advantage.

Empirical evidence

Strategic investment decisions are major commitments of current resources made in anticipation of generating future payoffs. By definition, such decisions involve a current resource outflow and an uncertain payback. Therefore, any significant corporate investment depresses current earnings and increases uncertainty about the firm's future performance. Only three empirical studies have investigated the relationship between strategic investment announcements and stock prices. One study examined the relationship between joint-venture formation and announcement-day stock prices (McConnell and Nantell, 1985). It treated joint ventures as one type of capital expenditure, a special form of intercorporate 'merger,' in which only a subset of the resources of two (or more) firms are joined together to accomplish some strategic objective. The sample was 210 firms involved in 136 joint ventures during 1972–79. Joint-venture formations were positively and significantly correlated with announcement-day returns. This finding was consistent with the Shareholder Value Maximization hypothesis.

Another study analyzed the relationship between research and development (R&D) projects and stock prices (Jarrell, Lehn, and Marr, 1985). The sample was 62 R&D announcements made in the *Wall Street Journal* during 1973–83. The primary hypothesis was that a negative stock price reaction to R&D expenditure announcements would support the 'short-term argument' or the Institutional Investors hypothesis. Research and development announcements were found to be significantly associated with positive stock returns. This finding refuted the 'short-term argument' about the stock market.

The third study examined the reaction of stock prices to 658 announcements of increases or decreases in the dollar amount of planned capital expenditures (McConnell and Muscarella, 1985). Announcements of increases (decreases) in capital budgets were significantly associated with positive (negative) abnormal stock returns for industrial firms but not for public utilities. The overall conclusion was that, for industrial firms, the stock market's reaction was consistent with the Shareholder Value Maximization hypothesis. For

---

[1] An alternative interpretation of negative stock returns is that managers may be engaging in activities with negative net present values. These may result from traditional agency problems in which managers' interests conflict with those of stockholders. For example, it has been argued that managers may enact mergers simply to increase the size of their firms rather than create value for stockholders (Malatesta, 1983). This would be especially true in the area of capital expenditures, since these appear on the balance sheet (unlike joint ventures or R&D expenditures). Therefore, the 'size maximization' hypothesis would be supported in the present study if stock prices are discovered to react negatively to capital expenditures announcements.

public utilities, on the other hand, regulatory pricing mechanisms reduced the likelihood that capital projects with positive net present values would be available.

Thus, for three different types of strategic investment decisions (joint ventures, R&D projects, and major capital expenditures), the empirical evidence conforms most closely to the Shareholder Value Maximization hypothesis. That is, when corporations announce their strategic investment plans, the stock market usually reacts positively. The present study attempted to add to this emerging research stream in three ways: (a) considerably expand the size of the empirical data base; (b) examine stock market reaction to an additional type of strategic decision (diversification into new products and/or markets); and (c) determine the impact on stock prices of two important contingency variables, the size and duration of corporate investments.

HYPOTHESES

There are three general hypotheses that pertain to the relationship between strategic investment announcements and stock market reaction. Each hypothesis has a corollary prediction concerning investment size and duration.

Hypothesis 1 (Shareholder Value Maximization): The stock market will react positively to corporate announcements of strategic investment decisions.

Hypothesis 1a: There will be positive abnormal returns for both small and large investments with little or no difference between the two size categories. There will be positive abnormal returns for both short- and long-term investments with little or no difference between the two duration categories.

Hypothesis 2 (Institutional Investors): The stock market will react negatively to corporate announcements of strategic investment decisions.

Hypothesis 2a: There will be negative abnormal returns for both small and large investments with large investments having greater negative returns. There will be negative abnormal returns for both short- and long-term investments with

long-term investments having greater negative returns.

Hypothesis 3 (Rational Expectations): The stock market will not react to corporate announcements of strategic investment decisions.

Hypothesis 3a: There will be insignificant abnormal returns for all investments whether small, large, short-run, or long-run.

There is as yet no direct evidence that relates the size and duration of corporate investments to changes in stock price. The Shareholder Value Maximization and Rational Expectations hypotheses do not differentiate among corporate investments by either their size or duration. The former hypothesis predicts that all investments will be positively valued by the stock market; the latter hypothesis predicts no stock market response because investments are required to maintain competitive fitness. Because institutional investors are presumed to focus on short-term profitability, the Institutional Investors hypothesis predicts that the stock market will react negatively to larger and longer-term investments because (a) larger investments have a more detrimental effect on short-run profitability and (b) profits from longer-run investments will be realized in the more distant future.

METHODOLOGY

Data and sample

To examine the relationship between investment announcements and stock prices, a sample of corporate investment decisions was developed from articles that appeared in the *Wall Street Journal* during June 1972–December 1987. This 15-year span showed substantial variation in economic activity and stock market behavior. The 'What's News' column of the paper was surveyed for announcements that described corporate investment decisions, specifically those pertaining to joint ventures, R&D projects, capital expenditures, and product/market diversification. If an announcement was found in the 'What's News' column, then the full article was consulted to confirm the type of investment decision and to see whether other information about the company was also published. If the announcement included information about the firm's sales or earnings, or if another announcement concerning the firm's sales, earnings, personnel changes, etc. appeared in the paper within one day (before or after) of the investment decision announcement, it was excluded from the sample. This procedure was used to minimize the effect of extraneous influences on stock prices. The final sample contained 767 announcements made by 248 companies in 102 industries.

Method of analysis

The impact of an event on the value of a firm's common stock is usually assessed by measuring the difference between the actual and expected returns on the stock during a relevant time period surrounding the event. The analytic method used in this study is known as the market-adjusted returns approach (MARA).[2] Using this approach, the return for security i on day t (r_{it}) is specified as:

$$r_{it} = u_{it} + e_{it}$$

where u_{it} is the expected return on security i on day t, and e_{it} represents a stochastic error term that has an expected value of zero and is uncorrelated over time. Solving for e_{it} in the above equation yields the following:

$$e_{it} = r_{it} - u_{it}$$

In MARA, r_{it} is the actual return on security i on day t, and u_{it} is estimated as the mean return on the stock market (the Standard and Poor 500) for day t. Since u_{it} is the expected return on security i on day t, the error term (e_{it}) represents the abnormal or unexpected return. Hence, the impact of new information on the price of security i on day t can be discovered through an evaluation of the e_{it} values.

To investigate the effect of strategic investment announcements on stock prices, the sample of investment decisions was arranged in 'event time' around the day that the announcement appeared

in the *Wall Street Journal*. In the analyses below, day 0 is the *Wall Street Journal* announcement date, and e_{it} represents the actual return on security i minus the return on the Standard and Poor 500 for that day. The average abnormal return (AR$_t$) across announcements of strategic investment decisions (where the number equals n) for event day t is computed as follows:

$$AR_t = \sum_{i=1}^{n} \frac{e_{it}}{n}$$

To assess information effects over time, these abnormal returns typically are cumulated over event days. The cumulative abnormal return (CAR$_n$) as of event day n is expressed as:

$$CAR_n = \sum_{t=1}^{n} AR_t$$

All stock return data were obtained from the daily returns file of the Center for Research in Security Prices' (CRSP) data base.

RESULTS

Daily stock returns during a period surrounding the announcement of a corporate investment were analyzed for the four types of strategic decisions. In all cases, announcements appeard in the *Wall Street Journal* on day 0. However, most announcements actually were made prior to the close of trading on the previous day (day −1). Therefore, the mean and cumulative abnormal returns on these two days (−1 and 0) were used to evaluate the market's reaction to a strategic investment announcement. These two days are referred to as the 'announcement period.' In addition, returns were calculated for the succeeding two trading weeks in order to ensure that the full announcement effect was captured. The cumulative abnormal returns (beginning with day −1) are reported for days 5 and 10. Mean abnormal returns (AR), cross-sectional T-tests (T), and cumulative abnormal returns (CAR) are shown in Tables 1 and 2. For descriptive purposes, mean unadjusted returns (R) and the percentage of unadjusted returns greater than zero are also shown.

---

[2] This approach is a variant of the well-known event-study methodology pioneered by Fama, Fisher, Jensen, and Roll (1969). Brown and Warner (1985) have shown that the MARA is as powerful as other more restrictive models of expected stock returns in detecting significant stock price movement associated with specific events.

All strategic investment announcements

Summary statistics for the daily stock returns of the entire sample of 767 strategic investment decision announcements are given in Section A of Table 1 for days −1, 0, 5, and 10. The average ARs for days −1 and 0—the announcement period—were 0.30 percent (T = 3.46, $p < 0.01$) and 0.35 percent (T = 4.55, $p < 0.01$), respectively. These were the two largest ARs over the 12-day period (−1 through 10). The CAR for the 2-day announcement period was 0.64 percent. Through day 10, the CAR was 0.57 percent, which indicated that ARs subsequent to the announcement period were negligible. The average unadjusted returns (Rs) were consistent with these positive announcement-period results, with day −1 and 0 averages of 0.38 percent and 0.35 percent, respectively, and a relatively higher percentage of daily returns greater than zero.

Whereas the T-tests indicate the statistical significance of the results, the practical or economic significance of these findings can be illustrated in two ways. First, the annual return equivalent of a 2-day abnormal return of 0.64 percent is 220 percent. Second, the 0.64 percent abnormal return for a large company with a market value of, say, $25 billion, results in an increase in market value (adjusted for overall market movements) of $160 million in 2 days.

The overall results strongly supported the Shareholder Value Maximization hypothesis. That is, when corporations announced their strategic investment decisions, the stock market usually reacted quickly and positively. In some cases, however, investors reacted negatively to corporate announcements of strategic decisions. Thus, it appeared that the stock market attempted to differentiate between good and bad investment decisions; it did not behave monolithically.[3]

Specific types of investment announcements

Section B of Table 1 contains the summary statistics for the daily stock returns associated with

the announcements of joint venture formations, research and development projects, captial expenditures, and product/market diversifications. These broad investment decisions were further classified into appropriate subcategories as shown.

Both the ARs and CARs indicated that the stock market responded positively to the announcement of joint venture formations. The ARs for days −1 and 0 were 0.42 percent (T = 2.45, $p < 0.01$) and 0.38 percent (T = 2.17, $p < 0.05$), respectively. There was no evidence of stock price declines during the 10 days following the announcement of a joint venture (the CAR over the entire 12-day period was 1.27 percent). As shown in Table 2, joint ventures were formed for three main purposes: research and development, shared assets/resources, and asset construction. Of the three types of joint venture, the 2-day CAR associated with firms that announced plans to share assets or other resources was the largest (1.40 percent).

The ARs for days −1 and 0 of R&D projects were 0.80 percent (T = 2.36, $p < 0.05$) and 0.33 percent (T = 1.34, ns), respectively. There was no evidence of stock price declines for the subsequent 10 days, with the CAR growing from 1.13 to 1.53 percent. As shown in Table 2, R&D expenditures were announced for ongoing as well as new projects. The 2-day CAR associated with additional allocations to ongoing R&D programs was 1.68 versus 0.69 for allocations to new projects.

For the 277 announcements of major capital expenditures, the ARs for days −1 and 0 were 0.06 percent (T = 0.38, ns) and 0.31 percent (T = 2.64, $p < 0.01$), respectively. Between days 0 and 10, the CAR declined a mere 0.07 percent (from 0.36 to 0.29). As shown in Table 2, capacity expansion and capital budget increases were evaluated most positively by investors.[4]

The last part of Section B, Table 1 shows the daily stock returns associated with announcements of product and/or market diversification. For all 241 announcements the ARs for days −1 and 0 were positive (0.33 and 0.35 percent, respectively) and significant (T = 2.41, $p < 0.01$ and T = 2.59, $p < 0.01$, respectively). Between days 0 and 10, however, the CARs declined; over the

---

[3] A negative reaction perhaps is best exemplified by the stock market response to oil companies' announcements of their exploration and development programs in the early 1980s. At that time the petroleum industry was generating tremendous cash flow from high crude oil prices and was investing the cash in expanded exploration and development. Investors, however, regarded the price of crude to be artificially high and therefore responded negatively to these R&D announcements.

[4] The positive returns associated with capital expenditure announcements, and especially the results for the capacity expansion subsample, did not support the size-maximization hypothesis discussed by Malatesta (1983)—see footnote 1.

Table 1. Strategic investment announcements and stock returns

	Day	Mean unadjusted return (R)	Percentage unadjusted return greater than zero	Mean abnormal return (AR)	T-test (T)	Cumulative abnormal return (CAR)
Section A: Overall results						
All investment announcements ($n=767$)						
	−1	0.38	48.01	0.30	3.46**	0.30
	0	0.35	51.74	0.35	4.55**	0.64
	5					0.66
	10					0.57
Section B: Specific types of investment announcements						
Joint venture ($n=197$)						
	−1	0.55	50.25	0.42	2.45**	0.42
	0	0.40	52.79	0.38	2.17*	0.80
	5					1.05
	10					1.27
R&D project ($n=52$)						
	−1	0.90	53.85	0.80	2.36*	0.80
	0	0.43	46.15	0.33	1.34	1.13
	5					0.81
	10					1.53
Capital expenditure ($n=277$)						
	−1	0.12	41.52	0.06	0.38	0.06
	0	0.23	50.54	0.31	2.64**	0.36
	5					0.63
	10					0.29
Product/market diversification ($n=241$)						
	−1	0.43	51.87	0.33	2.41**	0.33
	0	0.41	52.70	0.35	2.59**	0.69
	5					0.26
	10					0.01

*$p < 0.05$; **$p < 0.01$.

entire 12-day period they were nearly zero. The results for the three subcategories—old products targeted toward new markets, new products developed for old markets, and new products announced for new markets—are shown in Table 2. These results indicated that investors responded positively to new product introductions, both in new and old markets (2-day CARs of 0.86 and 0.78 percent, respectively), but not to expansion into new markets with old products (2-day CAR of −0.08 percent). However, one could argue that the latter type of diversification is the one most easily predicted by investors. Therefore, the fact that no significant price reaction was detected may indicate that investors anticipated such moves and stock prices already reflected this information.

Size and duration of investment

For some of the investment announcements, the *Wall Street Journal* article provided information on the size or the duration of the investment. In 365 of the 767 cases, information about the dollar size of the investment was given. To incorporate investment size into the analysis, the dollar amount of the investment was first divided by the total assets of the firm so that each investment was expressed as a relative percentage. Then the entire subsample of 365 investment announcements was dichotomized at the median (5.3 percent). This permitted the assessment of stock market reaction to announcements of small versus large investments (i.e. less than or greater than 5.3 percent of total firm assets).

Table 2. Strategic investment announcements and 2-day cumulative abnormal returns

	Number of announcements	Two-day cumulative abnormal returns (percentage)
All investment announcements	767	0.64
Joint venture formation	197	0.80
R&D	40	0.40
Shared assets/resources	68	1.40
Asset construction	89	0.52
R&D project	52	1.13
Ongoing	23	1.68
New	29	0.69
Capital expenditure	277	0.36
Capacity expansion	204	0.33
Plant modernization	36	0.13
Capital budget increase	37	0.75
Product/market diversification	241	0.69
Old product/new market	30	−0.08
New product/old market	168	0.78
New product/new market	43	0.86

The expected life span or duration of a corporate investment was provided in 287 cases. This subsample was divided into two categories, short-term (less than 3 years) and long-term (more than 3 years), and the stock market valuation of each group was calculated. It should be noted that in both the size and duration subsamples, over 95 percent of the investments came from the R&D and capital expenditures categories. Very few joint venture and diversification announcements contained size or duration information.

Summary statistics for the stock returns on the size and duration subsamples are given in Table 3. The 2-day ARs for small and large investments were 0.37 percent ($T = 2.95$, $p < 0.01$) and 0.34 percent ($T = 2.14$, $p < 0.05$), respectively. The 2-day CARs for small and large investments were 0.47 and 0.46 percent, respectively, both of which were of substantial practical or economic import. The 2-day ARs for short- and long-term invest- ments were 0.26 percent ($T = 1.90$, $p < 0.05$) and 0.46 percent ($T = 2.21$, $p < 0.05$), respectively. The 2-day CAR of long-term invest- ments (0.59 percent) was especially strong. Given that the stock market's reaction to small and large investments was positive and virtually identical, and that the market reacted positively and significantly to long-run investments, these results provided additional support for the Share- holder Value Maximization hypothesis and clearly refuted the Institutional Investors hypothesis.

DISCUSSION

The findings have several implications for strategic management research and practice. They indicate a very clear and strong relationship between strategic investment decision announcements and stock market valuation. However, the study dealt with stock market reactions to *announcements* of corporate decisions and not to the *outcomes* of those decisions. Using Mintzberg's (1978) terminology, announcements are intended strat- egies that can either be realized or unrealized. Further, intended strategies may be modified during implementation (Mintzberg and Waters, 1985; Quinn, 1980). It would be helpful for future researchers to track a set of announced decisions, determine the outcomes of those decisions, and attempt to assess when and by how much market valuation changed. Such research would measure the effectiveness of strategy implementation as well as formulation.

In some cases the stock market reacted negatively to a firm's investment announcement. The market may have lacked confidence in that firm's strategy or future prospects, management's ability to implement the investment project successfully, or the timing of the proposed investment. Future research that sought to identify investment characteristics that differen- tiated positive from negative stock returns would help managers understand better how the market assesses strategic decision-making.

From an economic standpoint the objective of corporate strategy is the selection of industries to participate in, whereas the purpose of business strategy is to achieve a sustainable advantage over competitors *in* an industry (Porter, 1985). The study of investment announcements can aid in understanding relationships among industry,

Table 3. Size and duration of strategic investment announcements and stock returns

	Day	Mean unadjusted return (R)	Percentage unadjusted return greater than zero	Mean abnormal return (AR)	T-test (T)	Cumulative abnormal return (CAR)
Section A: Investment size						
Small (n=183)	−1	0.17	43.2	0.11	0.84	0.11
	0	0.33	50.3	0.37	2.95**	0.47
Large (n=182)	−1	0.16	42.3	0.12	0.58	0.12
	0	0.28	51.7	0.34	2.14*	0.46
Section B: Investment duration						
Short (n=194)	−1	−0.02	43.3	−0.04	−0.22	−0.04
	0	0.16	47.4	0.26	1.90*	0.23
Long (n=93)	−1	0.16	41.9	0.13	0.69	0.13
	0	0.31	52.7	0.46	2.21*	0.59

*$p < 0.05$; **$p < 0.01$.

strategy, and firm performance. The apparent methodology for this type of research is a matched-pair sample of companies. Those companies that made investment decisions could be compared in key ways to competitors that did not make such decisions during the same time interval. Relevant matching factors might include type of industry, industry profitability, market shares of the matched firms, type of corporate strategy, type of investment announcement, and the business strategies of the units to which the announcement applies. This methodology would facilitate more fine-grained analyses of the stock market's reaction to corporate investment announcements.

With the exception of capital expenditures, which can be undertaken by any type of firm, favorably received investment announcements tended to involve actions taken by firms that Miles and Snow (1978) called prospectors (early movers) and analyzers (fast followers). This was especially true of diversification decisions, where new product and market development generated significantly more returns than the extension of current products to new markets. Even though empirical studies have indicated that the stock market's assessment of information is unbiased and rational (Fama, 1970, 1976), analysts may generally prefer prospector and analyzer strategies over defender strategies. Future research could be directed at this issue. If this observation is found to be correct, then defender firms, which have been shown to be highly profitable (Hambrick, 1983), may need to engage in joint

ventures or other strategic alliances in order to be viewed more favorably by the stock market.

The results of this study also have implications for practitioners. The most obvious implication is that managers of successful companies need not worry unduly about the stock market as they formulate corporate and business strategies. As evidenced in the diverse array of industries and companies examined in this study, announcements of large, long-run investment projects created, on average, substantial value for stockholders. To be sure, managers cannot ignore the market's expectations of short-run earnings, but it is clear that they are not being compelled to develop short-term strategies aimed only at producing profits.

The stock market appeared to favor announcements regarding investments in R&D and joint ventures over those in product/market diversification and capital expenditures. This suggests that the market may be in favor of lowering mobility barriers among firms because these forms of investment often involve alliances with other companies (including domestic or foreign competitors). Traditional business strategy is predicated largely on how firms within an industry should attempt to erect mobility barriers in order to achieve competitive advantages over their rivals (Caves and Porter, 1977). Managers have been encouraged to understand how firms in their strategic group operate, and to read the signals and moves of firms in other strategic groups (Porter, 1980, 1985). In the future, managers may be able to generate greater returns by developing collective strategies (Astley, 1984), network organizations (Miles and Snow, 1986; Thorelli, 1986), and other corporate alliances that compete in nontraditional ways.

It may appear at first glance that corporate strategists could make an investment announcement merely to increase the firm's market value and then not implement the decision. Whereas this study only evaluated the immediate stock-price impact of corporate announcements, management's performance over time is a major factor in investors' assessments of future strategic directions and objectives. Therefore, any attempt to manipulate the market in this manner potentially seems unwise.

CONCLUSION

Today's corporate strategists have a considerable challenge to meet the demands of a wide variety of constituents. One very important constituent is the stock market. Recently, the stock market has been characterized as misguided and even hostile, supposedly forcing managers to make strategic decisions that are not in the best long-run interests of their companies and the total economy. The findings from this study indicate that the stock market does not penalize managements for making well-conceived, long-run strategic decisions. In fact, it rewards them for doing so. Moreover, it appears that managers do not have to forsake other important constituents, such as customers, as they contemplate strategic investments.

ACKNOWLEDGEMENTS

We would like to thank Patrick Cusatis for his assistance with the data analysis, and we are grateful to Grant Miles, Mark Sharfman, John Slocum, Scott Snell, and James Thomas for their helpful comments on an earlier version of this paper. The two anonymous *SMJ* reviewers made several very helpful suggestions for revising the paper.

REFERENCES

Astley, W. G. 'Toward an appreciation of collective strategy', *Academy of Management Review*, July 1984, pp. 526–535.

Brealey, R. A. and S. C. Myers. *Principles of Corporate Finance*, 3rd edn, McGraw-Hill, New York, 1988.

Brown, S. and J. Warner. 'Using daily stock returns: The case of event studies', *Journal of Financial Economics*, March 1985, pp. 3–31.

Business Week. 'Will money managers wreck the economy?', 13 August 1984, pp. 86–93.

Caves, R. E. and M. E. Porter. 'From entry barriers to mobility barriers', *Quarterly Journal of Economics*, May 1977, pp. 241–262.

Drucker, P. F. 'A crisis of capitalism', *Wall Street Journal*, 30 September 1986, p. 31.

Ellsworth, E. 'Capital markets and competitive decline', *Harvard Business Review*, September/October 1985, pp. 171–183.

Fama, E. F., L. Fisher, M. Jensen and R. Roll. 'The adjustment of stock prices to new information', *International Economic Review*, February 1969, pp. 1–21.

Fama, E. F. 'Efficient capital markets: A review of theory and empirical work', *Journal of Finance*, May 1970, pp. 383–417.

Fama, E. F. *Foundations of Finance*, Basic Books, New York, 1976.

Fama, E. F. and M. Jensen. 'Organizational forms and investment decisions', *Journal of Financial Economics*, April 1985, pp. 101–119.

Hambrick, D. C. 'Some tests of the effectiveness and functional attributes of Miles and Snow's strategic types', *Academy of Management Journal*, March 1983, pp. 5–26.

Hayes, R. H. and W. J. Abernathy. 'Managing our way to economic decline', *Harvard Business Review*, July–August 1980, pp. 67–77.

Hector, G. 'Yes, you *can* manage long term', *Fortune*, 21 November 1988, pp. 64–76.

Jarrell, G., K. Lehn and W. Marr. 'Institutional ownership, tender offers and long-term investments', The Office of the Chief Economist, Securities and Exchange Commission, 19 April 1985.

Malatesta, P. 'The wealth effect of merger activity and the objective functions of merging firms', *Journal of Financial Economics*, April 1983, pp. 155–181.

McConnell, J. and C. Muscarella. 'Corporate capital expenditures decisions and the market value of the firm', *Journal of Financial Economics*, July 1985, pp. 399–422.

McConnell, J. and T. Nantell. 'Corporate combinations and common stock returns: The case of joint ventures', *Journal of Finance*, June 1985, pp. 519–536.

Miles, R. E. and C. C. Snow. *Organizational Strategy, Structure and Process*, McGraw-Hill, New York, 1978.

Miles, R. E. and C. C. Snow. 'Network organizations: New concepts for new forms', *California Management Review*, Spring 1986, pp. 62–73.

Mintzberg, H. 'Patterns in strategy formulation', *Management Science*, May 1978, pp. 934–948.

Mintzberg, H. and J. A. Waters. 'Of strategies, deliberate and emergent', *Strategic Management Journal*, July–September 1985, pp. 257–272.

Pennar, K. 'Is the financial system shortsighted?', *Business Week*, 3 March 1986, pp. 82–83.

Porter, M. E. *Competitive Strategy*, Free Press, New York, 1980.

Porter, M. E. *Competitive Advantage*, Free Press, New York, 1985.

Quinn, J. B. *Strategies for Change: Logical Incrementalism*, Irwin, Homewood, IL, 1980.

Rappaport, A. *Creating Shareholder Value*, Free Press, New York, 1986.

Reimann, B. C. *Managing for Value*, The Planning Forum, Oxford, OH, 1987.

Shapiro, A. 'Corporate strategy and the capital budgeting decision', *Midland Corporate Finance Journal*, Spring 1985, pp. 22–36.

Thorelli, H. B. 'Networks: Between markets and hierarchies', *Strategic Management Journal*, January–February 1986, pp. 37–51.

Wall Street Journal, 'Business bulletin', 12 June 1986, p. 1.

Article 29

A NEW LOOK AT THE RETURNS AND RISKS TO PHARMACEUTICAL R&D*

HENRY GRABOWSKI AND JOHN VERNON

Department of Economics, Duke University, Durham, North Carolina 27706

This study investigates the returns to R&D for 100 new drugs introduced into the United States during the decade of the 1970s. In contrast to prior studies, it incorporates several significant structural changes that have occurred in the pharmaceutical industry during the 1980s. These include higher real drug prices and a greater degree of generic competition. A major finding is that the return on R&D for the average new drug is approximately equal to the 9 percent industry cost of capital. However, the performance of new drugs introduced during the latter half of the 1970s was markedly better than that of early 1970s introductions. This latter finding is consistent with the more rapid rate of industry growth in real R&D expenditures. The study also finds that the variation in returns is highly skewed, with only the top 30 drugs covering mean R&D costs on a fully allocated basis. Finally, it is shown that real drug price increases in the 1980s were necessary for the average new drug introduction to recover its R&D costs.
(PHARMACEUTICALS; DRUGS; R&D; RETURNS; RISK)

A number of past studies have been performed on the returns to pharmaceutical R&D activity. These studies indicate that the rate of return to pharmaceutical R&D fell significantly during the 1960s and early 1970s. They find a mean real return of between 4 to 6 percent for post-1962 new drug introductions. Overall, existing studies present a picture of declining and low real returns to pharmaceutical R&D over the past few decades.

Lower returns on new drug introductions during the 1960s and 1970s can be traced to various factors, including more stringent health and safety regulations (Grabowski and Vernon 1983). Nevertheless, one would expect the industry to adapt to an unfavorable regulatory environment through changes in research strategy, product prices, firm attrition and other means.[1] Although the adjustment process may take several years, returns on R&D should eventually come back in line with the industry's cost of capital.

Investment behavior in pharmaceuticals suggests a more favorable environment for R&D activity has emerged in recent years. While R&D investment in drugs slowed markedly during the 1970s, it has been growing at a rapid rate during the 1980s. In particular, U.S. pharmaceutical industry R&D expenditures have been growing at an annual rate in excess of ten percent over the current decade (Grabowski 1989).

A new look at the returns to pharmaceutical R&D therefore would appear timely. Existing rate of return studies predate several developments that are relevant to assessing the returns to pharmaceutical R&D. First, beginning in the latter half of the 1970s, the industry experienced the introduction of several important new drug products from a therapeutic standpoint. Second, there has been a major change in drug pricing patterns during the 1980s. Third, product life cycles have changed during the 1980s, particularly in the post-patent period where generic competition is now more intense than in the past. Fourth, the trends in foreign market sales experienced by U.S. new drug introductions have also changed significantly in the current decade.

In the present analysis, we consider the economic performance of new drugs introduced during the 1970s. We are interested in seeing whether these new product introductions

---

* Accepted by Alok K. Chakrabarti; received April 4, 1989. This paper has been with the authors 1 month for 1 revision.

[1] With regard to the issue of firm attrition, a number of studies have shown that increased regulation had a particularly adverse effect on smaller sized firms. This group of firms now account for a much smaller fraction of industry R&D than in the pre-1962 period (Grabowski and Vernon 1976) (Thomas 1988).

have obtained higher returns than in earlier periods. In addition, it is instructive to examine how returns are affected by the drug pricing patterns which emerged in the 1980s. Real price increases in pharmaceuticals have received increasing attention by policymakers, including recent congressional hearings (U.S. Congress 1985, 1987). Another important objective is to analyze the effects of several policy developments, such as evolving cost containment programs. Insights into the potential impact of these changes on R&D returns can be obtained from a sensitivity analysis of our main results.

The next section of the paper discusses prior studies and recent trends in the pharmaceutical industry in more detail. The following one covers the major assumptions and basic methodology of the analysis. The final two sections present the main findings and the results of various sensitivity analyses.

1. Prior Studies and Recent Trends

Most studies of the returns to pharmaceutical R and D have found low yields in the post-1962 Drug Amendment period. On the basis of an econometric analysis, Baily (1972) estimated *nominal pre-tax* returns to pharmaceutical R&D dropped from over 30 percent pre-1962 to less than 15 percent post-1962. Using a somewhat different methodological approach, Statman (1983) found *nominal after tax* returns on pharmaceutical R and D declined from 20 percent in the mid 1950s to about 10 percent in the late 1970s. Schwartzman (1975) estimated *real after tax* returns were between 3.3 to 7.5 percent for the 1966 to 1972 period. Joglekar and Patterson (1986) have performed the most recent and comprehensive study on this subject. Their best estimate of the *real after tax* returns on pharmaceutical R&D was approximately 6 percent for a new drug compound beginning R&D in the mid 1970s.

A major limitation of all the current studies is that they employ data and extrapolate drug industry trends from the 1960s and 1970s. None employ any data from the 1980s.[2] However the investment and product life cycles for new pharmaceuticals span several decades of time. Moreover, the industry has experienced important changes in recent years that have potentially significant implications for the returns to R&D.

First, there appears to be a distinct improvement in research opportunities within the last decade.[3] There has been an explosive growth in basic biomedical knowledge and research. Consistent with this situation, pharmaceutical R&D is increasingly characterized by a "discovery by design" approach. This in contrast to the random screening approach which was more prevalent in the earlier post World War II period (Grabowski and Vernon 1983, Chapter 2). In addition, research is now increasingly directed to chronic rather than acute health care problems. Drug therapies for chronic use have accounted for an increasing share of the major new drug introductions of recent periods.

There have also been important changes in the life cycle pattern of expected revenues for new product introductions during the 1980s. There is some evidence that product lifetimes are becoming shorter. A more rapid introduction of close substitutes to the pioneer drug compound in various therapeutic groupings is taking place.[4] This apparently

[2] The most recent study by Joglekar and Patterson (1986) examines 218 new chemical entities introduced between 1962 and 1977. The latest year for which sales data were utilized was 1981 in this study. Their sensitivity analysis considers some of the emerging trends in the 1980s, such as increased generic competition and changing drug price behavior.

[3] This is also suggested by a recent analysis of the new products achieving 100 million dollars of U.S. sales by the fifth year of market life. There were 11 such products introduced between 1977 and 1982 as opposed to only 3 such products introduced between 1970 and 1976 (Grabowski 1989).

[4] A good example of this phenomenon is the case of Tagamet, the leading product introduction in terms of U.S. sales in the 1970s. Since its introduction in 1978, there have been three anti-ulcer product substitutes introduced and one of these products, Zantac, now has a larger share of the market. A regression analysis that we performed on the sales of new product introductions in our sample indicates that peak sales are generally occurring sooner after the date of introduction than was the case for older products.

reflects several factors. These include increased diversification of R&D programs by major firms and the ability of firms to use the discovery by design approach to produce closely substitutive as well as pioneer products.

The most significant change in product life cycles, however, is the much greater generic competition experienced in the post-patent period. Traditionally in pharmaceuticals, when the patent of a pioneering brand expired, the loss of sales to less expensive generic products occurred only very gradually (Statman 1981). However, this situation has changed dramatically in the 1980's. The repeal of state anti-substitution laws and the passage of the 1984 Drug Price Competition and Patent Restoration Act have been important factors in this regard.[5] In preliminary research covering 18 drug compounds in which a patented brand name product was first subjected to generic competition in the 1983–1987 period, we have found that generics achieved an average unit market share of 49 percent by two years after market entry (Grabowski and Vernon 1989).

There has also been an important change in industry pricing behavior. During the 1970s, U.S. drug prices lagged overall economy wide inflation. At the end of the 1970s, however, drug firms began increasing product prices significantly faster than inflation. This pattern has persisted throughout the 1980s. This has important implications for drug profit margins, as discussed below.

Another significant change during the 1980s relates to sales of U.S. introductions in foreign markets. Throughout the previous decade, an upward trend was observable in the ratio of foreign to domestic sales for U.S. drug firms. However, during the 1980s, foreign sales have not increased relative to U.S. drug sales. This reflects the oscillating movements in exchange rates as well as the moderating growth rates of pharmaceuticals in foreign markets.

In sum, there have been major structural changes in recent years influencing both the inputs and outputs from pharmaceutical R&D. Hence studies of the returns to R&D which simply extrapolate the trends of the 1960s and 1970s to future periods are likely to have significant limitations.[6] A re-examination of the returns to R&D utilizing more recent industry experiences and data would therefore appear appropriate.

2. Data Samples and Methodology

A. *Overview*

As discussed, the first objective is to measure the historical performance of New Chemical Entities (NCEs) introduced during the 1970s. The basic sample is 100 NCEs approved by the FDA and introduced into the United States between 1970 and 1979.[7] For each NCE, annual cash flows are estimated over the compound's projected product life. A key question analyzed is whether the present value of cash flows from the average NCE covers average R&D investment costs, including the opportunity cost of capital. This

---

[5] The Drug Price Competition and Patent Restoration Act allows easier approval of generic products by the FDA and also results in longer effective patent lifetimes for new drug introductions. However, the primary short-run effect of the Act is to facilitate generic competition for drugs now coming off patents. A preliminary analysis of these developments and the economic impacts of the Act is presented in Grabowski and Vernon (1986).

[6] In this regard, Joglekar and Patterson (1986) assume in their base case analysis that the ratio of worldwide sales to U.S. sales would increase steadily and that drug prices would lag overall inflation during the rest of the century, based on an extrapolation of trends observed in the 1960s and 1970s. If one modifies these assumptions to take account of the 1980s experience in pharmaceuticals, rates of returns are influenced in both a positive and negative manner.

[7] Our sample excludes new drugs in the cancer area because they are typically developed jointly with the National Institutes of Health. Similarly drugs discovered and developed by nonprofit institutions and universities are excluded because the R&D costs of these compounds would not be representative of drugs emanating from the pharmaceutical industry.

analysis is performed on a real after-tax basis. Both cash flows and R&D expenditures are expressed in constant 1986 after-tax dollars, utilizing a tax rate appropriate to the pharmaceutical industry.

The analysis is performed from the perspective of a long-run capital investment decision. Hence, cash flows are compared to fully allocated R&D investment expenditures. The latter include discovery costs common to all NCEs and the costs associated with R&D failures. It is, of course, rational for firms to continue to make incremental investments as long as cash inflows are expected to cover all future cash outflows on a net present value basis. Over the long run, however, a firm's total portfolio of new drug introductions must cover all investment costs, including "dry holes" and opportunity costs, if R&D is to remain a viable enterprise. In this regard, it is therefore instructive to ask whether the full portfolio of drugs emanating from the pharmaceutical industry over a period of several years covers the industry's opportunity cost of capital. This is a principal issue to be considered in the first half of the paper.

B. *Opportunity Cost of Capital*

The cost of capital for pharmaceuticals in this study is based on an analysis of the capital asset pricing model (CAPM) estimated at various points in time between mid-70s and mid 80s.[8] An analysis of investment riskiness was first undertaken for a representative portfolio of pharmaceutical firms. This indicated that pharmaceutical firms had comparable riskiness to the market over this period (i.e., betas approximately equal to one). Long-term estimates on the risk free rates and the market equity risk premia were then obtained using the analysis of Ibbotson (1987). Using these inputs to the CAPM, the estimated cost of equity capital for pharmaceuticals exhibited a central tendency around 9 percent for the time period studied.[9] This value is utilized therefore to capitalize R&D costs and all cash flows in the present analysis.[10]

C. *R&D Costs*

The most comprehensive analyses of R&D expenditures in pharmaceuticals was performed by Ron Hansen (1979, 1980). He utilized cost data from a significant sample of

---

[8] Since the capital structure of pharmaceuticals is overwhelmingly equity financed (in excess of 90 percent), the cost of equity capital provides a good proxy for the overall cost of capital. This issue has been examined in Statman (1983). Joglekar and Patterson (1986) compare R&D returns in pharmaceuticals with the returns on corporate bonds. As the authors recognize, this is a very conservative approach, in that the returns on corporate bonds have been significantly below that for equities over the relevant time period.

[9] The return on long-term government bonds rather than the return on short-term bills was used to compute the risk free rate (and the market equity risk premia) since we are dealing here with long term investment projects. The basic Capital Asset Pricing Model formula is

$$\text{Cost of Equity Capital} = \text{Risk Free Rate} + (\text{Beta})(\text{Market Risk Premium}).$$

Setting Beta for pharmaceuticals equal to one and using values published in Ibbotson (1987) to obtain the market equity risk premia and risk free rates (in real terms) yields the following results for 1974 and 1986:

$$\text{Real Cost of Equity Capital (1974)} = 1.3 + (1)7.5 = 8.8\%,$$

$$\text{Real Cost of Equity Capital (1986)} = 1.6 + (1)7.4 = 9.0\%.$$

The values for intervening years also cluster around 9 percent.

[10] An alternate approach to estimating the cost of capital would be to utilize the "hurdle rates" derived from surveys of U.S. industrial firms. These hurdle rates are significantly higher than the cost of capital values estimated from the CAPM, especially for R&D oriented industries like pharmaceuticals (Gitman and Mecurio 1982, Scherer 1983). Some recent research has attempted to reconcile these different findings by generalizing the CAPM in a number of directions (Bernhein and Shoven 1989). This research, while preliminary in nature, points to cost of capital values that are more in line with revealed U.S. corporate hurdle rates. From this perspective, the 9 percent value utilized in this study may be viewed as a conservative estimate of the equity cost of capital for pharmaceuticals.

new drug candidates undergoing clinical development in the period 1963 to 1975. Hansen's work is a useful starting point for estimating R&D costs for our sample of new drugs. However, his R&D cost estimates cannot be used directly here without adjustment. This is because his study is centered on a time period which predates our sample period. There are several factors that have caused R&D costs to increase in real terms over time. These include rising real costs for pharmaceutical R&D inputs,[11] a longer R&D process,[12] and increasing concentration of R&D on chronic disease problems.[13] At the same time, there is some indication that success rates in clinical development have improved over time.[14]

In the current study, we utilize two separate approaches to estimate R&D costs. The first approach uses Hansen's R&D costs by therapeutic class as a starting point. Annual costs by therapeutic class are then adjusted to take account of the net growth in real R&D costs resulting from the various factors mentioned above (R&D input inflation, longer R&D times, etc.). The second approach relies on total R&D expenditures and NCE introductions for the pharmaceutical industry. Specifically this approach employs a variable lag analysis between aggregate R&D expenditures and introductions to estimate average R&D costs in the 1970s. The two approaches are described in greater detail in a separately available appendix.

The results of these two approaches yield very similar values for average R&D costs over the 1970s. In particular they indicate the average R&D costs for 1970–79 introductions, capitalized at 9 percent and expressed in 1986 dollars is in the neighborhood of 125 million dollars.[15] By way of comparison, Hansen's original average R&D cost estimate, capitalized at 9 percent and updated for inflation, would be equal to 100 million dollars in 1986 dollars. The difference between these values provide a measure of the net increase in real R&D costs during the 1970s. A recent study by Wiggins (1987) also finds that R&D costs have increased significantly in real terms over time.[16]

We also found that there is a considerable *variance* around our mean R&D cost estimate. In particular, the year to year fluctuations can be 20 percent above or below the average. Recognizing this, we examine a range around the baseline value in the sensitivity analysis.

---

[11] An analysis of this issue for several industrial sectors was performed by Mansfield, Romeo and Switzer (1983). Pharmaceuticals was subsumed in the broader chemicals class in their analysis. This latter sector experienced a 122 percent price increase over 1969–1979 as compared to an 88 increase for the GNP price deflator. This type of analysis also has been generalized and extended to more recent time periods by Mansfield (1987).

[12] Mattison, Trimble and Lasagna (1988) show that total R&D times for self-originated NCEs of U.S. firms have increased from approximately 9 years in 1970 to 14 years by 1981. This factor by itself results in an approximately 2 percent annual increase in real R&D costs.

[13] In this regard, data collected annually by the Pharmaceutical Manufacturers Association show that cardiovascular research has accounted for an increasing percentage of total industry R&D, while research on anti-infectives, has experienced corresponding declines (*PMA Statistical Factbook* 1988). The analysis of Hansen (1980) indicates significantly lower R&D costs for acute indications compared to categories involving chronic diseases.

[14] Mattison, Trimble and Lasagna (1988) provide an analysis of this issue. They find that success rates for drugs in clinical development in the United States are increasing over time, but a major reason for this fact is that more drugs are being pre-screened abroad before entering U.S. clinical testing. Preliminary results from an updated analysis of pharmaceutical R&D by Hansen et al. (1989) also suggest an improving success rate over time, but at the same time indicate that R&D costs per new drug introduction are growing significantly faster than inflation. On the basis of these new survey data, our adjustments to Hansen's original R&D costs for the 1970s would appear on balance to be conservative.

[15] The first approach yielded mean R&D costs per 1970s introduction between 120 and 132 (pre-tax) million dollars, using alternative assumptions for the net effect of the different factors leading to higher real cost over time. The second approach yielded a mean R&D cost of 123 million dollars with a substantial year to year variation. For further details, see the appendix which is available on request from the authors.

[16] Wiggins' study is not strictly comparable to ours in that it focuses on a longer time period (1960–1975) and utilizes a somewhat different methodological approach (i.e. a short fixed time lag between aggregate R&D costs and NCE introductions). However, his findings are qualitatively consistent as indicated above.

In addition, NCE introductions in the latter half of the 1970s have significantly higher mean R&D costs than those introduced in the first half of the 1970s. This is relevant when we examine particular time cohorts in our analysis of R&D performance.

D. *Domestic Sales Revenues and Product Life Cycles*

We next turn to the issue of estimating cash flows for our sample of NCE introductions. The first step in this estimation process was to assemble data on the U.S. sales for each new product introduction. For each of the NCEs first marketed between 1970 to 1979, annual drugstore and hospital sales through 1986 were obtained from audit data sources. From this data base, there were 17 years of sales data for the 1970 NCE introductions, 16 years for the 1971 cohort, 15 years for 1972 NCE introductions and so on down to 8 years of sales data available for the 1979 cohort.

The next task is to extrapolate future sales over the market life of each product. On the basis of prior studies and the sales patterns observed in this sample, 25 years was chosen as the market life for the present sample of drugs.[17] In order to project sales for the full product life of 25 years, a standard life cycle pattern for drugs sales was utilized (Thomas 1981, Stauffer 1975). Our procedures are illustrated in Figures 1-A and 1-B where the sales data and projections from two representative drugs, selected from the top few deciles of sample compounds, are presented.

The compound in Figure 1-A is one in which 17 years of actual sales are available from audit sources. This compound is beyond its point of peak sales and already has experienced patent expiration. Sales in the first year after patent expiration have begun to decline sharply due to generic competition. In projecting sales in this post-patent period, we assume that drug products in our sample will experience a cumulative loss of 60 percent in sales to generic competitors within a five-year period. This is in line with recent empirical analyses (Grabowski and Vernon 1989, Drexel et al. 1988).

By contrast, the drug compound in Figure 1-B is a more recent introduction. It has many fewer years of actual sales data available (9 years). This drug is in the peak sales portion of its product life cycle. Using our representative life cycle curve, this product is projected to have relatively stable sales until year 12. This is the year when its patent expires and generic entry occurs. A significant decline in sales is projected after that point due to both generic competition and product obsolescence.

Our procedures produce a representative life cycle sales pattern for each new drug introduction that is related to its specific patent date and other economic factors. The amount of error introduced into our present value analysis from the extrapolated sales values should be minimal. This is because we have actual sales data for most compounds through their period of peak sales. Furthermore, the later segments of the product life cycle are not only subject to intensive generic competition, but are also heavily discounted in present value terms.

Figure 2 shows the life cycle sales estimates for the mean, median and the top few deciles of our sample. This figure illustrates the highly skewed distribution of sales which exists for new product introductions in pharmaceuticals. In particular, the peak sales of the top decile are several times that of the next ranked decile of drugs. In addition the mean values are much higher than the median. This high degree of skewness has important implications for the returns to pharmaceutical R&D.

E. *Worldwide Sales Revenues*

To obtain estimates of worldwide dollar sales, we utilize a foreign sales "multiplier." In an earlier paper, we examined domestic and worldwide sales for a representative

---

[17] As noted (see fn. 6), there are indications that product life cycles have been shortening. As a consequence, many of the introductions made toward the end of the 1970s may experience shorter market lifetimes than 25 years. This issue is considered in the sensitivity analysis.

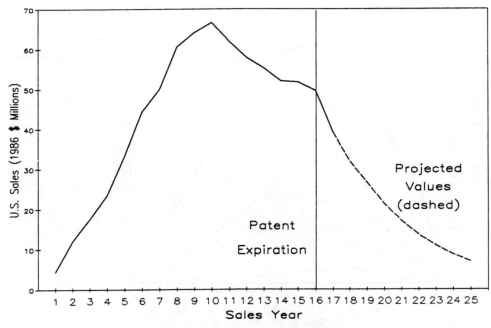

FIGURE 1-A.   Historical/Projected Sales Values—Product A.

sample of U.S. NCE introductions during the mid 1970s (Grabowski and Vernon 1982).
The relevant multiplier for global to U.S. sales was found to be 1.75 for this period. There
is also evidence that this multiplier was increasing throughout the 1970s and reached a
value of just over 2.00 by the end of the decade (PMA 1988).

The 1980s have witnessed contrasting trends in this multiplier, primarily as a consequence of exchange rate fluctuations. Consistent with the strong appreciation of the

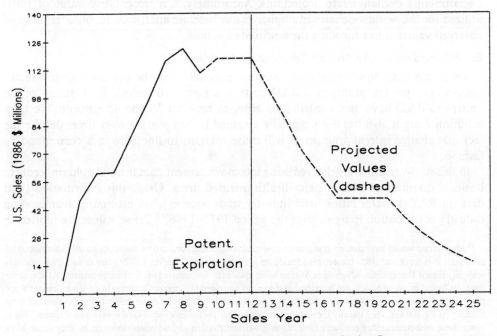

FIGURE 1-B.   Historical/Projected Sales Values—Product B.

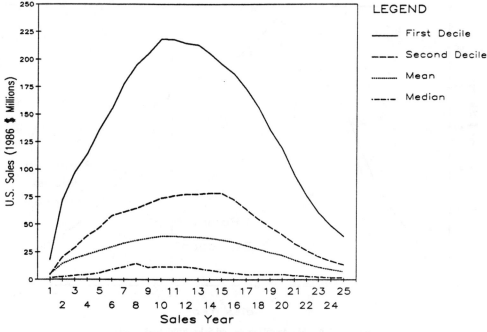

FIGURE 2. Sales profile of 1970–79 Cohort.

dollar in the years prior to 1985, the ratio of worldwide sales to U.S. declined significantly until the mid-1980s. It has partially recovered in value since that point. This pattern is borne out by balance sheet data on U.S. and foreign sales of multinational pharmaceutical firms as well as other data sources.

These different data sources indicate that the ratio of worldwide to U.S. sales has fluctuated between 1.75 to just over 2.0 for the decade of the 1970s and 1980s. This would also appear to be a relevant range for the immediate future using U.S. Treasury Department's exchange rate projections. Accordingly, a representative value of 1.9 is utilized for the worldwide sales multiplier in our baseline analysis. The broader range of observed values is examined in the sensitivity analysis.

F. *Pricing Trends and Pre-tax Contribution Margins*

To obtain cash flows from sales, sales are multiplied by the pre-tax "contribution" margin (i.e., pre-tax profits plus R&D costs as a percent of sales). Past studies of the returns to R&D have used contribution margins between 25 and 45 percent. The contribution margin also has been typically assumed to be constant over time, despite the fact that change in real drug prices will cause margins to fluctuate in a corresponding fashion.

In this study, margins are derived using income statement data from the pharmaceutical business divisions of twelve major health oriented firms. Using this information (and data on R&D to sales ratios from industry trade sources), we estimated average drug industry contribution margins over the period 1973–1986.[18] These values are plotted in

[18] Ideally, one would have data on margins on new product introductions rather than data for all pharmaceutical products. It is not clear what biases this introduces into the analysis. Reekie (1979) has found that products with significant therapeutic advantages over existing products will command a price premium. At the same time, he found many products are launched at discounts compared to market leaders. In addition, recent work suggests that older drugs experiencing generic competition do not typically lower prices to match those of their cheaper rivals. Rather, they usually increase prices while their unit sales erode (Grabowski and Vernon 1989). Since these post-patent drug products have much lower distribution and administrative costs, they could have higher margins than a representative grouping of newer products.

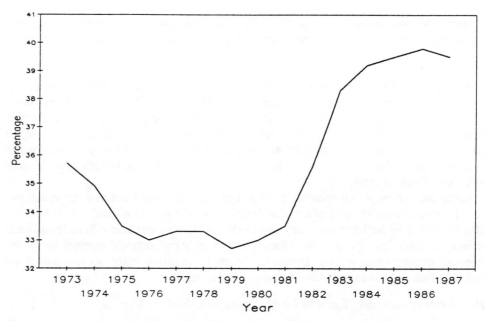

FIGURE 3. Margins Used as Inputs in the Baseline Case: 1973–1987.

Figure 3. The observed time pattern on margins corresponds directly with the behavior of domestic prices. Prices lagged inflation until the late 1970s. They began increasing faster than general inflation in 1981, which is also the year when profit margins in Figure 3 begin significantly increasing. We tested the hypothesis that the changes in margins over this time period could be primarily explained by domestic prices, using a statistical regression analysis. The analysis provided strong formal support for this hypothesis.[19]

We use the pre-tax margins shown in Figure 3 to estimate the pre-tax cash flows generated by each product's sales in a given year. Hence, in contrast to past work, our analysis utilizes time dependent margins. A product launched in the early 1970s would thus have moderately declining margins on its sales until the late 1970s, at which point its margins would begin significantly increasing as one comes forward in time to 1987. In this way, our analysis incorporates the changes in real prices that have occurred in pharmaceuticals since the early 1970s.

For future years, we assume in the baseline case that margins will remain fixed at the 40 percent level observed over recent years.[20] One might alternatively postulate that margins in the 1990s will decline as a result of increased cost containment pressures in the U.S. and abroad. A number of financial industry reports have projected this kind of

[19] In particular, a "backcasting" model for predicting margins was first constructed. Margins were estimated based on the assumption that U.S. drug output prices change in accordance with the pharmaceutical producer price index, while U.S. product input costs increase with the GNP price deflator. For foreign markets, prices were assumed to move proportionally with costs. Using these assumptions, along with an assumed value of 40 percent for margins in 1985, values were estimated back to 1973. The estimates produced by this procedure were highly correlated with the margins based on industry accounting data shown in Figure 3. The correlation coefficient, R, between the two series is 0.93. This implies that domestic real price increases explain 87 percent of the variation in contribution margins using this model.

[20] The plateauing of profit margins in the 1985 to 1987 period at 40 percent is perhaps surprising, given the fact that domestic prices are still increasing faster than economy wide prices. However, in recent years, prices in a number of key foreign markets, such as Japan, have been significantly restrained (OECD, 1987). Foreign sales account for nearly half of the total sales of U.S. firms and hence have nearly equal weight in the determination of margins. The last few years have been characterized by a situation of rising margins domestically and falling ones internationally, apparently leading to relatively stable profit margins for the U.S. pharmaceutical industry.

scenario (Mabon, Nugent and Co. 1987). Alternative scenarios, with both declining and increasing trends for future margins, are considered as part of the sensitivity analysis.

G. Tax Rates

An analysis of historical data since 1970 indicates that the average effective tax rate for most drug firms has been in the range of 30 to 45 percent. This is below the statutory rate and reflects various credits available in federal laws which lower average effective rates.[21] The recently enacted Federal tax reform reduces the federal statutory rate for corporations in future periods, but also curtails the ability of firms to utilize particular credits to lower effective tax rates. It is not clear at this point whether effective tax rates will change significantly.

Based on our empirical analysis, a 35 percent tax rate is utilized as a representative baseline tax rate for the pharmaceutical industry for the period of study. This rate was also employed by Joglekar and Patterson (1986) in their recent study. Since both R&D inputs and cash flow revenues are affected in a roughly proportional manner by the tax rate, our present value analysis should not be highly sensitive to the tax rate parameter utilized. This issue is examined in the sensitivity analysis.

H. Outlays for Product Launch, Fixed Capital and Working Capital

Pharmaceutical products typically experience heavy promotional expenditures in the first few years of product launch. In the current analysis we assume promotional expenditures equal to sales in year one, declining to 50 percent and then 25 percent of sales respectively in year two and three after product launch. This is based on a separate analysis of drug promotion expenditures for new products using audit data from IMS. These upfront promotional expenditures result in realized pre-tax margins below the assumed steady state values in the first few years of market life, in accordance with general industry experience.

In our analysis, total plant and equipment expenditures are assumed to be equal to 50 percent of tenth year sales for each new product introduction.[22] This ratio was based on balance sheet data of firms with a high degree of specialization in pharmaceuticals. For working capital, it is assumed that accounts receivable represent 1.3 months of annual sales and inventories are 5 months of sales (valued at the product's manufacturing cost). All working capital is recovered in the final year of product life.

After-tax cash flows are also affected by differences in book and tax depreciation methods. Book depreciation is based on a straight line accounting method, while tax depreciation is based on an accelerated schedule in accordance with the U.S. tax code. The more rapid depreciation for tax purposes results in positive cash flow in earlier years in the form of deferred taxes, which then reverses in later years.

3. Results

A. Average Investment Returns

Using the above data and assumptions, we first examine the performance of the mean NCE introduction during the 1970s. The results are presented in Table 1. A major finding is that the present value of cash flows and R&D investment are approximately the same

---

[21] Both the investment tax credit (repealed by the 1986 Tax Reform Act) and research and development tax credit (reduced by this Act) are reflected directly in the average effective tax rate of the pharmaceutical industry. A more refined analysis would investigate the effects of these factors separately rather than combining them in a net effective tax parameter. However, as shown below, the results are not highly sensitive to tax rates.

[22] Approximately two-thirds of the required capital expenditures are allocated in the two years prior to product launch. The remaining outlays are allocated between year two and ten of product life and are used for maintenance and replacement capital.

TABLE 1

Investment Performance of the Average New Product Introduction During the 1970s

Cohort[1]	Case	Present Value[2] Cash Flows	Present Value[2] R & D Costs	Year When NPV Becomes Positive
1970–79	Baseline[3]	83.5	81	23
1970–74	Baseline	49.0	72	Never
1975–79	Baseline	111.7	92	17
1970–79	Constant Margins[4]	69.8	81	Never
1970–74	Constant Margins	43.7	72	Never
1975–79	Constant Margins	91.2	92	Never

[1] There are 100 new drug introductions in the full sample (1970–79); There are 43 introductions in the 1970–74 subsample and 57 introductions in the 1975–79 subsample.

[2] Cash Flows and R & D Costs are after-tax and are expressed in millions of 1986 dollars. They are discounted at 9% from the date of marketing.

[3] Baseline parameters assume a 25 year market life, a tax rate of 35 percent, a worldwide sales multiplier of 1.9, and variable pre-tax tax margins by calendar year (see text).

[4] Margins are assumed constant at 33 percent value after 1979 (i.e. no real price increases in pharmaceuticals). All other parameters are assumed to be the same as in the baseline case.

over the 1970 to 1979 sample period. The first entry of Table 1 shows the present value of after-tax cash flows (exclusive of R&D) for the mean compound is equal to 83.5 million dollars. The second column shows that the average after-tax R&D investment for 1970s introductions, also capitalized at 9 percent, is 81 million dollars. This approximate equality between the present value of cash flows and R&D costs implies that the average new product introduction in the 1970s earned a return in the neighborhood of 9 percent, in line with the industry's cost of capital.

The results in Table 1 also indicate that the average investment for the 1970–79 period takes 23 years from the date of marketing introduction to achieve a positive net discounted present value. This is illustrated in Figure 4. The cumulative present value curve for the mean compound achieves equality with R&D investment (81 million dollars) in year 23 of market life. This is close to the assumed product life of 25 years. If new products in the future are characterized by shorter effective lifetimes (e.g., 20 years), then, ceteris paribus, the average NCE would not produce a discounted payback over its lifetime. This issue is considered further below in the sensitivity analysis.

B. *Performance in the 1970–74 Period Compared to 1975–79*

Table 1 also provides present values and discounted payback periods for the two subperiods 1970 to 1974 and 1975 to 1979. This shows that the performance of the average NCE in the first half of the 1970s was very different from the second half. In particular, the average NCE in the 1970–74 period has an estimated present value significantly below its R&D investment and experiences a loss of over 20 million dollars. At the same time, the average NCE introduction in the second half of the 1970s has an estimated present value which significantly exceeds its R&D investment and achieves a positive discounted payback by the 17th year after introduction.[23]

While the observed positive change in performance between the first and second half of the 1970s may be the result of normal statistical fluctuations, it is also consistent with

[23] We also examined the internal rate of return for these two subperiods. This analysis is subject to the qualification that there is uncertainty about the time pattern of R&D costs applicable to these sample periods. However, if one essentially utilizes a time pattern for R&D identical to Hansen's (with proprotional adjustments in annual costs), the internal rate of return is equal to 7.1 percent for the 1970–74 period, while it is 10 percent for the 1975–79 period.

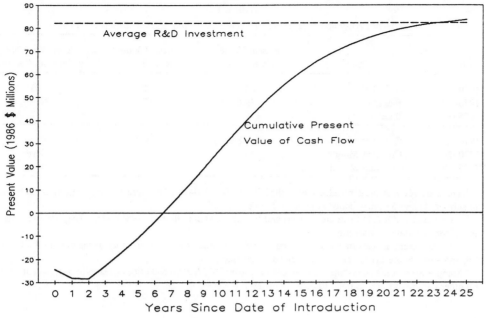

FIGURE 4. Present Value of Cash Flow vs. R&D Investment for the Mean New Product Introduction over 1970–79 Period.

the observed behavior of the pharmaceutical industry's R&D expenditures. Over the period 1977 to 1987, real R&D expenditures in pharmaceuticals have more than doubled. This is a much faster rate of growth than in the previous decade and also than for other developed countries (Grabowski 1989). The upward shift in the growth of U.S. R&D expenditures dovetails with our finding of a positive shift in returns for the average new product introduction in the latter part of the 1970s.

C. The Distribution of NCE Revenues

In Figure 5, the present value distribution of returns by deciles for NCEs introduced during the 1970 to 1979 period is presented. As this figure illustrates, this is a highly skewed distribution. The top decile has an estimated present value of 457 million dollars. This is several times the average present value of R&D costs (81 million dollars). At the same time, only the top few deciles have present values in excess of average R&D costs.[24]

The skewed distribution of returns presented in Figure 5 point up the importance of the top decile drugs to drug industry performance. This can be also illustrated by analyzing how average present values change when the top decile of compounds is excluded. This results in a decrease in the present value of the mean compound by approximately 50 percent. Indeed, if we exclude only the single largest selling compound introduced during the 1970s, Tagamet, the mean present value for the remaining 99 compounds declines from the baseline value in Table 1 by 14 percent. These computations illustrate the

---

[24] We investigated the issue of whether R&D costs were positively related to a compound's decile class. We found there was a slight positive (but statistically insignificant) relationship between a compound's decile class and its R&D costs. However, our analysis was able to formally analyze only two components of the variance in R&D costs—those associated with therapeutic class and year of introduction. It is possible that other factors contribute to a positive relationship between R&D costs and sales. This is an important issue for further research. However, it seems clear from the analysis that sales are much more skewed than R&D costs.

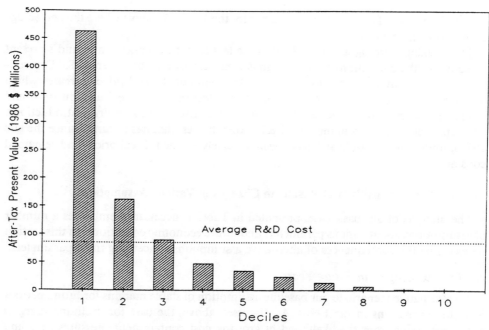

FIGURE 5. Present Values by Decile for the 1970–79 Cohort.

central importance of the top decile compounds to the economic viability of the pharmaceutical industry.[25]

The distribution of present values exhibited in Figure 5 indicate that the majority of new drug introductions in our sample have present values below average R&D costs. While many of these lower decile products will be contributors to firm profits (in the sense that incremental expected cash flows exceed incremental development and capital investment cost), a firm's fully allocated R&D costs must also be covered over the long run. In this regard, the results indicate that a firm must have an occasional "blockbuster" compound from the top deciles of the sales distribution, if it is to cover the large fixed costs which characterizes the drug development process.

D. The Effect of Changing Prices on Present Values

In this section, our analytical framework is utilized to examine how present values have been affected by the real pharmaceutical price increases that have occurred since 1980. To accomplish this objective, present values are calculated under the hypothetical assumption that contribution margins would have remained constant at their minimum value of the late 1970s. In our analysis, this is tantamount to the assumption that drug prices since 1980 rose only at the rate of inflation (i.e., no real price increases), rather than experiencing net price increases over this period.[26]

The results are reported in the lower half of Table 1. They clearly demonstrate that there is a rather dramatic effect on the computed present values. For the 1970 to 1979 sample, there is a decline of 13.7 million dollars or a 16 percentage point decline from

---

[25] It is also important to note in this regard that eight of the ten drugs which make up the top decile during the 1970s come from the 1975 to 1979 sub-period. Hence, a large factor in the observed upward shift in the economic performance of NCE introductions was the increased number of "blockbuster" products introduced in the latter part of the 1970s.

[26] In this regard, real price increases were found to explain over 87 percent of the variance in pre-tax margins over the period 1973 to 1985. See the discussion of this point in footnote 19.

the baseline value. The impact is even larger for the 1975–79 cohort where the percentage decline is over 18 percent.

These changes are significant in light of the fact that the average compound's present value under the constant margin scenario is considerably less than average R&D investment cost. The analysis therefore indicates that without the real price increases which have occurred since 1980, and holding all other factors the same, the drug industry would not have recovered total allocated costs from their portfolio of 1970s drug introductions. The rapid rate of growth in industry R&D expenditures, that has occurred since the late 1970s, undoubtedly would also have been adversely affected if real prices had remained constant.

4. Sensitivity of Results to Changes in Various Assumptions

The analysis of our basic case, presented in Table 1, necessarily embodies a number of assumptions about various parameters and future economic conditions. In this section we examine the consequences of alternative assumptions concerning these parameters.

A. *Pre-tax Margins in Future Years*

An alternative scenario to our baseline assumption of stable margins for future periods is declining margins in the 1990s. As discussed above, the case for declining margins over time stems from the likelihood of growing cost containment pressures here and abroad.[27] Under this case, margins are projected to decline, beginning in 1990, from 40 percent to a steady state value of 36 percent. The latter value is representative of the mean experience for our sample of observed values (Figure 3).

The opposite scenario, increasing contribution margins over future periods, is also examined. This could occur if U.S. drug prices in the 1990s were to outpace inflation by an amount sufficiently large enough to dominate the effect of declining real prices abroad. We view this as very unlikely for the reasons cited. Nevertheless, the case of increasing margins is considered in order to see how sensitive the results are to this scenario. Specifically, for this case, it is assumed that contribution margins will steadily rise through the early 1990s, until they reach a steady state value of 44 percent.

The results for these alternative scenarios are presented in the first two rows of Table 2. We focus on the 1970 to 1979 cohort in these sensitivity analyses. There is not a large impact on the estimated present values for either the increasing or declining margin cases. The new values are within a few percent of previous estimates. This is perhaps surprising, but it reflects the fact that the changes in assumptions about future contribution margins affect only the later years of the life cycle for our sample, and these years are also heavily discounted in economic terms. There would be much greater effects, of course, for new product introductions just beginning their market life at the present time.

B. *Greater Generic Competition and Shorter Product Life*

Our basic case embodies assumptions on sales erosion of the pioneer brands to generic competitors that are consistent with current experience. However, there appears to be a strong dynamic trend toward intensifying generic competition. The next decade is likely to witness significantly greater market penetration of generic drugs, consistent with the evolution of cost containment programs in both the public and private sectors. There is currently a strong movement toward increased generic drug usage by HMOs and other managed health care institutions.

In order to test the sensitivity of our results to the prospects of increased generic competition, a scenario was examined in which pioneer sales erode faster over time and

---

[27] Drug prices in recent years have lagged inflation for established drug therapies in all major markets outside the United States. These same cost containment pressures are likely to be increasingly felt in the U.S. market in coming periods.

TABLE 2
Sensitivity of Findings to Changes in Assumptions 1970–79 Cohort

Case-Baseline Assumptions Except:	Present Value[1] Cash Flows (% Change)	Present Value[1] R & D Costs (% Change)	Year When NPV Becomes Positive
1) Declining Margins[2] in 1990s	81.7 (−2.2)	81 (—)	25
2) Increasing Margins[3] in 1990s	85.3 (2.4)	81 (—)	22
3) Increasing Generic Use & Shorter Life	75.8 (−9.2)	81 (—)	Never
4) Case (1) and (3) combined	74.6 (−10.7)	81 (—)	Never
5) R & D Investment Increased by 20%	83.5 (—)	98 (20)	Never
6) R & D Investment Decreased by 20%	83.5 (—)	65 (−20)	16
7) 1.75 Worldwide Sales Multiplier	76.9 (−7.9)	81 (—)	Never
8) 2.05 Worldwide Sales Multiplier	90.1 (7.9)	81 (—)	19
9) 40% Tax Rate	75.7 (−9.3)	75 (−7.7)	25
10) 30% Tax Rate	91.3 (9.6)	88 (7.7)	22

[1] Percent changes are computed from the baseline cases values presented in Table 1 (1970–79 cohort).

[2] Declining margin case assumes that margins drop by one percent a year beginning in 1990 until they reach an equilibrium value of 36 percent in 1993 and then remain constant.

[3] Increasing margin case assumes that margins increase by one percent a year beginning in 1990 until they reach an equilibrium value of 44 percent in 1993 and then remain constant.

lose 80 percent of the total market to generics within six years after patent expiration. This is in contrast to the base case which assumes an equilibrium share for generics of 60 percent after five years. Under the increased generic competition scenario, we also assume a shortened product life of 20 years, reflecting the lower sales values associated with the back end of the product life cycle curve.

The results are presented in the third row of Table 2. Increased generic competition and shorter product life reduce the present value of returns in the basic cohort by approximately 9 percent. A breakeven also does not occur within the assumed commercial life for the average drug product.

The same cost containment pressures that are likely to increase generic usage will also probably operate to constrain future prices and margins in future periods. Hence it is useful to consider the case of declining margins and increased generic usage in combination. This case is considered in the fourth row of Table 2. The results show that these factors are largely additive in nature. The present value of cash flows in this case are reduced by over 10 percent below the base case and the gap between returns and R&D costs is further widened. Once again, the impact of these factors is moderated by the fact that they occur relatively late in the product life cycle here and are significantly discounted for 1970s introductions. If cost containment measures affect future introductions earlier in the life cycle, their impact will be substantially increased.

C. *R&D Investment*

The next sensitivity analysis involves R&D investment expenditures. The baseline utilized a pre-tax average R&D investment of 125 million dollars for 1970s introductions. This translates into an after tax value of 81 million dollars given the assumed 35 percent tax rate. However there is considerable variability around this average value. Our analysis of year to year fluctuations during the 1970s suggest a plus or minus 20 percent bound would be a plausible range for a sensitivity analysis on this parameter.

In Table 2, rows 5 and 6, results are presented assuming these alternative values for R&D investment. As one might expect, our findings are quite sensitive to the R&D investment variable. An increase of 20 percent in the present value of R&D outlays creates a significant shortfall between the after tax cash flows and R&D investment. The average introduction fails to achieve breakeven on a discounted payback basis. On the other hand, a decrease of 20 percent from baseline values has the opposite effect. In particular, the average introduction would then earn almost 20 million dollars and achieve breakeven discounted payback in year 16 of market life. This is 7 years sooner than in the baseline case.

These results point up the importance of upfront R&D investment to economic performance and breakeven lifetimes. Since FDA regulations and review times are one of the primary factors influencing R&D investment outlays, this also highlights the important effect that regulatory developments can have on the returns to pharmaceutical R&D. This is also a principal finding of an earlier study on breakeven lifetimes (Grabowski and Vernon 1982).[28]

D. *Foreign Sales Multiplier*

The next sensitivity analysis presented in Table 2 concerns the foreign sales multiplier. Worldwide sales were set in the baseline analysis at 1.9 times domestic sales based on an analysis of individual product as well as balance sheet data. Table 2 shows the consequences of alternatively assuming worldwide sales at 1.75 and 2.05 times U.S. sales. Present values are changed by approximately 8 percent from the baseline case values. Since these values involve the high and low ends of the spectrum, our results do not appear highly sensitive to this parameter.

E. *Effective Tax Rate*

The final two rows of Table 2 show the sensitivity of the results to alternative tax rate assumptions. A representative tax rate of 35 percent is utilized in our base case. Table 2 shows the effect of alternatively assuming tax rates of 30 and 40 percent over the full market life of each NCE introduction. The average present value of returns would be decreased by 9.3 percent if a tax rate of 40 percent is employed. At the same time, however, the present value of the mean R&D investment would decrease by a comparable amount of 7.7 percent, given that R&D costs are tax deductible. Consequently, breakeven lifetimes change only marginally from the baseline case and overall, our results are little affected by tax rates changes of this magnitude.

F. *Overview*

In general, the results in Table 2 show our findings are quite robust to changes of various parameters within a plausible range around the baseline values.[29] The most sensitive factor is R&D investment outlays. Given this result, further analyses of pharmaceutical R&D costs and how these costs have been changing over time would appear to be a high priority for future work.[30] Another factor to which returns were sensitive was

[28] In our earlier paper, we found that one year reduction in upfront regulatory review time will result in three or more years reduction in the breakeven lifetime (Grabowski and Vernon 1982).

[29] In addition to the sensitivity analyses reported in Table 2, we also considered alternative scenarios for other parameters such as the required investment in physical capital for a typical new drug. The findings of the baseline case were robust to plausible variations in this and other factors.

[30] The 125 million dollar R&D cost figure for this study is based on the mid-1970's, corresponding to our sample of the 1970's introductions. Given the continuing upward trend in real R&D costs observed here, the mean R&D cost of a new drug introduction at the present time should be substantially higher than this value. Preliminary results from a new study of R&D costs by Hansen et al. (1989) suggest this is the case.

the industry's ability to achieve price increases, especially in the first several years after product launch. This is highlighted by our findings on the effect of changes in the product margins in Table 1.

5. Summary and Conclusions

A major finding of this study is that new drug product introductions in the 1970s realized returns in line with the 9 percent industry cost of capital. Our finding in this regard represents a departure from prior work which has generally found lower returns to pharmaceutical R&D, both in absolute terms and relative to the industry's cost of capital. One explanation for this difference in findings is that our study considers a more recent sample of NCE introductions and utilizes time trends on sales and cost data through the mid 1980s.

Another important finding is that the economic performance of new drugs introduced during the latter half of the 1970s was markedly better than that of the early 1970s introductions. In this regard, eight of the ten drugs in the top decile of sales during the 1970s represented introductions which occurred after 1974. This fact suggests a possible improving situation in terms of technological opportunities in the pharmaceutical industry which become manifest in the latter half of the 1970s. This hypothesis is consistent with the behavior of industry R&D expenditures. The industry's growth in real R&D expenditures has been on the order of 10 percent since 1977, more than double the growth rate of the prior decade. Very preliminary research also suggests that the new drugs introduced during the 1980s experienced sales patterns in their early years of market life that are consistent with the strong economic performance of the late 1970s introductions.[31]

In comparison to past work, our study considers the effects of a number of significant economic changes that have occurred in the pharmaceutical industry over the past decade. Specifically, our analysis indicates that higher real drug prices in the 1980s had an especially important effect in allowing firms to cover R&D investments. A sensitivity analysis performed in the paper indicated that, if no real price increases had occurred, and drug contribution margins correspondingly remained at their minimum values of the late 1970s, the present value of returns would have been reduced by 16 percent for the average 1970s new drug introduction. Under this scenario, and holding other factors constant, the typical new drug introduction would not have been able to cover average R&D costs.

Our sensitivity analysis also considered the effects of evolving cost containment pressures in the pharmaceutical industry. These pressures are likely to result in a greater degree of generic competition, shorter product lives and lower margins than assumed in our baseline case estimates. If these factors become increasingly significant during the 1990s, they would have a negative effect on the returns earned by past introductions. This effect would be moderated by the fact that these events would affect only the later years of market life. However, these changes would have a much larger impact on future new drug candidates. A prospective analysis of the effects of evolving policy changes on future introductions is an important task for further study.

---

[31] Average sales for new drug introductions during the 1980s are generally equal to or higher than those observed at comparable points in the life cycle of 1970s introductions. At the same time, mean R&D costs would also be expected to be greater for these 1980s introductions.

References

BAILY, MARTIN N., "Research and Development Costs and Returns: The U.S. Pharmaceutical Industry," *J. Political Economy*, (January/February 1972).

BERNHEIM, R. DOUGLAS AND JOHN SHOVEN, "Comparison of the Cost of Capital in the U.S. and Japan: the Roles of Risk and Taxes," presented to a Conference of the Center for Economic Policy Research, Stanford University, September 1989.

DREXEL, BURNHAM AND LAMBERT, "Drug Industry Review," New York, December 1988.

GITMAN, LAWRENCE J. AND VINCENT A. MERCURIO, "Cost of Capital Techniques Used by Major U.S. Firms," *Financial Management*, (Winter 1982).

GRABOWSKI, HENRY, "Medicaid Patients' Access to New Drugs," *Health Affairs*, (Winter 1988).

———, "An Analysis of U.S. International Competitiveness in Pharmaceuticals," *Managerial and Decision Economics*, (Spring 1989).

——— AND JOHN VERNON, "Structural Effects of Regulation on Innovation in the Ethical Drug Industry." In *Essays on Industrial Organization in Honor of Joe S. Bain*, ed. R. T. Masson and P. Qualls (Cambridge, Mass: Ballinger, 1976).

——— AND ———, "A Sensitivity Analysis of Expected Profitability of Pharmaceutical R&D," *Managerial and Decision Economics*, (March 1982).

——— AND ———, *The Regulation of Pharmaceuticals: Balancing the Benefits and Risks*, American Enterprise Institute, Washington, D.C., 1983.

——— AND ———, "Longer Patents for Lower Imitation Barriers: The 1986 Drug Act," *Amer. Economic Rev.*, (May 1986).

——— AND ———, "The Effect of Generic Entry on Market Prices in the Pharmaceutical Industry," Duke University, June 1989.

HANSEN, RONALD W., "The Pharmaceutical Development Process: Estimates of Current Development Costs and Times and the Effects of Regulatory Changes," in *Issues in Pharmaceutical Economics*, R. I. Chien (ed.), Lexington Books, Cambridge, MA, 1979.

———, "Pharmaceutical Development Cost by Therapeutic Categories," University of Rochester Graduate School of Management Working Paper No. GPB-80-6, March 1980.

———, JOSEPH DIMASI, HENRY GRABOWSKI AND LOUIS LASAGNA, "Preliminary Findings on R&D costs per NCE Taken into Humans between 1970 and 1982," Mimeographed Tables, Center for the Study of Drug Development, 1989.

IBBOTSON ASSOCIATES, *Stocks, Bonds, Bills and Inflation: 1987 Yearbook*, Ibbotson Associates Inc., Chicago, IL, 1987.

JOGLEKAR, PRAFULLA AND MORTON PATERSON, "A Closer Look at the Returns and Risks of Pharmaceutical R&D," *J. Health Economics*, (1986).

MABON, NUGENT AND CO., "New Gatekeepers and the Slide Toward Price Competition in the Pharmaceutical Industry," New York, June 1987.

MANSFIELD, EDWIN, "Price Indexes for R and D Inputs," *Management Sci.*, 33 (January 1987).

———, ANTHONY ROMEO AND LORNA SWITZER, "R&D Price Indexes and Real R&D Expenditures in the United States," *Research Policy*, (April 1983).

MATTISON, NANCY, A. GENE TRIMBLE AND LOUIS LASAGNA, "New Drug Development in the United States, 1963 through 1984," *Clinical Pharmacology and Therapeutics*, (March 1988).

OECD, "La Santé, Financement et Prestations," Paris, 1987.

PMA, *Statistical Fact Book*, Pharmaceutical Manufacturers Association, Washington, D.C., 1988.

REEKIE, W. DUNCAN, "Price and Quality Competition in the United States Drug Industry," *J. Industrial Economics*, (March 1979).

SCHERER, F. M., "Inflation, Capital Budgeting and the Long View," Unpublished manuscript, 1983.

SCHWARTZMAN, DAVID, "Pharmaceutical R&D Expenditures and Rates of Return," in *Drug Development and Marketing*, R. B. Helms (ed.), American Enterprise Institute, Washington, D.C., 1975.

STATMAN, MEIR, *Competition in the Pharmaceutical Industry: The Declining Profitability of Drug Innovation*, American Enterprise Institute, Washington, D.C., 1983.

———, "The Effect of Patent Expiration on the Market Position of Drugs," in Robert Helms (Ed.), *Drugs and Health*, American Enterprise Institute, Washington D.C., 1981.

STAUFFER, THOMAS, "Profitability Measures in the Pharmaceutical Industry" in Robert Helms (ed.), *Drug Development and Marketing*, American Enterprise Institute, Washington, D.C., 1975.

THOMAS, CELIA, "The Return To Research and Development in the Pharmaceutical Industry," Unpublished Ph.D Dissertation, Duke University, 1981.

THOMAS, LACY GLENN, "Regulation and Firm Size: FDA Impacts on Innovation," Columbia University Graduate School of Business, First Boston Working Paper Series, FB-87-24, September 1987.

U.S. Congress, House, Subcommittee on Health and the Environment of the Committee on Energy and Commerce, *Prescription Drug Price Increases*, 99th Congress, First Session, July 15, 1985.

U.S. Congress, House, Subcommittee on Health and the Environment of the Committee on Energy and Congress, *Medical Devices and Drug Issues*, 100th Congress, First Session, April 21, 1987 and May 4, 1987.

WIGGINS, STEVEN, *The Cost of Developing a New Drug*, Pharmaceutical Manufacturers Association, Washington, D.C., June 1987.

Article 30

Benefit-Cost Analysis of the Perry Preschool Program and Its Policy Implications

W. Steven Barnett
Utah State University

Benefit-cost analysis is applied to the Perry Preschool Program and its long-term follow-up in order to examine preschool education as a social investment. Economic values are estimated for program cost, child care provided, later education cost reductions, increased higher education cost, delinquency and crime cost reductions, earnings increases, and welfare cost reductions. The net present value of benefits and costs is positive, indicating that the program was a profitable social investment. Analysis of the distribution of effects revealed that taxpayers obtained most of the economic benefits and that their benefits exceeded costs. Generalizability of the findings and their implications for public policy are examined.

The purpose of this paper is to present a benefit-cost analysis of the Perry Preschool Program and its long-term effects, and to examine the analysis as a basis for U.S. public policy decisions regarding the provision of early childhood education. Research on the Perry Preschool Program has been conducted since 1962, and its very positive findings have been widely reported. This research constitutes one of the strongest and best known sources of support for the long-term efficacy of early intervention with disadvantaged children. Benefit-cost analysis uses the theories and methods of economics to explore the implications of the Perry Preschool findings for society as a whole. Such analyses are relatively rare and unfamiliar in early intervention research. Thus, we have attempted to provide a report that is accessible to early intervention researchers and yet meets generally accepted standards for benefit-cost analysis.

Background

The Perry Preschool Project is a study conducted in Ypsilanti, Michigan, with children born between 1958 and 1962. The study's participants were 123 three- and four-year-old black children with no discernible physical handicaps. Participants were selected on the basis of low parental educational attainment and socioeconomic status, and the participants' low IQ test scores (61–88 on the Stanford-Binet). Participants were assigned either to an experimental group that received the preschool program or to a control group that did not. This assignment was performed in such a way that these groups can be treated as independent samples

Preparation of this manuscript was supported by funds from the U.S. Department of Education (Contract No. 300-82-0367) to the Early Intervention Research Institute at Utah State University.

The author is grateful to John Berrueta-Clement, Ellen Frede, and Gerald Musgrave for their comments on this manuscript. Many people have contributed to the Perry Preschool Study over the past 20 years, none more important than David Weikart, whose commitment and guidance have been responsible for its continuing success.

drawn from the same population. Thus, differences between the experimental and control group can safely be attributed to the preschool program and are not attributable to initial differences between the two groups.

The 123 children entered the study in five waves. The first two waves began in 1962, one wave at age 4 and the other at age 3. The remaining waves entered at age 3, one wave in each of the following three years. The number of experimental and control participants in each wave is shown in Table I.

The 13 experimental group participants in Wave Zero received only one year of the preschool program at age 4. The remaining 45 experimental group participants received two years of the program, one at age 3 and one at age 4. Thus, the study provides some information about the costs and benefits of one year of preschool as opposed to two years, but based on a very small sample for one year.

In this paper, the benefits of preschool are compared to both the cost of one year and the cost of two years of preschool. It is important to note that the benefits for both comparisons are estimated based on the entire sample because the sample size for Wave Zero is too small to provide meaningful estimates by itself, and we cannot statistically differentiate the effects of one year of preschool from the effects of two years. The only substantial difference in the comparison of one and two years is the cost difference, which is estimated based on the actual costs of one year for all waves and of two years for Waves One through Four.

The preschool program provided to the experimental group was operated for a relatively short school year (October through May) and had three elements. One element was a center-based program for 2½ hours each morning 5 days a week. The curriculum gradually evolved from a fairly traditional nursery school approach to a more cognitively oriented Piagetian approach. The child-teacher ratio was relatively low, about 5:1. The teachers were trained in both special education and early childhood and were relatively well paid. Another element of the program was home visiting. The teachers were to visit each child's home once a week in the afternoon for 1½ hours. The final element was group meetings of parents. Actual attendance by the children and participation in home visits and group meetings by the parents varied considerably within the experimental group. More detailed descriptions of the program and curriculum are provided in Weikart (1967) and Weikart, Bond, and McNeil (1978).

The Perry Project collected data on both the experimental and control groups during the years of the preschool program, through their early elementary school years, at age 15, and most recently at age 19. Analysis of these data shows that the preschool program had a variety of significant positive effects on the lives of the experimental group. These positive effects are the basis for estimating economic benefits. They have been reported in great detail elsewhere (Berrueta-Clement, Schweinhart, Barnett, Epstein, & Weikart, 1984). Some of the most important findings, including those that are crucial to the benefit-cost analysis, are presented in Table II.

Method

From the perspective of economics, the Perry Preschool Program was an invest-

TABLE I
Number of Participants in the Perry Preschool Project

Wave	Entry year	Number of experimentals	Number of controls	Total
Zero	1962	13	15	28
One	1962	8	9	17
Two	1963	12	14	26
Three	1964	13	14	27
Four	1965	12	13	25
Total		58	65	123

TABLE II

Findings of the Perry Preschool Project

Category	Experimental	Control	p	N
Early childhood: IQ at age 5	95	83	<.01	93
Late childhood				
School years in special education	16%	28%	.04	112
Ever classified mentally retarded	15%	35%	.01	112
Adolescence/early adulthood				
Age 15 mean achievement test score	122.2	94.5	<.01	95
High school graduation	67%	49%	.03	121
Post-secondary education	38%	21%	.03	121
Arrested or detained	31%	51%	.02	121
Employed at age 19	50%	32%	.03	121
Receiving welfare at age 19	18%	32%	.04	121

ment by the larger society in the lives of children whose chances for educational success, and thus for economic success, were relatively poor. Benefit-cost analysis is a tool for evaluating the profitability and fairness of this preschool investment and its long-term effects from the perspective of society as a whole. Profitability can be completely assessed in a benefit-cost analysis. In the case of fairness, benefit-cost analysis merely provides the informational basis for ethical judgments. A brief introduction to benefit-cost analysis, and the specific approach taken in this work, is provided in the full report (Barnett, 1985).

In the benefit-cost analysis summarized here, profitability is evaluated based on net discounted present value, and distributional consequences are considered for two groups. One group is participants and their families; the other is "taxpayers," an abstract representation of those who paid for the preschool program. The participants were from low-income families, were black, and had relatively poor educational prognoses at an early age. A program that aids people in these circumstances may decrease inequality in the national distribution of income and in the national distribution of educational experiences and outcomes. Taxpayers paid most of the direct costs of the preschool program, and fairness to them can be assessed in the benefits preschool yields to taxpayers. In addition, as a practical matter, the benefits and costs to taxpayers affect the chances that a program will be adopted as a public policy.

Findings

The benefit-cost analysis enabled an estimate to be made of the economic value of significant program effects (based on group differences) in seven categories: (a) immediate program costs, (b) child care, (c) elementary and secondary education, (d) higher education, (e) delinquency and crime, (f) earnings and employment, and (g) welfare. Best estimates of costs or benefits are presented for each category, and some of the more important limitations of these estimates are indicated. Details of estimation and explorations of the alternative assumptions are presented in the full report (Barnett, 1985). Each category is considered in a separate section below. For comparability, all money estimates are presented in undiscounted 1981 dollars. The "Conclusions" section brings together all of the estimated costs and benefits to present an overall view of profitability and fairness using a range of discount rates.

Program Cost

The Perry Preschool Program's estimated average cost per child was $4,963 for one year and $9,708 for two years. These cost estimates are based on detailed data for the program and the school district in which it operated. Cost includes both operating and capital costs. The Perry Preschool Program's cost is not unusually high when compared to typical public school preschool programs for mildly handicapped children (Kakalik, Furry, Thomas, & Carney, 1981). However, it is higher than the costs of many preschool programs currently operating. This is because of the Perry Program's relatively low child-teacher ratio, which ranged from 4:1 to 6.5:1.

Child Care

The Perry Program provided child care to the families of the children enrolled, and this child care had economic value apart from any long-term benefits to the children. The child care allowed parents to pursue other activities and provided an enjoyable and enriching experience for the children. Based on national survey data regarding parents' payments for day-care, the value of child care was estimated to be $300 per child for one school year. This estimate will seem low to many, but it should be remembered that it represents the value to low-income parents of the "custodial" aspect of the program alone and that the program was only part of a day. The $300 figure probably is best considered a lower bound estimate of the program's immediate benefits.

Elementary and Secondary Education

The preschool program had several important effects on the elementary and secondary education of the participants. They were more successful and more committed to schooling. This produced economic benefits for both the participants and the schools that they attended. For participants, we were able to estimate only the resulting earnings benefits (discussed in a later section), and not the value they placed on greater success in their school years per se. The benefits estimated are the cost reductions that resulted because those who attended preschool were less expensive to educate.

The effect of the Perry Program on educational cost was estimated from cost histories constructed for each study participant based on type of educational services received in each year. Data were sufficient to construct histories for 112 participants. Major influences on cost were remedial and special educational placement and number of years of schooling. Overall, preschool reduced total elementary and secondary school costs by an estimated $7,082 per child. This estimate, however, combines two opposing effects. On the one hand, former preschool stu-

dents required less costly placements, which tended to lower total cost. On the other hand, former preschool students had higher educational attainment, which tended to increase total cost. Viewing education as a production process, we would say that preschool produced both cost reductions and output increases. One way to isolate the effect on cost is to look at the cost per unit of output. The estimated reduction in cost per year of educational attainment was $800 per child. This effect on unit cost is roughly 20% greater than the effect on total cost.

Higher Education

Former preschool students had obtained signficantly more higher education by age 19. Some of this education was vocational and some academic. Only the costs for college attendance could be estimated from the available data, however. (Consistent with this, only college attendance was used in estimating future earnings.) The Perry Program was estimated to increase expenditures for higher education by $1,168 per child.

Delinquency and Crime

Juvenile delinquency and adult crime were significantly reduced as a result of the preschool program. This was evinced in both self-report and official police and court records of the study participants. Financial data for the criminal justice system, estimates of the costs of crimes to victims, and official records of the study participants' involvement with the law through age 20 were used to estimate the economic value of this effect through age 20. National data on the patterns of arrests by age were used to project this estimate beyond age 20. The estimated reduction in cost of crime and delinquency was $1,574 per child through age 20 and $5,320 per child over the participants' remaining lifetimes. While these estimates are the best that could be produced, we are concerned that they fail to account for most of the human costs of crime. Our estimates neglect the pain and suffering of victims, the fears and curtailed activities of potential victims, and even the costs of locks, alarms, and private security forces.

Earnings and Employment

Differences in annual earnings account for most of the financial implications of preschool's effects on earnings and employment. Estimates of earnings through age 19 are based on interviews with participants. Estimates of earnings beyond age 19 are based on national cross-sectional data and study participants' educational attainment at age 19. We have more confidence in the pre-19 estimates, but the estimation procedure for lifetime earnings beyond age 19 is quite defensible and rests on assumptions that seem likely to yield lower bound estimates of the effects of preschool (Barnett, 1985).

Median earnings of those who had attended preschool were $1,702 higher at age 19. Earnings at earlier ages did not significantly differ between preschool and no-preschool groups. This suggests that if any earnings were forgone by the preschool group because of their greater commitment to schooling, they were simultaneously offset by earnings increases associated with greater ability, commitment to schooling, or a related variable.

The estimated effect of the Perry Program on lifetime earnings beyond age 19 was $59,871 per person. In addition, it was judged important to estimate the effect on fringe benefits and nonpecuniary benefits provided by formal employment beyond the teenage years. The effect on fringes and nonpecuniary benefits was estimated to be 30% of the effect on earnings (Duncan, 1976). The effect on nonpecuniary benefits is more than mere conjecture; at age 19 the preschool group scored higher on a job-satisfaction scale than did the no-preschool group.

Welfare

Data were more limited for welfare assistance than for any other area of estimation. In part, this was because the participants' adult welfare histories were necessarily short at age 19. Thus, while the Perry Program's effect on welfare at age 19 is based on self-report and we consider it to be relatively reliable, it provides a narrow base for projecting lifetime reductions. Moreover, although the literature leads us to expect substantial long-term decreases in welfare assistance (based on the other effects observed by age 19), it gives little specific guidance for extrapolation beyond age 19 (Bane & Ellwood, 1983a, 1983b; Coe, 1981; Plotnick, 1983). Faced with this situation, we explored a range of simple extrapolations and incorporated the most theoretically plausible into the analysis.

The estimated effect on annual welfare assistance payments at age 19 was $820 per person. The estimated effect on lifetime payments beyond age 19 was $31,430 per person. The benefit to society as a whole is equal to only a small fraction of the reduction in payments, however, because welfare primarily shifts income among people. Only the administrative costs of welfare are a net cost from a national perspective. Based on budget data from federal welfare programs, we estimate that average administrative costs equal approximately 10% of payments. Thus, the estimated benefits to society from welfare assistance reductions were about $82 per person at age 19 and $3,143 beyond age 19.

Omitted Benefits

Three general types of omissions should be taken into account in the final assessment of the program's profitability. One is peer effects that have not been measured because benefits are estimated from the differences between control and experimental groups. For example, other students may learn more because their classmates are more competent. The increased productivity of the experimental group may have increased the quality of life and productivity of their associates generally.

Another type of omission is long-term benefits that we have been unable to measure or to value monetarily, but that are associated with higher educational attainment. These include better health and improvements in the quality of household management, parenting, marital success, and other non-labormarket activities (Haveman & Wolfe, 1984). Fertility is one important family-life variable associated with education that was measured. Women in the preschool group had only half as many children by age 19. This suggests a reduction in the medical costs and risks to infants associated with teenage births. There are also benefits to the family from improved timing and spacing of births, including higher family income per capita in the early years of family formation.

Finally, throughout this analysis we have ignored the issue of excess burden attributable to taxes that support government expenditures, including transfer payments. Its magnitude and importance relative to inefficiencies in the private sector is a matter of considerable debate in which we do not wish to become embroiled. Instead, we simply note that, because the Perry Program produced a net decrease in government spending, the omission of excess burden tends to underestimate the program's benefits.

Conclusions

This section brings together the estimated costs and benefits to assess the profitability (net present value) and distributional consequences of the Perry Preschool Program. All costs and benefits have been discounted at a real rate of 5%. In the detailed report (Barnett, 1985), a range of discount rates was considered, but for brevity this paper is limited to one intermediate rate. Table III presents the results in two sections so that estimates that depend only on observed effects through age 19 can be examined separately from those requiring projections. The results are presented for society as a whole and distributed between participants and taxpayers.

Profitability

From the "To society" column in Table III it can be seen that estimated benefits through age 19 alone exceeded the cost of one year of the Perry Program, but not the cost of two years. When benefits projected beyond age 19 are added, benefits exceed even the costs of two years by a considerable margin. Thus, our best estimates yield a substantial positive net present value, indicating that the Perry Program was a highly profitable social investment.

The degree of confidence that should be placed in this conclusion depends on the precision of our estimates and on their robustness with respect to changes in basic assumptions. Standard errors were estimated for benefits through age 19. The results are presented in Table IV. Benefits are significantly different from zero at the .10 level of confidence. However, even one year's costs falls within a one standard error confidence interval. Thus, confidence in the program's profitability must depend on the addition of some benefits beyond age 19. Although there are no estimated confidence intervals for post-19 projections, confidence can be judged in other ways. The vast majority of post-19 benefits are earnings, the variable with the strongest methodology for projection. When pre- and post-19 benefit estimates are combined, even a 50% reduction in all benefits leaves benefits exceeding two years' costs.

The effects of alternative analytical assumptions were considered at length in the full report. The assumption with the greatest impact was the discount rate chosen. Real rates as high as 7% are plausible, and detailed analyses were conducted using rates of 3%, 5%, and 7%. Within this range the findings regarding profitability did not vary. In order to test the strength of the findings, even higher real discount rates were considered. The estimated benefits of the program were found to exceed one year's cost at rates up to 11% and to exceed two years' cost at rates as high as 8%.

Distribution

Returning to Table III, it can be seen that taxpayers received most of the net benefits from the program. The discounted benefits to taxpayers more than offset the costs of one or two years of the program, although recouping costs for two years required benefits beyond age 19. It is also apparent that the returns to participants and their families were insufficient to have made the program profitable for them if it had not been publicly funded. In this case, the only way for both groups to profit from the program was to have taxpayers pay for it.

The distributional findings are less robust than those regarding overall social profitability. Projected welfare payments play a much larger role, and we consider their projection to be the least reliable of our estimates. Nevertheless, the overwhelming majority of benefits through

TABLE III
Estimated Net Benefits Per Child[a]

Category	To society Preschool attendance 1 year	To society Preschool attendance 2 years	To participants Preschool attendance 1 year	To participants Preschool attendance 2 years	To taxpayers and potential crime victims Preschool attendance 1 year	To taxpayers and potential crime victims Preschool attendance 2 years
Preschool program	−4,726	−9,027	0	0	−4,726	−9,027
Child care	284	555	284	555	0	0
School cost savings	4,148	3,950	0	0	4,148	3,950
Crime reduction	950	905	0	0	950	905
Earnings increase	469	446	352	335	117	111
Welfare reduction	38	36	−376	−358	414	394
Benefits to age 19	1,163	−3,135	260	532	903	−3,778
College costs[b]	−502	−483	0	0	−502	−483
Crime reduction	1,131	1,077	0	0	1,131	1,077
Earnings increase	11,755	11,194	9,495	9,041	2,260	2,153
Welfare reduction	810	772	−8,104	−7,718	8,914	8,490
Benefits beyond age 19	13,194	12,560	1,391	1,323	11,803	11,237
Total net benefits	14,357	9,425	1,651	1,855	12,706	7,459

[a] Present value discounted at a 5% real rate. All figures adjusted for inflation to 1981 dollars.
[b] All attended state institutions and most of the cost was borne by the public. Except for "forgone earnings," which are accounted for in the "Earnings increase" category, we were unable to estimate costs to the students.

TABLE IV
Estimated Benefits to Society Through Age 19 ($)[a]

1-Year preschool[b] Estimate	1-Year preschool[b] Standard error	2-Year preschool[b] Estimate	2-Year preschool[b] Standard error
5,525	3,200	4,987	2,936

[a] Benefit estimates differ slightly from those in Table III because estimates in Table III are based on all cases for each benefit category, whereas estimates in Table IV are based on only the 109 cases with complete data for all benefit categories.
[b] Present values discounted at 5%, adjusted to 1981 dollars.

age 19 accrue to taxpayers, and pre-19 benefits to taxpayers are estimated to exceed the cost of one year of the program. Interestingly, as higher discount rates are employed in the analysis, the proportion of discounted benefits received becomes even more favorable to taxpayers because they receive relatively more of their benefits in earlier years.

Policy Implications

We emphatically conclude that the Perry Program was a good investment for society at the cost of one year and that there is relatively strong evidence that it was a good investment at the cost of two

years. The difference in cost between one and two years is the most crucial factor in assessing the potential payoff to the program. We found no significant differences in long-term effects between one and two years. However, the Perry study's relatively small sample provides little precision when estimating the effects of one and two years separately. In our analysis, all benefits except child care were estimated based on average effects for one and two years. Given the importance of duration for costs, it should be a primary subject of future research on early childhood programs.

For our conclusions regarding the Perry

Program to have significant implications for public policy, they must be generalizable. Three domains of generalizability are important: the program, the population, and the context. Each of these three domains is discussed below.

The characteristics that are required for a preschool program to yield long-term effects similar to those of the Perry Program have not yet been precisely defined. Lawrence Schweinhart and David Weikart addressed this issue in the report of the Perry study's findings at age 19 (Berrueta-Clement et al., 1984, chap. 7). From a review of the literature, they concluded that, *within limits*, program duration, parent involvement, type of curriculum, and teacher-child ratio were unrelated to program effectiveness. They went on to speculate that the key to preschool's long-term effectiveness is style of program operation, which suggests that program management and direction may be the most important factor in effectiveness. Presently, there is little evidence to support this speculation. However, the suggestion that researchers and program providers take a holistic view rather than focus on program components individually has merit, and it might prove fruitful to develop a definition of style of operation that has the precision needed to formulate a testable hypothesis.

Another attempt to address the issue of the relation of program characteristics to long-term effectiveness is the meta-analysis of existing literature being conducted by the Early Intervention Research Institute at Utah State University. Early findings from this study (Casto, White, & Taylor, 1983) indicated that a range of different types of preschool programs have substantive short-term effects on disadvantaged children. However, they found little evidence regarding either long-term effectiveness or the effects of variations in program characteristics generally believed to be important determinants of program outcomes.

A special concern for program generalizability arises because, as an experiment, the Perry Program had some characteristics that are not likely to be replicated in preschool programs generally. Just being part of an experiment can stimulate and motivate staff and requires that programs be exceptionally well planned, monitored, and managed. The Perry research staff worked with the program staff in analyzing and developing the program, and research staff offered consulting services on all aspects of the program. Weekly seminars with visiting experts were held for the entire preschool staff (Weikart, 1967). The effects and costs of these experiment-related activities are unknown, but we cannot rule out their potential importance.

The issue of the populations for which preschool programs are likely to be effective is also a difficult one. The participants in the Perry study were black, had low IQ scores as preschoolers, and had parents with relatively low educational attainment and income. The literature indicates that preschool intervention's effectiveness generalizes to other children of low-income families and to handicapped children, although there are few studies of severely handicapped children. There is a substantial overlap between low-income and mildly handicapped populations. Existing research does not preclude the possibility that there are significant benefits to all children. It is plausible, however, that the use of screening criteria, such as IQ and income, may increase program effectiveness. Note that the literature provides information mostly about short-term effectiveness, and that there there is very little information regarding the kinds of long-term effects measured in the Perry study, especially for handicapped children.

We now turn to the issue of context. The Perry study began in 1962. Much in society has changed since then, and this has altered the system in which preschool functions. In our opinion, the structure of school and society has not changed sufficiently to threaten the generalizability of the Perry study's conclusions. Despite economic progress, the Civil Rights movement, and PL 94-142 (Education of All Handicapped Children Act), minority and poor children still have relatively poor educational prognoses and a high probability of special education placement. More children are living in poverty, in single parent families, and with working mothers. Finally, it should be considered that other studies have found preschool programs to be effective in both more and less urban settings and in the southern as well as northern United States.

The conclusion that preschool programs are likely to be a good investment for some children, and may be a good investment for all children, is not sufficient reason to urge *public funding* of preschool on economic grounds. The rationale for public funding is found in our analysis of the distribution of costs and benefits. The Perry Program was estimated to yield the vast majority of its economic benefits to taxpayers, especially in the early years. Participants and their families also gain, but only if they do not have to bear the preschool program's cost. If taxpayers are to obtain the benefits, they will have to bear the costs.

In generalizing from the Perry study, the case for public funding is strongest for disadvantaged children who can be expected to have the same kinds of social experiences as the Perry participants. It is also potentially strong for handicapped children because of the high costs of their special education programs. The economic rationale does not readily generalize to public funding for universal preschool programs, however. Even if preschool programs produced strong cognitive and other gains for higher income nonhandicapped children, these children are unlikely to impose the kinds of high costs on taxpayers that were reduced by the Perry Program. Most benefits would accrue to higher-income participants themselves. Thus, the case for public funding of preschool programs for all children must be made on other grounds.

There is a great need for replication of the Perry study. for well-designed research studies that focus on long-term effects of preschool with "real life" importance, and for studies that explore the relationships between preschool program characteristics and effectiveness. Based on their meta-analysis, White and Casto (in press) concluded that the Perry study "stands out in stark contrast to the trend . . . for effects to wash out over time." Most other studies found little evidence of long-term effects. As they point out, the greatest concern is that there are few studies on which to base such conclusions. Even fewer studies have truly strong designs for drawing valid conclusions about long-term effectiveness.

The need for further research does not lessen the need for action. Society must weigh the likely costs of delay against the potential benefits from awaiting further information. In our opinion, we have shown that the social costs of delay are likely to be quite high. In proceeding, the safest course would be to provide programs that do not vary in the extreme from the Perry Program and others that have evidenced effectiveness. Despite the lack of evidence that these programs' characteristics are necessary for success, they are likely to be sufficient. If society implements only programs that have 1:20 teacher-child ratios, little organization, and a lack of training, it may not learn much about program effectiveness. As a guide, the National Academy of Early Childhood Programs (1984) has established standards regarding characteristics generally believed to be related to effectiveness.

Finally, when public preschool programs are provided, they should be accompanied by careful evaluation. Otherwise, it will not be possible to determine whether they are producing the predicted long-term effects. Program provision and evaluation should both be planned with a willingness to experiment that is based on our acknowledged ignorance about the relation of program characteristics to effectiveness. If research and practice are not combined in these ways, we will learn little about best practices and the costs and benefits of preschool programs. The stakes are too high to continue to rely on the Perry study alone.

References

BANE, M. J., & ELLWOOD, D. (1983a). *Slipping into and out of poverty: The dynamics of spells* (Working Paper No. 1199). Cambridge. MA: National Bureau of Economic Research.

BANE, M. J., & ELLWOOD, D. (1983b). *The dynamics of dependence: The routes to self-sufficiency* (Final report to the Assistant Secretary for Planning and Evaluation, Department of Health and Human Services) (mimeographed). Cambridge. MA: Harvard University.

BARNETT, W. S. (1985). The Perry Preschool Program and its long-term effects: A benefit-cost analysis. Ypsilanti, MI: High/Scope Press.

BERRUETA-CLEMENT, J. R., SCHWEINHART. L. J.. BARNETT. W. S.. EPSTEIN, A. S., & WEIKART. D. P.

(1984). Changed lives: The effects of the Perry Preschool program through age 19. *Monographs of the High/Scope Educational Research Foundation, 8.*

CASTO, G., WHITE, K. R., & TAYLOR, C. (1983). *Final report 1982–83 workscope.* Logan: Utah State University, Early Intervention Research Institute.

COE, R. D. (1981). A preliminary empirical investigation of the dynamics of welfare use. In M. S Hill, D. H. Hill, & J. N. Morgan (Eds.), *Five thousand American families—Patterns of economic progress: Vol. 9. Analyses of the first twelve years of the panel study of income dynamics.* Ann Arbor: University of Michigan, Institute for Social Research.

DUNCAN, G. J. (1976). Earnings functions and nonpecuniary benefits. *Journal of Human Resources, 11(4),* 462–483.

HAVEMAN, R., & WOLFE, B. (1984). Schooling and economic well-being: The role of non-market effects. *Journal of Human Resources, 19(3),* 377–407.

KAKALIK, J. S., FURRY, W. S., THOMAS, M. A., & CORNEY, M. F. (1981). *The cost of special education* (Report No. N-1792-ED). Santa Monica, CA: The Rand Corporation.

National Academy of Early Childhood Programs (1984). *Accreditation criteria and procedures.* Washington, DC: National Association for the Education of Young Children.

PLOTNICK, R. (1983). Turnover in the AFDC population: An event history analysis. *Journal of Human Resources, 18(1),* 65–81.

WEIKART, D. P. (ED.). (1967). *Preschool intervention: Preliminary results of the Perry Preschool Project.* Ann Arbor, MI: Campus Publishers.

WEIKART, D. P., BOND, J. T., & McNEIL, J. T. (1978). The Ypsilanti Perry Preschool Project: Preschool years and longitudinal results through fourth grade. *Monographs of the High/Scope Educational Research Foundation, 3.*

WHITE, K. R., & CASTO, G. (in press). An integrative review of early intervention efficacy studies with at-risk children: Implications for the handicapped. *Analysis and Intervention in Developmental Disabilities.*

Author

W. STEVEN BARNETT, Research Associate, Early Intervention Research Institute, Utah State University, Logan, UT 84322. *Specializations:* Policy analysis, economics of education, early childhood education.

Article 31

"Just Say No?" The Economic and Political Realities of a Small City's Investment in Minor League Baseball

Mark S. Rosentraub
David Swindell
Indiana University

Mark S. Rosentraub is Professor and Associate Dean in the School of Public and Environmental Affairs, Indiana University. His research interests include urban development and policy, urban service delivery and financing, and health services delivery. His research has appeared in Urban Affairs Quarterly, Journal of Urban Affairs, Nonprofit Sector Quarterly, Public Productivity Review, Policy Studies Review, *and numerous other journals and collections. Currently, he is working on an analysis of the impact of older populations on local budgets.*

David Swindell is a doctoral student in the School of Public and Environmental Affairs. His areas of interest include public management, research methodology and statistics, and urban affairs. He has recently completed a needs assessment of elders in Indiana.

The magical aura which encases sports in our society continues to encourage cities to offer inducements to attract franchises. Now, even minor league franchises have become coveted assets by smaller cities seeking the same "glamour" that major league teams give larger cities. Smaller cities are seemingly mesmerized by the idea, "build it and they will come." The "they" is the anticipated economic impact and benefits of the team. This article analyzed one city's decision by measuring the substitution effects and real growth impact of a team on the local economy. Given the tax structure in the community and the marginal impact of the team, the city and the private sector made the correct decision in not offering substantial inducements; net gains were too small for all concerned. The small impact also suggests no natural constituency existed to support the needed investments. Finally, some have argued economic analyses are not the most important element in considering whether or not to invest in sports since baseball is a form of escapism and publicity. If these are valued ideas it remains for city councils and voters to decide if the "Boys of Summer" really define a community's image, culture, placement in the fabric of American society, and the quality of life. Or, is a minor league baseball team simply an example of "big boys wanting big toys" at someone else's expense.

The magical aura which encases sports in our society continues, virtually unaffected by challenges to its image. At the collegiate level, the popularity of sports was unscathed even by detailed reports of the litany of criminal actions involving football athletes at several universities. Further, the possible participation of members of a major university's board of trustees in the channeling of payments to football athletes also had no appreciable impact on the popularity of college football. At the professional level, the blatant shopping of the football Raiders to several cities in California brought little criticism of the management of professional sports.[1] Indeed, at the same time the ownership of the Los Angeles Raiders sought the best deal for their team, the National Football League was able to negotiate its most lucrative media package with the three major television networks and two cable television networks. Baseball, too, was able to negotiate its best-ever media contract and seems to have been unaffected by its recent labor problems. Professional leagues are not the only entities enjoying favored treatment from fans, the media, and society. Individual college teams now find themselves able to sign lucrative local, regional, and national broadcast

AUTHORS' NOTE: An earlier version of this article was presented at the 20th annual meeting of the Urban Affairs Association, April 18-21, 1990, Charlotte, North Carolina.

contracts. With a regularity that seems to be annualized, the inducements given teams to relocate, and the amount of money paid to teams for media rights, continue to escalate.

With professional and collegiate sports enjoying this unprecedented level of attention from our larger metropolitan cities, the media, and society in general, it comes as no surprise that minor league sports franchises have become coveted assets by smaller cities. Minor league teams offer to smaller cities much of the same "glamour" that major league (or professional) teams appear to give larger cities. The presence of a minor league team gives a smaller city a stake in the "Sports World."[2] Cities and society have become convinced that sports teams help define a community's image.[3] If a city is home to a team, then it is a major player in the sports world and part of the larger fabric of American society. The absence of a team means one is not part of this very important dimension of life in America.[4] Minor league baseball, and baseball in smaller communities, has been further lionized by the recent movie sensations *Bull Durham* and *Field of Dreams*. From all vantage points, then, smaller cities are seemingly mesmerized by the idea, "build it and they will come." In this instance, the "they" are fans, businesses, major league glamour, and economic development.

There are other reasons smaller cities seek minor league teams. Civic and local fan support for a minor league team can also be used as evidence of a community's potential commitment to support a major league team. The city of Buffalo's strategy to convince Major League Baseball of its willingness to support a team has included building a new facility for its minor league team (which could be expanded for a major league team) which helped attract more than 1,000,000 fans each season. Lastly, of course, the justification for bringing any team to a city, including a minor league team to a smaller city, is the anticipated economic impact and benefits of the team. Sports, after all, means money for cities, and minor league sports means money and benefits for smaller cities. Or does it?

In 1989, a group of investors from the city of Fort Wayne, Indiana, bought the Class A minor league team, the Wausau (Wisconsin) Timbers. The objective of the investors was to relocate the team to Fort Wayne. However, to bring the team to Fort Wayne, the investors needed a place for the team to play, and they wanted the city or the community to help pay for the stadium. Asking communities to build playing facilities, and then making them available to teams on extremely favorable terms, is a virtual requirement for participation in the sports world. Since the movement of the Brooklyn Dodgers to Los Angeles, the New York (baseball) Giants to San Francisco, and the Milwaukee Braves to Atlanta, extremely attractive rental agreements for the use of playing facilities are the accepted initiation point for attracting and retaining a team.[5] From this perspective, it could have been expected that the new owners would ask the city of Fort Wayne to assist in the development of a playing facility. Indeed, if the supposition were true that the city of Fort Wayne would earn money because of the location of the team, then one could argue with sound logic that the city's expenditures for a playing facility would represent a valid and wise investment.

The basic issue for the city of Fort Wayne, and community groups in that area, in considering whether or not to invest in an appropriate playing facility, and the question addressed here is, "would the city of Fort Wayne or the Fort Wayne economy benefit from the relocation of the Timbers to the city?" When the Fort Wayne owners acquired the Timbers, the city did not have a facility for a minor league team. To construct a new stadium appeared to be a long-term solution; however, the owners wanted to move the team to Fort Wayne within 15 months. To meet this objective, the owners and the city looked at renovations to an existing city park and stadium used for community leagues.

This facility was located in the midst of Fort Wayne's busiest retail/commercial area, 1.5 miles east of Indiana's largest enclosed mall (approximately 130 stores) and 2.5 miles south of Indiana's largest outdoor mall (approximately 75 stores). In addition, the facility was across from the regional campus of Indiana University and Purdue University (enrollment 10,000) and adjacent to the county's Coliseum (home of a minor league hockey team) and convention center. Although this location would afford the stadium the parking necessary for fans' cars, traffic control and congestion was already a major concern to the city and the business community.

Plans were developed to renovate the existing facility and the total cost of the project was estimated to be $1,950,201. After considerable discussions, the city of Fort Wayne offered to give the Timbers owners a 15-year loan for $1,200,000 (at 6.48%). The team, however, would be responsible for repaying the loan, and providing the additional $750,201 needed for reconstruction. The team would pay no rent for use of the facility, and the city would assume responsibility for maintaining the stadium. In reaction to this proposal, the Mayor of Fort Wayne and the Timbers owners tried to find private groups who would either guarantee the loan or provide the needed $750,201. In Fort Wayne, there are at least two foundations which could have provided the funds, guaranteed the loan, or provided some financial assistance. There were also several large financial institutions which were approached to gauge their interest in helping to finance the stadium for the Timbers. In the end, no financial guarantees could be found from the private sector or from the foundations, and the Timbers owners elected not to move the team to Fort Wayne. Less than 12 months later, the Fort Wayne owners of the Timbers sold the franchise and ended their interest in bringing minor league baseball to Fort Wayne.

The city of Fort Wayne could have offered to build the stadium for the Timbers and absorb all the costs of providing a playing facility. Instead, they choose to offer a loan and require a substantial investment from the Timbers owners or other private interests. Did the city of Fort Wayne make the right decision in offering to provide a loan for some of the cost of the stadium, and requiring a substantial investment from the team's owners or some other actors in the city? Did the private sector, community groups and businesses make the right decision in refusing to support construction of the stadium? Should a city similar to Fort Wayne invest in minor league sports? To answer these questions this article examines the anticipated economic impact of the team and the conditions under which an investment in the sports world is feasible for a city similar to Fort Wayne.

MEASURING THE IMPACT OF SPORTS ON LOCAL ECONOMIES

Considering the economic impact of a baseball team is no different from assessing the influence of any business on a community. As a recreational activity, the economic impact of baseball can be analyzed or segregated into several different tiers (see Figure 1). The primary tier involves new spending by consumers which results from the presence of a team in the community. New spending is not equal to the total spending or economic impact related to the presence of a team. Prior to the existence of a baseball team in any community, people attend concerts and movies, dine out at restaurants, buy books, go to skating rinks, and the like. In short, recreational spending occurs whether or not a baseball team exists. If a baseball team moves to a community and consumers simply *shift* their spending patterns from other recreational activities to baseball, there is no real economic growth or impact of the team on the local economy. The presence of the baseball team could simply represent a shift in recreational spending. Estimating the impact of a team without subtracting the transfer of recreational spending from other activities is equivalent to assuming that no recreational activity occurs without the presence of sports in a community. Similarly, if the presence of a baseball team transfers spending patterns from other activities (education, food, transportation, etc.) to recreational spending, no real growth occurs. For example, if a consumer elects to attend baseball games and uses funds that would have been used to dine out, buy an additional car, attend school, etc., there is no new economic growth, but a transfer of resources between sectors of the economy. Transfers of spending between sectors of the economy do not represent economic growth and should not be included in any assessment of the economic growth related to the presence of a baseball team in an economy. Transfers of spending within a city or community as a result of the presence of a baseball team do represent an impact, but economic impacts do not necessarily imply economic growth.

If transfers within the recreational sector and between the sectors of an economy in a city or community do not represent economic growth, how does a baseball team increase economic activity? There are four possible ways. First, if the team attracts recreational spending away from other geographical areas, then a positive impact is identified. For example, if baseball fans from

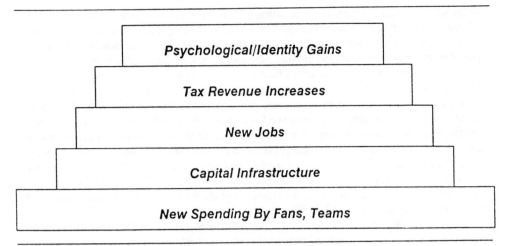

Figure 1: The Tiers of the Economic Impact of Minor League Baseball Teams

communities outside of the city that hosts a team came to games instead of attending movies, in their communities or elsewhere, the host city registers an important economic impact. This impact is not limited to simple attendance at the game. If fans came from outside of a community to attend a game, they will make ancillary purchases (food, overnight lodging, souvenirs, etc.) which can be quite substantial. Second, if the presence of a baseball team in a city deflects residents from going elsewhere for baseball games or recreation, the host city again gains from direct and ancillary spending activities. Third, visiting teams, through their expenditures in the city, also bring new economic activity to a community because of the presence of a baseball team. The location of a minor league baseball team in a community does mean approximately 70 home games which involves the temporary presence of a visiting team. The players on these teams will need hotel rooms, they will use the recreational facilities of the city to a limited extent, and they will eat several meals in the city. Each of those actions represents new economic growth because the teams would not come to the city if there was no baseball team in residence. Similarly, there will be some small impact from scouts from major league teams that will come to games to recruit and evaluate minor league players. Lastly, if the presence of a baseball team in a city actually increases aggregate spending (by consumers decreasing their savings or increasing their income through higher levels of productivity permitting more spending), real economic growth occurs. (The impact of decreased savings in a community could be offset by a negative impact on lending activities or higher interest rates. This point should also be considered in any analysis.)

The second tier of economic growth results from the construction of the playing facility and related transportation improvements. These activities add to the demand for construction workers and create jobs, if only for a short period. Regardless, the impact of construction is real growth in a community. However, there can also be a negative impact from this growth. If there is a shortage of construction workers and materials, the construction of playing facility could increase costs for other businesses seeking these workers.

The third tier of economic benefits includes the creation of permanent and seasonal jobs. Baseball teams, directly and indirectly, employ both full-time workers (office staff) and part-time or seasonal workers (players, stadium personnel, etc.). These new jobs do represent a positive impact on the community (if no jobs are ended elsewhere in the community because of shifting patterns of recreational consumption), although some representation has to be made for the proportion of players' salaries that will be spent outside the city as they may not have a permanent home in a minor league city. The fourth tier, which could be subsumed within each of the existing tiers, is the changes in tax revenues which result from the team's presence in a community. Spending by fans, players, and others can result in increased sales- and property-tax revenues, increased user fees, and, where local income taxes exist, there can be an increase in revenues from this tax source as a result of incomes earned. The last tier of benefits involves any psychological value received from the presence of a team which helps define a community's identity. Any assessment of economic growth resulting from a baseball team's location in a city, then, must look at each tier to determine the total growth and impact which results from a team's locational decision.

In consideration of each of these potential benefits, some have argued that cities, similar to Fort Wayne, should build a stadium for a professional sports team. If the economic impact of the team is more than the cost of the stadium, then construction of the facility is a benefit to the community. Cities must be careful to determine if these extra benefits exist, because direct revenues from the stadium are not likely to cover its costs. Baade and Dye[6] note:

> When the costs of paying interest and amortizing principle are included, stadium revenues cover only 70% of the stadium costs. Okner goes on to argue that publicly owned stadia have an additional implicit cost from not collecting property taxes on would-be private development of the parcel. When his estimate of foregone taxes is included, the average stadium covers only 60% of total costs.

Consequently, estimating the economic impact of the team is critical to any decision because stadium operations are unlikely to cover the public sector's investment in the stadium.

In producing an estimate of the economic growth associated with each tier cited in Figure 1, there are a set of standardized procedures which can be followed to measure each level of impact. The area served by the baseball team is defined as the Basic Trade Area (BTA), which is somewhat larger than the standard metropolitan statistical areas (SMSAs) defined by the Bureau of the Census. BTAs recognize the dependence of rural or smaller communities on larger urban centers for recreation, transportation, and other services. As such, in calculating attendance at games and spending, it is common to use BTAs as the geographical area of reference, and not the SMSA.

Second, after accurate attendance figures are discerned, the next step in calculating economic impact is to apply the attendance figures to project sales figures for in-park and out-of-park spending (primary and secondary-direct, respectively). Secondary spending is further refined into direct and indirect categories. The secondary-direct spending is the money spent directly related to the team's presence in a city (i.e., stopping before or after the game for a meal, etc.). The secondary-indirect spending is inferred from the secondary-direct spending. This indirect spending is the money from direct spending, spent and respent, as it circulates through the local economy before "leaking" out of the community. This respending can be calculated by applying an appropriate multiplier to the direct spending value. In calculating the effect of total spending, the multiplier chosen is an important factor. An inflated estimate of impacts can result if an artificially high multiplier is chosen. Similarly, an inaccurate estimate emerges if a small figure is chosen. There are a number of empirical studies which exist to guide one's choice. Generally, the smaller the community the smaller the multiplier because these areas have greater difficulty containing all spending than do larger areas. A study of the Pittsburgh Pirates found multipliers of 1.2 and 1.6 were accurate measures of the impact of the team on the Pittsburgh economy. For a study of sports in Philadelphia, a multiplier of 1.7 was used based on the Wharton School's econometric model of the city.[7] A study of the economic impact of the Atlanta Falcons used a multiplier of 2.2.[8] A detailed study of recreational spending in San Diego found multipliers as high as 3.36 if fans stayed in hotels, but as low as 1.0 if fans did not stay overnight.[9] For one study of South Bend's minor league team a multiplier of 3 was used,[10] while other studies of recreational spending have used multipliers of approximately 1.5.[11] Bergstrom, et al.[12] also looked at the multiplier effects of recreational investments and found multipliers in rural areas ranging from 1.48 to 1.97. In a rural area, one would expect the lowest multiplier effects because of the greater possibility for the leakage of economic impacts to other areas. A review of regional input-output literature and research performed by the U.S. Department of Commerce produced additional support for the idea that a multiplier similar to those used in Philadelphia and Pittsburgh would be appropriate.[13]

With each of these studies in mind, a conservative approach was taken in the use of a multiplier of 2 for this study. This seems appropriate given the relative mix of fans likely to use hotels, and the varied multiplier rates determined to exist by the other studies. A multiplier of 2 is clearly larger than the number used in other large cities, and greater than the recreational spending impacts found in other rural areas. However, the work of Bergstrom, et al.[14] also raises the possibility that the estimates were too low in Philadelphia and Pittsburgh because they found multiplier effects ranging as high as 1.79 and 1.97 in rural areas. Given the ability of larger cities to capture more spending, perhaps multipliers greater than 1.2 and 1.6 should be used. There is value in considering a greater multiplier to examine what the effects of the Timbers's move to Fort Wayne would be if one assumed a very large impact from spending. If the spending level predicted, even with a robust multiplier, is small, then the actual impact of the team would be less. For this analysis, based on other studies, a multiplier effect of 2 seems reasonable to estimate effects. However, impacts resulting from a "higher" multiplier of 3 will also be discussed.

THE ECONOMIC IMPACT OF MINOR LEAGUE BASEBALL IN FORT WAYNE

Tier 1 Impacts

Expenditures by fans, the Timbers baseball team itself, and expenditures by visiting teams (including media and scouts) each represent potential new economic activity for Fort Wayne. In terms of the expenditures by fans, however, it is first necessary to estimate the number of fans likely to attend games and the proportion of their spending that is likely to be new economic activity for Fort Wayne. These expenditures could then be added to the spending by the Timbers and the expenditures made by visiting teams to estimate the impact of the team on the local economy.

Attendance levels. Estimating attendance levels is both important and difficult. The importance of this task lies in its connection to overall spending levels. If attendance levels are inflated, or deflated, the impact on spending or economic change is substantial. Supporters of a team usually prefer larger estimates, while opponents seek lower estimates. Three different techniques were used to establish a valid estimate of the number of fans likely to attend games in Fort Wayne. The initial measure was derived from data provided by the Midwest League (the league in which the Timbers would play). For the 1988 season, the league office provided a complete tabulation of: (1) attendance at each game for each team in the league, (2) the win-loss percentage of each team, (3) stadium capacities, and (4) the number of years each team had been in the league. These data were supplemented with interviews with 7 of the 14 team's owners or general managers who were contacted to better understand each team's operating costs. Seven of the team's owners or general managers refused to be interviewed. As a result, when necessary, the averages for the seven teams were used to estimate league figures. Among the data collected during the interviews were the number of persons employed in part-time and full-time positions, the number of season tickets sold in the 1988 season, and current ticket prices.

The data supplied by the Midwest League was used to calculate average game attendance. Attendance levels ranged from a high of 2,961 (Peoria) to a low of 789 (Wausau), and a mean of 1,691 for the league. Using the BTAs for each team, an average attendance figure per 1,000 population was calculated. This figure was then used to forecast the attendance of a team in Fort Wayne at 3,749 fans per game. Fort Wayne's attendance would be the highest in the league. In part, this higher average is a function of the larger BTA which would be served by the Fort Wayne team. Notice that the team in Madison, Wisconsin, was located in a market area almost as large as Fort Wayne, with 8 of the teams in markets less than one-half the size of Fort Wayne (see Table 1).

Projecting attendance levels from league averages is sometimes not the best method to use because attendance is affected by many factors. For example, attendance is clearly related to market size, and using the 14 cities in Table 1, market size itself accounted for 38% of the variance in attendance. Other factors including income, proximity to alternate entertainment outlets, and, to some extent, the performance of the team could also affect attendance. Although there is debate

TABLE 1
Projected Attendance for a Fort Wayne Baseball Team

Team	Total Attendance	Average Per Game	BTA Population (in 000s)	Average Attendance Per 1,000
Appleton Foxes	85,310	1,219	390.6	3.12
Beloit Brewers	96,616	1,380	211.5	6.53
Burlington Braves	78,308	1,119	147.2	7.60
Cedar Rapids Reds	166,121	2,373	246.2	9.64
Clinton Giants	127,251	1,818	158.4	11.48
Kenosha Twins	64,285	918	292.3	3.14
Madison Muskies	88,343	1,262	578.2	2.18
Peoria Chiefs	207,294	2,961	477.8	6.20
Quad City Angels	115,459	1,649	446.9	3.69
Rockford Expos	158,674	2,267	415.7	5.45
South Bend White Sox	171,144	2,449	325.1	7.53
Springfield Cardinals	155,413	2,220	262.8	8.45
Waterloo Diamonds	87,819	1,254	272.1	4.61
Wausau Timbers	55,255	789	222.6	3.55
Midwest League	1,657,595	1,691	317.7	5.79
Fort Wayne projection	262,430	3,749	647.5	5.79

... attendance at minor league games may be affected by a team's performance; similar results have been found involving major league baseball teams. However, others argue that minor league attendance is not related to a team's performance but is more dependent on the "show" in the stands and the promotions team owners offer.

on the extent to which winning teams attract more fans,[15] winning records did account for 15% of the variance in attendance in the Midwest League. Therefore, attendance at minor league games may be affected by a team's performance; similar results have been found involving major league baseball teams.[16] However, others argue that minor league attendance is not related to a team's performance but is more dependent on the "show" in the stands and the promotions team owners offer. This observation results from the recognition of the lack of control minor league owners have over players whose contracts are owned by the major league club. Because minor league owners cannot control what takes place on the field (players can be assigned to any team by the Major League affiliate), owners affect attendance by making it "fun" to be at minor league baseball games.[17] In Fort Wayne's situation, market size itself accounts for much of the robust nature of the projected attendance. If the Timbers' record declined, it is possible attendance levels in Fort Wayne would not be as large as those forecast. However, it is also possible that successful marketing could overcome field performance.

Two other estimates of attendance at Fort Wayne Timbers games were made. First, an analysis was made of the attendance at two other professional sports teams in Fort Wayne, the Fort Wayne Komets and the Fort Wayne Flames. The Komets are a hockey team with a long history in the International Hockey League. The Flames are a charter member of the 3-year-old American Indoor Soccer Association. In 1988, the Komets's average attendance per 1,000 residents of the BTA was 5.23; the corresponding figure for the Flames was 5.06. Given the popularity of baseball, the Timbers might be expected to draw as well as the Komets. Using 5.23 as the average attendance per 1,000 residents, the projected attendance would be 3,386/game, or 237,050 people for a 70-game season. If won/lost performance had its maximum negative impact, a baseball team in Fort Wayne could expect to draw 201,492 people for a 70-game season based on the performance of the Komets hockey team. Second, a survey was conducted in randomly selected households in Fort Wayne to determine how many games people would attend if tickets were $2.50. Based on survey responses, a projected attendance from Fort Wayne residents was 191,000. Fort Wayne's county is about one-half of the BTA. The 191,000 projected attendance from Allen County (Fort Wayne) cannot be projected across the counties in the region because of differential costs of attendance (travel) and lower incomes in the areas surrounding Fort Wayne. However, the survey data indicates that an attendance level of 225,000 to 240,000 people could be expected. These figures would suggest an average attendance of 232,500. For the balance of this analysis, this mean figure will be increased to 235,000 and used as an estimate of annual attendance.

In accepting this estimate of possible attendance, one also must take notice of the possible impact the other sports teams could have on attendance. Baade and Tiehen[19] have noted that competition from other sports activities is a statistically significant variable in projecting attendance. No adjustment was made for the projected Fort Wayne attendance for three reasons. First, the overlap between the hockey and soccer schedules with the schedule for the Timbers would have involved only the playoffs for the hockey team and only if the Komets were in the final or championship series. Second, even if this overlap took place it would occur when weather is very unpredictable and cold in the upper Midwest. This means attendance at baseball games, at this time of the year (April and early May), is likely to be very low even if there was no overlap with the hockey playoffs. Third, if attendance at minor league baseball is a function of the "show" rather than the quality of team play,[19] then the absence or presence of a hockey game would probably have very little effect on attendance.

In selecting the figure of 235,000 from the three different estimates produced, it should be remembered that during the first year of operation at least, a "honeymoon" effect should be anticipated. That is, in the first year of operation, it is reasonable to expect that attendance would be somewhat higher since residents of Fort Wayne and the region might be attracted to more games because of the relative "newness" of minor league baseball. An adjustment for this honeymoon period will be made in the assessment of the economic impact of the team. This extra boost in attendance is anticipated for one year.

Expenditures by fans: Ticket sales. Calculating revenue from ticket sales must account for variations in prices within the park and promotions. Indeed, even determining average price per ticket is difficult. The owners of the Timbers were planning to charge an average ticket price of $2.50, and this figure was used when surveying fans concerning their expected attendance at games. However, minor league teams often use promotions to increase attendance. In 1985, the Midwest League's adjusted price per ticket (including promotions) was $0.81.[20] It may be reasonable to expect that a similar level of promotions would take place in Fort Wayne; for this analysis then, an adjusted ticket price of $1.00 to $1.25 multiplied against the total expected attendance was used to estimate that revenues from tickets sold would generate $235,000 to $293,750 (this higher figure was used to account for inflation and the anticipated price of tickets). The owners of the Timbers were planning to charge $2.50 as an average ticket price, but clearly that average was not sustained anywhere else in the league, given the number of promotions that were used. Indeed, promotions are an integral part of minor league attendance. As noted, minor league players, unlike their major leagues counterparts, are not under contract to the team. Minor league players contract with the major league team, and are then assigned to minor league teams. The players can be moved to other teams, at higher or lower levels, without the approval of the minor league team. Promotions to attract attendance are very important since fans do not know which players will be at any game. Further, fan loyalty to a particular player is not an asset owners can rely upon. Whereas the owners of the Texas Rangers know Nolan Ryan will draw fans to the stadium (as will a Michael Jordon or Magic Johnson), minor league owners must build loyalty to the team and to the "good times" at the stadium. Promotions are sometimes very effective ways to attract fans to the stadium to spend their money on souvenirs, beverages, and food, even if average ticket prices decline.

It seems prudent to expect ticket revenues would probably produce approximately $265,000. Further, spending at the stadium which includes food, beverages, parking, and souvenirs was estimated to be $1.58 per fan by the consulting firm retained by the city of Fort Wayne. This figure was also accepted as valid by the Timbers owners.[21] If 235,000 fans came to games, $371,300 would be spent. Total revenues at the stadium, then, could be expected to be $636,300 each season. With this figure in mind, two central issues need to be established. First, how much of this money is likely to be from outside the city of Fort Wayne brought in by visitors and thus potential real growth? Second, how much of the money from Fort Wayne residents is simply a reallocation of funds from existing recreational spending and how much represents new economic growth?

To answer the first question, some measure of the extent to which Fort Wayne already attracts recreational dollars from residents of surrounding counties is necessary. Fort Wayne, as the central service city in a BTA of 647,000 people, could already expect to receive a great deal of revenue from residents outside of the city. Virtually all movie theaters, plays, shows, and concerts in the region are staged or located in Fort Wayne. Substantial attendance at these events and programs from people outside the city is already expected and part of the revenue flows in the city. To estimate the proportion of recreational consumption in Fort Wayne that comes from residents who do not live in the county, a survey of cars was performed at one of Fort Wayne's movie theater complexes. Indiana license plates designate the county of residence, so it is relatively easy to ascertain where consumers live. A survey of more than 500 cars at a theater complex indicated that 55.6% were from inside the county in which Fort Wayne is located, and 44.6% were from other counties. In other words, Fort Wayne's recreational economy is already based on extensive participation by nonresidents of the area. Of the $636,000 that would be spent at the stadium it is reasonable to assume that $283,790 would come from nonresidents. If baseball was to bring additional revenue to the city, the proportion of nonresidents attending games would have to exceed 44.6% since that is what Fort Wayne's economy already expects. Could Fort Wayne exceed this ratio? The South Bend minor league team expects that only 20% of their attendees are not from the region. The Indianapolis Indians, a AAA team, have found that 60% of the fans at their games are not from Indianapolis. A 1976 study of fans attending Pittsburgh Pirate games found 38.7% were from outside of the Pittsburgh area.[22] If Fort Wayne replicated Indianapolis's success, 15.4% of expenditures by fans in the stadium and for tickets would be new income for the city's economy. If Fort Wayne's experience was closer to South Bend's or Pittsburgh's, the city's economy would realize no new economic gain from increased recreational spending from people outside of the county.

To address the second point—how much of the funds spent by Fort Wayne residents is a reallocation of existing recreational dollars—one assumption was made and a survey was performed of baseball fans attendance patterns. The assumption involves households' marginal propensity to consume and their demand for recreation. With savings rates no higher in Fort Wayne than in other parts of the country, the assumption was made that consumer spending is unlikely to increase simply for another recreational activity. People will certainly go to games, but with spending levels in excess of 95% of income, it is unlikely to expect reduced savings simply to attend minor league baseball games or the assumption of debt to finance trips to games. This assumption does not mean that there will be no redirection of recreational dollars as a result of the presence of the team. Baseball fans in Fort Wayne might now travel to Indianapolis, South Bend, Chicago, or Cincinnati to see baseball games since there is no team in Fort Wayne. A survey of 786 randomly selected households found that 39.9% (314) of the households had made a trip to another city to attend a sporting event. This attendance represents a loss for Fort Wayne's economy and if these people elected to stay in Fort Wayne to see baseball games instead of making a trip, new economic growth would be generated.

The respondents who indicated they did make trips to other cities for sporting events were then asked if they would reduce their trips if a team was in Fort Wayne. A total of 40 respondents, 12.7% of the group that went to out-of-town games, indicated they would cancel some of their trips if a team was located in Fort Wayne; this group also indicated they would attend seven games in Fort Wayne.[23] These 40 respondents represent 5.1% of the total sample.

If this group actually canceled 50% of their out-of-town trips, attended seven games in Fort Wayne with at least two people at each game, and the patterns of their spending were projected to all households in the county, then this group would account for 28,000 of the seats purchased to games. With an expected attendance level of 235,000, it might be anticipated that 11.9% of the revenues are new growth deflected from recreational spending in other communities. In terms of economic activity generated by the team, the analysis here suggests 11.9% would be deflected from losses to other counties and, at a maximum, 15.4% of the revenues generated would be from new spending from outside of the community. At a maximum, then, 27.3% of the revenues resulting from the baseball team represent new growth for the Fort Wayne economy. Put another way, at least 72.6% of the recreational spending by fans to attend baseball games would be simple redistribution of recreational dollars.

At a maximum . . . 27.3% of the revenues resulting from the baseball team represent new growth for the Fort Wayne economy. Put another way, at least 72.6% of the recreational spending by fans to attend baseball games would be a simple redistribution of recreational dollars.

Expenditures by fans: Other spending. In terms of the first tier of benefits, then, it is estimated that a total of $636,300 would be spent by fans at the stadium. To these expenditures is added an estimate of $8.00 per fan spending for purchases resulting from attendance at the game, but taking place outside the playing facility. This estimate was taken from surveys in Illinois and Denver of fans attending minor league games[24] and adjusted for inflation. Total fan expenditures are estimated to be $2,831,500 of which no more than $775,839 would be new growth for the Fort Wayne economy. Further, if Fort Wayne was only as successful as South Bend and Pittsburgh in attracting out-of-town fans, the real gain would be less than $336,952, as those cities reported less out-of-town attendance than Fort Wayne's recreational sector already enjoys. It also should be noted that this is an optimistic estimate of spending outside of the stadium, as other reviews of spending indicate a hotel occupancy rate that is half of what is anticipated for Fort Wayne.

Expenditures by the Fort Wayne Timbers. The expenditures by the team itself also adds to the local economy. In addition to the creation of jobs and office expenses of $100,000, there are the income payments to the players. A portion of this money would be spent in the city, and some would be spent elsewhere as the players probably would not live in Fort Wayne for the entire year. Player salaries were estimated from the league average to be $316,000. Of this money, its seems reasonable to argue that approximately 50% would be spent in the city for living expenses.

Expenditures by visiting teams. To estimate the new spending generated by the visits of baseball teams to play a Fort Wayne team, studies by the El Paso Diablos, Sumter Braves, Riverside Red Wave, and the Springfield (Illinois) Economic Development Council were reviewed. From these studies, an estimate of $85 per player for each visit could be used to project new spending in Fort Wayne at a level of $178,500 based on 70 home games.

Tier 2 Benefits: Capital Infrastructure

The Fort Wayne Timbers would play in an existing field which would be improved to meet the needs of a minor league team. The cost of the improvements, as agreed to by the City and the owners of the Timbers, was $1,950,201. No other construction plans were involved as the existing street/road system was deemed adequate and parking facilities at an adjacent facility (the Coliseum) would be used for fans attending the Timbers games.

Tier 3 Benefits: Jobs Created

Each team in the Midwest League was surveyed to learn how many full-time equivalent positions were created. The reports received listed both annual and seasonal employees, and the average number of jobs created by the 14 teams was 21.53. These jobs would be classified as service industry positions, and in Indiana, the average pay for this job classification is $18,500.[25] The net impact of the team in terms of job creation is $398,305. However, as Johnson[26] has noted, most of the jobs with minor league teams are only seasonal or half-time. For this reason, the dollar impact of the jobs created by the Timbers is valued at $200,00.

Tier 4 Benefits: Tax Dollars Received

The ability of any local government to capture the benefits of professional sports is a function of the taxing instruments available. The city of Fort Wayne has a property tax, and it also shares in the revenue from a county-wide income tax. The city does not have an add-on to the state's sales tax (no city in Indiana is authorized to levy such a tax) but the county does have a 5% hotel tax and a 1% tax on food and beverages consumed in restaurants. The latter tax is for support of the county's Coliseum. With the income and expenditure patterns identified in the previous tiers, the total revenue local governments could expect from the Timbers' operation in Fort Wayne is between $21,396 and $36,456 (see Table 2). This is based on the .002% income tax against all new incomes (50% for players as they would not be full year residents), the application of the 5% hotel tax and 1% food and beverage tax to spending by fans and visiting teams, and a multiplier of 2.

There are other sources of income which could accrue to local governments. If the stadium was rented to the team, the city could earn as much as $100,000. In addition, the city (or county) should expect to net an additional $100,000 in parking revenues from cars. Although the exact terms of the contract with the Timbers might have eliminated rental payments, at a minimum, local government would earn the $100,000 from parking operations.

Tier 5 Benefits: Psychological/Identity Gains

The economic impact of sports may pale in comparison to the importance of sports in American society. Lipsyte[27] was certainly one of the earliest writers to discuss the phenomenon of sports in America, and Edwards's *The Sociology of Sport* in 1973 clearly articulated the important role sports assumes in reflecting and defining American life. Michener[28] underscored this emphasis on sports in life by noting the stadia and arenas we have built for our teams and heroes might be similar to the facilities and edifices built by other civilizations (Romans and Greeks) to honor their heroes and idols. Indeed, even the mayor of Fort Wayne believed a baseball team could market the city quite well, and serve the city's identity in the sense that people would associate more with Fort Wayne, and know where the city is, and know that the city does exist.[29] More recently, Noll and others have argued that investments to attract teams should not even be defined in economic terms, but in the psychological and social gains and losses given the critical dimensions of sports in America.[30]

Within this context, different actors in Fort Wayne clearly had different perceptions of the value of a class A, minor league baseball team. Surveys of business leaders indicate that the presence or absence of a major league franchise has a very small impact on locational decisions.[31] It would not be surprising, then, that decision makers in Fort Wayne were not very attracted to the Timbers. In addition, Fort Wayne leaders, seeing the city as the largest city in the Midwest League, may have believed a class A team would have underscored the image of Fort Wayne as a minor league community. The city may have believed its longer term image would be better served by trying to attract a AAA team, or no team at all. Because these sentiments are difficult to measure and quantify, they were not included in the fiscal impact analysis. However the issue of the image of the city and A-level baseball is addressed in the conclusions.

The Fiscal Realities of the Fort Wayne Timbers

With the economic impact of the team identified for each of the tiers, except for the construction of the stadium, it is now possible to assess elements of the fiscal viability of the team. The total economic impact of the team, without the cost of the stadium, is summarized in Table 2. Whereas the total annual economic impact of the team is more than $7,000,000, the new economic activity generated by team, with a multiplier of 2 applied, would be between $1.77 and $2.67 million. At first, then, it might appear that the building of the stadium as a cost for getting the Timbers to move to Fort Wayne would be a worthwhile investment. But who should make the investment?

The original proposal for the development of an adequate playing field for the Timbers in Fort Wayne would have required an investment of $1,950,201. (This was the projected cost of the renovation to the existing field. The cost projection was made by an architect retained by the Timbers management. However, the city of Fort Wayne's staff reviewed the estimates and verified the cost projections. As such, both the city and the owners agreed on the price of the renovations.) The city had proposed loaning the team $1,200,000 at 6.48% interest, and requiring a $750,000 investment from the owners or some other group in the community. At the proposed interest rate, the annual payments to retire the loan in 15 years would be $125,282. These costs would have to be borne by the owners, assumed by the public sector, or supplied by other actors in the area's economy. If the ownership of the Timbers assumed the cost of the loan, the $125,282 in loan payments would have to be added to the cost of employee salaries and office expenses, $300,000 (see Table 2). To this figure would have to be added transportation costs to get the team to the other cities in the league. This is estimated at $100,000. Operating costs, then, would be approximately $400,000. The cost of the stadium, together with other operating costs of the Timbers would then

TABLE 2
Economic Impact of the Fort Wayne Timbers (Excluding Construction of New Stadium)

Revenue Source	Total Impact	New Revenue Estimate		Local Government Income	
		11.9%	27.3%	11.9%	27.3%
Fans' spending					
Ticket sales	$265,000	$31,535	$72,345	$ 315	$ 726
In stadium[a]	371,300	44,185	101,365	442	1,017
Outside stadium[b]	1,880,000	223,720	513,240	4,027[d]	9,273
"1st year"	315,230	37,512	86,058	771	1,976
Subtotal	2,831,530	336,952	773,008	5,555	12,992
Timbers' spending					
Players' salaries	316,000[c]	158,000	158,000	316	316
Jobs created	200,000	200,000	200,000	400	400
Operations	100,000	11,900	27,300	71	164
Subtotal	616,000	369,900	385,300	787	880
Visiting teams	178,500	178,500	178,500	4,356[e]	4,356
Parking revenues				100,000	100,000
Total spending	3,626,030	885,352	1,336,808	110,698	118,228
Multiplier	2X	2X	2X	2X	2X
Total spending	$7,252,060	$1,770,704	$2,673,616	$121,396	$136,456[f]
Total spending (Multiplier = 3)	$10,878,090	$2,656,056	$4,010,424	$132,094	$154,684

a. Includes advertising revenues.
b. Includes parking fees.
c. Players' salaries, while paid by the major league affiliate, do have a direct impact on the Fort Wayne economy.
d. Assumes 20% of expenses subject to 5% hotel tax; 80% of expenditures subject to 1% food and beverage tax.
e. Assumes half of the expenditures subject to 5% hotel tax; half of the expenditures subject to 1% food and beverage tax.
f. Multiplier not applied to direct local government income from parking, but is included in calculation of additional income and sales tax dollars through the new revenue columns.

be $525,282. The projected income of the team is $636,000 for a projected net income of $110,718 unless a subsidy was received from the major league affiliate or income was received in excess of the travel costs for playing games in other cities.[32] This projection is optimistic because the renovations to the stadium would still require a down payment of $750,000. Without a subsidy from the major league affiliate or local businesses or government, the Timbers would have to invest all profits for at least 7 years to cover this cost and hope for increased profits in the future. Only with additional support would the team generate enough profit to support the construction of the stadium. In short, the owners of the Timbers could not afford to build the stadium.

Notice that local government in Fort Wayne could also not afford to pay for the stadium. As noted, the city of Fort Wayne does not have a local option sales tax. As a result, its only source of revenue from the team is from a local income tax, currently at .002% of gross income, and increases in the property tax. It is very unlikely that the team would bring any changes in the property tax as the area of town proposed for the stadium is already well-developed as Fort Wayne's prime commercial district. An income tax at two-tenths of 1% would not produce enough revenue for a stadium. Allen County government does administer a 1% food and beverage tax for its sports coliseum, and also levies a 5% hotel tax. Adding the revenues from these taxes to the income tax revenues received means the most optimistic estimate of new revenue for city and county government would be slightly more than $100,000 with a multiplier of 2 (see Table 2). Local government could not afford to build a stadium for the Fort Wayne Timbers.

It is also possible to look at the economic impacts if a multiplier of 3 is used. Notice, however, even with this inflated view of the impact of the team, local government would net approximately $150,000 and new revenue generation would range from $2.66 to $4.01 million (see Table 2).

Without a subsidy from the major league affiliate or local businesses or government, the Timbers would have to invest all profits for at least 7 years to cover this cost and hope for increased profits in the future. Only with additional support would the team generate enough profit to support the construction of the stadium.

CONCLUSIONS

Given the tax structure that exists in Indiana for local government, Fort Wayne's decision not to finance the stadium was correct. In declining to finance the stadium through the public sector — and thus saying no to the owners of the Timbers — Fort Wayne made the right decision. Indeed, the final loan proposal to the team was the very most the city should have offered to the owners of the team. The net gains to all local governments would preclude both the city and the county from financing a baseball stadium without assuming a very large fiscal loss. It is even difficult to envision the circumstances under which the owners of the Timbers could accept the loan from the city to renovate the existing facility. Certainly even optimistic measures of their income would not sustain the costs of operation of team, renovation of the stadium, and any return on the investment. Without a high level of support from their major league affiliate or financing for the stadium from the community, they also made the prudent decision in electing not to move to Fort Wayne.

With both local government and the owners making the correct decision, is minor league baseball for Fort Wayne and similar cities a "tragedy of the commons" issue? In other words, the owners of the Timbers and local government do what is in their own self-interest — neither could afford to build the stadium — and the Fort Wayne economy loses between $2.67 million and $1.77 million (multiplier equals 2). Is this an instance where everyone does what is in his or her own self-interest and the community loses? The answer to this question is also no.

The most favorable projection of the economic gain for the local economy was $2.67 million. Although this is a large sum of money, it is not a very substantial portion of the income of the Fort Wayne BTA. For 1985, the Indiana Business Research Center reported that the total income in the eight countries within the Fort Wayne BTA was $7,299,167,000.[33] If the economic impact of the Fort Wayne Timbers was $2,673,616, this would mean an increase of less than one-half of 1% in total income for the area. If the new growth was $1.77 million, the increase in income would be 0.024%. Although this figure seems very small, it is actually quite similar to the impact figures generated for other areas. A study of economic impacts in Chicago concluded all professional sports (Bears, Bulls, Black Hawks, Cubs, and White Sox) spending represented but 0.024% of the total income of Cook County.[34] In terms of Fort Wayne, then, minor league baseball, at least as represented by the Fort Wayne Timbers, would have too small an impact to warrant a substantial level of risk and investment by the public sector. Indeed, the private sector, by refusing to make the needed investments without public-sector involvement, implicitly verified what has been enumerated here. Minor league baseball does not make enough money to warrant the investment.

A contrary position could be argued because new growth would occur if the team located in Fort Wayne. However, similar to other investments, expenditures for minor league baseball in Fort Wayne generate returns that spread or spillover through the entire economy. The problem is that the benefits diffuse quickly and without any perceptible concentration; no natural constituency develops to support the needed investments. There is no economic constituency in the public sector because neither the city nor the county would earn a sufficient return to warrant their participation. Likewise, actors in the private sector (business leaders, recreation industry leaders, restaurant and hotel operators, etc.) could not realize a return sufficient to galvanize their political and economic support for an investment in sports. The size of the Fort Wayne BTA economy is so large that galvanization of support requires a concentration of benefits which the small impact of the Fort Wayne Timbers would not accomplish. Although few if any of the actors in the decision making system may have quantified their decision as was done here, their explicit actions were nevertheless sustained by the data.

There are circumstances, however, where the investment would make economic and political sense for Fort Wayne, and where it might have been possible to galvanize support for the team. As noted, the field where the team was to have played was located in Fort Wayne's most intensively developed commercial region. As such, the presence or absence of the team was not seen as a substantial positive factor in affecting traffic flows which would impact the economy. Indeed, given existing street traffic patterns, many business leaders may have opposed the location of another activity with such a limited potential or impact in an area as congested as the site selected.

The field proposed for the renovation was directly across from the Fort Wayne campus of Indiana and Purdue Universities (enrollment exceeds 10,000); one mile east of Indiana's largest enclosed shopping mall (more than 150 stores) and 2.5 miles south of Indiana's largest open mall (70 stores). In addition to these stores, more than 100 other retail establishments are located within a three-mile radius of the field, and the field is adjacent to the Allen County Coliseum and Convention Center. From a traffic perspective, there is no worse location for the team and traffic flows in Fort Wayne.

Although the proposed location is quite a prosperous section of Fort Wayne, like other cities, Fort Wayne has declining areas and strives to keep its downtown center vibrant. In this regard, then, there is a real "opportunity cost" associated with the development of a stadium in an area where no new stimulus for development is needed from the public sector. Indeed, some merchants could argue the placement of the stadium would increase traffic and reduce the value of existing private investments. Developing a facility for a team in the downtown area, however, could mean that more than one-quarter of a million people would come to that part of the city each year. This would represent very real growth for that part of Fort Wayne. If property values increased, Fort Wayne could realize an important increase in its property tax levels. As a result, Fort Wayne could have an economic stake in bringing a team to downtown Fort Wayne. When South Bend developed its downtown stadium, property values within a one mile radius of the park increased.[35]

The building of a facility downtown would also receive considerable support from business leaders in the downtown area as well as operators of hotels and restaurants. Indeed, the knowledge that as many as 225,000 would be coming downtown could enhance the image of that part of the city and convince other businesses to locate in the area or stay in downtown Fort Wayne. This is not to suggest that the location of the stadium downtown could lead to the development of the downtown area. Certainly sufficient evidence exists to suggest a stadium by itself cannot lead to development.[36] However, downtown in Fort Wayne is still "home" to several of the region's largest employers. This development and maintenance of a commercial center could be enhanced by a stadium that promised to bring traffic to the area to supplement the extensive daytime and other recreational traffic Fort Wayne's downtown already enjoys. In short, the location of the team in the downtown area could create a natural constituency which would concentrate benefits sufficiently to galvanize support for the team and its needs.

The case of the Fort Wayne Timbers highlights several very important points for minor league baseball. First, whereas the minor league teams in smaller cities may well bring real growth to the community, the overall impact of the team is usually so small that a natural constituency to support the team may be hard to find. Owners of minor league teams and public officials must appreciate the very small dimensions of the economic impact of minor league sports on local economies and the difficulty in containing these benefits such that any group is willing to invest in the infrastructure needed by a team. Minor league owners and city officials might need to carefully court the corporate sector to explain to this group the entertainment benefits of the stadium and to use this group to help finance the kind of luxury boxes which generate sufficient profit to offset the costs of the stadium. Interviews with Fort Wayne officials indicate that some actors in the corporate sector do see a benefit to having a minor league team and are willing to help finance the team in a way that benefits their organizations. These actors want luxury suites, and they appear to be willing to pay a price for these suites that can help to offset the cost of construction. Second, with a very diffused economic impact from minor league teams, baseball owners and public officials must strive to geographically concentrate the benefits in such a way that political and economic constituencies form to support the team. Fort Wayne is not a large market as compared with major cities, but with an annual income in excess of $7 billion, business and local government leaders could hardly be expected to invest substantial sums of money in an enterprise which would increase incomes by less than one-half of 1%. Economically and politically, their support would have to be contingent on a sufficient concentration of the benefits to make investments economically and politically viable.

Should Fort Wayne and similar cities "just say no" to minor league teams? If the decision is made on purely economic grounds, yes they should. There are circumstances under which the investment would make sense for a local government, even with the tax structure of cities and counties in Indiana. First, if team owners are willing to locate where cities need to increase development and recreation, then minor league baseball would be a good investment. A second scenario under which investment in sports would be economically viable is if a sufficient level of corporate support exists which can be used to finance the stadium. This would involve the careful pricing of luxury suites, and seems to be an option which was possible in Fort Wayne. Sufficient time was needed to develop this constituency, but the city could not meet a deadline imposed by the Timbers owners.[37]

Finally, it must be remembered that some have argued economic analyses are not the most important element in considering whether or not to invest in sports.[38] If a city or its leadership decides that participation in the sports world and the larger fabric of American society is necessary for the city's identification, then perhaps the investment should be made and considered a marketing or development expense. The economic impact of a class A minor league team will never be as large as the impact of numerous other activities. However, none of those other activities offer the escapism and publicity of sports. If a city hosts a team, then in many newspapers they receive some level of publicity each day the team plays. If that level of exposure is valued by a city, then studies of this nature at least define their risks and the small level of economic impact. However, given the level of economic data regarding labor, land, capital, and utilities that companies can access,[39] it seems difficult to argue that one needs a baseball team to supplement the economic image available from Standard and Poor's, or Moody's. Further, it is this actual economic identity, and not the sports image of a city, which drives locational decision-making by private firms.[40] In the end, it remains for city councils and voters to decide if the "Boys of Summer" really define a community's image, culture, placement in the fabric of American society, and the quality of life, or whether a class A minor league baseball team is simply an example of "big boys wanting big toys" at someone else's expense.

NOTES

1. Ilana DeBare, "Investors Say They're Risking $335 Million on Raiders," *The Sacramento Bee*, September 1, 1989, p. 1; idem, "Raiders Would Bring Capital $1.4 Billion Boost, Study Says," *The Sacramento Bee*, September 3, 1989, p. 22; idem, "Some Economists Skeptical that Raiders Mean A Bonanza," *The Sacramento Bee*, September 3, 1989, p. 1.

2. Robert Lipsyte, *Sports World: An American Dreamland* (New York: Quandrangle Books, 1977).

3. John Bale, *Sports Geography* (New York: Routledge Chapman & Hall, 1989); DeBare, "Some Economists Skeptical."

4. Bale, *Sports Geography*.

5. Mark S. Rosentraub, "Financial Incentives, Locational Decision-Making, and Professional Sports: The Case of the Texas Ranger Baseball Network and the City of Arlington, Texas," in *Financing Local Government: New Approaches to Old Problems*, ed. Mark S. Rosentraub (Fort Collins, CO: The Western Social Science Association, 1977).

6. Robert A. Baade and Richard F. Dye, "Sports Stadiums and Area Development: A Critical Review," *Economic Development Quarterly* 2 (1988): 265-75.

7. Ibid.

8. Bale, *Sports Geography*.

9. Ibid.

10. John E. Peck, "An Economic Impact Analysis of South Bend's Proposed Class A Baseball Stadium," mimeo (South Bend: Bureau of Business and Economic Research, Indiana University at South Bend, 1985).

11. Roger R. Stough, *The Indiana Tourism Report: An Assessment of Visitor Expenditures on the Indiana Economy in 1987* (Indianapolis, IN: Tourism Development Division, 1987).

12. John C. Bergstrom, H. Ken Cordell, Gregory A. Ashley, and Alan E. Watson, "Economic Impacts of Recreational Spending on Rural Areas: A Case Study," *Economic Development Quarterly* 4 (1990): 29-39.

13. U.S. Department of Commerce, *Regional Multipliers* (Washington, DC: Bureau of Economic Analysis, U.S. Department of the Commerce, 1986).

14. Bergstrom et al. "Economic Impacts."

15. Roger Noll, ed., *Government and the Sports Business* (Washington, DC: Brookings Institutions, 1974).

16. Robert A. Baade and Laura Tiehen, "An Analysis of Major Baseball Attendance, 1969-1987," *Journal of Sports and Social Issues*, forthcoming.

17. Art Johnson, *Local Government in the Business of Minor League Baseball: A Guide for Decision-Making* (Washington, DC: International City Management Association, 1990).

18. Baade and Tiehen, "An Analysis of Major League Baseball."

19. Johnson, *Local Government*.

20. Peck, "An Economic Impact Analysis."

21. William L. Haralson and Associates, "Feasibility of Developing A Stadium for Minor League Baseball in Fort Wayne," unpublished mimeo (Dallas: Haralson and Associates, Inc., 1988).

22. Edward Malloy, *The Impact of Baseball on the Pittsburgh Economy* (Pittsburgh PA: Pittsburgh Chamber of Commerce and the Department of Economics, the University of Pittsburgh, 1977).

23. In estimating the attendance which would be deflected away from visits to other cities, respondents were asked the number of people likely to go to games with them. Respondents were not asked to separate household members from friends. Is it possible, therefore, that the estimate produced was higher than what would take place as some respondents might have counted other respondents in other households. This methodological problem is not seen as serious since the estimate produced through the techniques used actually would inflate the number of fans at games. Given the lack of profitability of the venture, it seemed prudent to inflate the attendance levels since even with this higher estimate the investment may not be warranted.

24. Peck, "An Economic Impact Analysis."

25. U.S. Department of Commerce, *Regional Multipliers*.

26. Johnson, *Local Government*.

27. Lipsyte, *Sports World*.

28. James A. Michener, *Sports in America* (New York: Random House, 1976).

29. Paul Mayor Helmke, interview conducted by C. James Owen, July 7, 1989.

30. DeBare, "Raiders Would Bring Capital"; idem, "Some Economists Skeptical."

31. Samuel Nunn, *Suburban Cities, Professional Sports, and the Recapturement of Economic Activity: The Case of Arlinton and Irving, Texas*, unpublished master's thesis, University of Texas at Arlington Graduate School (1977).

32. In projecting this estimate, no entry was made for the cost of getting the team to other cities. This would make the fiscal position of the team even weaker unless revenues from games in other cities was sufficient to meet all travel costs.

33. Terry K. Creeth, ed., *The Indiana Factbook* (Bloomington: Indiana University School of Business, 1989).

34. Baade and Dye, "Sports Stadiums and Area Development."

35. Peck, "An Economic Impact Analysis."

36. Baade and Dye, "Sports Stadiums and Area Development."

37. Helmke, interview.

38. DeBare, "Some Economists Skeptical."

39. Robert Warren and Mark S. Rosentraub, "Information, Space, and the Control of Local Decisions," *Journal of Urban Affairs* 8 (1986): 40-50.

40. R. Schmenner, *Making Business Location Decisions* (Englewood Cliffs, NJ: Prentice-Hall, 1982).

Article 32

Benefits from a Baseball Franchise: An Alternative Methodology

John P. Blair
Wright State University

Rosentraub and Swindell presented a fiscal impact study of a minor league franchise in Fort Wayne, Indiana. They concluded that it would not be advisable for the city to provide a substantial subsidy to the franchise because the extra tax revenues generated by the team would be insufficient to justify the subsidy. Their conclusions rest on faulty methodology. The largest benefit from the franchise is the additional income that Fort Wayne residents would receive due to extra spending. These important benefits were treated as negligible in the Rosentraub and Swindell study. A benefit-cost approach provided a framework for a more complete accounting of the benefits to Fort Wayne residents. When all the benefits to local residents are considered, a larger subsidy could have been justified. Had a larger subsidy induced the team to locate in Fort Wayne, citizen welfare could have been enhanced.

John P. Blair is a Professor of Economics at Wright State University. He has written numerous books and articles in the fields of urban development and public policy. His latest book, Urban and Regional Economics (1991) published by Irwin, is designed for undergraduate economics and urban studies students. Blair received his Ph.D. from West Virginia University in 1974. In addition to his teaching and research, he is a member of the Montgomery County Planning Commission.

Occasionally, urban planners mistakenly evaluate the feasibility of specific projects based only on fiscal impact analysis. Fiscal impact studies provide a framework for determining how new projects will affect governmental revenues and expenditures. Such evaluative criteria support projects that bolster the public treasury.[1]

Benefit-cost studies provide an alternative evaluative criteria. Benefit-cost studies examine all of the relevant costs and benefits regardless of whether they accrue to the treasury or to citizens in other ways. The logic of benefit-cost studies suggests that projects may be subsidized even if they deplete the public treasury as long as the costs are offset by benefits to citizens.

Rosentraub and Swindell's[2] (hereafter R and S's) analysis of a proposed minor league baseball team in Fort Wayne, Indiana provides a springboard for comparing the fiscal impact approach with

TABLE 1
Revenue Estimates of Timbers in Fort Wayne

Revenue Source	New Revenue Estimate 11.9% of Spending (dollars)	Local Government Income (dollars)
I. Fans' spending		
a. Ticket sales	31,535	315
b. In stadium[a]	44,185	442
c. Outside stadium[b]	223,720	4,027
d. "1st year"	37,512	771
e. Subtotal	336,952	5,555
II. Timbers' spending		
a. Players' salaries	158,000	316
b. Jobs created	200,000	400
c. Operations	11,900	71
d. Subtotal	369,900	787
III. Visiting teams	178,500	4,356
IV. Parking revenues		100,000
V. Total spending	885,352	110,698
VI. Multiplier	2×	2×
a. Total spending	1,770,704	121,396
Timbers' financial position		
Gross annual income	$636,000	
Operating costs	$400,000	
Net operating income (excluding stadium construction costs)	$236,000	
Cost of stadium = $1,950,201		

SOURCE: Rosentraub and Swindell, " 'Just Say No?' The Economic and Political Realities of a Small City's Investment in Minor League Baseball," *Economic Development Quarterly* 5 (1991): 152-67.

benefit-cost analysis. This article explains why benefit-cost analysis is the preferred methodology in this case and shows how the policy implications would be affected by the benefit-cost approach.

R and S analyzed the advisability of Fort Wayne providing a subsidy to induce the Timbers, a minor league class A baseball team, to locate in the city. They concluded that, "Given the tax structure in the community and the marginal impact of the team, the city and the private sector made the correct decision in not offering substantial inducements; the net gains were too small for all concerned" (p. 152). The authors based their conclusion almost exclusively on a comparison of the increased local government revenues attributable to the location of the Timbers in Fort Wayne with the expenditures needed to attract the franchise. Benefits to residents were mentioned only in passing. .

Table 1 is a summary of some of the principal data used by R and S. The authors were explicit in describing the assumptions used to develop their data. The revenue figures in column 2 were adjusted to account for the fact that most spending on the new franchise would be at the expense of other local spending. Their lowest estimate is that only 11.9% of spending on the Timbers will be new to the area. Local government income, shown in column 3, was estimated based on the existing tax structure. The local spending multiplier of 2 was based on studies in similar communities. The data in Table 1 are R and S's most conservative estimates. They are the basis for a scenario that will make the case for subsidizing the Timbers the most difficult. Anyone interested in the derivations is referred to the original article.

Based on the anticipated governmental revenue increase of $121,396 annually, R and S concluded that Fort Wayne could "not afford to pay for the stadium." Similarly, the authors concluded that the Timbers' projected net income of $236,000 was insufficient to allow the owners of the minor league franchise to bear a significant portion of the construction costs. Their reasoning was that a 7-year pay back period was too long to warrant the investment.

FISCAL IMPACTS RECONSIDERED

Before applying a benefit-cost test to R and S's data, it is worth reconsidering their conclusion that it would not be in the interest of either Fort Wayne or the franchise owner to build the stadium. R and S did not answer this fundamental question rigorously. Most feasibility studies use the discounted value of future benefits to estimate the value of a project such as the location of the Timbers. If the discounted value of the increase in income is greater than the cost of acquiring the income flow (in this instance, the subsidy for the stadium), then the investment is feasible.

Determining an appropriate discount rate is necessary to establish the present value of the future returns. It accounts for the fact that a dollar today is worth more than a dollar in the future. There are several techniques for estimating the discount rate. Factors to be considered include the current interest rate, returns on other investments, and risk.[3]

For illustration, let's assume (as implicit in the R and S article) that the Timbers' franchise was just breaking even at their current location. Also assume: (1) a 15-year life of the facility, (2) the team would stay in Fort Wayne for at least the length of the facility's economic life, and (3) the discount rate is 15% for the franchise owners and 9% for the city of Fort Wayne. These are reasonable discount rates considering the economic conditions and the nature of the project.

Accordingly, the present value of the income flow for Fort Wayne's treasury and the franchise owners would be:[4]

present value of $121,396 to city (at .09 for 15 years)	$ 978,452
present value of $236,000 to Timbers (at .15 for 15 years)	$1,379,892
	$2,358,344

Clearly an asset with a present value of $2,358,344 is just barely sufficient to warrant an investment of $1,950,201. Although neither party could afford to bear the entire cost, there was potential for a cost-sharing deal in which both parties could gain.

The combined flow of future benefits is worth only slightly more than the costs of the stadium, so it is a close call given the conservative assumptions. However, if the more optimistic assumptions of R and S had been used, the combined income of the franchise and the city's revenue increase clearly would have been sufficient to justify construction of the stadium.

In reality, most locational negotiations are more complex than determining whether the city could provide a subsidy large enough to allow the franchise to earn an adequate rate of return. From the point of view of the Timbers' owner(s), the issue is whether the franchise could earn the highest possible return when alternative locations are considered. To resolve this issue, analysts must know the opportunities and incentive (subsidy) packages at other locations. Not surprisingly, such an analysis was missing from the R and S study because local policymakers seldom have such knowledge. Parenthetically, lack of knowledge about alternative locational opportunities often places local officials at a disadvantage when negotiating with firms.

THE BENEFIT COST APPROACH

How large of a subsidy could Fort Wayne have offered the Timbers? R and S contended that a $1,200,000 loan at 6.48% interest was about the maximum the city of Fort Wayne could have offered the Timbers based on the project's increases in tax revenues. However, if benefits to residents as well as to the Fort Wayne treasury had been considered, the estimate of value of the Timbers to Fort Wayne would have been greatly enhanced.

R and S asked the critical benefit-cost question in their conclusion:

With both local government and the owners making the correct decision, is minor league baseball for Fort Wayne and similar cities a "tragedy of the commons" issue? In other words, the Timbers owners and local government do what is in their own self-interest — neither could afford to build the stadium — and the Fort Wayne economy loses between $2.67 million and $1.77 million (multiplier equals 2). Is this an instance where everyone does what is in his or her own self-interest and the community loses? The answer to this question is no. (p. 164)[5]

R and S explained that because professional sports teams account for only a small percentage of the income in a community, the benefits to residents could not be significant. "In terms of Fort Wayne, then, minor league baseball . . . would have too small an impact to warrant a substantial level of risk and investment by the public sector" (p. 164). In fact, the benefit-cost analysis described below indicates that the increased income to Fort Wayne residents is the most significant benefit of the franchise.

Table 1 includes important community benefits that were excluded from R and S's fiscal impact study. These include benefits of outside-of-stadium spending, the impact of local spending by Timbers' players, income from nonplayer jobs that would be created, benefits from operating spending, and income created by the spending of visiting teams.

One difficulty in determining the income generated by additional spending is that local spending does not translate dollar for dollar into local income. For instance, if a fan from out of the area spent $1.50 for a beer at a ball game, some portion of the $1.50 would go to the beer manufacturer, perhaps located in Chicago.

In order to convert spending into local income, four sectors that represent typical sources of out-of-area spending were examined — hotels and motels (standard industrial classification [SIC] 70), personal services (SIC 72), eating and drinking places (SIC 58) and general merchandise (SIC 53).[6] The ratio of payrolls to receipts was calculated from national averages for each respective type of establishment. R and S provide no indication of the portion of spending that would be accounted for by the likely spending categories. Therefore, the categories were weighted equally. An overall estimate of the portion of receipts attributable to payrolls of .28 was derived. In other words, it is estimated that for each extra dollar of local spending attributable to the Timbers, 28 cents of wage and salary income for local residents will be created.

Other income such as profits and rents may also flow to Fort Wayne residents. Nationwide proprietors' income and rental income to persons is about 8.6% of wage and salary income.[7] Accordingly, the portion of receipts attributable to payrolls was increased by 8.6%. Therefore, the portion of new spending that will be transformed into local income can be estimated at 30%.

Another difficulty in determining income increases for residents of Fort Wayne is that not all of the jobs created due to the Timbers will accrue to residents of the city. Residents of suburban areas may also receive some of the benefits if they got jobs created by the Timbers. Because the stadium will be in Fort Wayne and because most of the jobs will be moderate or low-paying, part-time employment, they are likely to go to the residents of the city.[8] The population of Fort Wayne is about half of the population of the surrounding area. Consequently, it was assumed that 60% of the income generated by the Timbers would flow to Fort Wayne residents.

R and S found $772,120 of annual income generating spending that could be attributable to the Timbers. This figure is the sum of the spending categories that will create local income — items Ic, IIa, IIb, IIc, and III. Applying the 30% local income-to-spending ratio and the assumption that 60% of the income will flow to Fort Wayne residents leads to the conclusion that $138,982 ($772,120 × .30 × .60) of additional local income can be attributed to the Timbers annually.

In order to determine the present value of the future benefits of the $138,982 annual increase in income, three adjustments are necessary. First, the multiplier effect must be considered. For this step the R and S "conservative" multiplier of 2 will be used. Second, the extra local income taxes should be deducted from citizen benefits because they have already been included in the governmental revenue estimate. Third, the future annual income flow should be discounted to determine the present value. A 15-year economic life and a 10% discount factor are used for this step.

A multiplier of 2 would bring the annual income flow to $277,964. R and S reported that the county had a ".002% income tax against all new incomes." (This may have been a misprint. County officials reported a rate of .2%) Therefore, the benefits to residents should be reduced by .2% to account for the local taxes. Annual benefits to residents net of income taxes will be $277,408. Applying a 10%, 15-year discount factor provides an estimate of the value of the future income flow of $2,109,965.[9]

The total benefits to Fort Wayne residents are:

present value benefits to Fort Wayne treasury	$ 978,452
present value benefits to Fort Wayne residents	$2,109,965
	$3,088,417

Because the stadium cost was $1,950,201, it appears that Fort Wayne officials could have offered more than the $1,200,000 low interest loan to attract the team. In fact, they could have financed the entire stadium and still received net benefits. Further, monetary values were not assigned to the intangible benefits—"the psychological/identity" gains mentioned by R and S in passing. If the Timbers had located in Fort Wayne, these benefits would have been icing on the cake.

CONCLUSION

There are numerous appropriate uses for fiscal impact studies. However, when local officials are considering how much bait to use to hook a potential business, they should consider benefits beyond those that accrue to the treasury. In the case of the Timbers, the largest benefit was to residents who would have experienced income increases had the team located in Fort Wayne. If the city officials fully considered the benefits that accrue to residents rather than focusing only on the health of their treasury, they would probably have offered a more attractive incentive package to the Timbers than they did.

Of course, negotiating such arrangements require skill and political savvy. If one party tries to capture too high a portion of the benefits, negotiations can, and often do, fail. Consequently, it is important that policymakers be as informed as possible about the benefits of a new business.

NOTES

1. Fiscal impact studies have clear philosophic links to mercantilism. Mercantilism was the economic system that dominated Western economies from the end of feudalism to the rise of capitalism. The principal tenant of mercantilism was that the economy's function is to build a strong state. Accordingly, mercantilists evaluated economic activity by considering whether it bolstered the government's treasury.

Adam Smith rejected mercantilism in *The Wealth of Nations* (New York: Random House, Modern Library Edition, 1937). The intellectual founder of capitalism argued that the economy should enhance the welfare of the citizens of the state. According to Smith, the function of the polity should be to assist in building a strong economy that will in turn enhance citizen welfare.

2. Mark S. Rosentraub and David Swindell, " 'Just Say No?' The Economic and Political Realities of a Small City's Investment in Minor League Baseball," *Economic Development Quarterly* 5 (1991): 152-67.

3. John P. Blair, *Urban and Regional Economics* (Homewood, IL: Irwin, 1991): 532-33.

4. The present value of $1 per year for 15 years discounted at 9% is 8.060 and 5.847 at 15%.

5. R and S's phrase "the government's own self interest" is interesting. It suggests, as would the mercantilist philosophy, that the government has an interest separate from that of residents.

6. U.S. Department of Commerce, *1987 Census of Service Industries* (Washington, DC: U.S. Government Printing Office, 1988), Table 2; and idem *1988 Census of Retail Trade* (Washington, DC: U.S. Government Printing Office, 1989), Table 2a.

7. U.S. Bureau of Economic Analysis, "The U.S. National Income and Product Accounts: Revised Estimates," *Survey of Current Business*, July 1990, p. 73.

8. Robert A. Baade and Richard F. Dye, "Sports Stadiums and Area Development: A Critical Review" *Economic Development Quarterly* 2 (1988): 265-75.

9. The present value of $1 per year for 15 years discounted at 10% is 7.606. $2,109,965 = 7.606 × $277,408.

Article 33

Hammers and Their Use:
Some Issues Involved in the Selection of
Appropriate Tools for Public Policy Analysis

David Swindell
Mark S. Rosentraub
Indiana University

Following is the original abstract to the Rosentraub and Swindell article " 'Just Say No?' The Economic and Political Realities of a Small City's Investment in Minor League Baseball."

David Swindell is a doctoral student in the School of Public and Environmental Affairs. His areas of interest include public management, research methodology and statistics, and urban affairs. He has recently completed a needs assessment of elders in Indiana.

Mark S. Rosentraub is Professor and Associate Dean in the School of Public and Environmental Affairs, Indiana University. His research interests include urban development and policy, urban service delivery and financing, and health services delivery. His research has appeared in Urban Affairs Quarterly, Journal of Urban Affairs, Nonprofit Sector Quarterly, Public Productivity Review, Policy Studies Review, *and numerous other journals and collections. Currently, he is working on an analysis of the impact of older populations on local budgets.*

The magical aura which encases sports in our society continues to encourage cities to offer inducements to attract franchises. Now, even minor league franchises have become coveted assets by smaller cities seeking the same "glamour" that major league teams give larger cities. Smaller cities are seemingly mesmerized by the idea, "build it and they will come." The "they" is the anticipated economic impact and benefits of the team. This article analyzed one city's decision by measuring the substitution effects and real growth impact of a team on the local economy. Given the tax structure in the community and the marginal impact of the team, the city and the private sector made the correct decision in not offering substantial inducements; net gains were too small for all concerned. The small impact also suggests no natural constituency existed to support the needed investments. Finally, some have argued economic analyses are not the most important element in considering whether or not to invest in sports since baseball is a form of escapism and publicity. If these are valued ideas it remains for city councils and voters to decide if the "Boys of Summer" really define a community's image, culture, placement in the fabric of American society, and the quality of life. Or, is a minor league baseball team simply an example of "big boys wanting big toys" at someone else's expense.

Public officials who are often confronted with difficult policy choices in the management of cities also must consider the issues involved with the selection of any of several different research tools available to analyze various subjects. Abraham Kaplan[1] cautioned students of research to be sensitive to the issues associated with the selection of any research tool through the observation that a child with a hammer quickly concludes everything needs hammering. For the public policy researcher, the selection of any research strategy involves a careful consideration of the implicit and explicit issues, assumptions, and limitations within each method. This methodological consideration is designed to select the most appropriate tool for each problem, and to be sure we do not select a hammer simply because everything needs hammering.

Professor John Blair's alternative methodological approach to considering the benefits from a baseball franchise presents us with an excellent opportunity to expand on our original contribution and to explore methodological issues we did not include in our original article. Benefit-cost analysis is, indeed, an important public policy tool, but we purposely decided to use a fiscal impact approach to study the implications of a city's decision not to invest in professional sports. A careful reconsideration of our logic, prompted by Professor Blair's well-written commentary, still suggests to us that a fiscal impact approach to the analysis is more appropriate than a benefit-cost analysis. We believe the benefit-cost analysis performed by Professor Blair is inadequate because it failed to consider (1) opportunity costs, (2) the distribution of benefits, and (3) the costs associated with the decision-making process involving the team. Further, we anticipate no psychological or identity benefits from the team's location. These limitations are common in many benefit-cost analyses used to evaluate public investments in professional sports. As a result of our recognition of these limitations, we decided to use a simple fiscal impact method. It too does not include these facets, but it is the more preferred technique as it looks at the return on the investment from the two investors perspective of the city and the owners. For students of public policy, the more detailed description of our considerations, which now follows, will permit readers to evaluate the merits of both approaches to the assessment of the public sector's investment in professional sports.

PROFESSIONAL SPORTS AS PUBLIC POLICY

Professional sports occupies a unique place in American society, city management, and economic development. Its central point in our culture results from the very special entertainment and psychological benefits it provides. This importance is underscored by the common use of sports analogies and metaphors in politics and management, the socialization of children through sports and team building, the role model, images, and profile levels accorded to players and teams, and the identity many believe is conveyed by teams to cities.[2] Perhaps as a result of this very special emphasis on sports, public-private partnerships between cities and team owners have become commonplace as communities strive to become part of "sportsworld."[3] Because cities are now routinely expected to subsidize the development of playing facilities, sports is an important facet of city management and city politics. Within the last year, municipal investment and the management of professional sports facilities have become political issues in Oakland, Sacramento, Los Angeles, Philadelphia, Arlington (Texas), St. Petersburg, and Salem (Oregon).

In many of the political discussions in these cities, the economic development aspect of sports becomes the "60-second sound bite" used to convince people to support public subsidies. The anticipated economic returns, combined with the cultural romanticism of sports, place urban managers and citizens in the difficult position of deciding whether or not to favor public investment in professional sports and in creating their place in the sportsworld of American culture.

Our article[4] was designed to draw attention to the economic impacts and growth resulting from investments in sports facilities. To accomplish this, we executed a simple fiscal impact analysis instead of a benefit-cost analysis for one city, Fort Wayne, Indiana. A benefit-cost analysis that enumerated all costs would be a fine tool for analysis, but the frequent omission of critical costs and the distribution of benefits, as a result of the cultural and social affinity for sports in our society, makes classical cost-benefit analyses impractical. Similar to the analysis presented by Professor Blair, many cost-benefit analyses involving sports fail to carefully evaluate the opportunity costs of an investment in professional sports, the distribution of economic benefits that results from the public's investment in sports, and the implications associated with decision-making when communities must decide to enter or expand a city's role in sportsworld. In understanding our decision to use a simple fiscal impact model it is best to identify each of the costs that were not enumerated in Professor Blair's presentation.

The Economic Limitations of Benefit-Cost Analyses of Professional Sports Teams

When communities are asked to support an investment in professional sports, the issue is rarely framed in the context that "City X is considering a $Y investment to enhance economic development or create jobs; what investment would yield the greatest return, and to whom?" Indeed, communities usually frame the issue in terms of the notion that if we do not make a deal for the team, the owners will simply select another city who will. In this regard, the choice of pursuing one investment in lieu of another is rarely considered, but the foregone investment is the lost opportunity cost. In Professor Blair's benefit-cost analysis, he makes reference to the inclusion of opportunity costs in reaching any final decision or calculations for a benefit-cost analysis. He noted the difficulty of this task and, as is frequently done in many benefit-cost analyses, made no measure of the opportunity costs.

The issue of opportunity costs, however, is the fundamental social issue associated with municipal investment in professional sports. If a benefit-cost analysis is used to evaluate an investment, the question is not whether an investment in sports is profitable, but if more benefits would be generated from any number of other opportunities. The city, for example, could invest a similar level of resources in a local university, public schools, its transportation infrastructure, health programs, or seek to attract another industry or business. All too often, advocates of public subsidies for sports avoid the impacts of alternative investments, even when the returns from professional sports investments are found to be quite small and lead to the creation of few jobs. In this manner, proponents of professional sports capitalize on the sportsworld mentality and use incomplete benefit-cost analyses to validate their positions. The error would not be so egregious if the economic impact of the investment was large, or if the benefits were distributed in such a manner as to make the public's investment a "quasi public good." Neither of these positions exist with regard to the public's investment in professional sports. The economic return from sports is slight; sports is not a public good, but a private good; and the benefits of the investment are not progressively distributed.[5] An incomplete benefit-cost analysis that has ignored opportunity costs and distributional issues is not as effective a tool for public policy analysis as a more simplified fiscal impact approach.

In our fiscal impact analysis, we identified a less than .5% increase in total income for the Fort Wayne area as a result of the public sector's investment in professional sports. Further, the value of the investment may increase to approximately $978,452 as tabulated by Professor Blair, but who actually benefits? Policy analysts cannot use benefit-cost analyses to hide behind regressive subsidies that transfer public resources to higher income individuals in the form of subsidized entertainment (fans paying less than the cost of production to watch a game) or reduced costs to benefit wealthy owners and major and minor league players. Professional sports, as we and others have noted, simply creates too few jobs for middle or lower income groups to rationalize public subsidies.[6] Implicitly, then, we question the use of public subsidies to subsidize economic activities that are private goods, create few jobs, have very small economic impacts, and are not part of any overall plan or strategy. If public subsidies are to be used, the distribution of benefits should be far more progressive, a point not lost on many students of benefit-cost analysis.[7] Students of urban policy, city management, and economic development must continue to look beyond the "discounted value of the increase in income [even if it] is greater than the cost of acquiring the income flow."[8] The feasibility of any such investment, as numerous scholars in economic development have noted, does indeed require a consideration of the distribution of benefits and costs when the public's money is involved.[9] Professor Blair's failure to include these issues in his analysis leads us to strongly disagree with his assertion that "benefit-cost studies examine all of the relevant costs and benefits."

In terms of Professor Blair's benefit-cost analysis, he also failed to consider the source of the money for Fort Wayne's investment. The money for the city's investment would have come from the utility improvement fund. The locational decision-making literature indicates that the presence of a sound infrastructure is a far more enticing factor than the presence of a Class A minor league baseball team.[10] Indirectly, money spent on infrastructure improvements could have helped draw several more businesses whose net impact would have dwarfed that of the ball club and provided far more jobs than a professional sports franchise. This was another "opportunity cost" issue obscured in Professor Blair's analysis. Lastly, benefit-cost analyses cannot ignore the observation that the public's investment in sports facilities amounts to a subsidy for upper income groups with far too few returns for others. Although this criticism can certainly be directed toward other forms of public-private partnerships,[11] the diminutive dimensions of the economic impact of sports on jobs created and dollars generated requires special attention to fiscal impact analyses rather than benefit-cost assessments. Finally, the distribution of the costs must also be considered given the number of communities that rely on more regressive taxes to finance their investment in sports.[12]

The Political Limitations of Benefit-Cost Analyses of Professional Sports

The political pressure that usually accompanies requests for public investments in professional sports involves the psychological and identity benefits from a team's locational decisions. Professor Blair refers to these benefits as "icing on the cake." Because these benefits are difficult to enumerate, both we and Professor Blair omitted them from our analyses. We did note the potential for psychological or identity gains from being the home of a sports team as a fifth source of impact that a sports team might have on a local area. Although this impact can be icing on the cake, cities could also find this icing can cause substantial indigestion.

There is anecdotal evidence to suggest that the importance of identity gains may render any economic arguments inconsequential if a team helps a city's or a region's view of itself or the view others have of it. In Fort Wayne's case, however, the likely gains may have been quite speculative. Fort Wayne would have been, by far, the largest host city in the Class A Midwest Minor League. Attracting a team with a higher class ranking (i.e., AA or AAA) would place Fort Wayne in the newspapers of more comparable cities, increasing the residents' sense of worth as gauged against other host cities. This is not to detract from the other Midwest League host cities. Rather, it is a recognition that being listed in a league with Indianapolis, Buffalo, and Oklahoma City in the Class AAA league, for instance, would probably be preferred by Fort Wayne residents to listing the city with smaller, less known cities and economic regions in the Class A league. Choosing to wait and making an effort to attract a team in a higher league is an example of an alternative investment that could yield larger psychological as well as economic benefits. This is an alternative opportunity cost that also should be evaluated. In addition, Fort Wayne could have as easily suffered as gained from attracting a Class A baseball team because the city is already home to a higher level hockey team and was once home to the NBA Pistons. There may have been no icing on the cake but indigestion, if Fort Wayne was viewed as a minor league city which could do no better than subsidize Class A baseball. In addition, if the city had subsidized Class A baseball as the owners of the Timbers wanted, the city might have placed itself in a dangerous negotiating position with the International Hockey League franchise in the city which is the equivalent of a AAA baseball team. Those owners could have sought a larger subsidy given what the city proposed for a Class A baseball team. As such, the city stood to lose a substantial amount in its negotiating position from Professor Blair's icing on the cake.

These losses are in addition to other risks the city would have taken in terms of identity issues. The argumentation of the benefits of team location is based on the assumption that newspaper coverage in other cities' sports pages leads to some form of payoff. However, minor league baseball scores are probably not the strongest method of municipal advertising available, although it could supplement a larger overall campaign. There is also another assumption present. Those who use city awareness arguments in support of public subsidies to sports expect that the coverage will be positive. They discount the possibility that the host city could suffer negative press from a potential "loser image" or from being seen as a low, minor league city. If this were to happen, the psychological/identity gains would not be gains at all, but losses. Charlotte, North Carolina, officials argue that the presence of the NBA Hornets has created a more cohesive community and regional spirit. Juxtaposed, Cleveland has had to fight the "loser image" associated with baseball's American League Indians. Thus, the awareness or identity argument is a potentially double-edged sword that represents another risk a city faces in the decision to subsidize sports.

Who Decides? Who Gains?

The various issues involved with decisions regarding urban development are difficult to examine in isolation. Situational contexts and variable interactions impact the outcome of evaluation criteria. Professor Blair suggests that we premised our conclusion (that Fort Wayne made the right decision) solely on the increase in local governmental revenues and not on the fiscal return to the economy as a whole. Given the gains he identified, the investment by the city was seen as worthwhile in terms of the income benefits that would accrue to residents. In pronouncing the investment wise, Professor Blair's arguments failed to identify as a cost or issue the way in which decisions regarding the baseball team would have been made.

The owners of the Timbers, in their "offer" to Fort Wayne, actually dictated where the city was to build the stadium. They informed city officials that the ball field in Fort Wayne's most intensively developed commercial/retail region, across from the campus of a state university, should be renovated to league standards so the team could relocate in accordance with the owners' time-frame. This site was not part of the city's plans for enhanced or future development. This location offered no help in revitalization efforts as there was nothing that needed revitalizing at that location. If anything, that location for the team would have had a negative impact because of the increased traffic which would result. Finally, the team's action could be seen to represent an effort by a private business to make city planning decisions as opposed to city planners and citizens making decisions considering the returns from sports and other programs and priorities. As we noted in the original article, there were many sites in and around the downtown area that were in need of some form of revitalization effort. A baseball stadium and team could have helped these areas by increasing local traffic by approximately 250,000 people annually. The opportunity cost lost by not locating the stadium in one of these areas is of absolute and fundamental importance to decision-making in urban economic development.

With the entire adjusted value of approximately $3.1 million (including the discount factor), Professor Blair argues that such a figure warranted the $1.95 million investment in stadium construction costs by the city. This cost could have been borne by both the city and the team, but neither alone. The issue of the distribution of benefits is again raised by these figures. Under this program, the city would invest $1.2 million for a $0.9 million return while the team invested $0.75 million and would net almost $1.4 million. Implicitly, Professor Blair argues the city's subsidy is compensated by the return to citizens in the area, returns that many have found to be diminutive, creating few, if any, full-time jobs. Given these outcomes, it seems prudent to compare the returns that accrue to the two principal investors, the city and the owners of the team, as we did in our fiscal impact approach. With these points in mind, what should the city have given away to insure an "adequate rate of return" to another business? Making investments in propositions which do not generate sufficient tax revenues are an increasingly unsatisfactory option for public officials given the political climate of opposition to increased property and income taxes, especially in Indiana where local governments do not share in general sales tax revenues. Without an adequate return on its investment, a city's capacity to invest in other development strategies which generate greater growth and are more equitably distributed, is considerably reduced. As such, contrary to Professor Blair's conclusion, there is indeed the necessity for a city to insure its return on its own investments to guarantee its future ability to further development activities.

CONCLUSIONS

Professor Blair has provided a valuable opportunity to consider the issues involved with the selection of a policy analysis tool when evaluating the public's investment in economic development. There are, as Abraham Kaplan reminds his students, numerous tools. For some tasks hammers are appropriate; for others, drills and screwdrivers may be better suited. The emotionalism that is always associated with investments in professional sports mandates that decision-makers and analysts carefully consider which tool they use. Selection of the wrong tool can make a task more difficult, and sometimes using two tools provides a more complete view of an issue.

When communities consider investments in professional sports, a complete benefit-cost analysis that considers all costs and the distribution of benefits is the best tool to use. However, when all the substantial costs cannot be enumerated, when the distribution of benefits is not tabulated, and when urban decision-making costs are ignored, a benefit-cost analysis will provide a very biased view of outcomes. This is especially dangerous because professional sports is a very small component of any city's economic sphere. As we illustrated, the vast majority of revenues associated with sports would be spent in the community whether the team existed or not. In addition, utility improvement, the original source of the funds in Fort Wayne, will have been foregone, perhaps reducing other investments that could have increased job opportunities for lower income individuals. The identity gains from teams are also speculative, and in many instances have more potential to be negative than positive. The economic impact of sports teams is too small, and few new jobs will be created. Further, the majority of these new jobs are seasonal and part-time. Lastly, there is sufficient evidence to suggest the benefits of subsidies to professional sports are regressively distributed with many communities relying on less than progressive revenue sources to provide the subsidies. As a result, it is better to use a limited fiscal impact model that compares returns to the city to those accruing to owners who seek subsidies from the city.

In comparing the two different conclusions generated by our interchange, we oppose the investment that Professor Blair would support, and we underscore our belief that the role of cities is not to subsidize investors to create a few, low-skill jobs while increasing the opportunities for entrepreneurs to make profits. Municipal governments can be seen to have a responsibility to provide a stable framework for entrepreneurship to flourish. They provide, and sometimes produce, urban services. Many times these services are the "public goods" that residents rely on cities to provide because private producers find it difficult to realize substantial profits due to scale issues. However, baseball is not a public good. If the returns to the city for any investment are too speculative, then it, like any entrepreneur should look for investments which generate greater benefits for all its residents, or greater tax revenues for itself.

NOTES

1. Abraham Kaplan, *The Conduct of Inquiry* (Scranton, PA: Chandler, 1964).

2. Robert Lipsyte, *Sportsworld: An American Dreamland* (New York: Quadrangle, 1977).

3. Ibid.

4. Mark Rosentraub and David Swindell, " 'Just Say No?' The Economic and Political Realities of a Small City's Investment in Minor League Baseball," *Economic Development Quarterly* 5 (1991): 152-67.

5. Robert A. Baade and Richard F. Dye, "Sports Stadiums and Area Development: A Critical Review," *Economic Development Quarterly* 2 (1988): 265-75; Art Johnson, *Local Government in the Business of Minor League Baseball: A Guide for Decision-Making* (Washington, DC: International City Management Association, 1990).

6. Ibid.

7. I.D.M. Little, *A Critique of Welfare Economics* (Oxford: Clarendon, 1957); Vilfredo Pareto, *Manual d'economic politique* (Paris; M. Giard, 1927).

8. John Blair, "Benefits from a Baseball Franchise: An Alternative Methodology," *Economic Development Quarterly* 6 (1992 [this issue]): 91-95.

9. Timothy Barnekov and Daniel Rich, "Privatism and the Limits of Local Economic Development Policy," *Urban Affairs Quarterly* 25 (1989): 212-38; Dennis Judd, *The Politics of American Cities: Private Power and Public Policy* (Boston: Scott, Foresman, 1988); Susan Fainstein, Norman Fainstein, Richard Hill, Dennis Judd, and Michael Smith, *Restructuring the City: The Political Economy of Urban Redevelopment* (New York: Longman, 1983); Little, *A Critique of Welfare Economics* Pareto, *Manual d'economic politique*; William Tabb and Larry Sawers, *Marxism and the Metropolis: New Perspectives in Urban Political Economy* (New York: Oxford University Press, 1984).

10. Roger Schmenner, *Making Business Location Decisions* (Englewood Cliffs, NJ: Prentice-Hall, 1982).

11. Barnekov and Rich, "Privatism and the Limits of Local Economic Development Policy."

12. City of Arlington, Texas, "Master Agreement Regarding Ballpark Complex Development." Proposed by the city and passed by the citizens, January 19, 1991.

Section VIII
International Issues

The growth in activity on foreign exchange markets and the growth in the volume of imports and exports attests to the need for managers to understand international finance and international trade issues. This section includes articles that are concerned with issues of both international finance and trade. In "A Guide to Foreign Exchange Markets," K. Alec Chrystal provides an introduction to the way foreign exchange markets operate. In addition to the discussion of spot and forward markets, foreign exchange futures and options markets are described.

Protectionist trade policies are the subject of "Protectionist Trade Policies: A Survey of Theory, Evidence and Rationale," by Cletus C. Coughlin, K. Alec Chrystal, and Geoffrey E. Wood. The authors first show the gains to nations that participate in international trade. The effects of the trade policies of tariffs, quotas, regulatory barriers, subsidies, and exchange controls are then described. The authors present estimates of the magnitude of the gains to domestic producers and losses to consumers from protectionist trade policies. Arguments used to justify protectionist trade policies conclude the article.

Two domestic industries strongly influenced by international competition are the textiles industry and the apparel industry. In "The Effect of Exchange Rate Variation on U.S. Textile and Apparel Imports," Christine Chmura examines empirically the hypothesis that variations in the exchange rate influence U.S. textile and apparel imports. Using data from 1977 through 1986 she finds evidence to support the view that U.S. dollar appreciation (depreciation) is associated with increases (decreases) in U.S. textile and apparel imports.

Comparisons of Japan and the U.S. regarding industrial innovation in a number of industries is the subject of Edwin Mansfield's article, "Industrial Innovation in Japan and the United States." Among the findings he reports is that Japanese firms are more efficient than U.S. firms at developing new products and processes based on externally developed technology. Also, Japanese firms emphasize tooling, equipment, and manufacturing facilities more than U.S. firms. Marketing start–up is emphasized more by U.S. firms.

Article 34

A Guide to Foreign Exchange Markets

K. Alec Chrystal

$\mathbf{T}$HE economies of the free world are becoming increasingly interdependent. U.S. exports now amount to almost 10 percent of Gross National Product. For both Britain and Canada, the figure currently exceeds 25 percent. Imports are about the same size. Trade of this magnitude would not be possible without the ability to buy and sell currencies. Currencies must be bought and sold because the acceptable means of payment in other countries is not the U.S. dollar. As a result, importers, exporters, travel agents, tourists and many others with overseas business must change dollars into foreign currency and/or the reverse.

The trading of currencies takes place in foreign exchange markets whose major function is to facilitate international trade and investment. Foreign exchange markets, however, are shrouded in mystery. One reason for this is that a considerable amount of foreign exchange market activity does not appear to be related directly to the needs of international trade and investment.

The purpose of this paper is to explain how these markets work.[1] The basics of foreign exchange will first

be described. This will be followed by a discussion of some of the more important activities of market participants. Finally, there will be an introduction to the analysis of a new feature of exchange markets — currency options. The concern of this paper is with the structure and mechanics of foreign exchange markets, not with the determinants of exchange rates themselves.

THE BASICS OF FOREIGN EXCHANGE MARKETS

There is an almost bewildering variety of foreign exchange markets. Spot markets and forward markets abound in a number of currencies. In addition, there are diverse prices quoted for these currencies. This section attempts to bring order to this seeming disarray.

Spot, Forward, Bid, Ask

Virtually every major newspaper, such as the *Wall Street Journal* or the *London Financial Times*, prints a daily list of exchange rates. These are expressed either as the number of units of a particular currency that exchange for one U.S. dollar or as the number of U.S. dollars that exchange for one unit of a particular currency. Sometimes both are listed side by side (see table 1).

For major currencies, up to four different prices typically will be quoted. One is the "spot" price. The others may be "30 days forward," "90 days forward,"

K. Alec Chrystal, professor of economics-elect; University of Sheffield, England, is a visiting scholar at the Federal Reserve Bank of St. Louis. Leslie Bailis Koppel provided research assistance. The author wishes to thank Joseph Hempen, Centerre Bank, St. Louis, for his advice on this paper.

[1]For further discussion of foreign exchange markets in the United States, see Kubarych (1983). See also Dufey and Giddy (1978) and McKinnon (1979).

Table 1

Foreign Exchange Rate Quotations

Foreign Exchange

Wednesday, September 7, 1983

The New York foreign exchange selling rates below apply to trading among banks in amounts of $1 million and more, as quoted at 3 p.m. Eastern time by Bankers Trust Co. Retail transactions provide fewer units of foreign currency per dollar.

Country	U.S. $ equiv. Wed.	U.S. $ equiv. Tues.	Currency per U.S. $ Wed.	Currency per U.S. $ Tues.
Argentina (Peso)	.09652	.09652	10.36	10.36
Australia (Dollar)	.8772	.8777	1.1340	1.1393
Austria (Schilling)	.05296	.0560	18.88	17.84
Belgium (Franc)				
Commercial rate	.01851	.01855	54.01	53.90
Financial rate	.01841	.01846	54.21	54.15
Brazil (Cruzeiro)	.001459	.00149	685.	671.00
Britain (Pound)	1.4910	1.5000	.6707	.6666
30-Day Forward	1.4915	1.5004	.6704	.6664
90-Day Forward	1.4930	1.5010	.6697	.6662
180-Day Forward	1.4952	1.5028	.6688	.6654
Canada (Dollar)	.8120	.8123	1.2315	.2310
30-Day Forward	.8125	.8128	1.2307	1.2303
90-Day Forward	.8134	.8137	1.2293	1.2289
180-Day Forward	.8145	.8147	1.2277	1.2274
Chile (Official rate)	.01246	.01246	80.21	80.21
China (Yuan)	.50499	.50489	1.9802	1.9806
Colombia (Peso)	.01228	.01228	81.4	81.40
Denmark (Krone)	.10362	.10405	9.65	9.6100
Ecuador (Sucre)				
Official rate	.02082	.02082	48.03	48.03
Floating rate	.010917	.010917	91.60	91.60
Finland (Markka)	.17424	.17485	5.7390	5.7190
France (Franc)	.1238	.1238	8.0750	8.0750
30-Day Forward	.1235	.1230	8.0955	8.1300
90-Day Forward	.1224	.1223	8.1695	8.1725
180-Day Forward	.1203	.1202	8.3100	8.3150
Greece (Drachma)	.01075	.01078	93.	92.70
Hong Kong (Dollar)	.1297	.13089	7.71	7.6400
India (Rupee)	.0980	.0980	10.20	10.20
Indonesia (Rupiah)	.001015	.001015	985.	985.
Ireland (Punt)	1.1715	1.1775	.8536	.8493
Israel (Shekel)	.0173	.0173	57.80	57.80
Italy (Lira)	.000624	.0006255	1602.	1598.50
Japan (Yen)	.004072	.004067	245.55	245.85
30-Day Forward	.004083	.004079	244.88	245.15
90-Day Forward	.004107	.004102	243.48	243.75
180-Day Forward	.004147	.004142	241.10	241.39
Lebanon (Pound)	.20618	.20618	4.85	4.85
Malaysia (Ringgit)	.42462	.42489	2.3550	2.3535
Mexico (Peso)				
Floating rate	.00665	.00666	150.25	150.00
Netherlands (Guilder)	.33288	.3333	3.0040	3.000
New Zealand (Dollar)	.6497	.6505	1.5397	1.5327
Norway (Krone)	.13368	.1340	7.48	7.4625
Pakistan (Rupee)	.07518	.07518	13.30	13.30
Peru (Sol)	.0005105	.0005105	1958.89	1958.89
Philippines (Peso)	.09085	.09085	11.007	11.007
Portugal (Escudo)	.00804	.00807	124.35	123.90
Saudi Arabia (Riyal)	.28735	.28735	3.48	3.48
Singapore (Dollar)	.46609	.4664	2.1455	2.1440
South Africa (Rand)	.8870	.8900	1.1273	1.1236
South Korea (Won)	.001285	.001285	778.20	778.20
Spain (Peseta)	.00655	.00658	152.60	151.90
Sweden (Krona)	.12635	.12666	7.9140	7.8950
Switzerland (Franc)	.4596	.4591	2.1755	2.1780
30-Day Forward	.4619	.4615	216.46	2.1666
90-Day Forward	.4662	.4657	2.1449	2.1470
180-Day Forward	.4728	.4723	2.1150	2.1172
Taiwan (Dollar)	.02489	.02489	40.17	40.17
Thailand (Baht)	.043459	.043459	23.01	23.01
Uruguay (New Peso)				
Financial	.02798	.02798	35.73	35.73
Venezuela (Bolivar)				
Official rate	.23256	.23256	4.30	4.30
Floating rate	.07194	.07272	13.90	13.75
W. Germany (Mark)	.3726	.3726	2.6835	2.6835
30-Day Forward	.3740	.3741	2.6731	2.6728
90-Day Forward	.3767	.3768	2.6540	2.6538
180-Day Forward	.3808	.3808	2.6260	2.6259
SDR	1.04637	1.04903	.955685	.953625

Special Drawing Rights are based on exchange rates for the U.S., West German, British, French and Japanese currencies. Source: International Monetary Fund.

z-Not quoted.

The Dollar Spot and Forward

Sept 7	Day's spread	Close	One month	% p.a.	Three months	% p.a.
UK†	1.4860-1.4975	1.4910-1.4920	0.02-0.07c dis	−0.36	0.17-0.22dis	−0.52
Ireland†	1.1665-1.1720	1.1710-1.1720	0.36-0.30c pm	3.39	0.88-0.78 pm	2.84
Canada	1.2305-1.2320	1.2310-1.2315	0.09-0.06c pm	0.73	0.24-0.21 pm	0.73
Nethlnd.	3.0050-3.0150	3.0050-3.0070	1.12-1.02c pm	4.26	3.00-2.90 pm	3.92
Belgium.	54.06-54.20	54.06-54.08	7-6c pm	1.44	14-11 pm	0.92
Denmark	9.6400-9.6800	9.6400-9.6450	2-2$^1_2$ore dis	−2.79	par-$^1_2$ dis	−0.10
W. Ger.	2.6850-2.6980	2.6865-2.6875	1.07-1.02pf pm	4.66	3.00-2.95 pm	4.42
Portugal	124.20-125.00	124.40-124.70	115-290c dis	−19.51	330-790dis	−17.98
Spain	152.40-152.70	152.50-152.60	170-220c dis	−15.33	675-775dis	−18.99
Italy	1604-1608	1605-1606	10-10$^1_2$lire dis	−7.65	29$^1_2$-31 dis	−7.53
Norway	7.4730-7.4940	7.4730-7.4780	1.90-2.20ore dis	−3.29	5.90-6.20ds	−3.23
France	8.0775-8.1225	8.0825-8.0875	2.02-2.12c dis	−3.07	9.65-9.85ds	−4.81
Sweden	7.9120-7.9265	7.9120-7.9170	0.90-1.10ore dis	−1.51	2.25-2.45ds	−1.19
Japan	245.50-246.50	245.65-245.75	0.69-0.64y pm	3.24	2.11-2.03 pm	3.36
Austria	18.89-18.95$^1_2$	18.89-18.90	7.50-6.70gro pm	4.50	21.00-18.50 pm	4.17
Switz.	2.1770-2.1875	2.1800-2.1810	1.10-1.05c pm	5.91	3.10-3.05 pm	5.63

†UK and Ireland are quoted in U.S. currency. Forward premiums and discounts apply to the U.S. dollar and not to the individual currency.

Belgian rate is for convertible francs. Financial franc 54.40-54.45.

London Financial Times, September 8, 1983

Wall Street Journal, September 8, 1983

and "180 days forward." These may be expressed either in "European Terms" (such as number of $ per £) or in "American Terms" (such as number of £ per $). (See the glossary for further explanation.)

The spot price is what you must pay to buy currencies for immediate delivery (two working days in the interbank market; over the counter, if you buy bank notes or travelers checks). The forward prices for each currency are what you will have to pay if you sign a contract today to buy that currency on a specific future date (30 days from now, etc.). In this market, you pay for the currency when the contract matures.

Why would anyone buy and sell foreign currency forward? There are some major advantages from having such opportunities available. For example, an exporter who has receipts of foreign currency due at some future date can sell those funds forward now, thereby avoiding all risks associated with subsequent adverse exchange rate changes. Similarly, an importer who will have to pay for a shipment of goods in foreign currency in, say, three months can buy the foreign exchange forward and, again, avoid having to bear the exchange rate risk.

The exchange rates quoted in the financial press (for example, those in table 1) are not the ones individuals would get at a local bank. Unless otherwise specified, the published prices refer to those quoted by banks to other banks for currency deals in excess of $1 million. Even these prices will vary somewhat depending upon whether the bank buys or sells. The difference between the buying and selling price is sometimes known as the "bid-ask spread." The spread partly reflects the banks' costs and profit margins in transactions; however, major banks make their profits more from capital gains than from the spread.[2]

The market for bank notes and travelers checks is quite separate from the interbank foreign exchange market. For smaller currency exchanges, such as an individual going on vacation abroad might make, the spread is greater than in the interbank market. This presumably reflects the larger average costs — including the exchange rate risks that banks face by holding bank notes in denominations too small to be sold in the interbank market — associated with these smaller exchanges. As a result, individuals generally pay a higher price for foreign exchange than those quoted in the newspapers.

Table 2

Dollar Price of Deutschemarks and Sterling at Various Banks

	Deutschemark		Sterling	
	Buy	Sell	Buy	Sell
Retail				
Local (St. Louis) banks (avg.)	.3572–.3844		1.4225–1.5025	
Wholesale				
New York banks	.3681–.3683		1.4570–1.4580	
European banks (high)	.3694–.3696		1.4573–1.4583	
European banks (low)	.3677–.3678		1.4610–1.4620	
Bankers trust	.3681		1.4588	

Note: These prices were all quoted on November 28, 1983, between 2:00 p.m. and 2:45 p.m. (Central Standard Time). Prices for local banks were acquired by telephoning for their price on a $10,000 transaction. The prices quoted were reference rates and not the final price they would offer on a firm transaction. Figure for Bankers Trust is that given in the *Wall Street Journal*, November 29, 1983, as priced at 2:00 p.m. (Central Standard Time) on November 28, 1983. Other prices were taken from the Telerate information system at 2:35 p.m. New York prices were the latest available (Morgan and Citibank, respectively). European prices were the last prices quoted before close of trading in Europe by various banks. Deutschemark prices were actually quoted in American terms. The sell prices above have been rounded up. The difference between buy and sell prices for DM in the interbank market actually worked out at $0.00015.

An example of the range of spot exchange rates available is presented in table 2, which shows prices for deutschemarks and sterling quoted within a one-hour period on November 28, 1983. There are two important points to notice. First, all except those in the first line are prices quoted in the interbank, or wholesale, market for transactions in excess of $1 million. The sterling prices have a bid-ask spread of only 0.1 cent (which is only about 0.07 percent of the price, or $7 on $10,000). On DM, the spread per dollars worth works out to be about half that on sterling ($4 on $10,000).[3]

Second, the prices quoted by local banks for small, or retail, transactions, which serve only as a guide and do not necessarily represent prices on actual deals, involve a much larger bid-ask spread. These retail spreads vary from bank to bank, but are related to (and larger than) the interbank rates. In some cases, they

---

[2]Notice the *Wall Street Journal* quotes only a bank selling price at a particular time. The *Financial Times* quotes the bid-ask spread and the range over the day.

[3]In practice, the spread will vary during the day, depending upon market conditions. For example, the sterling spread may be as little as 0.01 cents at times and on average is about 0.05 cents. Spreads generally will be larger on less widely traded currencies.

may be of the order of 4 cents or less on sterling, though the prices quoted in St. Louis involved average spreads of 8 cents on sterling. The latter represents a spread of about 5½ percent (about $550 per $10,000 transaction). The equivalent spread for DM was 7 percent ($700 per $10,000 transaction).

The spread on forward transactions will usually be wider than on spot, especially for longer maturities. For interbank trade, the closing spread on one and three months forward sterling on September 8, 1983, was .15 cents, while the spot spread was .10 cents. This is shown in the top line of the *Financial Times* report in table 1. Of course, like the spot spread, the forward spread varies with time of day and market conditions. At times it may be as low as .02 cents. No information is available for the size of spread on the forward prices typically offered on small transactions, since the retail market on forward transactions is very small.

HOW DOES "THE" FOREIGN EXCHANGE MARKET OPERATE?

It is generally not possible to go to a specific building and "see" the market where prices of foreign exchange are determined. With few exceptions, the vast bulk of foreign exchange business is done over the telephone between specialist divisions of major banks. Foreign exchange dealers in each bank usually operate from one room; each dealer has several telephones and is surrounded by video screens and news tapes. Typically, each dealer specializes in one or a small number of markets (such as sterling/dollar or deutschemark/dollar). Trades are conducted with other dealers who represent banks around the world. These dealers typically deal regularly with one another and are thus able to make firm commitments by word of mouth.

Only the head or regional offices of the larger banks actively deal in foreign exchange. The largest of these banks are known as "market makers" since they stand ready to buy or sell any of the major currencies on a more or less continuous basis. Unusually large transactions, however, will only be accommodated by market makers on more favorable terms. In such cases, foreign exchange brokers may be used as middlemen to find a taker or takers for the deal. Brokers (of which there are four major firms and a handful of smaller ones) do not trade on their own account, but specialize in setting up large foreign exchange transactions in return for a commission (typically 0.03 cents or less on the sterling spread). In April 1983, 56 percent of spot transactions by value involving banks in the United States were channeled through brokers.[4] If all interbank transactions are included, the figure rises to 59 percent.

Most small banks and local offices of major banks do not deal directly in the interbank foreign exchange market. Rather they typically will have a credit line with a large bank or their head office. Transactions will thus involve an extra step (see figure 1). The customer deals with a local bank, which in turn deals with a major bank or head office. The interbank foreign exchange market exists between the major banks either directly or indirectly via a broker.

FUTURES AND OPTION MARKETS FOR FOREIGN EXCHANGE

Until very recently, the interbank market was the only channel through which foreign exchange transactions took place. The past decade has produced major innovations in foreign exchange trading. On May 16, 1972, the International Money Market (IMM) opened under the auspices of the Chicago Mercantile Exchange. One novel feature of the IMM is that it provides a trading floor on which deals are struck by brokers face to face, rather than over telephone lines. The most significant difference between the IMM and the interbank market, however, is that trading on the IMM is in futures contracts for foreign exchange, the typical business being contracts for delivery on the third Wednesday of March, June, September or December. Activity at the IMM has expanded greatly since its opening. For example, during 1972, 144,336 contracts were traded; the figure for 1981 was 6,121,932.

There is an important distinction between "forward" transactions and "futures" contracts. The former are individual agreements between two parties, say, a bank and customer. The latter is a contract traded on an organized market of a standard size and settlement date, which is resalable at the market price up to the close of trading in the contract. These organized markets are discussed more fully below.

While the major banks conduct foreign exchange deals in large denominations, the IMM trading is done in contracts of standard size which are fairly small. Examples of the standard contracts at present are £25,000; DM125,000; Canadian $100,000. These are actually smaller today than in the early days of the IMM.

Further, unlike prices on the interbank market, price movements in any single day are subject to specific

---

[4]See Federal Reserve Bank of New York (1983).

Figure 1
Structure of Foreign Exchange Markets

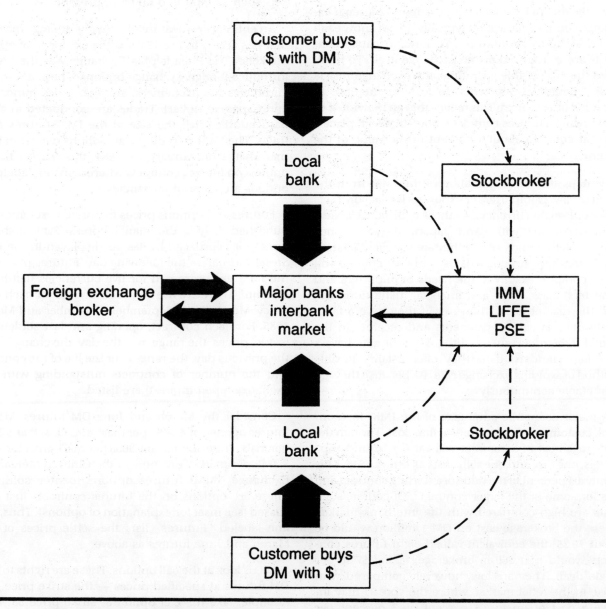

NOTE: The International Money Market (IMM) Chicago trades foreign exchange futures and DM futures options.
The London International Financial Futures Exchange (LIFFE) trades foreign exchange futures.
The Philadelphia Stock Exchange (PSE) trades foreign currency options.

limits at the IMM. For example, for sterling futures, prices are not allowed to vary more than $.0500 away from the previous day's settlement price; this limit is expanded if it is reached in the same direction for two successive days. The limit does not apply on the last day a contract is traded.

Unlike the interbank market, parties to a foreign exchange contract at the IMM typically do not know each other. Default risk, however, is minor because contracts are guaranteed by the exchange itself. To minimize the cost of this guarantee, the exchange insists upon "margin requirements" to cover fluctuations in the value of a contract. This means that an individual or firm buying a futures contract would, in effect, place a deposit equal to about 4 percent of the value of the contract.[5]

Perhaps the major limitation of the IMM from the point of view of importers or exporters is that contracts cover only eight currencies — those of Britain, Canada, West Germany, Switzerland, Japan, Mexico, France and the Netherlands — and they are specified in standard sizes for particular dates. Only by chance will these conform exactly to the needs of importers and exporters. Large firms and financial institutions will find the market useful, however, if they have a fairly continuous stream of payments and receipts in the traded foreign currencies. Although contracts have a specified standard date, they offer a fairly flexible method of avoiding exchange rate risk because they are marketable continuously.

A major economic advantage of the IMM for non-bank customers is its low transaction cost. Though the brokerage cost of a contract will vary, a "round trip" (that is, one buy and one sell) costs as little as $15. This is only .04 percent of the value of a sterling contract and less for some of the larger contracts. Of course, such costs are high compared with the interbank market, where the brokerage cost on DM 1 million would be about $6.25 (the equivalent-valued eight futures contracts would cost $60 in brokerage, taking $7.50 per single deal). They are low, however, compared with those in the retail market, where the spread may involve a cost of up to 2.5 percent or 3 percent per transaction.

A market similar to the IMM, the London International Financial Futures Exchange (LIFFE), opened in September 1982. On LIFFE, futures are traded in sterling, deutschemarks, Swiss francs and yen in identical bundles to those sold on the IMM. In its first year, the foreign exchange business of LIFFE did not take off in a big way. The major provider of exchange rate risk coverage for business continues to be the bank network. Less than 5 percent of such cover is provided by markets such as IMM and LIFFE at present.

An entirely new feature of foreign exchange markets that has arisen in the 1980s is the existence of option markets.[6] The Philadelphia Exchange was the first to introduce foreign exchange options. These are in five currencies (deutschemark, sterling, Swiss franc, yen and Canadian dollar). Trades are conducted in standard bundles half the size of the IMM futures contracts. The IMM introduced an options market in German marks on January 24, 1984; this market trades options on futures contracts whereas the Philadelphia options are for spot currencies.

Futures and options prices for foreign exchange are published daily in the financial press. Table 3 shows prices for February 14, 1984, as displayed in the *Wall Street Journal* on the following day. Futures prices on the IMM are presented for five currencies (left-hand column). There are five contracts quoted for each currency: March, June, September, December and March 1985. For each contract, opening and last settlement (settle) prices, the range over the day, the change from the previous day, the range over the life of the contract and the number of contracts outstanding with the exchange (open interest) are listed.

Consider the March and June DM futures. March futures opened at $.3653 per mark and closed at $.3706 per mark; June opened at $.3698 per mark and closed at $.3746 per mark. Turn now to the Chicago Mercantile Exchange (IMM) futures options (center column). These are options on the futures contracts just discussed (see inset for explanation of options). Thus, the line labeled "Futures" lists the settle prices of the March and June futures as above.

Let us look at the call options. These are rights to buy DM futures at specified prices — the strike price. For example, take the call option at strike price 35. This means that one can purchase an option to buy DM 125,000 March futures up to the March settlement date for $.3500 per mark. This option will cost 2.05 cents per mark, or $2,562.50, plus brokerage fees. The June option to buy June futures DM at $.3500 per mark will cost 2.46 cents per mark, or $3,075.00, plus brokerage fees.

---

[5]A bank may also insist upon some minimum deposit to cover a forward contract, though there is no firm rule.

[6]For a discussion of options in commodities, see Belongia (1983).

Table 3
Futures and Options Markets

Wall Street Journal, February 15, 1984

Futures Prices

Tuesday, February 14, 1984
Open Interest Reflects Previous Trading Day.

	Open	High	Low	Settle	Change	Lifetime High	Lifetime Low	Open Interest
BRITISH POUND (IMM)—25,000 pounds; $ per pound								
Mar	1.4150	1.4400	1.4150	1.4370	+ .0170	1.6010	1.3930	17,694
June	1.4175	1.4435	1.4175	1.4395	+ .0170	1.5520	1.3950	3,251
Sept	1.4285	1.4410	1.4220	1.4410	+ .0160	1.5240	1.3980	157
Dec	1.4280	1.4435	1.4245	1.4435	+ .0160	1.4650	1.3990	75
Mar85	1.4280	1.4460	1.4270	1.4470	+ .0170	1.4625	1.4000	65

Est vol 10,651; vol Mon 1,987; open int 21,242, +78.

	Open	High	Low	Settle	Change	Lifetime High	Lifetime Low	Open Interest
CANADIAN DOLLAR (IMM)—100,000 dlrs.; $ per Can $								
Mar	.8010	.8024	.8010	.8020	....	.8169	.7979	4,033
June	.8014	.8029	.8013	.8023	....	.8168	.7983	740
Sept				.8026	....	.8147	.7988	312
Dec	.8021	.8031	.8021	.8029	....	.8040	.8021	152
Mar85	.8035	.8035	.8035	.8032	....	.8035	.8023	50

Est vol 1,087; vol Mon 535; open int 5,287, −103.

	Open	High	Low	Settle	Change	Lifetime High	Lifetime Low	Open Interest
JAPANESE YEN (IMM) 12.5 million yen; $ per yen (.00)								
Mar	.4276	.4297	.4276	.4294	+ .0011	.4396	.4125	25,730
June	.4315	.4337	.4312	.4334	+ .0011	.4435	.4180	3,908
Sept	.4354	.4375	.4354	.4374	+ .0012	.4450	.4354	974
Dec	.4416	.4420	.4400	.4415	+ .0012	.4493	.4395	271

Est vol 9,133; vol Mon 3,306; open int 30,883, +534.

	Open	High	Low	Settle	Change	Lifetime High	Lifetime Low	Open Interest
SWISS FRANC (IMM)—125,000 francs; $ per franc								
Mar	.4495	.4556	.4486	.4549	+ .0047	.5230	.4470	24,164
June	.4564	.4629	.4557	.4622	+ .0051	.5045	.4536	3,165
Sept	.4632	.4692	.4632	.4688	+ .0052	.5020	.4598	153
Dec	.4705	.4780	.4705	.4747	+ .0049	.4880	.4665	71
Mar85				.4830	+ .0050	.4840	.4755	5

Est vol 30,610; vol Mon 8,466; open int 27,558, +296.

	Open	High	Low	Settle	Change	Lifetime High	Lifetime Low	Open Interest
W. GERMAN MARK (IMM)—125,000 marks; $ per mark								
Mar	.3653	.3713	.3650	.3706	+ .0036	.4100	.3537	30,974
June	.3698	.3754	.3688	.3746	+ .0037	.4002	.3568	4,911
Sept	.3743	.3790	.3743	.3780	+ .0034	.4030	.3602	362
Dec	.3780	.3825	.3780	.3825	+ .0043	.3825	.3640	204
Mar85				.3838	+ .0035	.3699	.3699	1

Est vol 30,248; vol Mon 9,045; open int 36,452, +680.

Futures Options

Chicago Mercantile Exchange

W. GERMAN MARK—125,000 marks, cents per mark

Strike Price	Calls—Settle Mar	Calls—Settle Jun	Puts—Settle Mar	Puts—Settle Jun
34	....	....	0.01	0.01
35	2.05	2.46	0.01	0.09
36	1.11	1.66	0.06	0.25
37	0.38	1.00	0.33	0.57
38	0.10	0.54	1.00	1.02
39	0.01	0.27	....	....
Futures	.3706	.3746		

Estimated total vol. 2,187.
Calls: Mon vol. 180; open int. 2,416.
Puts: Mon vol. 73; open int. 1,841.

Foreign Currency Options

Philadelphia Exchange

Option & Underlying Price	Strike	Calls—Last Mar	Calls—Last Jun	Calls—Last Sep	Puts—Last Mar	Puts—Last Jun	Puts—Last Sep
12,500 British Pounds-cents per unit.							
BPound	140	3.40	r	5.70	0.40	1.85	r
143.00	.145	0.70	2.40	r	3.40	r	r
50,000 Canadian Dollars-cents per unit.							
CDollar	.80	r	r	0.68	r	r	r
62,500 West German Marks-cents per unit.							
DMark	.34	2.67	r	r	r	r	r
36.88	.35	1.99	2.18	r	r	r	r
36.88	.36	1.04	1.59	r	0.05	0.35	r
36.88	.37	0.38	1.00	r	0.37	0.56	r
36.88	.38	0.10	0.62	0.85	r	r	r
36.88	.39	r	0.28	s	r	r	s
36.88	.40	0.01	0.11	s	r	r	s
6,250,000 Japanese Yen-100ths of a cent per unit.							
JYen	.42	0.95	1.49	2.04	r	r	r
42.75	.43	0.30	0.90	r	0.50	0.60	r
42.75	.44	0.04	0.45	0.99	r	r	r
62,500 Swiss Francs-cents per unit.							
SFranc	.44	r	r	3.15	r	0.24	r
45.18	.45	0.65	r	r	0.26	r	r
45.18	.46	0.28	1.09	1.82	r	1.00	r
45.18	.47	0.06	r	r	r	r	r
45.18	.48	0.02	0.28	r	r	r	r

Total call vol.   2,271   Call open int.   37,349
Total put vol.   799   Put open int.   26,173
r—Not traded.   s—No option offered.   o—Old.
Last is premium (purchase price).

The March call option at strike price $.3900 per mark costs only 0.01 cents per mark or $12.50. These price differences indicate that the market expects the dollar price of the mark to exceed $.3500, but not to rise substantially above $.3900.

Notice that when you exercise a futures call option you buy the relevant futures contract but only fulfill that futures contract at maturity. In contrast, the Philadelphia foreign currency options (right column) are options to buy foreign exchange (spot) itself rather than futures. So, when a call option is exercised, foreign currency is obtained immediately.

The only difference in presentation of the currency option prices as compared with the futures options is that, in the former, the spot exchange rate is listed for comparison rather than the futures price. Thus, on the Philadelphia exchange, call options on March DM 62,500 at strike price $.3500 per mark cost 1.99 cents per mark or $1,243.75, plus brokerage. Brokerage fees here would be of the same order as on the IMM, about $16 per transaction round trip, per contract.

We have seen that there are several different markets for foreign exchange — spot, forward, futures, options on spot, options on futures. The channels through which these markets are formed are, however, fairly straightforward (see figure 1). The main channel is the interbank network, though for large interbank transactions, foreign exchange brokers may be used as middlemen.

FOREIGN EXCHANGE MARKET ACTIVITIES

Much foreign exchange market trading does not appear to be related to the simple basic purpose of allowing businesses to buy or sell foreign currency in order, say, to sell or purchase goods overseas. It is certainly easy to see the usefulness of the large range of foreign exchange transactions available through the interbank and organized markets (spot, forward, futures, options) to facilitate trade between nations. It is also clear that there is a useful role for foreign exchange brokers in helping to "make" the interbank market. There are several other activities, however, in foreign exchange markets that are less well understood and whose relevance is less obvious to people interested in understanding what these markets accomplish.

Foreign Exchange Options

An option is a contract specifying the right to buy or sell — in this case foreign exchange — within a specific period (American option) or at a specific date (European option). A call option confers the right to buy. A put option confers the right to sell. Since each of these options must have a buyer and a seller, there are four possible ways of trading a single option: buy a call, sell a call, buy a put, sell a put.

The buyer of an option has the right to undertake the contract specified but may choose not to do so if it turns out to be unprofitable. The seller of the option *must* fulfill the contract if the buyer desires. Clearly, the buyer must pay the seller some premium (the option price) for this privilege. An option that would be profitable to exercise at the current exchange rate is said to be "in the money." The price at which it is exercised is the "exercise" or "strike" price.

Consider a call option on £1000 (although options of this size are not presently available on organized exchanges, it is used to present a simple illustration of the principles involved). Suppose this costs $0.03 per pound or $30 and the exercise price is $1.50 per pound. The option expires in three months. This means that the buyer has paid $30 for the right to buy £1000 with dollars at a price of $1.50 per pound any time in the next three months. If the current spot price of sterling is, say, $1.45, the option is "out of the money" because sterling can be bought cheaper on the spot market. However, if the spot price were to rise to, say, $1.55, the option would be in the money. If sold at that time, the option buyer would get a $50 return (1000 × $0.05), which would more than cover the cost of the option ($50 − $30 = $20 profit). In contrast, a put option at the same terms would be in the money at the current spot price of $1.45, but out of the money at $1.55.

Figure 2 presents a diagrammatic illustration of how the profitability of an option depends upon the relationship between the exercise price and the current spot price.[1] Figure 2a illustrates the profit avail-

---

[1]The pricing of options has been the subject of a large theoretical literature with a major contribution being made by Black and Scholes (1973). The Black-Scholes formula has been modified for foreign exchange options by Garman and Kohlhagen (1983) [see also Giddy (1983)], but the Black-Scholes formula is complex and beyond the scope of the present paper.

Figure 2
Profit from Options

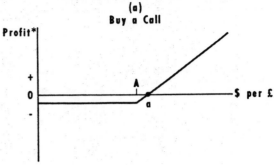

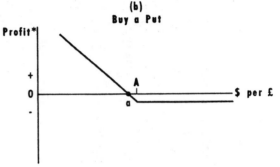

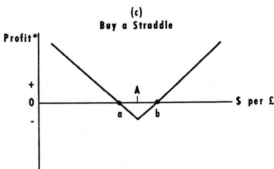

*Profit from exercise of option at current spot exchange rate.

One simple relationship which is of interest may be called "option price parity." This arises because arbitrage will ensure that the difference between a call option price (per unit) and a put option price (per unit) at the same exercise price will be equal to the present value of the difference between the exercise price and the forward exchange rate at maturity of the options (if the options are marketable, it will also hold for any date to maturity). The relationship may be expressed:

$$C - P = \frac{F - E}{1 + r},$$

when C and P are the call and put option prices at exercise price E. F is the forward exchange rate and r is the interest rate per period of the contracts. This arises because the simultaneous buying of a call and selling of a put is equivalent to buying currency forward at price E. The forward contract, however, would be paid for at the end of the period, whereas the options are transacted at the beginning. Hence, the forward contract has to be discounted back to the present.

able from buying a call option at exercise price A. At spot exchange rate A and anything lower, the option will not be exercised so the loss will equal the price of the option. At a spot exchange rate above a, the option is sufficiently in the money to more than cover its cost. Between A and a, the option is in the money but not by enough to cover cost. The profit from *selling* a call could be illustrated by reversing the + and − signs in figure 2a, or by flipping the profit line about the horizontal axis.

Figure 2b illustrates the profit from buying a put option. At spot exchange rates below a, the option with exercise price A will show a profit.

Figure 2c illustrates the profit from a simultaneous purchase of a put and call at the same exercise price. This combination will show a profit at exercise price A if the spot price goes *either* above b or below a. It is known as a "straddle." The straddle is of special interest because it makes clear the role of options as a hedge against risk. The price of a straddle can be regarded as the market valuation of the variability of the exchange rate. That is, the buyer of the straddle will show a profit if the spot price moves from some central value (the exercise price) by more than plus or minus some known percentage. The seller of the straddle accepts that risk for a lump sum. More complicated "multiple strategies" are also possible.[2]

---

[2]See Giddy (1983).

Two major classes of activity will be discussed. First, the existence of a large number of foreign exchange markets in many locations creates opportunities to profit from "arbitrage." Second, there is implicitly a market in (foreign exchange) risk bearing. Those who wish to avoid foreign exchange risk (at a price) may do so. Those who accept the risk in expectation of profits are known as "speculators."

Triangular Arbitrage

Triangular arbitrage is the process that ensures that all exchange rates are mutually consistent. If, for example, one U.S. dollar exchanges for one Canadian dollar, and one Canadian dollar exchanges for one British pound, then the U.S. dollar-pound exchange rate should be one pound for one dollar. If it differs, then there is an opportunity for profit making. To see why this is so, suppose that you could purchase two U.S. dollars with one British pound. By first buying C$1 with U.S.$1, then purchasing £1 with C$1, and finally buying U.S.$2 with £1, you could double your money immediately. Clearly this opportunity will not last for long since it involves making large profits with certainty. The process of triangular arbitrage is exactly that of finding and exploiting profitable opportunities in such exchange rate inconsistencies. As a result of triangular arbitrage, such inconsistencies will be eliminated rapidly. Cross rates, however, will only be roughly consistent given the bid-ask spread associated with transaction costs.

In the past, the possibility of making profits from triangular arbitrage was greater as a result of the practice of expressing exchange rates in American terms in the United States and in European terms elsewhere. The adoption of standard practice has reduced the likelihood of inconsistencies.[7] Also, in recent years, such opportunities for profit making have been greatly reduced by high-speed, computerized information systems and the increased sophistication of the banks operating in the market.

Arbitrage of a slightly different kind results from price differences in different locations. This is "space" arbitrage. For example, if sterling were cheaper in London than in New York, it would be profitable to buy in London and sell in New York. Similarly, if prices in the interbank market differed from those at the IMM, it would be profitable to arbitrage between them. As a result of this activity, prices in different locations will be brought broadly into line.

Interest Arbitrage

Interest arbitrage is slightly different in nature from triangular or space arbitrage; however, the basic motive of finding and exploiting profitable opportunities still applies. There is no reason why interest rates denominated in different currencies should be equal. Interest rates are the cost of borrowing or the return to lending for a specific period of time. The relative price (exchange rate) of money may change over time so that the comparison of, say, a U.S. and a British interest rate requires some allowance for expected exchange rate changes. Thus, it will be not at all unusual to find

---

[7]All except U.K. and Irish exchange rates are expressed in American terms. Futures and options contracts are expressed in European terms.

interest rates denominated in dollars and interest rates denominated in, say, pounds being somewhat different. However, real returns on assets of similar quality should be the same if the exchange rate risk is covered or hedged in the forward market. Were this not true, it would be possible to borrow in one currency and lend in another at a profit with no exchange risk.

Suppose we lend one dollar for a year in the United States at an interest rate of r_{us}. The amount accumulated at the end of the year per dollar lent will be $1 + r_{us}$ (capital plus interest). If, instead of making dollar loans, we converted them into pounds and lent them in the United Kingdom at the rate r_{uk}, the amount of pounds we would have for each original dollar at the end of the year would be $S(1 + r_{uk})$, where S is the spot exchange rate (in pounds per dollar) at the beginning of the period. At the outset, it is not known if $1 + r_{us}$ dollars is going to be worth more than $S(1 + r_{uk})$ pounds in a year's time because the spot exchange rate in a year's time is unknown. This uncertainty can be avoided by selling the pounds forward into dollars. Then the relative value of the two loans would no longer depend on what subsequently happens to the spot exchange rate. By doing this, we end up with $\frac{S}{F}(1 + r_{uk})$ dollars per original dollar invested. This is known as the "covered," or hedged, return on pounds.

Since the covered return in our example is denominated in dollars, it can reasonably be compared with the U.S. interest rate. If these returns are very different, investors will move funds where the return is highest on a covered basis. This process is interest arbitrage. It is assumed that the assets involved are equally safe and, because the returns are covered, all exchange risk is avoided. Of course, if funds do move in large volume between assets or between financial centers, then interest rates and the exchange rates (spot and forward) will change in predictable ways. Funds will continue to flow between countries until there is no extra profit to be made from interest arbitrage. This will occur when the returns on both dollar- and sterling-denominated assets are equal, that is, when

(1) $\quad (1 + r_{us}) = \frac{S}{F}(1 + r_{uk})$.

This result is known as covered interest parity. It holds more or less exactly, subject only to a margin due to transaction costs, so long as the appropriate dollar and sterling interest rates are compared.[8]

---

[8]Since there are many different interest rates, it obviously cannot hold for all of them. Where (1) does hold is if the interest rates chosen are eurocurrency deposit rates of the same duration. In other words, if for

Speculation

Arbitrage in the foreign exchange markets involves little or no risk since transactions can be completed rapidly. An alternative source of profit is available from outguessing other market participants as to what future exchange rates will be. This is called speculation. Although any foreign exchange transaction that is not entirely hedged forward has a speculative element, only deliberate speculation for profit is discussed here.

Until recently, the main foreign exchange speculators were the foreign exchange departments of banks, with a lesser role being played by portfolio managers of other financial institutions and international corporations. The IMM, however, has made it much easier for individuals and smaller businesses to speculate. A high proportion of IMM transactions appears to be speculative in the sense that only about 5 percent of contracts lead to ultimate delivery of foreign exchange. This means that most of the activity involves the buying and selling of a contract *at different times* and possibly different prices prior to maturity. It is possible, however, that buying and selling of contracts before maturity would arise out of a strategy to reduce risk. So it is not possible to say that all such activity is speculative.

Speculation is important for the efficient working of foreign exchange markets. It is a form of arbitrage that occurs across time rather than across space or between markets at the same time. Just as arbitrage increases the efficiency of markets by keeping prices consistent, so speculation increases the efficiency of forward, futures and options markets by keeping those markets liquid. Those who wish to avoid foreign exchange risk may thereby do so in a well-developed market. Without speculators, risk avoidance in foreign exchange markets would be more difficult and, in many cases, impossible.[9]

Risk Reduction

Speculation clearly involves a shifting of risk from one party to another. For example, if a bank buys for-

---

[9]r_{us} we take, say, the three-month eurodollar deposit rate in Paris and for r_{uk} we take the three-month eurosterling deposit rate in Paris, then (1) will hold just about exactly. Indeed, if we took the interest rate and exchange rate quotes all from the same bank, it would be remarkable if (1) did not hold. Otherwise the bank would be offering to pay you to borrow from it and lend straight back! That is, the price of borrowing would be less than the covered return on lending. A margin between borrowing and lending rates, of course, will make this even less likely so that in reality you would lose.

[9]This is not to say that all speculative activity is necessarily beneficial.

Covered Interest Parity: An Example

The following interest rate and exchange rate quotations are taken from the *London Financial Times* of September 8, 1983 (table 1).

Closing
Exchange Rate:	Spot	3-Month Forward
dollars per pound	1.4910–1.4920	.17–.22 discount

Interest Rates:	Eurosterling	Eurodollar
3-Month Offer Rate	9¹³⁄₁₆	10¼

The interest rate on the three-month eurodollar deposit is a little higher (.7 percent) than that on an eurosterling deposit. If the exchange rate remains unchanged, it would be better to hold dollars; if the exchange rate falls, the eurosterling deposit would be preferable. Suppose you decide to cover the exchange risk by selling the dollars forward into pounds. Let us compare the return to holding a sterling deposit with the return to holding a dollar deposit sold forward into sterling (assuming that you start with sterling).

Two important points need to be clarified about the above data. First, the interest rates are annualized so they are not what would actually be earned over a three-month period. For example, the three-month rate equivalent to an annual rate of 10¼ percent is 2.47 percent.

Second, the forward exchange rates need some explanation. The dollar is at a discount against sterling. This means the forward dollar buys less sterling. So we have to *add* the discount onto the spot price to get the forward price (because the price is the number of dollars per pound, not the reverse). Notice also that the discount is measured in fractions of a cent, not fractions of a dollar! So the bid-ask spread on the forward rate would be 1.4927 – 1.4942.

Now let us see if we would do better to invest in a three-month eurosterling deposit or a three-month eurodollar deposit where the dollars to be received were sold forward into sterling. The return per £100 invested in eurosterling is £2.369 (annual interest rate of 9¹³⁄₁₆), whereas the return on a covered eurodollar deposit is

$$£2.251 = (100 \times \frac{1.4910}{1.4942} \, 1.0247) - 100.$$

Thus, we could not make a profit out of covered interest arbitrage. Despite the fact that dollar interest rates are higher, the discount on forward dollars in the forward market means they buy fewer forward pounds. As a result, there is no benefit to the operation. Transaction costs for most individuals would be even greater than those above as they would face a larger bid-ask spread than that quoted on the interbank market.

Consequently, there is no benefit for the typical investor from making a covered or hedged eurocurrency deposit. The return will be at least as high on a deposit in the currency in which you start and wish to end up. That is, if you have dollars and wish to end up with dollars, make a eurodollar deposit. If you have sterling and wish to end up with sterling, make a eurosterling deposit. If you have sterling and wish to end up in dollars, there is likely to be little or no difference between holding a eurosterling deposit sold forward into dollars or buying dollars spot and holding a eurodollar deposit. Of course, if you hold an "uncovered" deposit and exchange rates subsequently change, the result will be very different.

ward foreign exchange from a customer, it increases its exposure to risk while the customer reduces his. However, there is not a fixed amount of risk that has to be "shared out." Some strategies may involve a net reduction of risk all around.

As a general rule, financial institutions (or other firms), operating in a variety of currencies, will try to minimize the risk of losses due to unexpected exchange rate changes. One simple way to do this is to ensure that assets and liabilities denominated in each operating currency are equal. This is known as "matching." For example, a bank that sells sterling forward to a customer may simultaneously buy sterling forward. In this event, the bank is exposed to zero exchange rate risk.

Why Is the Dollar the "Money" of Foreign Exchange Markets?

One interesting aspect of the organization of the foreign exchange markets is that the "money" used in these markets is generally the U.S. dollar. This is generally true for spot markets and universally true for forward markets. "Cross-markets" between many currencies are very thin, and future cross markets are virtually nonexistent. For example, the bulk of foreign exchange trading between £s and cruzeiro will involve dollar-£ and dollar-cruzeiro transactions instead of direct £-cruzeiro trading. The only exception to this is the transactions involving the major Organization for Economic Cooperation and Development (OECD) currencies, especially within Europe. Of the $702.5 billion turnover in foreign exchange reported by U.S. banks in April 1983, only $1.5 billion did not involve U.S. dollars.

There are two explanations for this special role of the dollar in foreign exchange markets. Both rely upon the fact that transaction costs are likely to be lower if the dollar is used as a medium. Krugman shows that the clearing of foreign exchange markets requires some "intermediary" currency.[1] Even if every country is in payments balance vis a vis the rest of the world, it will not necessarily be in bilateral balance with each other country. Because some currency has to be used to cover this residual finance, it is natural to choose the currency that has the lowest transaction costs. Chrystal shows there are economic reasons why cross-markets between many currencies do not exist.[2] It typically will be easier and cheaper to set up a deal in two steps via the dollar than in a single step (cruzeiro-dollar, dollar-drachma rather than cruzeiro-drachma). This is because these cross-markets, if they existed, would be fairly thin and hence relatively costly for such transactions. The two markets with the dollar, on the other hand, are well developed.

These analyses refer to the role of the dollar in the interbank market. In the development of the trading places such as the IMM in Chicago and LIFFE in London to date, it is also true that all currency futures are traded against the dollar.

---

[1] See Krugman (1980).

[2] See Chrystal (1982).

Banks often use "swaps" to close gaps in the maturity structure of their assets and liabilities in a currency. This involves the simultaneous purchase and sale of a currency for *different* maturity dates. In April 1983, 33 percent of U.S. banks' foreign exchange turnover involved swaps as compared with 63 percent spot contracts and only 4 percent outright forward contracts.[10]

Suppose a bank has sold DM to a customer three months forward and bought the same amount of DM from a different customer six months forward. There are two ways in which the bank could achieve zero foreign exchange risk exposure. It could either undertake two separate offsetting forward transactions, or it could set up a single swap with another bank that has the opposite mismatch of dollar-DM flows whereby it receives DM in exchange for dollars in three months and receives back dollars in exchange for DM in six

months. Once the swap is set up, the bank's net profits are protected against subsequent changes in spot exchange rates during the next six months.

Within the limits imposed by the nature of the contracts, a similar effect can be achieved by an appropriate portfolio of futures contracts on the IMM. Thus, a bank would buy and sell futures contracts so as to match closely its forward commitments to customers. In reality, banks will use a combination of methods to reduce foreign exchange risk.

Markets that permit banks, firms and individuals to hedge foreign exchange risk are essential in times of fluctuating exchange rates. This is especially important for banks if they are to be able to provide efficient foreign exchange services for their customers. In the absence of markets that permit foreign exchange risk hedging, the cost and uncertainty of international transactions would be greatly increased, and international specialization and trade would be greatly reduced.

---

[10] See Federal Reserve Bank of New York (1983).

CONCLUSION

The foreign exchange markets are complex and, for the outsider, hard to comprehend. The primary function of these markets is straightforward. It is to facilitate international transactions related to trade, travel or investment. Foreign exchange markets can now accommodate a large range of current and forward transactions.

Given the variability of exchange rates, it is important for banks and firms operating in foreign currencies to be able to reduce exchange rate risk whenever possible. Some risk reduction is achieved by interbank swaps, but some is also taken up by speculation. Arbitrage and speculation both increase the efficiency of spot and forward foreign exchange markets and have enabled foreign exchange markets to achieve a high level of efficiency. Without the successful operation of these markets, the obstacles to international trade and investment would be substantial and the world would be a poorer place.

Glossary

American option — an option that can be exercised any time up to maturity.

American terms — an exchange rate expressed as number of currency units per dollar.

arbitrage — the simultaneous purchase and sale of currency in separate markets for a profit arising from a price discrepancy between the markets.

bid-ask spread — the difference between the buying (bid) and selling (ask) price.

covered interest arbitrage — buying a country's currency spot, investing for a period, and selling the proceeds forward in order to make a net profit due to the higher interest rate in that country. This act involves "hedging" because it guarantees a covered return without risk. The opportunities to profit in this way seldom arise because covered interest differentials are normally close to zero.

covered interest parity — the gap between interest rates in foreign and domestic currencies will be matched by the forward exchange rate differential, such that the "covered" interest rate differential will be close to zero.

eurodollar deposits — bank deposits, generally bearing interest and made for a specific time period, that are denominated in dollars but are in banks outside the United States. Similarly, euro-sterling deposits would be denominated in sterling but outside the United Kingdom.

European option — an option that can be exercised only on a specified date.

European terms — an exchange rate expressed as number of dollars per currency unit.

floating exchange rate — an exchange rate that is allowed to adjust freely to the supply of and demand for foreign exchange.

foreign exchange speculation — the act of taking a net position in a foreign currency with the intention of making a profit from exchange rate changes.

forward exchange rate — the price of foreign currency for delivery at a future date agreed to by a contract today.

futures market — a market in which contracts are traded to buy or sell a standard amount of currency in the future at a particular price.

hedging — or covering exchange risk, means that foreign currency is sold forward into local currency so that its value is not affected by subsequent exchange rate changes. Say an exporter knows he will be paid £10,000 in two months. He can wait until he gets the money and convert it into dollars at whatever the spot rate turns out to be. This outcome is uncertain as the spot rate may change. Alternatively, he can sell £10,000 two months forward at today's two-month forward price. Suppose this is $1.5 per £. In two months, he will receive £10,000, fulfill his forward contract and receive $15,000. This export contract has been hedged or covered in the forward market.

matching — equating assets and liabilities denominated in each currency so that losses due to foreign exchange rate changes are minimized.

options market — a market in which contracts are traded that gives a purchaser the right but no obligation to buy (call) or to sell (put) a currency in the future at a given price.

spot exchange rate — the price paid to exchange currencies for immediate delivery (two business days in the interbank market, or over the counter in the retail and travelers check market).

swap — the simultaneous purchase and sale of a currency for different maturity dates that closes the gaps in the maturity structure of assets and liabilities in a currency.

REFERENCES

Belongia, Michael T. "Commodity Options: A New Risk Management Tool for Agricultural Markets," this *Review* (June/July 1983), pp. 5–15.

Black, Fisher, and Myron Scholes. "The Pricing of Options and Corporate Liabilities," *Journal of Political Economy* (May/June 1973), pp. 637–54.

Chrystal, K. Alec. "On the Theory of International Money" (paper presented to U.K. International Economics Study Group Conference, September 1982, Sussex, England). Forthcoming in J. Black and G. S. Dorrance, eds., *Problems of International Finance* (London: Macmillan, 1984).

Dufey, Gunter, and Ian H. Giddy. *The International Money Market* (Prentice-Hall, 1978).

Federal Reserve Bank of New York. "Summary of Results of U.S. Foreign Exchange Market Turnover Survey Conducted in April 1983" (September 8, 1983).

Garman, Mark B., and Steven W. Kohlhagen. "Foreign Currency Option Values," *Journal of International Money and Finance* (December 1983), pp. 231–37.

Giddy, Ian H. "Foreign Exchange Options," *Journal of Futures Markets* (Summer 1983), pp. 143–66.

Krugman, Paul. "Vehicle Currencies and the Structure of International Exchange," *Journal of Money, Credit and Banking* (August 1980), pp. 513–26.

Kubarych, Roger M. *Foreign Exchange Markets in the United States.* (Federal Reserve Bank of New York, 1983).

McKinnon, Ronald I. *Money in International Exchange: The Convertible Currency System* (Oxford University Press, 1979).

Article 35

Protectionist Trade Policies: A Survey of Theory, Evidence and Rationale

Cletus C. Coughlin, K. Alec Chrystal and Geoffrey E. Wood

PROTECTIONIST pressures have been mounting worldwide during the 1980s. These pressures are due to various economic problems including the large and persistent balance of trade deficits in the United States; the hard times experienced by several industries; and the slow growth of many foreign countries.[1] Proponents of protectionist trade policies argue that international trade has contributed substantially to these problems and that protectionist trade policies will lead to improved results. Professional economists in the United States, however, generally agree that trade restrictions such as tariffs and quotas substantially reduce a nation's economic well-being.[2]

This article surveys the theory, evidence and rationale concerning protectionist trade policies. The first section illustrates the gains from free trade using the concept of comparative advantage. Recent developments in international trade theory that emphasize other reasons for gains from trade are also reviewed. The theoretical discussion is followed by an examination of recent empirical studies that demonstrate the large costs of protectionist trade policies. Then, the rationale for restricting trade is presented. The concluding section summarizes the paper's main arguments.

Cletus C. Coughlin is a senior economist at the Federal Reserve Bank of St. Louis. K. Alec Chrystal is the National Westminster Bank Professor of Personal Finance at City University, London. Geoffrey E. Wood is a professor of economics at City University, London. This article was written while Chrystal was a professor of economics at the University of Sheffield, Sheffield, England. Thomas A. Pollmann provided research assistance.

[1] See Page (1987) for a detailed examination of trade protectionism since 1974.

[2] This consensus was found in a survey published in the late 1970s (Kearl et al., 1979). Recent developments in international trade theory, which can be used to justify governmental intervention in trade policy, have not altered the consensus (Krugman, 1987).

THE GAINS FROM FREE TRADE

The most famous demonstration of the gains from trade appeared in 1817 in David Ricardo's *Principles of Political Economy and Taxation*. We use his example involving trade between England and Portugal to demonstrate how both countries can gain from trade. The two countries produce the same two goods, wine and cloth, and the only production costs are labor costs. The figures below list the amount of labor (e.g., worker-days) required in each country to produce one bottle of wine or one bolt of cloth.

	Wine	Cloth
England	3	7
Portugal	1	5

Since both goods are more costly to produce in England than in Portugal, England is absolutely less efficient at producing both goods than its prospective trading partner. Portugal has an absolute advantage in both wine and cloth. At first glance, this appears to rule out mutual gains from trade; however, as we demonstrate below, absolute advantage is irrelevant in discerning whether trade can benefit both countries.

The ratio of the production costs for the two goods is different in the two countries. In England, a bottle of wine will exchange for 3/7 of a bolt of cloth because the labor content of the wine is 3/7 of that for cloth. In Portugal, a bottle of wine will exchange for 1/5 of a bolt of cloth. Thus, wine is relatively cheaper in Portugal than in England and, conversely, cloth is relatively cheaper in England than in Portugal. The example indicates that Portugal has a comparative advantage in wine production and England has a comparative advantage in cloth production.

The different relative prices provide the basis for

both countries to gain from international trade. The gains arise from both exchange and specialization.

The gains from *exchange* can be highlighted in the following manner. If a Portuguese wine producer sells five bottles of wine at home, he receives one bolt of cloth. If he trades in England, he receives more than two bolts of cloth. Hence, he can gain by exporting his wine to England. English cloth-producers are willing to trade in Portugal; for every 3/7 of a bolt of cloth they sell there, they get just over two bottles of wine. The English gain from exporting cloth to (and importing wine from) Portugal, and the Portuguese gain from exporting wine to (and importing cloth from) England. Each country gains by exporting the good in which it has a comparative advantage and by importing the good in which it has a comparative disadvantage.

Gains from *specialization* can be demonstrated in the following manner. Initially, each country is producing some of both goods. Suppose that, as a result of trade, 21 units of labor are shifted from wine to cloth production in England, while, in Portugal, 10 units of labor are shifted from cloth to wine production. This reallocation of labor does not alter the total amount of labor used in the two countries; however, it causes the production changes listed below.

	Bottles of Wine	Bolts of Cloth
England	− 7	+ 3
Portugal	+10	− 2
Net	+ 3	+ 1

The shift of 21 units of labor to the English cloth industry raises cloth production by three bolts, while reducing wine production by seven bottles. In Portugal, the shift of 10 units of labor from cloth to wine raises wine production by 10 bottles, while reducing cloth production by two bolts. This reallocation of labor increases the total production of both goods: wine by three bottles and cloth by one bolt. This increased output will be shared by the two countries. Thus, the consumption of both goods and the wealth of both countries are increased by the specialization brought about by trade based on comparative advantage.

TRADE THEORY SINCE RICARDO

Since 1817, numerous analyses have generated insights concerning the gains from trade. They chiefly examine the consequences of relaxing the assumptions used in the preceding example. For example,

labor was the only resource used to produce the two goods in the example above; yet, labor is really only one of many resources used to produce goods. The example also assumed that the costs of producing additional units of the goods are constant. For example, in England, three units of labor are used to produce one bottle of wine regardless of the level of wine production. In reality, unit production costs could either increase or decrease as more is produced. A third assumption was that the goods are produced in perfectly competitive markets. In other words, an individual firm has no effect on the price of the good that it produces. Some industries, however, are dominated by a small number of firms, each of which can affect the market price of the good by altering its production decision. Some of these extensions are discussed in the appendix.

These theoretical developments generally have strengthened the case for an open trading system. They suggest three sources of gains from trade. First, as the market potentially served by firms expands from a national to a world market, there are gains associated with declining per unit production costs. A second source of gains results from the reduction in the monopoly power of domestic firms. Domestic firms, facing more pressure from foreign competitors, are forced to produce the output demanded by consumers at the lowest possible cost.[3] Third is the gain to consumers from increased product variety and lower prices. Generally speaking, the gains from trade result from the increase in competitive pressures as the domestic economy becomes less insulated from the world economy.

The gains from free trade can also be illustrated graphically. The shaded insert on pages 14 and 15 examines the gains from trade in perfectly competitive markets using supply and demand analysis. The insert also analyzes the effects of trade restrictions, a topic that we discuss below.

COSTS OF TRADE PROTECTIONISM

Protectionist trade policies can take numerous forms, some of which are discussed in the shaded insert on pages 16 and 17. All forms of protection are

---

[3]A profit-maximizing firm produces its output at minimum cost. When firms are insulated from competition, costs are not necessarily being minimized. This situation, which is called X-efficiency, has been stressed by Leibenstein (1980). The increase in competitive pressures due to international trade reduces the probability that costs are not minimized.

A Supply and Demand Analysis of the Gains from Free Trade and the Effects of a Tariff

A standard illustration of the gains from free trade and the effects of a tariff is presented below. The analysis assumes perfectly competitive markets throughout.

Gains From Free Trade

In figure 1 the lines S_{us} and D_{us} are the U.S. supply and demand curves for a hypothetical good. Their intersection at B results in the equilibrium values for price and quantity of P_{us} and Q_{us}. Assuming the United States has a comparative disadvantage in the production of this good, the price will be lower abroad than in the United States. Let this lower world price be P_w, and assume that U.S. purchases do not affect this world price. Graphically, this is represented by the horizontal world supply curve S_w. If one allows for free trade, this lower world price has two effects. First, U.S. consumers will increase their consumption to D'_{us}. Second, U.S. producers will contract their production to S'_{us}. The excess of U.S. consumption over production is U.S. purchases from foreign producers (that is, imports).

The lower price simultaneously benefits U.S. consumers and harms U.S. producers, a fact that underlies the recent controversial discussions of U.S.

trade policy. The magnitude of these gains and losses using the concepts of consumer and producer surplus can be seen in figure 1. Consumers gain in two ways. Initially, consumers purchased Q_{us} at a price per unit of P_{us}. With free trade, they purchase Q_{us} at the lower price per unit of P_w. This gain is represented by the rectangle P_{us} BE P_w. In addition, the lower price induces consumers to increase their purchases from Q_{us} to D'_{us}. This gain is represented by the triangle BCE. The total gain to consumers is P_{us} BC P_w or, using the lower case letters to represent areas, a + b + c. Analogously, producers lose due to the lower price they receive for their output, S'_{us}, and due to their contraction of production from Q_{us} to S'_{us}. The total loss to producers is P_{us} BF P_w or a.

The nation as a whole gains because the consumer gains of a + b + c exceed the producer losses of a by b + c. This analysis can also be viewed using a good that the United States exports. In other words, the United States will have a comparative advantage in the production of a good. For the export good, the change to free trade will cause producer gains that exceed consumer losses.

The Effects of a Tariff

To make the analysis of protectionist trade policy as straightforward as possible, the impact of a tariff is analyzed. (One can view any protectionist trade policy, however, in an analogous manner.) For convenience, the free trade results in figure 1 are duplicated in figure 2. Given the free trade world price of P_w, U.S. consumption, production and imports are D'_{us}, S'_{us}, and S'_{us} D'_{us}. Assume a tariff is imposed, causing the price in the United States to increase to P_T. The price in the United States now exceeds price in the world by the amount of the tariff, $P_w P_T$.

The higher U.S. price causes consumer purchases to decrease from D'_{us} to D''_{us}, domestic production to increase from S'_{us} to S''_{us}, and imports to decrease from $S'_{us} D'_{us}$ to $S''_{us} D''_{us}$. By imposing the tariff, consumers lose the area $P_T JCP_w$ or d + e + f + g and producers gain the area $P_T IFP_w$ or d. Do-

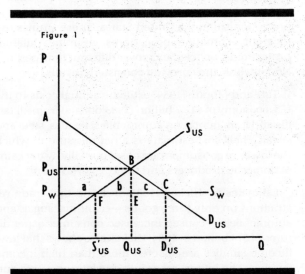

Figure 1

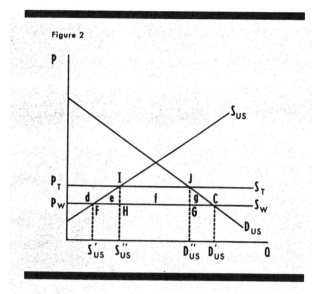

Figure 2

mestic producers are protected at the expense of domestic consumers.

One complication stems from tariff revenue. Tariff revenue, which can be viewed as a gain for the government, equals the tariff, $P_w P_T$, times the quantity of imports, $S''_{us} D''_{us}$. This revenue is equal to area IJGH or f.

Overall, the nation loses because the consumers' losses of d + e + f + g exceed the producers' gains of d and the government gains of f by e + g. Area e is called a "deadweight production loss" and can be viewed as a loss resulting from inefficient (excess) domestic production, while area g is called a "deadweight consumption loss" and can be viewed as a loss resulting from inefficient (too little) consumption.

intended to improve the position of domestic relative to foreign producers. This can be done through policies that increase the home market price of the foreign product, decrease the production costs of domestic firms, or somehow restrict the access of foreign producers to the domestic market.

The specific goal of protectionist trade policies is to expand domestic production in the protected industries, benefiting the owners, workers and suppliers of resources to the protected industry. The government imposing protectionist trade policies may also benefit, for example, in the form of tariff revenue.

The expansion of domestic production in protected industries is not costless; it requires additional resources from other industries. Consequently, output in other domestic industries is reduced. These industries also might be made less competitive because of higher prices for imported inputs. Since protectionist trade policies frequently increase the price of the protected good, domestic consumers are harmed. They lose in two ways. First, their consumption of the protected good is reduced because of the associated rise in its price. Second, they consume less of other goods, as their output declines and prices rise.

The preceding discussion highlights the domestic winners and losers due to protectionist trade policies. Domestic producers of the protected good and the government (if tariffs are imposed) gain; domestic consumers and other domestic producers lose. Foreign interests are also affected by trade restrictions. The protection of domestic producers will harm some foreign producers; oddly enough, other foreign producers may benefit. For example, if quotas are placed on imports, some foreign producers may receive higher prices for their exports to the protected market.

There have been numerous studies of the costs of protectionism. We begin by examining three recent studies of protectionism in the United States, then proceed to studies examining developed and, finally, developing countries.

Costs of Protectionism in the United States

Recent studies by Tarr and Morkre (1984), Hickok (1985) and Hufbauer et al. (1986) estimated the costs of protectionism in the United States. These studies use different estimation procedures, examine different protectionist policies and cover different time periods. Nonetheless, they provide consistent results.

Tarr and Morkre (1984) estimate annual costs to the U.S. economy of $12.7 billion (1983 dollars) from all tariffs and from quotas on automobiles, textiles, steel and sugar. Their cost estimate is a net measure in which the losses of consumers are offset partially by the gains of domestic producers and the U.S. government.

Estimates by Hickok (1985) indicate that trade restrictions on only three goods — clothing, sugar, and automobiles — caused increased consumer expenditures of $14 billion in 1984. Hickok also shows that low-income families are affected more than high-income families. The import restraints on clothing, sugar and automobiles are calculated to be equivalent to a 23 percent income tax surcharge (that is, an additional

Forms Of Protectionism

Protection may be implemented in numerous ways. All forms of protection are intended to improve the position of a domestic relative to foreign producer. This can be done by policies that increase the home market price of the foreign product, decrease the costs of domestic producers or restrict the access of foreign producers to the home market in some other way.

Tariffs

Tariffs, which are simply taxes imposed on goods entering a country from abroad, result in higher prices and have been the most common form of protection for domestic producers. Tariffs have been popular with governments because it appears that the tax is being paid by the foreigner who wishes to sell his goods in the home economy and because the tariff revenue can be used to finance government services or reduce other taxes.

In the 20th century, U.S. tariff rates peaked as a result of the Smoot-Hawley Tariff of 1930. For example, in 1932, tariff revenue as a percentage of total imports was 19.6 percent. An identical calculation for 1985 yields a figure of 3.8 percent. The decline was due primarily to two reasons. First, since many of the tariffs under Smoot-Hawley were set as specific dollar amounts, the rising price level in the United States eroded the effective tariff rate. Second, since World War II, numerous tariff reductions have been negotiated under the General Agreement on Tariffs and Trade.

On the other hand, various other forms of protection, frequently termed non-tariff barriers, have become increasingly important. A few of the more frequently used devices are discussed below.

Quotas

A quota seems like a sensible alternative to a tariff when the intention is to restrict foreign producers' access to the domestic market. Importers typically are limited to a maximum number of products that they can sell in the home market over specific periods. A quota, similar to a tariff, cause prices to increase in the home market. This induces domestic producers to increase production and consumers to reduce consumption. One difference between a tariff and a quota is that the tariff generates revenue for the government, while the quota generates a revenue gain to the owner of import licenses. Consequently, foreign producers might capture some of this revenue.

In recent years, a slightly different version of quotas, called either orderly marketing agreements or voluntary export restraints, has been used. In an orderly marketing agreement, the domestic government asks the foreign government to restrict the quantity of exports of a good to the domestic country. The request can be viewed as a demand, like the U.S.-Japan automobile agreement in the 1980s, because the domestic country makes it clear that more restrictive actions are likely unless the foreign government "voluntarily" complies. In effect, the orderly marketing agreement is a mutually agreed-upon quota.

Regulatory Barriers

There are many other ways of restricting foreigners' access to domestic markets. Munger (1983) has noted that the tariff code itself tends to limit trade. The 1983 *Tariff Schedules of the United States Annotated* consists of 792 pages, plus a 78-page appendix. Over 200 tariff rates pertain to watches and clocks. Simply ascertaining the appropriate tariff classification, which requires legal assistance and can be subject to differences of opinion, is a deterrent.

Product standards are another common regulatory barrier. These standards appear in various forms and are used for many purposes. The standards can be used to serve the public interest by ensuring that imported food products are processed according to acceptable sanitary standards and that drugs have been screened before their introduction in the United States. In other cases, the standards, sometimes intentionally, protect domestic producers. An example of unintended restrictions may be the imposition of safety or pollution standards that were not previously being met by foreign cars.

Subsidies

An alternative to restricting the terms under which foreigners can compete in the home market is to subsidize domestic producers. Subsidies may be focused upon an industry in general or upon the export activities of the industry. An example of the former, discussed by Morici and Megna (1983), is the combination of credit programs, special tax incentives and direct subsidy payments that benefit the U.S. shipbuilding industry. An example of the latter is the financial assistance to increase exports provided by the U.S. Export-Import Bank through direct loans, loan guarantees and insurance, and discount loans. In either case, production will expand.

An important difference between subsidies and tariffs involves the revenue implications for government. The former involves the government in paying out money, whereas tariffs generate income for the government. The effect on domestic production and welfare, however, can be the same under subsidies as under tariffs and quotas. In all cases, the protected industry is being subsidized by the rest of the economy.

Exchange Controls

All of the above relate directly to the flow of goods. A final class of restrictions works by restricting access to the foreign money required to buy foreign goods. For example, a government that wished to protect its exporting and import-competing industries may try to hold its exchange rate artificially low. As a result, foreign goods would appear expensive in the home market while home goods would be cheap overseas. Home producers implicitly are subsidized and home consumers implicitly are taxed. This policy is normally hard to sustain. The central bank, in holding the exchange rate down has to buy foreign exchange with domestic currency. This newly issued domestic currency increases the domestic money stock and eventually causes inflation. Inflationary policies are not normally regarded as a sensible way of protecting domestic industry.

There is another aspect to exchange controls. The justification is that preventing home residents from investing overseas benefits domestic growth as it leads to greater domestic real investment. In reality, it could do exactly the opposite. Restricting access to foreign assets may raise the variance and lower the return to owners of domestic wealth. In the short run, it also may appreciate the domestic exchange rate and, thereby, make domestic producers less competitive.

tax added to the normal income tax) for families with incomes less than $10,000 in 1984 and a 3 percent income tax surcharge for families with incomes exceeding $60,000.

Hufbauer et al. (1986) examined 31 cases in which trade volumes exceeded $100 million and the United States imposed protectionist trade restrictions.[4] They generated estimates of the welfare consequences for each major group affected (see table 1). The figures in the table indicate that annual consumer losses exceed $100 million in all but six of the cases. The largest losses, $27 billion per year, come from protecting the textiles and apparel industry. There also are large

consumer losses associated with protection in carbon steel ($6.8 billion), automobiles ($5.8 billion) and dairy products ($5.5 billion).

The purpose of protectionism is to protect jobs in specific industries. A useful approach to gain some perspective on consumer losses is to express these losses on a per-job-saved basis. In 18 of the 31 cases, the cost per-job-saved is $100,000 or more per year; the consumer losses per-job-saved in benzenoid chemicals, carbon steel (two separate periods), specialty steel, and bolts, nuts and screws exceeded $500,000 per year.

Table 1 also reveals that domestic producers were the primary beneficiaries of protectionist policies; however, there are some noteworthy cases where foreign producers realized relatively large gains. For the U.S.-Japanese voluntary export agreement in automobiles, foreign producers gained 38 percent of what domestic consumers lost, while a similar computation

---

[4]While there were cases in which the industry adjusted to its new competitive position and the protection was terminated, these cases were more the exception than the rule. In far more cases, protectionist policies were maintained indefinitely or removed because of favorable demand changes.

Table 1

Distribution of Costs and Benefits from Special Protection

Case	Consumer Losses Totals (million dollars)	Consumer Losses Per job saved[1] (dollars)	Producer Gains Totals (million dollars)	Welfare Costs of Restraints Gain to foreigners (million dollars)	Welfare Costs of Restraints Tariff revenue (million dollars)	Welfare Costs of Restraints Efficiency loss (million dollars)
Manufacturing						
Book manufacturing	$ 500	$ 100,000	$ 305	neg.	$ 0	$ 29
Benzenoid chemicals	2,650	over 1 million	2,250	neg.	252	14
Glassware	200	200,000	130	neg.	54	13
Rubber footwear	230	30,000	90	neg.	139	33
Ceramic articles	95	47,500	25	neg.	69	6
Ceramic tiles	116	135,000	62	neg.	55	11
Orange juice	525	240,000	390	neg.	128	130
Canned tuna	91	76,000	74	$ 7	10	4
Textiles and apparel: Phase I	9,400	22,000	8,700	neg.	1,158	1,100
Textiles and apparel: Phase II	20,000	37,000	18,000	350	2,143	3,100
Textiles and apparel: Phase III	27,000	42,000	22,000	1,800	2,535	4,850
Carbon steel: Phase I	1,970	240,000	1,330	330	290	50
Carbon steel: Phase II	4,350	620,000	2,770	930	556	120
Carbon steel: Phase III	6,800	750,000	3,800	2,000	560	330
Ball bearings	45	90,000	21	neg.	18	neg.
Specialty steel	520	1,000,000	420	50	32	30
Nonrubber footwear	700	55,000	250	220	262	16
Color televisions	420	420,000	190	140	77	7
CB radios	55	93,000	14	neg.	32	5
Bolts, nuts, large screws	110	550,000	60	neg.	16	1
Prepared mushrooms	35	117,000	13	neg.	25	0.8
Automobiles	5,800	105,000	2,600	2,200	790	200
Motorcycles	104	150,000	67	neg.	21	17
Services						
Maritime industries	3,000	270,000	2,000	neg.	10[2]	1,000
Agriculture and fisheries						
Sugar	930	60,000 690/acre	550	410	5	130
Dairy products	5,500	220,000 1,800/cow	5,000	250	34	1,370
Peanuts	170	1,000/acre	170	neg.	9	14
Meat	1,800	160,000 225/head	1,600	135	44	145
Fish	560	21,000	200	170	177	15
Mining						
Petroleum	6,900	160,000	4,800	2,000[3]	70	3,000
Lead and zinc	67	30,000	46	4	11	5

Neg. = negligible.
[1]Unless otherwise specified, figures are per worker.
[2]Estimated duties collected on ship repairs performed abroad.
[3]In this case, because of the way the quotas were allocated, the gains to importers accrued to domestic refiners rather than foreign exporters.
SOURCE: Trade Protection in the United States: 31 Case Studies.

for the latest phase of protection for carbon steel was 29 percent.

Finally, table 1 indicates that the efficiency losses are small in comparison to the total losses borne by consumers. These efficiency losses, which are defined precisely and illustrated in the first shaded insert, result from the excess domestic production and the reduction in consumption caused by protectionist trade policies. In large cases such as textiles and apparel, petroleum, dairy products and the maritime industries, these losses equal or exceed $1 billion. It is likely that these estimates understate the actual costs because they do not capture the secondary effects that occur as production and consumption changes in one industry affect other industries.[5] In addition, restrictive trade policies generate additional costs because of bureaucratic enforcement costs and efforts by the private sector to influence these policies for their own gain as well as simply comply with administrative regulations.

Costs of Protectionism Throughout the World

In 1982, the Organization for Economic Co-operation and Development (OECD) began a project to analyze the costs and benefits of protectionist policies in manufacturing in OECD countries. The OECD (1985) highlighted a number of ways that protectionist policies have generated costs far in excess of benefits. Since protectionist policies increase prices, the report concludes that the attainment of sustained non-inflationary growth is hindered by such price-increasing effects. Moreover, economic growth is potentially reduced if the uncertainty created by varying trade policies depresses investment.

Wood and Mudd (1978), and many others, have shown that imports do not cause higher unemployment. Conversely, the OECD study stresses the fact that a reduction in imports via trade restrictions does not cause greater employment. A reduction in the value of imports results in a similar reduction in the

value of exports. One rationale for this finding is that a reduction in the purchases of foreign goods reduces foreign incomes and, in turn, causes reduced foreign purchases of domestic goods.

While the reduction in imports increases employment in industries that produce products similar to the previously imported goods, the reduction in exports decreases employment in the export industries. In other words, while some jobs are saved, others are lost; however, this economic reality may not be obvious to businessmen, labor union leaders, politicians and others. Luttrell (1978) has stressed that the jobs saved by protectionist legislation are more readily observed than the jobs lost due to protectionist legislation. In other words, the jobs that are protected in, say, the textiles industry by U.S. import restrictions on foreign textiles are more readily apparent (and publicized) than the jobs in agriculture and high technology industries that do not materialize because of the import restrictions. These employment effects will net to approximately zero.[6]

The OECD study also stresses that developing countries need exports to offset their debts. Thus, protectionist trade policies by developed countries affect not only the economic activity of the developing countries, but the stability of the international financial system as debtor nations find it increasingly difficult to service their debts.

Not only does a free trade policy by developed countries benefit developing countries, but a free trade policy by developing countries benefits developing countries. A recent World Bank study (1987) of 41 developing countries compared the performance of countries following a free trade policy with countries following a restricted trade policy.[7] Table 2 lists the

---

[6]Recent evidence shows that protectionist legislation actually may reduce employment. Denzau (1987) estimated that 35,600 manufacturing jobs were lost as a result of the September 1984 voluntary export restraints that limited the level of U.S. steel imports. Despite an increased employment for producers of steel (14,000) and producers of inputs for steel producers (2,800), these increases were more than offset by the 52,400 job losses by steel-using firms. These losses are due to the higher steel prices that cause steel-using firms to be less competitive in export markets and subject them to more foreign competition in the U.S. market.

[7]The World Bank study divides trade strategies into two groups: outward oriented and inward oriented. An outward-oriented strategy, which we call a free trade policy, is one in which trade and industrial policies do not discriminate between production for the domestic market and exports, nor between purchases of domestic and foreign goods. An inward-oriented strategy, which we call a restricted trade policy, is one in which trade and industrial policies are biased toward production for the domestic market relative to the export market.

---

[5]Recent estimates of the costs of protectionist policies using general equilibrium models suggest that the secondary effects, to the limited extent they are measurable, are substantial. For example, Grais, de Melo and Urata (1986) estimate that the elimination of quotas in Turkey in 1978 would have caused a 5.4 percent rise in gross domestic product, while Clarete and Whalley (1985) estimate that the elimination of tariffs, quotas and export taxes in the Philippines in 1978 would have caused a 5.2 percent rise in gross national product.

Table 2

Annual Average Growth of Per Capita Real Gross National Product

| Period | Free Trade | | | | Restricted Trade | | | |
	Strongly		Moderately		Moderately		Strongly	
1963–73	Singapore	9.0%	Brazil	5.5%	Yugoslavia	4.9%	Turkey	3.5%
	South Korea	7.1	Israel	5.4	Mexico	4.3	Dominican Republic	3.4
	Hong Kong	6.0	Thailand	4.9	Nigeria	4.2	Burundi	3.2
			Indonesia	4.6	Tunisia	4.0	Argentina	3.1
			Costa Rica	3.9	Kenya	3.9	Pakistan	3.1
			Malaysia	3.8	Philippines	2.2	Tanzania	2.7
			Ivory Coast	3.5	Bolivia	2.0	Sri Lanka	2.3
			Colombia	3.3	Honduras	1.9	Ethiopia	1.9
			Guatemala	2.7	El Salvador	1.4	Chile	1.7
			Cameroon	−0.1	Madagascar	1.1	Peru	1.5
					Nicaragua	1.1	Uruguay	1.5
					Senegal	−0.6	Zambia	1.2
							India	1.1
							Ghana	0.4
							Bangladesh	−1.4
							Sudan	−1.9
1973–85	Singapore	6.5	Malaysia	4.1	Cameroon	5.6	Bangladesh	2.0
	Hong Kong	6.3	Thailand	3.8	Indonesia	4.0	India	2.0
	South Korea	5.4	Tunisia	2.9	Sri Lanka	3.3	Burundi	1.2
			Brazil	1.5	Pakistan	3.1	Dominican Republic	0.5
			Turkey	1.4	Yugoslavia	2.7	Ethiopia	−0.4
			Israel	0.4	Colombia	1.8	Sudan	−0.4
			Uruguay	0.4	Mexico	1.3	Peru	−1.1
			Chile	0.1	Philippines	1.1	Tanzania	−1.6
					Kenya	0.3	Argentina	−2.0
					Honduras	−0.1	Zambia	−2.3
					Senegal	−0.8	Nigeria	−2.5
					Costa Rica	−1.0	Bolivia	−3.1
					Guatemala	−1.0	Ghana	−3.2
					Ivory Coast	−1.2	Madagascar	−3.4
					El Salvador	−3.5		
					Nicaragua	−3.9		

SOURCE: World Development Report 1987 and *The Economist* (1987).

annual average growth in real per capita gross national product for each of the 41 countries for 1963–73 and 1973–85. Those countries that did not bias industrial production toward the domestic market by trade restrictions grew at faster rates than those that did. For example, the average annual growth rate in real per capita income for 1963–73 was 6.9 percent in the economies strongly oriented to free trade and 1.6 percent in the economies strongly oriented to restricted trade. For 1973–85 these growth rates were 5.9 percent and −0.1 percent, respectively.

The study proceeds to identify the macroeconomic reason for the general finding. A given amount of new investment generated more additional output in countries following a free trade policy than a restricted trade policy. The reason is that a free trade environment allows capital to flow to its most highly valued uses, while a restricted trade environment distorts economic incentives.

ARGUMENTS FOR RESTRICTING TRADE

If protectionism is so costly, why is protectionism so pervasive? This section reviews the major arguments for restricting trade and provides explanations for the existence of protectionist trade policies.

National Defense

The national defense argument says that import barriers are necessary to ensure the capacity to produce crucial goods in a national emergency. While this argument is especially appealing for weapons during a war, there will likely be demands from other industries that deem themselves essential. For example, the footwear industry will demand protection because military personnel need combat boots.[8]

The national defense argument ignores the possibility of purchases from friendly countries during the emergency. The possibilities of storage and depletion raise additional doubts about the general applicability of the argument. If crucial goods can be stored, for example, the least costly way to prepare for an emergency might be to buy the goods from foreigners at the low world price before an emergency and store them. If the crucial goods are depletable mineral resources, such as oil, then the restriction of oil imports before an emergency will cause a more rapid depletion of domestic reserves. Once again, stockpiling might be a far less costly alternative.

Income Redistribution

Since protectionist trade policies affect the distribution of income, a trade restriction might be defended on the grounds that it favors some disadvantaged group. It is unlikely, however, that trade policy is the best tool for dealing with the perceived evils of income inequality, because of its bluntness and adverse effects on the efficient allocation of resources. Attempting to equalize incomes directly by tax and transfer payments is likely less costly than using trade policy. In addition, as Hickok's (1985) study indicates, trade restrictions on many items increase rather than decrease income inequality.

Optimum Tariff Argument

The optimum tariff argument applies to situations in which a country has the economic power to alter world prices. This power exists because the country (or a group of countries acting in consort like the Organization of Petroleum Exporting Countries) is such a large producer or consumer of a good that a change in its production or consumption patterns influences world prices. For example, by imposing a tariff, the country can make foreign goods cheaper. Since a tariff reduces the demand for foreign goods, if the tariff-imposing country has some market power, the world price for the good will fall.[9] The tariff-imposing country will gain because the price per unit of its imports will have decreased.

There are a number of obstacles that preclude the widespread application of this argument. Few countries possess the necessary market power and, when they do, only a small number of goods is covered. Secondly, in a world of shifting supply and demand, calculating the optimum tariff and adjusting the rate to changing situations is difficult. Finally, the possibility of foreign retaliation to an act of economic warfare is likely. Such retaliation could leave both countries worse off than they would have been in a free trade environment.

Balancing the Balance of Trade

Many countries enact protectionist trade policies in the hope of eliminating a balance of trade deficit or increasing a balance of trade surplus. The desire to increase a balance of trade surplus follows from the mercantilist view that larger trade surpluses are beneficial from a national perspective.

This argument is suspect on a number of grounds. First, there is nothing inherently undesirable about a trade deficit or desirable about a surplus.[10] For example, faster economic growth in the United States than in the rest of the world would tend to cause a trade deficit. In this case, the trade deficit is a sign of a healthy economy. Second, protectionist policies that reduce imports will cause exports to decrease by a comparable amount. Hence, an attempt to increase exports permanently relative to imports will fail. It is doubtful that the trade deficit will be reduced even temporarily because import quantities do not decline quickly in response to the higher import prices and the revenues of foreign producers might rise.

---

[9]If a country such as the United States has no market power, the world price is fixed. Consequently, the price faced by U.S. consumers and producers rises by the full amount of the tariff. In the optimum tariff case, the price faced by U.S. consumers and producers rises, but not by the full amount of the tariff. This must be the case because the world price falls and the amount of the tariff is the difference between the world price and the U.S. price.

[10]See Chrystal and Wood (1988) earlier in this issue.

---

[8]See Pine (1984).

Protection of Jobs — Public Choice

The protection of jobs argument is closely related to the balance of trade argument. Since a reduction in imports via trade restrictions will result in a similar reduction in exports, the overall employment effects, as found in the OECD (1985) study and many others, are negligible. While the *overall* effects are negligible, workers (and resource owners) in specific industries are affected differently.

A domestic industry faced with increased imports from its foreign competition is under pressure to reduce production and lower costs. Productive resources must move from this industry to other domestic industries. Workers must change jobs and, in some cases, relocate to other cities. Since this change is forced upon these workers, these workers bear real costs that they are likely to resist. A similar statement can be made about the owners of capital in the affected industry.

Workers and other resource owners will likely resist these changes by lobbying for trade restrictions. The previously cited studies on the costs of protectionism demonstrated that trade restrictions entail substantial real costs as well. These costs likely exceed the adjustment costs because the adjustment costs are one-time costs, while the costs of protectionism continue as long as trade restrictions are maintained.

An obvious question is why politicians supply the protectionist legislation demanded by workers and other resource owners. A branch of economics called public choice, which focuses on the interplay between individual preferences and political outcomes, provides an answer. The public choice literature views the politician as an individual who offers voters a bundle of governmentally supplied goods in order to win elections.[11] Many argue that politicians gain by providing protectionist legislation. Even though the national economic costs exceed the benefits, the politician faces different costs and benefits.

Those harmed by a protectionist trade policy for a domestic industry, especially household consumers, will incur a small individual cost that is difficult to identify. For example, a consumer is unlikely to ponder how much extra a shirt costs because of protectionist legislation for the textiles and apparel industry.

Even though the aggregate effect is large, the harm to each consumer may be small. This small cost, of which an individual may not even be aware, and the costs of organizing consumers deter the formation of a lobby against the legislation.

On the other hand, workers and other resource owners are very concerned about protectionist legislation for their industry. Their benefits tend to be large individually and easy to identify. Their voting and campaign contributions assist politicians who support their positions and penalize those who do not. Thus, politicians are likely to respond to their demands for protectionist legislation.[12]

Infant Industries

The preceding argument is couched in terms of protecting a domestic industry. A slightly different argument, the so-called infant industry case, is couched in terms of *promoting* a domestic industry. Suppose an industry, already established in other countries, is being established in a specific country. The country might not be able to realize its comparative advantage in this industry because of the existing cost and other advantages of foreign firms. Initially, owners of the fledgling firm must be willing to suffer losses until the firm develops its market and lowers its production costs to the level of its foreign rivals. In order to assist this entrant, tariff protection can be used to shield the firm from some foreign competition.

After this temporary period of protection, free trade should be restored; however, the removal of tariff protection frequently is resisted. As the industry develops, its political power to thwart opposing legislation also increases.

Another problem with the infant industry argument is that a tariff is not the best way to intervene. A production subsidy is superior to a tariff if the goal is to expand production. A subsidy will do this directly, while a tariff has the undesirable side effect of reducing consumption.

In many cases, intervention might not be appropriate at all. If the infant industry is a good candidate for being competitive internationally, borrowing from the

---

[11]The role of pressure groups, acting in their economic self-interest, has been stressed by Stigler (1971) and Peltzman (1976). For references, as well as an example of an international trade study focused on the interaction of politicians and interest groups, see Coughlin (1985).

[12]Special interests benefiting from trade will likely resist the forces for protectionist legislation. Destler and Odell (1987) identify exporters, industrial import users, retailers of imported products, businesses providing trade-related services, foreign exporters, and foreign governments as interest groups capable of exerting some anti-protection pressure. Decisions about protectionist legislation result from the interaction of both pro-protection and anti-protection forces.

private capital markets can finance the expansion. Investors are willing to absorb losses *temporarily* if the prospects for future profits are sufficiently good.

Spillover Effects

The justification for protecting an industry, infant or otherwise, frequently entails a suggestion that the industry generates spillover benefits for other industries or individuals for which the industry is not compensated. Despite patent laws, one common suggestion is that certain industries are not fully compensated for their research and development expenditures. This argument is frequently directed toward technologically progressive industries where some firms can capture the results of other firms' research and development simply by dismantling a product to see how it works.

The application of this argument, however, engenders a number of problems. Spillovers of knowledge are difficult to measure. Since spillovers are not market transactions, they do not leave an obvious trail to identify their beneficiaries. The lack of market transactions also complicates an assessment of the value of these spillovers. To determine the appropriate subsidy, one must be able to place a dollar value on the spillovers generated by a given research and development expenditure. Actually, the calculation requires much more than the already difficult task of reconstructing the past. It requires complex estimates of the spillovers' future worth as well. Since resources are moved from other industries to the targeted industry, the government must understand the functioning of the entire economy.

Finally, there are political problems. An aggressive application of this argument might lead to retaliation and a mutually destructive trade war. In addition, as interest groups compete for the governmental assistance, there is no guarantee that the right groups will be assisted or that they will use the assistance efficiently.

Strategic Trade Policy

Recent theoretical developments have identified cases in which so-called strategic trade policy is superior to free trade. As we discussed earlier, decreasing unit production costs and market structures that contain monopoly elements are common in industries involved in international trade. Market imperfections immediately suggest the potential benefits of governmental intervention. In the strategic trade policy argument, government policy can alter the terms of competition to favor domestic over foreign firms and shift the excess returns in monopolistic markets from foreign to domestic firms.

Krugman (1987) illustrates an example of the argument. Assume that there is only one firm in the United States, Boeing, and one multinational firm in Europe, Airbus, capable of producing a 150-seat passenger aircraft. Assume also that the aircraft is produced only for export, so that the returns to the firm can be identified with the national interest. This export market is profitable for either firm if it is the only producer; however, it is unprofitable for both firms to produce the plane. Finally, assume the following payoffs are associated with the four combinations of production: 1) if both Boeing and Airbus produce the aircraft, each firm loses $5 million; 2) if neither Boeing nor Airbus produces the aircraft, profits are zero; 3) if Boeing produces the aircraft and Airbus does not, Boeing profits by $100 million and Airbus has zero profits; and 4) if Airbus produces the aircraft and Boeing does not, Airbus profits by $100 million and Boeing has zero profits.

Which firm(s) will produce the aircraft? The example does not yield a unique outcome. A unique outcome can be generated if one firm, say Boeing, has a head start and begins production before Airbus. In this case, Boeing will reap profits of $100 million and will have deterred Airbus from entering the market because Airbus will lose $5 million if it enters after Boeing.

Strategic trade policy, however, suggests that judicious governmental intervention can alter the outcome. If the European governments agree to subsidize Airbus' production with $10 million no matter what Boeing does, then Airbus will produce the plane. Production by Airbus will yield more profits than not producing, no matter what Boeing does. At the same time, Boeing will be deterred from producing because it would lose money. Thus, Airbus will capture the entire market and reap profits of $110 million, $100 million of which can be viewed as a transfer of profits from the United States.

The criticisms of a strategic trade policy are similar to the criticisms against protecting a technologically progressive industry that generates spillover benefits.[13] There are major informational problems in applying a

---

[13]A recent volume edited by Paul Krugman (1986) examines the policy implications of the new trade literature. See Grossman's article in that volume for a discussion of the information requirements.

strategic trade policy. The government must estimate the potential payoff of each course of action. Economic knowledge about the behavior of industries that have monopoly elements is limited. Firms may behave competitively or cooperatively and may compete by setting prices or output. The behavior of rival governments also must be anticipated. Foreign retaliation must be viewed as likely where substantial profits are at stake. In addition, many interest groups will compete for the governmental assistance. Though only a small number of sectors can be considered potentially strategic, many industries will make a case for assistance.

Reciprocity and the "Level Playing Field"

Bhagwati and Irwin (1987) note that U.S. trade policy discussions in recent years have frequently stressed the importance of "fair trade." The concept of fair trade, which is technically referred to as reciprocity, means different things to different people.

Under the General Agreement on Tariffs and Trade, negotiations to reduce trade barriers focus upon matching concessions. This form of reciprocity, known as first-difference reciprocity, attempts to reduce trade barriers by requiring a country to provide a tariff reduction of value comparable to one provided by the other country. In this case, reciprocity is defined in terms of matching changes.

Recent U.S. demands, exemplified by the Gephardt amendment to the current trade legislation, reveal an approach that is called full reciprocity. This approach seeks reciprocity in terms of the level of protection bilaterally and over a specific range of goods. Reciprocity requires equal access and this access can be determined by bilateral trade balances. A trade deficit with a trading partner is claimed to be *prima facie* evidence of unequal access. Examples abound. For example, U.S. construction firms have not had a major contract in Japan since 1965, while Japanese construction firms did $1.8 billion worth of business in the United States in 1985 alone. Recent legislation bars Japanese participation in U.S. public works projects until the Japanese offer reciprocal privileges.

As the name suggests, the fundamental argument for fair trade is one of equity. Domestic producers in a free trade country argue that foreign trade barriers are unfair because it places them at a competitive disadvantage. In an extreme version, it is asserted that this unfair competition will virtually eliminate U.S. manufacturing, leaving only jobs that consist primarily of flipping hamburgers at fast food restaurants or, as Bhagwati and Irwin have said, rolling rice cakes at Japanese-owned sushi bars. While domestic pro-

ducers *are* relatively disadvantaged, the wisdom of a protectionist response is doubtful. Again, the costs of protectionism exceed substantially the benefits from a national perspective.

In an attempt to reinforce the argument for fair trade, proponents also argue that retaliatory threats, combined with changes in tariffs and non-tariff barriers, allow for the simultaneous protection of domestic industries against unequal competition and induce more open foreign markets. This more flexible approach is viewed as superior to a "one-sided" free trade policy. The suggestion that a fair trade policy produces a trading environment with fewer trade restrictions allows proponents to assert that such a policy serves to promote both equity and efficiency. In other words, not only will domestic and foreign producers in the same industry be treated equally, but the gains associated with a freer trading environment will be realized.

On the other hand, critics of a fair trade policy argue that such a policy is simply disguised protectionism — it simply achieves the goals of specific interest groups at the expense of the nation at large. In many cases, fair traders focus on a specific practice that can be portrayed as protectionist while ignoring the entire package of policies that are affecting a nation's competitive position. In these cases, the foreign country is more likely either not to respond or retaliate by increasing rather than reducing their trade barriers. In the latter case, the escalation of trade barriers causes losses for both nations, which is exactly opposite to the alleged effects of an activist fair trade policy.

Critics of fair trade proposals are especially bothered by the use of bilateral trade deficits as evidence of unfair trade. In a world of many trading countries, the trade between two countries need not be balanced for the trade of each to be in global balance. Differing demands and productive capabilities across countries will cause a specific country to have trade deficits with some countries and surpluses with other countries. These bilateral imbalances are a normal result of countries trading on the basis of comparative advantage.[14] Thus, the focus on the bilateral trade deficit can produce inappropriate conclusions about fairness and, more importantly, policies attempting to eliminate bilateral trade deficits are likely to be very costly because they eliminate the gains from a multilateral trading system.

---

[14] Bergsten and Cline (1985) estimate an equilibrium U.S.-Japanese bilateral trade deficit of $20–$25 billion annually.

CONCLUSION

The proliferation of protectionist trade policies in recent years provides an impetus to reconsider their worth. In the world of traditional trade theory, characterized by perfect competition, a definitive recommendation in favor of free trade can be made. The gains from international trade result from a reallocation of productive resources toward goods that can be produced less costly at home than abroad and the exchange of some of these goods for goods that can be produced at less cost abroad than at home.

Recent developments in international trade theory have examined the consequences of international trade in markets where there are market imperfections, such as monopoly and technological spillovers. Do these imperfections justify protectionist trade policies? The answer continues to be no. While protectionist trade policies may offset monopoly power overseas or advantageously use domestic monopoly power, trade restrictions tend to reduce the competition faced by domestic producers, protecting domestic producers at the expense of domestic consumers.

The empirical evidence is clear-cut. The costs of protectionist trade policies far exceed the benefits. The losses suffered by consumers exceed the gains reaped by domestic producers and government. Low-income consumers are relatively more adversely affected than high-income consumers. Not only are there inefficiencies associated with excessive domestic production and restricted consumption, but there are costs associated with the enforcement of the protectionist legislation and attempts to influence trade policy.

The primary reason for these costly protectionist policies relies on a public choice argument. The desire to influence trade policy arises from the fact that trade policy changes benefit some groups, while harming others. Consumers are harmed by protectionist legislation; however, ignorance, small individual costs, and the high costs of organizing consumers prevent the consumers from being an effective force. On the other hand, workers and other resource owners in an industry are more likely to be effective politically because of their relative ease of organizing and their individually large and easy-to-identify benefits. Politicians interested in re-election will most likely respond to the demands for protectionist legislation of such an interest group.

The empirical evidence also suggests that the adverse consumer effects of protectionist trade policies are not short-lived. These policies generate lower economic growth rates than the rates associated with free trade policies. In turn, slow growth contributes to additional protectionist pressures.

Interest group pressures from industries experiencing difficulty and the general appeal of a "level playing field" combine to make the reduction of trade barriers especially difficult at the present time in the United States. Nonetheless, national interests will be served best by such an admittedly difficult political course. In light of the current Uruguay Round negotiations under the General Agreement on Tariffs and Trade, as well as numerous bilateral discussions, this fact is especially timely.

REFERENCES

Bergsten, C. Fred, and William R. Cline. *The United States-Japan Economic Problem* (Institute for International Economics, October 1985).

Bhagwati, Jagdish N., and Douglas A. Irwin. "The Return of the Reciprocitarians — U.S. Trade Policy Today," *World Economy* (June 1987), pp. 109–30.

Brander, James A. "Intra-Industry Trade in Identical Commodities," *Journal of International Economics* (February 1981), pp. 1–14.

Brander, James A., and Paul R. Krugman. "A 'Reciprocal Dumping' Model of International Trade," *Journal of International Economics* (November 1983), pp. 313–21.

Chrystal, K. Alec, and Geoffrey E. Wood. "Are Trade Deficits a Problem?" this *Review* (January/February 1988), pp. 5–13.

Clarete, Ramon L., and John Whalley. "Interactions Between Trade Policies and Domestic Distortions," Center for the Study of International Economic Relations Working Paper 8522C (London, Ontario: University of Western Ontario, 1985).

Coughlin, Cletus C. "Domestic Content Legislation: House Voting and the Economic Theory of Regulation," *Economic Inquiry* (July 1985), pp. 437–48.

Denzau, Arthur T. "How Import Restraints Reduce Employment," Washington University Center for the Study of American Business, Formal Publication #80 (June 1987).

Destler, I. M., and John S. Odell. *Anti-Protection: Changing Forces in United States Trade Politics* (Institute for International Economics, 1987).

Dixit, Avinash K., and Victor D. Norman. *Theory of International Trade* (Cambridge University Press, 1980).

Dixit, Avinash K., and Joseph E. Stiglitz. "Monopolistic Competition and Optimum Product Diversity," *American Economic Review* (June 1977), pp. 297–308.

The Economist. July 4, 1987, p.74.

Grais, Wafik, Jaime de Melo, and Shujiro Urata. "A General Equilibrium Estimation of the Effects of Reductions in Tariffs and Quantitative Restrictions in Turkey in 1978," in T. N. Srinivasan and John Whalley, eds. *General Equilibrium Trade Policy Modeling* (MIT Press, 1986).

Grossman, Gene M. "Strategic Export Promotion: A Critique," *Strategic Trade Policy and the New International Economics* in Paul R. Krugman, ed. (MIT Press, 1986), pp. 47–68.

Helpman, Elhanan. "International Trade in the Presence of Product Differentiation, Economies of Scale and Monopolistic Competition," *Journal of International Economics* (August 1981), pp. 305–40.

Hickok, Susan. "The Consumer Cost of U.S. Trade Restraints," Federal Reserve Bank of New York *Quarterly Review* (Summer 1985), pp. 1–12.

Hufbauer, Gary Clyde, Diane T. Berliner, and Kimberly Ann Elliott. *Trade Protection in the United States: 31 Case Studies* (Institute for International Economics, 1986).

Kearl, James R., Clayne L. Pope, Gordon C. Whiting, and Larry T. Wimmer. "A Confusion of Economists?" *American Economic Review, Papers and Proceedings* (May 1979), pp. 28–37.

Kierzkowski, Henry K. "Recent Advances in International Trade Theory: A Selective Survey," *Oxford Review of Economic Policy* (Spring 1987), pp. 1–19.

Krugman, Paul R. "Is Free Trade Passé?" *Journal of Economic Perspectives* (Fall 1987), pp. 131–44.

_____. *Strategic Trade Policy and the New International Economics* (MIT Press, 1986).

Lancaster, Kelvin. "Intra-Industry Trade Under Perfect Monopolistic Competition," *Journal of International Economics* (May 1980), pp. 151–75.

_____. *Variety, Equity, and Efficiency* (Columbia University Press, 1979).

Leibenstein, Harvey. *Beyond Economic Man* (Harvard University Press, 1980).

Luttrell, Clifton B. "Imports and Jobs — The Observed and the Unobserved," this *Review* (June 1978), pp. 2–10.

Mill, John Stuart. *Principles of Political Economy*, W. J. Ashley, ed. (Longman, 1909).

Morici, Peter, and Laura L. Megna. *U.S. Economic Policies Affecting Industrial Trade: A Quantitative Assessment* (National Planning Association, 1983).

Munger, Michael C. "The Costs of Protectionism: Estimates of the Hidden Tax of Trade Restraint," Washington University Center for the Study of American Business, Working Paper #80 (July 1983).

Organization for Economic Co-Operation and Development (OECD). *Costs and Benefits of Protection* (1985).

Page, Sheila. "The Rise in Protection Since 1974," *Oxford Review of Economic Policy* (Spring 1987), pp. 37–51.

Peltzman, Sam. "Toward a More General Theory of Regulation," *Journal of Law and Economics* (August 1976), pp. 211–40.

Pine, Art. "Footwear Industry Tells Congress 'Shoe Gap' Threatens U.S. Defense," *Wall Street Journal*, August 24, 1984.

Ricardo, David. *The Principles of Political Economy and Taxation* (Penguin, 1971).

Stigler, George J. "The Theory of Economic Regulation," *Bell Journal of Economics and Management Science* (Spring 1971), pp. 3–21.

Stolper, Wolfgang, and Paul A. Samuelson. "Protection and Real Wages," *Review of Economic Studies* (November 1941), pp. 58–73.

Tarr, David G., and Morris E. Morkre. *Aggregate Costs to the United States of Tariffs and Quotas on Imports: General Tariff Cuts and Removal of Quotas on Automobiles, Steel, Sugar, and Textiles*, Bureau of Economics Staff Report to the Federal Trade Commission (December 1984).

Venables, Anthony, and Alasdair Smith. "Trade and Industrial Policy Under Imperfect Competition," *Economic Policy* (October 1986), pp. 621–72.

Wood, Geoffrey E., and Douglas R. Mudd. "The Recent U.S. Trade Deficit — No Cause for Panic," this *Review* (April 1978), pp. 2–7.

World Bank. *World Development Report 1987* (Oxford University Press, 1987).

Appendix
Developments in International Trade Theory and the Gains from Trade

Since 1817, numerous developments have taken place in international trade theory. The consequences of more than one factor of production, increasing and decreasing unit production costs, and imperfectly competitive markets are examined in this appendix. Special attention is focused on developments in international trade theory in the last decade.

Increasing the Number of Factors of Production

Assume that, in the United States, two resources, labor and capital (e.g., machines), are used in the production of two goods, automobiles and airplanes. The prices of these resources will be affected differently by trade. As trade develops, demand for the exported good (that is, the good in which the United States has a comparative advantage) will increase and demand for U.S. production of the imported good will fall. This demand shift causes the price of the exported good to rise relative to the price of the imported good. Similarly, the shift may also produce changes in the prices of resources; however, these price changes are not always obvious.

Initially, assume that the resources cannot be transferred across industries. For example, the labor and capital used to produce automobiles, the good imported into the United States, cannot be used to produce airplanes, the exported good. Consequently, as the price of airplanes rises in the United States, the compensation for labor and capital in the airplane industry will rise; meanwhile, the decline in automobile prices causes a decline in compensation for labor and capital in the industry. It would not be surprising if labor and owners of capital in the industry would resist such changes by asking for trade protection.

While resources may not be easily transferred across industries in the short run, workers can change jobs and capital can be moved as time passes. If resources are mobile, then the longer-run consequences for labor and owners of capital are different from those described above. Even if labor and capital are perfectly mobile, however, one set of resource owners may benefit while another group is harmed by trade.[1]

The real world is more complicated than this discussion has allowed. There are more than two factors of production and varying degrees of mobility for these factors. For example, the U.S. labor force contains scientists and engineers as well as short-order cooks. Nonetheless, the underlying analysis does suggest some generalizations. When trade occurs, owners of the resources that are more specialized in the production of export goods will tend to become weal-

---

[1]Who wins and who loses? It depends on the U.S. endowment of capital to labor relative to other countries. If the United States has relatively larger amounts of capital to labor relative to other countries, then owners of capital would benefit, while labor would be harmed. This result follows from the Stolper-Samuelson Theorem (Stolper and Samuelson, 1941). In the example, the United States is defined to be capital-abundant. The example also implicitly assumes that airplanes are produced by capital-intensive methods and automobiles by labor-intensive methods. Thus, the production of airplanes requires the use of more capital relative to labor than automobiles. Since the United States is relatively well-endowed with capital and the production of airplanes is capital intensive, the United States will have a comparative advantage in the production of airplanes. With the elimination of trade barriers, the relative price of airplanes to automobiles will increase. The Stolper-Samuelson Theorem shows that an increase in the relative price of the capital intensive good will increase the return to capital relative to the prices of both goods and reduce the return to labor relative to the prices of both goods.

thier; those who own resources more specialized in the production of import-competing goods will tend to lose wealth. People also gain or lose, however, depending on what happens to the prices of the goods they buy. Individuals who chiefly consume imported goods will benefit, while those who prefer consuming the exported goods will lose. Thus, the net effect on any individual depends on both the gains or losses associated with the price changes on the goods that he consumes and the effect of trade on his wealth (or income).

Increasing Unit Production Costs

A second assumption underlying the Ricardian example of the gains from trade is that unit production costs are constant. If unit production costs rise as more is produced, however, the general conclusions about the gains from trade remain essentially unchanged. The major difference is that rising unit production costs limit the extent to which specialization occurs.

Decreasing Unit Production Costs and Imperfect Competition

On the other hand, if unit production costs decrease as production increases, the extent to which actual trade patterns can be explained by comparative advantage becomes unclear. It also forces trade theory to deal with numerous characteristics of international trade in the real world. The market structure of industries engaged in trade is frequently highly concentrated. In other words, the individual firms in an industry, contrary to those in a perfectly competitive industry, can affect the market price of their good by their production and advertising decisions. In addition, trade statistics show that intra-industry trade (i.e., the simultaneous export and import of the output of the same industry) accounts for increasingly larger shares of world trade.

In the last decade, trade theorists have developed numerous models to deal with these facts. An exhaustive review of this rapidly expanding literature is beyond the scope of this appendix; however, a few illustrative articles are discussed in order to establish some key points. Brander (1981) and Brander and Krugman (1983) developed models using a homogeneous good to highlight how imperfect competition can cause intra-industry trade and how intra-industry trade can arise in the absence of cost differences.

Assume two countries with one firm in each country. The firms are producing a homogeneous good under identical cost situations and there are no trans-

portation costs. Each firm operates under what is termed a "Cournot conjecture," meaning that each firm assumes its production decision will not affect its rival's production decision. Before international trade, each firm has a monopoly position in its home market. Allowing for free trade induces each firm to enter the other firm's market, because price exceeds marginal cost in each country. Thus, the same good will flow to and from each country.

Kierzkowski (1987) has noted that the bulk of intra-industry trade involves differentiated rather than homogeneous goods. Two approaches, Lancaster's (1979) characteristics approach and Dixit and Stiglitz's (1977) "love of variety" approach, have provided the foundation for trade models involving differentiated goods.

In the characteristics approach, individuals have preferences for the characteristics of goods rather than for collections of the goods themselves. A group of goods is defined as goods possessing the same characteristics but in different proportions. A diversity in consumer preferences causes different consumers to prefer different products (i.e., varieties) of a group of goods.

Helpman (1981) and Lancaster (1980) used the characteristics approach to show how intra-industry trade results from combining the demand for variety with economies of scale. The change from autarchy to free trade enlarges the market and causes output of the existing varieties to increase and the production of new varieties to begin. Consumers gain from the production of more varieties and lower prices as economies of scale are realized.

The sources of gains from trade are identical using the love-of-variety and characteristics approaches. In the love-of-variety approach, which is used by Dixit and Norman (1980), consumers have identical tastes and prefer to consume as many types of the differentiated product as possible.

The introduction of imperfect competition and declining unit production costs suggest three sources of gain from free trade. As the market potentially served by firms expands from a national to a world market, there will be gains due to declining unit production costs. The second is the reduction in monopoly power of firms faced with foreign competitors. The third is the gain to consumers from lower prices and increased product variety. Generally speaking, gains from trade result from the increase in competitive pressures as the domestic economy becomes less insulated from the world economy. Nonetheless, the numerous market structures and firm behaviors possible under imperfect competition preclude a definitive statement about the optimality of free trade.

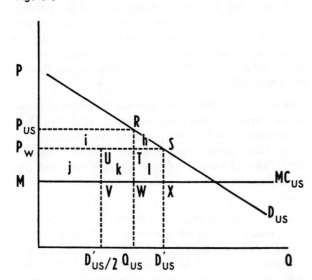

Figure 3

The demand curve is D_{us} and the marginal cost curve is MC_{us}. (The marginal revenue curve associated with D_{us} is omitted.) The monopoly price and output are P_{us} and Q_{us}.

The change from autarchy to free trade transforms the national monopolies into a world duopoly. Assuming the firms follow a Cournot strategy, price declines from P_{us} to P_w, sales in the United States increase from Q_{us} to D'_{us}, and consumers gain area P_{us} RS P_w or $h + i$. Profits (ignoring fixed costs) in the United States decline from area P_{us} RWM or $i + j + k$ to area P_w SXM or $j + k + l$. The domestic firm has one-half of the domestic market, so its profits are j with $k + l$ going to the foreign firm. The domestic firm's exports allow it to capture one-half of the foreign market. If the foreign market is identical to the domestic market, the firm's profits on foreign sales will equal $k + l$. Therefore, the net reduction in the domestic firm's profits is $i - l$ and the overall welfare gain to the economy is $h + l$.

If the assumption of identically sized domestic and foreign markets is dropped, then a different conclusion is possible. If the foreign market is smaller than the domestic, the profits of the domestic firm in the foreign market will be less than $k + l$. Assuming zero exports, the domestic gains from trade are $h - k$, and the domestic economy could lose from free trade. In this case, consumer gains can be more than offset by the shifting of profits from the domestic to the foreign economy. This shifting reflects the contraction of an activity that is already too little to an even smaller level.

Sometimes the benefits of expanded consumption resulting from free trade are less than the costs associated with distorted production. Venables and Smith (1986) provide a graphical illustration, duplicated in figure 3, of the preceding point using the Brander-Krugman duopoly model. Assume the U.S. market and the market in the rest of the world for a specific good are monopolies, the good is produced at a constant marginal cost, and there are no transportation costs.

Article 36

THE EFFECT OF EXCHANGE RATE VARIATION ON U.S. TEXTILE AND APPAREL IMPORTS

Christine Chmura [*]

In the past 12 years, textile and apparel imports have risen nearly six fold, from $4.3 billion in 1974 to $24.7 billion in 1986. During this time, foreign textile producers increased their U.S. market share from 5 percent to 12 percent while foreign apparel producers increased theirs from 8 percent to 24 percent.

The increase of textiles and apparel imports has often been attributed to the appreciation of the U.S. dollar and the resulting fall in the relative price of foreign goods that occurred from 1981 through 1985. The purpose of this study is to test this hypothesis. More specifically, this study seeks to determine if exchange rate variations significantly influenced the level of U.S. textile and apparel imports during the period from 1977 to 1986.

This study begins with a description of the textile and apparel industries. The specific characteristics of these industries are then related to their competitiveness. Subsequently, two earlier studies of the impact of foreign competition on U.S. textile and apparel industries are reviewed. Finally, we present and explain the results of empirical tests of the effect of exchange rate variation on textile and apparel imports.

INDUSTRY PROFILES

The textile and apparel industries are in some ways similar but in other ways quite different. These similarities and differences figure importantly in determining the susceptibility of these industries to import competition.

Standard Industrial Classification

The textile, or "textile mill products," industry is composed of nine groups of firms that weave fiber into fabric and process fabric into intermediate products. The textile groups include mills weaving cotton, wool, and synthetic fibers. About one-third of textile production is used by the apparel, or "apparel and other textile products," industry. The apparel industry is also composed of nine industry groups among which are manufacturers of clothing, curtains and draperies, and automotive and apparel trimmings.

Characteristics

The U.S. textile and apparel industries are highly competitive. Each is composed of a large number of small manufacturers. In 1984, the U.S. apparel industry comprised about 23,000 establishments employing a total of 1.2 million production workers, and the U.S. textile industry consisted of about 6,000 establishments employing 724,000 production workers. Sixty percent of the textile firms and 75 percent of the apparel establishments employ fewer than 50 employees.[1] Moreover, textile and apparel firms are located all over the world. Textile manufacturing is often one of the first major industries formed in a developing country. Consequently, nearly every country has a textile industry, and apparel industries are also common to most countries.[2]

The textile industry exists in a more competitive environment than the apparel industry because textile products are more standardized than apparel products. Buyers of textiles can easily switch from a firm that sells a standard good at a higher price to one that sells virtually the same good at a lower price. Because they are more differentiated, the products of competing apparel firms are viewed as more distinct and are likely to be less sensitive than textile goods to changes in prices.

Textile and apparel production are labor intensive, giving a competitive edge to producers in low-wage

[*] The author gratefully acknowledges helpful comments from Dan M. Bechter and Michael T. Belongia.

[1] U.S. Department of Commerce, Bureau of the Census, *County Business Patterns 1984, United States*, 1986. An establishment is defined as a single physical location where business is conducted or where services or industrial operations are performed.

[2] Brian Toyne, Jeffrey S. Arpan, Andy H. Barnett, et al., *The U.S. Textile Mill Products Industry: Strategies for the 1980's and Beyond* (The University of South Carolina Press: Columbia, 1983), p. 4-2.

foreign countries. Apparel production is considerably more labor intensive than textile production. The relative labor intensities of the textile and apparel industries as well as their low capital barriers to entry are apparent in the value of capital equipment per worker. In the U.S. textile industry, the net value of capital equipment per worker in 1980 was $9,020, slightly below the average for all manufacturing. In apparel, however, the net value of capital equipment per worker was $1,909, one-fifth of the U.S. average.[3]

Effects of Economic Conditions

The demand for textiles and apparel is sensitive to the business cycle. Sales of textiles and apparel rise during economic expansions and decline during economic contractions. This procyclical behavior characterizes the major users of textiles: the home furnishing industry, the automobile and marine industries, and the apparel industry. Because of the sensitivity of textile and apparel sales to the business cycle, competition in these industries is intense during a general economic downturn.

The demand for textiles and apparel is also influenced by long-term economic conditions. As income has steadily risen in the United States, apparel and textile consumption has also risen. For example, in 1974 U.S. apparel consumption in real terms was $178 per capita while real disposable personal income was $703. By 1985, real apparel consumption had risen 52 percent to $270 per capita while real disposable personal income had risen 25 percent to $878.[4]

TWO RECENT STUDIES

This section reviews two recent reports on the effect of the dollar's value in foreign exchange markets on U.S. textile and apparel industries. The first report, by the Economic Consulting Services (ECS), studies the impact of the exchange rate on U.S. imports of textiles and apparel. The second report, by the Congressional Budget Office (CBO), considers the effect of the exchange rate on production levels of U.S. manufacturing industries, including textiles and apparel.

The ECS Report

A report prepared by ECS examines the effect of the U.S. dollar appreciation during the years 1981 through 1984 on the increase in U.S. imports of textiles and apparel.[5] The study focuses on the 25 countries supplying the largest quantities of U.S. imports of textiles and apparel. The ECS study uses a nominal exchange rate rather than a real exchange rate.[6]

The ECS study begins by identifying a "control" group of countries. The logic is that in countries where the currencies have maintained a stable rate of exchange with the dollar or have appreciated against the dollar, the growth in textile and apparel imports cannot be attributed to the appreciating U.S. dollar. Six "exchange rate neutral" countries comprise this control group.[7] These six countries were responsible for 11 percent of textiles and 27 percent of apparel imported from the 25 top suppliers.

The U.S. imports of textiles from the exchange rate neutral countries rose 84 percent during 1981 through 1984, while imports of apparel from these countries rose 48 percent. The remaining countries, whose currencies depreciated against the U.S. dollar between 1981 and 1984, showed a 98 percent increase in textile imports and a 49 percent increase in apparel imports. These figures seemed to indicate little difference between the two cases. Therefore, ECS concluded that U.S. dollar appreciation had only a small impact on the increase in U.S. imports of textiles and had a negligible impact on the increase in U.S. imports of apparel. In country by country comparisons, however, the ECS study found that the U.S. dollar appreciation had a greater effect on imports from countries with wage rates comparable to those in the United States.

CBO Study

In a report prepared by Elliot Schwartz for the CBO, quarterly data from 1973.3 through 1985.1

---

[3] *Statistical Abstract of the United States 1985*, pp. 413, 525, and U.S. Department of Commerce, unpublished data in Daniel P. Kaplan, *Has Trade Protection Revitalized Domestic Industries?* (Washington, D.C.: Congressional Budget Office, 1986), p. 17.

[4] Numbers are deflated by the consumer price index (CPI) for all items and for the "apparel and upkeep" expenditure class where 1967 = 100.

[5] Economic Consulting Services Incorporated, *The Impact of the Appreciation of the Dollar on U.S. Imports of Textiles and Apparel*, (Washington, D.C., 1985). This study was prepared for the American Textile Manufacturers Institute.

[6] For an explanation of the importance of using a real exchange rate to determine international competitiveness, see Dallas S. Batten and Michael T. Belongia, "The Recent Decline in Agricultural Exports: Is the Exchange Rate the Culprit?" The Federal Reserve Bank of St. Louis, *Review* 66 (October 1984), pp.5-14.

[7] They are the Dominican Republic, Haiti, Malaysia, Singapore, Taiwan, and Egypt.

are used to study the effects of imports on production.[8] Schwartz's regression equations contain explanatory variables for the nominal exchange rate, income effects, and price effects.

His results suggest that nominal exchange rate changes have no effect on U.S. textile and apparel production. None of the explanatory variables are significant in his textile regression equation. The only significant variable in his apparel regression is the income effect, included to capture short-term changes in the business cycle.

REEXAMINATION OF THE EVIDENCE

This section describes the method used here to estimate the impact of exchange rate variation and other factors on the level of U.S. imports of textiles and apparel.

Scope of the Study

The period chosen for the empirical tests extends from the first quarter of 1977 through the first quarter of 1986. This period is chosen for three reasons. First, the Multifiber Arrangement was in effect during the entire period, therefore there were few changes in foreign trade arrangements.[9] Second, the period includes pronounced variations in the exchange rate. The foreign exchange value of the dollar declined between the second quarter of 1976 and the first quarter of 1979, appreciated between the fourth quarter of 1979 and the first quarter of 1985, then declined through the first quarter of 1986. Third, the volume of textile imports increased 256 percent and the volume of apparel imports increased 380 percent over this period. (See Chart 1.)

Real Exchange Rate Changes

The importance of using real, rather than nominal, exchange rates in studies of import competition is well documented.[10] The nominal exchange rate is

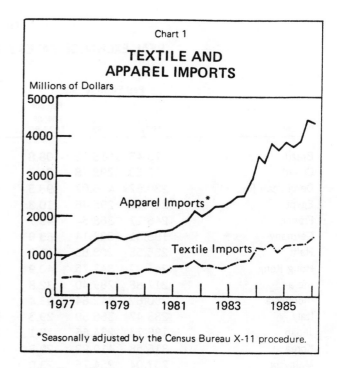

Chart 1

TEXTILE AND APPAREL IMPORTS

Millions of Dollars

*Seasonally adjusted by the Census Bureau X-11 procedure.

simply the amount of one foreign currency that can be obtained for a unit of another currency. The real exchange rate, however, is the nominal exchange rate adjusted for the difference in price levels in the two countries. It shows the real quantity of imports the country gets per unit of export given up. (See Appendix A.)

Table I provides comparisons of the percentage changes in individual countries' real exchange rates with their associated percentage changes in textile and apparel imports to the United States. Inspection of these percentage changes, does not, however, suggest any strong correlation between real exchange rates and textile and apparel imports. Indeed, the correlation coefficient between percentage changes in the real exchange rates and textile imports is only 50 percent, and for apparel only 56 percent, for these 24 countries over the period examined.[11]

As Michael Belongia has argued, however, it is misleading to consider only individual countries because changes in relative prices cause many forms of substitution among users. Thus, a number of bilateral exchange rate movements will not capture the substitution possibilities as well as a single measure of changes in the dollar's value relative to

---

[8] Elliot Schwartz, "The Dollar in Foreign Exchange and U.S. Industrial Production," Staff Working Paper, The Congress of the United States, Congressional Budget Office, December 1985.

[9] The Multifiber Arrangement (MFA) established a set of rules for developed countries to regulate imports of textiles and apparel made of cotton, wool, and man-made fiber. Although such barriers to trade interfere with estimations of the effect of exchange rate changes on imports, the constancy of these barriers is less damaging than frequent changes in the barriers.

[10] Belongia, op. cit.

[11] The correlation coefficients are distorted by the large percentage changes in textile and apparel imports from Sri Lanka and Indonesia. When these two countries are deleted from the comparison, the correlation coefficient between percentage changes in the real exchange rates and textile imports is only 7 percent, and for apparel only 37 percent.

Table I

REAL EXCHANGE RATES AND IMPORTS BY COUNTRY

| | Real Exchange Rate* | | | Million SYE** | | | | | |
| | | | | Textile Imports | | | Apparel Imports | | |
Country	1977	1985	Percent change 1977-85	1977	1985	Percent change 1977-85	1977	1985	Percent change 1977-85
Brazil	773.43	1615.12	108.8	38.3	157.3	310.7	6.4	41.9	554.7
Canada	245.60	298.78	21.7	68.9	239.3	247.3	6.9	14.6	111.6
Dominican Republic	239.62	475.07	98.3	2.1	12.2	481.1	25.5	107.2	320.4
Egypt	267.77	295.46	10.3	8.7	42.5	388.5	0.2	0.8	300.0
France	246.17	368.54	49.7	99.9	100.4	0.5	12.9	22.8	76.7
Germany	198.31	327.14	65.0	191.7	326.7	70.4	3.9	10.3	164.1
Haiti	235.56	208.85	-11.3	0.8	4.2	425.0	43.0	80.6	87.4
Hong Kong	246.87	347.75	40.9	214.3	222.9	4.0	601.0	824.9	37.3
India	217.88	289.40	32.8	115.1	153.9	33.7	50.5	116.2	130.1
Indonesia	280.62	542.64	93.4	0.2	130.8	65300.0	2.7	136.3	4948.1
Italy	283.47	366.59	29.3	153.5	455.1	196.5	37.7	73.3	94.4
Japan	198.75	234.66	18.1	773.8	593.0	-23.4	169.3	130.2	-23.1
Korea	316.58	410.92	29.8	84.8	472.1	456.7	439.6	671.0	52.6
Malaysia	207.04	254.75	23.0	11.6	60.3	419.8	9.1	91.9	909.9
Mexico	326.77	347.76	6.4	76.3	135.2	77.2	78.7	109.6	39.3
Pakistan	233.58	365.27	56.4	57.2	219.4	283.6	10.2	70.1	587.3
Peru	890.06	1460.00	64.0	19.7	68.2	246.2	0.1	1.6	1500.0
Philippines	269.90	318.04	17.8	14.0	13.4	-4.3	128.0	257.4	101.1
Singapore	212.92	245.59	15.3	18.9	7.7	-59.3	42.3	152.8	261.2
Sri Lanka	297.84	584.52	96.3	0.01	11.9	118900.0	4.1	110.6	2597.6
Spain	320.70	447.70	39.6	10.1	106.4	953.5	4.2	4.9	16.7
Taiwan	168.72	182.33	8.1	91.2	644.6	606.8	547.5	957.9	75.0
Thailand	257.79	337.57	30.9	23.5	145.2	517.9	22.0	130.6	493.6
United Kingdom	258.40	304.28	17.8	122.3	176.1	44.0	8.1	27.1	234.6

* Units of foreign exchange per U.S. dollar, adjusted for inflation.

** Standard yard equivalents.

Note: Import numbers are for cotton, wool, and man-made fibers textiles and apparel.

Sources: See Appendix A.

multiple currencies.[12] For that reason, aggregate imports and a trade-weighted exchange rate are used in the regression equations in this paper.

Comprehensive real trade-weighted exchange rates covering all exported and imported goods are available.[13] Because of their breadth of coverage,

however, such indexes are not appropriate for studies of imports of specific types of goods. For that reason, this study uses a specially constructed index composed of trade-weighted data from countries that accounted for an average 84 percent of U.S. textile and apparel imports during the period 1977 through 1986. Chart 2 shows how the behavior of this special index for textiles and apparel differs from the behavior of the Federal Reserve's comprehensive index designed to cover all goods. (See Appendix A for a description of the textile and apparel index.)

[12] Michael T. Belongia, "Estimating Exchange Rate Effects on Exports: A Cautionary Note," The Federal Reserve Bank of St. Louis, *Review* 68 (January 1986), p. 5.

[13] One such index is published monthly by the Board of Governors of the Federal Reserve System. The countries used in this index were collectively responsible for only 22 percent of U.S. imports of textiles and apparel in 1984.

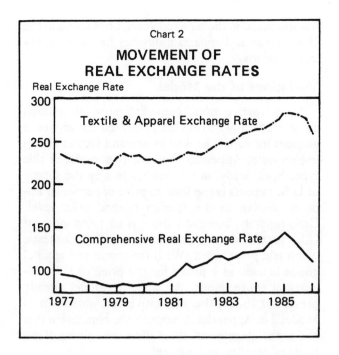

Chart 2

**MOVEMENT OF
REAL EXCHANGE RATES**

Real Exchange Rate

The Model

The model used below to test the exchange rate's affect on import demand focuses on the principal factors likely to affect the U.S. demand for imports of textiles and apparel. In addition to the real exchange rate, the model includes an explanatory variable for shifts in U.S. income. The primary purpose of the model is, of course, to determine if real exchange rate changes affect textile and apparel imports. A second purpose is to see if imports of textiles are affected differently from imports of apparel by changes in real exchange rates.

The model used in this paper posits a linear relationship between the dependent variable, imports (real dollar volume), and two independent ones, namely the real trade-weighted exchange value of the dollar, and the level of income (real GNP). In equation form:

$$\text{imports} = b_1 + b_2(\text{real exchange rate}) + b_3(\text{real GNP}) + \text{error term}$$

where the import variable is in terms of textiles or apparel.[14]

The independent variables are lagged by one quarter to capture the effect of time delays occurring before import levels respond to changes in

[14] Import data were obtained from the American Textile Manufacturers Institute, Inc., *Textile Hi-Lights,* various issues, and unpublished data. See appendix for real exchange rate data. GNP data (1982 = 100) were obtained from the Department of Commerce.

income and real exchange rates.[15] All variables are in the form of their natural logarithms.[16] Therefore, their coefficients can be interpreted as elasticities. In other words, the coefficient value of a particular explanatory variable represents the percent change in the imports of the textile or apparel industry with respect to a 1 percent change in the explanatory variable, holding other variables constant.

The explanatory variable representing the exchange rate is the real trade-weighted exchange value of the U.S. dollar. It is expected to be related positively to the quantity of textile and apparel imports. As the dollar appreciates in value, imports should rise, all else equal.

The explanatory variable for shifts in income (real GNP) should be positively related to imports. The higher the level of U.S. real economic activity, the higher the demand for textile and apparel goods (including imports), all else equal.

The Results

As shown in Table II, all of the coefficients of the explanatory variables for both the textile and apparel regression equations are statistically significant. Results for both textiles and apparel indicate that changes in the exchange value of the dollar affect the quantity of imports. For both textiles and apparel, a 1 percent increase in the exchange rate is associated with about a 1.4 percent increase in imports.[17]

These findings suggest that the exchange value of the dollar has the same effect on imports of apparel as on imports of textiles. At first blush, this result may seem surprising because imports of the more standardized textile goods might be expected to be more sensitive to price changes via the exchange rate than the more differentiated apparel goods. On the other hand, the high labor intensity of the apparel industry might lead one to expect a greater influence of the exchange rate on this industry's import competition. It might be easier to combat the import-

[15] Alternatively, when the delay is specified as a second-degree polynomial distributed lag, the effect of the exchange rate changes are shown to persist for a period of four quarters for both textile and apparel imports. In the textile equation, the effect of real GNP is shown to persist for four quarters; lagged effects were not found for the real GNP variable in the apparel equation.

[16] The dependent variable, imports, increases at different percentage rates over the time period studied. For that reason, the natural logarithms are a better measure than the natural numbers.

[17] Statistically significant results were obtained using the Board of Governors real exchange rate in the regression. However, the coefficients for the real exchange rate varibles were much lower (0.004 for textiles and 0.78 for apparel).

Table II

REGRESSION RESULTS FOR THE PERIOD 1977.1 TO 1986.1

Variable	Textiles*	Apparel*
Intercept	−29.41	−35.09
	(−11.20)†	(−11.35)†
Log of Real Exchange Rate	1.33	1.40
	(3.54)†	(3.39)†
Log of Real GNP	2.91	3.69
	(5.94)†	(7.23)†
R-Square	.87	.84

* A two-step full transform method was used to correct for first order autocorrelation.

† T-statistic significant at the 1 percent level.

promoting effects of increases in the value of the dollar in a capital intensive industry where equipment can be modernized to lower cost than in a labor intensive industry. In a labor intensive industry in which there is little available capital to substitute for labor, it is probably harder to cut costs because it is difficult to decrease wages.[18]

In both regression equations, the income variable (real GNP) has a positive effect on imports. This result was expected as textile and apparel consumption have historically risen with increases in income. In addition, the income variable has a greater effect on textile and apparel imports than does the exchange rate. In other words, if the economy were to continue to grow at its trend rate of 2 percent and real exchange rates did not vary, then the dollar volume of imports of textiles would double by the year 2011 and the dollar volume of imports of apparel would double by 2006. However, an increase in the volume of imports does not necessarily mean production in the United States will decline by the same amount. In fact, although the market share of foreign imports

[18] Indeed, the evidence on capital investment in the textile and apparel industries in the last few years lends credence to this argument. As a result of the dollar appreciation in the 1980s, domestically produced textiles and apparel became more expensive than their foreign-produced counterparts. Because of increased capital expenditures and modernization in the textile industry, productivity in that industry rose 14 percent from 1981 through 1985. In the apparel industry, however, productivity rose only 6 percent during the same period. The industries' consequent loss in competitiveness with foreign producers is apparent in the share of the U.S. market gained by foreign producers: foreign market share in the textile industry increased from 5 percent in 1977 to 12 percent in 1986 while in the apparel industry foreign market share increased from 10 percent to 24 percent over the same period.

has increased in the past ten years, production in the U.S. textile and apparel industries has held steady in real terms.

Variations of the Model

An alternative model providing more information about trade flows than that presented above would account for supply as well as demand factors affecting imports. Appendix B contains a model of this type. Specifically, one variable affecting the supply of U.S. imports is the foreign price of particular imports relative to the foreign general price level. Unfortunately, however, there is no price index of U.S. textile and apparel imports. The domestic wholesale price index (WPI) for textile and apparel goods is used as a proxy for the price of U.S. imports of those goods. As with the model already presented above, the alternative version shown as Model 2 in Appendix B supports the conclusion that real exchange rate variations affect the volume of imports of textiles and apparel.

Still another way to measure the effect of exchange rate variations on imports is to use a commodity-specific real exchange rate. Such a measure was employed in the third version of the model, designated Model 3 in Appendix B. The results of this version again support the conclusion that exchange rate variations affect the volume of imports of textiles and apparel.

SUMMARY AND CONCLUDING COMMENTS

Although two recent studies indicate that exchange rate variations do not influence overall textile and apparel imports or production, the empirical tests conducted here suggest to the contrary that exchange rate variations do indeed have a significant effect on textile and apparel imports. Changes in income are found to have a greater impact than changes in the exchange rate on textile and apparel imports.

The results reported here are good news for the U.S. textile and apparel industries. If, as our study indicates, the exchange value of the dollar does affect imports, then the recent exchange rate depreciation should cause a decline in the quantity of imports. In addition, as our study indicates that textile and apparel imports are related to income and thus demand increases, part of the reason why imports are rising may be that the U.S. demand is expanding. If so, then the potential exists for domestic production to expand with a rise in demand. Consequently, although the market share of foreign imports has increased, production in the U.S. textile and apparel industry has held steady in real terms.

APPENDIX A

Calculating a Real Exchange Rate for Textile and Apparel Imports

The multilateral real exchange rate for this study consists of 24 foreign countries that supplied the United States with an average of 84 percent of its textile and apparel imports from 1977 through 1986.[1]

The index is constructed on a quarterly basis for the period 1977.1 through 1986.1 by using the following formula:

$$I_t = \left[\prod_{i=1}^{24} \left(\frac{E_t^i}{E_B^i} \cdot \frac{CPI_t^{US}}{CPI_t^i} \right)^{W_t^i} \right] 100$$

where

I_t = the textile and apparel index in quarter t,

E_t^i = the number of units of currency i per U.S. dollar in quarter t,

E_B^i = the number of units of currency i per U.S. dollar in the base period (first quarter 1977),

CPI_t^i = the consumer price index of country i in quarter t,

CPI_t^{US} = the consumer price index of the U.S. in quarter t,

$W_t^i = \dfrac{M_t^i}{\sum\limits_{i=1}^{24} M_t^i}$ trade weight,

M_t^i = U.S. imports from country i in year t.

---

[1] These countries are: Taiwan, Korea, Hong Kong, Japan, Italy, Pakistan, Mexico, Canada, Germany, Philippines, Indonesia, India, Thailand, United Kingdom, Brazil, Malaysia, Singapore, Dominican Republic, Sri Lanka, France, Haiti, Spain, Egypt, and Peru. Although the People's Republic of China provides the second largest quantity of textile and apparel imports to the United States, it is not included in the exchange rate computation because CPI data is not available on a quarterly basis.

Sources: Exchange rates and CPIs were obtained from International Monetary Fund, *International Financial Statistics*, various issues; Taiwan exchange rate was obtained from Board of Governors, *Annual Statistical Digest*, various issues; Taiwan CPI was obtained from Central Bank of China, *Financial Statistics*, Taiwan District, The Republic of China, various issues; the U.S. CPI was obtained from U.S. Department of Labor, Bureau of Labor Statistics; and imports of cotton, wool, and man-made fibers textiles and apparel were obtained from U.S. Department of Commerce, *Major Shippers Report*.

APPENDIX B

Variations of the Model for the Period 1977.1 to 1986.1

Model 2

Variable	Textiles*	Apparel*
Intercept	−24.75	−16.10
	(−3.71)†	(−2.42)†
Log of Real Exchange Rate	1.14	0.83
	(2.49)†	(2.05)‡
Log of Real GNP	2.58	2.19
	(3.91)†	(3.32)†
Log of Real Price Index	−0.18	−0.75
	(−0.76)	(−3.14)†
R-Square	.87	.88

$$\text{Real Price Index} = \left[\prod_{i=1}^{24} \left(\frac{WPI_t^{US}}{CPI_t^i} \right)^{W_t^i} \right] 100$$

Model 3

Variable	Textiles*	Apparel*
Intercept	−25.89	−19.63
	(−5.24)†	(−3.85)†
Log of Commodity-Specific Real Exchange Rate	1.13	0.99
	(3.79)†	(3.29)†
Log of Real GNP	2.63	2.05
	(4.36)†	(3.38)†
Time Trend	0.01	0.02
	(2.88)†	(5.46)†
R-Square	.91	.93

Commodity-Specific Real Exchange Rate =

$$\left[\prod_{i=1}^{24} \left(\frac{E_t^i}{E_B^i} \cdot \frac{WPI_t^{US}}{CPI_t^i} \right)^{W_t^i} \right] 100$$

$W_t^i = \dfrac{M_t^i}{\sum\limits_{i=1}^{24} M_t^i}$ trade weight,

M_t^i = U.S. imports from country i in year t.

Time trend = the trend that may be attributed to variables that are not in the regression equation, such as a relative price variable.

---

* A two-step full transform method was used to correct for first order autocorrelation.

† T-statistic significant at the 1 percent level.

‡ T-statistic significant at the 5 percent level.

Article 37

Industrial Innovation in Japan and the United States

EDWIN MANSFIELD

Japanese firms tend to be quicker and more economical than U.S. firms at developing and introducing new products and processes, but this advantage seems to exist only among innovations based on external technology, rather than internal technology. Whereas U.S. firms put more emphasis on marketing start-up, they put much less emphasis on tooling, equipment, and manufacturing facilities than do Japanese firms. Applied R&D in Japan, which focuses more on processes than in the United States, seems to have yielded a handsome return; but there is no evidence that the rate of return from basic research has been relatively high in Japan. In robotics, the Japanese edge seems to increase as one moves from R&D toward the market.

AMERICAN TECHNOLOGICAL LEADERSHIP IS BEING SEVERE-ly challenged in many high-technology industries by the Japanese (1). Yet very little systematic investigation has been carried out to determine how much of an advantage, if any, Japan has over the United States in developing and commercially introducing the new products and processes that are central to success in these industries. Intensive empirical studies have not been conducted to compare the extent, composition, and effectiveness of the research and development (R&D) activities of Japanese firms with those of comparable U.S. firms. We do not have an adequate understanding of the differences between Japan and the United States in the rates of diffusion of many new technologies (2).

In this article, I summarize some of the principal results of a 2-year study, based largely on data obtained from carefully selected samples of several hundred Japanese and U.S. firms, which shed new light on these important topics. Differences between the two countries in the quickness and cost of developing and introducing new products and processes are evaluated, and the size, composition, and effects of industrial R&D expenditures in the two countries are compared. Also, the introduction and diffusion in both countries of a particular new technology, the industrial robot, are analyzed.

Time and Cost Differentials

In the chemical, rubber, machinery, instruments, metals, and electrical equipment industries (3), firms from both countries tend to agree that the Japanese develop and commercially introduce new products and processes more quickly than the Americans, although their advantage in this respect is not as great as is sometimes claimed. This finding is based on detailed data obtained from a random sample of 50 Japanese and 75 U.S. firms. Averaged over all six industries, the time differential in 1985 was about 18%, according to the Japanese firms, or 6%, according to the U.S. firms (Table 1). However, the picture varies from industry to industry. In some industries, like machinery, both the Japanese and U.S. firms indicate that there was a substantial differential. In other industries, like instruments, the Japanese firms indicate that there was a substantial differential, whereas the U.S. firms do not. In still other industries, notably chemicals, both the Japanese and U.S. firms indicate that there was no large differential. These data pertain to the length of time elapsing from the beginning of applied research (if there was any) by the innovator on a new product or process to the date of the new product's or process's first commercial introduction (4).

On the average, the Japanese also develop and commercially introduce new products and processes more cheaply than the Americans. Averaged over all six industries, the resource cost differential in 1985 was 23%, according to the Japanese firms, or 10%, according to the U.S. firms. Here too, the situation varies from industry to industry. For example, in machinery and instruments, based on both the Japanese and U.S. estimates, the cost differential seemed substantial; in chemicals, on the other hand, the U.S. firms do not indicate that any substantial differential existed. The cost figures used here include all costs to the innovator of developing and introducing the innovation. Specifically, they include the costs (before the innovation's first commercial introduction) of applied research, preparation of project requirements and basic specifications, prototype or pilot plant, tooling and manufacturing equipment and facilities, manufacturing start-up, and market-

Table 1. Mean ratio of U.S. to Japanese innovation times and of U.S. to Japanese innovation costs, from data provided by 50 Japanese and 75 U.S. firms for 1985 (5).

Industry	Mean ratio of innovation times		Mean ratio of innovation costs	
	U.S. estimates	Japanese estimates	U.S. estimates	Japanese estimates
Chemicals	1.04	0.96	1.02	1.14
Rubber	1.16	1.10	1.16	1.22
Machinery	1.17	1.23	1.21	1.28
Metals	0.99	1.18	0.95	1.10
Electrical	1.03	1.42	1.04	1.32
Instruments	1.00	1.38	1.23	1.40
All industries	1.06	1.18	1.10	1.23

The author is director of the Center for Economics and Technology and professor of Economics at the University of Pennsylvania, Philadelphia, PA 19104. This article is adapted from his talk at the 25th anniversary of the School of Management at Rensselaer Polytechnic Institute, Troy, NY, 27 February 1988, and from his testimony before the Joint Economic Committee of Congress, Washington, DC, 2 December 1987.

ing start-up. Because the Japanese cost figures were converted to dollars on the basis of purchasing power parities for resources used in the innovation process, they indicate approximately how much the resources used in Japan would have cost in the United States.

To understand the factors responsible for these cost and time differentials, one must recognize that some innovations are based largely on external technology (that is, technology developed outside the innovating firm), whereas others are based largely on internal technology (that is, technology developed within the innovating firm). To see whether these cost and time differentials depend on whether innovations are based on internal or external technology, I picked a random sample of 60 major Japanese and U.S. firms in the chemical industry (defined broadly to include pharmaceuticals and petroleum), the machinery industry (including computers), and the electrical equipment and instruments industries. The sample is composed of 30 matched pairs; each pair consists of a U.S. and a Japanese firm of roughly comparable size in the same industry. Every firm indicated how much time and money it devoted, on the average, to the development and commercialization of each of the new products it introduced from 1975 to 1985, depending on whether the product was based on external or internal technology. According to expert opinion, the new products introduced by each pair of firms were reasonably comparable.

Like the estimates obtained from the 125-firm sample described above, the results indicate that the Japanese tend to have significant cost and time advantages over U.S. firms. However, these advantages seem to be confined to innovations based on external technology (where the cost and time differentials are greater than those indicated above). Among innovations based on internal technology, there seems to be no significant difference in average cost or time between Japan and the United States (5).

Innovations Based on External Technology

As a first step toward understanding why the Japanese have cost and time advantages over U.S. firms with respect to innovations based on external technology, it is important to recognize that, according to the above data, U.S. firms take almost as long, and spend almost as much money, to carry out an innovation based on external technology as one based on internal technology. In the development part of the innovation process (beginning at the start of R&D and ending when the product is developed), a U.S. innovation based on external technology takes less time and money than one based on internal technology; but in the commercialization part (beginning when the product is developed and ending when it is first introduced commercially), the time and cost are at least as great as one based on internal technology.

In Japan, on the other hand, firms take about 25% less time, and spend about 50% less money, to carry out an innovation based on external technology than one based on internal technology. Moreover, this is true in all industries included in my study. The contrast between Japanese and U.S. firms in the commercialization part of the innovation process is particularly striking. Whereas in the United States the commercialization of an innovation based on external technology takes more time and about as much money as the commercialization of one based on internal technology, in Japan it takes about 10% less time and over 50% less money than the commercialization of an internal technology–based innovation.

Many innovations based on external technology are new products that imitate others in important respects. The relatively higher commercialization cost for innovations based on external technology in the United States than in Japan seems to have been due in part

to the fact that the Japanese, in carrying out such innovations, have been more likely than the Americans to make significant technical adaptations of the imitated product and to reduce its production costs substantially. The Americans have been more inclined than the Japanese to invest heavily in marketing start-up costs in an effort to position such innovations optimally in the market, the emphasis being more on marketing strategies than on technical performance and production cost. On balance, despite the Japanese emphasis on tooling, equipment, and facilities, this seems to have resulted in relatively high commercialization costs for such innovations in the United States.

Resource Allocation in the Innovation Process

Japanese firms, in carrying out an innovation, allocate their resources quite differently than do U.S. firms. Table 2 shows the proportion of the total cost of developing and introducing a new product (introduced in 1985) that was incurred in each of the following stages of the innovation process: applied research, preparation of project requirements and basic specifications, prototype or pilot plant, tooling and manufacturing equipment and facilities, manufacturing start-up, and marketing start-up. My sample was chosen from the chemical, machinery, electrical equipment, instruments, rubber, and metals industries (3). It contains 50 matched pairs, in which each pair consists of a U.S. and Japanese firm of roughly comparable size in the same industry.

The percentage of total innovation cost devoted in Japan to

Table 2. Percentage distribution of innovation costs, 100 firms, Japan and the United States, 1985 (5).

Stage of innovation process	Japan* (%)	United States (%)
Applied research	14	18
Preparation of product specifications	7	8
Prototype or pilot plant	16	17
Tooling and manufacturing equipment and facilities	44	23
Manufacturing start-up	10	17
Marketing start-up	8	17
Total	100	100

*Due to rounding, numbers do not sum to total.

Table 3. Company R&D funds as a percentage of net sales, Japan and the United States (12).

Industry	Japan (1986)	United States (1985)
Food	0.8	0.4
Textiles	1.2	0.5
Paper	0.7	1.3
Chemicals	3.8	4.7
Petroleum	0.4	0.7
Rubber	2.9	2.2
Ferrous metals	1.9	0.5
Nonferrous metals	1.9	1.4
Fabricated metal products	1.6	1.3
Machinery	2.7	5.8
Electrical equipment	5.1	4.8
Motor vehicles	3.0	3.2
Other transportation equipment	2.6	1.2
Instruments	4.5	9.0
Total manufacturing	2.7	2.8

tooling and manufacturing equipment and facilities is almost double that in the United States. (Moreover, this difference is found in practically every industry in the sample.) This reflects, of course, Japan's emphasis on process engineering and efficient manufacturing facilities. On the other hand, the percentage of total innovation cost devoted to manufacturing start-up is significantly higher in the United States than in Japan. This may reflect greater difficulties in attaining desired quality levels in the United States than in Japan and the tendency of Japanese engineers to work more closely and directly with their work force than American engineers do (6).

Particularly striking is the difference in marketing start-up costs—that is, the expenses of pre-introduction marketing activities. In every industry in the sample, the percentage of total innovation cost devoted to marketing start-up in the United States is almost double that in Japan. If U.S. firms could reduce this percentage to the Japanese level (while holding constant the amount they spend on other stages of the innovation process), it appears that about 60% of the Japanese cost advantage would be eliminated (7).

Industrial R&D

Many observers are impressed by the efficiency of Japanese industrial R&D. Indeed, the president of the Semiconductor Research Corporation has gone so far as to state that: "The United States may never match Japan's R&D efficiency" (8, p. 40). If one is willing to accept a highly simplified, but frequently employed, econometric model (9), the results are consistent with the contention that applied R&D in Japan has yielded a higher rate of return (10) than in the United States. This contention seems reasonable, given Japan's greater emphasis on commercial (rather than government-financed) projects and its reliance on advanced technology from the West, which could be adapted and improved at relatively low cost. On the other hand, the econometric results provide no indication that basic research has been particularly effective in Japan (11). Based on these findings, the Japanese advantage has been confined largely to applied R&D, particularly R&D concerned with the adaptation and improvement of existing technology.

Comparison of official data in both countries shows that the R&D intensity of manufacturing firms has increased more rapidly in Japan than in the United States, which is not surprising, given the previous finding that the rate of return from applied R&D has been higher there than here. In 1986, company-financed R&D expenditures in manufacturing were about 2.7% of sales in Japan, in comparison with about 2.8% in 1985 in the United States (Table 3) (12). In 1970, the corresponding figures were 1.3% for Japan and

2.2% for the United States. In all industries other than machinery, instruments, paper, and petroleum, Japan has narrowed the gap substantially. In some industries (food, textiles, metals, and rubber) Japan now leads; in other industries (paper, petroleum, machinery, and instruments) the United States now leads; and in the rest there is a relatively small difference in R&D intensity.

Japanese firms seem to give users of their R&D results a more important role in shaping their R&D programs than do U.S. firms. Japanese firms seem to base about one-third of their R&D projects on suggestions from their production personnel and customers, whereas only about one-sixth of U.S. projects come from these sources. Both production personnel and customers tend to be users of a firm's R&D results. In contrast, U.S. firms seem to put more emphasis than do the Japanese on the R&D function as a generator of R&D projects. Particularly in the electrical equipment industry, U.S. firms tend to base a larger percentage of their R&D projects on suggestions from R&D personnel than do Japanese firms.

Composition of Industrial R&D

Because R&D projects are so heterogeneous, it is important to look behind the total R&D figures at the composition of firms' R&D expenditures. Fifty Japanese firms were chosen at random in the chemical, electrical equipment, instrument, machinery, rubber, and metals industries, and for each Japanese firm I picked at random a U.S. firm of the same industry and approximate size. The firms in this sample carry out about 25% of the R&D in each country in these industries. Based on detailed information obtained from each of these 100 firms (50 matched pairs), the Japanese seem to devote about as large a percentage of their R&D expenditures to relatively risky and long-term projects as do U.S. firms (Table 4). This differs greatly from the early 1970s, when Peck and Tamura characterized Japanese industrial R&D as composed very largely of "low-risk and short-term projects" (13).

However, it is by no means true that Japanese and U.S. industrial R&D have become essentially the same. Whereas U.S. firms report that almost one-half of their R&D expenditures are going for projects aimed at entirely new products and processes, Japanese firms report that only about one-third of their R&D expenditures go for this purpose (14). (Outside the chemical industry, in which there is little difference in this regard, the gap is even wider.) Of course, this is in accord with a great deal of anecdotal information to the effect that the Japanese devote more of their R&D resources to the improvement and adaptation of existing products and processes (rather than to the development of entirely new products and

Table 4. Composition of R&D expenditures, 100 firms (50 matched pairs), Japan and the United States, 1985 (9).

Industry	Percentage of R&D expenditures					
	Basic research	Applied research	Products (rather than processes)	Entirely new products and processes	Projects with <0.5 estimated chance of success	Projects expected to last >5 years
All industries combined						
Japan	10	27	36	32	26	38
United States	8	23	68	47	28	38
*Chemicals**						
Japan	11	42	48	42	24	39
United States	11	39	74	43	39	41
Machinery,† instruments, metals, and rubber						
Japan	9	23	32	28	26	37
United States	4	9	62	51	16	36

*Including drugs.   †Including electrical equipment and computers.

processes) than do U.S. firms.

Even more striking is the difference between Japanese and U.S. firms in their allocation of R&D resources between projects aimed at improved product technology and projects aimed at improved process technology. The U.S. firms in this sample devote about two-thirds of their R&D expenditures to improved product technology (new products and product changes) and about one-third to improved process technology (new processes and process changes). Among the Japanese firms, on the other hand, the proportions are reversed, two-thirds going for improved process technology and one-third going for improved product technology (15).

These results shed new light on a major issue concerning industrial R&D in the United States. Many observers have criticized U.S. industry for neglecting process innovation. As the President's Commission on Industrial Competitiveness puts it, "It does us little good to design state-of-the-art products, if within a short time our foreign competitors can manufacture them more cheaply" (16, p. 20). Contrary to the common impression that U.S. firms have in recent years begun to react to such criticism by paying more attention to process innovation than in the past, my results do not indicate that there was any perceptible increase between 1976 and 1985 in the proportion of their R&D expenditures devoted to new or improved processes. Thus, in terms of the allocation of their R&D funds, U.S. firms do not seem to have put more emphasis on processes, despite this criticism.

Industrial Robots: A Case Study

An important industry in which the Japanese are often cited as being ahead of the United States is industrial robots. Given that this is the case, it is interesting to compare the innovation process in the two countries in this industry. From data obtained from a sample of U.S. and Japanese robot producers that account for almost 90% of U.S. robot output and about 20% of Japanese robot output, it appears that the Japanese tend to be faster (by about 20 to 30%) and use less resources (by about 10%) than their U.S. rivals in developing and introducing a new robot (of comparable novelty, importance, and complexity). U.S. firms devote a much larger percentage

37% versus 10%) of innovation cost to marketing start-up, and a much lower percentage (4% versus 23%) to tooling and manufacturing equipment and facilities than do Japanese firms (17).

The composition of innovation costs differs between high-growth and low-growth robot producers. In both countries, high-growth robot producers tend to devote a much higher proportion of innovation costs to tooling and manufacturing facilities than do low-growth robot producers, and the proportion devoted to marketing start-up seems to be much lower among high-growth than low-growth robot producers. In this industry at least, it appears that the more successful firms in both countries, like the Japanese, tend to emphasize manufacturing in the innovation process, not marketing.

Given the oft-stated assertion that Japanese managers are often more patient than their U.S. counterparts, it is interesting to note that the proportion of R&D expenditure devoted to relatively long-term projects (those expected to last more than 5 years) does not differ significantly between the two countries—and the sample proportion is higher in the United States than in Japan (Table 5). Moreover, in contrast to other industries (as shown in Table 4), the share of R&D expenditure devoted to new products and product improvements (rather than new processes and process improvements) is higher for Japanese robot firms than for U.S. robot firms. Perhaps this is an indication that, as their technology becomes more advanced and they become world leaders in particular areas, Japanese firms will devote more resources to product R&D (relative to process R&D), and become more like U.S. firms in this respect.

In both countries, high-growth robot producers tend to be more research-intensive and technologically ambitious in their R&D programs than low-growth robot producers. The percentage of sales devoted to R&D was about two or three times as great among high-growth as among low-growth producers. The percentage of R&D expenditures devoted to research (rather than development), and the percentage aimed at entirely new products and processes, was at least twice as high among high-growth as among low-growth producers. In the robot industry, the more successful firms seem to devote a larger share of their R&D to more fundamental and technologically ambitious projects, which is likely to have contributed to their success (18).

Table 5. Composition of R&D expenditures, Japanese and U.S. robot producers, 1985 (18).

Characteristics of firms*	Percentage of R&D expenditures				
	Basic research	Applied research	New products and product improvements	Entirely new products and processes	Projects expected to last >5 years
Japanese firms	12	23	65	51	10
Large	12	24	65	53	8
Small	11	17	73	10	34
High growth	15	32	73	63	6
Low growth	6	11	51	34	12
U.S. firms	13	21	39	46	17
Large	15	23	41	44	11
Small	2	8	25	56	50
High growth	14	29	48	52	12†
Low growth	15	4	22	19	11†

*In the United States, a small robot producer is one with 1984 sales below $5 million; a large robot producer is one with 1984 sales of $5 million or more. In Japan, a small robot producer is one with 1983 sales below 800 million yen; a large robot producer is one with 1983 sales of 800 million yen or more. In the United States, high-growth producers are defined as those that had more than a 50% average annual increase in robot sales from 1982 to 1985; low-growth producers are those that had a 50% increase or less. (Of course, this is a short period, but the robot industry is very young. In one case where data were unavailable for 1982 to 1985, the growth rate had to be based on only part of the period.) In Japan, high-growth producers are those that had an average annual growth rate of sales of more than 50% during 1979 to 1984; low-growth producers are those that had an average annual growth rate of 50% or less. (In cases where data were unavailable for 1979 to 1984, the growth rates had to be based on only part of the period.) For lack of data, not all of the sample can be classified as "high growth" or "low growth." Joint ventures between U.S. and Japanese firms are omitted, since they are neither purely American nor purely Japanese. †Because of lack of data, not all of the sample can be classified as "high growth" or "low growth." This explains why both these percentages are below the figure of 17% given in this column for all U.S. firms.

The Diffusion of Industrial Robots

Although the industrial robot was largely an American invention, the rate of imitation for industrial robots in the United States was slow, relative to other major industrial innovations. On the basis of data I obtained from a random sample of 100 major firms, it took, on the average, about 12 years (from the date of first use in the relevant industry) for half of the major potential users in ten industries—autos, auto parts, electrical equipment, appliances, steel, nonferrous metals, aerospace, farm machinery, machine tools, and other machinery—to begin using robots (Table 6). In contrast, it took only about 5 years, on the average, for half of the potential users in an industry to begin using numerically controlled machine tools, an important precursor of robots (19).

In Japan, where U.S. robotics technology began to be transferred in the 1960s, the rate of imitation was faster than in the United States. On the basis of data I obtained from a random sample of 75 firms, it took, on the average, about 8 years (from the date of first use in the relevant industry) for half of the major potential users in four industries—autos, electrical equipment, metals, and machinery—to begin using robots. In both the United States and Japan, the imitation process can be represented reasonably well by a simple econometric model I suggested a number of years ago (20). According to the results, Japan's higher rate of imitation can be explained entirely by its later start, which enabled it to use earlier experience in the United States and elsewhere.

Turning from the rate of imitation (the growth over time in the number of firms using robots) to the intrafirm rate of diffusion (the growth over time in the number of robots used by a firm), it seems clear that the intrafirm rate of diffusion has tended to be much greater in Japan than in the United States. In my sample, the number of robots used per 10,000 employees in 1985 was about four to eight times as great (depending on the industry) in Japan as in the United States (21).

In considerable part, this observed difference in robot use between Japan and the United States seems to be due to differences in the minimum rate of return required to justify investing in robots. Whereas the Japanese often invest in robots yielding returns of 20%, U.S. firms frequently insist on 30% or more. This difference in minimum required rates of return has been noted in other studies as well, and it may reflect a tendency, cited by Kaplan (22) and others, for U.S. firms to exaggerate their cost of capital. On the basis of data I obtained from the Japanese firms in the sample, it seems that, if they had applied the same "hurdle rates" as their U.S. rivals, their robot use would have fallen by 50% or more.

Conclusions

At least five conclusions seem to follow from the studies described above. First, with respect to the differences between the two countries in innovation cost and time, the situation is much more varied and complex than is generally portrayed by the largely anecdotal accounts that have begun to appear. Whereas the Japanese have substantial advantages in this regard in some industries (notably machinery), they do not seem to have any substantial advantage in others (notably chemicals). Whereas they have very great advantages in carrying out innovations based on external technology, they do not seem to have any in carrying out innovations based on internal technology.

Second, a large part of America's problem in this regard seems to be due to its apparent inability to match the Japanese as quick and effective users of external technology. As Brooks has warned, "The United States, so long accustomed to leading the world, may have

Table 6. Number of years before half of major potential users introduced robots, Japan and United States, by industry (19).

Industry	Number of years
United States	
Autos and trucks	15
Auto parts and equipment	8
Electrical equipment	17
Appliances	19
Nonferrous metals	20
Steel	3
Farm and construction machinery	18
Machine tools and industrial machinery	16
Other machinery*	1
Aerospace	7
Mean	12
Japan	
Autos	6
Electrical equipment	2
Metals	9
Machinery	15
Mean	8

*Because the sample in this industry is small, this result should be treated with considerable caution.

lost the art of creative imitation" (23, p. 17). This is not to deny that part of the Japanese advantage may be due to factors like their propensity to overlap various stages of the innovation process, their subcontractor network, and their fewer organizational barriers and better communication between functional departments of firms. But the fact that the Japanese advantage tends to be limited to innovations based on external technology suggests that it is in this area that many central problems lie.

Third, part of these problems may be related to the differences between Japan and the United States in the way resources are allocated in the industrial innovation process. Whereas U.S. firms emphasize marketing start-up to a much greater degree than do the Japanese, they put much less emphasis on tooling, equipment, and manufacturing facilities than do Japanese firms. Perhaps U.S. firms might consider whether they safely can reduce the cost and time devoted to marketing start-up without impairing the vital interface between R&D and marketing. Although it would be foolish for the United States, which has long been at the forefront of industrial innovation, to attempt mindlessly to mimic the Japanese, it would also be foolish not to try to learn from them.

Fourth, my results, which are subject to many limitations detailed elsewhere (9), support the contention that applied R&D in Japan has yielded a handsome return, higher than in the United States. In large part, this can be explained by Japan's greater emphasis on commercial (rather than government-financed) projects, by its ability to obtain Western technology that was more advanced than its own, and which could be adapted and improved at relatively low cost, and by its emphasis on process technology, which according to many experts has tended to be neglected in the United States. On the other hand, there is no evidence that the rate of return from basic research has been relatively high in Japan. Apparently, the Japanese advantage has been confined largely to applied R&D, particularly R&D concerned with the adaptation and improvement of existing technology.

Fifth, my results concerning robotics, an important area where the Japanese currently seem to have an edge, suggest that the Japanese advantage increases as one moves from R&D toward the market. Whereas the Japanese seem to be quicker and more efficient innovators, they do not seem to be more effective at R&D. Whereas they have introduced many more robots than U.S. firms, they have not been quicker to begin using them (when account is taken of their later start). If, as many observers claim, U.S. industry has not used robots as fully as it should, the principal fault does not seem to lie with U.S. R&D. Instead, this case seems to illustrate the contention that, in those areas where the United States is falling behind competitively, it is due frequently to problems not so much in R&D or inventiveness, but in the commercial application of science and technology.

REFERENCES AND NOTES

1. For important studies of the relation between technological change and economic growth, see E. Denison [*Trends in American Economic Growth* (Brookings Institution, Washington, DC, 1985)] and J. Kendrick [J. Kendrick, Ed., *International Comparisons of Productivity and Causes of the Slowdown* (American Enterprise Institute/Ballinger, Washington, DC, 1984)].
2. For two articles dealing with the competitiveness of U.S. industry, see S. Cohen and J. Zysman [*Science* 239, 1110 (1988)] and L. C. Thurow [*ibid.* 238, 1659 (1987)].
3. The chemical industry referred to in this section includes pharmaceuticals; the machinery industry includes computers.
4. The overall U.S.–Japanese differences in Table 1 are highly significant in a statistical sense; the all-industry mean ratios differ from 1.00 at the 0.01 probability level. This is also true for many of the figures in the machinery, instruments, and chemical industries, but in other industries like metals and rubber, many of the figures are based on relatively few observations. Note too that, although the estimates in Table 1 were based on reasonably precise data concerning the firms' own times and costs, they sometimes had to be based on the best judgment of the firms' leading executives concerning their rivals' times and costs. The data in my 60-firm sample described later in this article are free of this problem.
5. For a more detailed account of the studies in this and the next two sections, see E. Mansfield (*Manage. Sci.*, in press).
6. It may also be related to the fact that the percentage of innovation cost devoted to tooling and manufacturing equipment and facilities is lower in the United States than in Japan.
7. For all industries combined, the difference between Japanese and U.S. firms in the percentage of innovation cost devoted to tooling and manufacturing cost and facilities, as well as the difference between them in the percentage devoted to marketing start-up costs, is statistically significant at the 0.01 probability level.
8. L. W. Sumney and R. M. Burger, *Issues Sci. Technol.* 3, 32 (summer 1987).
9. For this model as well as a more detailed account of the studies described in this and the next section, see E. Mansfield [*Am. Econ. Rev.* 78, 223 (1988)].
10. As pointed out in (9), this rate of return pertains to entire industries, not to particular firms, in Japan and the United States.
11. The National Science Foundation's definitions of basic research, applied research, and development are used here.
12. Bureau of Statistics, *Report of the Survey of Research and Development in Japan* (Bureau of Statistics, Tokyo, 1987); National Science Foundation, *National Patterns of Science and Technology Resources, 1987* (Government Printing Office, Washington, DC, 1988). G. Saxonhouse translated the Japanese material.
13. M. J. Peck and S. Tamura, in *Asia's New Giant*, H. Patrick and H. Rosovsky, Eds. (Brookings Institution, Washington, DC, 1976).
14. Of course, the distinction between an entirely new product or process and an improved or modified product or process is often arbitrary (although it frequently is used).
15. Among the large R&D spenders (top 20%), this difference between U.S. and Japanese firms is significant at the 0.01 probability level. From the point of view of the economy as a whole, a large proportion of the resources allocated to product technology in the United States really goes for processes, since one firm's products frequently are parts of another firm's processes. Thus, this difference between Japan and the United States reflects a difference in how much of the process R&D for a given product is carried out by the producers of the product and how much is done by equipment producers and other suppliers of the producers of the product. As many observers have stressed, there can be disadvantages in leaving this sort of R&D to the latter firms. (Of course, the observed U.S.-Japan difference in this regard is due partly to differences in industrial and firm structure.)
16. President's Commission on Industrial Competitiveness, *Global Competition: The New Reality* (Government Printing Office, Washington, DC, 1985).
17. These U.S.–Japanese differences are statistically significant. For a more detailed account, see E. Mansfield (paper presented at Symposium on Research and Development, Industrial Change and Economic Policy, University of Karlstad, Sweden, June 1987). Also, see R. Ayres, L. Lynn, and S. Miller [in C. Uyehara, Ed., *Technological Exchange: The U.S.–Japanese Experience* (University Press of America, Washington, DC, 1982), pp. 77–115].
18. E. Mansfield, *Manage. Decis. Econ.*, in press. For the statistical significance of these differences, see E. Mansfield in (17).
19. ———, "The diffusion of industrial robots in Japan and the United States" (working paper, Center for Economics and Technology, University of Pennsylvania, Philadelphia, 1987).
20. ———, *Econometrica* 29, 741 (1961).
21. Also see K. Flamm [*International Differences in Industrial Robot Use* (Brookings Institution and Development Research Department, World Bank, Washington, DC, May 1986)].
22. R. Kaplan, *Harv. Bus. Rev.* 64, 87 (1986). According to some economists, the cost of capital is higher in the United States than in Japan. This too might account for the higher hurdle rates in the United States than in Japan.
23. H. Brooks, *Japanese Technological Advances and Possible United States Responses Using Research Joint Ventures*. Testimony before Subcommittee on Science, Research and Technology of the House Committee on Science, Space, and Technology, 98th Cong., 1st sess., 29 to 30 June 1983.
24. The research on which this article is based was supported by grants from the National Science Foundation, which, of course, is not responsible for the views expressed here.

Sources

1. "An Economist's Perspective on the Theory of the Firm," Oliver Hart, *Columbia Law Review,* November 1989, pp. 1757–1774. Reprinted by permission.

2. "Eclipse of the Public Corporation," Michael C. Jensen, *Harvard Business Review,* September–October 1989, pp. 61–74. Reprinted by permission.

3. "CEO Incentives—It's Not How Much You Pay, But How," Michael C. Jensen and Kevin J. Murphy, *Harvard Business Review,* May–June 1990, pp. 138–153. Reprinted by permission.

4. "The Business Economist at Work: Atlantic Richfield Company," Anthony Finizza, *Business Economics,* April 1991, pp. 57–59. Reprinted by permission.

5. "Advertising and the U.S. Market Demand for Beer," Byunglak Lee and Victor J. Tremblay, *Applied Economics,* January 1992, pp. 69–76. Reprinted by permission of Chapman & Hall, London.

6. "An Economic Analysis of the Demand for Abortions," Marshall H. Medoff, *Economic Inquiry,* April 1988, pp. 353–359. Reprinted by permission of Western Economic Association International.

7. "Search Costs and Apartment Rents," John D. Benjamin and Kenneth M. Lusht, *Journal of Real Estate Finance and Economics,* 6:2, March 1993, pp. 189–197. Reprinted by permission of Kluwer Academic Publishers.

8. "Price Concessions, Time on the Market, and the Actual Sale Price of Homes," Paul K. Asabere and Forrest E. Huffman, *Journal of Real Estate Finance and Economics,* 6:2, March 1993, pp. 167–174. Reprinted by permission of Kluwer Academic Publishers.

9. "Economic Forecasting in the Private and Public Sectors," Alan Greenspan, *Business Economics,* January 1991, pp. 52–55. Reprinted by permission.

10. "Corporate Forecasting Practices in the Manufacturing Industry," Nada R. Sanders, *Production and Inventory Management Journal,* Third Quarter 1992, pp. 54–57. Reprinted by permission of American Production and Inventory Control Society, Inc.

11. "Predicting Interest Rates: A Comparison of Professional and Market–Based Forecasts," Michael T. Belongia, Federal Reserve Bank of St. Louis, *Review,* March 1987, pp. 9–15. Reprinted by permission.

12. "Educational Cost Factors and Student Achievement in Grades 3 and 6: Some New Evidence," David Stern, *Economics of Education Review,* 8:2, 1989, pp. 149–58. Reprinted by permission from Pergamon Press Ltd., Oxford, England.

13. "The Effect of Chain Ownership on Nursing Home Costs," Niccie L. McKay, *Health Services Research,* April 1991, pp. 109–124. Reprinted with permission from the Hospital Research and Educational Trust.

14. "Scale Economies, Capacity Utilization, and School Costs: A Comparative Analysis of Secondary and Elementary Schools," John Riew, *Journal of Education Finance,* Spring 1986, pp. 433–446. Reprinted by permission.

15. "Financial Restraint in the Free Agent Labor Market for Major League Baseball: Players Look at Strike Three," Thomas H. Bruggink and David R. Rose, Jr., *Southern Economic Journal,* April 1990, pp. 1029–1043. Reprinted by permission.

16. "Learning Curves in Manufacturing," Linda Argote and Dennis Epple, *Science,* February 23, 1990, pp. 920–924. Reprinted by permission of the American Association for the Advancement of Science.

17. "A Classroom Exercise Using Linear Programming in the Construction of Duration–Matched Dedicated Portfolios," Robert A. Strong and Kent D. Carter, *Journal of Financial Education,* November 1991, pp. 69–75. Reprinted by permission.

18. "The Determinants of Direct Air Fares to Cleveland: How Competitive?" Paul W. Bauer and Thomas J. Zlatoper, Federal Reserve Bank of Cleveland, *Economic Review,* Quarter 1, 1989, pp. 2–9. Reprinted by permission.

19. "Cable Television and Competition: Theory, Evidence and Policy," Stanford L. Levin and John B. Meisel, *Telecommunications Policy,* December 1991, pp. 519–528. Reprinted by permission of Butterworth–Heinemann, Oxford, UK.

20. "The Behavior of Retail Gasoline Prices: Symmetric or Not?" Jeffrey D. Karrenbrock, Federal Reserve Bank of St. Louis, *Review,* July–August 1991, pp. 19–29. Reprinted by permission.

21. "The Takeover Wave of the 1980s," Andrei Shleifer and Robert W. Vishny, *Science,* August 17, 1990, pp. 745–749. Reprinted by permission of the American Association for the Advancement of Science.

22. "Economic Incentives and the Containment of Global Warming," Wallace E. Oates and Paul R. Portney, *Eastern Economic Journal,* Winter 1992, pp. 85–98. Reprinted by permission.

23. "What Can Regulators Regulate? The Case of Electric Utility Rates of Return," Walter J. Primeaux, Jr., *Managerial and Decision Economics,* June 1988, pp. 145–152. Reprinted by permission of John Wiley & Sons Ltd.

24. "The Effect of Lead Paint Abatement Laws on Rental Property Values," Deborah Ann Ford and Michele Gilligan, *American Real Estate and Urban Economics Journal,* Spring 1988, pp. 84–94. Reprinted by permission.

25. "The Effect of Gasoline Taxes on Highway Fatalities," J. Paul Leigh and James T. Wilkinson, *Journal of Policy Analysis and Management,* Summer 1991, pp. 474–481. Reprinted by permission of John Wiley & Sons, Inc.

26. "The Capital Budgeting Process: Theory and Practice," Tarun K. Mukherjee and Glenn V. Henderson, *Interfaces,* March–April 1987, pp. 78–90. Reprinted by permission of the Operations Research Society of America and The Institute of Management Sciences, 290 Westminster Street, Providence, RI 02903.

27. "Capital Budgeting Forecast Biases: Evidence from the *Fortune 500,*" Stephen W. Pruitt and Lawrence J. Gitman, *Financial Management,* Spring 1987, pp. 46–51. Reprinted by permission of the Financial Management Association.

28. "Stock Market Reaction to Strategic Investment Decisions," J. Randall Woolridge and Charles C. Snow, *Strategic Management Journal,* September 1990, pp. 353–363. Reprinted by permission of John Wiley & Sons Ltd.

29. "A New Look at the Returns and Risks to Pharmaceutical R&D," Henry Grabowski and John Vernon, *Management Science,* July 1990, pp. 804–821. Reprinted by permission of The Institute of Management Sciences, 290 Westminster Street, Providence, RI 02903.

30. "Benefit–Cost Analysis of the Perry Preschool Program and Its Policy Implications," W. Steven Barnett, *Educational Evaluation and Policy Analysis,* Winter 1985, pp. 333–342. Reprinted by permission of the American Educational Research Association.

31. " 'Just Say No?' The Economic and Political Realities of a Small City's Investment in Minor League Baseball," Mark S. Rosentraub and David Swindell, *Economic Development Quarterly,* May 1991, pp. 152–167. Reprinted by permission of Sage Publications, Inc.

32. "Benefits from a Baseball Franchise: An Alternative Methodology," John P. Blair, *Economic Development Quarterly,* February 1992, pp. 91–95. Reprinted by permission of Sage Publications, Inc.

33. "Hammers and Their Use: Some Issues Involved in the Selection of Appropriate Tools for Public Policy Analysis," David Swindell and Mark S. Rosentraub, *Economic Development Quarterly,* February 1992, pp. 96–101. Reprinted by permission of Sage Publications, Inc.

34. "A Guide to Foreign Exchange Markets," K. Alec Chrystal, Federal Reserve Bank of St. Louis, *Review,* March 1984, pp. 5–18. Reprinted by permission.

35. "Protectionist Trade Policies: A Survey of Theory, Evidence and Rationale," Cletus C. Coughlin, K. Alec Chrystal, and Geoffrey E. Wood, Federal Reserve Bank of St. Louis, *Review,* January–February 1988, pp. 12–29. Reprinted by permission.

36. "The Effect of Exchange Rate Variation on U.S. Textile and Apparel Imports," Christine Chmura, Federal Reserve Bank of Richmond, *Economic Review,* May–June 1987, pp. 17–23. Reprinted by permission.
37. "Industrial Innovation in Japan and the United States," Edwin Mansfield, *Science,* September 30, 1988, pp. 1769–74. Reprinted by permission of the American Association for the Advancement of Science.